THE
KERNER
REPORT

THE

KERNER REPORT

THE 1968 REPORT
OF THE
NATIONAL ADVISORY
COMMISSION
ON CIVIL DISORDERS

with a preface by Fred R. Harris
and a new introduction by Tom Wicker

Pantheon Books · New York

Contents

Foreword by Fred R. Harris ix
Introduction to the 1988 Edition by Tom Wicker xii
Original Introduction by Tom Wicker xv
Foreword xxii
The National Advisory Commission on Civil Disorders xxiii
Advisory Panels to the Commission xxiv
Professional Staff xxvi
Summary 1
Preface 31

PART I. WHAT HAPPENED?

Chapter 1 / Profiles of Disorder 35
    Introduction 35
  I. Tampa 42
  II. Cincinnati 47
  III. Atlanta 52
  IV. Newark 56
  V. Northern New Jersey 69
  VI. Plainfield 75
  VII. New Brunswick 82
  VIII. Detroit 84
    Methodology 108

Chapter 2 / Patterns of Disorder 109
    Introduction 109
  I. The Pattern of Violence and Damage 112
  II. The Riot Process 116
  III. The Riot Participant 127
  IV. The Background of Disorder 135
  V. The Aftermath of Disorder 151
    Notes 158

Chapter 3 / Organized Activity 201

PART II. WHY DID IT HAPPEN?

Chapter 4 / The Basic Causes   203

Chapter 5 / Rejection and Protest: An Historical Sketch   206
  Introduction 206
  The Colonial Period 207
  The Revolution 208
  The Constitution and the Laws 208
  Discrimination as Doctrine 209
  The Path Toward Civil War 210
  Civil War and "Emancipation" 212
  Reconstruction 213
  The End of Reconstruction 214
  Segregation by Law 214
  Booker T. Washington 216
  The Niagara Movement 216
  The NAACP 217
  The Federal Government 217
  East St. Louis, 1917 217
  World War I 218
  Postwar Violence 219
  The 1920's and the New Militancy 219
  Separatism 221
  The Depression 221
  The New Deal 222
  World War II 223
  The Postwar Period 224
  The Persistence of Discrimination 226
  Revolution of Rising Expectations 226
  Student Involvement 227
  Organizational Rivalries 228
  The Role of Whites 228
  The Black Muslims 229
  "Freedom Now!" 229
  The March on Washington 230
  Failures of Direct Action 230
  New Directions 231
  "Black Power" 232
  Old Wine in New Bottles 234
  The Meaning 235

Chapter 6 / The Formation of The Racial Ghettos   236
  Major Trends in Negro Population 236
  The Growth Rate of the Negro Population 237
  The Migration of Negroes from the South 239
  The Concentration of Negro Population
    in Large Cities 242

Chapter 7 / Unemployment, Family Structure, and
Social Disorganization 251
     Recent Economic Trends 251
     Unemployment and Underemployment 252
     The Low-Status and Low-Paying Nature of
        Many Negro Jobs 253
     The Magnitude of Poverty in Disadvantaged
        Neighborhoods 258
     The Social Impact of Employment Problems
        in Disadvantaged Negro Areas 260
     Note—Calculation of Nonwhite Subemployment
        in Disadvantaged Areas of All Central
        Cities 264

Chapter 8 / Conditions of Life in the Racial Ghetto 266
  I. Crime and Insecurity 266
  II. Health and Sanitation Conditions 269
 III. Exploitation of Disadvantaged Consumers
       by Retail Merchants 274

Chapter 9 / Comparing the Immigrant and Negro
Experience 278
     The Maturing Economy..........................278
     The Disability of Race...........................278
     Entry Into the Political System....................279
     Cultural Factors 280
     The Vital Element of Time.......................281

PART III. WHAT CAN BE DONE?

Chapter 10 / The Community Response 283
     Introduction 283
     Basic Strategy and Goals.........................288
     Programs: First Phase Actions.....................289
     Second Phase Actions...........................294
     Conclusion 298

Chapter 11 / The Police and The Community 299
     Introduction 299
  I. Police Conduct and Patrol Practices 301
  II. The Problem of Police Protection 307
 III. The Problem of Grievance Mechanisms 310
 IV. The Need for Policy Guidelines 312
  V. Community Support for Law Enforcement 315

Chapter 12 / Control of Disorder 323
     Introduction 323
  I. The Initial Incident 324
  II. Control Capabilities 327

  III. The Use of Force 329
  IV. Community Assistance in Disorder Control 331
   V. Danger of Overreaction 334
  VI. Funding of Recommendations 335

Chapter 13 / The Administration of Justice Under
Emergency Conditions   337
    I. The Conditon in Our Lower Courts 337
   II. The Experience of Summer 1967 338
  III. Guidelines for the Future 344
  IV. Summary of Recommendations 357

Chapter 14 / Damages: Repair and Compensation   358
       Amending the Federal Disaster Act 358
       Compensating for Individual Losses—Insurance 360

Chapter 15 / The News Media and the Disorders   362
       Introduction 362
    I. News Coverage of Civil Disorders—
        Summer 1967 368
   II. A Recommendation to Improve Riot Coverage 378
  III. Reporting of Racial Problems in
        the United States 382
  IV. Institute of Urban Communications 386

Chapter 16 / The Future of the Cities   389
       Introduction 389
    I. The Key Trends 390
   II. Choices for the Future 395
  III. The Present Policies Choice 396
  IV. The Enrichment Choice 401
   V. The Integration Choice 406
  VI. Conclusions 407
       On Population Growth 408

Chapter 17 / Recommendations for National Action   410
       Introduction 410
    I. Employment 413
   II. Education 424
  III. The Welfare System 457
  IV. Housing 467
       Conclusion 483

Remarks Of The President, July 29, 1967 484

Biographical Materials on Commissioners 486

Index   490

Preface to the 1988 Edition

BY FRED R. HARRIS

Newark blew up in the summer of 1967. Detroit burst into flames. Police and national guard—virtually all-white, mostly poorly trained, and tragically overreacting—struggled to contain the violence within the black ghettos where it began, but, for a long time, they were unable to quell it. On Monday, July 24, President Lyndon B. Johnson ordered U.S. troops into Detroit.

This was the "long hot summer," during which terrible riots, looting, and burning devastated the black sections of so many of America's cities.

What happened? Why did it happen? What can be done to prevent it from happening again? These were the questions President Johnson asked when, on July 28, 1967, he appointed the National Advisory Commission on Civil Disorders (called the Kerner Commission, after its chairman). Johnson was speaking for most people. He wanted answers, but he also wanted to reassure white people that violence would not be tolerated or allowed to spread. And he wanted to demonstrate to black people his concern about the "conditions that breed despair and violence," as he put it.

Serving on that commission was, for me and all of us, a searing experience. We had known the figures on urban poverty, but now we saw the dull eyes of the inner-city children. We had known the rates of unemployment, but now we heard the bitter frustrations of those who had been made idle. We had known the facts of racism, but now we experienced firsthand the hostility of the oppressed. In the 1950s and 1960s, before the era of the riots, it was possible for most middle-class Americans to live without any contact with—or awareness of—the realities of urban poverty. Now, just seven months after it was created, moved by a deepened sense of urgency and concern, the Kerner Commission made its report—on March 1, 1968.

"This has been a working commission," we said in the report's Foreword. Indeed, that had been true. Under the direction of a dedicated and sensitive executive director, Washington attorney David Ginsburg, and aided by a superb staff and con-

ix

sultant corps, we first held twenty days of formal hearings in Washington—from August through November. The 130 witnesses who appeared before us ranged all the way from civil-rights leader Dr. Martin Luther King, Jr., to FBI Director J. Edgar Hoover.

Staff members and consultants undertook field surveys in twenty-three cities, involving some twelve hundred interviews, attitude (or opinion) surveys, and other serious studies of conditions and causes—and wrote up their findings. Commissioners divided into teams and made site visits to eight cities where riots had occurred. John V. Lindsay and I walked the "mean streets" of Milwaukee and Cincinatti's black ghettos together. We encountered young black men, idling on the streets, who implored us to help them find work, and other blacks who were so angry that they could not bear to shake hands with us or look us in the face. We saw, close up, the human cost of wretched poverty and harsh racism.

Back in Washington, shaken, moved, commission members met for forty-four intense days, from December through February, to craft our report, every word of which was read aloud, debated and revised before finally being approved by a majority vote, when there was any division.

We took up the questions the president had asked us in order, deciding to answer each one as truthfully as we could before going on to the next:

What happened? We knew that the riots had not been the result of a conspiracy, as President Johnson had thought. We said so: *The urban disorders of the summer of 1967 were not caused by, nor were they the consequence of, any organized plan or "conspiracy."*

Why did it happen? We did not know why violence occurred in one place and not another, but we could describe with particularity these conditions and said, straight out, that they were the direct result of racism and poverty: *Segregation and poverty have created in the racial ghettos a destructive environment totally unknown to most white Americans.*

What can be done to prevent it from happening again? When we arrived at this last question, it was clear to all of us, including the commission's more conservative members, that our earlier answers had already locked us into an answer: great sustained national efforts were required to combat racism, unemployment, and poverty. There was no doubt about that. We said: *It is time to make good the promises of American democracy to all citizens—urban and rural, white and black, Spanish-surname, American Indian and every minority group.*

And, for a time after the Kerner Report, through the mid-1970s, America made progress on almost all fronts that the report had covered. Then came a series of recessions and other economic blows that were most severe for poor people and minorities; these were accompanied by federal cutbacks in jobs, training, and other social programs most important to the poor. Just a few years after the bitter lessons of the sixties, the government lost interest in, and even became hostile towards, affirmative-action programs and civil-rights laws.

So poverty is worse today than it was twenty years ago. More people are poor. Poor people are poorer—and less able to escape their poverty. Unemployment is worse. There is a growing American urban underclass, principally black and Hispanic. "Quiet riots" of high unemployment and poverty, segregation, family deterioration, social disorganization, narcotics use, and crime characterize today's central cities. These quiet riots are not as noticeable or alarming to outsiders as the violent riots of the 1960s, but they are more destructive of human life.

The Kerner Report was a milestone, an honest measure of these problems of the inner city, and of their terrible consequences.

Perhaps by reissuing it now we can put "the promises of American democracy" back on our national agenda.

June 1, 1988

Introduction to the 1988 Edition

BY TOM WICKER

As I read my introduction to the report of the National Advisory Commission on Civil Disorders twenty years later, what struck me most forcefully about what I had written was that its prevailing tone of doubt had been so largely sustained by events.

That doubt, repeatedly expressed, was not about the report's conclusion that pervasive white racism was the underlying cause of the black riots that rocked American cities in the 1960s. Nor did I express doubt, as some were doing, about the credentials of those who had made such a powerful judgment.

"Perhaps the one hopeful note," I suggested, was that "what had to be said has been said at last, and by representatives of that white, moderate, responsible America that, alone, needed to say it."

No, what daunted me then, and still does, was—first—the size of the task the commission set before President Lyndon Johnson and the American people: the long, expensive, largely uncharted course of dispersing poor blacks from isolated urban ghettos and integrating them fully into the national life and economy, while progressively easing "the grinding life of the urban poor" so graphically exposed in the report.

Equally daunting was the implication of the report's basic premise: if the cause of the trouble was the society that white racism had created, obviously racism would also be the major obstacle to the "great commitment of money and effort" that same society was asked to make in order to attack the trouble—a vicious circle indeed.

No wonder I wrote that the commission's "monumental prescription" propounded "a task that beggars any other planned social evolution known to human history." After the passage of two decades, five presidents, the post-New Deal political order, American economic preeminence, and the nation's faith in its government's ability to act effectively against social problems—an ability taken for granted in the Kerner Report—my doubts remain, and so does the divided society the commission aptly described.

It's true that black voting and political participation have greatly increased, especially in local government, owing mostly the Voting Rights Act; and that's a good portent for the future. It also may be an improvement that the word "Negro"—which I routinely used in 1968—is rarely heard or written anymore; at least there's no longer an excuse of sloth or dialect for the corrupt and corrupting word "nigger."

But the urban ghetto is, if anything, more populous, confining, and poverty-ridden than in 1968. Despite the rise of a small and tenuous black "middle class," the overall economic position of blacks is little improved. Black median family income, which rose to 61.5 percent of the white median in 1975, had dropped back to 57.5 percent by 1985, almost no gain since the 1950s. Black unemployment continues to measure approximately twice that of whites.

Only the southern states are noticeably more "integrated" today than in the 1960s. Housing discrimination persists everywhere, only 44 percent of black high-school graduates were enrolled in college in 1985, and there still are too many incidents such as the death of one black man and the beating of another when an enraged mob of white youths chased them out of Howard Beach, a New York City neighborhood, in 1986.

Worse, the national desire to act—never robust—is greatly diminished. The urban riots that generated so much alarmed attention twenty years ago have long since vanished—rather as if a wave had risen momentarily on the sea of events and then subsided. The alarmed attention, too, has subsided—but not the need to take action. The most visible target for action—state-supported segregation in the South—has been dismantled, with little effect on de facto segregation elsewhere. The easiest remedies, which were embodied in the various civil rights acts—had been approved *before* the commission's report. And "affirmative action," though occasionally helpful, has created its own backlash.

In the 1980s, a President of the United States who made his first campaign speech in Philadelphia, Mississippi,* led the nation to its biggest income-tax reduction in history—and thus to the deadening of what the commission had called for: "the will to tax ourselves to the extent necessary to meet the vital need of the nation."

Nothing has persuaded me, in the twenty years since the Kerner Report appeared, to change my original judgments about

* The small town where three young civil rights workers were killed by whites, in 1964.

the rioters of the 1960s—that they were "a time-bomb ticking in the heart of the . . . nation" and "the personification of that nation's shame, of its deepest failure, of its greatest challenge." In the teeming ghettos that persist in our cities, the lot of their children is little changed.

Rochester, Vermont
June 3, 1988

Introduction

BY TOM WICKER

This report is a picture of one nation, divided. It is a picture that derives its most devastating validity from the fact that it was drawn by representatives of the moderate and "responsible" Establishment—not by black radicals, militant youth or even academic leftists. From it rises not merely a cry of outrage; it is also an expression of shocked intelligence and violated faith.

President Johnson, in appointing his Commission on Civil Disorders on July 27, 1967, was severely criticized for its moderate character. Where, the critics demanded, were Stokely Carmichael, Floyd McKissick, Martin Luther King, such white radicals as Tom Hayden or such fiery evangelists as James Baldwin?

How could the Commission's report be comprehensive or acceptable without the participation of such men? The inclusion of Senator Edward Brooke of Massachusetts and Roy Wilkins of the NAACP hardly answered the question; they represented inter-racial moderation, not radical militance.

But just as it sometimes takes a hawk to settle a war—Eisenhower in Korea, de Gaulle in Algeria—so did it take bona fide moderates to validate the case that had to be made. A commission made up of militants, or even influenced by them, could not conceivably have spoken with a voice so effective, so sure to be heard in white, moderate, responsible America. And the importance of this report is that it makes plain that white, moderate, responsible America is where the trouble lies.

The Commission seemed an unpromising group, when it was first convened in the Indian treaty room of the Old State, War and Navy Building—the room where Dwight Eisenhower held his news conferences and steadfastly insisted that it was none of the business of the President of the United States to endorse the Supreme Court's school desegregation decision. Even the staff director chosen by President Johnson, David Ginsburg, was a prosperous Washington attorney without visible qualifications for understanding the uneasy ghetto.

Governor Otto Kerner of Illinois, the designated chairman, had done much to integrate his state's National Guard and a tenuous racial peace had generally been maintained in Chicago during his administration; but he was not a nationally renowned figure. John Lindsay, the Republican-Liberal Mayor of New York had exhibited a deep interest in civil rights matters during his several terms in Congress, and had worked long and hard to keep his city quiet; he was clearly an asset to the Commission, and its most glamorous member.

Senator Fred Harris, Democrat of Oklahoma; Rep. James Corman, Democrat of California; Rep. William M. McCulloch, Republican of Ohio; Miss Katherine G. Peden, the former Commissioner of Commerce of Kentucky; I. W. Abel, President of the United Steelworkers of America; Herbert Jenkins, Chief of Police in Atlanta, Ga.; Charles B. Thornton, the Chairman of Litton Industries, Inc.; Brooke and Wilkins—this did not seem to be a group likely to break new social ground. What, for instance, was Harris of Oklahoma likely to know of urban affairs?

But those acquainted with the Commission's work say that Harris of Oklahoma—who had served earlier in Senator Abraham Ribicoff's inquiry into the problems of cities—proved one of the ablest, most sensitive members. His long experience with underprivileged and ill-treated Indians in his home state gave him a depth of understanding that not all the other members reached.

On the other hand, Corman of California and McCulloch of Ohio, both of whom had excellent civil rights records in Congress, proved more cautious when discussion moved beyond civil rights to the social and economic questions into which the Commission inevitably intruded. Jenkins, the policeman, surprised other members with his acute sensitivity to such matters, and his progressive and compassionate approach.

In general, a rough division often was visible among members of the Commission—Kerner, Lindsay, Harris, Jenkins, Wilkins and Brooke on the one hand, and Corman, McCulloch, Thornton and Miss Peden on the other. Accounts vary as to Abel and in fact such division as there was did not produce a hard-and-fast voting lineup.

It was rather that some members were more willing than others to recommend massive economic programs—for instance, 600,000 housing units in the next year were twice as many as proposed by President Johnson; and the more liberal group worked to give the over-all report a more militant tone, particularly on the urgency of the situation.

Thus, one member of the Commission steadfastly resisted advocacy of Federal "open housing" legislation. Why, he kept asking, "can't a man sell his own house to whomever he pleases?" Ultimately, he supported the open housing section because it was softened somewhat, not because he had really changed his view. In such ways, the Commission itself reflected the inability of American society, dominantly white, to see and treat its Negro citizens fairly.

Yet, surely it must be a hopeful thing—perhaps the one hopeful note in recent years—that ultimately even such a divided and representative Commission could not and did not blink the fact that the single overriding cause of rioting in the cities was not any one thing commonly adduced—unemployment, lack of education, poverty, exploitation—but that it was all of those things and more, expressed in the insidious and pervasive white sense of the inferiority of black men. Here is the essence of the charge: "What white Americans have never fully understood—but what the Negro can never forget—is that white society is deeply implicated in the ghetto. *White institutions created it, white institutions maintain it, and white society condones it.*" (italics added)

But if it is hopeful that a group of representatives of those institutions and that society could recognize unanimously this central and devastating fact, there is nothing hopeful at all about the fact itself. What kind of program can be advanced to cope with the sheer humanness of racism?

Conceivably the nation could continue its present failing efforts toward an integrated society, including the present proportion of its resources devoted to social and economic programs; or it could abandon integration as a goal and commit increased resources to "enrichment" of life in the ghetto— thus presumably making it bearable without producing violence against white society.

The first of these is hopeless; not only will it tend to produce more and more ghetto violence but it is an obvious fraud, in terms of its ability to produce anything like integration. As the Commission points out, if achieving that goal is difficult now, what will it be when the Negro population of the central cities has risen from the present 12.5 million to the 21 million projected for 1985?

The second course is rejected here with equal frankness, as simply another method of producing a permanently divided society. For who can deny what is insisted upon in these pages: "In a country where the economy and particularly the resources of employment are predominantly white, a policy of separation can only relegate Negroes to a permanently inferior economic status."

Having thus disposed of both white "moderation" and black "separatism," the Commission concluded that the only possible course for a sensible and humane nation was "a policy which combines ghetto enrichment with programs designed to encourage integration of substantial numbers of Negroes into the society outside the ghetto."

But—even with the best of will—what a monumental prescription this is. In 1910, 91 percent of American Negroes lived in the old South; by 1966, while the Negro population had doubled to 21.5 million, the number living in metropolitan areas had risen to 14.6 million and the number living outside the South had increased *elevenfold* to 9.7 million. That is what created the black ghetto but by now natural increase has replaced migration as the major cause of Negro population growth in the cities—and almost all Negro population growth *is* taking place in the cities.

In combination with an almost equally rapid white exodus from the cities, these statistics mean that one-third of American Negroes live in our 12 largest cities (two-thirds of non-Southern Negroes).

Obviously, this is not a situation that can be reversed or even substantially changed in a short period of time; one has only to contemplate the controversies over bussing students from the ghetto to white neighborhoods, and vice versa, and the not infrequent white violence that results when a Negro moves into white man's country.

While the slow process of dispersing the residents of the ghetto—which, for all practical purposes, has not even been started—goes on, therefore, something also is going to have to be done about the grinding life of the urban poor—a life documented by this Report in terms both harsh and heartbreaking. Because the brutal fact is that for millions of Negroes now living, and perhaps for some unborn, the ghetto is all they are ever going to know.

What the Commission recommends—from specifics on jobs, housing, schools, police procedures, newspaper practices, to large abstractions like community attitudes—is best told in the Commission's own words, backed by its own accounts of its findings. But it is again of the highest importance that these recommendations come from the moderate Establishment.

That is because, whatever the fate of its specific proposals, the Commission has minced no words about the prime necessity:

"Only a commitment to national action on an unprecedented scale can shape a future compatible with the historic ideals of American society . . . The major need is to generate new will—the will to tax ourselves to the extent necessary to meet the vital needs of the nation."

That kind of recommendation gets little attention when it comes from "liberals" and "radicals" and "intellectual bleeding hearts"; but when it comes from men like Thornton and McCulloch and Abel and Jenkins, it is not easy to doubt the urgency of the case, the shock of the findings, the truth of the need.

And still—this report can only provide, as its profoundly disturbed authors concede, "an honest beginning" on a task that beggars any other planned social evolution known to human history.

It can only be a beginning because, patently, until the fact of white racism is admitted, it cannot conceivably be expunged; and until it is far more nearly eliminated than this Commission—or any fair man—could find today, how can that great commitment of money and effort here recommended even be approached, much less made?

And in the vicious circle in which the nation is so nearly trapped, how can the conditions of life in the ghetto be improved to the point—not merely of preventing violence—where its present and prospective victims can have the kind of education, housing, income and social experience that, practically speaking, are the prerequisites of equality? Only by the great commitment that—even if there were no war in Vietnam, no gold drain, no Federal budgetary crisis—seems now so remote.

But a journey of a thousand miles, President Kennedy used to say, must begin with a single step. And perhaps that step has been taken in this Report—this indictment.

It is, at the least, an extraordinary document. We are not likely to get a better view of socially directed violence—what underlies it, what sets it off, how it runs its course, what follows. There are novels here, hidden in the Commission's understated prose; there are a thousand doctoral theses germinating in its statistics, its interviews, its anecdotes and "profiles."

Myths, naturally, are exploded. There was not, after all, much evidence of Negro snipers in the 1967 rioting; most of the shooting came from scared guardsmen and policemen and some of it was only fireworks. Nor was there—as President

Johnson was inclined to believe when he appointed the Commission—an organized conspiracy. The Commission staff even ran Stokely Carmichael's comings and goings through a computer in its effort to find conspiratorial traces; in the end, the staff found lots of "incitement"—mostly oratorical—and no conspiracy.

The report also disposes of white middle-class insistence that if immigrants from Europe could rise from the ghetto, so could today's Negroes. As that cliché is analyzed here, the unskilled labor the black immigrant from the cotton fields can offer is in nothing like the demand that once there was for the unskilled labor of the arriving Italian, Irishman or eastern European. Moreover, the power of the urban political machine has declined for many reasons, and today's ghetto resident can exert less organized political pressure than could yesterday's.

Above all, the ghetto today is black. Since white society is far more prejudiced against black men than against mere foreigners, jobs and social acceptance are harder for them to get. Thus, precisely because today's black immigrant has less chance to "get ahead" than his white predecessor, he also has less incentive to do so.

As for the rioters—those ominous looters and arsonists whose eruption into violence precipitated this massive study—they tended, curiously, to be somewhat more educated than the "brothers" who remained uninvolved. By and large, the rioters were young Negroes, natives of the ghetto (not of the South), hostile to the white society surrounding and repressing them, and equally hostile to the middle-class Negroes who accommodated themselves to that white dominance. The rioters were mistrustful of white politics, they hated the police, they were proud of their race, and acutely conscious of the discrimination they suffered. They were and they are a time-bomb ticking in the heart of the richest nation in the history of the world.

But more than that, the rioters are the personification of that nation's shame, of its deepest failure, of its greatest challenge. They will not go away. They can only be repressed or conceded their humanity, and the choice is not theirs to make. They can only force it upon the rest of us, and what this Report insists upon is that they are already doing it, and intend to keep on.

Thus, there is not really in these pages a rebuke to any president, any administration, any political party, any state or group of states. There is no finger pointed in scorn. Save for a tacit insistence upon the enormous role the Federal government, of necessity, must have in raising and spending the sums required, there is no preference for any political philosophy.

The Commission's members insist that they had no guidance from the White House, and suffered no restrictions by it. They went out and saw for themselves; they heard the voices of the ghetto; in a basement in Cincinnati, Fred Harris and John Lindsay were spat upon. Through 24 full days of executive session, most of them from nine in the morning until ten at night, they worked on this document.

In the end, not without dispute and travail and misgiving, in the clash and spark of human conflict and human pride, against the pressures of time and ignorance, they produced not so much a report on the riots as a report on America—one nation, divided.

Reading it is an ugly experience but one that brings, finally, something like the relief of beginning. What had to be said has been said at last, and by representatives of that white, moderate, responsible America that, alone, needed to say it.

March 1, 1968

Foreword

This report of The National Advisory Commission on Civil Disorders responds to Executive Order 11365 issued by President Lyndon B. Johnson on July 29, 1967, and to the personal charge given to us by the President.

"Let your search," he said, "be free . . . As best you can, find the truth and express it in your report."

We have sought to do so.

"This matter," he said, "is far, far too important for politics."

This was a bipartisan Commission and a nonpartisan effort.

"Only you," he said, "can do this job. Only if you . . . put your shoulders to the wheel can America hope for the kind of report it needs and will take to its heart."

This has been a working Commission.

To our staff, headed by David Ginsburg, Executive Director, to his deputy, Victor H. Palmieri, and to all those in government and private life who helped us, we are grateful.

/s/ Otto Kerner
Chairman

/s/ John V. Lindsay
Vice Chairman

/s/ Fred R. Harris
/s/ James C. Corman
/s/ I. W. Abel
/s/ Roy Wilkins

/s/ Edward W. Brooke
/s/ William M. McCulloch
/s/ Charles B. Thornton
/s/ Katherine G. Peden

/s/ Herbert Jenkins

THE NATIONAL ADVISORY COMMISSION ON CIVIL DISORDERS

Chairman
Otto Kerner
Governor of Illinois

Vice Chairman
John V. Lindsay
Mayor of New York City

PROFESSIONAL STAFF

Executive Director
David Ginsburg
   David L. Chambers,
      Spec. Asst.

Deputy Executive Director
Victor H. Palmieri
   John A. Koskinen, Spec. Asst.

Deputy Director for Operations
Stephen Kurzman
   Lee A. Satterfield, Spec. Asst.

General Counsel
Merle M. McCurdy
   Nathaniel Jones,
      Asst. Gen. Counsel
   David E. Birenbaum,
      Asst. Gen. Counsel
   Roger L. Waldman,
      Asst. Gen. Counsel

Assistant Deputy Director—Research
Robert Shellow, Ph.D.

Associate Director for Public Safety
Arnold Sagalyn
   Paul G. Bower, Asst. Dir.

Associate Director for Program Research
Richard P. Nathan, Ph.D.,

Director of Investigations
Milan C. Miskovsky
   Stanley P. Hebert, Deputy

Director of Program Operations
Charles E. Nelson
   Herman Wilson, Deputy
   George Trask, Spec. Asst.

Director of Congressional Relations
Henry B. Taliaferro, Jr.

Director of Information
Alvin A. Spivak
   Lawrence A. Still, Deputy

Director of Research Services
Melvin L. Bergheim

Special Consultants
Robert Conot
Jacob Rosenthal

Executive Officer
Norman J. McKenzie

* * *

James D. Arthur
*Dennis E. Barrett
Patricia Bennett
Leslie Berkowitz
Eric D. Blanchard
David Boesel
*John I. Boswell
Harry M. Bratt
Louis B. Brickman
Anna Byus
Sarah Carey
Esther Carter
Theodore Chamberlain
John M. Christman
Martin J. Connell
Florence F. Conot
Bernard Dobranski
Walter Dukes, Jr.

Harvey Friedman
Geraldine L. Furth
Barbara Garcia-Dobles
Lucy Gilbert
Mildred Glasgow
Louis Goldberg
Melvin Goldstein
Luis Guinot
Harold H. Hair
William H. Hayden
William R. Hill, Jr.
Richard B. Holcomb
Andrew B. Horgan
*Isaac Hunt
Wilbur H. Jenkins
Anthony L. Jones
Hannah J. Kaiser
Robert G. Kelly

Charles E. King
Jane Korff
Karen Krueger
Carl B. Liebman
Eleanor J. McGee
Phyllis K. Mensh
Robert Moss
Barbara P. Newman
Constance Newman
Lloyd Oliver
William Oxley
Jane Pasachoff
Daniel Pearlman
Haywood L. Perry
Diane Phillips
*Thomas Popp
James Porter
John Pride

James Raschard
Norbert C. Rayford
Eleanor Robbins
Salvador A. Romero
Allen Ross
Louise Sagalyn
John K. Scales
Suzanne Schilling
Arlene Shadoan
*Francis Sharp
*Ira T. Simmons
Shedd H. Smith
*Bruce R. Thomas
John Ursu
Leona Vogt
Steven Waldhorn
Everett Waldo
*B. J. Warren

*Field Team Leaders

*Special Assistants to
Commissioners*

William L. Cowin
Kyran McGrath
William A. Smith
Donald W. Webb
Stephen S. Weiner

Personal Assistants

Doris Claxton:
    Executive Director
Vivian A. Bullock:
    Deputy Executive Director
Claudette Johnson:
    The Commission

Student Assistants

Rene Berblinger
Gerold F. Berger
John Davis
Jesse Epstein
Oliver Holmes
Merry Hudson
Elizabeth Jamison
Richard Lane
Norris D. Wolff

. . . . The only genuine, long-range solution for what has happened lies in an attack—mounted at every level—upon the conditions that breed despair and violence. All of us know what those conditions are: ignorance, discrimination, slums, poverty, disease, not enough jobs. We should attack these conditions—not because we are frightened by conflict, but because we are fired by conscience. We should attack them because there is simply no other way to achieve a decent and orderly society in America. . . .

Lyndon Baines Johnson
Address to the Nation
July 27, 1967

REPORT OF THE
NATIONAL ADVISORY
COMMISSION
ON CIVIL
DISORDERS

SUMMARY

INTRODUCTION

The summer of 1967 again brought racial disorders to American cities, and with them shock, fear and bewilderment to the nation.

The worst came during a two-week period in July, first in Newark and then in Detroit. Each set off a chain reaction in neighboring communities.

On July 28, 1967, the President of the United States established this Commission and directed us to answer three basic questions:

What happened?

Why did it happen?

What can be done to prevent it from happening again?

To respond to these questions, we have undertaken a broad range of studies and investigations. We have visited the riot cities; we have heard many witnesses; we have sought the counsel of experts across the country.

This is our basic conclusion: Our nation is moving toward two societies, one black, one white—separate and unequal.

Reaction to last summer's disorders has quickened the movement and deepened the division. Discrimination and segregation have long permeated much of American life; they now threaten the future of every American.

This deepening racial division is not inevitable. The movement apart can be reversed. Choice is still possible. Our principal task is to define that choice and to press for a national resolution.

To pursue our present course will involve the continuing polarization of the American community and, ultimately, the destruction of basic democratic values.

The alternative is not blind repression or capitulation to lawlessness. It is the realization of common opportunities for all within a single society.

This alternative will require a commitment to national

action—compassionate, massive and sustained, backed by the resources of the most powerful and the richest nation on this earth. From every American it will require new attitudes, new understanding, and, above all, new will.

The vital needs of the nation must be met; hard choices must be made, and, if necessary, new taxes enacted.

Violence cannot build a better society. Disruption and disorder nourish repression, not justice. They strike at the freedom of every citizen. The community cannot—it will not—tolerate coercion and mob rule.

Violence and destruction must be ended—in the streets of the ghetto and in the lives of people.

Segregation and poverty have created in the racial ghetto a destructive environment totally unknown to most white Americans.

What white Americans have never fully understood—but what the Negro can never forget—is that white society is deeply implicated in the ghetto. White institutions created it, white institutions maintain it, and white society condones it.

It is time now to turn with all the purpose at our command to the major unfinished business of this nation. It is time to adopt strategies for action that will produce quick and visible progress. It is time to make good the promises of American democracy to all citizens—urban and rural, white and black, Spanish-surname, American Indian, and every minority group.

Our recommendations embrace three basic principles:

- To mount programs on a scale equal to the dimension of the problems;
- To aim these programs for high impact in the immediate future in order to close the gap between promise and performance;
- To undertake new initiatives and experiments that can change the system of failure and frustration that now dominates the ghetto and weakens our society.

These programs will require unprecedented levels of funding and performance, but they neither probe deeper nor demand more than the problems which called them forth. There can be no higher priority for national action and no higher claim on the nation's conscience.

We issue this Report now, five months before the date called for by the President. Much remains that can be learned. Continued study is essential.

As Commissioners we have worked together with a sense of the greatest urgency and have sought to compose whatever differences exist among us. Some differences remain. But the gravity of the problem and the pressing need for action are too clear to allow further delay in the issuance of this Report.

2

PART I—WHAT HAPPENED?

Chapter 1—Profiles of Disorder

The report contains profiles of a selection of the disorders that took place during the summer of 1967. These profiles are designed to indicate how the disorders happened, who participated in them, and how local officials, police forces, and the National Guard responded. Illustrative excerpts follow:

NEWARK

. . . It was decided to attempt to channel the energies of the people into a nonviolent protest. While Lofton promised the crowd that a full investigation would be made of the Smith incident, the other Negro leaders began urging those on the scene to form a line of march toward the city hall.

Some persons joined the line of march. Others milled about in the narrow street. From the dark grounds of the housing project came a barrage of rocks. Some of them fell among the crowd. Others hit persons in the line of march. Many smashed the windows of the police station. The rock throwing, it was believed, was the work of youngsters; approximately 2,500 children lived in the housing project.

Almost at the same time, an old car was set afire in a parking lot. The line of march began to disintegrate. The police, their heads protected by World War I-type helmets, sallied forth to disperse the crowd. A fire engine, arriving on the scene, was pelted with rocks. As police drove people away from the station, they scattered in all directions.

A few minutes later a nearby liquor store was broken into. Some persons, seeing a caravan of cabs appear at city hall to protest Smith's arrest, interpreted this as evidence that the disturbance had been organized, and generated rumors to that effect.

However, only a few stores were looted. Within a short period of time, the disorder appeared to have run its course.

* * *

. . . On Saturday, July 15, [Director of Police Dominick] Spina received a report of snipers in a housing project. When he arrived he saw approximately 100 National Guardsmen and police officers crouching behind vehicles, hiding in corners and lying on the ground around the edge of the courtyard.

Since everything appeared quiet and it was broad daylight, Spina walked directly down the middle of the street. Nothing happened. As he came to the last building of the complex, he heard a shot. All around him the troopers jumped, believing themselves to be under sniper fire. A moment later a young Guardsman ran from behind a building.

The Director of Police went over and asked him if he had fired the shot. The soldier said yes, he had fired to scare a man away from a window; that his orders were to keep everyone away from windows.

3

Spina said he told the soldier: "Do you know what you just did? You have now created a state of hysteria. Every Guardsman up and down this street and every state policeman and every city policeman that is present thinks that somebody just fired a shot and that it is probably a sniper."

A short time later more "gunshots" were heard. Investigating, Spina came upon a Puerto Rican sitting on a wall. In reply to a question as to whether he knew "where the firing is coming from?" the man said:

"That's no firing. That's fireworks. If you look up to the fourth floor, you will see the people who are throwing down these cherry bombs."

By this time four truckloads of National Guardsmen had arrived and troopers and policemen were again crouched everywhere looking for a sniper. The Director of Police remained at the scene for three hours, and the only shot fired was the one by the Guardsman.

Nevertheless, at six o'clock that evening two columns of National Guardsmen and state troopers were directing mass fire at the Hayes Housing Project in response to what they believed were snipers. . . .

DETROIT

. . . A spirit of carefree nihilism was taking hold. To riot and destroy appeared more and more to become ends in themselves. Late Sunday afternoon it appeared to one observer that the young people were "dancing amidst the flames."

A Negro plainclothes officer was standing at an intersection when a man threw a Molotov cocktail into a business establishment at the corner. In the heat of the afternoon, fanned by the 20 to 25 m.p.h. winds of both Sunday and Monday, the fire reached the home next door within minutes. As residents uselessly sprayed the flames with garden hoses, the fire jumped from roof to roof of adjacent two- and three-story buildings. Within the hour the entire block was in flames. The ninth house in the burning row belonged to the arsonist who had thrown the Molotov cocktail. . . .

*　　*　　*

. . . Employed as a private guard, 55-year-old Julius L. Dorsey, a Negro, was standing in front of a market when accosted by two Negro men and a woman. They demanded he permit them to loot the market. He ignored their demands. They began to berate him. He asked a neighbor to call the police. As the argument grew more heated, Dorsey fired three shots from his pistol into the air.

The police radio reported: "Looters, they have rifles." A patrol car driven by a police officer and carrying three National Guardsmen arrived. As the looters fled, the law enforcement personnel opened fire. When the firing ceased, one person lay dead.

He was Julius L. Dorsey . . .

*　　*　　*

. . . As the riot alternately waxed and waned, one area of the ghetto remained insulated. On the northeast side the residents of some 150 square blocks inhabited by 21,000 persons had, in 1966, banded together in the Positive Neighborhood Action Com-

4

mittee (PNAC). With professional help from the Institute of Urban Dynamics, they had organized block clubs and made plans for the improvement of the neighborhood. . . .

When the riot broke out, the residents, through the block clubs, were able to organize quickly. Youngsters, agreeing to stay in the neighborhood, participated in detouring traffic. While many persons reportedly sympathized with the idea of a rebellion against the "system," only two small fires were set—one in an empty building.

* * *

. . . According to Lt. Gen. Throckmorton and Col. Bolling, the city, at this time, was saturated with fear. The National Guardsmen were afraid, the citizens were afraid, and the police were afraid. Numerous persons, the majority of them Negroes, were being injured by gunshots of undetermined origin. The general and his staff felt that the major task of the troops was to reduce the fear and restore an air of normalcy.

In order to accomplish this, every effort was made to establish contact and rapport between the troops and the residents. The soldiers—20 percent of whom were Negro—began helping to clean up the streets, collect garbage, and trace persons who had disappeared in the confusion. Residents in the neighborhoods responded with soup and sandwiches for the troops. In areas where the National Guard tried to establish rapport with the citizens, there was a similar response.

NEW BRUNSWICK

. . . A short time later, elements of the crowd—an older and rougher one than the night before—appeared in front of the police station. The participants wanted to see the mayor.

Mayor [Patricia] Sheehan went out onto the steps of the station. Using a bullhorn, she talked to the people and asked that she be given an opportunity to correct conditions. The crowd was boisterous. Some persons challenged the mayor. But, finally, the opinion, "She's new! Give her a chance!" prevailed.

A demand was issued by people in the crowd that all persons arrested the previous night be released. Told that this already had been done, the people were suspicious. They asked to be allowed to inspect the jail cells.

It was agreed to permit representatives of the people to look in the cells to satisfy themselves that everyone had been released.

The crowd dispersed. The New Brunswick riot had failed to materialize.

Chapter 2—Patterns of Disorder

The "typical" riot did not take place. The disorders of 1967 were unusual, irregular, complex and unpredictable social processes. Like most human events, they did not unfold in an orderly sequence. However, an analysis of our survey information leads to some conclusions about the riot process.

In general:

- The civil disorders of 1967 involved Negroes acting against local symbols of white American society, authority and property in Negro neighborhoods—rather than against white persons.
- Of 164 disorders reported during the first nine months of 1967, eight (5 percent) were major in terms of violence and damage; 33 (20 percent) were serious but not major; 123 (75 percent) were minor and undoubtedly would not have received national attention as riots had the nation not been sensitized by the more serious outbreaks.
- In the 75 disorders studied by a Senate subcommittee, 83 deaths were reported. Eighty-two percent of the deaths and more than half the injuries occurred in Newark and Detroit. About 10 percent of the dead and 38 percent of the injured were public employees, primarily law officers and firemen. The overwhelming majority of the persons killed or injured in all the disorders were Negro civilians.
- Initial damage estimates were greatly exaggerated. In Detroit, newspaper damage estimates at first ranged from $200 million to $500 million; the highest recent estimate is $45 million. In Newark, early estimates ranged from $15 to $25 million. A month later damage was estimated at $10.2 million, 80 percent in inventory losses.

In the 24 disorders in 23 cities which we surveyed:

- The final incident before the outbreak of disorder, and the initial violence itself, generally took place in the evening or at night at a place in which it was normal for many people to be on the streets.
- Violence usually occurred almost immediately following the occurrence of the final precipitating incident, and then escalated rapidly. With but few exceptions, violence subsided during the day, and flared rapidly again at night. The night-day cycles continued through the early period of the major disorders.
- Disorder generally began with rock and bottle throwing and window breaking. Once store windows were broken, looting usually followed.
- Disorder did not erupt as a result of a single "triggering" or "precipitating" incident. Instead, it was generated out of an increasingly disturbed social atmosphere, in which typically a series of tension-heightening incidents over a period of weeks or months became linked in the minds of many in the Negro community with a reservoir of underlying grievances. At some point in the mounting tension, a further incident—in itself often routine or trivial—became the breaking point and the tension spilled over into violence.
- "Prior" incidents, which increased tensions and ultimately led to violence, were police actions in almost half the cases; police actions were "final" incidents before the outbreak of violence in 12 of the 24 surveyed disorders.
- No particular control tactic was successful in every situation. The varied effectiveness of control techniques emphasizes the need for advance training, planning, adequate intelligence systems, and knowledge of the ghetto community.

- Negotiations between Negroes—including young militants as well as older Negro leaders—and white officials concerning "terms of peace" occurred during virtually all the disorders surveyed. In many cases, these negotiations involved discussion of underlying grievances as well as the handling of the disorder by control authorities.
- The typical rioter was a teenager or young adult, a lifelong resident of the city in which he rioted, a high school dropout; he was, nevertheless, somewhat better educated than his nonrioting Negro neighbor, and was usually underemployed or employed in a menial job. He was proud of his race, extremely hostile to both whites and middle-class Negroes and, although informed about politics, highly distrustful of the political system.

A Detroit survey revealed that approximately 11 percent of the total residents of two riot areas admitted participation in the rioting, 20 to 25 percent identified themselves as "bystanders," over 16 percent identified themselves as "counter-rioters" who urged rioters to "cool it," and the remaining 48 to 53 percent said they were at home or elsewhere and did not participate. In a survey of Negro males between the ages of 15 and 35 residing in the disturbance area in Newark, about 45 percent identified themselves as rioters, and about 55 percent as "noninvolved."

- Most rioters were young Negro males. Nearly 53 percent of arrestees were between 15 and 24 years of age; nearly 81 percent between 15 and 35.
- In Detroit and Newark about 74 percent of the rioters were brought up in the North. In contrast, of the noninvolved, 36 percent in Detroit and 52 percent in Newark were brought up in the North.
- What the rioters appeared to be seeking was fuller participation in the social order and the material benefits enjoyed by the majority of American citizens. Rather than rejecting the American system, they were anxious to obtain a place for themselves in it.
- Numerous Negro counter-rioters walked the streets urging rioters to "cool it." The typical counter-rioter was better educated and had higher income than either the rioter or the noninvolved.
- The proportion of Negroes in local government was substantially smaller than the Negro proportion of population. Only three of the 20 cities studied had more than one Negro legislator; none had ever had a Negro mayor or city manager. In only four cities did Negroes hold other important policy-making positions or serve as heads of municipal departments.
- Although almost all cities had some sort of formal grievance mechanism for handling citizen complaints, this typically was regarded by Negroes as ineffective and was generally ignored.
- Although specific grievances varied from city to city, at least 12 deeply held grievances can be identified and ranked into three levels of relative intensity:

First Level of Intensity

1. Police practices
2. Unemployment and underemployment
3. Inadequate housing

Second Level of Intensity

4. Inadequate education
5. Poor recreation facilities and programs
6. Ineffectiveness of the political structure and grievance mechanisms

Third Level of Intensity

7. Disrespectful white attitudes
8. Discriminatory administration of justice
9. Inadequacy of federal programs
10. Inadequacy of municipal services
11. Discriminatory consumer and credit practices
12. Inadequate welfare programs

• The results of a three-city survey of various federal programs—manpower, education, housing, welfare and community action—indicate that, despite substantial expenditures, the number of persons assisted constituted only a fraction of those in need.

The background of disorder is often as complex and difficult to analyze as the disorder itself. But we find that certain general conclusions can be drawn:

• Social and economic conditions in the riot cities constituted a clear pattern of severe disadvantage for Negroes compared with whites, whether the Negroes lived in the area where the riot took place or outside it. Negroes had completed fewer years of education and fewer had attended high school. Negroes were twice as likely to be unemployed and three times as likely to be in unskilled and service jobs. Negroes averaged 70 percent of the income earned by whites and were more than twice as likely to be living in poverty. Although housing cost Negroes relatively more, they had worse housing—three times as likely to be overcrowded and substandard. When compared to white suburbs, the relative disadvantage is even more pronounced.

A study of the aftermath of disorder leads to disturbing conclusions. We find that, despite the institution of some post-riot programs:

• Little basic change in the conditions underlying the outbreak of disorder has taken place. Actions to ameliorate Negro grievances have been limited and sporadic; with but few exceptions, they have not significantly reduced tensions.
• In several cities, the principal official response has been to train and equip the police with more sophisticated weapons.
• In several cities, increasing polarization is evident, with continuing breakdown of inter-racial communication, and growth of white segregationist or black separatist groups.

8

The President directed the Commission to investigate "to what extent, if any, there has been planning or organization in any of the riots."

To carry out this part of the President's charge, the Commission established a special investigative staff supplementing the field teams that made the general examination of the riots in 23 cities. The unit examined data collected by federal agencies and congressional committees, including thousands of documents supplied by the Federal Bureau of Investigation, gathered and evaluated information from local and state law enforcement agencies and officials, and conducted its own field investigation in selected cities.

On the basis of all the information collected, the Commission concludes that:

> The urban disorders of the summer of 1967 were not caused by, nor were they the consequence of, any organized plan or "conspiracy."

Specifically, the Commission has found no evidence that all or any of the disorders or the incidents that led to them were planned or directed by any organization or group, international, national or local.

Militant organizations, local and national, and individual agitators, who repeatedly forecast and called for violence, were active in the spring and summer of 1967. We believe that they sought to encourage violence, and that they helped to create an atmosphere that contributed to the outbreak of disorder.

We recognize that the continuation of disorders and the polarization of the races would provide fertile ground for organized exploitation in the future.

Investigations of organized activity are continuing at all levels of government, including committees of Congress. These investigations relate not only to the disorders of 1967 but also to the actions of groups and individuals, particularly in schools and colleges, during this last fall and winter. The Commission has cooperated in these investigations. They should continue.

PART II—WHY DID IT HAPPEN?

Chapter 4—The Basic Causes

In addressing the question "Why did it happen?" we shift our focus from the local to the national scene, from the particular events of the summer of 1967 to the factors within the society at large that created a mood of violence among many urban Negroes.

These factors are complex and interacting; they vary significantly in their effect from city to city and from year to year; and the consequences of one disorder, generating new grievances and new demands, become the causes of the next. Thus was created the "thicket of tension, conflicting evidence and extreme opinions" cited by the President.

Despite these complexities, certain fundamental matters are clear. Of these, the most fundamental is the racial attitude and behavior of white Americans toward black Americans.

Race prejudice has shaped our history decisively; it now threatens to affect our future.

White racism is essentially responsible for the explosive mixture which has been accumulating in our cities since the end of World War II. Among the ingredients of this mixture are:

- *Pervasive discrimination and segregation* in employment, education and housing, which have resulted in the continuing exclusion of great numbers of Negroes from the benefits of economic progress.
- *Black in-migration and white exodus,* which have produced the massive and growing concentrations of impoverished Negroes in our major cities, creating a growing crisis of deteriorating facilities and services and unmet human needs.
- *The black ghettos* where segregation and poverty converge on the young to destroy opportunity and enforce failure. Crime, drug addiction, dependency on welfare, and bitterness and resentment against society in general and white society in particular are the result.

At the same time, most whites and some Negroes outside the ghetto have prospered to a degree unparalleled in the history of civilization. Through television and other media, this affluence has been flaunted before the eyes of the Negro poor and the jobless ghetto youth.

Yet these facts alone cannot be said to have caused the disorders. Recently, other powerful ingredients have begun to catalyze the mixture:

- *Frustrated hopes* are the residue of the unfulfilled expectations aroused by the great judicial and legislative victories of the Civil Rights Movement and the dramatic struggle for equal rights in the South.
- *A climate that tends toward approval and encouragement of violence* as a form of protest has been created by white terrorism directed against nonviolent protest; by the open defiance of law and federal authority by state and local officials resisting desegre-

gation; and by some protest groups engaging in civil disobedience who turn their backs on nonviolence, go beyond the constitutionally protected rights of petition and free assembly, and resort to violence to attempt to compel alteration of laws and policies with which they disagree.

● *The frustrations of powerlessness* have led some Negroes to the conviction that there is no effective alternative to violence as a means of achieving redress of grievances, and of "moving the system." These frustrations are reflected in alienation and hostility toward the institutions of law and government and the white society which controls them, and in the reach toward racial consciousness and solidarity reflected in the slogan "Black Power."

● *A new mood* has sprung up among Negroes, particularly among the young, in which self-esteem and enhanced racial pride are replacing apathy and submission to "the system."

● *The police are not merely a "spark" factor.* To some Negroes police have come to symbolize white power, white racism and white repression. And the fact is that many police do reflect and express these white attitudes. The atmosphere of hostility and cynicism is reinforced by a widespread belief among Negroes in the existence of police brutality and in a "double standard" of justice and protection—one for Negroes and one for whites.

*   *   *

To this point, we have attempted to identify the prime components of the "explosive mixture." In the chapters that follow we seek to analyze them in the perspective of history. Their meaning, however, is clear:

In the summer of 1967, we have seen in our cities a chain reaction of racial violence. If we are heedless, none of us shall escape the consequences.

Chapter 5—Rejection and Protest: An Historical Sketch

The causes of recent racial disorders are embedded in a tangle of issues and circumstances—social, economic, political and psychological—which arise out of the historic pattern of Negro-white relations in America.

In this chapter we trace the pattern, identify the recurrent themes of Negro protest and, most importantly, provide a perspective on the protest activities of the present era.

We describe the Negro's experience in America and the development of slavery as an institution. We show his persistent striving for equality in the face of rigidly maintained social, economic and educational barriers, and repeated mob violence. We portray the ebb and flow of the doctrinal tides— accommodation, separatism, and self-help—and their relationship to the current theme of Black Power. We conclude:

The Black Power advocates of today consciously feel that they are the most militant group in the Negro protest movement. Yet they have retreated from a direct confrontation with American society on the issue of integration and, by preaching separatism, unconsciously function as an accommodation to white racism. Much of their economic program, as well as their interest in Negro history, self-help, racial solidarity and separation, is reminiscent of Booker T. Washington. The rhetoric is different, but the ideas are remarkably similar.

Chapter 6—The Formation Of the Racial Ghettos[1]

Throughout the 20th century the Negro population of the United States has been moving steadily from rural areas to urban and from South to North and West. In 1910, 91 percent of the nation's 9.8 million Negroes lived in the South and only 27 percent of American Negroes lived in cities of 2,500 persons or more. Between 1910 and 1966 the total Negro population more than doubled, reaching 21.5 million, and the number living in metropolitan areas rose more than fivefold (from 2.6 million to 14.8 million). The number outside the South rose eleven-fold (from 880,000 to 9.7 million).

Negro migration from the South has resulted from the expectation of thousands of new and highly paid jobs for unskilled workers in the North and the shift to mechanized farming in the South. However, the Negro migration is small when compared to earlier waves of European immigrants. Even between 1960 and 1966, there were 1.8 million immigrants from abroad compared to the 613,000 Negroes who arrived in the North and West from the South.

As a result of the growing number of Negroes in urban areas, natural increase has replaced migration as the primary source of Negro population increase in the cities. Nevertheless, Negro migration from the South will continue unless economic conditions there change dramatically.

Basic data concerning Negro urbanization trends indicate that:

• Almost all Negro population growth (98 percent from 1950 to 1966) is occurring within metropolitan areas, primarily within central cities.[2]
• The vast majority of white population growth (78 percent from 1960 to 1966) is occurring in suburban portions of metropolitan areas. Since 1960, white central-city population has declined by 1.3 million.

[1] The term "ghetto" as used in this report refers to an area within a city characterized by poverty and acute social disorganization, and inhabited by members of a racial or ethnic group under conditions of involuntary segregation.

[2] A "central city" is the largest city of a standard metropolitan statistical area, that is, a metropolitan area containing at least one city of 50,000 or more inhabitants.

- As a result, central cities are becoming more heavily Negro while the suburban fringes around them remain almost entirely white.
- The twelve largest central cities now contain over two-thirds of the Negro population outside the South, and one-third of the Negro total in the United States.

Within the cities, Negroes have been excluded from white residential areas through discriminatory practices. Just as significant is the withdrawal of white families from, or their refusal to enter, neighborhoods where Negroes are moving or already residing. About 20 percent of the urban population of the United States changes residence every year. The refusal of whites to move into "changing" areas when vacancies occur means that most vacancies eventually are occupied by Negroes.

The result, according to a recent study, is that in 1960 the average segregation index for 207 of the largest United States cities was 86.2. In other words, to create an unsegregated population distribution, an average of over 86 percent of all Negroes would have to change their place of residence within the city.

Chapter 7—Unemployment, Family Structure, and Social Disorganization

Although there have been gains in Negro income nationally, and a decline in the number of Negroes below the "poverty level," the condition of Negroes in the central city remains in a state of crisis. Between 2 and 2.5 million Negroes—16 to 20 percent of the total Negro population of all central cities— live in squalor and deprivation in ghetto neighborhoods.

Employment is a key problem. It not only controls the present for the Negro American but, in a most profound way, it is creating the future as well. Yet, despite continuing economic growth and declining national unemployment rates, the unemployment rate for Negroes in 1967 was more than double that for whites.

Equally important is the undesirable nature of many jobs open to Negroes and other minorities. Negro men are more than three times as likely as white men to be in low-paying, unskilled or service jobs. This concentration of male Negro employment at the lowest end of the occupational scale is the single most important cause of poverty among Negroes.

In one study of low-income neighborhoods, the "subemployment rate," including both unemployment and underemployment, was about 33 percent, or 8.8 times greater than the overall unemployment rate for all United States workers.

Employment problems, aggravated by the constant arrival of new unemployed migrants, many of them from depressed

13

rural areas, create persistent poverty in the ghetto. In 1966, about 11.9 percent of the nation's whites and 40.6 percent of its nonwhites were below the "poverty level" defined by the Social Security Administration (in 1966, $3,335 per year for an urban family of four). Over 40 percent of the nonwhites below the poverty level live in the central cities.

Employment problems have drastic social impact in the ghetto. Men who are chronically unemployed or employed in the lowest status jobs are often unable or unwilling to remain with their families. The handicap imposed on children growing up without fathers in an atmosphere of poverty and deprivation is increased as mothers are forced to work to provide support.

The culture of poverty that results from unemployment and family breakup generates a system of ruthless, exploitative relationships within the ghetto. Prostitution, dope addiction, and crime create an environmental "jungle" characterized by personal insecurity and tension. Children growing up under such conditions are likely participants in civil disorder.

Chapter 8—Conditions of Life In the Racial Ghetto

A striking difference in environment from that of white, middle-class Americans profoundly influences the lives of residents of the ghetto.

Crime rates, consistently higher than in other areas, create a pronounced sense of insecurity. For example, in one city one low-income Negro district had 35 times as many serious crimes against persons as a high-income white district. Unless drastic steps are taken, the crime problems in poverty areas are likely to continue to multiply as the growing youth and rapid urbanization of the population outstrip police resources.

Poor health and sanitation conditions in the ghetto result in higher mortality rates, a higher incidence of major diseases, and lower availability and utilization of medical services. The infant mortality rate for nonwhite babies under the age of one month is 58 percent higher than for whites; for one to 12 months it is almost three times as high. The level of sanitation in the ghetto is far below that in high income areas. Garbage collection is often inadequate. Of an estimated 14,000 cases of rat bite in the United States in 1965, most were in ghetto neighborhoods.

Ghetto residents believe they are exploited by local merchants; and evidence substantiates some of these beliefs. A study conducted in one city by the Federal Trade Commission showed that higher prices were charged for goods sold in ghetto stores than in other areas.

Lack of knowledge regarding credit purchasing creates special pitfalls for the disadvantaged. In many states garnishment practices compound these difficulties by allowing creditors to deprive individuals of their wages without hearing or trial.

Chapter 9—Comparing the Immigrant and Negro Experience

In this chapter, we address ourselves to a fundamental question that many white Americans are asking: why have so many Negroes, unlike the European immigrants, been unable to escape from the ghetto and from poverty. We believe the following factors play a part:

- *The Maturing Economy:* When the European immigrants arrived, they gained an economic foothold by providing the unskilled labor needed by industry. Unlike the immigrant, the Negro migrant found little opportunity in the city. The economy, by then matured, had little use for the unskilled labor he had to offer.
- *The Disability of Race:* The structure of discrimination has stringently narrowed opportunities for the Negro and restricted his prospects. European immigrants suffered from discrimination, but never so pervasively.
- *Entry into the Political System:* The immigrants usually settled in rapidly growing cities with powerful and expanding political machines, which traded economic advantages for political support. Ward-level grievance machinery, as well as personal representation, enabled the immigrant to make his voice heard and his power felt.

  By the time the Negro arrived, these political machines were no longer so powerful or so well equipped to provide jobs or other favors, and in many cases were unwilling to share their influence with Negroes.
- *Cultural Factors:* Coming from societies with a low standard of living and at a time when job aspirations were low, the immigrants sensed little deprivation in being forced to take the less desirable and poorer-paying jobs. Their large and cohesive families contributed to total income. Their vision of the future—one that led to a life outside of the ghetto—provided the incentive necessary to endure the present.

  Although Negro men worked as hard as the immigrants, they were unable to support their families. The entrepreneurial opportunities had vanished. As a result of slavery and long periods of unemployment, the Negro family structure had become matriarchal; the males played a secondary and marginal family role —one which offered little compensation for their hard and unrewarding labor. Above all, segregation denied Negroes access to good jobs and the opportunity to leave the ghetto. For them, the future seemed to lead only to a dead end.

Today, whites tend to exaggerate how well and quickly they escaped from poverty. The fact is that immigrants who came from rural backgrounds, as many Negroes do, are only now, after three generations, finally beginning to move into the middle class.

By contrast, Negroes began concentrating in the city less than two generations ago, and under much less favorable conditions. Although some Negroes have escaped poverty, few have been able to escape the urban ghetto.

PART III—WHAT CAN BE DONE?

Chapter 10—The Community Response

Our investigation of the 1967 riot cities establishes that virtually every major episode of violence was foreshadowed by an accumulation of unresolved grievances and by widespread dissatisfaction among Negroes with the unwillingness or inability of local government to respond.

Overcoming these conditions is essential for community support of law enforcement and civil order. City governments need new and more vital channels of communication to the residents of the ghetto; they need to improve their capacity to respond effectively to community needs before they become community grievances; and they need to provide opportunity for meaningful involvement of ghetto residents in shaping policies and programs which affect the community.

The Commission recommends that local governments:

- Develop Neighborhood Action Task Forces as joint community-government efforts through which more effective communication can be achieved, and the delivery of city services to ghetto residents improved.
- Establish comprehensive grievance-response mechanisms in order to bring all public agencies under public scrutiny.
- Bring the institutions of local government closer to the people they serve by establishing neighborhood outlets for local, state and federal administrative and public service agencies.
- Expand opportunities for ghetto residents to participate in the formulation of public policy and the implementation of programs affecting them through improved political representation, creation of institutional channels for community action, expansion of legal services, and legislative hearings on ghetto problems.

In this effort, city governments will require state and federal support.

The Commission recommends:

- State and federal financial assistance for mayors and city councils to support the research, consultants, staff and other resources needed to respond effectively to federal program initiatives.

• State cooperation in providing municipalities with the jurisdictional tools needed to deal with their problems; a fuller measure of financial aid to urban areas; and the focusing of the interests of suburban communities on the physical, social and cultural environment of the central city.

Chapter 11—Police and the Community

The abrasive relationship between the police and the minority communities has been a major—and explosive—source of grievance, tension and disorder. The blame must be shared by the total society.

The police are faced with demands for increased protection and service in the ghetto. Yet the aggressive patrol practices thought necessary to meet these demands themselves create tension and hostility. The resulting grievances have been further aggravated by the lack of effective mechanisms for handling complaints against the police. Special programs for bettering police-community relations have been instituted, but these alone are not enough. Police administrators, with the guidance of public officials, and the support of the entire community, must take vigorous action to improve law enforcement and to decrease the potential for disorder.

The Commission recommends that city government and police authorities:

• Review police operations in the ghetto to ensure proper conduct by police officers, and eliminate abrasive practices.
• Provide more adequate police protection to ghetto residents to eliminate their high sense of insecurity, and the belief in the existence of a dual standard of law enforcement.
• Establish fair and effective mechanisms for the redress of grievances against the police, and other municipal employees.
• Develop and adopt policy guidelines to assist officers in making critical decisions in areas where police conduct can create tension.
• Develop and use innovative programs to ensure widespread community support for law enforcement.
• Recruit more Negroes into the regular police force, and review promotion policies to ensure fair promotion for Negro officers.
• Establish a "Community Service Officer" program to attract ghetto youths between the ages of 17 and 21 to police work. These junior officers would perform duties in ghetto neighborhoods, but would not have full police authority. The federal government should provide support equal to 90 percent of the costs of employing CSOs on the basis of one for every ten regular officers.

Chapter 12—Control of Disorder

Preserving civil peace is the first responsibility of government. Unless the rule of law prevails, our society will lack

17

not only order but also the environment essential to social and economic progress.

The maintenance of civil order cannot be left to the police alone. The police need guidance, as well as support, from mayors and other public officials. It is the responsibility of public officials to determine proper police policies, support adequate police standards for personnel and performance, and participate in planning for the control of disorders.

To maintain control of incidents which could lead to disorders, the Commission recommends that local officials:

- Assign seasoned, well-trained policemen and supervisory officers to patrol ghetto areas, and to respond to disturbances.
- Develop plans which will quickly muster maximum police manpower and highly qualified senior commanders at the outbreak of disorders.
- Provide special training in the prevention of disorders, and prepare police for riot control and for operation in units, with adequate command and control and field communication for proper discipline and effectiveness.
- Develop guidelines governing the use of control equipment and provide alternatives to the use of lethal weapons. Federal support for research in this area is needed.
- Establish an intelligence system to provide police and other public officials with reliable information that may help to prevent the outbreak of a disorder and to institute effective control measures in the event a riot erupts.
- Develop continuing contacts with ghetto residents to make use of the forces for order which exist within the community.
- Establish machinery for neutralizing rumors, and enabling Negro leaders and residents to obtain the facts. Create special rumor details to collect, evaluate, and dispel rumors that may lead to a civil disorder.

The Commission believes there is a grave danger that some communities may resort to the indiscriminate and excessive use of force. The harmful effects of overreaction are incalculable. The Commission condemns moves to equip police departments with mass destruction weapons, such as automatic rifles, machine guns and tanks. Weapons which are designed to destroy, not to control, have no place in densely populated urban communities.

The Commission recommends that the federal government share in the financing of programs for improvement of police forces, both in their normal law enforcement activities as well as in their response to civil disorders.

To assist government authorities in planning their response to civil disorder, this report contains a Supplement on Control of Disorder. It deals with specific problems encountered during riot-control operations, and includes:

- Assessment of the present capabilities of police, National Guard and Army forces to control major riots, and recommendations for improvement;
- Recommended means by which the control operations of those forces may be coordinated with the response of other agencies, such as fire departments, and with the community at large;
- Recommendations for review and revision of federal, state and local laws needed to provide the framework for control efforts and for the call-up and interrelated action of public safety forces.

Chapter 13—The Administration of Justice Under Emergency Conditions

In many of the cities which experienced disorders last summer, there were recurring breakdowns in the mechanisms for processing, prosecuting and protecting arrested persons. These resulted mainly from long-standing structural deficiencies in criminal court systems, and from the failure of communities to anticipate and plan for the emergency demands of civil disorders.

In part, because of this, there were few successful prosecutions for serious crimes committed during the riots. In those cities where mass arrests occurred many arrestees were deprived of basic legal rights.

The Commission recommends that the cities and states:

- Undertake reform of the lower courts so as to improve the quality of justice rendered under normal conditions.
- Plan comprehensive measures by which the criminal justice system may be supplemented during civil disorders so that its deliberative functions are protected, and the quality of justice is maintained.

Such emergency plans require broad community participation and dedicated leadership by the bench and bar. They should include:

- Laws sufficient to deter and punish riot conduct.
- Additional judges, bail and probation officers, and clerical staff.
- Arrangements for volunteer lawyers to help prosecutors and to represent riot defendants at every stage of proceedings.
- Policies to ensure proper and individual bail, arraignment, pretrial, trial and sentencing proceedings.
- Adequate emergency processing and detention facilities.

Chapter 14—Damages: Repair and Compensation

The Commission recommends that the federal government:

- Amend the Federal Disaster Act—which now applies only to natural disasters—to permit federal emergency food and medical assistance to cities during major civil disorders, and provide long-term economic assistance afterwards.
- With the cooperation of the states, create incentives for the private insurance industry to provide more adequate property-insurance coverage in inner-city areas.

The Commission endorses the report of the National Advisory Panel on Insurance in Riot-Affected Areas: "Meeting the Insurance Crisis of our Cities."

Chapter 15—The News Media and the Disorders

In his charge to the Commission, the President asked: "What effect do the mass media have on the riots?"

The Commission determined that the answer to the President's question did not lie solely in the performance of the press and broadcasters in reporting the riots. Our analysis had to consider also the overall treatment by the media of the Negro ghettos, community relations, racial attitudes, and poverty—day by day and month by month, year in and year out.

A wide range of interviews with government officials, law enforcement authorities, media personnel and other citizens, including ghetto residents, as well as a quantitative analysis of riot coverage and a special conference with industry representatives, leads us to conclude that:

- Despite instances of sensationalism, inaccuracy and distortion, newspapers, radio and television tried on the whole to give a balanced, factual account of the 1967 disorders.
- Elements of the news media failed to portray accurately the scale and character of the violence that occurred last summer. The overall effect was, we believe, an exaggeration of both mood and event.
- Important segments of the media failed to report adequately on the causes and consequences of civil disorders and on the underlying problems of race relations. They have not communicated to the majority of their audience—which is white—a sense of the degradation, misery and hopelessness of life in the ghetto.

These failings must be corrected, and the improvement must come from within the industry. Freedom of the press is not the issue. Any effort to impose governmental restrictions would be inconsistent with fundamental constitutional precepts.

We have seen evidence that the news media are becoming aware of and concerned about their performance in this field. As that concern grows, coverage will improve. But much more must be done, and it must be done soon.

The Commission recommends that the media:

- Expand coverage of the Negro community and of race problems through permanent assignment of reporters familiar with urban and racial affairs, and through establishment of more and better links with the Negro community.
- Integrate Negroes and Negro activities into all aspects of coverage and content, including newspaper articles and television programming. The news media must publish newspapers and produce programs that recognize the existence and activities of Negroes as a group within the community and as a part of the larger community.
- Recruit more Negroes into journalism and broadcasting and promote those who are qualified to positions of significant responsibility. Recruitment should begin in high schools and continue through college; where necessary, aid for training should be provided.
- Improve coordination with police in reporting riot news through advance planning, and cooperate with the police in the designation of police information officers, establishment of information centers, and development of mutually acceptable guidelines for riot reporting and the conduct of media personnel.
- Accelerate efforts to ensure accurate and responsible reporting of riot and racial news, through adoption by all news gathering organizations of stringent internal staff guidelines.
- Cooperate in the establishment of a privately organized and funded Institute of Urban Communications to train and educate journalists in urban affairs, recruit and train more Negro journalists, develop methods for improving police-press relations, review coverage of riots and racial issues, and support continuing research in the urban field.

Chapter 16—The Future of the Cities

By 1985, the Negro population in central cities is expected to increase by 68 percent to approximately 20.3 million. Coupled with the continued exodus of white families to the suburbs, this growth will produce majority Negro populations in many of the nation's largest cities.

The future of these cities, and of their burgeoning Negro populations, is grim. Most new employment opportunities are being created in suburbs and outlying areas. This trend will continue unless important changes in public policy are made.

In prospect, therefore, is further deterioration of already inadequate municipal tax bases in the face of increasing demands for public services, and continuing unemployment and poverty among the urban Negro population:

Three choices are open to the nation:

- We can maintain present policies, continuing both the proportion of the nation's resources now allocated to programs for the unemployed and the disadvantaged, and the inadequate and failing effort to achieve an integrated society.
- We can adopt a policy of "enrichment" aimed at improving dramatically the quality of ghetto life while abandoning integration as a goal.
- We can pursue integration by combining ghetto "enrichment" with policies which will encourage Negro movement out of central city areas.

The first choice, continuance of present policies, has ominous consequences for our society. The share of the nation's resources now allocated to programs for the disadvantaged is insufficient to arrest the deterioration of life in central city ghettos. Under such conditions, a rising proportion of Negroes may come to see in the deprivation and segregation they experience, a justification for violent protest, or for extending support to now isolated extremists who advocate civil disruption. Large-scale and continuing violence could result, followed by white retaliation, and, ultimately, the separation of the two communities in a garrison state.

Even if violence does not occur, the consequences are unacceptable. Development of a racially integrated society, extraordinarily difficult today, will be virtually impossible when the present black central city population of 12.1 million has grown to almost 21 million.

To continue present policies is to make permanent the division of our country into two societies; one, largely Negro and poor, located in the central cities; the other, predominantly white and affluent, located in the suburbs and in outlying areas.

The second choice, ghetto enrichment coupled with abandonment of integration, is also unacceptable. It is another way of choosing a permanently divided country. Moreover, equality cannot be achieved under conditions of nearly complete separation. In a country where the economy, and particularly the resources of employment, are predominantly white, a policy of separation can only relegate Negroes to a permanently inferior economic status.

We believe that the only possible choice for America is the third—a policy which combines ghetto enrichment with programs designed to encourage integration of substantial numbers of Negroes into the society outside the ghetto.

Enrichment must be an important adjunct to integration, for no matter how ambitious or energetic the program, few Negroes now living in central cities can be quickly integrated.

22

In the meantime, large-scale improvement in the quality of ghetto life is essential.

But this can be no more than an interim strategy. Programs must be developed which will permit substantial Negro movement out of the ghettos. The primary goal must be a single society, in which every citizen will be free to live and work according to his capabilities and desires, not his color.

Chapter 17—Recommendations For National Action

INTRODUCTION

No American—white or black—can escape the consequences of the continuing social and economic decay of our major cities.

Only a commitment to national action on an unprecedented scale can shape a future compatible with the historic ideals of American society.

The great productivity of our economy, and a federal revenue system which is highly responsive to economic growth, can provide the resources.

The major need is to generate new will—the will to tax ourselves to the extent necessary to meet the vital needs of the nation.

We have set forth goals and proposed strategies to reach those goals. We discuss and recommend programs not to commit each of us to specific parts of such programs but to illustrate the type and dimension of action needed.

The major goal is the creation of a true union—a single society and a single American identity. Toward that goal, we propose the following objectives for national action:

- Opening up opportunities to those who are restricted by racial segregation and discrimination, and eliminating all barriers to their choice of jobs, education and housing.
- Removing the frustration of powerlessness among the disadvantaged by providing the means for them to deal with the problems that affect their own lives and by increasing the capacity of our public and private institutions to respond to these problems.
- Increasing communication across racial lines to destroy stereotypes, to halt polarization, end distrust and hostility, and create common ground for efforts toward public order and social justice.

We propose these aims to fulfill our pledge of equality and to meet the fundamental needs of a democratic and civilized society—domestic peace and social justice.

Pervasive unemployment and underemployment are the most persistent and serious grievances in minority areas. They are inextricably linked to the problem of civil disorder.

Despite growing federal expenditures for manpower development and training programs, and sustained general economic prosperity and increasing demands for skilled workers, about two million—white and nonwhite—are permanently unemployed. About ten million are underemployed, of whom 6.5 million work full time for wages below the poverty line.

The 500,000 "hard-core" unemployed in the central cities who lack a basic education and are unable to hold a steady job are made up in large part of Negro males between the ages of 18 and 25. In the riot cities which we surveyed, Negroes were three times as likely as whites to hold unskilled jobs, which are often part time, seasonal, low-paying and "dead end."

Negro males between the ages of 15 and 25 predominated among the rioters. More than 20 percent of the rioters were unemployed, and many who were employed held intermittent, low status, unskilled jobs which they regarded as below their education and ability.

The Commission recommends that the federal government:

- Undertake joint efforts with cities and states to consolidate existing manpower programs to avoid fragmentation and duplication.
- Take immediate action to create 2,000,000 new jobs over the next three years—one million in the public sector and one million in the private sector—to absorb the hard-core unemployed and materially reduce the level of underemployment for all workers, black and white. We propose 250,000 public sector and 300,000 private sector jobs in the first year.
- Provide on-the-job training by both public and private employers with reimbursement to private employers for the extra costs of training the hard-core unemployed, by contract or by tax credits.
- Provide tax and other incentives to investment in rural as well as urban poverty areas in order to offer to the rural poor an alternative to migration to urban centers.
- Take new and vigorous action to remove artificial barriers to employment and promotion, including not only racial discrimination but, in certain cases, arrest records or lack of a high school diploma. Strengthen those agencies such as the Equal Employment Opportunity Commission, charged with eliminating discriminatory practices, and provide full support for Title VI of the 1964 Civil Rights Act allowing federal grant-in-aid funds to be withheld from activities which discriminate on grounds of color or race.

The Commission commends the recent public commitment of the National Council of the Building and Construction Trades Unions, AFL-CIO, to encourage and recruit Negro membership in apprenticeship programs. This commitment should be intensified and implemented.

Education in a democratic society must equip children to develop their potential and to participate fully in American life. For the community at large, the schools have discharged this responsibility well. But for many minorities, and particularly for the children of the ghetto, the schools have failed to provide the educational experience which could overcome the effects of discrimination and deprivation.

This failure is one of the persistent sources of grievance and resentment within the Negro community. The hostility of Negro parents and students toward the school system is generating increasing conflict and causing disruption within many city school districts. But the most dramatic evidence of the relationship between educational practices and civil disorders lies in the high incidence of riot participation by ghetto youth who have not completed high school.

The bleak record of public education for ghetto children is growing worse. In the critical skills—verbal and reading ability—Negro students are falling further behind whites with each year of school completed. The high unemployment and underemployment rate for Negro youth is evidence, in part, of the growing educational crisis.

We support integration as the priority education strategy; it is essential to the future of American society. In this last summer's disorders we have seen the consequences of racial isolation at all levels, and of attitudes toward race, on both sides, produced by three centuries of myth, ignorance and bias. It is indispensable that opportunities for interaction between the races be expanded.

We recognize that the growing dominance of pupils from disadvantaged minorities in city school populations will not soon be reversed. No matter how great the effort toward desegregation, many children of the ghetto will not, within their school careers, attend integrated schools.

If existing disadvantages are not to be perpetuated, we must drastically improve the quality of ghetto education. Equality of results with all-white schools must be the goal.

To implement these strategies, the Commission recommends:

● Sharply increased efforts to eliminate de facto segregation in our

25

schools through substantial federal aid to school systems seeking to desegregate either within the system or in cooperation with neighboring school systems.

- Elimination of racial discrimination in Northern as well as Southern schools by vigorous application of Title VI of the Civil Rights Act of 1964.
- Extension of quality early childhood education to every disadvantaged child in the country.
- Efforts to improve dramatically schools serving disadvantaged children through substantial federal funding of year-round compensatory education programs, improved teaching, and expanded experimentation and research.
- Elimination of illiteracy through greater federal support for adult basic education.
- Enlarged opportunities for parent and community participation in the public schools.
- Reoriented vocational education emphasizing work-experience training and the involvement of business and industry.
- Expanded opportunities for higher education through increased federal assistance to disadvantaged students.
- Revision of state aid formulas to assure more per student aid to districts having a high proportion of disadvantaged school-age children.

THE WELFARE SYSTEM

Our present system of public welfare is designed to save money instead of people, and tragically ends up doing neither. This system has two critical deficiencies:

First, it excludes large numbers of persons who are in great need, and who, if provided a decent level of support, might be able to become more productive and self-sufficient. No federal funds are available for millions of unemployed and underemployed men and women who are needy but neither aged, handicapped nor the parents of minor children.

Second, for those included, the system provides assistance well below the minimum necessary for a decent level of existence, and imposes restrictions that encourage continued dependency on welfare and undermine self-respect.

A welter of statutory requirements and administrative practices and regulations operate to remind recipients that they are considered untrustworthy, promiscuous and lazy. Residence requirements prevent assistance to people in need who are newly arrived in the state. Searches of recipients' homes violate privacy. Inadequate social services compound the problems.

The Commission recommends that the federal government, acting with state and local governments where necessary, reform the existing welfare system to:

- Establish, for recipients in existing welfare categories, uniform

26

national standards of assistance at least as high as the annual "poverty level" of income, now set by the Social Security Administration at $3,335 per year for an urban family of four.

- Require that all states receiving federal welfare contributions participate in the Aid to Families with Dependent Children— Unemployed Parents program (AFDC-UP) that permits assistance to families with both father and mother in the home, thus aiding the family while it is still intact.
- Bear a substantially greater portion of all welfare costs—at least 90 percent of total payments.
- Increase incentives for seeking employment and job training, but remove restrictions recently enacted by the Congress that would compel mothers of young children to work.
- Provide more adequate social services through neighborhood centers and family-planning programs.
- Remove the freeze placed by the 1967 welfare amendments on the percentage of children in a state that can be covered by federal assistance.
- Eliminate residence requirements.

As a long-range goal, the Commission recommends that the federal government seek to develop a national system of income supplementation based strictly on need with two broad and basic purposes:

- To provide, for those who can work or who do work, any necessary supplements in such a way as to develop incentives for fuller employment;
- To provide, for those who cannot work and for mothers who decide to remain with their children, a minimum standard of decent living, and to aid in the saving of children from the prison of poverty that has held their parents.

A broad system of supplementation would involve substantially greater federal expenditures than anything now contemplated. The cost will range widely depending on the standard of need accepted as the "basic allowance" to individuals and families, and on the rate at which additional income above this level is taxed. Yet if the deepening cycle of poverty and dependence on welfare can be broken, if the children of the poor can be given the opportunity to scale the wall that now separates them from the rest of society, the return on this investment will be great indeed.

HOUSING

After more than three decades of fragmented and grossly underfunded federal housing programs, nearly six million substandard housing units remain occupied in the United States.

27

The housing problem is particularly acute in the minority ghettos. Nearly two-thirds of all non-white families living in the central cities today live in neighborhoods marked with substandard housing and general urban blight. Two major factors are responsible.

First: Many ghetto residents simply cannot pay the rent necessary to support decent housing. In Detroit, for example, over 40 percent of the non-white occupied units in 1960 required rent of over 35 percent of the tenants' income.

Second: Discrimination prevents access to many non-slum areas, particularly the suburbs, where good housing exists. In addition, by creating a "back pressure" in the racial ghettos, it makes it possible for landlords to break up apartments for denser occupancy, and keeps prices and rents of deteriorated ghetto housing higher than they would be in a truly free market.

To date, federal programs have been able to do comparatively little to provide housing for the disadvantaged. In the 31-year history of subsidized federal housing, only about 800,-000 units have been constructed, with recent production averaging about 50,000 units a year. By comparison, over a period only three years longer, FHA insurance guarantees have made possible the construction of over ten million middle and upper-income units.

Two points are fundamental to the Commission's recommendations:

First: Federal housing programs must be given a new thrust aimed at overcoming the prevailing patterns of racial segregation. If this is not done, those programs will continue to concentrate the most impoverished and dependent segments of the population into the central-city ghettos where there is already a critical gap between the needs of the population and the public resources to deal with them.

Second: The private sector must be brought into the production and financing of low and moderate rental housing to supply the capabilities and capital necessary to meet the housing needs of the nation.

The Commission recommends that the federal government:

- Enact a comprehensive and enforceable federal open housing law to cover the sale or rental of all housing, including single family homes.
- Reorient federal housing programs to place more low and moderate income housing outside of ghetto areas.
- Bring within the reach of low and moderate income families within the next five years six million new and existing units of decent housing, beginning with 600,000 units in the next year.

To reach this goal we recommend:

- Expansion and modification of the rent supplement program to permit use of supplements for existing housing, thus greatly increasing the reach of the program.
- Expansion and modification of the below-market interest rate program to enlarge the interest subsidy to all sponsors and provide interest-free loans to nonprofit sponsors to cover pre-construction costs, and permit sale of projects to nonprofit corporations, cooperatives, or condominiums.
- Creation of an ownership supplement program similar to present rent supplements, to make home ownership possible for low-income families.
- Federal writedown of interest rates on loans to private builders constructing moderate-rent housing.
- Expansion of the public housing program, with emphasis on small units on scattered sites, and leasing and "turnkey" programs.
- Expansion of the Model Cities program.
- Expansion and reorientation of the urban renewal program to give priority to projects directly assisting low-income households to obtain adequate housing.

CONCLUSION

One of the first witnesses to be invited to appear before this Commission was Dr. Kenneth B. Clark, a distinguished and perceptive scholar. Referring to the reports of earlier riot commissions, he said:

I read that report . . . of the 1919 riot in Chicago, and it is as if I were reading the report of the investigating committee on the Harlem riot of '35, the report of the investigating committee on the Harlem riot of '43, the report of the McCone Commission on the Watts riot.

I must again in candor say to you members of this Commission —it is a kind of Alice in Wonderland—with the same moving picture re-shown over and over again, the same analysis, the same recommendations, and the same inaction.

These words come to our minds as we conclude this report. We have provided an honest beginning. We have learned much. But we have uncovered no startling truths, no unique insights, no simple solutions. The destruction and the bitterness of racial disorder, the harsh polemics of black revolt and white repression have been seen and heard before in this country.

It is time now to end the destruction and the violence, not only in the streets of the ghetto but in the lives of people.

Preface

The summer of 1967 brought racial disorder again to American cities, deepening the bitter residue of fear and threatening the future of all Americans.

We are charged by the President with the responsibility to examine this condition and to speak the truth as we see it. Two fundamental questions confront us:

How can we as a people end the resort to violence while we build a better society?

How can the nation realize the promise of a single society —one nation indivisible—which yet remains unfulfilled?

Violence surely cannot build that society. Disruption and disorder will nourish not justice but repression. Those few who would destroy civil order and the rule of law strike at the freedom of every citizen. They must know that the community cannot and will not tolerate coercion and mob action.

We have worked together these past months with a sense of the greatest urgency. Although much remains that can be learned, we have determined to say now what we have learned. We do this in the hope that the American public will understand the nature and gravity of the problem and that those who have power to act—at all levels of government and in all sections of the community—will listen and respond.

This sense of urgency has led us to consolidate in this single report the interim and final reports called for by the President. To accomplish this, it has been necessary to do without the benefit of some studies still under way which will not be completed for months to come. Certain of these studies—a 15-city survey of Negro and white attitudes, a special survey of attitudes of community leaders, elected officials, administrators and teachers, a report on the application of mediation techniques, and a further analysis of riot arrestees—will be issued later, with other materials, as supplemental reports.

We believe that to wait until mid-summer to present our findings and recommendations may be to forfeit whatever

31

opportunity exists for this report to affect this year the dangerous climate of tension and apprehension that pervades our cities.

II

Last summer nearly 150 cities reported disorders in Negro—and in some instances, Puerto Rican—neighborhoods. These ranged from minor disturbances to major outbursts involving sustained and widespread looting and destruction of property. The worst came during a two-week period in July when large-scale disorders erupted first in Newark and then in Detroit, each setting off a chain reaction in neighboring communities.

It was in this troubled and turbulent setting that the President of the United States established this Commission. He called upon it "to guide the country through a thicket of tension, conflicting evidence and extreme opinions."

In his charge, the President framed the Commission's mandate in these words:

> "We need to know the answers to three
> basic questions about these riots:
> —What happened?
> —Why did it happen?
> —What can be done to
>   prevent it from happen-
>   ing again and again?"

The three parts of this report offer answers to these questions.

Part I tells "What happened?" Chapter 1 is a profile of the 1967 disorders told through a narrative of the summer's events in 10 of the 23 cities surveyed by the Commission. Chapter 2 calls on data from all 23 cities to construct an analytical profile. Chapter 3 is the report of the Commission on the issue of conspiracy.

Part II responds to the question "Why did it happen?" Early in our investigation it became clear that the disorders were not the result of contemporary conditions alone; Chapter 5 identifies some of the historical factors that are an essential part of the background of last summer's outbreaks. Chapters 6 through 9 deal with present conditions, examining the impact of ghetto formation, unemployment, and family structures, and conditions of life in the ghettos, and the differences between

32

the Negro experience and that of other urban immigrant groups.

Part III contains our answer to the question "What can be done?" Our recommendations begin with organizing the community to respond more effectively to ghetto needs and then proceed with police-community relations, control of disorders, the administration of justice under emergency conditions, compensation for property damage, the role of the news media, and national action in the critical areas of employment, education, welfare and housing.

In formulating this report, we have attempted to draw on all relevant sources. During closed hearings held from August through December, we heard over 130 witnesses, including federal, state and local officials, experts from the military establishment and law enforcement agencies, universities and foundations, Negro leaders and representatives of the business community. We personally visited eight cities in which major disturbances had occurred. We met together for 24 days to review and revise the several drafts of our report. Through our staff we also undertook field surveys in 23 cities in which disorders occurred during the summer of 1967, and took sworn testimony in nine of the cities investigated and from Negro leaders and militants across the country. Expert consultants and advisors supplemented the work of our staff in all the areas covered in our report.

III

Much of our report is directed to the condition of those Americans who are also Negroes and to the social and economic environment in which they live—many in the black ghettos of our cities. But this nation is confronted with the issue of justice for all its people—white as well as black, rural as well as urban. In particular, we are concerned for those who have continued to keep faith with society in the preservation of public order—the people of Spanish surname, the American Indian and other minority groups to whom this country owes so much.

We wish it to be clear that in focusing on the Negro, we do not mean to imply any priority of need. It will not do to fight misery in the black ghetto and leave untouched the reality of injustice and deprivation elsewhere in our society. The first priority is order and justice for all Americans.

In speaking of the Negro, we do not speak of "them."

We speak of us—for the freedoms and opportunities of all Americans are diminished and imperiled when they are denied to some Americans. The tragic waste of human spirit and resources, the unrecoverable loss to the nation which this denial has already caused—and continues to produce—no longer can be ignored or afforded.

Two premises underlie the work of the Commission:

- that this nation cannot abide violence and disorder if it is to ensure the safety of its people and their progress in a free society.

- that this nation will deserve neither safety nor progress unless it can demonstrate the wisdom and the will to undertake decisive action against the root causes of racial disorder.

This report is addressed to the institutions of government and to the conscience of the nation, but even more urgently, to the minds and hearts of each citizen. The responsibility for decisive action, never more clearly demanded in the history of our country, rests on all of us.

We do not know whether the tide of racial disorder has begun to recede. We recognize as we must that the conditions underlying the disorders will not be obliterated before the end of this year or the end of the next and that, so long as these conditions exist, a potential for disorder remains. But we believe that the likelihood of disorder can be markedly lessened by an American commitment to confront those conditions and eliminate them—a commitment so clear that Negro citizens will know its truth and accept its goal. The most important step toward domestic peace is an act of will; this country can do for its people what it chooses to do.

The pages that follow set forth our conclusions and the facts upon which they are based. Our plea for civil order and our recommendations for social and economic change are a call to national action. We are aware of the breadth and scope of those recommendations but they neither probe deeper nor demand more than the problems which call them forth.

PART I

WHAT HAPPENED?

Chapter 1 / Profiles of Disorder

INTRODUCTION

The President directed the Commission to produce "a profile of the riots—of the rioters, of their environment, of their victims, of their causes and effects."

In response to this mandate the Commission constructed profiles of the riots in 10 of the 23 cities under investigation. Brief summaries of what were often conflicting views and perceptions of confusing episodes, they are, we believe, a fair and accurate picture of what happened.

From the profiles, we have sought to build a composite view of the riots as well as of the environment out of which they erupted.

*   *   *

The summer of 1967 was not the beginning of the current wave of disorders. Omens of violence had appeared much earlier.

1963-64

In 1963, serious disorders, involving both whites and Negroes, broke out in Birmingham, Savannah, Cambridge, Md., Chicago, and Philadelphia. Sometimes the mobs battled each other; more often they fought the police.

The most violent encounters took place in Birmingham. Police used dogs, firehoses and cattle prods against marchers, many of whom were children. White racists shot at Negroes and bombed Negro residences. Negroes retaliated by burning white-owned businesses in Negro areas. On a quiet Sunday morning, a bomb exploded beneath a Negro church. Four young girls in a Sunday school class were killed.

In the spring of 1964, the arrest and conviction of civil

rights demonstrators provoked violence in Jacksonville. A shot fired from a passing car killed a Negro woman. When a bomb threat forced evacuation of an all-Negro high school, the students stoned policemen and firemen and burned the cars of newsmen. For the first time, Negroes used Molotov cocktails in setting fires.

Two weeks later, at a demonstration protesting school segregation in Cleveland, a bulldozer accidentally killed a young white minister. When police moved in to disperse a crowd composed primarily of Negroes, violence erupted.

In late June, white segregationists broke through police lines and attacked civil rights demonstrators in St. Augustine, Florida. In Philadelphia, Mississippi, law enforcement officers were implicated in the lynch murders of three civil rights workers. On July 10 Ku Klux Klansmen shot and killed a Negro United States Army lieutenant colonel, Lemuel Penn, as he was driving through Georgia.

On July 16, in New York City, several young Negroes walking to summer school classes became involved in a dispute with a white building superintendent. When an off-duty police lieutenant intervened, a 15-year-old boy attacked him with a knife. The officer shot and killed the boy.

A crowd of teenagers gathered and smashed store windows. Police arrived in force, and dispersed the group.

On the following day, the Progressive Labor Movement, a Marxist-Leninist organization, printed and passed out inflammatory leaflets charging the police with brutality.

On the second day after the shooting, a rally called by the Congress of Racial Equality to protest the Mississippi lynch murders developed into a march on a precinct police station. The crowd clashed with the police; one person was killed, and 12 police officers and 19 citizens were injured.

For several days thereafter the pattern was repeated: despite exhortations of Negro community leaders against violence, protest rallies became uncontrollable. Police battled mobs in Harlem and in the Bedford Stuyvesant section of Brooklyn. Firemen fought fires started with Molotov cocktails. When bricks and bottles were thrown, police responded with gunfire. Widespread looting followed and many persons were injured.

A week later a riot broke out in Rochester when police tried to arrest an intoxicated Negro youth at a street dance. After two days of violence, the National Guard restored order.

During the first two weeks of August, disorders took place in three New Jersey communities: Jersey City, Elizabeth, and Paterson.

On August 15, when a white liquor store owner in the Chicago suburb of Dixmoor had a Negro woman arrested for stealing a bottle of whiskey, he was accused of having man-handled her. A crowd gathered in front of the store, broke the store window, and threw rocks at passing cars. The police restored order. The next day, when the disturbance was renewed, a Molotov cocktail set the liquor store afire. Several persons were injured.

The final violence of the summer occurred in Philadelphia. A Negro couple's car stalled at an intersection in an area known as "The Jungle"—where, with almost 2,000 persons living in each block, there is the greatest incidence of crime, disease, unemployment, and poverty occurs in the city. When two police officers, one white and one black, attempted to move the car, the wife of the owner became abusive and the officers arrested her. Police officers and Negro spectators gathered at the scene. Two nights of rioting, resulting in extensive damage.

1965

In the spring of 1965, the nation's attention shifted back to the South. When civil rights workers staged a nonviolent demonstration in Selma, Alabama, police and state troopers forcibly interrupted their march. Within the next few weeks racists murdered a white clergyman and a white housewife active in civil rights.

In the small Louisiana town of Bogalusa, when Negro demonstrators attacked by whites received inadequate police protection, the Negroes formed a self-defense group called the "Deacons for Defense and Justice."

As late as the second week of August, there had been few disturbances outside the South. But, on the evening of August 11, as Los Angeles sweltered in a heat wave, a highway patrolman halted a young Negro driver for speeding. The young man appeared intoxicated, and the patrolman arrested him. As a crowd gathered, law enforcement officers were called to the scene. A highway patrolman mistakenly struck a bystander with his billy club. A young Negro woman, who was accused of spitting on the police, was dragged into the middle of the street.

When the police departed, members of the crowd began hurling rocks at passing cars, beating white motorists, and overturning cars and setting them on fire. The police reacted hesitantly. Actions they did take further inflamed the people on the streets.

The following day the area was calm. Community leaders attempting to mediate between Negro residents and the police received little cooperation from municipal authorities. That evening the previous night's pattern of violence was repeated.

37

Not until almost 30 hours after the initial flareup did window smashing, looting, and arson begin. Yet the police utilized only a small part of their forces.

Few police were on hand the next morning when huge crowds gathered in the business district of Watts, two miles from the location of the original disturbance, and began looting. In the absence of police response, the looting became bolder and spread into other areas. Hundreds of women and children from five housing projects clustered in or near Watts took part. Around noon, extensive firebombing began. Few white persons were attacked; the principal intent of the rioters now seemed to be to destroy property owned by whites, in order to drive white "exploiters" out of the ghetto.

The chief of police asked for National Guard help, but the arrival of the military units was delayed for several hours. When the Guardsmen arrived, they, together with police, made heavy use of firearms. Reports of "sniper fire" increased. Several persons were killed by mistake. Many more were injured.

Thirty-six hours after the first Guard units arrived, the main force of the riot had been blunted. Almost 4,000 persons were arrested. Thirty-four were killed and hundreds injured. Approximately $35 million in damage had been inflicted.

The Los Angeles riot, the worst in the United States since the Detroit riot of 1943, shocked all who had been confident that race relations were improving in the North, and evoked a new mood in the Negro ghettos around the country.

1966

The events of 1966 made it appear that domestic turmoil had become part of the American scene.

In March, a fight between several Negroes and Mexican-Americans resulted in a new flareup in Watts. In May, after a police officer accidentally shot and killed a Negro, demonstrations by Negro militants again increased tension in Los Angeles.

Evidence was accumulating that a major proportion of riot participants were youths. Increasing race pride, skepticism about their job prospects, and dissatisfaction with the inadequacy of their education, caused unrest among students in Negro colleges and high schools throughout the country. Students and youths were the principal participants in at least six of the 13 spring and early summer disorders of 1966.

July 12, 1966, was a hot day in Chicago. Negro youngsters were playing in water gushing from an illegally opened fire hydrant. Two police officers, arriving on the scene closed the hydrant. A Negro youth turned it on again, and the police officers arrested him. A crowd gathered. Police reinforcements arrived. As the crowd became unruly, seven Negro youths were arrested.

Rumors spread that the arrested youths had been beaten, and that police were turning off fire hydrants in Negro neighborhoods but leaving them on in white areas. Sporadic window breaking, rock throwing, and firebombing lasted for several hours. Most of the participants were teenagers.

In Chicago, as in other cities, the long-standing grievances of the Negro community needed only minor incidents to trigger violence.

In 1961 when Negroes, after being evacuated from a burning tenement, had been sheltered in a church in an all-white area, a crowd of residents had gathered and threatened to attack the church unless the Negroes were removed.

Segregated schools and housing had led to repeated picketing and marches by civil rights organizations. When marchers had gone into white neighborhoods, they had been met on several occasions by KKK signs and crowds throwing eggs and tomatoes. In 1965, when a Chicago fire truck had killed a Negro woman in an accident, Negroes had congregated to protest against the fire station's all-white complement. Rock throwing and looting had broken out. More than 170 persons were arrested in two days.

On the evening of July 13, 1966, the day after the fire hydrant incident, rock throwing, looting and fire-bombing began again. For several days thereafter the pattern of violence was repeated. Police responding to calls were subjected to random gunfire. Rumors spread. The press talked in highly exaggerated terms of "guerrilla warfare" and "sniper fire."

Before the police and 4,200 National Guardsmen managed to restore order, scores of civilians and police had been injured. There were 533 arrests, including 155 juveniles. Three Negroes were killed by stray bullets, among them a 13-year-old boy and a 14-year-old pregnant girl.

Less than a week later, Ohio National Guardsmen were mobilized to deal with an outbreak of rioting that continued for four nights in the Hough section of Cleveland. It is probable that Negro extremists, although they neither instigated nor organized the disorder, exploited and enlarged it. Amidst widespread reports of "sniper fire," four Negroes, including one young woman, were killed; many others, several children among them, were injured. Law enforcement officers were responsible for two of the deaths, a white man firing from a car for a third, and a group of young white vigilantes for the fourth.

Some news media keeping "tally sheets" of the disturbances

began to apply the term "riot" to acts of vandalism and relatively minor disorders.

At the end of July, the National States Rights Party, a white extremist organization that advocates deporting Negroes and other minorities, preached racial hatred at a series of rallies in Baltimore. Bands of white youths were incited into chasing and beating Negroes. A court order halted the rallies.

Forty-three disorders and riots were reported during 1966. Although there were considerable variations in circumstances, intensity, and length, they were usually ignited by a minor incident fueled by antagonism between the Negro population and the police.

Spring 1967

In the spring of 1967 disorders broke out at three Southern Negro universities at which SNCC (Student Non-Violent Coordinating Committee), a militant anti-white organization, had been attempting to organize the students.

On Friday, April 7, learning that Stokely Carmichael was speaking at two primarily Negro universities, Fisk and Tennessee A&I, in Nashville, and receiving information that some persons were preparing to riot, the police adopted an emergency riot plan. On the following day Carmichael and others, including South Carolina Senator Strom Thurmond, spoke at a symposium at Vanderbilt University.

That evening the Negro operator of a restaurant located near Fisk University summoned police to arrest an allegedly intoxicated Negro soldier.

Within a few minutes students, many of them members of SNCC, began to picket the restaurant. A squad of riot police arrived and soon became the focus of attention. Spectators gathered. When a city bus was halted and attacked by members of the crowd, a Negro police lieutenant fired five shots into the air.

Rocks and bottles were thrown, and additional police were called into the area. Officers fired a number of shots over the heads of the crowd. The students and spectators gradually dispersed.

On the following evening, after negotiations between students and police broke down, crowds again began forming. Police fired over their heads, and shots were fired back at the police. On the fringes of the campus several white youths aimed shots at a police patrol wagon.

A few days later, when police raided the home of several young Negro militants, they confiscated a half dozen bottles prepared as Molotov cocktails.

About a month later, students at Jackson State College, in Jackson, Mississippi, were standing around after a political rally when two Negro police officers pursued a speeding car, driven by a Negro student, onto the campus. When the officers tried to arrest the driver, the students interfered. The police called for reinforcements. A crowd of several hundred persons quickly gathered, and a few rocks were thrown.

On the following evening, an even larger crowd assembled. When police attempted to disperse it by gunfire, three persons were hit. One of them, a young Negro, died the next day. The National Guard restored order.

Six days later, on May 16, two separate Negro protests were taking place in Houston. One group was picketing a garbage dump in a Negro residential neighborhood, where a Negro child had drowned. Another was demonstrating at a junior high school on the grounds that Negro students were disciplined more harshly than white.

That evening college students who had participated in the protests returned to the campus of Texas Southern University. About 50 of them were grouped around a 21-year-old student, D. W., a Vietnam veteran, who was seeking to stimulate further protest action. A dispute broke out, and D. W. reportedly slapped another student. When the student threatened D. W. he left, armed himself with a pistol, and returned.

In response to the report of a disturbance, two unmarked police cars with four officers arrived. Two of the officers questioned D. W., discovered he was armed with a pistol, and arrested him.

A short time later, when one of the police cars returned to the campus, it was met by rocks and bottles thrown by students. As police called for reinforcements, sporadic gunshots reportedly came from the men's dormitory. The police returned the fire.

For several hours, gunfire punctuated unsuccessful attempts by community leaders to negotiate a truce between the students and the police.

When several tar barrels were set afire in the street and shooting broke out again, police decided to enter the dormitory. A patrolman, struck by a ricocheting bullet, was killed. After clearing all 480 occupants from the building, police searched it and found one shotgun and two .22 caliber pistols. The origin of the shot that killed the officer was not determined.

As the summer of 1967 approached, Americans, conditioned by three years of reports of riots, expected violence. But they had no answers to hard questions: What was causing the turmoil? Was it organized and, if so, by whom? Was there a pattern to the disorders?

41

I. TAMPA

On Sunday, June 11, 1967, Tampa, Florida, sweltered in the 94-degree heat. A humid wind ruffled the bay, where thousands of persons watched the hydroplane races. Since early morning the Police Department's Selective Enforcement Unit, designed as a riot control squad, had been employed to keep order at the races.

At 5:30 P.M., a block from the waterfront, a photo supply warehouse was broken into. Forty-five minutes later two police officers spotted three Negro youths as they walked near the State Building. When the youths caught sight of the officers, they ducked into an alley. The officers gave chase. As they ran, the suspects left a trail of photographic equipment scattered from yellow paper bags they were carrying.

The officers transmitted a general broadcast over the police radio. As other officers arrived on the scene, a chase began through and around the streets, houses, and alleys of the neighborhood. When Negro residents of the area adjacent to the Central Park Village Housing Project became aware of the chase, they began to participate. Some attempted to help the officers in locating the suspects.

R. C. Oates, one of 17 Negros on the 511-man Tampa police force, spotted 19-year-old Martin Chambers, bare to the waist, wriggling away beneath one of the houses. Oates called for Chambers to surrender. Ignoring him, Chambers emerged running from beneath the house. A white officer, J. L. Calvert, took up the pursuit.

Pursuing Calvert, in turn, were three young Negroes, all spectators. Behind one of the houses a high cyclone fence created a two-foot wide alley twenty-five feet in length.

As Chambers darted along the fence, Officer Calvert rounded the corner of the house. Calvert yelled to him to halt. Chambers ignored him. Calvert pointed his .38 revolver and fired. The slug entered the back of Chambers and passed completely through his body. Raising his hands over his head, he clutched at the cyclone fence.

When the three youths running behind Officer Calvert came upon the scene, they assumed Chambers had been shot standing in the position in which they saw him. Rumor quickly spread through the neighborhood that a white police officer had shot a Negro youth who had had his hands over his head and was trying to surrender.

The ambulance that had been summoned became lost on the way. The gathering crowd viewing the bloody, critically injured youth grew increasingly belligerent.

Finally, Officer Oates loaded Chambers into his car and drove him to the hospital. The youth died shortly thereafter.

As officers were leaving the scene, a thunderstorm broke. Beneath the pelting rain, the spectators scattered. When an officer went back to check the area he found no one on the streets.

A few minutes after 7:00 P.M., the Selective Enforcement Unit, tired and sun-parched, reported in from the races. A half hour later a report was received that 500 persons were gathering. A police car was sent into the area to check the report. The officers could find no one. The men of the Selective Enforcement Unit were told to go home.

The men in the scout car had not, however, penetrated into the Central Park Village Housing complex where, as the rain ended, hundreds of persons poured from the apartments. At least half were teenagers and young adults. As they began to mill about and discuss the shooting, old grievances, both real and imagined, were resurrected: discriminatory practices of local stores, advantages taken by white men of Negro girls, the kicking in the face of a Negro boy by a white man as the Negro lay handcuffed on the ground, blackballing of two Negro high schools by the athletic conference.

Although officials prided themselves on supposedly good race relations and relative acceptance by whites of integration of schools and facilities, Negroes, composing almost 20 percent of the population,[1] had had no one of their own race to represent them in positions of policy or power, nor to appeal to for redress of grievances.

There was no Negro on the city council; none on the school board: none in the fire department; none of high rank on the police force. Six of every 10 houses inhabited by Negroes were unsound. Many were shacks with broken window panes, gas leaks, and rat holes in the walls. Rents averaged $50 to $60 a month. Such recreational facilities as did exist lacked equipment and supervisors. Young toughs intimidated the children who tried to use them.

The majority of Negro children never reached the eighth grade. In the high schools, only 3 to 4 percent of Negro seniors attained the minimum passing score on the State's college entrance examination, one-tenth the percentage of white students.

A difference of at least three-and-a-half years in educational attainment separated the average Negro and white. Fifty-five

[1] Throughout the report, in the presentation of statistics *Negro* is used interchangeably with *non-white*. Wherever available, current data are used. Where no updating has been possible, figures are those of the 1960 census. Sources are the U.S. Bureau of the Census and other government agencies, and, in a few instances, special studies.

percent of the Negro men in Tampa were working in unskilled jobs. More than half of the families had incomes of less than $3,000 a year. The result was that 40 percent of the Negro children lived in broken homes, and the city's crime rate ranked in the top 25 percent in the nation.

About a month before, police-community relations had been severely strained by the actions of a pair of white officers who were subsequently transferred to another beat.

When Officer Oates returned to the area he attempted to convince the crowd to disperse by announcing that a complete investigation would be made into the shooting. He seemed to be making headway when a young woman came running down the street screaming that the police had killed her brother. Her hysteria galvanized the crowd. Rock throwing began. Police cars driving into the area were stoned. The police, relying on a previous experience when, after withdrawal of their units, the crowd had dispersed, decided to send no more patrol cars into the vicinity.

This time the maneuver did not work. From nearby bars and tawdry night spots patrons joined the throng. A window was smashed. Haphazard looting began. As fluid bands of rioters moved down the Central Avenue business district, stores whose proprietors were particularly disliked were singled out. A grocery store, a liquor store, a restaurant were hit. The first fire was set.

Because of the dismissal of the Selective Enforcement Unit and the lack of accurate intelligence information, the police department was slow to react. Although Sheriff Malcolm Beard of Hillsborough County was in contact with the Department throughout the evening, it was not until after 11:00 P.M. that a request for deputies was made to him

At 11:30 P.M. a recall order, issued earlier by the police department, began to bring officers back into the area. By this time, the streets in the vicinity of the housing project were lighted by the flames of burning buildings.

Falling power lines whipped sparks about the skirmish line of officers as they moved down the street. The popping noise of what sounded to the officers like gunshots came from the direction of the housing project.

The officers did not return the fire. Police announced from a sound car that anyone caught armed would be shot. The firing ceased. Then, and throughout the succeeding two days, law enforcement officers refrained from the use of firearms. No officer or civilian suffered a gunshot wound during the riot.

Driving along the expressway, a young white couple, Mr. and Mrs. C. D., were startled by the fires. Deciding to investigate, they took the off-ramp into the midst of the riot. The car was swarmed over. Its windows were shattered. C. D. was dragged into the street.

As he emerged from a bar in which he had spent the evening, 19-year old J. C., a Negro fruit-picker from Arkansas, was as surprised by the riot as Mr. and Mrs. C. D. Rushing toward the station wagon in which the young woman was trapped, he interposed himself between her and the mob. Although rocks and beer cans smashed the windows, she was able to drive off. J. C. pushed through to where the white man lay. With the hoots and jeers of rioting youths ringing in his ears, J. C. helped him, also, to escape.

By 1:00 A.M., police officers and sheriff's deputies had surrounded an area several blocks square. Firemen began to extinguish the flames which, by this time, had spread to several other establishments from the three stores in which they had, originally, been set. No resistance was met. Control was soon re-established.

Governor Claude Kirk flew to Tampa. Since the chief of police was absent, and since the Governor regarded the sheriff as his "direct arm," Sheriff Beard was placed in charge of the combined forces of the police and sheriff's departments.

For the next 12 hours the situation remained quiet but tense. By afternoon of Monday, June 12, the sheriff's and police forces both had been fully committed. The men were tired. There were none in reserve.

As a precaution, the Sheriff requested that a National Guard contingent be made available.

Late in the afternoon Governor Kirk met with the residents at a school in the Central Park Village area. It was a tense meeting. Most speakers, whether white or Negro, were booed and hissed. The meeting broke up without concrete results. Nevertheless, the Governor believed it had enabled the residents to let off steam.

That evening, as National Guard troops began to supplant local forces in maintaining a perimeter and establishing roving patrols, anti-poverty workers went from door to door, urging citizens to stay off the streets.

A reported attempt by Black Muslims to incite further violence failed. Although there were scattered reports of trouble from several areas of the city, and a few fires were set—largely in vacant buildings—there were no major incidents. Several youths with a cache of Molotov cocktails were arrested. They were white.

All the next day false reports poured into Police Headquarters. Everyday scenes took on menacing tones. Twenty Negro men, bared to the waist and carrying clubs were reported to be gathering. They turned out to be construction workers.

Mayor Nuccio met with residents. At their suggestion that the man most likely to carry weight with the youngsters was Coach Jim Williams, he placed a call to Tallahassee, where Williams was attending a coaching clinic.

An impressive-looking man with graying hair, Williams arrived in Tampa almost 48 hours after the shooting of Martin Chambers. Together with another coach he went to an eatery called The Greek Stand, behind which he found a number of youngsters fashioning an arsenal of bottles, bricks, and Molotov cocktails. As in the crowds that were once more beginning to gather, the principal complaint was the presence of the National Guard, which, the residents asserted, gave them a feeling of being hemmed in. Williams decided to attempt to negotiate the removal of the National Guard if the people would agree to keep the peace and to disperse.

When Sheriff Beard arrived at a meeting called for the College Hill Elementary School, Robert Gilder of the NAACP was speaking to leaders of the Negro youth. Some were college students who had been unable to get summer jobs. One was a Vietnam veteran who had been turned down for a position as a swimming pool lifeguard. The youths believed that discrimination had played a part in their failure to find jobs.

The suggestion was made to Sheriff Beard that the National Guard be pulled out of the Negro areas, and that these young men, as well as others, be given the opportunity to keep order. The idea, which was encouraged by James Hammond, Director of the Commission of Community Relations, made sense to the Sheriff. He decided to take a chance on the Youth Patrol.

In another part of the city, West Tampa, two Negro community leaders, Dr. James O. Brookins and attorney Delano S. Stewart, were advised by acquaintances that, unless the intensive patrolling of Negro neighborhoods ceased, people planned to set fires in industrial districts that evening. Like Coach Williams, Dr. Brookins and Stewart contacted neighborhood youths, and invited Sheriff Beard to a meeting. The concept of the Youth Patrol was expanded. Participants were identified first by phosphorescent arm bands, and later by white hats.

During the next 24 hours 126 youths, some of whom had participated in the riot, were recruited into the patrol. Many were high school dropouts.

On Wednesday, the inquiry into the death of Martin Chambers was concluded. With the verdict that Officer Calvert had fired the shot justifiably and in the line of duty, apprehension rose that trouble would erupt again. The leaders of the Youth Patrol were called in. The Sheriff explained the law to them, and pointed out that the verdict was in conformance with the law. Despite the fact that the verdict was not to their liking, the White Hats continued to keep order.

II. CINCINNATI

On Monday, June 12, before order had been restored in Tampa, trouble erupted 940 miles away in Cincinnati.

Beginning in October, 1965, assaults on middle-aged white women, several of whom were murdered, had generated an atmosphere of fear. When the "Cincinnati Strangler" was tentatively identified as a Negro, a new element of tension was injected into relations between the races.

In December, 1966, a Negro jazz musician named Posteal Laskey was arrested and charged with one of the murders. In May of 1967 he was convicted and sentenced to death. Two of the principal witnesses against Laskey were Negroes. Nevertheless, many Negroes felt that, because of the charged atmosphere, he had not received a fair trial.

They were further aroused when, at about the same time, a white man, convicted of manslaughter in the death of his girlfriend, received a suspended sentence. Although the cases were dissimilar, there was talk in the Negro community that the difference in the sentences demonstrated a double standard of justice for white and for black.

A drive began in the Negro community to raise funds for an appeal. Laskey's cousin, Peter Frakes, began walking the streets on behalf of this appeal carrying a sandwich board declaring: "Cincinnati Guilty—Laskey Innocent." After warning him several times, police arrested Frakes on a charge of blocking pedestrian traffic.

Many Negroes viewed his arrest as evidence of police harassment, similar to the apparently selective enforcement of the city's anti-loitering ordinance. Between January, 1966, and June, 1967, 170 of some 240 persons arrested under the ordinance were Negro.

Frakes was arrested at 12:35 A.M. on Sunday, June 11. That evening, concurrently with the commencement of a Negro Baptist Convention, it was announced in one of the churches that a meeting to protest the Frakes arrest and the anti-loitering ordinance would be held the following night on the grounds of a junior high school in the Avondale District.

Part of the significance of such a protest meeting lay in the context of past events. Without the city's realizing what was occurring, over the years protest through political and nonviolent channels had become increasingly difficult for Negroes. To young, militant Negroes, especially, such protest appeared to have become almost futile.

Although the city's Negro population had been rising swiftly —in 1967, 135,000 out of the city's 500,000 residents were Negroes—there was only one Negro on the city council. In the 1950's, with a far smaller Negro population, there had been two. Negroes attributed this to dilution of the Negro vote through abolition of the proportional representation system of electing the nine councilmen.

Although, by 1967, 40 percent of the school children were Negro, there was only one Negro on the Board of Education. Of more than 80 members of various city commissions, only three or four were Negro.

Under the leadership of the NAACP, picketing, to protest lack of Negro membership in building trades unions, took place at the construction site of a new city convention hall. It produced no results. When the Reverend Fred Shuttlesworth, who had been one of the leaders of the Birmingham demonstrations of 1963, staged a protest against alleged discriminatory practices at the County Hospital, he and his followers were arrested and convicted of trespassing.

Traditional Negro leaders drawn from the middle class lost influence as promises made by the city produced petty results. In the spring of 1967, a group of 14 white and 14 Negro business and community leaders, called the Committee of 28, talked about 2,000 job openings for young Negroes. Only 65 materialized. Almost one out of every eight Cincinnati Negroes was unemployed. Two of every five Negro families were living on or below the border of poverty.

A study of the West End section of the city indicated that one out of every four Negro men living there was out of work. In one public housing area two-thirds of the fathers were missing. Of private housing occupied by Negroes, one-fourth was overcrowded, and half was deteriorated or dilapidated.

In the 90-degree temperature of Monday, June 12th, as throughout the summer, Negro youngsters roamed the streets. The two swimming pools available to them could accommodate only a handful. In the Avondale section—once a prosperous white middle class community, but now the home of more than half the city's Negro population—Negro youths watched white workers going to work at white-owned stores and businesses. One youth began to count the number of delivery trucks being driven by Negroes. During the course of the afternoon, of the 52 trucks he counted, only one had a Negro driver. His sampling was remarkably accurate. According to a study conducted by the Equal Employment Opportunities Commission, less than 2 percent of truck drivers in the Cincinnati area are Negro.

Late in the afternoon the youths began to interfere with deliveries being made by white drivers. Dr. Bruce Green, president of the local NAACP chapter, was notified. Dr. Green asked his colleague, Dr. Robert Reid, the director of the Opportunities Industrialization Center, to go and try to calm the youngsters. Dr. Reid found several whom he knew, and convinced them to go with him to the Avondale Special Services Office to talk things over.

They were drawing up plans for a meeting with merchants of the Avondale area when word came of an altercation at a nearby drugstore. Several of the youths left the meeting and rushed over to the store. Dr. Reid followed them. The owner of the store was complaining to the police that earlier the youths had been interfering with his business; he declared that he wasn't going to stand for it.

Dr. Reid was attempting to mediate when a police sergeant arrived and asked the officers what was going on. One allegedly replied that they had been called in because "young nigger punks were disrupting deliveries to the stores."

A dispute arose between Dr. Reid and the sergeant as to whether the officer had said "nigger." After further discussion the sergeant told the kids to "break it up!" Dr. Reid, together with some of the youngsters, returned to the Special Services Office. After talking to the youngsters again, Dr. Reid left to attend a meeting elsewhere.

Soon after, some of the youngsters headed for the junior high school, where the meeting protesting the Frakes arrest and the anti-loitering ordinance was scheduled to take place.

The police department, alerted to the possibility of a disturbance, mobilized. However, the police were wary of becoming, as some Negro militants had complained, an inciting factor. Some months earlier, when Ku Klux Klansmen had been attracted to the scene of a speech by Stokely Carmichael, a Negro crowd, reacting to the heavy police patrolling, had gathered about the car of a plainclothesman and attempted to overturn it. On Monday, June 12, the department decided to withhold its men from the immediate area of the meeting.

It appeared for a time as if this policy might be rewarded. Near the end of the rally, however, a Negro real estate broker arose to defend the police and the anti-loitering ordinance. The crowd, including the youngsters who had had the encounter with the police officers only a short time earlier, was incensed. When the meeting broke up, a missile was hurled through the window of a nearby church. A small fire was set in the street. A Molotov cocktail was thrown through the window of a drug store.

The police were able to react quickly. There was only one major confrontation between them and the mob. Little resistance was offered.

Although windows were broken in some two dozen stores, there was virtually no looting. There were 14 arrests, some unconnected with the disturbance. Among those arrested was a community worker, now studying for a doctorate at Brandeis University. When he went to the area to help get people off the streets, he was arrested and charged with loitering.

The next morning a judge of the Municipal Court, before whom most of the persons charged were to be brought, said he intended to mete out the maximum sentence to anyone found guilty of a riot-connected offense. Although the judge later told the Commission that he knew his statement was a "violation of judicial ethics," he said that he made it because the "city was in a state of siege," and he intended it to act as a deterrent against further violence.

Maximum sentences were, in fact, pronounced by the judge on all convicted in his court, regardless of the circumstances of the arrest, or the background of the persons arrested. Police were charging most white persons arrested with disorderly conduct—for which the maximum sentence is 30 days in jail and a $100 fine. Many Negroes, however, were charged with violation of the Riot Act—for which the maximum sentence is one year in jail plus a $500 fine. Consequently, a major portion of the Negro community viewed this as an example of discriminatory justice.

Tuesday morning Negro leaders presented a list of 11 demands and grievances stemming from the Monday night meeting to the municipal government. Included were demands for repeal of the anti-loitering law, release of all prisoners arrested during the disturbance, full employment for Negroes, and equal justice in the courts.

Municipal officials agreed that the city council would consider the demands. However, they rejected a suggestion that they attend an open-air meeting of residents in the Avondale section. City leaders did not want to give stature to the militants by recognizing them as the *de facto* representatives of the community. Yet, by all indications, the militants were the only persons with influence on the people on the streets.

Mayor Walton H. Bachrach declared that he was "quite surprised" by the disturbance because the council had "worked like hell" to help Negroes. Municipal officials, whose contacts were, as in other cities, generally with a few middle-class Negroes, appeared not to realize the volatile frustrations of Negroes in the ghetto.

Early in the evening a crowd, consisting mostly of teenagers and young adults, began to gather in the Avondale District. When, after a short time, no one appeared to give direction, they began to mill about. A few minutes before 7:00 P.M. cars were stoned and windows were broken. Police moved in to disperse the gathering.

Fires were set. When firemen reached the scene they were barraged with rocks and bottles. A full-scale confrontation took place between police riot squads and the Negro crowd. As police swept the streets, people scattered. According to the chief of police, at approximately 7:15, "All hell broke loose."

The disorder leaped to other sections of the city. The confusion and rapidity with which it spread made it almost impossible to determine its scope.

Many reports of fires set by Molotov cocktails, cars being stoned, and windows being broken were received by the police. A white motorist—who died three weeks later—and a Negro sitting on his porch suffered gunshot wounds. Rumors spread of Negro gangs raiding white neighborhoods, of shootings, and of organization of the riot. Nearly all of them were determined later to be unfounded.

At 9:40 P.M., following a request for aid to surrounding communities, Mayor Bachrach placed a call to the Governor asking for mobilization of the National Guard.

At 2:30 A.M., Wednesday the first Guard units appeared on the streets. They followed a policy of restraint in the use of weapons. Few shots were fired. Two hours later, the streets were quiet. Most of the damage was minor. Of 40-odd fires reported before dawn, only 11 resulted in a loss of more than $1,000. The fire department log listed four as having caused major damage.

That afternoon the city council held an open session. The chamber was jammed with Negro residents, many of whom gave vociferous support as their spokesmen criticized the city administration. When the audience became unruly, a detail of National Guardsmen was stationed outside the council chamber. Their presence resulted in a misunderstanding, causing many of the Negroes to walk out, and the meeting to end.

Wednesday night there were virtually no reports of riotous activity until 9:00 P.M., when scattered incidents of violence again began to take place. One person was injured by a gunshot.

Despite fears of a clash between Negroes and SAMS—white

Southern Appalachian migrants whose economic conditions paralleled those of Negroes—such a clash was averted.

H. "Rap" Brown, arriving in the city on Thursday, attempted to capitalize on the discontent by presenting a list of 20 "demands." Their principal effect would have been total removal of all white persons, whatever their capacity, from the ghetto area. Demand No. 18 stated that "at any meeting to settle grievances . . . any white proposal or white representative objected to by black representatives must be rejected automatically." No. 20 demanded a veto power over police officers patrolling the community.

His appearance had no galvanizing effect. Although scattered incidents occurred for three days after the arrival of the National Guard, the disorder never returned to its early intensity.

Of 63 reported injuries, 12 were serious enough to require hospitalization; 56 of the persons injured were white. Most of the injuries resulted from thrown objects and glass splinters. Of the 107 persons arrested Tuesday night, when the main disturbance took place, 75 were 21 years of age or younger. Of the total of 404 persons arrested, 128 were juveniles, and 338 were 26 years of age or younger. Of the adults arrested, 29 percent were unemployed.

III. ATLANTA

On Saturday, June 17, as the National Guard was being withdrawn from Cincinnati, the same type of minor police arrest that had initiated the Cincinnati riot took place in Atlanta.

Rapid industrialization following World War II, coupled with annexations that quadrupled the area of the city, had made Atlanta a vigorous and booming community. Pragmatic business and political leaders worked to give it a reputation as the moderate stronghold of the Deep South.

Nevertheless, despite acceptance, in principle, of integration of schools and facilities, the fact that the city is headquarters both for civil rights organizations and segregationist elements created a strong and ever-present potential for conflict.

The rapidly growing Negro population, which, by the summer of 1967 had reached an estimated 44 percent, and was scattered in several ghettos throughout the city, was maintaining constant pressure on surrounding white residential areas. Some real estate agents engaged in "blockbusting tactics"[2] to

___
[2] A block is considered to have been "busted" when one Negro family has been sold a home in a previously all-white area.

stimulate panic sales by white homeowners. The city police were continually on the alert to keep marches and countermarches of civil rights and white supremacist organizations from flaring into violence.

In September 1966, following a fatal shooting by a police officer of a Negro auto thief who was resisting arrest, only the dramatic ghetto appearance of Mayor Ivan Allen, Jr. had averted a riot.

Boasting that Atlanta had the largest KKK membership in the country, the Klan, on June 4, 1967, marched through one of the poorer Negro sections. A massive police escort prevented a racial clash.

According to Mayor Allen, 55 percent of municipal employees hired in 1967 were Negroes, bringing their proportion of the city work force to 28 percent. Of 908 police department employees, 85 are Negro—a higher proportion of Negroes than in most major city police departments in the nation.

To the Negro community, however, it appeared that the progress made served only to reduce the level of inequality. Equal conditions for blacks and whites remained a hope for the future. Different pay scales for black and white municipal employees performing the same jobs had been only recently eliminated.

The economic and educational gap between the black and white populations may, in fact, have been increasing. The average white Atlantan was a high school graduate; the average Negro Atlantan had not completed the eighth grade.

In 1960 the median income of a Negro family was less than half of the white's $6,350 a year, and 48 percent of Negro families earned less than $3,000 a year. Fifty percent of the men worked in unskilled jobs, and many more Negro women than men, 7.9 percent as against 4.9 percent of the respective work forces, held well-paying, white collar jobs.

Living on marginal incomes in cramped and deteriorating quarters—one-third of the housing was overcrowded and more than half substandard—families were breaking up at an increasing rate. In approximately four out of every 10 Negro homes the father was missing. In the case of families living in public housing projects, more than 60 percent are headed by females.

Mayor Allen estimated there were 25,000 jobs in the city waiting to be filled because people lacked the education or skills to fill them. Yet overcrowding in many Negro schools forced the scheduling of extended and double sessions. Although Negroes comprised 60 percent of the school population, there were 14 "white" high schools compared to 9 Negro.

The city has integrated its schools, but *de facto* segregation as a result of housing patterns has had the effect of continuing separate schooling of nearly all white and Negro pupils. White high school students attended classes 6½ hours a day; Negroes in high schools with double sessions attended 4½.

One Atlanta newspaper continued to advertise jobs by race, and in some industrial plants there were "Negro" jobs and "white" jobs, with little chance for advancement by Negroes.

Shortly after 8:00 P.M. on Saturday, June 17, a young Negro, E. W., carrying a can of beer, attempted to enter the Flamingo Grill in the Dixie Hills Shopping Center. When a Negro security guard told the youth he could not enter, a scuffle ensued. Police officers were called to the guard's aid. E. W. received help from his 19-year-old sister, who flailed away at the officers with her purse. Another 19-year-old Negro youth entered the fray. All three were arrested.

Although some 200 to 300 persons had been drawn to the scene of the incident, when police asked them to disperse, they complied.

Because the area is isolated from the city in terms of transportation, and there are few recreational facilities, the shopping center is a natural gathering place. The next night, Sunday, an even bigger crowd was on hand.

As they mingled, residents discussed their grievances. They were bitter about their inability to get the city government to correct conditions and make improvements. Garbage sometimes was not picked up for two weeks in succession. Overflowing garbage cans, littered streets, and cluttered empty lots were breeding grounds for rats. Inadequate storm drains led to flooded streets. Although residents had obtained title to several empty lots for use as playgrounds, the city failed to provide the equipment and men necessary to convert them.

The area lacked a swimming pool. A nearby park was inaccessible because of the lack of a road. Petitions submitted to the mayor's office for the correcting of these and other conditions were acknowledged, but not acted upon.

Since only one of the 16 aldermen was a Negro, and a number of black wards were represented by white aldermen, many Negroes felt they were not being properly represented on the city government. The small number of elected Negro officials appeared to be due to a system in which aldermen are elected at large, but represent specific wards, and must reside in the wards from which they are elected. Because of the quilted pattern of black-white housing, white candidates were able to meet the residency requirements for running from predominantly Negro wards. Since, however, candidates are dependent upon the city-wide vote for election, and the city has a white majority, few Negroes had been able to attain office.

A decision was made by the Dixie Hills residents to organize committees and hold a protest meeting the next night.

The headquarters of the Student Nonviolent Coordinating Committee (SNCC) is located in Atlanta. Its former president, Stokely Carmichael, wearing a green Malcolm X sweatshirt, appeared, together with several companions. Approaching a police captain, Carmichael asked why there were so many police cars in the area. Informed that they were there to make sure there was no disturbance, Carmichael, clapping his hands, declared in a sing-song voice that there might have to be a riot if the police cars were not removed. When Carmichael refused to move on as requested, he was arrested.

Soon released on bail, the next morning Carmichael declared that the black people were preparing to resist "armed aggression" by the police by whatever means necessary.

Shortly thereafter in the Dixie Hills Shopping Center, which had been closed down for the day, a Negro youth, using a broom handle, began to pound on the outside bell of a burglar alarm that had been set off, apparently, by a short circuit. Police officers responded to the alarm and ordered him to stop hitting the bell. A scuffle ensued. Several bystanders intervened. One of the officers drew his service revolver and fired, superficially wounding the young man.

Tension rose. Approximately 250 persons were present at that evening's meeting. When a number of Negro leaders urged the submission of a petition of grievances through legal channels, the response was lukewarm. When Carmichael took to the podium, urging Negroes "to take to the streets and force the police department to work until they fall in their tracks," the response was tumultous.

The press quoted him as saying: "It's not a question of law and order. We are not concerned with peace. We are concerned with the liberation of black people. We have to build a revolution."

As the people present at the meeting poured into the street, they were joined by others. The crowd soon numbered an estimated 1,000. From alleys and rooftops rocks and bottles were thrown at the nine police officers on the scene. Windows of police cars were broken. Firecrackers exploded in the darkness. Police believe they may have been fired on.

Reinforced by approximately 60 to 70 officers, the police, firing over the heads of the crowd, quickly regained control. Of the 10 persons arrested, six were 21 years of age or younger; only one was in his thirties.

The next day city equipment appeared in the area to begin work on the long-delayed playgrounds and other projects demanded by the citizens. It was announced that a Negro Youth

Patrol would be established along the lines of the Tampa White Hats.

SNCC responded that volunteers for the patrol would be selling their "Black brothers out," and would be viewed as "Black Traitors," to be dealt with in the "manner we see fit." Nevertheless, during the course of the summer the 200 youths participating in the corps played an important role in preventing a serious outbreak. The police believe that establishment of the youth corps became a major factor in improving police-community relations.

Another meeting of area residents was called for Tuesday evening. At its conclusion 200 protesters were met by 300 police officers. As two police officers chased several boys down the street, a cherry bomb or incendiary device exploded at the officers' feet. In response, several shots were fired from a group of police consisting mostly of Negro officers. The discharge from a shotgun struck in the midst of several persons sitting on the front porch of a house. A 46-year old man was killed; a 9-year old boy was critically injured.

Because of the efforts of neighborhood and anti-poverty workers who circulated through the area, and the later appearance of Mayor Allen, no further violence ensued.

When H. "Rap" Brown, who had returned to the city that afternoon, went to other Negro areas in an attempt to initiate a demonstration against the shooting of the Negroes on the porch, he met with no response.

Within the next few days a petition was drawn up by State Senator Leroy Johnson and other moderate Negro leaders demanding that Stokely Carmichael get out of the community and allow the people to handle their own affairs. It was signed by more than 1,000 persons in the Dixie Hills area.

IV. Newark

The last outburst in Atlanta occurred on Tuesday night, June 20. That same night, in Newark, New Jersey, a tumultuous meeting of the Planning Board took place. Until 4 A.M., speaker after speaker from the Negro ghetto arose to denounce the city's intent to turn over 150 acres in the heart of the Central Ward as a site for the state's new medical and dental college.

The growing opposition to the city administration by vocal black residents had paralyzed both the Planning Board and the Board of Education. Tension had been rising so steadily throughout the northern New Jersey area that, in the first week of June, Colonel David Kelly, head of the state police, had met with municipal police chiefs to draw up plans for state police support of city police wherever a riot developed. Nowhere was the tension greater than in Newark.

Founded in 1666, the city, part of the Greater New York City port complex, rises from the salt marshes of the Passaic River. Although in 1967 Newark's population of 400,000 still ranked it thirtieth among American municipalities, for the past 20 years the white middle class had been deserting the city for the suburbs.

In the late 1950's the desertions had become a rout. Between 1960 and 1967, the city lost a net total of more than 70,000 white residents. Replacing them in vast areas of dilapidated housing where living conditions, according to a prominent member of the County Bar Association, were so bad that "people would be kinder to their pets," were Negro migrants, Cubans and Puerto Ricans. In six years the city switched from 65 percent white to 52 percent Negro and 10 percent Puerto Rican and Cuban.

The white population, nevertheless, retained political control of the city. On both the City Council and the Board of Education seven of nine members were white. On other key boards the disparity was equal or greater. In the Central Ward, where the medical college controversy raged, the Negro constituents and their white councilman found themselves on opposite sides of almost every crucial issue.

The municipal administration lacked the ability to respond quickly enough to navigate the swiftly changing currents. Even had it had great astuteness, it would have lacked the financial resources to affect significantly the course of events.

In 1962, seven-term Congressman Hugh Addonizio had forged an Italian-Negro coalition to overthrow long-time Irish control of the City Hall. A liberal in Congress, Addonizio, when he became mayor, had opened his door to all people. Negroes, who had been excluded from the previous administration, were brought into the government. The police department was integrated.

Nevertheless, progress was slow. As the Negro population increased, more and more of the politically oriented found the progress inadequate.

The Negro-Italian coalition began to develop strains over the issue of the police. The police were largely Italian, the persons they arrested largely Negro. Community leaders agreed that, as in many police forces, there was a small minority of officers who abused their responsibility. This gave credibility to the cries of "Brutality!" voiced periodically by ghetto Negroes.

In 1965 Mayor Addonizio, acknowledged that there was "a small group of misguided individuals" in the department, declared that "it is vital to establish once and for all, in the minds of the public, that charges of alleged police brutality will be thoroughly investigated and the appropriate legal or punitive action be taken if the charges are found to be substantiated."

Pulled one way by the Negro citizens who wanted a Police Review Board, and the other by the police, who adamantly opposed it, the mayor decided to transfer "the control and investigation of complaints of police brutality out of the hands of both the police and the public and into the hands of an agency that all can support—the Federal Bureau of Investigation;" and to send "a copy of any charge of police brutality . . . directly to the Prosecutor's office." However, the FBI could act only if there had been a violation of a person's federal civil rights. No complaint was ever heard of again.

Nor was there much redress for other complaints. The city had no money with which to redress them.

The city had already reached its legal bonding limit, yet expenditures continued to outstrip income. Health and welfare costs, per capita, were 20 times as great as for some of the surrounding communities. Cramped by its small land area of 23.6 square miles—one-third of which was taken up by Newark Airport and unusable marshland—and surrounded by independent jurisdictions, the city had nowhere to expand.

Taxable property was contracting as land, cleared for urban renewal, lay fallow year after year. Property taxes had been increased, perhaps, to the point of diminishing return. By the fall of 1967 they were to reach $661.70 on a $10,000 house—double that of suburban communities.[3] As a result, people were refusing either to own or to renovate property in the city. Seventy-four percent of white and 87 percent of Negro families lived in rental housing. Whoever was able to move to the suburbs, moved. Many of these persons, as downtown areas were cleared and new office buildings were constructed, continued to work in the city. Among them were a large proportion of the people from whom a city normally draws its civic leaders, but who, after moving out, tended to cease involving themselves in the community's problems.

During the daytime Newark more than doubled its population—and was, therefore, forced to provide services for a large number of people who contributed nothing in property taxes. The city's per capita outlay for police, fire protection and other municipal services continued to increase. By 1967 it was twice that of the surrounding area.

---

[3] The legal tax rate is $7.76 per $100 of market value. However, because of inflation, a guideline of 85.27 percent of market value is used in assessing, reducing the true tax rate to $6.617 per $100.

Consequently, there was less money to spend on education. Newark's per capita outlay on schools was considerably less than that of surrounding communities. Yet within the city's school system were 78,000 children, 14,000 more than 10 years earlier.

Twenty thousand pupils were on double sessions. The dropout rate was estimated to be as high as 33 percent. Of 13,600 Negroes between the ages of 16 and 19, more than 6,000 were not in school. In 1960 over half of the adult Negro population had less than an eighth grade education.

The typical ghetto cycle of high unemployment, family breakup, and crime was present in all its elements. Approximately 12 percent of Negroes were without jobs. An estimated 40 percent of Negro children lived in broken homes. Although Newark maintained proportionately the largest police force of any major city, its crime rate was among the highest in the nation. In narcotics violations it ranked fifth nationally. Almost 80 percent of the crimes were committed within two miles of the core of the city, where the Central Ward is located. A majority of the criminals were Negro. Most of the victims, likewise, were Negro. The Mafia was reputed to control much of the organized crime.

Under such conditions a major segment of the Negro population became increasingly militant. Largely excluded from positions of traditional political power, Negroes, tutored by a handful of militant social activists who had moved into the city in the early 1960's, made use of the anti-poverty program, in which poor people were guaranteed representation, as a political springboard. This led to friction between the United Community Corporation, the agency that administered the anti-poverty program, and the city administration.

When it became known that the secretary of the Board of Education intended to retire, the militants proposed for the position the city's budget director, a Negro with a master's degree in accounting. The mayor, however, had already nominated a white man. Since the white man had only a high school education, and at least 70 percent of the children in the school system were Negro, the issue of who was to obtain the secretaryship, an important and powerful position, quickly became a focal issue.

Joined with the issue of the 150-acre medical school site, the area of which had been expanded to triple the original request—an expansion regarded by the militants as an effort to dilute the black political power by moving out Negro residents —the Board of Education battle resulted in a confrontation between the mayor and the militants. Both sides refused to alter their positions.

Into this impasse stepped a Washington Negro named Albert Roy Osborne. A flamboyant, 42-year-old former wig salesman who called himself Colonel Hassan Jeru-Ahmed and wore a black beret, he presided over a mythical "Blackman's Volunteer Army of Liberation." Articulate and magnetic, the self-commissioned "Colonel" proved to be a one-man show. He brought Negro residents flocking to Board of Education and Planning Board meetings. The Colonel spoke in violent terms, and backed his words with violent action. At one meeting he tore the tape from the official stenographic recorder.

It became more and more evident to the militants that, though they might not be able to prevail, they could prevent the normal transaction of business. Filibustering began. A Negro former state assemblyman held the floor for more than four hours. One meeting of the Board of Education began at 5:00 P.M. and did not adjourn until 3:23 A.M. Throughout the months of May and June speaker after speaker warned that if the mayor persisted in naming a white man as Secretary to the Board of Education, and in moving ahead with plans for the medical school site, violence would ensue. The city administration played down the threats.

On June 27th, when a new secretary to the Board of Education was to be named, the state police set up a command post in the Newark armory.

The militants, led by the local CORE (Congress of Racial Equality) chapter, disrupted and took over the Board of Education meeting. The outcome was a stalemate. The incumbent secretary decided to stay on another year. No one was satisfied.

At the beginning of July there were 24,000 unemployed Negroes within the city limits. Their ranks were swelled by an estimated 20,000 teenagers, many of whom, with school out and the summer recreation program curtailed due to a lack of funds, had no place to go.

On July 8, Newark and East Orange Police attempted to disperse a group of Black Muslims. In the melee that followed, several police officers and Muslims suffered injuries necessitating medical treatment. The resulting charges and countercharges heightened the tension between police and Negroes.

Early on the evening of July 12, a cab driver named John Smith began, according to police reports, tailgating a Newark police car. Smith was an unlikely candidate to set a riot in motion. Forty years old, a Georgian by birth, he had attended college for a year before entering the Army in 1950. In 1953 he had been honorably discharged with the rank of corporal. A chess-playing trumpet player, he had worked as a musician and a factory hand before, in 1963, becoming a cab driver.

As a cab driver, he appeared to be a hazard. Within a relatively short period of time he had eight or nine accidents. His license was revoked. When, with a woman passenger in his cab, he was stopped by the police, he was in violation of that revocation.

From the high-rise towers of the Reverend William P. Hayes Housing Project, the residents can look down on the orange-red brick facade of the Fourth Precinct Police Station and observe every movement. Shortly after 9:30 P.M., people saw Smith, who either refused or was unable to walk, being dragged out of a police car and into the front door of the station.

Within a few minutes at least two civil rights leaders received calls from a hysterical woman declaring a cab driver was being beaten by the police. When one of the persons at the station notified the cab company of Smith's arrest, cab drivers all over the city began learning of it over their cab radios.

A crowd formed on the grounds of the housing project across the narrow street from the station. As more and more people arrived, the description of the beating purportedly administered to Smith became more and more exaggerated. The descriptions were supported by other complaints of police malpractice that, over the years, had been submitted for investigation—but had never been heard of again.

Several Negro community leaders, telephoned by a civil rights worker and informed of the deteriorating situation, rushed to the scene. By 10:15 P.M. the atmosphere had become so potentially explosive that Kenneth Melchior, the senior police inspector on the night watch, was called. He arrived at approximately 10:30 P.M.

Met by a delegation of civil rights leaders and militants who requested the right to see and interview Smith, Inspector Melchior acceded to their request.

When the delegation was taken to Smith, Melchior agreed with their observations that, as a result of injuries Smith had suffered, he needed to be examined by a doctor. Arrangements were made to have a police car transport him to the hospital.

Both within and outside of the police station the atmosphere was electric with hostility. Carloads of police officers arriving for the 10:45 P.M. change of shifts were subjected to a gauntlet of catcalls, taunts and curses.

Joined by Oliver Lofton, administrative director of the Newark Legal Services Project, the Negro community leaders inside the station requested an interview with Inspector Melchior. As they were talking to the inspector about initiating an investigation to determine how Smith had been injured, the crowd outside became more and more unruly. Two of the Negro spokesmen went outside to attempt to pacify the people.

There was little reaction to the spokesmen's appeal that the people go home. The second of the two had just finished speaking from atop a car when several Molotov cocktails smashed against the wall of the police station.

With the call of "Fire!" most of those inside the station, police officers and civilians alike, rushed out of the front door. The Molotov cocktails had splattered to the ground; the fire was quickly extinguished.

Inspector Melchior had a squad of men form a line across the front of the station. The police officers and the Negroes on the other side of the street exchanged volleys of profanity.

Three of the Negro leaders, Timothy Still of the United Community Corporation, Robert Curvin of CORE, and Lofton, requested they be given another opportunity to disperse the crowd. Inspector Melchior agreed to let them try, and provided a bullhorn. It was apparent that the several hundred persons who had gathered in the street and on the grounds of the housing project were not going to disperse. Therefore, it was decided to attempt to channel the energies of the people into a nonviolent protest. While Lofton promised the crowd that a full investigation would be made of the Smith incident, the other Negro leaders urged those on the scene to form a line of march toward the city hall.

Some persons joined the line of march. Others milled about in the narrow street. From the dark grounds of the housing project came a barrage of rocks. Some of them fell among the crowd. Others hit persons in the line of march. Many smashed the windows of the police station. The rock throwing, it was believed, was the work of youngsters; approximately 2,500 children lived in the housing project.

Almost at the same time, an old car was set afire in a parking lot. The line of march began to disintegrate. The police, their heads protected by World War I-type helmets, sallied forth to disperse the crowd. A fire engine, arriving on the scene, was pelted with rocks. As police drove people away from the station, they scattered in all directions.

A few minutes later a nearby liquor store was broken into. Some persons, seeing a caravan of cabs appear at city hall to protest Smith's arrest, interpreted this as evidence that the disturbance had been organized, and generated rumors to that effect.

However, only a few stores were looted. Within a short period of time the disorder ran its course.

The next afternoon, Thursday, July 13, the mayor described it as an isolated incident. At a meeting with Negro leaders to discuss measures to defuse the situation, he agreed to appoint the first Negro police captain, and announced that he would set up a panel of citizens to investigate the Smith arrest. To one civil rights leader this sounded like"the playback of a record," and he walked out. Other observers reported that the mayor seemed unaware of the seriousness of the tensions.

The police were not. Unknown to the mayor, Dominick Spina, the director of police, had extended shifts from eight hours to 12, and was in the process of mobilizing half the strength of the department for that evening. The night before, Spina had arrived at the Fourth Precinct Police Station at approximately midnight, and had witnessed the latter half of the disturbance. Earlier in the evening he had held the regular weekly "open house" in his office. This was intended to give any person who wanted to talk to him an opportunity to do so. Not a single person had shown up.

As director of police, Spina had initiated many new programs: police-precinct councils, composed of the police precinct captain and business and civic leaders, who would meet once a month to discuss mutual problems; Junior Crimefighters; a Boy Scout Explorer program for each precinct; mandatory human relations training for every officer; a Citizens' Observer Program, which permitted citizens to ride in police cars and observe activities in the stations; a Police Cadet program; and others.

Many of the programs initially had been received enthusiastically, but—as was the case with the "open house"—interest had fallen off. In general, the programs failed to reach the hard-core unemployed, the disaffected, the school dropouts —of whom Spina estimates there are 10,000 in Essex County —that constitute a major portion of the police problem.

Reports and rumors, including one that Smith had died, circulated through the Negro community. Tension continued to rise. Nowhere was the tension greater than at the Spirit House, the gathering place for Black Nationalists, Black Power advocates, and militants of every hue. Black Muslims, Orthodox Muslims, and members of the United Afro-American Association, a new and growing organization that follows, in general, the teachings of the late Malcolm X, came regularly to mingle and exchange views. Anti-white playwright LeRoi Jones held workshops. The two police-Negro clashes, coming one on top of the other, coupled with the unresolved political issues, had created a state of crisis.

On Thursday, inflammatory leaflets were circulated in the neighborhoods of the Fourth Precinct. A "Police Brutality Protest Rally" was announced for early evening in front of the Fourth Precinct Station. Several television stations and newspapers sent news teams to interview people. Cameras were set up. A crowd gathered.

A picket line was formed to march in front of the police station. Between 7:00 and 7:30 P.M. James Threatt, Executive Director of the Newark Human Rights Commission, arrived to announce to the people the decision of the mayor to form a citizens group to investigate the Smith incident, and to elevate a Negro to the rank of captain.

The response from the loosely milling mass of people was derisive. One youngster shouted "Black Power!" Rocks were thrown at Threatt, a Negro. The barrage of missiles that followed placed the police station under siege.

After the barrage had continued for some minutes, police came out to disperse the crowd. According to witnesses, there was little restraint of language or action by either side. A number of police officers and Negroes were injured.

As on the night before, once the people had been dispersed, reports of looting began to come in. Soon the glow of the first fire was seen.

Without enough men to establish control, the police set up a perimeter around a two-mile stretch of Springfield Avenue, one of the principal business districts, where bands of youths roamed up and down smashing windows. Grocery and liquor stores, clothing and furniture stores, drug stores and cleaners, appliance stores and pawnshops were the principal targets. Periodically police officers would appear and fire their weapons over the heads of looters and rioters. Laden with stolen goods, people began returning to the housing projects.

Near midnight, activity appeared to taper off. The Mayor told reporters the city had turned the corner.

As news of the disturbance had spread, however, people had flocked into the streets. As they saw stores being broken into with impunity, many bowed to temptation and joined the looting.

Without the necessary personnel to make mass arrests, police were shooting into the air to clear stores. A Negro boy was wounded by a .22 caliber bullet said to have been fired by a white man riding in a car. Guns were reported stolen from a Sears, Roebuck store. Looting, fires, and gunshots were reported from a widening area. Between 2:00 and 2:30 A.M. on Friday, July 14, the mayor decided to request Governor Richard J. Hughes to dispatch the state police, and National Guard troops. The first elements of the state police arrived with a sizeable contingent before dawn.

During the morning the governor and the mayor, together with police and National Guard officers, made a reconnaissance of the area. The police escort guarding the officials arrested looters as they went. By early afternoon the National Guard had set up 137 roadblocks, and state police and riot teams were beginning to achieve control. Command of anti-riot operations was taken over by the governor, who decreed a "hard line" in putting down the riot.

As a result of technical difficulties, such as the fact that the city and state police did not operate on the same radio wavelengths, the three-way command structure—city police, state police and National Guard—worked poorly.

At 3:30 P.M. that afternoon, the family of Mrs. D. J. was standing near the upstairs windows of their apartment, watching looters run in and out of a furniture store on Springfield Avenue. Three carloads of police rounded the corner. As the police yelled at the looters, they began running.

The police officers opened fire. A bullet smashed the kitchen window in Mrs. D. J.'s apartment. A moment later she heard a cry from the bedroom. Her 3-year old daughter, Debbie, came running into the room. Blood was streaming down the left side of her face: the bullet had entered her eye. The child spent the next two months in the hospital. She lost the sight of her left eye and the hearing in her left ear.

Simultaneously, on the street below, Horace W. Morris, an associate director of the Washington Urban League who had been visiting relatives in Newark, was about to enter a car for the drive to Newark Airport. With him were his two brothers and his 73-year old step-father, Isaac Harrison. About 60 persons had been on the street watching the looting. As the police arrived, three of the looters cut directly in front of the group of spectators. The police fired at the looters. Bullets plowed into the spectators. Everyone began running. As Harrison, followed by the family, headed toward the apartment building in which he lived, a bullet kicked his legs out from under him. Horace Morris lifted him to his feet. Again he fell. Mr. Morris' brother, Virgil, attempted to pick the old man up. As he was doing so, he was hit in the left leg and right forearm. Mr. Morris and his other brother managed to drag the two wounded men into the vestibule of the building, jammed with 60 to 70 frightened, angry Negroes.

Bullets continued to spatter against the walls of the buildings. Finally, as the firing died down, Morris—whose stepfather died that evening—yelled to a sergeant that innocent people were being shot.

"Tell the black bastards to stop shooting at us," the sergeant, according to Morris, replied.

"They don't have guns; no one is shooting at you," Morris said.

"You shut up, there's a sniper on the roof," the sergeant yelled.

A short time later, at approximately 5:00 P.M., in the same vicinity a police detective was killed by a small caliber bullet. The origin of the shot could not be determined. Later during the riot a fireman was killed by a .30 caliber bullet. Snipers were blamed for the deaths of both.

At 5:30 P.M., on Beacon Street, W. F. told J. S., whose 1959 Pontiac he had taken to the station for inspection, that his front brake needed fixing. J. S., who had just returned from work, went to the car which was parked in the street, jacked up the front end, took the wheel off and got under the car.

The street was quiet. More than a dozen persons were sitting on porches, walking about, or shopping. None heard any shots. Suddenly several state troopers appeared at the corner of Springfield and Beacon. J. S. was startled by a shot clanging into the side of the garbage can next to his car. As he looked up he saw a state trooper with his rifle pointed at him. The next shot struck him in the right side.

At almost the same instant, K. G., standing on a porch, was struck in the right eye by a bullet. Both he and J. S. were critically injured.

At 8:00 P.M., Mrs. L. M. bundled her husband, her husband's brother, and her four sons into the family car to drive to a restaurant for dinner. On the return trip her husband, who was driving, panicked as he approached a National Guard roadblock. He slowed the car, then quickly swerved around. A shot rang out. When the family reached home, everyone began piling out of the car. Ten-year-old Eddie failed to move. Shot through the head, he was dead.

Although, by nightfall, most of the looting and burning had ended, reports of sniper fire increased. The fire was, according to New Jersey National Guard reports, "deliberately or otherwise inaccurate." Major General James F. Cantwell, Chief of Staff of the New Jersey National Guard, testified before an Armed Services Subcommittee of the House of Representatives that "there was too much firing initially against snipers" because of "confusion when we were finally called on for help and our thinking of it as a military action."

"As a matter of fact," Director of Police Spina told the Commission, "down in the Springfield Avenue area it was so bad that, in my opinion, Guardsmen were firing upon police and police were firing back at them . . . I really don't believe there was as much sniping as we thought . . . We have since compiled statistics indicating that there were 79 specified instances of sniping."

Several problems contributed to the misconceptions regarding snipers: the lack of communications; the fact that one shot might be reported half a dozen times by half a dozen different persons as it caromed and reverberated a mile or more through the city; the fact that the National Guard troops lacked riot training. They were, said a police official, "young and very scared," and had had little contact with Negroes.

Within the Guard itself contact with Negroes had certainly been limited. Although, in 1949, out of a force of 12,529 men there had been 1,183 Negroes, following the integration of the Guard in the 1950's the number had declined until, by July of 1967, there were 303 Negroes in a force of 17,529 men.

On Saturday, July 15, Spina received a report of snipers in a housing project. When he arrived he saw approximately 100 National Guardsmen and police officers crouching behind vehicles, hiding in corners and lying on the ground around the edge of the courtyard.

Since everything appeared quiet and it was broad daylight, Spina walked directly down the middle of the street. Nothing happened. As he came to the last building of the complex, he heard a shot. All around him the troopers jumped, believing themselves to be under sniper fire. A moment later a young Guardsman ran from behind a building.

The director of police went over and asked him if he had fired the shot. The soldier said yes, he had fired to scare a man away from a window; that his orders were to keep everyone away from windows.

Spina said he told the soldier: "Do you know what you just did? You have now created a state of hysteria. Every Guardsman up and down this street and every State Policeman and every city policeman that is present thinks that somebody just fired a shot and that it is probably a sniper."

A short time later more "gunshots" were heard. Investigating, Spina came upon a Puerto Rican sitting on a wall. In reply to a question as to whether he knew "where the firing is coming from?" the man said:

"That's no firing. That's fireworks. If you look up to the fourth floor, you will see the people who are throwing down these cherry bombs."

By this time four truckloads of National Guardsmen had arrived and troopers and policemen were again crouched everywhere, looking for a sniper. The director of police remained at the scene for three hours, and the only shot fired was the one by the Guardsman.

Nevertheless, at six o'clock that evening two columns of National Guardsmen and state troopers were directing mass fire at the Hayes Housing Project in response to what they believed were snipers.

On the tenth floor, Eloise Spellman, the mother of several children, fell, a bullet through her neck.

Across the street a number of persons, standing in an apartment window, were watching the firing directed at the housing project. Suddenly several troopers whirled and began firing in the general direction of the spectators. Mrs. Hattie Gainer, a grandmother, sank to the floor.

A block away Rebecca Brown's 2-year old daughter was standing at the window. Mrs. Brown rushed to drag her to safety. As Mrs. Brown was, momentarily, framed in the window, a bullet spun into her back.

All three women died.

A number of eye witnesses, at varying times and places, reported seeing bottles thrown from upper story windows. As these would land at the feet of an officer he would turn and fire. Thereupon, other officers and Guardsmen up and down the street would join in.

In order to protect his property, B. W. W., the owner of a Chinese laundry, had placed a sign saying "Soul Brother" in his window. Between 1:00 and 1:30 A.M., on Sunday, July 16, he, his mother, wife, and brother, were watching television in the back room. The neighborhood had been quiet. Suddenly B. W. W. heard the sound of jeeps, then shots.

Going to an upstairs window he was able to look out into the street. There he observed several jeeps, from which soldiers and state troopers were firing into stores that had "Soul Brother" signs in the windows. During the course of three nights, according to dozens of eye witness reports, law enforcement officers shot into and smashed windows of businesses that contained signs indicating they were Negro owned.

At 11.00 P.M., on Sunday, July 16th, Mrs. Lucille Pugh looked out of the window to see if the streets were clear. She then asked her 11-year-old son, Michael, to take the garbage out. As he reached the street and was illuminated by a street light, a shot rang out. He died.

By Monday afternoon, July 17, state police and National Guard forces were withdrawn. That evening, a Catholic priest saw two Negro men walking down the street. They were carrying a case of soda and two bags of groceries. An unmarked car with five police officers pulled up beside them. Two white officers got out of the car. Accusing the Negro men of looting, the officers made them put the groceries on the sidewalk, then kicked the bags open, scattering their contents all over the street.

Telling the men, "Get out of here," the officers drove off.

The Catholic priest went across the street to help gather up the groceries. One of the men turned to him: "I've just been back from Vietnam two days," he said, "and this is what I get. I feel like going home and getting a rifle and shooting the cops."

Of the 250 fire alarms, many had been false, and 13 were considered by the city to have been "serious." Of the $10,-251,000 damage total, four-fifths was due to stock loss. Damage to buildings and fixtures was less than $2 million.

Twenty-three persons were killed—a white detective, a white fireman, and 21 Negroes. One was 73-year-old Isaac Harrison. Six were women. Two were children.

V. NORTHERN NEW JERSEY

Reports of looting, sniping, fire and death in Newark wove a web of tension over other Negro enclaves in northern New Jersey. Wherever Negro ghettos existed—Elizabeth, Englewood, Jersey City, Plainfield, New Brunswick—people had friends and relatives living in Newark. Everywhere the telephone provided a direct link to the scenes of violence. The telephoned messages frequently were at variance with reports transmitted by the mass media.

As reports of the excessive use of firearms in Newark grew, so did fear and anger in the Negro ghettos. Conversely, rumors amplified by radio, television and the newspapers—especially with regard to guerrilla bands roaming the streets—created a sense of danger and terror within the white communities. To Mayor Patricia Q. Sheehan of New Brunswick, it seemed "almost as if there was a fever in the air." She went on to say: "Rumors were coming in from all sides on July 17th. Negroes were calling to warn of possible disturbances; whites were calling; shop owners were calling. Most of the people were concerned about a possible bloodbath."

Her opinion was: "We are talking ourselves into it."

Everywhere there was the same inequality with regard to education, job opportunities, income, and housing. Everywhere, partly because the Negro population was younger than the white, Negroes were under-represented on the local government. In six New Jersey communities[4] with sizeable Negro populations, of a total of 50 councilmen, six were Negro. In a half-dozen school systems in which Negro children comprised as much as half of the school population, of a total of 42 members on boards of education, seven were Negro.

In each of the ghettos the Negro felt himself surrounded by an intransigent wall of whites. In four suburban cities—

[4] Jersey City, Elizabeth, Englewood, Plainfield, Paterson, New Brunswick.

Bloomfield, Harrison, Irvington, and Maplewood—forming an arc about Newark, out of a total population of more than 150,000, only 1,000 were Negroes. In the six cities surrounding Plainfield, out of a population of more than 75,000, only 1,500 were Negro.

Three northern New Jersey communities, Jersey City, Paterson, and Elizabeth, had had disorders in previous years, the first two in 1964, Elizabeth in both 1964 and 1965. In general, these seem to have developed from resentment against the police. The most serious outbreak had occurred in Jersey City after police had arrested a woman, and a rumor circulated that the woman had been beaten.

As early as May, 1967, the authorities in Jersey City and Elizabeth had started receiving warnings of trouble in the summer ahead. Following the Newark outbreak, rumors and reports, as in New Brunswick, became rampant. The police, relying on past experiences, were in no mood to take chances. In both Jersey City and Elizabeth patrols were augmented, and the departments were placed in a state of alert.

The view from Jersey City is that of the New York skyline. Except for a few imposing buildings, such as the high-rise New Jersey Medical Center, much of the city is a collection of factories and deteriorating houses, cut up by ribbons of super-highways and railroads.

As one of the principal freight terminals for New York City, Jersey City's decline has paralleled that of the railroads. As railroad lands deteriorated in value and urban renewal lands were taken off the tax rolls, assessed valuation plummeted from $464 million in 1964 to $367 million in 1967. The tax rate, according to Mayor Thomas J. Whelan, has "reached the point of diminishing returns."

Urban renewal projects, which were intended to clear slums and replace them with low-cost housing, in fact, resulted in a reduction of 2,000 housing units. On one area, designated for urban renewal six years before, no work had been done, and it remained as blighted in 1967 as it had been in 1961. Ramshackle houses deteriorated, no repairs were made, yet people continued to inhabit them. "Planners make plans and then simply tell people what they are going to do," Negroes complained in their growing opposition to such projects.

Wooden sewers serve residents of some sections of the city. Collapsing brick sewers in other sections back up the sewage. The population clamors for better education, but the school system has reached its bonding capacity. By 1975 it is estimated that there will be a net deficit of 10 elementary schools and one high school.

Recently the mayor proposed to the Ford Foundation that

it take over the operation of the entire educational system. The offer was declined.

Many whites send their children to parochial schools. Possibly as a result, white residents have been slower to move to the suburbs than in other cities.

The exodus, however, is accelerating. Within the past 10 years the Negro population has almost doubled, and now comprises an estimated 20 percent of the total. The little Negro political leadership that exists is fragmented and indecisive. The county in which Jersey City is located is run by an old-line political machine that has given Negroes little opportunity for participation.

Although the amount of schooling whites and Negroes have had is almost equal, in 1960 the median family income of whites was $1,500 more than that of Negroes.

The police department, like Newark's, one of the largest in the nation for a city of its size, has a reputation for toughness. A successful white executive recalled that in his childhood: "We were accustomed to the Special Service Division of the Police Department. If we were caught hanging around we were picked up by the police, taken to a nearby precinct, and beaten with a rubber hose."

A city official, questioned about Negro representation on the 825-man police force, replied that it was 34 times greater than 20 years ago. Twenty years ago it had consisted of one man.

During the four days of the Newark riot, when Jersey City was flooded with tales of all description, Mayor Whelan announced that if there were any disturbances he would "meet force with force." The ghetto area was saturated with police officers.

On Monday and Tuesday, July 17 and 18, when crowds gathered and a few rocks were thrown, mass arrests were made. Only one store was broken into, and pilferage was limited to items such as candy and chewing gum.

One man died. He was a Negro passenger in a cab into which a Negro boy threw a Molotov cocktail.

In Elizabeth, as in Jersey City, police had beefed up their patrols, and the very presence of so many officers contributed to the rising tensions. Residents of the 12-block by 3-block ghetto, jammed between the New Jersey Turnpike and the waterfront, expressed the opinion that: "We are being punished but we haven't done anything."

"The community," another said later, "felt it was in a concentration camp."

Youths from the two high-density housing projects concentrated in the area were walking around saying: "We're next, we might as well go."

Between 10:00 and 10:30 p.m. Monday, July 17, a window was broken in a drugstore across the street from a housing project. A businessman commented: "Down here in the port it's business as usual when one store window is broken each week. What is normal becomes abnormal at a time like this."

When the window was broken, three extra police cars were sent to the area. Shortly after 11:00 p.m., the field supervisor dispatched three more cars and, observing the crowd gathering at the housing project, requested an additional 30 patrolmen. The department activated its emergency recall plan.

Since there are almost no recreational facilities, on any summer night scores of youths may be found congregating on the streets near the housing projects. As more and more police cars patrolled the streets, rocks and bottles were thrown at them.

Store windows were broken. Fires were set in trash cans and in the middle of the street. An expectation of impending violence gripped the crowd.

Arriving on the scene, Human Rights Commission Executive Director Hugh Barbour requested that, in order to relieve tension, the extra police be withdrawn from the immediate vicinity of the crowd. The officer in command agreed to pull back the patrols.

Workers from the anti-poverty agency and the Human Relations Commission began circulating through the area, attempting to get kids off the street. Many of the residents had relatives and friends in Newark. Based on what had happened there, they feared that, if the disturbance were not curbed, it would turn into a bloodbath.

The peacemakers were making little headway when a chicken fluttered out of the shattered window of a poultry market. One youth tried to throw gasoline on it and set it afire. As the gasoline sloshed onto the pavement, the chicken leaped. The flames merely singed its feathers. A gangling six-foot youth attempted to stomp the chicken. The bird, which had appeared dead, reacted violently. As it fluttered and darted out of his way, the youth screamed, slipped, and tumbled against a tree.

The stark comedy reduced the tension. People laughed. Soon some began to drift home.

A short time later a Molotov cocktail was thrown against the front of a tavern. Fire engines met with no opposition as they extinguished the flames before they could do much damage.

The chief of police ordered the area cleared. As the officers moved in, the persons who remained on the street scattered. Within 15 minutes the neighborhood was deserted.

72

Both municipal authorities and Negro leaders feared that, if the disorder followed the pattern of other disturbances, there would be an intensification of action by youths the next day. Therefore, the next evening, police patrolled the 36 square blocks with more than 100 men, some of them stationed on rooftops. Tension mounted as residents viewed the helmeted officers, armed with shotguns and rifles.

Early in the evening the mayor agreed to meet with a delegation of 13 community leaders. When they entered his office, the chief of police was already present. The mayor read him an order that, if he were faced with sniping or flagrant looting, his men were to: "Shoot to kill. . . . Force will be met with superior force." An officer's deviation from this order, the mayor said, would be considered dereliction of duty.

Some of the members of the delegation believed that the mayor had staged the reading of this order for their benefit, and were not pleased by his action. They proposed a "peace-keeper task force." The mayor agreed to let them try. One hundred stickers with the word "Peacekeeper" were printed.

One of those who agreed to be a peacemaker was Hesham Jaaber. Jaaber, who officiated at Malcolm X's funeral and has made two pilgrimages to Mecca, is a leader of a small sect of Orthodox Moslems. A teacher of Arabic and the Koran at the Spirit House in Newark, he is a militant who impressed the mayor with his sense of responsibility.

Although Jaaber believed that certain people were sucking the life blood out of the community—"Count the number of taverns and bars in the Elizabeth port area and compare them with the number of recreation facilities"—he had witnessed the carnage in Newark and believed it could serve no purpose to have a riot. Two dozen of his followers, in red fezzes, took to the streets to urge order. He himself traveled about in a car with a bullhorn.

As the peacekeepers began to make their influence felt, the police withdrew from the area. There was no further trouble.

Nevertheless, many white citizens reacted unfavorably to the fact that police had permitted Negro community leaders to aid in the dispersal of the crowd on the first night. The police were called "yellow," and accused of allowing the looting and damaging of stores.

In Englewood, a bedroom community of 28,000, astride the Palisades opposite New York, police had been expecting a riot by some of the city's 7,000 Negro residents since two weeks before Newark. As part of this expectation they had tested tear gas guns on the police firing range, situated in the middle of the Negro residential area. The wind had blown the tear gas into surrounding houses. The occupants had been enraged.

A continuing flow of rumors and anonymous tips to police of a riot in preparation had specified July 19 and July 28. However, the week following the Newark outbreak, the rumors began mentioning Friday, July 21, as the date. And it was on that day the chief of police became sufficiently concerned to alert the mayor, order mobilization of the police department, and request police assistance from Bergen County and nearby communities. The 160 officers who responded brought the total force in Englewood that evening to 220 men.

At approximately 9:00 p.m. a rock was thrown through a market in the lower class Negro area, resulting in the setting off of a burglar alarm at police headquarters. Two police cars responded. They were hit by rocks.

The tactical force of officers that had been assembled was rushed to the scene. A small number of persons, estimated in the official police report to be no more than 15 or 20, were standing in the street. When police formed a skirmish line, the loiterers, mostly youths, retreated into a large nearby park.

As the police remained in the vicinity, people, attracted by the presence of the officers, began drifting out of the park. Angry verbal exchanges took place between the residents and the police. The Negroes demanded to see the mayor.

The mayor arrived. The residents complained about the presence of so many police officers. Other grievances, many of them minor, began to be aired. According to the mayor, he became involved in a "shouting match," and departed. Shortly thereafter the police, too, left.

They returned after receiving a report that two markets had been hit by Molotov cocktails. Arriving, they discovered firemen fighting two small fires on the outside of the markets.

The police ordered the people on the street to disperse and return to their homes. A rock knocked out a streetlight. Darkness blanketed the area. From behind hedges and other places of concealment a variety of missiles were thrown at the police. The officer in charge was cut severely when a bottle broke the windshield of a car.

A fire department lighting unit was brought to the scene to illuminate the area. Except for some desultory rock throwing the neighborhood was quiet for the rest of the night. The only other disturbance occurred when a small band of youths made a foray into the city's principal business district two blocks away. Although a few windows were broken, there was no looting. Police quickly sealed off the area.

The same pattern of disorders continued for the next three nights. A relatively large number of police, responding to the breaking of windows or the setting of a fire, would come upon a small number of persons in the street. Fires repeatedly were set at or near the same two stores and a tavern. On one occasion two Negro youths threw Molotov cocktails at police officers, and the officers responded with gunfire.

Although sounds resembling gunshots were heard sporadically throughout the area, no bullets or expended shells were found. Lt. William Clark who, as the Bergen County Police Department's civil disorders expert, was on the scene, reported that teenagers, as a harassing tactic, had exploded cherry bombs and firecrackers over a widely scattered area. Another view is that there may have been shots, but that they were fired into the air.

Nevertheless, the press reported that: "Snipers set up a three-way crossfire at William and Jay Streets in the heart of the Fourth Ward Negro ghetto, and pinned down 100 policemen, four reporters and a photographer for more than an hour."

These reports were "very definitely exaggerated and overplayed," according to Deputy Chief William F. Harrington of the Englewood Police Department. What police termed a "disturbance" appeared in press reports as a "riot," and "was way out of proportion in terms of the severity of the situation."

" I feel strongly," the Chief said, "that the news media . . . actually inflamed the situation day by day."

VI. PLAINFIELD

New Jersey's worst violence outside of Newark was experienced by Plainfield, a pleasant, tree-shaded city of 45,000. A "bedroom community," more than a third of whose residents work outside the city, Plainfield had had relatively few Negroes until 1950. By 1967 the Negro population had risen to an estimated 30 percent of the total. As in Englewood, there was a division between the Negro middle class, which lived in the East side "gilded ghetto," and the unskilled, unemployed and underemployed poor on the West side.

Geared to the needs of a suburban middle class, the part-time and fragmented city government had failed to realize the change in character which the city had undergone, and was unprepared to cope with the problems of a growing disadvantaged population. There was no full-time administrator or city manager. Boards, with independent jurisdiction over such areas as education, welfare and health, were appointed by the part-time mayor, whose own position was largely honorary.

Accustomed to viewing politics as a gentleman's pastime, city officials were startled and upset by the intensity with which demands issued from the ghetto. Usually such demands were met obliquely, rather than head-on.

In the summer of 1966, trouble was narrowly averted over the issue of a swimming pool for Negro youngsters. In the summer of 1967, instead of having built the pool, the city began busing the children to the county pool a half-hour's ride distant. The fare was 25 cents per person, and the children had to provide their own lunch, a considerable strain on a frequent basis for a poor family with several children.

The bus operated only on three days in mid-week. On weekends the county pool was too crowded to accommodate children from the Plainfield ghetto.

Pressure increased upon the school system to adapt itself to the changing social and ethnic backgrounds of its pupils. There were strikes and boycotts. The track system created de facto segregation within a supposedly integrated school system. Most of the youngsters from white middle-class districts were in the higher track, most from the Negro poverty areas in the lower. Relations were strained between some white teachers and Negro pupils. Two-thirds of school dropouts were estimated to be Negro.

In February 1967 the NAACP, out of a growing sense of frustration with the municipal government, tacked a list of 19 demands and complaints to the door of the city hall. Most dealt with discrimination in housing, employment and in the public schools. By summer, the city's common council had not responded. Although two of the 11 council members were Negro, both represented the East side ghetto. The poverty area was represented by two white women, one of whom had been appointed by the council after the elected representative, a Negro, had moved away.

Relations between the police and the Negro community, tenuous at best, had been further troubled the week prior to the Newark outbreak. After being handcuffed during a routine arrest in a housing project, a woman had fallen down a flight of stairs. The officer said she had slipped. Negro residents claimed he had pushed her.

When a delegation went to city hall to file a complaint, they were told by the city clerk that he was not empowered to accept it. Believing that they were being given the run-around, the delegation, angry and frustrated, departed.

On Friday evening, July 14, the same police officer was moonlighting as a private guard at a diner frequented by Negro youths. He was, reportedly, number two on the Negro community's "ten most-wanted" list of unpopular police officers.

(The list was colorblind. Although out of 82 officers on the force only five were Negro, two of the 10 on the "most-wanted"

76

list were Negro. The two officers most respected in the Negro community were white.)

Although most of the youths at the diner were of high school age, one, in his mid-twenties, had a reputation as a bully. Sometime before 10 p.m., as a result of an argument, he hit a 16-year-old boy and split open his face. As the boy lay bleeding on the asphalt, his friends rushed to the police officer and demanded that he call an ambulance and arrest the offender. Instead, the officer walked over to the boy, looked at him, and reportedly said: "Why don't you just go home and wash up?" He refused to make an arrest.

The youngsters were incensed. They believed that, had the two participants in the incident been white, the older youth would have been arrested, the younger taken to the hospital immediately.

On the way to the housing project where most of them lived, the youths traversed four blocks of the city's business district. As they walked, they smashed three or four windows. An observer interpreted their behavior as a reaction to the incident at the diner, in effect challenging the police officer: "If you won't do anything about that, then let's see you do something about this!"

On one of the quiet city streets two young Negroes, D. H. and L. C., had been neighbors. D. H. had graduated from high school, attended Fairleigh Dickinson University and, after receiving a degree in psychology, had obtained a job as a reporter on the Plainfield *Courier-News*.

L. C. had dropped out of high school, become a worker in a chemical plant, and, although still in his twenties, had married and fathered seven children. A man with a strong sense of family, he liked sports and played in the local baseball league. Active in civil rights, he had, like the civil rights organizations, over the years, become more militant. For a period of time he had been a Muslim.

The outbreak of vandalism aroused concern among the police. Shortly after midnight, in an attempt to decrease tensions, D. H. and the two Negro councilmen met with the youths in the housing project. The focal point of the youths' bitterness was the attitude of the police—until 1966 police had used the word "nigger" over the police radio and one officer had worn a Confederate belt buckle and had flown a Confederate pennant on his car. Their complaints, however, ranged over local and national issues. There was an overriding cynicism and disbelief that government would, of its own accord, make meaningful changes to improve the lot of the lower class Negro. There was an overriding belief that there were two sets of policies by the people in power, whether law enforcement officers, newspaper editors, or government officials: one for white, and one for black.

There was little confidence that the two councilmen could exercise any influence. One youth said: "You came down here last year. We were throwing stones at some passing cars and you said to us that this was not the way to do it. You got us to talk with the man. We talked to him. We talked with him, and we talked all year long. We ain't got nothing yet!"

However, on the promise that meetings would be arranged with the editor of the newspaper and with the mayor later that same day, the youths agreed to disperse.

At the first of these meetings the youths were, apparently, satisfied by the explanation that the newspaper's coverage was not deliberately discriminatory. The meeting with the mayor, however, proceeded badly. Negroes present felt that the mayor was complacent and apathetic, and that they were simply being given the usual lip service, from which nothing would develop.

The mayor, on the other hand, told Commission investigators that he recognized that, "Citizens are frustrated by the political organization of the city," because he, himself, has no real power and "each of the councilmen says that he is just one of the 11 and therefore can't do anything."

After approximately two hours, a dozen of the youths walked out, indicating an impasse and signalling the breakup of the meeting. Shortly thereafter window smashing began. A Molotov cocktail was set afire in a tree. One fire engine, in which a white and Negro fireman were sitting side by side, had a Molotov cocktail thrown at it. The white fireman was burned.

As window smashing continued, liquor stores and taverns were especially hard hit. Some of the youths believed that there was an excess concentration of bars in the Negro section, and that these were an unhealthy influence in the community.

Because the police department had mobilized its full force, the situation, although serious, never appeared to get out of hand. Officers made many arrests. The chief of the fire department told Commission investigators that it was his conclusion that "individuals making fire bombs did not know what they were doing, or they could have burned the city."

At 3 o'clock Sunday morning a heavy rain began, scattering whatever groups remained on the streets.

In the morning police made no effort to cordon off the area. As white sightseers and churchgoers drove by the housing project there was sporadic rock throwing. During the early afternoon such incidents increased.

At the housing project, a meeting was convened by L.C. to draw up a formal petition of grievances. As the youths gathered it became apparent that some of them had been drinking. A few kept drifting away from the parking lot where the meeting was being held to throw rocks at passing cars. It was decided to move the meeting to a county park several blocks away.

Between 150 and 200 persons, including almost all of the rock throwers, piled into a caravan of cars and headed for the park. At approximately 3:30 p.m. the Chief of the Union County Park Police arrived to find the group being addressed by David Sullivan, Executive Director of the Human Relations Commission. He "informed Mr. Sullivan he was in violation of our park ordinance and to disperse the group."

Sullivan and L.C. attempted to explain that they were in the process of drawing up a list of grievances, but the chief remained adamant. They could not meet in the park without a permit, and they did not have a permit.

After permitting the group 10 to 15 minutes grace, the chief decided to disperse them. "Their mood was very excitable," he reported, and "in my estimation no one could appease them so we moved them out without too much trouble. They left in a caravan of about 40 cars, horns blowing and yelling and headed south on West End Avenue to Plainfield."

Within the hour looting became widespread. Cars were overturned, a white man was snatched off a motorcycle, and the fire department stopped responding to alarms because the police were unable to provide protection. After having been on alert until midday, the Plainfield Police Department was caught unprepared. At 6 p.m. only 18 men were on the streets. Checkpoints were established at crucial intersections in an effort to isolate the area.

Officer John Gleason, together with two reserve officers, had been posted at one of the intersections, three blocks from the housing project. Gleason was a veteran officer, the son of a former lieutenant on the police department. Shortly after 8 p.m. two white youths, chased by a 22-year-old Negro, Bobby Williams, came running from the direction of the ghetto toward Gleason's post.

As he came in sight of the police officers, Williams stopped. Accounts vary of what happened next, or why Officer Gleason took the action he did. What is known is that when D. H., the newspaper reporter caught sight of him a minute or two later, Officer Gleason was two blocks from his post. Striding after Williams directly into the ghetto area, Gleason already had passed one housing project. Small groups were milling about. In D.H.'s words: "There was a kind of shock and amazement," to see the officer walking by himself so deep in the ghetto.

Suddenly there was a confrontation between Williams and Gleason. Some witnesses report Williams had a hammer in his hand. Others say he did not. When D.H., whose attention momentarily had been distracted, next saw Gleason he had drawn his gun and was firing at Williams. As Williams, critically injured, fell to the ground Gleason turned and ran back toward his post.

Negro youths chased him. Gleason stumbled, regained his balance, then had his feet knocked out from under him. A score of youths began to beat him and kick him. Some residents of the apartment house attempted to intervene, but they were brushed aside. D. H. believes that, under the circumstances and in the atmosphere that prevailed at that moment, any police officer, black or white, would have been killed.

After they had beaten Gleason to death, the youths took D.H.'s camera from him and smashed it.

Fear swept over the ghetto. Many residents—both lawless and law-abiding—were convinced, on the basis of what had occurred in Newark, that law enforcement officers, bent on vengeance, would come into the ghetto shooting.

People began actively to prepare to defend themselves. There was no lack of weapons. Forty-six carbines were stolen from a nearby arms manufacturing plant and passed out in the street by a young Negro, a former newspaper boy. Most of the weapons fell into the hands of youths, who began firing them wildly. A fire station was peppered with shots.

Law enforcement officers continued their cordon about the area, but made no attempt to enter it except, occasionally, to rescue someone. National Guardsmen arrived shortly after midnight. Their armored personnel carriers were used to carry troops to the fire station, which had been besieged for five hours. During this period only one fire had been reported in the city.

Reports of sniper firing, wild shooting, and general chaos continued until the early morning hours.

By daylight Monday, New Jersey state officials had begun to arrive. At a meeting in the early afternoon, it was agreed that to inject police into the ghetto would be to risk bloodshed; that, instead, law enforcement personnel should continue to retain their cordon.

All during the day various meetings took place between government officials and Negro representatives. Police were anxious to recover the carbines that had been stolen from the arms plant. Negroes wanted assurances against retaliation. In the afternoon, L.C., an official of the Human Relations Commission, and others drove through the area urging people to be calm and to refrain from violence.

At 8 p.m., the New Jersey attorney general, commissioner of community affairs, and commander of the state police, accompanied by the mayor, went to the housing project and spoke to several hundred Negroes. Some members of the crowd were hostile. Others were anxious to establish a dialogue. There were demands that officials give concrete evidence that they were prepared to deal with Negro grievances. Again, the meeting was inconclusive. The officials returned to City Hall.

At 9:15 p.m., L.C. rushed in claiming that—as a result of the failure to resolve any of the outstanding problems, and reports that people who had been arrested by the police were being beaten—violence was about to explode anew. The key demand of the militant faction was that those who had been arrested during the riot should be released. State officials decided to arrange for the release on bail of 12 arrestees charged with minor violations. L.C., in turn, agreed to try to induce return of the stolen carbines by Wednesday noon.

As state officials were scanning the list of arrestees to determine which of them should be released, a message was brought to Colonel Kelly of the state police that general firing had broken out around the perimeter.

The report testified to the tension: an investigation disclosed that one shot of unexplained origin had been heard. In response, security forces had shot out street lights, thus initiating the "general firing."

At 4:00 o'clock Tuesday morning, a dozen prisoners were released from jail. Plainfield police officers considered this a "sellout."

When, by noon on Wednesday, the stolen carbines had not been returned, the governor decided to authorize a mass search. At 2:00 p.m., a convoy of state police and National Guard troops prepared to enter the area. In order to direct the search as to likely locations, a handful of Plainfield police officers were spotted throughout the 28 vehicles of the convoy.

As the convoy prepared to depart, the state community affairs commissioner, believing himself to be carrying out the decision of the governor not to permit Plainfield officers to participate in the search, ordered their removal from the vehicles. The basis for his order was that their participation might ignite a clash between them and the Negro citizens.

As the search for carbines in the community progressed, tension increased rapidly. According to witnesses and newspaper reports, some men in the search force left apartments in shambles.

The search was called off an hour and a half after it was begun. No stolen weapons were discovered. For the Plainfield police, the removal of the officers from the convoy had been a humiliating experience. A half hour after the conclusion of the search, in a meeting charged with emotion, the entire department threatened to resign unless the state community affairs commissioner left the city. He acceded to the demand.

On Friday, seven days after the first outbreak, the city began returning to normal.

VII. NEW BRUNSWICK

Although New Brunswick has about the same population as Plainfield, New Brunswick is a county seat and center of commerce, with an influx of people during the day. No clearly defined Negro ghetto exists. Substantial proportions of the population are Puerto Rican, foreign-born, and Negro.

All during the weekend, while violence sputtered, flared, subsided, then flared again in Plainfield, less than 10 miles away, there were rumors that "New Brunswick was really going to blow." Dissatisfaction in the Negro community revolved around several issues: the closing of a local teenage coffee house by the police department, the lack of a swimming pool and other recreation facilities, and the release of a white couple on very low bond after they had been arrested for allegedly shooting at three Negro teenagers. As elsewhere, there was a feeling that the law was not being applied equally to whites and Negroes.

By Monday, according to Mayor Patricia Sheehan, the town was "haunted by what had happened in Newark and Plainfield." James E. Amos, the associate director of the anti-poverty program in Middlesex County, said there was a "tenseness in the air" that "got thicker and thicker."

Staff members of the anti-poverty agency met with the mayor and city commissioners to discuss what steps might be taken to reduce the tension. The mayor, who had been elected on a reform platform two months previously, appointed a Negro police officer, Lieutenant John Brokaw, as community liaison officer. He was authorized to report directly to the mayor.

Negro officers in the department went into the streets in plain clothes to fight rumors and act as counter-rioters. Uniformed police officers were counseled to act with restraint to avoid the possibility of a police action setting off violence. The radio station decided on its own initiative to play down rumors and news of any disturbance.

The anti-poverty agency set up a task force of workers to go into all of the communities; white, Puerto Rican, and Negro, to report information and to try to cool the situation.

The chief of police met with the chiefs of surrounding communities to discuss cooperation in case a disorder broke out.

The streets remained quiet until past 9 p.m. Then scattered reports of windows being broken began to be received by police. At 10:30 p.m. Amos noticed 100 youngsters marching in a column of twos down the street. A tall Negro minister stepped from the office of the anti-poverty agency and placed himself in the street in order to head them off.

"Brothers! Stop! Let me talk to you!" he called out.

The marchers brushed past him. A small boy, about 13 years old, looked up at the minister:

"Black power, baby!" he said.

The New Brunswick police were reinforced by 100 officers from surrounding communities. Roadblocks were set up on all principal thoroughfares into the city.

Wild rumors swept the city: reports of armed Negro and white gangs, shootings, fires, beatings, and deaths.

In fact, what was occurring was more in the nature of random vandalism. According to Mayor Sheehan, it was "like Halloween—a gigantic night of mischief."

Tuesday morning the mayor imposed a curfew, and recorded a tape, played periodically over the city's radio station, appealing for order. Most of the persons who had been picked up the previous night were released on their own recognizance or on low bail.

The anti-poverty agency, whose summer program had not been funded until a few days previously, began hiring youngsters as recreational aides. So many teenagers applied that it was decided to cut each stipend in half and hire twice as many as planned.

When the youngsters indicated a desire to see the mayor, she and the city commissioners agreed to meet with them. Although initially hostile, the 35 teenagers who made up the group "poured out their souls to the mayor." The mayor and the city commissioners agreed to the drawing up of a statement by the Negro youths attacking discrimination, inferior educational and employment opportunities, police harassment, and poor housing.

Four of the young people began broadcasting over the radio station, urging their "soul brothers and sisters" to "cool it, because you will only get hurt and the mayor has talked with us and is going to do something for us." Other youths circulated through the streets with the same message.

Despite these measures, a confrontation between the police and a crowd that gathered near a public housing project occurred that evening. The crowd was angry at the massive show of force by police in riot dress. "If you don't get the cops out of here," one man warned, "we are all going to get our guns." Asked to return to their homes, people replied: "We will go home when you get the police out of the area."

Requested by several city commissioners to pull back the uniformed police, the Chief at first refused. He was then told it was a direct order from the mayor. The police were withdrawn.

A short time later, elements of the crowd—an older and rougher one than the night before—appeared in front of the police station. The participants wanted to see the mayor.

Mayor Sheehan went out onto the steps of the station. Using a bullhorn, she talked to the people and asked that she be given an opportunity to correct conditions. The crowd was boisterous. Some persons challenged the mayor. But, finally, the opinion, "She's new! Give her a chance!" prevailed.

A demand was issued by people in the crowd that all persons arrested the previous night be released. Told that this already had been done, the people were suspicious. They asked to be allowed to inspect the jail cells.

It was agreed to permit representatives of the people to look in the cells to satisfy themselves that everyone had been released.

The crowd dispersed. The New Brunswick riot had failed to materialize.

VIII. DETROIT

On Saturday evening, July 22, the Detroit Police Department raided five "blind pigs." The blind pigs had had their origin in prohibition days, and survived as private social clubs. Often, they were after-hours drinking and gambling spots.

The fifth blind pig on the raid list, the United Community and Civic League at the corner of 12th Street and Clairmount, had been raided twice before. Once 10 persons had been picked up; another time, 28. A Detroit Vice Squad officer had tried but failed to get in shortly after 10 o'clock Saturday night. He succeeded, on his second attempt, at 3:45 Sunday morning.

The Tactical Mobile Unit, the Police Department's Crowd Control Squad, had been dismissed at 3:00 A.M. Since Sunday morning traditionally is the least troublesome time for police in Detroit—and all over the country—only 193 officers were patrolling the streets. Of these, 44 were in the 10th Precinct where the blind pig was located.

Police expected to find two dozen patrons in the blind pig. That night, however, it was the scene of a party for several servicemen, two of whom were back from Vietnam. Instead of two dozen patrons, police found 82. Some voiced resentment at the police intrusion.

An hour went by before all 82 could be transported from the scene. The weather was humid and warm—the temperature that day was to rise to 86—and despite the late hour, many people were still on the street. In short order, a crowd of about 200 gathered.

In November of 1965, George Edwards, Judge of the United States Court of Appeals for the Sixth Circuit, and Commissioner of the Detroit Police Department from 1961 to 1963, had written in the *Michigan Law Review:*

> It is clear that in 1965 no one will make excuses for any city's inability to foresee the possibility of racial trouble. . . . Although local police forces generally regard themselves as public servants with the responsibility of maintaining law and order, they tend to minimize this attitude when they are patrolling areas that are heavily populated with Negro citizens. There, they tend to view each person on the streets as a potential criminal or enemy, and all too often that attitude is reciprocated. Indeed, hostility between the Negro communities in our large cities and the police departments, is the major problem in law enforcement in this decade. It has been a major cause of all recent race riots.

At the time of Detroit's 1943 race riot, Judge Edwards told Commission investigators, there was "open warfare between the Detroit Negroes and the Detroit Police Department." As late as 1961, he had thought that "Detroit was the leading candidate in the United States for a race riot."

There was a long history of conflict between the police department and citizens. During the labor battles of the 1930's, union members had come to view the Detroit Police Department as a strike-breaking force. The 1943 riot, in which 34 persons died, was the bloodiest in the United States in a span of two decades.

Judge Edwards and his successor, Commissioner Ray Girardin, attempted to restructure the image of the department. A Citizens Complaint Bureau was set up to facilitate the filing of complaints by citizens against officers. In practice, however, this Bureau appeared to work little better than less enlightened and more cumbersome procedures in other cities.

On 12th Street, with its high incidence of vice and crime, the issue of police brutality was a recurrent theme. A month earlier the killing of a prostitute had been determined by police investigators to be the work of a pimp. According to rumors in the community the crime had been committed by a Vice Squad officer.

At about the same time, the killing of Danny Thomas, a 27-year-old Negro Army veteran, by a gang of white youths had inflamed the community. The city's major newspapers played down the story in hope that the murder would not become a cause for increased tensions. The intent backfired. A banner story in the *Michigan Chronicle,* the city's Negro newspaper, began: "As James Meredith marched again Sunday to prove a Negro could walk in Mississippi without fear, a young woman who saw her husband killed by a white gang, shouting: 'Niggers keep out of Rouge Park,' lost her baby.

"Relatives were upset that the full story of the murder was not being told, apparently in an effort to prevent the incident from sparking a riot."

Some Negroes believed that the daily newspapers' treatment of the story was further evidence of the double standard: playing up crimes by Negroes, playing down crimes committed against Negroes.

Although police arrested one suspect for murder, Negroes questioned why the entire gang was not held. What, they asked, would have been the result if a white man had been killed by a gang of Negroes? What if Negroes had made the kind of advances toward a white woman that the white men were rumored to have made toward Mrs. Thomas?

The Thomas family lived only four or five blocks from the raided blind pig. A few minutes after 5:00 A.M., just after the last of those arrested had been hauled away, an empty bottle smashed into the rear window of a police car. A litter basket was thrown through the window of a store. Rumors circulated of excess force used by the police during the raid. A youth, whom police nicknamed "Mr. Greensleeves" because of the color of his shirt, was shouting: "We're going to have a riot!" and exhorting the crowd to vandalism.

At 5:20 A.M. Commissioner Girardin was notified. He immediately called Mayor Jerome Cavanagh. Seventeen officers from other areas were ordered into the 10th Precinct. By 6:00 A.M. police strength had grown to 369 men. Of these, however, only 43 were committed to the immediate riot area. By that time the number of persons on 12th Street was growing into the thousands and widespread window-smashing and looting had begun.

On either side of 12th Street were neat, middle-class districts. Along 12th Street itself, however, crowded apartment houses created a density of more than 21,000 persons per square mile, almost double the city average.

The movement of people when the slums of "Black Bottom" had been cleared for urban renewal had changed 12th Street from an integrated community into an almost totally black one, in which only a number of merchants remained white. Only 18 percent of the residents were homeowners. Twenty-five percent of the housing was considered so substandard as to require clearance. Another 19 percent had major deficiencies.

The crime rate was almost double that of the city as a whole. A Detroit police officer told Commission investigators that prostitution was so widespread that officers made arrests only when soliciting became blatant. The proportion of broken families was more than twice that in the rest of the city.

By 7:50 A.M., when a 17-man police commando unit attempted to make the first sweep, an estimated 3,000 persons were on 12th Street. They offered no resistance. As the sweep moved down the street, they gave way to one side, and then flowed back behind it.

A shoe store manager said he waited vainly for police for two hours as the store was being looted. At 8:25 A.M. someone in the crowd yelled "The cops are coming!" The first flames of the riot billowed from the store. Firemen who responded were not harassed. The flames were extinguished.

By mid-morning, 1,122 men—approximately a fourth of the police department—had reported for duty. Of these, 540 were in or near the six-block riot area. One hundred and eight officers were attempting to establish a cordon. There was, however, no interference with looters, and police were refraining from the use of force.

Commissioner Girardin said: "If we had started shooting in there . . . not one of our policemen would have come out alive. I am convinced it would have turned into a race riot in the conventional sense."

According to witnesses, police at some roadblocks made little effort to stop people from going in and out of the area. Bantering took place between police officers and the populace, some still in pajamas. To some observers, there seemed at this point to be an atmosphere of apathy. On the one hand, the police failed to interfere with the looting. On the other, a number of older, more stable residents, who had seen the street deteriorate from a prosperous commercial thoroughfare to one ridden by vice, remained aloof.

Because officials feared that the 12th Street disturbance might be a diversion, many officers were sent to guard key installations in other sections of the city. Belle Isle, the recreation area in the Detroit River that had been the scene of the 1943 riot, was sealed off.

In an effort to avoid attracting people to the scene, some broadcasters cooperated by not reporting the riot, and an effort was made to downplay the extent of the disorder. The facade of "business as usual" necessitated the detailing of numerous police officers to protect the 50,000 spectators that were expected at that afternoon's New York Yankees-Detroit Tigers baseball game.

Early in the morning a task force of community workers went into the area to dispel rumors and act as counter-rioters. Such a task force had been singularly successful at the time of the incident in the Kercheval district in the summer of 1966, when scores of people had gathered at the site of an arrest. Kercheval, however, has a more stable population, fewer stores, less population density, and the city's most effective police-community relations program.

The 12th Street area, on the other hand, had been determined, in a 1966 survey conducted by Dr. Ernest Harburg of the Psychology Department of the University of Michigan, to be a community of high stress and tension. An overwhelming majority of the residents indicated dissatisfaction with their environment.

Of those interviewed, 93 percent said they wanted to move out of the neighborhood; 73 percent felt that the streets were not safe; 91 percent believed that a person was likely to be robbed or beaten at night; 58 percent knew of a fight within the last 12 months in which a weapon had been employed; 32 percent stated that they themselves owned a weapon; 57 percent were worried about fires.

A significant proportion believed municipal services to be inferior: 36 percent were dissatisfied with the schools; 43 percent with the city's contribution to the neighborhood; 77 percent with the recreational facilities; 78 percent believed police did not respond promptly when they were summoned for help.

United States Representative John Conyers, Jr., a Negro, was notified about the disturbance at his home, a few blocks from 12th Street, at 8:30 A.M. Together with other community leaders, including Hubert G. Locke, a Negro and assistant to the commissioner of police, he began to drive around the area. In the side streets he asked people to stay in their homes. On 12th Street, he asked them to disperse. It was, by his own account, a futile task.

Numerous eyewitnesses interviewed by Commission investigators tell of the carefree mood with which people ran in and out of stores, looting and laughing, and joking with the police officers. Stores with "Soul Brothers" signs appeared no more immune than others. Looters paid no attention to residents who shouted at them and called their actions senseless. An epidemic of excitement had swept over the persons on the street.

Congressman Conyers noticed a woman with a baby in

her arms; she was raging, cursing "whitey" for no apparent reason.

Shortly before noon Congressman Conyers climbed atop a car in the middle of 12th Street to address the people. As he began to speak he was confronted by a man in his fifties whom he had once, as a lawyer, represented in court. The man had been active in civil rights. He believed himself to have been persecuted as a result, and it was Conyers' opinion that he may have been wrongfully jailed. Extremely bitter, the man was inciting the crowd and challenging Conyers: "Why are you defending the cops and the establishment? You're just as bad as they are!"

A police officer in the riot area told Commission investigators that neither he nor his fellow officers were instructed as to what they were supposed to be doing. Witnesses tell of officers standing behind saw-horses as an area was being looted —and still standing there much later, when the mob had moved elsewhere. A squad from the commando unit, wearing helmets with face-covering visors and carrying bayonet-tipped carbines, blockaded a street several blocks from the scene of the riot. Their appearance drew residents into the street. Some began to harangue them and to question why they were in an area where there was no trouble. Representative Conyers convinced the police department to remove the commandos.

By that time a rumor was threading through the crowd that a man had been bayoneted by the police. Influenced by such stories, the crowd became belligerent. At approximately 1:00 P.M. stonings accelerated. Numerous officers reported injuries from rocks, bottles, and other objects thrown at them. Smoke billowed upward from four fires, the first since the one at the shoe store early in the morning. When firemen answered the alarms, they became the target for rocks and bottles.

At 2:00 P.M. Mayor Cavanagh met with community and political leaders at police headquarters. Until then there had been hope that, as the people blew off steam, the riot would dissipate. Now the opinion was nearly unanimous that additional forces would be needed.

A request was made for state police aid. By 3:00 P.M. 360 officers were assembling at the armory. At that moment looting was spreading from the 12th Street area to other main thoroughfares.

There was no lack of the disaffected to help spread it. Although not yet as hard-pressed as Newark, Detroit was, like Newark, losing population. Its prosperous middle-class whites were moving to the suburbs and being replaced by unskilled Negro migrants. Between 1960 and 1967 the Negro population rose from just under 30 percent to an estimated 40 percent of the total.

In a decade the school system had gained 50,000 to 60,000 children. Fifty-one percent of the elementary school classes were overcrowded. Simply to achieve the statewide average, the system needed 1,650 more teachers and 1,000 additional classrooms. The combined cost would be $63 million.

Of 300,000 school children, 171,000, or 57 percent, were Negro. According to the Detroit Superintendent of Schools, 25 different school districts surrounding the city spent up to $500 more per pupil per year than Detroit. In the inner city schools, more than half the pupils who entered high school became dropouts.

The strong union structure had created excellent conditions for most working men, but had left others, such as civil service and government workers, comparatively disadvantaged and dissatisfied. In June the "Blue Flu" had struck the city as police officers, forbidden to strike, had staged a sick-out. In September, the teachers were to go on strike. The starting wages for a plumber's helper were almost equal to the salary of a police officer or teacher.

Some unions, traditionally closed to Negroes, zealously guarded training opportunities. In January of 1967 the school system notified six apprenticeship trades it would not open any new apprenticeship classes unless a large number of Negroes were included. By fall, some of the programs were still closed.

High school diplomas from inner city schools were regarded by personnel directors as less than valid. In July, unemployment was at a five-year peak. In the 12th Street area it was estimated to be between 12 and 15 percent for Negro men and 30 percent or higher for those under 25.

The more education a Negro had, the greater the disparity between his income and that of a white with the same level of education. The income of whites and Negroes with a seventh grade education was about equal. The median income of whites with a high school diploma was $1,600 more per year than that of Negroes. White college graduates made $2,600 more. In fact, so far as income was concerned, it made very little difference to a Negro man whether he had attended school for 8 years or for 12. In the fall of 1967, a study conducted at one inner city high school, Northwestern, showed that, although 50 percent of the dropouts had found work, 90 percent of the 1967 graduating class was unemployed.

Mayor Cavanagh had appointed many Negroes to key positions in his administration, but in elective offices the Negro population was still under-represented. Of nine councilmen, one was a Negro. Of seven school board members, two were Negroes.

Although federal programs had brought nearly $360 million to the city between 1962 and 1967, the money appeared to have had little impact at the grassroots. Urban renewal, for which $38 million had been allocated, was opposed by many residents of the poverty area.

Because of its financial straits, the city was unable to produce on promises to correct such conditions as poor garbage collection and bad street lighting, which brought constant complaints from Negro residents.

On 12th Street Carl Perry, the Negro proprietor of a drug store and photography studio, was dispensing ice cream, sodas, and candy to the youngsters streaming in and out of his store. For safekeeping he had brought the photography equipment from his studio, in the next block, to the drug store. The youths milling about repeatedly assured him that, although the market next door had been ransacked, his place of business was in no danger.

In mid-afternoon the market was set afire. Soon after, the drug store went up in flames.

State Representative James Del Rio, a Negro, was camping out in front of a building he owned when two small boys, neither more than 10 years old, approached. One prepared to throw a brick through a window. Del Rio stopped him: "That building belongs to me," he said.

"I'm glad you told me, baby, because I was just about to bust you in!" the youngster replied.

Some evidence that criminal elements were organizing spontaneously to take advantage of the riot began to manifest itself. A number of cars were noted to be returning again and again, their occupants methodically looting stores. Months later, goods stolen during the riot were still being peddled.

A spirit of carefree nihilism was taking hold. To riot and to destroy appeared more and more to become ends in themselves. Late Sunday afternoon it appeared to one observer that the young people were "dancing amidst the flames."

A Negro plainclothes officer was standing at an intersection when a man threw a Molotov cocktail into a business establishment at the corner. In the heat of the afternoon, fanned by the 20 to 25 m.p.h. winds of both Sunday and Monday, the fire reached the home next door within minutes. As residents uselessly sprayed the flames with garden hoses, the fire jumped from roof to roof of adjacent two and three-story buildings. Within the hour the entire block was in flames. The ninth house in the burning row belonged to the arsonist who had thrown the Molotov cocktail.

In some areas residents organized rifle squads to protect firefighters. Elsewhere, especially as the wind-whipped flames began to overwhelm the Detroit Fire Department and more and more residences burned, the firemen were subjected to curses and rock-throwing.

Because of a lack of funds, on a per capita basis the department is one of the smallest in the nation. In comparison to Newark, where approximately 1,000 firemen patrol an area of 16 square miles with a population of 400,000, Detroit's 1,700 firemen must cover a city of 140 square miles with a population of 1.6 million. Because the department had no mutual aid agreement with surrounding communities, it could not quickly call in reinforcements from outlying areas, and it was almost 9:00 P.M. before the first arrived. At one point, out of a total of 92 pieces of Detroit fire fighting equipment and 56 brought in from surrounding communities, only four engine companies were available to guard areas of the city outside of the riot perimeter.

As the afternoon progressed the fire department's radio carried repeated messages of apprehension and orders of caution:

> There is no police protection here at all; there isn't a policeman in the area. . . . If you have any trouble at all, pull out! . . . We're being stoned at the scene. It's going good. We need help! . . . Protect yourselves! Proceed away from the scene. . . . Engine 42 over at Linwood and Gladstone. They are throwing bottles at us so we are getting out of the area. . . . All companies without police protection—all companies without police protection—orders are to withdraw, do not try to put out the fires. I repeat—all companies without police protection orders are to withdraw, do not try to put out the fires!

It was 4:30 P.M. when the firemen, some of them exhausted by the heat, abandoned an area of approximately 100 square blocks on either side of 12th Street to await protection from police and National Guardsmen.

During the course of the riot firemen were to withdraw 283 times.

Fire Chief Charles J. Quinlan estimated that at least two-thirds of the buildings were destroyed by spreading fires rather than fires set at the scene. Of the 683 structures involved, approximately one-third were residential, and in few, if any, of these was the fire set originally.

Governor George Romney flew over the area between 8:30 and 9:00 P.M. "It looked like the city had been bombed on the west side and there was an area two-and-a-half miles by three-and-a-half miles with major fires, with entire blocks in flames," he told the Commission.

In the midst of chaos there were some unexpected individual responses.

Twenty-four-year-old E. G., a Negro born in Savannah, Georgia, had come to Detroit in 1965 to attend Wayne State University. Rebellion had been building in him for a long time because,

> You just had to bow down to the white man. . . . When the insurance man would come by he would always call out to my mother by her first name and we were expected to smile and greet him happily. . . . Man, I know he would never have thought of me or my father going to his house and calling his wife by her first name. Then I once saw a white man slapping a young pregnant Negro woman on the street with such force that she just spun around and fell. I'll never forget that.

When a friend called to tell him about the riot on 12th Street, E. G. went there expecting "a true revolt," but was disappointed as soon as he saw the looting begin: "I wanted to see the people really rise up in revolt. When I saw the first person coming out of the store with things in his arms, I really got sick to my stomach and wanted to go home. Rebellion against the white suppressors is one thing, but one measly pair of shoes or some food completely ruins the whole concept."

E. G. was standing in a crowd, watching firemen work, when Fire Chief Alvin Wall called out for help from the spectators. E. G. responded. His reasoning was: "No matter what color someone is, whether they are green or pink or blue, I'd help them if they were in trouble. That's all there is to it."

He worked with the firemen for four days, the only Negro in an all-white crew. Elsewhere, at scattered locations, a half dozen other Negro youths pitched in to help the firemen.

At 4:20 P.M. Mayor Cavanagh requested that the National Guard be brought into Detroit. Although a major portion of the Guard was in its summer encampment 200 miles away, several hundred troops were conducting their regular weekend drill in the city. That circumstance obviated many problems. The first troops were on the streets by 7:00 P.M.

At 7:45 P.M. the mayor issued a proclamation instituting a 9:00 P.M. to 5:00 A.M. curfew. At 9:07 P.M. the first sniper fire was reported. Following his aerial survey of the city, Governor Romney, at or shortly before midnight, proclaimed that "a state of public emergency exists" in the cities of Detroit, Highland Park, and Hamtramck.

At 4:45 P.M. a 68-year-old white shoe repairman, George Messerlian, had seen looters carrying clothes from a cleaning establishment next to his shop. Armed with a saber, he had rushed into the street, flailing away at the looters. One Negro youth was nicked on the shoulder. Another, who had not been on the scene, inquired as to what had happened. After he had been told, he allegedly replied: "I'll get the old man for you!"

Going up to Messerlian, who had fallen or been knocked to the ground, the youth began to beat him with a club. Two other Negro youths dragged the attacker away from the old man. It was too late. Messerlian died four days later in the hospital.

At 9:15 P.M. a 16-year-old Negro boy, superficially wounded while looting, became the first reported gunshot victim.

At midnight Sharon George, a 23-year-old white woman, together with her two brothers, was a passenger in a car being driven by her husband. After having dropped off two Negro friends, they were returning home on one of Detroit's main avenues when they were slowed by a milling throng in the street. A shot fired from close range struck the car. The bullet splintered in Mrs. George's body. She died less than two hours later.

An hour before midnight a 45-year-old white man, Walter Grzanka together with three white companions, went into the street. Shortly thereafter a market was broken into. Inside the show window a Negro man began filling bags with groceries and handing them to confederates outside the store. Grzanka twice went over to the store, accepted bags, and placed them down beside his companions across the street. On the third occasion he entered the market. When he emerged, the market owner, driving by in his car, shot and killed him.

In Grzanka's pockets police found seven cigars, four packages of pipe tobacco, and nine pairs of shoelaces.

Before dawn four other looters were shot, one of them accidentally while struggling with a police officer. A Negro youth and a National Guardsman were injured by gunshots of undetermined origin. A private guard shot himself while pulling his revolver from his pocket. In the basement of the 13th Precinct Police Station a cue ball, thrown by an unknown assailant, cracked against the head of a sergeant.

At about midnight three white youths, armed with a shotgun, had gone to the roof of their apartment building, located in an all-white block, in order, they said, to protect the building from fire. At 2:45 A.M. a patrol car, carrying police officers and National Guardsmen, received a report of "snipers on the roof." As the patrol car arrived, the manager of the building went to the roof to tell the youths they had better come down.

The law enforcement personnel surrounded the building,

some going to the front, others to the rear. As the manager, together with the three youths, descended the fire escape in the rear, a National Guardsman, believing he heard shots from the front, fired. His shot killed 23-year-old Clifton Pryor.

Early in the morning a young white fireman and a 49-year-old Negro homeowner were killed by fallen power lines.

By 2:00 A. M. Monday, Detroit police had been augmented by 800 State Police officers and 1,200 National Guardsmen. An additional 8,000 Guardsmen were on the way. Nevertheless, Governor Romney and Mayor Cavanagh decided to ask for federal assistance. At 2:15 A.M. the mayor called Vice President Hubert Humphrey, and was referred to Attorney General Ramsey Clark. A short time thereafter telephone contact was established between Governor Romney and the attorney general.[5]

There is some difference of opinion about what occurred next. According to the attorney general's office, the governor was advised of the seriousness of the request and told that the applicable federal statute required that, before federal troops could be brought into the city, he would have to state that the situation had deteriorated to the point that local and state forces could no longer maintain law and order. According to the governor, he was under the impression that he was being asked to declare that a "state of insurrection" existed in the city.

The governor was unwilling to make such a declaration, contending that, if he did, insurance policies would not cover the loss incurred as a result of the riot. He and the mayor decided to re-evaluate the need for federal troops.

Contact between Detroit and Washington was maintained throughout the early morning hours. At 9:00 A.M., as the disorder still showed no sign of abating, the governor and the mayor decided to make a renewed request for federal troops.

Shortly before noon the President of the United States authorized the sending of a task force of paratroops to Selfridge Air Force Base, near the city. A few minutes past 3:00 P.M., Lt. General John L. Throckmorton, commander of Task Force Detroit, met Cyrus Vance, former Deputy Secretary of Defense, at the air base. Approximately an hour later the first federal troops arrived at the air base.

After meeting with state and municipal officials, Mr. Vance, General Throckmorton, Governor Romney, and Mayor Cavanagh, made a tour of the city, which lasted until 7:15 P.M.

---

[5] A little over two hours earlier, at 11:55 P.M. Mayor Cavanagh had informed the U.S. Attorney General that a "dangerous situation existed in the city." Details are set forth in the Final Report of Cyrus R. Vance, covering the Detroit Riots, released on September 12, 1967.

During this tour Mr. Vance and General Throckmorton independently came to the conclusion that—since they had seen no looting or sniping, since the fires appeared to be coming under control, and since a substantial number of National Guardsmen had not yet been committed—injection of federal troops would be premature.

As the riot alternately waxed and waned, one area of the ghetto remained insulated. On the northeast side the residents of some 150 square blocks inhabited by 21,000 persons had, in 1966, banded together in the Positive Neighborhood Action Committee (PNAC). With professional help from the Institute of Urban Dynamics, they had organized block clubs and made plans for the improvement of the neighborhood. In order to meet the need for recreational facilities, which the city was not providing, they had raised $3,000 to purchase empty lots for playgrounds. Although opposed to urban renewal, they had agreed to co-sponsor with the Archdiocese of Detroit a housing project to be controlled jointly by the archdiocese and PNAC.

When the riot broke out, the residents, through the block clubs, were able to organize quickly. Youngsters, agreeing to stay in the neighborhood, participated in detouring traffic. While many persons reportedly sympathized with the idea of a rebellion against the "system," only two small fires were set —one in an empty building.

During the daylight hours Monday, nine more persons were killed by gunshots elsewhere in the city, and many others were seriously or critically injured. Twenty-three-year old Nathaniel Edmonds, a Negro, was sitting in his back yard when a young white man stopped his car, got out, and began an argument with him. A few minutes later, declaring that he was "going to paint his picture on him with a shotgun," the white man allegedly shotgunned Edmonds to death.

Mrs. Nannie Pack and Mrs. Mattie Thomas were sitting on the porch of Mrs. Pack's house when police began chasing looters from a nearby market. During the chase officers fired three shots from their shotguns. The discharge from one of these accidentally struck the two women. Both were still in the hospital weeks later.

Included among those critically injured when they were accidentally trapped in the line of fire were an 8-year-old Negro girl and a 14-year-old white boy.

As darkness settled Monday, the number of incidents re-reported to police began to rise again. Although many turned out to be false, several involved injuries to police officers, National Guardsmen, and civilians by gunshots of undetermined origin.

Watching the upward trend of reported incidents, Mr. Vance and General Throckmorton became convinced Federal troops should be used, and President Johnson was so advised. At 11:20 P.M. the President signed a proclamation federalizing the Michigan National Guard and authorizing the use of the paratroopers.

At this time there were nearly 5,000 Guardsmen in the city, but fatigue, lack of training, and the haste with which they had had to be deployed reduced their effectiveness. Some of the Guardsmen traveled 200 miles and then were on duty for 30 hours straight. Some had never received riot training and were given on-the-spot instructions on mob control—only to discover that there were no mobs, and that the situation they faced on the darkened streets was one for which they were unprepared.

Commanders committed men as they became available, often in small groups. In the resulting confusion, some units were lost in the city. Two Guardsmen assigned to an intersection on Monday were discovered still there on Friday.

Lessons learned by the California National Guard two years earlier in Watts regarding the danger of overreaction and the necessity of great restraint in using weapons had not, apparently, been passed on to the Michigan National Guard. The young troopers could not be expected to know what a danger they were creating by the lack of fire discipline, not only to the civilian population but to themselves.

A Detroit newspaper reporter who spent a night riding in a command jeep told a Commission investigator of machine guns being fired accidentally, street lights being shot out by rifle fire, and buildings being placed under siege on the sketchiest reports of sniping. Troopers would fire, and immediately from the distance there would be answering fire, sometimes consisting of tracer bullets.

In one instance, the newsman related, a report was received on the jeep radio that an Army bus was pinned down by sniper fire at an intersection. National Guardsmen and police, arriving from various directions, jumped out and began asking each other: "Where's the sniper fire coming from?" As one Guardsman pointed to a building, everyone rushed about, taking cover. A soldier, alighting from a jeep, accidentally pulled the trigger on his rifle. As the shot reverberated through the darkness an officer yelled: "What's going on?" "I don't know," came the answer. "Sniper, I guess."

Without any clear authorization or direction someone opened fire upon the suspected building. A tank rolled up and sprayed the building with .50 caliber tracer bullets. Law enforcement officers rushed into the surrounded building and discovered it empty. "They must be firing one shot and running," was the verdict.

The reporter interviewed the men who had gotten off the bus and were crouched around it. When he asked them about the sniping incident he was told that someone had heard a shot. He asked "Did the bullet hit the bus?" The answer was: "Well, we don't know."

Bracketing the hour of midnight Monday, heavy firing, injuring many persons and killing several, occurred in the southeastern sector, which was to be taken over by the paratroopers at 4:00 A.M. Tuesday, and which was, at this time, considered to be the most active riot area in the city.

Employed as a private guard, 55-year-old Julius L. Dorsey, a Negro, was standing in front of a market when accosted by two Negro men and a woman. They demanded he permit them to loot the market. He ignored their demands. They began to berate him. He asked a neighbor to call the police. As the argument grew more heated, Dorsey fired three shots from his pistol into the air.

The police radio reported: "Looters, they have rifles." A patrol car driven by a police officer and carrying three National Guardsmen arrived. As the looters fled, the law enforcement personnel opened fire. When the firing ceased, one person lay dead.

He was Julius L. Dorsey.

In two areas—one consisting of a triangle formed by Mack, Gratiot, and E. Grand Boulevard, the other surrounding Southeastern High School—firing began shortly after 10:00 P.M. and continued for several hours.

In the first of the areas, a 22-year-old Negro complained that he had been shot at by snipers. Later, a half dozen civilians and one National Guardsman were wounded by shots of undetermined origin.

Henry Denson, a passenger in a car, was shot and killed when the vehicle's driver, either by accident or intent, failed to heed a warning to halt at a National Guard roadblock.

Similar incidents occurred in the vicinity of Southeastern High School, one of the National Guard staging areas. As early as 10:20 P.M. the area was reported to be under sniper fire. Around midnight there were two incidents, the sequence of which remains in doubt.

Shortly before midnight Ronald Powell, who lived three blocks east of the high school and whose wife was, momentarily, expecting a baby, asked the four friends with whom he had been spending the evening to take him home. He, together with Edward Blackshear, Charles Glover, and John Leroy climbed into Charles Dunson's station wagon for the short drive. Some of the five may have been drinking, but none was intoxicated.

To the north of the high school they were halted at a National Guard roadblock, and told they would have to detour around the school and a fire station at Mack and St. Jean Streets because of the firing that had been occurring. Following orders, they took a circuitous route and approached Powell's home from the south.

On Lycaste Street, between Charlevoix and Goethe, they saw a jeep sitting at the curb. Believing it to be another roadblock, they slowed down. Simultaneously a shot rang out. A National Guardsman fell, hit in the ankle.

Other National Guardsmen at the scene thought the shot had come from the station wagon. Shot after shot was directed against the vehicle, at least 17 of them finding their mark. All five occupants were injured, John Leroy fatally.

At approximately the same time firemen, police, and National Guardsmen at the corner of Mack and St. Jean Streets, two and one-half blocks away, again came under fire from what they believed were rooftop snipers to the southeast, the direction of Charlevoix and Lycaste. The police and Guardsmen responded with a hail of fire.

When the shooting ceased, Carl Smith, a young firefighter, lay dead. An autopsy determined that the shot had been fired at street level, and, according to police, probably had come from the southeast.

At 4:00 A.M. when paratroopers, under the command of Col. A. R. Bolling, arrived at the high school, the area was so dark and still that the colonel thought, at first, that he had come to the wrong place. Investigating, he discovered National Guard troops, claiming they were pinned down by sniper fire, crouched behind the walls of the darkened building.

The colonel immediately ordered all the lights in the building turned on and his troops to show themselves as conspicuously as possible. In the apartment house across the street nearly every window had been shot out, and the walls were pockmarked with bullet holes. The colonel went into the building and began talking to the residents, many of whom had spent the night huddled on the floor. He reassured them no more shots would be fired.

According to Lt. Gen. Throckmorton and Colonel Bolling, the city, at this time, was saturated with fear. The National Guardsmen were afraid, the residents were afraid, and the police were afraid. Numerous persons, the majority of them Negroes, were being injured by gunshots of undetermined origin. The general and his staff felt that the major task of the troops was to reduce the fear and restore an air of normalcy.

In order to accomplish this, every effort was made to establish contact and rapport between the troops and the residents. Troopers—20 percent of whom were Negro—began helping to clean up the streets, collect garbage, and trace persons who had disappeared in the confusion. Residents in the neighborhoods responded with soup and sandwiches for the troops. In areas where the National Guard tried to establish rapport with the citizens, there was a similar response.

Within hours after the arrival of the paratroops the area occupied by them was the quietest in the city, bearing out General Throckmorton's view that the key to quelling a disorder is to saturate an area with "calm, determined, and hardened professional soldiers." Loaded weapons, he believes, are unnecessary. Troopers had strict orders not to fire unless they could see the specific person at whom they were aiming. Mass fire was forbidden.

During five days in the city, 2,700 Army troops expended only 201 rounds of ammunition, almost all during the first few hours, after which even stricter fire discipline was enforced. (In contrast, New Jersey National Guardsmen and State police expended 13,326 rounds of ammunition in three days in Newark.) Hundreds of reports of sniper fire—most of them false—continued to pour into police headquarters; the Army logged only 10. No paratrooper was injured by a gunshot. Only one person was hit by a shot fired by a trooper. He was a young Negro who was killed when he ran into the line of fire as a trooper, aiding police in a raid on an apartment, aimed at a person believed to be a sniper.

General Throckmorton ordered the weapons of all military personnel unloaded, but either the order failed to reach many National Guardsmen, or else it was disobeyed.

Even as the general was requesting the city to relight the streets, Guardsmen continued shooting out the lights, and there are reports of dozens of shots being fired to dispatch one light. At one such location, as Guardsmen were shooting out the street lights, a radio newscaster reported himself to be pinned down by "sniper fire."

On the same day that the general was attempting to restore normalcy by ordering street barricades taken down, Guardsmen on one street were not only, in broad daylight, ordering people off the street, but off their porches and away from the windows. Two persons who failed to respond to the order quickly enough were shot, one of them fatally.

The general himself reported an incident of a Guardsman "firing across the bow" of an automobile that was approaching a roadblock.

As in Los Angeles two years earlier, roadblocks that were

ill-lighted and ill-defined—often consisting of no more than a trash barrel or similar object with Guardsmen standing nearby —proved a continuous hazard to motorists. At one such roadblock, National Guard Sergeant Larry Post, standing in the street, was caught in a sudden cross fire as his fellow Guardsmen opened up on a vehicle. He was the only soldier killed in the riot.

With persons of every description arming themselves, and guns being fired accidentally or on the vaguest pretext all over the city, it became more and more impossible to tell who was shooting at whom. Some firemen began carrying guns. One accidentally shot and wounded a fellow fireman. Another injured himself.

The chaos of a riot, and the difficulties faced by police officers, are demonstrated by an incident that occurred at 2:00 A.M. Tuesday.

A unit of 12 officers received a call to guard firemen from snipers. When they arrived at the corner of Vicksburg and Linwood in the 12th Street area, the intersection was well-lighted by the flames completely enveloping one building. Sniper fire was directed at the officers from an alley to the north, and gun flashes were observed in two buildings.

As the officers advanced on the two buildings, Patrolman Johnie Hamilton fired several rounds from his machinegun. Thereupon, the officers were suddenly subjected to fire from a new direction, the east. Hamilton, struck by four bullets, fell, critically injured, in the intersection. As two officers ran to his aid, they too were hit.

By this time other units of the Detroit Police Department, state police, and National Guard had arrived on the scene, and the area was covered with a hail of gunfire.

In the confusion the snipers who had initiated the shooting escaped.

At 9:15 P.M. Tuesday, July 25, 38-year-old Jack Sydnor, a Negro, came home drunk. Taking out his pistol, he fired one shot into an alley. A few minutes later the police arrived. As his common-law wife took refuge in a closet, Sydnor waited, gun in hand, while the police forced open the door. Patrolman Roger Poike, the first to enter, was shot by Sydnor. Although critically injured, the officer managed to get off six shots in return. Police within the building and on the street then poured a hail of fire into the apartment. When the shooting ceased, Sydnor's body, riddled by the gunfire, was found lying on the ground outside a window.

Nearby, a state police officer and a Negro youth were struck and seriously injured by stray bullets. As in other cases where the origin of the shots was not immediately determinable, police reported them as "shot by sniper."

Reports of "heavy sniper fire" poured into police headquarters from the two blocks surrounding the apartment house where the battle with Jack Sydnor had taken place. National Guard troops with two tanks were dispatched to help flush out the snipers.

Shots continued to be heard throughout the neighborhood. At approximately midnight—there are discrepancies as to the precise time—a machine gunner on a tank, startled by several shots, asked the assistant gunner where the shots were coming from. The assistant gunner pointed toward a flash in the window of an apartment house from which there had been earlier reports of sniping.

The machine gunner opened fire. As the slugs ripped through the window and walls of the apartment, they nearly severed the arm of 21-year-old Valerie Hood. Her 4-year-old niece, Tonya Blanding, toppled dead, a .50 caliber bullet hole in her chest.

A few seconds earlier, 19-year-old Bill Hood, standing in the window, had lighted a cigarette.

Down the street, a bystander was critically injured by a stray bullet. Simultaneously, the John C. Lodge Freeway, two blocks away, was reported to be under sniper fire. Tanks and National Guard troops were sent to investigate. At the Harlan House Motel, ten blocks from where Tonya Blanding had died a short time earlier, Mrs. Helen Hall, a 51-year-old white businesswoman, opened the drapes of the fourth floor hall window. Calling out to other guests, she exclaimed: "Look at the tanks!"

She died seconds later as bullets began to slam into the building. As the firing ceased, a 19-year-old Marine, carrying a Springfield rifle, burst into the building. When, accidentally, he pushed the rifle barrel through a window, the firing commenced anew. A police investigation showed that the Marine, who had just decided to "help out" the law enforcement personnel, was not involved in the death of Mrs. Hall.

R. R., a white 27-year-old coin dealer, was the owner of an expensive, three-story house on "L" Street, an integrated middle class neighborhood. In May of 1966, he and his wife and child had moved to New York and had rented the house to two young men. After several months he had begun to have problems with his tenants. On one occasion he reported to his attorney that he had been threatened by them.

In March of 1967, R. R. instituted eviction proceedings. These were still pending when the riot broke out. Concerned about the house, R. R. decided to fly to Detroit. When he arrived at the house, on Wednesday, July 26, he discovered the tenants were not at home.

He then called his attorney, who advised him to take physical possession of the house and, for legal purposes, to take witnesses along.

Together with his 17-year-old brother and another white youth, R. R. went to the house, entered, and began changing the locks on the doors. For protection they brought a .22 caliber rifle, which R. R.'s brother took into the cellar and fired into a pillow in order to test it.

Shortly after 8:00 P.M., R. R. called his attorney to advise him that the tenants had returned, and he had refused to admit them. Thereupon, R. R. alleged, the tenants had threatened to obtain the help of the National Guard. The attorney relates that he was not particularly concerned. He told R. R. that if the National Guard did appear he should have the officer in charge call him (the attorney).

At approximately the same time the National Guard claims it received information to the effect that several men had evicted the legal occupants of the house, and intended to start sniping after dark.

A National Guard column was dispatched to the scene. Shortly after 9:00 P.M., in the half-light of dusk, the column of approximately 30 men surrounded the house. A tank took position on a lawn across the street. The captain commanding the column placed in front of the house an explosive device similar to a firecracker. After setting this off in order to draw the attention of the occupants to the presence of the column, he called for them to come out of the house. No attempt was made to verify the truth or falsehood of the allegations regarding snipers.

When the captain received no reply from the house, he began counting to 10. As he was counting, he said, he heard a shot, the origin of which he could not determine. A few seconds later he heard another shot and saw a "fire streak" coming from an upstairs window. He thereupon gave the order to fire.

According to the three young men, they were on the second floor of the house and completely bewildered by the barrage of fire that was unleashed against it. As hundreds of bullets crashed through the first and second-story windows and ricocheted off the walls, they dashed to the third floor. Protected by a large chimney, they huddled in a closet until, during a lull in the firing, they were able to wave an item of clothing out of the window as a sign of surrender. They were arrested as snipers.

The firing from rifles and machine guns had been so intense

that in a period of a few minutes it inflicted an estimated $10,000 worth of damage. One of a pair of stone columns was shot nearly in half.

Jailed at the 10th Precinct Station sometime Wednesday night R. R. and his two companions were taken from their cell to an "alley court," police slang for an unlawful attempt to make prisoners confess. A police officer, who has resigned from the force, allegedly administered such a severe beating to R. R. that the bruises still were visible two weeks later.

R. R.'s 17-year-old brother had his skull cracked open, and was thrown back into the cell. He was taken to a hospital only when other arrestees complained that he was bleeding to death.

At the preliminary hearing 12 days later the prosecution presented only one witness, the National Guard captain who had given the order to fire. The police officer who had signed the original complaint was not asked to take the stand. The charges against all three of the young men were dismissed.

Nevertheless, the morning after the original incident, a major metropolitan newspaper in another section of the country composed the following banner story from wire service reports:

DETROIT, July 27 (Thursday)—Two National Guard tanks ripped a sniper's haven with machine guns Wednesday night and flushed out three shaggy-haired white youths. Snipers attacked a guard command post and Detroit's racial riot set a modern record for bloodshed. The death toll soared to 36, topping the Watts bloodbath of 1966 in which 35 died and making Detroit's insurrection the most deadly racial riot in modern U. S. history.
. . .
In the attack on the sniper's nest, the Guardsmen poured hundreds of rounds of .50 caliber machine gun fire into the home, which authorities said housed arms and ammunition used by West Side sniper squads.

Guardsmen recovered guns and ammunition. A reporter with the troopers said the house, a neat brick home in a neighborhood of $20,000 to $50,000 homes, was torn apart by the machine gun and rifle fire.

Sniper fire crackled from the home as the Guard unit approached. It was one of the first verified reports of sniping by whites. . . .

A pile of loot taken from riot-ruined stores was recovered from the sniper's haven, located ten blocks from the heart of the 200-square block riot zone.

Guardsmen said the house had been identified as a storehouse of arms and ammunition for snipers. Its arsenal was regarded as an indication that the sniping—or at least some of it—was organized.

As hundreds of arrestees were brought into the 10th Precinct Station, officers took it upon themselves to carry on investigations and to attempt to extract confessions. Dozens of charges of police brutality emanated from the station as prisoners were brought in uninjured, but later had to be taken to the hospital.

In the absence of the precinct commander, who had transferred his headquarters to the riot command post at a nearby hospital, discipline vanished. Prisoners who requested that they be permitted to notify someone of their arrest were almost invariably told that: "The telephones are out of order." Congressman Conyers and State Representative Del Rio, who went to the station hoping to coordinate with the police the establishing of a community patrol, were so upset by what they saw that they changed their minds and gave up on the project.

A young woman, brought into the station, was told to strip. After she had done so, and while an officer took pictures with a Polaroid camera, another officer came up to her and began fondling her. The negative of one of the pictures, fished out of a waste basket, subsequently was turned over to the mayor's office.

Citing the sniper danger, officers throughout the department had taken off their bright metal badges. They also had taped over the license plates and the numbers of the police cars. Identification of individual officers became virtually impossible.

On a number of occasions officers fired at fleeing looters, then made little attempt to determine whether their shots had hit anyone. Later some of the persons were discovered dead or injured in the street.

In one such case police and National Guardsmen were interrogating a youth suspected of arson when, according to officers, he attempted to escape. As he vaulted over the hood of an automobile, an officer fired his shotgun. The youth disappeared on the other side of the car. Without making an investigation, the officers and Guardsmen returned to their car and drove off.

When nearby residents called police, another squad car arrived to pick up the body. Despite the fact that an autopsy disclosed the youth had been killed by five shotgun pellets, only a cursory investigation was made, and the death was attributed to "sniper fire." No police officer at the scene during the shooting filed a report.

Not until a Detroit newspaper editor presented to the police the statements of several witnesses claiming that the youth had been shot by police after he had been told to run did the department launch an investigation. Not until three weeks after the shooting did an officer come forward to identify himself as the one who had fired the fatal shot.

Citing conflicts in the testimony of the score of witnesses, the Detroit Prosecutor's office declined to press charges.

Prosecution is proceeding in the case of three youths in whose shotgun deaths law enforcement personnel were implicated following a report that snipers were firing from the Algiers Motel. In fact, there is little evidence that anyone fired from inside the building. Two witnesses say that they had seen a man, standing outside of the motel, fire two shots from a rifle. The interrogation of other persons revealed that law enforcement personnel then shot out one or more street lights. Police patrols responded to the shots. An attack was launched on the motel.

The picture is further complicated by the fact that this incident occurred at roughly the same time that the National Guard was directing fire at the apartment house in which Tonya Blanding was killed. The apartment house was only six blocks distant from and in a direct line with the motel.

The killings occurred when officers began on-the-spot questioning of the occupants of the motel in an effort to discover weapons used in the "sniping." Several of those questioned reportedly were beaten. One was a Negro ex-paratrooper who had only recently been honorably discharged, and had gone to Detroit to look for a job.

Although by late Tuesday looting and fire-bombing had virtually ceased, between 7:00 and 11:00 P.M. that night there were 444 reports of incidents. Most were reports of sniper fire.

During the daylight hours of July 26th, there were 534 such reports. Between 8:30 and 11:00 P.M. there were 255. As they proliferated, the pressure on law enforcement officers to uncover the snipers became intense. Homes were broken into. Searches were made on the flimsiest of tips. A Detroit newspaper headline aptly proclaimed: "Everyone's Suspect in No Man's Land."

Before the arrest of a young woman IBM operator in the city assessor's office brought attention to the situation on Friday, July 28th, any person with a gun in his home was liable to be picked up as a suspect.

Of the 27 persons charged with sniping, 22 had charges against them dismissed at preliminary hearings, and the charges against two others were dismissed later. One pleaded guilty to possession of an unregistered gun and was given a suspended sentence. Trials of two are pending.

In all, more than 7,200 persons were arrested. Almost 3,000 of these were picked up on the second day of the riot, and by midnight Monday 4,000 were incarcerated in makeshift jails.

Some were kept as long as 30 hours on buses. Others spent days in an underground garage without toilet facilities. An uncounted number were people who had merely been unfortunate enough to be on the wrong street at the wrong time. Included were members of the press whose attempts to show their credentials had been ignored. Released later, they were chided for not having exhibited their identification at the time of their arrests.

The booking system proved incapable of adequately handling the large number of arrestees. People became lost for days in the maze of different detention facilities. Until the later stages, bail was set deliberately high, often at $10,000 or more. When it became apparent that this policy was unrealistic and unworkable, the Prosecutor's office began releasing on low bail or on their own recognizance hundreds of those who had been picked up. Nevertheless, this fact was not publicized for fear of antagonizing those who had demanded a high-bail policy.

Of the 43 persons who were killed during the riot, 33 were Negro and 10 were white. Seventeen were looters, of whom two were white. Fifteen citizens (of whom four were white), one white National Guardsman, one white fireman, and one Negro private guard died as the result of gunshot wounds. Most of these deaths appear to have been accidental, but criminal homicide is suspected in some.

Two persons, including one fireman, died as a result of fallen power lines. Two were burned to death. One was a drunken gunman; one an arson suspect. One white man was killed by a rioter. One police officer was felled by a shotgun blast when his gun, in the hands of another officer, accidentally discharged during a scuffle with a looter.

Action by police officers accounted for 20 and, very likely, 21 of the deaths; action by the National Guard for seven, and, very likely, nine; action by the Army for one. Two deaths were the result of action by store owners. Four persons died accidentally. Rioters were responsible for two, and perhaps three of the deaths; a private guard for one. A white man is suspected of murdering a Negro youth. The perpetrator of one of the killings in the Algiers Motel remains unknown.

Damage estimates, originally set as high as $500 million, were quickly scaled down. The city assessor's office placed the loss—excluding business stock, private furnishings, and the buildings of churches and charitable institutions—at approximately $22 million. Insurance payments, according to the State Insurance Bureau, will come to about $32 million, representing an estimated 65 to 75 percent of the total loss.

By Thursday, July 27, most riot activity had ended. The paratroopers were removed from the city on Saturday. On Tuesday, August 1, the curfew was lifted and the National Guard moved out.

METHODOLOGY—PROFILES OF DISORDER

Construction of the Profiles of Disorder began with surveys by field teams in 23 cities. From an analysis of the documents compiled and field interviews, 10 of the 23, a fair cross section of the cities, were chosen for intensive further investigation.

A special investigating group was dispatched to each city under study to conduct in-depth interviews of persons previously questioned, and others that had come to our attention as a result of the analysis. Additional documents were obtained. In the process of acquisition, analysis, and distillation of information, the special investigating group made several trips to each city. In the meantime, the regular field teams continued to conduct their surveys and report additional information.

The approximately 1200 persons interviewed represent a cross section of officials, observers, and participants involved in the riot process: from mayors, police chiefs, and army officers to Black Power advocates and rioters. Experts in diverse fields, such as taxation, fire fighting, and psychology, were consulted. Testimony presented to the Commission in closed hearings was incorporated.

Many official documents were used in compiling chronologies and corroborating statements made by witnesses. These included but were not limited to police department and other law enforcement agencies' after-action reports, logs, incident reports, injury reports, and reports of homicide investigations; after-action reports of U.S. Army and National Guard units; FBI reports; fire department logs and reports; and reports from Prosecutors' offices and other investigating agencies.

About 1500 pages of depositions were taken from 90 witnesses to substantiate each of the principal items in the Profiles.

Since some information was supplied to the Commission on a confidential basis, a fully annotated, footnoted copy of the Profiles cannot be made public at this time, but will be deposited in the Archives of the United States.

Chapter 2 / Patterns of Disorder*

INTRODUCTION

The President asked the Commission to answer several specific questions about the nature of riots:

- The kinds of communities where they occurred;
- The characteristics—including age, education, and job history—of those who rioted and those who did not;
- The ways in which groups of lawful citizens can be encouraged to help cool the situation;
- The relative impact of various depressed conditions in the ghetto which stimulated people to riot;
- The impact of federal and other programs on those conditions;
- The effect on rioting of police-community relationships;
- The parts of the community which suffered the most as a result of the disorders.

The profiles in the foregoing chapter portray the nature and extent of 10 of the disorders which took place during the summer of 1967. This chapter seeks in these events and in the others which we surveyed a set of common elements to aid in understanding what happened and in answering the President's questions.

This chapter also considers certain popular conceptions about riots. Disorders are often discussed as if there were a single type. The "typical" riot of recent years is sometimes seen as a massive uprising against white people, involving widespread burning, looting, and sniping, either by all ghetto Negroes or by an uneducated, Southern-born Negro underclass of habitual criminals or "riffraff." An agitator at a protest demonstration, the coverage of events by the news media, or an isolated "triggering" or "precipitating" incident is often identified as the primary spark of violence. A uniform set of stages is sometimes posited, with a succession of confrontations and withdrawals by two cohesive groups, the police on one side and a riotous mob on the other. Often it is assumed that there was no effort within the Negro community to reduce the violence. Sometimes the only remedy prescribed is application of the largest possible police or control force, as early as possible.

What we have found does not validate these conceptions. We have been unable to identify constant patterns in all aspects of civil disorders. We have found that they are unusual,

* Notes appear at end of chapter.

irregular, complex and, in the present state of knowledge, unpredictable social processes. Like many human events, they do not unfold in orderly sequences.

Moreover, we have examined the 1967 disorders within a few months after their occurrence and under pressing time limitations. While we have collected information of considerable immediacy, analysis will undoubtedly improve with the passage and perspective of time and with the further accumulation and refinement of data. To facilitate further analysis we have appended much of our data to this report.

We have categorized the information now available about the 1967 disorders as follows.

- The pattern of violence over the nation: severity, location, timing, and numbers of people involved;
- The riot process in a sample of 24 disorders we have surveyed:* prior events, the development of violence, the various control efforts on the part of officials and the community, and the relationship between violence and control efforts;
- The riot participants: a comparison of rioters with those who sought to limit the disorder and those who remained uninvolved;
- The setting in which the disorders occurred: social and economic conditions, local governmental structure, the scale of federal programs, and the grievance reservoir in the Negro community;
- The aftermath of disorder: the ways in which communities responded after order was restored in the streets.

Based upon information derived from our surveys, we offer the following generalizations:

1. No civil disorder was "typical" in all respects. Viewed in a national framework, the disorders of 1967 varied greatly in terms of violence and damage: while a relatively small number were major under our criteria and a somewhat larger number were serious, most of the disorders would have received little or no national attention as "riots" had the nation not been sensitized by the more serious outbreaks.

2. While the civil disorders of 1967 were racial in character, they were not *inter*racial. The 1967 disorders, as well as earlier disorders of the recent period, involved action within Negro neighborhoods against symbols of white American society—authority and property—rather than against white persons.

3. Despite extremist rhetoric, there was no attempt to subvert the social order of the United States. Instead, most of those who attacked white authority and property seemed to be demanding fuller participation in the social order and the

* See the Statement on Methodology in the Appendix for a description of our survey procedures.

110

material benefits enjoyed by the vast majority of American citizens.

4. Disorder did not typically erupt without preexisting causes, as a result of a single "triggering" or "precipitating" incident. Instead, it developed out of an increasingly disturbed social atmosphere, in which typically a series of tension-heightening incidents over a period of weeks or months became linked in the minds of many in the Negro community with a shared reservoir of underlying grievances.

5. There was, typically, a complex relationship between the series of incidents and the underlying grievances. For example, grievances about allegedly abusive police practices, unemployment and underemployment, housing and other conditions in the ghetto, were often aggravated in the minds of many Negroes by incidents involving the police, or the inaction of municipal authorities on Negro complaints about police action, unemployment, inadequate housing or other conditions. When grievance-related incidents recurred and rising tensions were not satisfactorily resolved, a cumulative process took place in which prior incidents were readily recalled and grievances reinforced. At some point in the mounting tension, a further incident—in itself often routine or even trivial—became the breaking point, and tension spilled over into violence.

6. Many grievances in the Negro community result from the discrimination, prejudice and powerlessness which Negroes often experience. They also result from the severely disadvantaged social and economic conditions of many Negroes as compared with those of whites in the same city and, more particularly, in the predominantly white suburbs.

7. Characteristically, the typical rioter was not a hoodlum, habitual criminal, or riffraff; nor was he a recent migrant, a member of an uneducated underclass, or a person lacking broad social and political concerns. Instead, he was a teen-ager or young adult, a lifelong resident of the city in which he rioted, a high-school drop-out—but somewhat better educated than his Negro neighbor—and almost invariably underemployed or employed in a menial job. He was proud of his race, extremely hostile to both whites and middle-class Negroes and, though informed about politics, highly distrustful of the political system and of political leaders.

8. Numerous Negro counter-rioters walked the streets urging rioters to "cool it." The typical counter-rioter resembled in many respects the majority of Negroes, who neither rioted nor took action against the rioters, that is, the non-involved. But certain differences are crucial: the counter-rioter was

111

better educated and had higher income than either the rioter or the noninvolved.

9. Negotiations between Negroes and white officials occurred during virtually all the disorders surveyed. The negotiations often involved young, militant Negroes as well as older, established leaders. Despite a setting of chaos and disorder, negotiations in many cases involved discussion of underlying grievances as well as the handling of the disorder by control authorities.

10. The chain we have identified—discrimination, prejudice, disadvantaged conditions, intense and pervasive grievances, a series of tension-heightening incidents, all culminating in the eruption of disorder at the hands of youthful, politically-aware activists—must be understood as describing the central trend in the disorders, not as an explanation of all aspects of the riots or of all rioters. Some rioters, for example, may have shared neither the conditions nor the grievances of their Negro neighbors; some may have coolly and deliberately exploited the chaos created by others; some may have been drawn into the melee merely because they identified with, or wished to emulate, others. Nor do we intend to suggest that the majority of the rioters, who shared the adverse conditions and grievances, necessarily articulated in their own minds the connection between that background and their actions.

11. The background of disorder in the riot cities was typically characterized by severely disadvantaged conditions for Negroes, especially as compared with those for whites; a local government often unresponsive to these conditions; federal programs which had not yet reached a significantly large proportion of those in need; and the resulting reservoir of pervasive and deep grievance and frustration in the ghetto.

12. In the immediate aftermath of disorder, the status quo of daily life before the disorder generally was quickly restored. Yet, despite some notable public and private efforts, little basic change took place in the conditions underlying the disorder. In some cases, the result was increased distrust between blacks and whites, diminished interracial communication, and growth of Negro and white extremist groups.

I. The Pattern of Violence and Damage

Levels of Violence and Damage

Because definitions of "civil disorder" vary widely, between 51 and 217 disorders were recorded by various agencies as having occurred during the first nine months of 1967. From these sources we have developed a list of 164 disorders which occurred during that period.[1] We have ranked them in three categories of violence and damage utilizing such criteria as the degree and duration of violence, the number of active participants, and the level of law enforcement response:

Major Disorders—Eight disorders, 5 percent of the total, were major. These were characterized generally by a combination of the following factors: (1) many fires, intensive looting, and reports of sniping; (2) violence lasting more than two days; (3) sizeable crowds; and (4) use of National Guard or federal forces as well as other control forces.[2]

Serious Disorders—Thirty-three disorders, 20 percent of the total, were serious but not major. These were characterized generally by: (1) isolated looting, some fires, and some rock throwing; (2) violence lasting between one and two days; (3) only one sizeable crowd or many small groups; and (4) use of state police though generally not National Guard or federal forces.[3]

Minor Disorders—One hundred and twenty-three disorders, 75 percent of the total, were minor. These would not have been classified as "riots" or received wide press attention without national conditioning to a "riot" climate. They were characterized generally by: (1) a few fires and broken windows; (2) violence lasting generally less than one day; (3) participation by only small numbers of people; and (4) use, in most cases, only of local police or police from a neighboring community.[4]

The 164 disorders which we have categorized occurred in 128 cities. Twenty-five (20 percent) of the cities had two or more disturbances. New York had five separate disorders, Chicago had four, six cities had three and 17 cities had two.[5] Two cities which experienced a major disorder—Cincinnati and Tampa—had subsequent disorders; Cincinnati had two more. However, in these two cities the later disorders were less serious than the earlier ones. In only two cities were later disorders more severe.[6]

Three conclusions emerge from the data:

- The significance of the 1967 disorders cannot be minimized. The level of disorder was major or serious, in terms of our criteria, on 41 occasions in 39 cities.
- The level of disorder, however, has been exaggerated. Three-fourths of the disorders were relatively minor and would not have been regarded as nationally-newsworthy "riots" in prior years.
- The fact that a city had experienced disorder earlier in 1967 did not immunize it from further violence.

Distribution in Terms of Time, Area and Size of Community

Time—In 1967, disorders occurred with increasing frequency as summer approached and tapered off as it waned. More than 60 percent of the 164 disorders occurred in July alone.

Disorders by Month[7] and Level

Month—1967	Number of Major Disorders	Number of Serious Disorders	Number of Minor Disorders	Totals
January			1	1
February				
March		1		1
April		1	3	4
May		3	8	11
June	3	3	10	16
July	5	22	76	103
August		3	14	17
September			11	11
Totals	8	33	123	164

Area—The violence was not limited to any one section of the country.

Disorders by Region[8] and Level

Region	Number of Major Disorders	Number of Serious Disorders	Number of Minor Disorders	Total (Percent)
East	3	10	44	35
Midwest	4	11	44	36
South and Border	1	7	19	16
West		5	16	13
Totals	8	33	123	100

When timing and location are considered together, other relationships appear. Ninety-eight disorders can be grouped into 23 clusters, which consist of two or more disturbances occurring within two weeks and within a few hundred miles of each other.

"Clustering" was particularly striking for two sets of cities. The first, centered on Newark, consisted of disorders in 14 New Jersey cities. The second, centered on Detroit, consisted of disturbances in seven cities in Michigan and one in Ohio.[9]

Size of Community—The violence was not limited to large cities. Seven of the eight major disorders occurred in communities with populations of 250,000 or more. But 37 (23 percent) of the disorders reviewed occurred in communities with populations of 50,000 or less; and 67 disorders (41 percent) occurred in communities with populations of 100,000 or less, including nine (about 22 percent) of the 41 serious or major disturbances.

Disorders by Level and City Population[10]

City Population (in thousands)	Number of Major Disorders	Number of Serious Disorders	Number of Minor Disorders	Totals
0-50	1	5	31	37
50-100	0	3	27	30
100-250	0	8	23	31
250-500	5	10	15	30
500-1,000	1	4	10	15
over 1,000	1	3	13	17
Totals	8	33	119[11]	160[11]

Death, Injury and Damage

In its study of 75 disturbances in 67 cities, the Permanent Subcommittee on Investigations of the Senate Committee on Government Operations reported 83 deaths and 1,897 injuries.[12] Deaths occurred in 12 of these disturbances. More than 80 percent of the deaths and more than half the injuries occurred in Newark and Detroit. In more than 60 percent of the disturbances, no deaths and no more than 10 injuries were reported.[13]

Substantial damage to property also tended to be concentrated in a relatively small number of cities. Of the disorders which the Commission surveyed, significant damage resulted in Detroit ($40-45 million), Newark ($10.2 million), and Cincinnati (more than $1 million). In each of nine cities, damage was estimated at less than $100,000.[14]

Fire caused extensive damage in Detroit and Cincinnati, two of the three cities which suffered the greatest destruction of property.[15] Newark had relatively little loss from fire but extensive inventory loss from looting and damage to stock.[16]

Damage estimates made at the time of the Newark and Detroit disorders were later greatly reduced. Early estimates in Newark ranged from $15 to $25 million; a month later the estimate was revised to $10.2 million. In Detroit, newspaper damage estimates at first ranged from $200 million to $500 million, the highest recent estimate is $45 million.[17]

What we have said should not obscure three important factors. First, the dollar cost of the disorders should be increased by the `xtraordinary administrative expenses of municipal, state and Federal governments.[18] Second, deaths and injuries are not the sole measures of the cost of civil disorders in human terms. For example, the cost of dislocation of people—though clearly not quantifiable in dollars and cents—was a significant factor in Detroit, the one case in which many residences were destroyed.[19] Other human costs—fear, distrust, and alienation—were incurred in every disorder. Third, even a relatively low level of violence and damage in absolute terms may seriously disrupt a small or medium-sized community.

Victims of Violence

Of the 83 persons who died in the 75 disorders studied by the Permanent Subcommittee on Investigations, about 10 percent were public officials, primarily law officers and firemen. Among the injured, public officials made up 38 percent.[20] The overwhelming majority of the civilians killed and injured were Negroes.

Retail businesses suffered a much larger proportion of the damage during the disorders than public institutions, industrial properties, or private residences. In Newark, 1,029 establishments, affecting some 4,492 employers and employees, suffered damage to buildings or loss of inventory or both. Those which suffered the greatest loss through looting, in descending order of loss, were liquor, clothing, and furniture stores.

White-owned businesses are widely believed to have been damaged much more frequently than those owned by Negroes. In at least nine of the cities studied, the damage seems to have been, at least in part, the result of deliberate attacks on white-owned businesses characterized in the Negro community as unfair or disrespectful toward Negroes.[21]

Not all the listed damage was purposeful or was caused by rioters. Some was a by-product of violence. In certain instances police and fire department control efforts caused damage. The New Jersey commission on civil disorders has found that in Newark, retributive action was taken against Negro-owned property by control forces.[22] Some damage was accidental. In Detroit some fire damage, especially to residences, may have been caused primarily by a heavy wind.

Public institutions generally were not targets of serious attacks,[23] but police and fire equipment was damaged in at least 15 of the 23 cities.[24]

Of the cities surveyed, significant damage to residences occurred only in Detroit. In at least nine of the 22 other cities there was minor damage to residences, often resulting from fires in adjacent businesses.[25]

II. The Riot Process

The Commission has found no "typical" disorder in 1967 in terms of intensity of violence and extensiveness of damage. To determine whether, as is sometimes suggested, there was a typical "riot process," we examined 24 disorders which occurred during 1967 in 20 cities and three university settings.[26] We have concentrated on four aspects of that process:

- The accumulating reservoir of grievances in the Negro community;
- "Precipitating" incidents and their relationship to the reservoir of grievances;
- The development of violence after its initial outbreak;
- The control effort, including official force, negotiation, and persuasion.

We found a common social process operating in all 24 disorders in certain critical respects. These events developed similarly, over a period of time and out of an accumulation of grievances and increasing tension in the Negro community. Almost invariably, they exploded in ways related to the local community and its particular problems and conflicts. But once violence erupted, there began a complex interaction of many elements—rioters, official control forces, counter-rioters—in which the differences between various disorders were more pronounced than the similarities.

The Reservoir of Grievances in the Negro Community

Our examination of the background of the surveyed disorders revealed a typical pattern of deeply-held grievances which were widely shared by many members of the Negro community.[27] The specific content of the expressed grievances varied somewhat from city to city. But in general, grievances among Negroes in all the cities related to prejudice, discrimination, severely disadvantaged living conditions and a general sense of frustration about their inability to change those conditions.

Specific events or incidents exemplified and reinforced the shared sense of grievance. News of such incidents spread quickly throughout the community and added to the reservoir. Grievances about police practices, unemployment and underemployment, housing and other objective conditions in the ghetto were aggravated in the minds of many Negroes by the inaction of municipal authorities.

Out of this reservoir of grievance and frustration, the riot process began in the cities which we surveyed.

Precipitating Incidents

In virtually every case a single "triggering" or "precipitating" incident can be identified as having immediately preceded —within a few hours and in generally the same location—the outbreak of disorder.[28] But this incident was usually relatively minor, even trivial, by itself substantially disproportionate to

117

the scale of violence that followed. Often it was an incident of a type which had occurred frequently in the same community in the past without provoking violence.

We found that violence was generated by an increasingly disturbed social atmosphere, in which typically not one, but a series of incidents occurred over a period of weeks or months prior to the outbreak of disorders.[29] Most cities had three or more such incidents; Houston had 10 over a five-month period. These earlier or prior incidents were linked in the minds of many Negroes to the pre-existing reservoir of underlying grievances. With each such incident, frustration and tension grew until at some point a final incident, often similar to the incidents preceding it, occurred and was followed almost immediately by violence.

As we see it, the prior incidents and the reservoir of underlying grievances contributed to a cumulative process of mounting tension that spilled over into violence when the final incident occurred. In this sense the entire chain—the grievances, the series of prior tension-heightening incidents, and the final incident—was the "precipitant" of disorder.

This chain describes the central trend in the disorders we surveyed, and not necessarily all aspects of the riots or of all rioters. For example, incidents have not always increased tension; and tension has not always resulted in violence. We conclude only that both processes did occur in the disorders we examined.

Similarly, we do not suggest that all rioters shared the conditions or the grievances of their Negro neighbors: some may deliberately have exploited the chaos created out of the frustration of others; some may have been drawn into the melee merely because they identified with, or wished to emulate, others. Some who shared the adverse conditions and grievances did not riot.

We found that the majority of the rioters did share the adverse conditions and grievances. Although they did not necessarily articulate in their own minds the connection between that background and their actions.

Newark and Detroit presented typical sequences of prior incidents, a build-up of tensions, a final incident, and the outbreak of violence:

NEWARK

Prior Incidents

1965: A Newark policeman shot and killed an 18-year-old Negro boy. After the policeman had stated that he had fallen and his gun had discharged accidentally, he later claimed that the

118

youth had assaulted another officer and was shot as he fled. At a hearing it was decided that the patrolman had not used excessive force. The patrolman remained on duty, and his occasional assignment to Negro areas was a continuing source of irritation in the Negro community:

April, 1967: Approximately 15 Negroes were arrested while picketing a grocery store which they claimed sold bad meat and used unfair credit practices.

Late May, early June: Negro leaders had for several months voiced strong opposition to a proposed medical-dental center to be built on 150 acres of land in the predominantly Negro Central Ward. The dispute centered mainly around the lack of relocation provisions for those who would be displaced by the medical center. The issue became extremely volatile in late May when public "blight hearings" were held regarding the land to be condemned: The hearings became a public forum in which many residents spoke against the proposed center. The city did not change its plan.

Late May, June: The mayor recommended appointment of a white city councilman who had no more than a high school education to the position of secretary to the board of education. Reportedly, there was widespread support from both whites and Negroes for a Negro candidate who held a master's degree and was considered more qualified. The mayor did not change his recommendation. Ultimately, the original secretary retained his position and neither candidate was appointed.

July 8: Several Newark policemen, allegedly including the patrolman involved in the 1965 killing, entered East Orange to assist the East Orange police during an altercation with a group of Negro men.

Final Incident

July 12, approximately 9:30 p.m.: A Negro cab driver was injured during or after a traffic arrest in the heart of the Central Ward. Word spread quickly, and a crowd gathered in front of the Fourth Precinct station-house across the street from a large public housing project.

Initial Violence

Same day, approximately 11:30 p.m.: The crowd continued to grow until it reached 300 to 500 people. One or two Molotov cocktails were thrown at the station-house. Shortly after midnight the police dispersed the crowd, and window-breaking and looting began a few minutes later. By about 1:00 a.m., the peak level of violence for the first night was reached.

DETROIT

Prior Incidents

August 1966: A crowd formed during a routine arrest of several Negro youths in the Kercheval section of the city. Tensions were high for several hours, but no serious violence occurred.

June 1967: A Negro prostitute was shot to death on her front steps. Rumors in the Negro community attributed the killing to a vice squad officer. A police investigation later reportedly unearthed leads to a disgruntled pimp. No arrests were made.

119

June 26: A young Negro man on a picnic was shot to death while reportedly trying to protect his pregnant wife from assault by seven white youths. The wife witnessed the slaying and miscarried shortly thereafter. Of the white youths, only one was charged. The others were released.

Final Incident

July 23, approximately 3:45 a.m.: Police raided a "blind pig," a type of night club in the Negro area which served drinks after hours. Eighty persons were in the club—more than the police had anticipated—attending a party for several servicemen, two of whom had recently returned from Vietnam. A crowd of about 200 persons gathered as the police escorted the patrons into the police wagons.

Initial Violence

Approximately 5:00 a.m.: As the last police cars drove away from the "blind pig," the crowd began to throw rocks. By 8:00 a.m., looting had become widespread. Violence continued to increase throughout the day, and by evening reached a peak level for the first day.

In the 24 disorders surveyed, the events identified as tension-heightening incidents, whether prior or final, involved issues which generally paralleled the grievances we found in these cities.[30] The incidents identified were of the following types:

POLICE ACTIONS

Some 40 percent of the prior incidents involved allegedly abusive or discriminatory police actions.[31] Most of the police incidents began routinely and involved a response to, at most, a few persons rather than a large group.[32]

A typical incident occurred in Bridgeton, New Jersey five days before the disturbance when two police officers went to the home of a young Negro man to investigate a nonsupport complaint. A fight ensued when the officers attempted to take the man to the police station, and the Negro was critically injured and partially paralyzed. A Negro minister representing the injured man's family asked for suspension of the two officers involved pending investigation. This procedure had been followed previously when three policemen were accused of collusion in the robbery of a white-owned store. The Negro's request was not granted.

Police actions were also identified as the final incident preceding 12 of the 24 disturbances.[33] Again, in all but two cases, the police action which became the final incident began routinely.[34]

The final incident in Grand Rapids occurred when police attempted to apprehend a Negro driving an allegedly stolen car.

A crowd of 30 to 40 Negro spectators gathered. The suspect had one arm in a cast, and some of the younger Negroes in the crowd intervened because they thought the police were handling him too roughly.

PROTEST ACTIVITIES

Approximately 22 percent of the prior incidents involved Negro demonstrations, rallies, and protest meetings.[35] Only five involved appearances by nationally-known Negro militants.[36]

Protest rallies and meetings were also identified as the final incident preceding five disturbances. Nationally-known Negro militants spoke at two of these meetings; in the other three only local leaders were involved.[37] A prior incident involving alleged police brutality was the principal subject of each of these three rallies.[38] Inaction of municipal authorities was the topic for two other meetings.[39]

WHITE RACIST ACTIVITIES

About 17 percent of the prior incidents involved activities by whites intended to discredit or intimidate Negroes, or violence by whites against Negroes.[40] These included some 15 cross-burnings in Bridgeton, the harassment of Negro college students by white teenagers in Jackson, Mississippi, and, in Detroit, the slaying of a Negro by a group of white youths. No final incidents were classifiable as racist activity.

PREVIOUS DISORDERS IN THE SAME CITY

In this category were approximately 16 percent of the prior incidents, including seven previous disorders, the handling of which had produced a continuing sense of grievance.[41] There were other incidents, usually of minor violence, which occurred prior to seven disorders[42] and were seen by the Negro community as precursors of the subsequent disturbance. Typically, in Plainfield the night before the July disorder, a Negro youth was injured in an altercation between white and Negro teenagers. Tensions rose as a result. No final incidents were identified in this category.

DISORDERS IN OTHER CITIES

Local media coverage and rumors generated by the Newark and Detroit riots were specifically identified as prior incidents in four cases.[43] However, these major disorders appeared to be important factors in all the disorders which followed them.

Media coverage and rumors generated by the major riots in nearby Newark and Plainfield were the only identifiable final incidents preceding five nearby disorders.[44] In these cases there was a substantial mobilization of police and extensive patrolling of the ghetto area in anticipation of violence.

OFFICIAL CITY ACTIONS

Approximately 14 percent of the prior incidents were identified as action, or in some cases, inaction of city officials other than police or the judiciary.[45] Typically, in Cincinnati two months prior to the disturbance, approximately 200 representatives (mostly Negroes) of the inner-city community councils sought to appear before the city council to request summer recreation funds. The council permitted only one person from the group to speak, and then only briefly, on the ground that the group had not followed the proper procedure for placing the issue on the agenda.

No final incidents were identified in this category.

ADMINISTRATION OF JUSTICE

Eight of the prior incidents involved cases of allegedly discriminatory administration of justice.[46] Typical was a case in Houston a month and a half before the disorder. Three civil rights advocates were arrested for leading a protest and for their participation in organizing a boycott of classes at the predominantly Negro Texas Southern University. Bond was set at $25,000 each. The court refused for several days to reduce bond, even though TSU officials dropped the charges they had originally pressed.

There were no final incidents identified involving the administration of justice.

In a unique case, New Haven, the shooting of a Puerto Rican by a white man was identified as the final incident before violence.[47]

Finally, we have noted a marked relationship between prior and final incidents within each city. In most of the cities surveyed, the final incident was of the same type as one or more of the prior incidents. For example, police actions were identified as both the final incident and one or more prior incidents preceding seven disturbances.[48] Rallies or meetings to protest police actions involved in a prior incident were identified as the final incident preceding three additional disturbances.[49] The cumulative reinforcement of grievances and heightening of tensions found in all instances were particularly evident in these cases.

The Development of Violence

Once the series of precipitating incidents culminated in violence, the riot process followed no uniform pattern in the 24 disorders surveyed.[50] However, some similarities emerge.

The final incident before the outbreak of disorder, and the initial violence itself, generally occurred at a time and place in which it was normal for many people to be on the streets. In most of the 24 disorders, groups generally estimated at 50 or more persons were on the street at the time and place of the first outbreak.[51]

In all 24 disturbances, including the three university-related disorders, the initial disturbance area consisted of streets with relatively high concentrations of pedestrian and automobile traffic at the time. In all but two cases—Detroit and Milwaukee—violence started between 7:00 p.m. and 12:30 a.m., when the largest numbers of pedestrians could be expected. Ten of the 24 disorders erupted on Friday night, Saturday or Sunday.[52]

In most instances, the temperature during the day on which violence first erupted was quite high.[53] This contributed to the size of the crowds on the street, particularly in areas of congested housing.

Major violence occurred in all 24 disorders during the evening and night hours, between 6:00 p.m. and 6:00 a.m., and in most cases between 9:00 p.m. and 3:00 a.m.[54] In only a few disorders, including Detroit and Newark, did substantial violence occur or continue during the daytime.[55] Generally, the night-day cycles continued in daily succession through the early period of the disorder.[56]

At the beginning of disorder, violence generally flared almost immediately after the final precipitating incident.[57] It then escalated quickly to its peak level, in the case of one-night disorders, and to the first night peak in the case of continuing disorders.[58] In Detroit and Newark, the first outbreaks began within two hours and reached severe, although not the highest, levels within three hours.

In almost all of the subsequent night-day cycles, the change from relative order to a state of disorder by a number of people typically occurred extremely rapidly—within one or two hours at the most.[59]

Nineteen of the surveyed disorders lasted more than one night.[60] In 10 of these, violence peaked on the first night, and the level of activity on subsequent nights was the same or less.[61] In the other nine disorders, however, the peak was reached on a subsequent night.[62]

Disorder generally began with less serious violence against property, such as rock and bottle throwing and window breaking.[63] These were usually the materials and the targets closest to hand at the place of the initial outbreak.

Once store windows were broken, looting usually followed.[64] Whether fires were set only after looting occurred is unclear. Reported instances of fire-bombing and Molotov cocktails in the 24 disorders appeared to occur as frequently during one cycle of violence as during another in disorders which continued through more than one cycle.[65] However, fires seemed to break out more frequently during the middle cycles of riots lasting several days.[66] Gunfire and sniping were also reported more frequently during the middle cycles.[67]

The Control Effort

What type of community response is most effective once disorder erupts is clearly a critically important question. Chapter 12, "Control of Disorder," and the Supplement on Control of Disorder to this report consider this question at length. We consider in this section the variety of control responses, official and unofficial, which were utilized in the 24 surveyed disorders, including:

● Use or threatened use of local official force;
● Use or threatened use of supplemental official force from other jurisdictions;
● Negotiations between officials and representatives from the Negro community;
● On-the-street persuasion by "counter-rioters."

Disorders are sometimes discussed as if they consisted of a succession of confrontations and withdrawals by two cohesive groups, the police or other control force on one side and a riotous mob on the other. Often it is assumed that there was no effort within the Negro community to reduce the violence. Sometimes the only remedy prescribed is mobilization of the largest possible police or control force, as early as possible. None of these views are accurate. We found that:

● A variety of different control forces employed a variety of tactics, often at the same time, and often in a confused situation;
● Substantial non-force control efforts, such as negotiations and on-the-street persuasion by "counter-rioters," were usually under way, often simultaneously with forcible control efforts; counter-

rioter activity often was carried on by Negro residents of the disturbance area, sometimes with and often without official recognition;
- No single tactic appeared to be effective in containing or reducing violence in all situations.

LOCAL OFFICIAL FORCE

In 20 of the 24 disorders, the primary effort to restore order at the beginning of violence was made entirely by local police.[68] In 10 cases no additional outside force was called for after the initial response.[69] In only a few cases was the initial control force faced with crowds too large to control.[70]

The police approach to the initial outbreak of disorder in the surveyed cities was generally cautious.[71] Three types of response were employed. One was dispersal (clearing the area, either by arrests or by scattering crowds), used in 10 cases.[72] Another was reconnaissance (observing and evaluating developments), used in eight cases.[73] In half of these instances, they soon withdrew from the disturbance area, generally because they believed they were unable to cope with the disorder.[74] The third was containment (preventing movement in or out of a cordoned or barricaded area), used in six cases.[75]

No uniform result from utilization of any of the three control approaches is apparent. In at least half of the 24 cases it can reasonably be said that the approach taken by the police did not prevent the continuation of violence.[76] To the extent that their effectiveness is measurable, the conclusion appears to hold for subsequent police control responses as well.[77] There is also evidence, in some instances, of over-response in subsequent cycles of violence.[78]

The various tactical responses we have described are not mutually exclusive, and in many instances combinations were employed. The most common were attempts at dispersal in the disturbance area and a simultaneous cordon or barricade at the routes leading from the disturbance area to the central commercial area of the city, either to contain the disturbance or to prevent persons outside the area from entering it, or both.[79]

In 11 disorders a curfew was imposed at some time, either as the major dispersal technique or in combination with other techniques.[80]

In only four disorders was tear gas used at any point as a dispersal technique.[81]

Only Newark and New Haven used a combination of all three means of control, cordon, curfew and tear gas.[82]

125

In nine disturbances—involving a wide variation in the intensity of violence—additional control forces were brought in after there had been serious violence which local police had been unable to handle alone.[83] In every case further violence occurred, often more than once and often of equal or greater intensity than before.[84]

The result was the same where extra forces were mobilized prior to serious violence. In four cities where this was done,[85] violence nonetheless occurred, in most cases more than once,[86] and often of equal or greater intensity than in the original outbreak.[87]

In the remaining group of seven cities no outside control forces were called,[88] because the level and duration of violence were lower. Outbreaks in these cities nevertheless followed the same random pattern as in the cities which did use outside forces.[89]

NEGOTIATION

In 21 of the 24 disturbances surveyed, discussion or negotiation occurred during the disturbances. These took the form of relatively formal meetings between government officials and Negroes during which grievances and issues were discussed and means were sought to restore order.[90]

Such meetings were usually held either immediately before or soon after the outbreak of violence.[91] Meetings often continued beyond the first or second day of the disorder and, in a few instances, through the entire period of the disorder.[92]

The Negro participants in these meetings usually were established leaders in the Negro community, such as city councilmen or members of human relations commissions, ministers, or officers of civil rights or other community organizations.[93] However, Negro youths were participants in over one-third of these meetings.[94] In a few disorders both the youths and the adult Negro leaders participated,[95] sometimes without the participation of local officials.[96]

Employees of community action agencies occasionally participated, either as intermediaries or as participants. In some cases they provided the meeting place.[97]

Discussions usually included issues generated by the disorder itself, such as the treatment by the police of those arrested.[98] In 12 cases, prior ghetto grievances, such as unemployment and inadequate recreational facilities, were included as subjects.[99] Often both disorder-related and prior grievances were discussed [100] with the focus generally shifting from the former to the latter as the disorder continued.

How effective these meetings were is, as in the case of forcible response, impossible to gauge. Again, much depends on who participated, timing, and what other responses were being made at the same time.

COUNTER-RIOTERS

In all but six of the 24 disorders, Negro private citizens were active on the streets attempting to restore order primarily by means of persuasion.[101] In a Detroit survey of riot area residents over the age of 15, some 14 percent stated that they had been active as counter-rioters.[102]

Counter-rioters sometimes had some form of official recognition from either the mayor or a human relations council.[103] Police reaction in these cases varied from total opposition to close cooperation.[104] In most such cases some degree of official authorization was given before the activity of the counter-rioters began,[105] and in a smaller number of cases, their activity was not explicitly authorized but merely condoned by the authorities.[106]

Distinctive insignia were worn by the officially recognized counter-rioters in at least a few cities.[107] In Dayton and Tampa, the white helmets issued to the counter-rioters have made the name "White Hats" synonymous with counter-rioters.

Public attention has centered on the officially-recognized counter-rioters. However, counter-rioters are known to have acted independently, without official recognition, in a number of cities.[108]

Counter-rioters generally included young men, ministers, community action agency and other anti-poverty workers and well-known ghetto residents.[109]

Their usual technique was to walk through the disturbance area urging people to "cool it," although they often took other positive action as well, such as distributing food.[110]

How effective the counter-rioters were is difficult to estimate. Authorities in several cities indicated that they believed they were helpful.

III. The Riot Participant

It is sometimes assumed that the rioters were criminal types, overactive social deviants, or riffraff—recent migrants, members of an uneducated underclass—alienated from responsible

Negroes, and without broad social or political concerns. It is often implied that there was no effort within the Negro community to attempt to reduce the violence.

We have obtained data on participation from four different sources.[111]

- Eyewitness accounts, from more than 1,200 interviews in our staff reconnaissance survey of 20 cities;
- Interview surveys based on probability samples of riot area residents in the two major riot cities—Detroit and Newark—designed to elicit anonymous self-identification of participants as rioters, counter-rioters or non-involved;
- Arrest records from 22 cities;
- A special study of arrestees in Detroit.

Only partial information is available on the total numbers of participants. In the Detroit survey, approximately 11 percent of the sampled residents over the age of 15 in the two disturbance areas admittedly participated in rioting; another 20 to 25 percent admitted to having been bystanders but claimed that they had not participated; approximately 16 percent claimed they had engaged in counter-riot activity; and the largest proportion (48 to 53 percent) claimed they were at home or elsewhere and did not participate. However, a large proportion of the Negro community apparently believed that more was gained than lost through rioting, according to the Newark and Detroit surveys.[112]

Greater precision is possible in describing the characteristics of those who participated. We have combined the data from the four sources to construct a profile of the typical rioter and to compare him with the counter-rioter and the noninvolved.

The Profile of a Rioter

The typical rioter in the summer of 1967 was a Negro, unmarried male between the ages of 15 and 24. He was in many ways very different from the stereotype. He was not a migrant. He was born in the state and was a life-long resident of the city in which the riot took place. Economically his position was about the same as his Negro neighbors who did not actively participate in the riot.

Although he had not, usually, graduated from high school, he was somewhat better educated than the average inner-city Negro, having at least attended high school for a time.

Nevertheless, he was more likely to be working in a menial or low status job as an unskilled laborer. If he was employed, he was not working full time and his employment was frequently interrupted by periods of unemployment.

He feels strongly that he deserves a better job and that he is barred from achieving it, not because of lack of training, ability, or ambition, but because of discrimination by employers.

He rejects the white bigot's stereotype of the Negro as ignorant and shiftless. He takes great pride in his race and believes that in some respects Negroes are superior to whites. He is extremely hostile to whites, but his hostility is more apt to be a product of social and economic class than of race; he is almost equally hostile toward middle-class Negroes.

He is substantially better informed about politics than Negroes who were not involved in the riots. He is more likely to be actively engaged in civil rights efforts, but is extremely distrustful of the political system and of political leaders.

The Profile of the Counter-Rioter

The typical counter-rioter, who risked injury and arrest to walk the streets urging rioters to "cool it," was an active supporter of existing social institutions. He was, for example, far more likely than either the rioter or the noninvolved to feel that this country is worth defending in a major war. His actions and his attitudes reflected his substantially greater stake in the social system; he was considerably better educated and more affluent than either the rioter or the noninvolved. He was somewhat more likely than the rioter, but less likely than the noninvolved, to have been a migrant. In all other respects he was identical to the noninvolved.[113]

Characteristics of Participants

Race—Eighty-three percent of the arrestees were Negroes; 15 percent were whites.[114] Our interviews in 20 cities indicate that almost all rioters were Negroes.

Age—The survey data from Detroit, the arrest records, and our interviews in 20 cities, all indicate that the rioters were late teenagers or young adults.[115] In the Detroit survey, 61.3 percent of the self-reported rioters were between the ages of 15 and 24, and 86.3 percent were between 15 and 35. The arrest data indicate that 52.5 percent of the arrestees were between 15 and 24, and 80.8 percent were between 15 and 35.

Of the noninvolved, by contrast, only 22.6 percent in the Detroit survey were between 15 and 24, and 38.3 percent were between 15 and 35.

Sex—In the Detroit survey 61.4 percent of the self-reported rioters were male. Arrestees, however, were almost all male—89.3 percent.[116] Our interviews in 20 cities indicate that the majority of rioters were male. The large difference in proportion between the Detroit survey data and the arrestee figures probably reflects either selectivity in the arrest process or less dramatic, less provocative riot behavior by women.

Family Structure—Three sources of available information—the Newark survey, the Detroit arrest study, and arrest records from four cities—indicate a tendency for rioters to be single.[117] The Newark survey indicates that rioters were single—56.2 percent—more often than the noninvolved—49.6 percent.

The Newark survey also indicates that rioters were more likely to have been divorced or separated—14.2 percent—than the noninvolved—6.4 percent. However, the arrest records from four cities indicate that only a very small percentage of those arrested fall in this category.

In regard to the structure of the family in which he was raised, the self-reported rioter, according to the Newark survey, was not significantly different from many of his Negro neighbors who did not actively participate in the riot. Twenty-five and five tenths percent of the self-reported rioters and 23.0 percent of the noninvolved were brought up in homes where no adult male lived.[118]

Region of Upbringing—Both survey data[119] and arrest records[120] demonstrate unequivocally that those brought up in the region in which the riot occurred are much more likely to have participated in the riots. The percentage of self-reported rioters brought up in the North is almost identical for the Detroit survey—74.4 percent—and the Newark survey—74 percent. By contrast, of the noninvolved, 36 percent in Detroit and 52.4 percent in Newark were brought up in the region in which the disorder occurred.[121]

Data available from five cities on the birthplace of arrestees indicate that 63 percent of the arrestees were born in the North. Although birthplace is not necessarily identical with place of upbringing, the data are sufficiently similar to provide strong support for the conclusion.

Of the self-reported counter-rioters, however, 47.5 percent were born in the North, according to the Detroit survey, a figure which places them between self-reported rioters and the noninvolved. Apparently, a significant consequence of growing up in the South is the tendency toward noninvolvement in a riot situation, while involvement in a riot, either in support of or against existing social institutions, was more common among those born in the North.

Residence—Rioters are not only more likely than the noninvolved to have been born in the region in which the riot occurred, but they also more likely to have been long-term residents of the city in which the disturbance took place.[122] The Detroit survey data indicate that 59.4 percent of the self-reported rioters, but only 34.6 percent of the noninvolved, were born in Detroit. The comparable figures in the Newark survey are 53.5 percent and 22.5 percent.

Outsiders who temporarily entered the city during the riot might have left before the surveys were conducted and therefore may be underestimated in the survey data. However, the arrest data,[123] which is contemporaneous with the riot, suggest that few outsiders were involved: 90 percent of those arrested resided in the riot city. Seven percent lived in the same state. Only 1 percent were from outside the state. Our interviews in 20 cities also corroborate these conclusions.

Income—In the Detroit and Newark survey data, income level alone does not seem to correlate with self-reported riot participation.[124] The figures from the two cities are not directly comparable since respondents were asked for individual income in Detroit, and family income in Newark. More Detroit self-reported rioters (38.6 percent) had annual incomes under $5,000 per year than the noninvolved (30.3 percent), but even this small difference disappears when the factor of age is taken into account.

In the Newark data, in which the age distributions of self-reported rioters and the noninvolved are more similar, there is almost no difference between the rioters, 32.6 percent of whom had annual incomes under $5,000, and the noninvolved, 29.4 percent of whom had annual incomes under $5,000.

The similarity in income distribution should not, however, lead to the conclusion that more affluent Negroes are as likely to riot as poor Negroes. Both surveys were conducted in disturbance areas in which incomes are considerably lower than in the city as a whole and the surrounding metropolitan area.[125] Nevertheless, the data show that rioters are not necessarily the poorest of the poor.

While income fails to distinguish self-reported rioters from those who were not involved, it does distinguish counter-rioters from rioters and the noninvolved. Less than 9 percent of both those who rioted and those not involved earned more than $10,000 annually. Yet almost 20 percent of the counter-rioters earned this amount or more. In fact, there were no male self-reported counter-rioters in the Detroit survey who earned less than $5,000 annually. In the Newark sample there were seven respondents who owned their own homes; none of them participated in the riot. While extreme poverty does not necessarily move a man to riot, relative affluence seems at least to inhibit him from attacking the existing social order and may motivate him to take considerable risks to protect it.

Education—Level of schooling is strongly related to participation. Those with some high school education were more likely to riot than those who had only finished grade school.[126] In the Detroit survey 93 percent of the self-reported rioters had gone beyond grade school, compared with 72.1 percent of the noninvolved. In the Newark survey the comparable figures are 98.1 percent and 85.7 percent. The majority of self-reported rioters are not, however, high school graduates.

The counter-rioters were clearly the best educated of the three groups. Approximately twice as many counter-rioters had attended college as had the noninvolved, and half again as many counter-rioters had attended college as rioters. Considered with the information on income, this data suggests that counter-rioters were probably well on their way into the middle class.

Education and income are the only factors which distinguish the counter-rioter from the noninvolved. Apparently, a high level of education and income not only prevents rioting but is more likely to lead to active, responsible opposition to rioting.

Employment—The Detroit and Newark surveys, the arrest records from four cities, and the Detroit arrest study all indicate that there are no substantial differences in unemployment between the rioters and the noninvolved.[127]

Unemployment levels among both groups were extremely high. In the Detroit survey, 29.6 percent of the self-reported rioters were unemployed; in the Newark survey, 29.7 percent; in the four-city arrest data, 33.2 percent; and in the Detroit arrest study, 21.8 percent. The unemployment rates for the noninvolved in the Detroit and Newark surveys were 31.5 and 19.0 percent.

Self-reported rioters were more likely to be only intermittently employed, however, than the noninvolved. Respondents in Newark were asked whether they had been unemployed for as long as a month or more during the last year.[128] Sixty-one percent of the self-reported rioters, but only 43.4 percent of the noninvolved, answered, "Yes."

Despite generally higher levels of education, rioters are more likely than the noninvolved to be employed in unskilled jobs.[129] In the Newark survey, 50.0 percent of the self-reported rioters, but only 39.6 percent of the noninvolved, had unskilled jobs.

Attitudes About Employment—The Newark survey data indicate that self-reported rioters were more likely to feel dissatisfied with their present jobs than were the noninvolved.[130]

Only 29.3 percent of the rioters, compared with 44.4 percent of the noninvolved, thought their present jobs to be appropriate for them in responsibility and pay. Of the self-reported rioters, 67.6 percent, compared with 56.1 percent of the noninvolved, felt that it was impossible to obtain the kind of job they wanted.[131] Of the self-reported rioters, 69 percent, as compared with 50.0 percent of the noninvolved, felt that racial discrimination was the major obstacle to their finding better employment.[132] Despite this feeling, surprising numbers of rioters, (76.9 percent) responded that "getting what you want out of life is a matter of ability, not being in the right place at the right time." [133]

Racial Attitudes—The Detroit and Newark surveys indicate that rioters have strong feelings of racial pride, if not racial superiority.[134] In the Detroit survey, 48.6 percent of the self-reported rioters said that they felt Negroes were more dependable than whites. Only 22.4 percent of the noninvolved stated this. In Newark, the comparable figures were 45.0 and 27.8 percent. The Newark survey data indicate that rioters want to be called "black" rather than "Negro" or "colored" and are somewhat more likely than the noninvolved to feel that all Negroes should study African history and languages.[135]

To what extent this racial pride antedated the riot and to what extent it was produced by the riot is impossible to determine from the survey data. Certainly the riot experience seems to have been associated with increased pride in the minds of many of the participants. This was vividly illustrated by the statement of a Detroit rioter:

Interviewer: You said you were feeling good when you followed the crowds?
Respondent: I was feeling proud, man, at the fact that I was a Negro. I felt like I was a first class citizen. I didn't feel ashamed of my race because of what they did.

Similar feelings were expressed by an 18-year-old Detroit girl who reported that she had been a looter:

Interviewer: What is the Negro then if he's not American?
Respondent: A Negro, he's considered a slave to the white folks. But half of them know that they're slaves and feel that they can't do nothing about it because they're just going along with it. But most of them they seem to get it in their heads now how the white folks treat them and how they've been treating them and how they've been slaves for the white folks. . . .

Along with increased racial pride there appears to be intense hostility toward whites.[136] Self-reported rioters in both the Detroit and Newark surveys were more likely to feel that civil rights groups with white and Negro leaders would do better without the whites. In Detroit, 36.1 percent of the self-reported rioters thought that this statement was true, while only 21.1 percent of the noninvolved thought so. In the Newark survey, 51.4 percent of the self-reported rioters agreed; 33.1 percent of the noninvolved shared this opinion.

Self-reported rioters in Newark were also more likely to agree with the statement, "Sometimes I hate white people." Of the self-reported rioters, 72.4 percent agreed; of the noninvolved, 50.0 percent agreed.

The intensity of the self-reported rioters' racial feelings may suggest that the recent riots represented traditional interracial hostilities. Two sources of data suggest that this intepretation is probably incorrect.

First, the Newark survey data indicate that rioters were almost as hostile to middle-class Negroes as they were to whites.[137] Seventy-one and four-tenths percent of the self-reported rioters, but only 59.5 percent of the noninvolved, agreed with the statement, "Negroes who make a lot of money like to think they are better than other Negroes." Perhaps even more significant, particularly in light of the rioters' strong feelings of racial pride, is that 50.5 percent of the self-reported rioters agreed that "Negroes who make a lot of money are just as bad as white people." Only 35.2 percent of the noninvolved shared this opinion.

Second, the arrest data show that the great majority of those arrested during the disorders were generally charged with a crime relating to looting or curfew violations.[138] Only 2.4 percent of the arrests were for assault and 0.1 percent were for homicide, but 31.3 percent of the arrests were for breaking and entering—crimes directed against white property rather than against individual whites.

Political Attitudes and Involvement—Respondents in the Newark survey were asked about relatively simple items of political information, such as the race of prominent local and national political figures. In general, the self-reported rioters were much better informed than the noninvolved.[139] For example, self-reported rioters were more likely to know that one of the 1966 Newark mayoral candidates was a Negro. Of the rioters, 77.1 percent—but only 61.6 percent of the noninvolved—identified him correctly. The overall scores on a series of similar questions also reflect the self-reported rioters' higher levels of information.

Self-reported rioters were also more likely to be involved in activities associated with Negro rights.[140] At the most basic level of political participation, they were more likely than the noninvolved to talk frequently about Negro rights. In the Newark survey, 53.8 percent of the self-reported rioters, but only 34.9 percent of the noninvolved, said that they talked about Negro rights nearly every day.

The self-reported rioters also were more likely to have attended a meeting or participated in civil rights activity. Of the rioters, 39.3 percent—but only 25.7 percent of the noninvolved—reported that they had engaged in such activity.

In the Newark survey, respondents were asked how much they thought they could trust the local government.[141] Only 4.8 percent of the self-reported rioters, compared with 13.7 percent of the noninvolved, said that they felt they could trust it most of the time; 44.2 percent of the self-reported rioters and 33.9 percent of the noninvolved reported that they could almost never trust the government.

In the Detroit survey, self-reported rioters were much more likely to attribute the riot to anger about politicians and police than were the noninvolved.[142] Of the self-reported rioters, 43.2 percent—but only 19.6 percent of the noninvolved—said anger at politicians had a great deal to do with causing the riot. Of the self-reported rioters, 70.5 percent, compared with 48.8 percent of the noninvolved, believed that anger at the police had a great deal to do with causing the riot.

Perhaps the most revealing and disturbing measure of the rioters' anger at the social and political system was their response to a question asking whether they thought "the country was worth fighting for in the event of a major world war." [143] Of the self-reported rioters, 39.4 percent in Detroit and 52.8 percent in Newark shared a negative view. In contrast, 15.5 percent of the noninvolved in Detroit and 27.8 percent of the noninvolved in Newark shared this sentiment. Almost none of the self-reported counter-rioters in Detroit—3.3 percent— agreed with the self-reported rioters.

Some comments of interviewees are worthy of note:

Not worth fighting for—if Negroes had an equal chance it would be worth fighting for.
Not worth fighting for—I am not a true citizen so why should I?
Not worth fighting for—because my husband came back from Vietnam and nothing had changed.

IV. The Background of Disorder

In response to the President's questions to the Commission about the riot environment, we have gathered information on the pre-riot conditions in 20 of the cities surveyed.[144] We have sought to analyze the backgrounds of the disorders in terms of four basic groupings of information:

- The social and economic conditions as described in the 1960 census, with particular reference to the area of each city in which the disturbance took place;
- Local governmental structure and its organizational capacity to respond to the needs of the people, particularly those living in the most depressed conditions;
- The extent to which federal programs assisted in meeting these needs; and
- The nature of the grievances in the ghetto community.

It is sometimes said that conditions for Negroes in the riot cities have improved over the years and are not materially different from conditions for whites; that local government now seeks to accommodate the demands of Negroes and has created many mechanisms for redressing legitimate complaints; that federal programs now enable most Negroes who so desire, to live comfortably through welfare, housing, employment or anti-poverty assistance; and that grievances are harbored only by a few malcontents and agitators.

Our findings show the contrary. In the riot cities we surveyed, we found that Negroes are severely disadvantaged, especially as compared with whites; that local government is often unresponsive to this fact; that federal programs have not yet reached a significantly large proportion of those in need; and that these facts create a reservoir of unredressed grievances and frustration in the ghetto.[145]

The Pattern of Disadvantage

Social and economic conditions in the riot cities [146] constituted a clear pattern of severe disadvantage for Negroes as compared with whites, whether the Negroes lived in the disturbance area or outside it.[147] When ghetto conditions are compared with those for whites in the suburbs, the relative disadvantage for Negroes is even greater.

In all the cities surveyed, the Negro population increased between 1950 and 1960 at a median rate of 75 percent.[148]

Meanwhile, the white population decreased in more than half the cities—including six which experienced the most severe disturbances in 1967. The increase in nonwhite population in four of these cities was so great that their total population increased despite the decrease in white population.[149] These changes were attributable in large part to heavy inmigration of Negroes from rural poverty areas and movement of whites from the central cities to the suburbs.

In all the cities surveyed:

- The percentage of Negro population in the disturbance area exceeded the percentage of Negro population in the entire city.

136

In some cases it is twice, and in nine instances triple, the city-wide percentage.[150]

- The Negro population was invariably younger than the white population.[151]
- Negroes had completed fewer years of education and proportionately fewer had attended high school than whites.[152]
- A larger percentage of Negroes than whites were in the labor force.[153]
- Yet they were twice as likely to be unemployed as whites.[154]
- In cities where they had greater opportunities to work at skilled or semi-skilled jobs, proportionately more Negro men tended to be working, or looking for work, than white men. Conversely, the proportion of men working, or looking for work, tended to be lower among Negroes than whites in cities that offered the least opportunities for skilled or semi-skilled labor.[155]
- Among the employed, Negroes were more than three times as likely to be in unskilled and service jobs as whites.[156]
- Negroes earned less than whites in all the surveyed cities, averaging barely 70 percent of white income, and were more than twice as likely to be living in poverty.[157]
- A smaller proportion of Negro children than white children under 18 were living with both parents.[158]
- However, family "responsibility" was strongly related to opportunity. In cities where the proportion of Negro men in better-than-menial jobs was higher, median Negro family income was higher, and the proportion of children under 18 living with both parents was also higher. Both family income and family structure showed greater weakness in cities where job opportunities were more restricted to unskilled jobs.[159]
- Fewer Negroes than whites owned their own homes. Among non-home owners, Negroes paid the same rents, yet they paid a higher share of their incomes for rent than did whites. Although housing cost Negroes relatively more, their housing was three times as likely to be overcrowded and substandard as dwellings occupied by whites.[160]

Local Governmental Structure

In the riot cities surveyed, we found that:

- All major forms of local government were represented.
- In a substantial minority of instances, a combination of at-large election of legislators and a "weak-mayor" system resulted in fragmentation of political responsibility and accountability.
- The proportion of Negroes in government was substantially smaller than the Negro proportion of population.
- Almost all the cities had a formal grievance machinery, but typically it was regarded by most Negroes interviewed as ineffective, and generally ignored.

All major forms of municipal government were represented in the 20 cities examined.[161] Fourteen had a mayor-city coun-

137

cil form of government, five had a council-city manager, and one had a commission.[162]

The division of power between the legislative and executive branches varied widely from city to city. Of the mayor-council cities, eight could be characterized as "strong mayor/weak city council" systems in the sense that the mayor had broad appointive and veto powers.[163] Five could be characterized as "weak mayor/strong council" forms, where the city council had broad appointive and veto powers.[164] In one city, Milwaukee, such powers appeared to be evenly balanced.[165]

In 17 of the 20 cities, mayors were elected directly.[166] Mayors were parttime in eight cities.[167] Almost all the cities had a principal executive, either a mayor or a city manager, who earned a substantial annual salary.[168] Terms of office for mayors ranged from two to four years.[169]

In eight cities, all legislators were elected at large and therefore represented no particular legislative ward or district.[170] Six of these cities also had either a city manager or a "weak-mayor" form of government. In these cases, there was heavy reliance upon the city council as the principal elected policy-making authority. This combination of factors appeared to produce even less identification by citizens with any particular elected official than in the 12 cities which elected all legislators from wards or districts[171] or used a combination of election by districts and at large.[172]

The proportion of Negroes in the governments of the 20 cities was substantially smaller than the median proportion of Negro population—16 percent. Ten percent of the legislators in the surveyed cities were Negroes.[173] Only in New Brunswick and Phoenix was the proportion of legislators who were Negroes as great as the percentage of the total population that was nonwhite. Six cities had no Negro legislators.[174] Only three cities had more than one Negro legislator: Newark and Plainfield had two, and New Haven had five. None of the twenty cities had or had ever had a Negro mayor or city manager. In only four cities did Negroes hold other important policy-making positions or serve as heads of other municipal departments.[175] In seven cities Negro representatives had been elected to the state legislature.[176]

In 17 of the cities, however, Negroes were serving on boards of education.[177] In all 17 cities which had human relations councils or similar organizations, Negroes were represented on the boards of such organizations.

One of the most surprising findings is that in 17 of the 20 surveyed riot cities, some formal grievance machinery existed prior to the 1967 disorders—a municipal human relations

138

council or similar organization authorized to receive citizen complaints about racial or other discrimination by public and private agencies.[178] Existence of these formal channels, however, did not necessarily achieve their tension-relieving purpose. They were seldom regarded as effective by Negroes who were interviewed. The councils generally consisted of prominent citizens, including one or more Negroes, serving part time and with little or no salary.

With only one exception, the councils were wholly advisory and mediatory, with power to conciliate and make recommendations but not to subpoena witnesses or enforce compliance.[179] While most of the councils had full-time paid staff, they were generally organized only as loosely-affiliated departments of the city government.[180] The number of complaints filed with the councils was low considering both the size of the Negro populations and the levels of grievance which the disorders manifested. Only five councils received more than 100 complaints a year.[181] In almost all cases, complaints against private parties were mediated informally by these councils. But complaints against governmental agencies usually were referred for investigation to the agencies against whom the complaints were directed. For example, complaints of police misconduct were accepted by most councils and then referred directly to the police for investigation.

In only two cities did human relations councils attempt to investigate complaints against the police. In neither case did they succeed in completing the investigation.[182]

Where special channels for complaints against the police existed, the result appears to have been similar. In several of the cities police-community relations units had been established within the police department, in most instances within two years prior to the disorder.[183] However, complaints about police misconduct generally were forwarded to the police investigative unit, complaint bureau or police chief for investigation.

In all the cities which had a police-community relations unit, during the year preceding the disorder complaints against policemen had been filed with or forwarded to the police department.[184] In at least two of these cities the police department stated that the complaints had been investigated and disciplinary action taken in several cases.[185] Whether or not these departments in fact did take action on the complaints, the results were never disclosed either to the public or to complainants. The grievances on which the complaints were based often appeared to remain alive.

What was the pattern of governmental effort to relieve ghetto conditions and respond to needs in the cities which experienced disorders in 1967?

We have attempted no comprehensive answer to this large and complex question. Instead, we have surveyed only the key federal anti-poverty programs in Detroit, Newark and New Haven—cities which received substantial federal funds and also suffered severe disorders.

Of the large number of federal programs to aid cities, we have concentrated on five types, which relate to the most serious conditions and which involve sizeable amounts of federal assistance. We have sought to evaluate these amounts against the proportion of persons reached.[186]

We conclude that:

- While these three cities received substantial amounts of federal funds in 1967 for manpower, education, housing, welfare and community action programs, the number of persons assisted by those programs in almost all cases constituted only a fraction of those in need.
- In at least 11 of the 15 programs examined (five programs in each of the three cities), the number of people assisted in 1967 was less than half of those in need.
- In one of the 15 programs the percentage rose as high as 72 percent.
- The median was 33 percent.

Manpower—Our study included all major manpower and employment programs including basic and remedial education, skill training, on-the-job training, job counseling, and placement.[187]

A 1966 Department of Labor study of 10 slum areas, as well as our own survey of 20 disorder areas, indicate that underemployment may be an even more serious problem for ghetto residents than unemployment. However, our measurement of need for manpower programs is based on unemployment figures alone because underemployment data are not available for the three cities surveyed. The Department of Labor estimates that underemployment rates in major central city ghettos are a multiple of the unemployment rate.

In Detroit in the first three quarters of 1967, federal funds, obligated in the amount of $19.6 million, provided job training opportunities for less than one-half of the unemployed.

During the first nine months of 1967, the labor force in

Detroit totalled 650,000 persons, of whom 200,000 were Negroes. The average unemployment rate for that period was 2.7 percent for whites and 9.6 percent for Negroes. The total average number unemployed during that period was 31,350, of whom 19,200 (61 percent) were Negroes.

During the same period, there were 22 manpower programs (excluding MDTA institutional programs) in various stages of operation in Detroit. Twenty of the programs provided for 13,979 trainees.[188]

In Newark, in the first half of 1967, $2.6 million of federal funds provided job training opportunities for less than 20 percent of the unemployed.[189] And in New Haven, during the first three quarters of 1967, federal funds in the amount of $2.1 million provided job training opportunities for less than one-third of the unemployed.[190]

Education—For purposes of comparing funding to needs, we have limited our examination to two major federal education programs for the disadvantaged: the Title I program under the Elementary and Secondary Education Act of 1965 (ESEA) and the Adult Basic Education program. Title I provides assistance to schools having concentrations of educationally disadvantaged children, defined as children from families having annual incomes of less than $3,000 or supported by the Aid to Families with Dependent Children program (AFDC). Title I supports remedial reading, career guidance for potential dropouts, reduced pupil-teacher ratios, special teacher training, educational television and other teaching equipment, and specialized staff for social work, guidance and counseling, psychiatry and medicine. The Adult Basic Education program is designed to teach functionally illiterate adults to read.

In order to measure the total federal contributions to state and local educational expenditures, we have also included such other federal programs as Head Start, for disadvantaged preschool children; the larger institutional Manpower Development and Training Programs; the Teacher Corps; library material and supplementary education projects under Titles II and III of ESEA; and vocational education programs.

In Detroit, during the 1967-68 school year, $11.2 million of ESEA Title I funds assist only 31 percent of the eligible students. Adult Basic Education reaches slightly more than 2 percent of the eligible beneficiaries. Federal contributions to the Detroit public school system add about 10 percent to state and local expenditures.[191]

In Newark, during the 1967-68 school year, $4 million of ESEA Title I funds assist about 72 percent of the eligible students. The number of persons reached by the Adult Basic

141

Education program is only approximately 6 percent of the number of functionally illiterate adults. Federal contributions to the Newark public school system add about 11 percent to state and local expenditures.[192]

In New Haven, during the 1967-68 school year, ESEA Title I funds in the amount of $992,000 assist only 40 percent of the eligible students in the middle and senior high schools. Although all eligible beneficiaries in 14 target elementary schools are aided, none of the eligible beneficiaries in 19 non-target elementary schools are reached. Adult Basic Education reaches less than 4 percent of eligible beneficiaries. Federal contributions to the New Haven public school system add about 7 percent to state and local expenditures.[193]

Housing—The major federal programs we have examined which are, at least in part, designed to affect the supply of low-income housing, include urban renewal, low rent public housing, housing for the elderly and handicapped, rent supplements, and FHA below market interest rate mortgage insurance (BMIR).

To measure the extent of need for low-income housing we have used the number of substandard and over-crowded units.[194] In measuring the size of housing programs, we have included expenditures for years prior to 1967 because they affected the low-income housing supply available in 1967.

In Detroit, a maximum of 758 low-income housing units have been assisted through these programs since 1956. This amounts to 2 percent of the substandard units and 1.7 percent of the overcrowded units.[195] Yet, since 1960, approximately 8,000 low income units have been demolished for urban renewal.

Similarly, in Newark, since 1959, a maximum of 3,760 low-income housing units have been assisted through the programs considered. This amounts to 16 percent of the substandard units and 23 percent of the overcrowded units.[196] During the same period, more than 12,000 families, mostly low-income, have been displaced by such public uses as urban renewal, public housing and highways.

In New Haven, since 1952, a maximum of 951 low-income housing units have been assisted through the programs considered. This amounts to 14 percent of the substandard units and 20 percent of the overcrowded units.[197] Yet since 1956, approximately 6,500 housing units, mostly low-income, have been demolished for highway construction and urban renewal.

Welfare—We have considered four federally-assisted programs which provide monetary benefits to low-income persons: Old Age Assistance, Aid to the Blind, Aid to the Permanently

142

and Totally Disabled, and Aid to Families with Dependent Children (AFDC).[198]

In Detroit, the number of persons reached with $48.2 million of federal funds through the four welfare programs during fiscal year 1967 was approximately 19 percent of the number of poor persons.[199] In Newark, the number of persons reached with $15 million was approximately 54 percent.[200] In New Haven, the number reached with $3.9 million was approximately 40 percent.[201]

Community Action Programs—We have considered such community action programs as neighborhood service centers, consumer education, family counseling, low-cost credit services, small business development, legal services, programs for the aged, summer programs, home economics counseling, and cultural programs.[202]

In Detroit, the number of persons reached by $12.6 million of community action funds in 1967 was only about 30 percent of the number of poor persons. Federal funding of these programs averaged approximately $35 for each poor person.[203] In Newark, the number of persons reached by $1.9 million was about 44 percent. Federal funding of these programs averaged approximately $21 for each poor person.[204] In New Haven, the number reached by $2.3 million was approximately 42 percent. Federal funding averaged approximately $72 for each poor person.[205]

Grievances

To measure the present attitudes of people in the riot cities as precisely as possible, we are sponsoring two attitude surveys among Negroes and whites in 15 cities and four suburban areas, including four of the 20 cities studied for this chapter. These surveys are to be reported later.

In the interim we have attempted to draw some tentative conclusions based upon our own investigations and the more than 1200 interviews which we conducted relatively soon after the disorders.[206]

In almost all the cities surveyed, we found the same major grievance topics among Negro communities—although they varied in importance from city to city. The deepest grievances can be ranked into the following three levels of relative intensity:

First Level of Intensity

1. Police practices
2. Unemployment and underemployment
3. Inadequate housing

143

Second Level of Intensity

4. Inadequate education [207]
5. Poor recreation facilities and programs [208]
6. Ineffectiveness of the political structure and grievance mechanisms

Third Level of Intensity

7. Disrespectful white attitudes
8. Discriminatory administration of justice
9. Inadequacy of federal programs
10. Inadequacy of municipal services [209]
11. Discriminatory consumer and credit practices [210]
12. Inadequate welfare programs

Our conclusions for the 20 cities have been generally confirmed by a special interview survey in Detroit sponsored by the Detroit Urban League. [211]

Police practices were, in some form, a significant grievance in virtually all cities and were often one of the most serious complaints.[212] Included in this category were complaints about physical or verbal abuse of Negro citizens by police officers, the lack of adequate channels for complaints against police, discriminatory police employment and promotion practices, a general lack of respect for Negroes by police officers, and the failure of police departments to provide adequate protection for Negroes.

Unemployment and underemployment were found to be grievances in all 20 cities and also frequently appeared to be one of the most serious complaints.[213] These were expressed in terms of joblessness or inadequate jobs and discriminatory practices by labor unions, local and state governments, state employment services and private employment agencies.

Housing grievances were found in almost all of the cities studied and appeared to be one of the most serious complaints in a majority of them.[214] These included inadequate enforcement of building and safety codes, discrimination in sales and rentals, and overcrowding.

The educational system was a source of grievance in almost all the 20 cities and appeared to be one of the most serious complaints in half of them.[215] These grievances centered on the prevalence of *de facto* segregation, the poor quality of instruction and facilities, deficiencies in the curriculum in the public schools (particularly because no Negro history was taught), inadequate representation of Negroes on school boards, and the absence or inadequacy of vocational training.

Grievances concerning *municipal recreation programs* were found in a large majority of the 20 cities and appeared to be one of the most serious complaints in almost half.[216] Inadequate recreational facilities in the ghetto and the lack of organized programs were common complaints.

The *political structure* was a source of grievance in almost all of the cities and was one of the most serious complaints in several.[217] There were significant grievances concerning the lack of adequate representation of Negroes in the political structure, the failure of local political structures to respond to legitimate complaints and the absence of obscurity of official grievance channels.

Hostile or racist attitudes of whites toward Negroes appeared to be one of the most serious complaints in several cities.[218]

In three-quarters of the cities there were significant grievances growing out of beliefs that the *courts* administer justice on a double, discriminatory standard, and that a presumption of guilt attaches whenever a policeman testifies against a Negro.[219]

Significant grievances concerning *federal programs* were expressed in a large majority of the 20 cities, but appeared to be one of the most serious complaints in only one.[220] Criticism of the federal anti-poverty programs focused on insufficient participation by the poor, lack of continuity, and inadequate funding. Other significant grievances involved urban renewal, insufficient community participation in planning and decision-making, and inadequate employment programs.

Services provided by municipal governments—sanitation and garbage removal, health and hospital facilities, and paving and lighting of streets—were sources of complaint in approximately half of the cities, but appeared to be one of the most serious grievances in only one.[221]

Grievances concerning *unfair commercial practices* affecting Negro consumers were found in approximately half of the cities, but appeared to be one of the most serious complaints in only two.[222] Beliefs were expressed that Negroes are sold inferior quality goods (particularly meats and produce) at higher prices and are subjected to excessive interest rates and fraudulent commercial practices.

Grievances relating to the *welfare system* were expressed in more than half of the 20 cities, but were not among the most serious complaints in any of the cities. There were complaints related to the inadequacy of welfare payments, "unfair regulations," such as the "man in the house" rule, which governs welfare eligibility, and the sometimes hostile and contemptuous attitude of welfare workers. The Commission's recommendations for reform of the welfare system are based on the necessity of attacking the cycle of poverty and dependency in the ghetto.

CHART I

PERVASIVENESS OF GRIEVANCES

Grievances Found and Number of Cities
Where Mentioned as Significant

1. *EMPLOYMENT AND UNDEREMPLOYMENT*
   (found in at least one of the following forms in 20
   cities)
   Unemployment and underemployment
   (General lack of full-time jobs) 19
   Union discrimination 13
   Discrimination in hiring by local and state
   government 9
   Discrimination in placement by state employment
   service 6
   Discrimination in placement by private employment
   agencies 3

2. *POLICE PRACTICES* (found in at least one of the
   following forms in 19 cities)
   Physical abuse 15
   Verbal abuse 15
   Nonexistent or inadequate channels for the redress
   of grievances against police 13
   Discrimination in employment and promotion of
   Negroes 13
   General lack of respect for Negroes, i.e., using de-
   rogatory language short of threats 11
   Abuse of Negroes in police custody 10
   Failure to answer ghetto calls promptly where Negro
   is victim of unlawful act 8

3. *INADEQUATE HOUSING* (found in at least one
   of the following forms in 18 cities)
   Poor housing code enforcement 13
   Discrimination in sales and rentals 12
   Overcrowding 12

4. *INADEQUATE EDUCATION* (found in at least
   one of the following forms in 17 cities)
   De facto segregation 15
   Poor quality of instruction and facilities 12
   Inadequacy of curriculum (e.g., no Negro history) 10

Inadequate Negro representation on school board 10
Poor vocational education or none at all 9

5. *POLITICAL STRUCTURE AND GRIEVANCE MECHANISM* (found in at least one of the following forms in 16 cities)
Lack of adequate Negro representation 15
Lack of response to legitimate grievances of Negroes 13
Grievance mechanism nonexistent or inadequately publicized 11

6. *INADEQUATE PROGRAMS* (found in at least one of the following forms in 16 cities)
Poverty program (OEO) (e.g., insufficient participation of the poor in project planning; lack of continuity in programs; inadequate funding; and unfulfilled promises) 12
Urban renewal (HUD) (e.g., too little community participation in planning and decision-making; programs are not urban renewal but "Negro removal") 9
Employment Training (Labor-HEW) (e.g., persons are trained for jobs that are not available in the community) 7

7. *DISCRIMINATORY ADMINISTRATION OF JUSTICE* (found in at least one of the following forms in 15 cities)
Discriminatory treatment in the courts 15
Lower courts act as arm of police department rather than as an objective arbiter in truly adversary proceedings 10
Presumption of guilt when policeman testifies against Negro 8

8. *POOR RECREATION FACILITIES AND PROGRAMS* (found in at least one of the following forms in 15 cities)
Inadequate facilities (parks, playgrounds, athletic fields, gymnasiums and pools) 15
Lack of organized programs 10

9. *RACIST AND OTHER DISRESPECTFUL WHITE ATTITUDES* (found in at least one of the following forms in 15 cities)
Racism and lack of respect for dignity of Negroes 15
General animosity toward Negroes 10

10. *INADEQUATE AND POORLY ADMINISTERED WELFARE PROGRAMS* (found in at least one of the following forms in 14 cities)

Unfair qualification regulations (e.g., "man in the house" rule) — 6

Attitude of welfare workers toward recipients (e.g., manifestations of hostility and contempt for persons on welfare) — 6

11. *INADEQUATE MUNICIPAL SERVICES* (found in at least one of the following forms in 11 cities)

Inadequate sanitation and garbage removal — 9

Inadequate health and hospital facilities — 6

Inadequate street paving and lighting — 6

12. *DISCRIMINATORY CONSUMER AND CREDIT PRACTICES* (found in at least one of the following forms in 11 cities)

Inferior quality goods (especially meats and produce) — 11

Overpricing (especially on days welfare checks issued) — 8

Exorbitant interest rates (particularly in connection with furniture and appliance sales) — 7

Fraudulent practices — 6

CHART II.—WEIGHTED COMPARISON OF GRIEVANCE CATEGORIES*

	1st Place (4 Points)		2nd Place (3 Points)		3rd Place (2 Points)		4th Place (1 Point)		Total	
	Cities	Points	Cities	Points	Cities	Points	Cities	Points	Cities	Points
Police Practices............	8	31½	4	12	0	0	2	2	14	45½
Unemployment & Under-Employment............	3	11	7	21	4	7	3	3	17	42
Inadequate Housing........	5	18½	2	6	5	9½	2	2	14	36
Inadequate Education......	2	8	2	6	2	4	3	3	9	21
Poor Recreation Facilities...............	3	11	1	2½	4	7½	0	0	8	21
Political Structure and Grievance Mechanism..	2	3	1	3	1	2	1	1	5	14
White Attitudes...........	0	0	1	3	1	1½	2	2	4	6½
Administration of Justice..	0	0	0	0	2	3½	1	1	3	4½
Federal Programs.........	0	0	1	2½	0	0	0	0	1	2½
Municipal Services........	0	0	0	0	1	2	0	0	1	2
Consumer and Credit Practices...............	0	0	0	0	0	0	2	2	2	2
Welfare.................	0	0	0	0	0	0	0	0	0	0

*The total of points for each category is the product of the number of cities times the number of points indicated at the top of each double column except where two grievances were judged equally serious. In these cases the total points for the two rankings involved were divided equally (e.g., in case two were judged equally suitable for the first priority, the total points for first and second were divided, and each received 3½ points).

149

RESULTS OF WEIGHTED COMPARISON OF GRIEVANCE CATEGORIES*

Police Practices
Unemployment
Housing
Education
Recreation
Political Structure
White Attitudes
Admin. of Justice
Federal Programs
Municipal Services
Commercial Practices
Welfare

0   5   10   15   20   25   30   35   40   45

*See right hand column of Chart II (Part 1).

150

V. The Aftermath of Disorder

> "We will all do our best for a
> peaceful future together."

> "Next time we'll really get the so
> and so's."

> "It won't happen again."

> "Nothing much changed here—one
> way or the other."

We have sought to determine whether any of these expressions accurately characterizes events in the immediate aftermath of the 20 surveyed disorders. We are conducting continuing studies of the post-disorder climate in a number of cities.[223] But we have tried to make a preliminary judgment at this point. To do so, we considered:

- Changes in Negro and white organizations;
- Official and civic responses to the social and economic conditions and grievances underlying the disorders;
- Police efforts to increase capacity to control future outbreaks;
- Efforts to repair physical damage.

We conclude that:

- The most common reaction was characterized by the last of the quoted expressions—"nothing much changed";
- The status quo of daily life before the disorder was quickly restored;
- Despite some notable public and private efforts, particularly regarding employment opportunities, little basic change took place in the conditions underlying the disorder;
- In some cities disorder recurred within the same summer;[224]
- In several cities, the principal official response was to train and equip the police and auxiliary law enforcement agencies with more sophisticated weapons;
- In several cities, Negro communities sought to develop greater unity to negotiate with the larger community and to initiate self-help efforts in the ghetto;
- In several cities, there has been increased distrust between blacks and whites, less interracial communication, and growth of white segregationist or black separatist groups.

Often several of these developments occurred simultaneously within a city.

151

Detroit provides a notable example of the complexity of post-disorder events. Shortly after the riot, many efforts to ameliorate the grievances of ghetto residents and improve interracial communication were announced and begun by public and private organizations. The success of these efforts and their reception by the Negro community were mixed. More recently, militant separatist organizations of both races appear to be growing in influence.

Some of the most significant of the post-riot developments were:

Official and Other Community Actions

The New Detroit Committee (NDC), organized under the co-sponsorship of the Mayor of Detroit and the Governor of Michigan, originally had a membership ranging from top industrialists to leading black militant spokesmen. NDC was envisioned as the central planning body for Detroit's rejuvenation.

However, it had an early setback last fall when the state legislature rejected its proposals for a statewide fair housing ordinance and for more state aid for Detroit's schools.

In January, 1968 NDC's broad interracial base was seriously weakened when black militant members resigned in a dispute over the conditions set for a proposed NDC-supported grant of $100,000 to a black militant organization.

To deal with the employment problem, the Ford Motor Company and other major employers in Detroit promised several thousand additional jobs to Detroit's hard-core unemployed. At least 55,000 persons were hired by some 17 firms. Ford, for example, established two employment offices in the ghetto. Reports vary on the results of these programs.

Steps taken to improve education after the riot include the appointment of Negroes to seven out of eighteen supervisory positions in the Detroit school system. Before the summer of 1967 none of these positions was held by a Negro. Michigan Bell Telephone Company announced that it would "adopt" one of Detroit's public high schools and initiate special programs in it.

Detroit's school board failed to obtain increased aid from the state legislature and announced plans to bring a novel suit against the state to force higher per capita aid to ghetto schools.

There are signs of increased hostility toward Negroes in the white community. One white extremist organization reportedly proposes that whites arm themselves for the holocaust it prophesies. A movement to recall the mayor has gained strength since the riot, and its leader has also pressed to have the fair housing ordinance passed by the Detroit Common Council put to a referendum.

The police and other law enforcement agencies in Detroit are making extensive plans to cope with any future disorder. The mayor has proposed to the Common Council the purchase of some $2 million worth of police riot equipment, including tanks, armored personnel carriers, and Stoner rifles (a weapon which fires a particularly destructive type of bullet).

Negro Community Action

A broadly-based Negro organization, the City-Wide Citizens Action Committee (CCAC), was formed after the riot by a leading local militant and originally included both militant and moderate members. It stresses self-determination for the black community. For example, it is developing plans for Negro-owned cooperatives and reportedly has demanded Negro participation in planning new construction in the ghetto. CCAC lost some of its moderate members because it has taken increasingly militant positions, and a rival, more moderate Negro organization, the Detroit Council of Organizations, has been formed.

Post-Riot Incidents and Prospects for the Future

There appears to be a growing division between the black and white communities as well as within the black community itself. Some pawnshops and gun stores have been robbed of firearms, and gun sales reportedly have tripled since the riot. In late 1967 a rent strike took place, some fire bombings were reported and a new junior high school was seriously damaged by its predominantly Negro student body.

Many Negroes interviewed rejected the theory that the 1967 riot immunized Detroit against further disorders. Some believed that a new disturbance may well be highly organized and therefore much more serious.

Changes in Negro and White Organizations

In half the cities surveyed, new organizations concerned with race relations were established or old ones revitalized. No clear trend is apparent.

In a few cities the only apparent changes have been the increased influence of Negro militant separatist or white segregationist groups.[225]

In a few cities the organizations identified tended to follow more moderate and integrationist policies.[226] A youthful Negro who emerged as a leader during the riot in Plainfield started a new organization which, though militant, is cooperating with and influencing the established, more moderate Negro leadership in the city.

And in a few cities, organizations of white segregationists, Negro militants and moderate integrationists all emerged following the disturbances. In Newark, as in Detroit, both black and white extremist organizations have been active, as well as a prominent integrationist post-riot organization, the Committee of Concern. The committee was formed immediately after the riot and includes leading white businessmen, educators and Negro leaders. At the same time, leading black militants reportedly gained support among Negro moderates. And a white extremist group achieved prominence—but not success—in attempting to persuade the city council to authorize the purchase of police dogs.[227]

Official and Civic Response

Actions to ameliorate Negro grievances in the 20 cities surveyed were limited and sporadic. With few exceptions, these actions cannot be said to have contributed significantly to reducing the level of tension.

POLICE-COMMUNITY RELATIONS

In eight of the cities surveyed municipal administrations took some action to strengthen police-community relations.[228] In Atlanta, immediately after the riot, residents of the disturbance area requested that all regular police patrols be withdrawn because of hostility caused during the riot, when a resident was killed allegedly by policemen. The request was granted, and for a time the only officers in the area were police-community relations personnel. In Cincinnati, however, a proposal to increase the size of the police-community relations unit and to station the new officers in precinct stations has received little support.

EMPLOYMENT

Public and private organizations, often including business and industry, made efforts to improve employment opportunities in nine of the cities.[229]

In Tucson, a joint effort by public agencies and private industry produced 125 private and 75 city jobs. Since most of the city jobs ended with with the summer, some companies sought to provide permanent employment for some of those who had been hired by the city.

HOUSING

In nine cities surveyed, municipal administrations increased their housing programs.[230] In Cambridge, the Community Relations Commission supported the application of a local church to obtain federal funds for low and moderate income housing. The Commission also tried to interest local and national builders in constructing additional low-cost housing.

The Dayton city government initiated a program of concentrated housing code enforcement in the ghetto. The housing authority also adopted a policy of dispersing public housing sites and, at the request of Negroes, declared a moratorium on any new public housing in the predominantly Negro West Dayton area.

But in Newark, municipal and state authorities continued to pursue a medical center project designed to occupy up to 150 acres in the almost all-Negro Central Ward. The project, bitterly opposed by Negroes before the riot, would have required massive relocation of Negroes and was a source of great tension in the Negro community. However, with the persistent efforts of federal officials (HUD and HEW), an accommodation appears to have been reached on the issue recently, with reduction of the site to approximately 58 acres.

Private organizations attempted to improve the quality of ghetto housing in at least three of the cities surveyed. A Catholic charity in New Jersey announced a plan to build or rehabilitate 100 homes in each of five cities, including three of the cities surveyed (Elizabeth, Jersey City and Newark) and to sell the homes to low-income residents. The plan received substantial business backing.[231]

EDUCATION

In five of the cities surveyed, local governments have taken positive steps to alleviate grievances relating to education.[232] In Rockford, residents approved a bond referendum to increase teacher salaries, build schools and meet other needs. A portion of this money will be used, with matching state and federal funds, to construct a vocational and technical center for secondary schools in the Rockford area.

In two cities, private companies made substantial contributions to local school systems. The Standard Oil Company of New Jersey donated to the Elizabeth school board a building valued at $500,000 for use as an administrative center and for additional classrooms.[233]

In four of the cities surveyed, grievances concerning education increased.[234] In Cincinnati recent elections resulted in the seating of two new board of education members who belonged to a taxpayers' group which had twice in 1966 successfully opposed a school bond referendum. Also, racial incidents in the Cincinnati schools increased dramatically in number and severity during the school year.

RECREATION

In four cities, programs have been initiated to increase recreational facilities in ghetto communities.[235] A month and a half after the New Brunswick disturbance, local business-men donated five portable swimming pools to the city. A boat which the city will use as a recreation center was also donated and towed to the city by private companies.

NEGRO REPRESENTATION

The elections of Negro mayors in Cleveland—which experienced the Hough riot in 1966—and Gary have been widely interpreted as significant gains in Negro representation and participation in municipal political structures. In five of the six surveyed cities which have had municipal elections since the 1967 disturbances, however, there has been no change in Negro representation in city hall or in the municipal governing body.[236] In New Haven, the one city where there was change, the result was decreased Negro representation on the board of aldermen from five out of 35 to three out of 30.

Changes toward greater Negro representation occurred in three other cities in which Negroes were selected as president of the city council and as members of a local civil service commission, a housing authority and a board of adjustments.[237]

GRIEVANCE MACHINERY

There was a positive change in governmental grievance channels or procedures in two cities.[238] But in one case, an effort to continue use of counter-rioters as a communications channel was abandoned.[239]

FEDERAL PROGRAMS

There are at least ten examples, in eight cities, of federal programs being improved or new federal programs being instituted[240]; in two cities disputes have arisen in connection with federally-assisted programs.[241]

MUNICIPAL SERVICES

Four cities have tried to improve municipal services in disturbance areas.[242] In Dayton, the city began a program of additional garbage collection and alley cleaning in the disturbance area. In Atlanta, on the day after the disturbance ended, the city began replacing street lights, repaving streets and collecting garbage frequently in the disturbance area. However, the improved services were reportedly discontinued after a month and a half.

156

In one city, a consumer education program was begun.[243] In none of the 20 cities surveyed were steps taken to improve welfare programs. In two of the surveyed cities, plans were developed to establish new businesses in disturbance areas.[244]

Capacity to Control Future Disorders

Five of the surveyed cities planned to improve police control capability in the event of disorder.[245] Four cities developed plans for using counter-rioters,[246] but in one case the plans were later abandoned.[247] In Detroit, plans were made to improve the administration of justice in the event of future disorder by identifying usable detention facilities and assigning experienced clerks to process arrestees.

Repair of Physical Damage

Significant numbers of businessmen in the riot areas have reopened in several cities where damage was substantial. In Detroit, none of the businesses totally destroyed in the riot have been rebuilt, but many which suffered only minor damage have reopened. In Newark, 83 percent of the damaged businesses have reopened, according to official estimates.[248] In Detroit, the only city surveyed which suffered substantial damage to residences, there has been no significant residential rebuilding.

In two cities, Negro organizations insisted on an active role in decisions about rehabilitation of the disturbance area.[249]

In many of these footnotes where a series of disorders is mentioned we have indicated the number of disturbances which have been classified as "major," "serious" or "minor" in the section on "Levels of Violence and Damage" in Chapter 2-I *supra*.

1. Five sources for our compilation were: Department of Justice, Criminal Division; Federal Bureau of Investigation; U. S. Commission on Civil Rights; Lemberg Center for the Study of Violence, Brandeis University; and Congressional Quarterly, September 8, 1967.

2. Buffalo, N.Y.
   Cincinnati, Ohio (June)
   Detroit, Mich.
   Milwaukee, Wis.
   Minneapolis, Minn.
   Newark, N.J.
   Plainfield, N.J.
   Tampa, Fla. (June)

3. Albany, N.Y.
   Atlanta, Ga. (June)
   Birmingham, Ala.
   Boston, Mass.
   Cairo, Ill.
   Cambridge, Md. (July)
   Cincinnati, Ohio (July 3-5)
   Dayton, Ohio (June)
   Flint, Mich.
   Fresno, Calif.
   Grand Rapids, Mich.
   Houston, Texas (May)
   Jackson, Miss.
   Montclair, N.J.
   Nashville, Tenn.
   New Haven, Conn.
   New York, N.Y.
     (Bronx and E. Harlem)
   Omaha, Nebr.
   Paterson, N.J.
   Phoenix, Ariz.
   Pontiac, Mich.
   Portland, Ore.
   Riviera Beach, Fla.
   Rochester, N.Y. (July)
   Saginaw, Mich.
   San Francisco, Calif.
     (May 14-15, July)
   Syracuse, N.Y.
   Toledo, Ohio
   Waterloo, Iowa
   Wichita, Kan. (August)
   Wilmington, Del.

4. Alton, Ill.
   Asbury Park, N.J.
   Atlanta, Ga. (July)
   Aurora, Ill.
   Benton Harbor, Mich.
   Bridgeport, Conn.
   Bridgeton, N.J.
   Cambridge, Md. (June)
   Chicago, Ill.
     (4 disorders)
   Cincinnati, Ohio
     (July 27)
   Clearwater, Fla.
   Cleveland, Ohio
     (2 disorders)
   Columbus, Ohio
   Dayton, Ohio
     (September)
   Deerfield Beach, Fla.
     (2 disorders)
   Denver, Colo.
     (2 disorders)
   Des Moines, Iowa
     (2 disorders)
   Durham, N.C.
   East Orange, N.J.
     (2 disorders)
   E. Palo Alto, Calif.
   East St. Louis, Ill.
     (2 disorders)
   Elgin, Ill.
     (2 disorders)
   Elizabeth, N.J.
   Englewood, N.J.
   Erie, Penn.
     (2 disorders)
   Greensboro, N.C.
   Hamilton, Ohio
   Hammond, La.
   Hartford, Conn.
     (3 disorders)
   Houston, Texas
     (July, August)
   Irvington, N.J.
   Jackson, Mich.
   Jamesburg, N.J.
   Jersey City, N.J.
   Kalamazoo, Mich.

Kansas City, Mo.
Lackawanna, N.Y.
Lakeland, Fla.
Lansing, Mich.
Lima, Ohio
Long Beach, Calif.
Lorain, Ohio
Los Angeles, Calif.
Louisville, Ky.
Marin City, Calif.
Massillon, Ohio
Maywood, Ill.
 (2 disorders)
Middletown, Ohio
Mt. Clemens, Mich.
Mt. Vernon, N.Y.
Muskegon, Mich.
New Britain, Conn.
New Brunswick, N.J.
Newburgh, N.Y.
New Castle, Penn.
New London, Conn.
New Rochelle, N.Y.
New York, N.Y. (Fifth
 Avenue and 2 Brooklyn
 disorders)
Niagara Falls, N.Y.
Nyack, N.Y. (2 disorders)
Oakland, Calif.
Orange, N.J.
Pasadena, Calif.
Passaic, N.J.
Peekskill, N.Y.
Peoria, Ill.
Philadelphia, Penn.
 (3 disorders)

Pittsburgh, Penn.
Poughkeepsie, N.Y.
Prattville, Ala.
Providence, R.I.
Rahway, N.J.
Rochester, N.Y. (May 31-
 June 1)
Rockford, Ill. (2 disorders)
Sacramento, Calif.
St. Louis, Mo.
St. Paul, Minn.
St. Petersburg, Fla.
San Bernardino, Calif.
San Diego, Calif.
Sandusky, Ohio
San Francisco, Calif. (May 21)
Seaford, Del.
Seattle, Wash.
South Bend, Ind.
Springfield, Ohio
Spring Valley, N.Y.
Tampa, Fla. (July)
Texarkana, Ark.
Tucson, Ariz.
Vallejo, Calif.
 (2 disorders)
Wadesboro, N.C.
Washington, D.C.
Waterbury, Conn.
Waukegan, Ill.
West Palm Beach, Fla.
Wichita, Kansas
 (May and July)
Wyandanch, N.Y.
Youngstown, Ohio
Ypsilanti, Mich.

5. Three:
Cincinnati
Hartford
Houston

Philadelphia
San Francisco
Wichita

Two:
Atlanta
Cambridge
Cleveland
Dayton
Deerfield Beach
Denver
Des Moines
East Orange

East St. Louis
Elgin
Erie
Maywood
Nyack
Rochester
Rockford
Tampa
Vallejo

6. Cleveland and Rochester.

7. Disorders were counted in the month in which they began. Thus the Omaha disorder, for example, which began on March 31 and ended on April 2, was counted in the March total.

January: Chicago

March: Omaha

April: Cleveland, Louisville, Massillon and Nashville.

May: Two in Chicago, Houston, Jackson (Miss.) Philadelphia, Rochester, San Diego, two in San Francisco, Vallejo and Wichita.

June: Atlanta, Boston, Buffalo, Cambridge, Cincinnati, Clearwater, Dayton, Lansing, Los Angeles, Maywood, Middletown, Niagara Falls, Philadelphia, Prattville, St. Petersburg and Tampa.

July:
Albany
Alton
Asbury Park
Atlanta
Benton Harbor
Birmingham
Bridgeport
Bridgeton
Cairo
Cambridge
Chicago
Cincinnati (2)
Cleveland
Deerfield Beach
Denver
Des Moines (2)
Detroit
Durham
E. Orange (2)
E. Palo Alto
E. St. Louis
Elgin
Elizabeth
Englewood
Erie (2)
Flint
Fresno
Greensboro
Grand Rapids
Hamilton
Hartford
Houston
Irvington
Jersey City
Kalamazoo
Kansas City
Lackawanna
Lakeland
Lima
Long Beach
Lorain
Marin City
Maywood
Milwaukee
Minneapolis
Montclair
Mt. Clemens
Mt. Vernon

Muskegon
Newark
New Britain
New Brunswick
Newburgh
New Castle
New Rochelle
New York (4)
Nyack
Oakland
Orange
Pasadena
Passaic
Paterson
Peekskill
Philadelphia
Phoenix
Plainfield
Pontiac
Portland
Poughkeepsie
Providence
Rahway
Riviera Beach
Rochester
Rockford (2)
Sacramento
Saginaw
St. Paul
San Bernardino
San Francisco
Seaford
Seattle
South Bend
Springfield
Tampa
Toledo
Tucson
Wadesboro
Waterbury
Waterloo
Waukegan
W. Palm Beach
Wichita
Wilmington
Youngstown
Ypsilanti

August:
Denver
Elgin
Hammond
Houston
Jackson (Mich.)
Jamesburg
New Haven
Peoria

Pittsburgh
St. Louis
Sandusky
Spring Valley
Syracuse
Vallejo
Washington
Wichita
Wyandanch

September:
Aurora
Columbus
Dayton
Deerfield Beach
East St. Louis

Hartford (2)
New London
New York
Nyack
Texarkana

8. East:
Albany
Asbury Park
Boston
Bridgeport
Bridgeton

Buffalo
E. Orange (2)
Elizabeth
Englewood
Erie (2)
Hartford (3)

160

Irvington
Jamesburg
Jersey City
Lackawanna
Montclair
Mt. Vernon
Newark
New Britain
New Brunswick
Newburgh
New Castle
New Haven
New London
New Rochelle
New York (5)
Niagara Falls
Nyack (2)

Orange
Passaic
Paterson
Peekskill
Philadelphia (3)
Pittsburgh
Plainfield
Poughkeepsie
Providence
Rahway
Rochester (2)
Seaford
Spring Valley
Syracuse
Waterbury
Wilmington
Wyandanch

Midwest:
Alton
Aurora
Benton Harbor
Cairo
Chicago (4)
Cleveland (2)
Cincinnati (3)
Columbus
Dayton (2)
Des Moines (2)
Detroit
E. St. Louis (2)
Elgin (2)
Flint
Grand Rapids
Hamilton
Jackson (Mich.)
Kalamazoo
Kansas City
Lansing
Lima
Lorain

Massillon
Maywood (2)
Middletown
Milwaukee
Minneapolis
Mt. Clemens
Muskegon
Omaha
Peoria
Pontiac
Rockford (2)
Saginaw
St. Louis
St. Paul
Sandusky
South Bend
Springfield
Toledo
Waterloo
Waukegan
Wichita (3)
Youngstown
Ypsilanti

South and Border States:
Atlanta (2)
Birmingham
Cambridge (2)
Clearwater
Deerfield Beach (2)
Durham
Greensboro
Hammond
Houston (3)
Jackson (Miss.)

Lakeland
Louisville
Nashville
Prattville
Riviera Beach
St. Petersburg
Tampa (2)
Texarkana
Wadesboro
W. Palm Beach
Washington

West:
Denver (2)
E. Palo Alto
Fresno
Long Beach
Los Angeles
Marin City
Oakland
Pasadena

Phoenix
Portland
Sacramento
San Bernardino
San Diego
San Francisco (3)
Seattle
Tucson
Vallejo (2)

9. Newark: Plainfield, Paterson, Orange, Irvington, E. Orange, Rahway, Montclair, Elizabeth, Asbury Park, Jersey City, New Brunswick, Nyack, Bridgeton and Englewood.

Detroit: Kalamazoo, Pontiac, Toledo, Flint, Grand Rapids, Muskegon, Saginaw and Mt. Clemens.

The causal relationship between the Detroit and Newark riots and the disorders in their respective clusters is considered under Precipitating Incidents in Part II of this chapter.

The other 21 clusters, arranged by the month in which each cluster began' were:

April: —Cleveland, Massillon
          —Nashville, Louisville

May: —San Francisco, Vallejo

June: —Cincinnati, Dayton, Middletown
          —Buffalo, Niagara Falls
          —Clearwater, Tampa, St. Petersburg

July: —Tampa, Deerfield Beach, Lakeland,
            Riviera Beach, W. Palm Beach
          —Greensboro, Durham, Wadesboro
          —Bronx, E. Harlem, New York 5th Avenue,
            Mt. Vernon, Brooklyn, Peekskill,
            Lackawanna, Newburgh, Passaic,
            Poughkeepsie, New Rochelle, New Britain,
            Bridgeport, Waterbury
          —Rochester, Albany
          —Philadelphia, Wilmington
          —Des Moines, Waterloo, Des Moines
          —Minneapolis, St. Paul
          —Youngstown, Lima, Cleveland
          —Lorain, Springfield, Cincinnati,
            Hamilton, Sandusky
          —Waukegan, Chicago, South Bend, Elgin,
            Rockford, Peoria
          —Tucson, Phoenix
          —Sacramento, San Francisco, Oakland
          —E. Palo Alto, Long Beach, San Bernardino, Pasadena

August: —New Haven, New London, Hartford

September: —Dayton, Columbus

10. This table is based upon the estimated 1967 population of the 128 cities except for New York and Hartford, for which 1966 estimates were used, and 15 cities for which 1960 census figures were used (Deerfield Beach, East Orange, Englewood, Irvington, Lackawanna, Maywood, Montclair, Orange, Prattville, Rahway, Riviera Beach, Seaford, Spring Valley, Wadesboro and Waterloo).

11. Figures were unavailable for four communities (East Palo Alto, Jamesburg, Marin City and Wyandanch).

12. See Hearings before the Permanent Subcommittee on Investigations of the Senate Committee on Government Operations, *Riots, Civil and Criminal Disorders*, 90th Cong., 1st Sess., Part I, insert facing p. 14.

More recent data indicate that there were 23 riot-related deaths in Newark rather than 25 as reported by the Subcommittee. There are similiar variations for some cities with regard to the number injured. In addition, Atlanta, in which there was one death and at least nine injuries, was not included in the Subcommittee's list. Finally, two of the disturbances included in the Subcommittee's figures are not in our list of 164 disorders (Hattiesburg, Miss.—no deaths, five injuries; Montgomery, Ala.—no deaths, no injuries).

13. In 12 (16 percent) of the disturbances studied by the Permanent Subcommittee there were deaths. Sixty-eight (82 percent) of the deaths and 1,049 (55 percent) of the injuries occurred in two (3 percent) of the disturbances.

According to figures of the Permanent Subcommittee, Detroit experienced 43 deaths and 324 injuries, Newark experienced 25 deaths and 725 injuries.

In six (8 percent) of the disturbances, there were one to four deaths and 11 to 65 injuries reported:

	Deaths	*Injuries*
Cincinnati (6/12-18)	1	63
Jackson	1	43
Milwaukee	4	44*
New York (7/23-25)	2	45
New York (9/4-8)	1	58
Plainfield	1	55

*This figure represents only injuries to "Law Officers." No figure was reported for injuries to civilians.

In four (5 percent) of the disturbances, there were one to two deaths and one to ten injuries reported:

	Deaths	*Injuries*
Erie (7/18-20)	1	6
Houston (5/16-17)	1	6
Pontiac	2	2
Rochester	1	9

In 46 (61 percent) of the disturbances, there were injuries but no deaths reported. In 15 (20 percent) of the disturbances, there were no deaths and 11 to 60 injuries:

City	*Injuries*
Birmingham	11
Boston	60
Buffalo	15
Grand Rapids	26
Hartford	18
Nashville	17
New York (7/24-8/3)	11
New York (7/29-31)	58
Providence	45
Sacramento	16
San Francisco (5/14-15)	33
San Francisco (7/26-31)	16
Tampa	16
Wichita	23
Wilmington	13

In 31 (41 percent) of the disturbances, there were no deaths and from one to ten injuries:

	Injuries
Cambridge	2
Cincinnati (7/3-4)	1
Cincinnati (7/27-28)	3
Englewood	9
Erie (7/31-8/3)	6
Fresno	2
Greensboro	2
Hamilton	1
Hattiesburg	5
Kalamazoo	6
Long Beach	5
Massillon	5
Minneapolis	3
Mt. Vernon	10
New Britain	5
New Haven	3
Passaic	4
Peoria	4
Phoenix	8
Portland	1
Poughkeepsie	5
Rockford	4
Saginaw	10
San Bernardino	2
South Bend	5*
Syracuse	7
Toledo	6
Tucson	8
Waterbury	3
Waterloo	3
West Palm Beach	1

*This figure represents only injuries to "Law Officers." No figure was reported for injuries to civilians.

In 17 (23 percent) of the disturbances, there were no injuries and no deaths reported:

Albany	Montgomery
Chicago	Mt. Clemens
Dayton (6/14-15)	Omaha
Elgin	Paterson
Flint	Peekskill
Houston (8/15-17)	Riviera Beach
Kansas City	Washington
Lima	Wyandanch
Louisville	

14.
Atlanta	Paterson
Bridgeton	Phoenix
Elizabeth	Rockford
Jersey City	Tucson
New Brunswick	

15. The Detroit Fire Department has listed 682 riot-connected building fires. Of these, 412 buildings were completely demolished. The Cincinnati Fire Department has estimated over $1 million in damage from riot-connected fires during the June disturbance.

16. Of 250 fires during a six-day period, only 13 were considered serious by Newark authorities. In no case did a fire spread from its original source to other areas.

    More than $8 million of the loss in Newark was attributed to loss of inventory due to looting and damage to stock. Of the 889 business establishments damaged, 25 (3 percent) were demolished and 136 (15 percent) were heavily damaged. Damage to glass, fixtures and buildings was estimated at $1,976,140.

17. On August 15, 1967, it was reported that the State Insurance Commission estimated the property loss at $144 million and that the Detroit Fire Department's estimate was closer to $200 million, only $84 million of which was insured. A December, 1967, estimate by the State Insurance Commission was between $40 million and $45 million. The Insurance Commission indicated that almost $33 million will be covered by insurance.

18. The City of Detroit incurred over $5 million in extraordinary expenses, more than $3 million of which was for personnel costs. In Cincinnati, a disorder of one week cost three city departments more than $300,000 in extraordinary expenditures, principally for overtime for police and firemen.

19. In Detroit at least 274 families were displaced by the destruction of their homes.

20. Seventy-four (89 percent) of the persons reported killed were civilians. The person killed in Atlanta was also a civilian. Of the 1,897 persons reported injured 1,185 (62 percent) were civilians and 712 (38 percent) were public officials. There is evidence that many additional injuries to civilians were not reported to officials.

21.
Cincinnati	New Brunswick
Dayton	New Haven
Englewood	Paterson
Newark	Plainfield
	Tampa

22. The New Jersey Commission said:

    The damage caused within a few hours early Sunday morning, July 16, to a large number of stores marked with "Soul" signs to depict non-white ownership and located in a limited area reflects a pattern of police action for which there is no possible justification. Testimony strongly suggests that State Police elements were mainly responsible with some participation by National Guardsmen.

    Governor's Select Commission on Civil Disorder, State of New Jersey, Report for Action, February 1968, p. 304.

23. In at least three of the cities (Detroit, Newark and Plainfield) there was damage to police and/or fire stations. In Cambridge, a public elementary school building was burned. In two of the university settings, school buildings were damaged. There was extensive damage to two dormitories at Texas Southern University in Houston. The bulk of this damage was allegedly caused by police gunfire and subsequent searches of the buildings. At privately-owned Fisk University in Nashville, a plate glass door was broken. It is unclear whether this was done by police or students.

24.
Atlanta	Englewood
Cincinnati	Grand Rapids
Dayton	Houston
Detroit	Jackson
Elizabeth	New Haven

Newark   Rockford
Phoenix   Tucson
Plainfield

25. Cambridge   Newark
    Elizabeth   Rockford
    Englewood   Tampa
    Nashville   Tucson
    New Haven
    Other types of property damage included private cars, buses, and delivery
    trucks in at least 11 of the 23 cities studied.
    Cambridge   Newark
    Cincinnati   Phoenix
    Dayton   Plainfield
    Grand Rapids   Tampa
    Jersey City   Tucson
    Nashville

26. The 20 cities were Atlanta, Bridgeton, Cambridge, Cincinnati (the June
    disorder), Dayton (the June and September disorders), Detroit, Elizabeth,
    Englewood, Grand Rapids, Jersey City, Milwaukee, New Brunswick,
    Newark, New Haven, Paterson, Phoenix, Plainfield, Rockford, Tampa
    and Tucson.
    The three university settings were Houston, Texas (Texas Southern Uni-
    versity), Jackson, Mississippi (Jackson State College) and Nashville,
    Tennessee (Fisk University and Tennessee A. & I. State College).
    See Statement on Methodology, Appendix, for a description of our survey
    procedures.

27. See Part IV, THE BACKGROUND OF DISORDER, *infra;* and Part
    III, THE RIOT PARTICIPANT, *infra.*

28. A final incident was identifiable preceding all 24 surveyed disorders except
    Rockford. See Section II, "The Development of Violence," *infra,* for the
    time and place of each final incident and the outbreak of violence.

29. In our surveys at least 88 prior incidents were identified by Negro inter-
    viewees as having been widely known and remembered at the time of the
    outbreak of violence, as having been a source or exemplification of griev-
    ances, and as having contributed to the disorders. The number of such
    prior precipitating incidents in a given city cannot be stated with certainty.
    Different sources recalled different events or stressed different aspects of a
    single event. However, we have been able to identify multiple incidents in
    most of the cities surveyed. Such incidents were reported in all except two
    cities (Elizabeth and Tucson; both minor).
    At least 10 prior incidents were identified in Houston (serious); seven in
    Bridgeton (minor); six in Atlanta, Milwaukee and Nashville (one major,
    two serious); five in Cincinnati, Newark and Plainfield (all major); four in
    Cambridge and the June and September Dayton disorders (two serious,
    one minor); three in Detroit, Jersey City, New Haven and Phoenix (one
    major, two serious and one minor); two in Englewood, Grand Rapids, Jack-
    son, New Brunswick, Paterson, Rockford and Tampa (one major, three
    serious and three minor). Twenty-eight prior incidents occurred within a
    week preceding violence, nine occurred one month to one week prior, 36
    occurred six months to one month prior, eleven occurred one year to six
    months prior to the violence. One year was used as an arbitrary time limit for
    counting incidents, except when the incident was identified as particularly
    significant to the disorder in that city. Four such incidents were identified:
    In Newark (the 1965 shooting of a Negro by police), in Jersey City (a
    disturbance in 1964), in Englewood (a 1962 disturbance), and in Cambridge
    (racial tensions necessitating the presence of National Guardsmen from
    1963 to 1965).

30. See the section on "Grievances" in Part IV, *infra.*

31. Such actions were identified as prior incidents in 35 cases preceding 18
    disturbances (Atlanta, Bridgeton, Cincinnati, the June and September
    Dayton disturbances, Detroit, Englewood, Houston, Jersey City, Mil-
    waukee, Nashville, New Brunswick, New Haven, Newark, Paterson,
    Plainfield, Rockford and Tampa; six major, six serious and six minor).
    The percentages used for the frequency of the occurrence of type of inci-
    dents total more than 100 percent since a few incidents fell into more than
    one category.

32. Thirty-two incidents preceding all 18 disorders fit this pattern. Responses
    to a larger group constituted four incidents, all involving groups of demon-

strators (Cincinnati, Nashville, and twice in Houston; one major and two serious).

33. Bridgeton, Cambridge, Detroit, Grand Rapids, Houston, Jackson, Milwaukee, Nashville, Newark, Phoenix, Tampa and Tucson (four major, six serious and two minor).

34. The two exceptions were Cambridge and Houston (both serious). The incident in Cambridge occurred when police fired at a group of Negroes leaving a protest meeting, and in Houston when they arrested a Negro trying to address a group of demonstrators.

35. This was the case in 15 instances preceding nine disorders (Atlanta, Bridgeton, Cambridge, Houston, Milwaukee, Nashville, New Haven, Newark and Phoenix; two major, six serious and one minor).

36. This occurred in five cases preceding four disorders (Cambridge, the June Dayton disturbance, Houston and Nashville; all serious).

37. Atlanta and the June Dayton disturbance (both serious) featured nationally-known militants. Cincinnati, the September Dayton disturbance and Plainfield (two major and one minor) involved only local leaders.

38. Atlanta, Cincinnati and the September Dayton disturbance (one major, one serious and one minor).

39. The June Dayton and Plainfield disturbances (both serious).

40. This occurred in 15 cases preceding nine disturbances (Atlanta, Bridgeton, Cambridge, the June Dayton disorder, Detroit, Jackson, Milwaukee, Nashville and Tampa; three major, five serious, one minor).

41. Atlanta, the June and September Dayton disturbance, Detroit, Englewood, Jersey City and Paterson (one major, three serious and three minor). The previous disorder counted in Detroit was the "Kercheval incident" in August of 1966 mentioned in the text of this section, and not the 1943 Detroit riot. In Dayton, the June 1967 disorder was counted as a prior incident in relation to the September disorder.

42. Atlanta, Cincinnati, Grand Rapids, Houston, Jersey City, Milwaukee and Plainfield (three major, three serious and one minor).

43. The Newark disorder was specifically identified as a prior incident in Bridgeton and Plainfield (one major and one minor). The Detroit riot was so identified in Grand Rapids and Phoenix (both serious).

44. Elizabeth, Englewood, Jersey City, New Brunswick and Paterson (one serious, four minor).
See Part I of this Chapter for a discussion of the patterns of the disorders in terms of timing and geographic distribution. The impact of communications media on the propagation of disorders is discussed in Chapter 16.

45. This was the case in nine or more instances preceding six disturbances (Bridgeton, Cincinnati, Jackson, Milwaukee, Newark and Plainfield; four major, one serious and one minor). The initial refusal to fund or the cancellation of funding by officials responsible for federally-financed anti-poverty programs was included in this category. There were three cases preceding three disturbances (the June Dayton disorder, New Haven and Phoenix; all serious).

46. This was the case in eight instances preceding eight disorders (Cambridge, Cincinnati, the September Dayton disorder, Detroit, Houston, Milwaukee, New Brunswick, and Paterson; three major, three serious and two minor).

47. This incident was not included in the category of racist activities, since the shooting apparently was not motivated entirely by the victim's ethnic origin.

48. Bridgeton, Detroit, Houston, Milwaukee, Nashville, Newark and Tampa (four major, two serious and one minor).

49. Atlanta, Cincinnati and the September Dayton disturbance (one major and two serious).
Meetings to protest actions involved in prior incidents on the part of city officials other than the police were identified as the final incident preceding two disorders (the June Dayton disturbance and Plainfield; one major and one serious).

50. This is readily apparent from the charts annexed to this Report, which portray graphically the varying levels of violence during the period of each of the 24 surveyed disorders.

51. All except Bridgeton, Cambridge, Elizabeth, Jersey City, New Brunswick and New Haven (two serious and four minor disturbances). In eight of the 18 cases the estimated size of the groups ranged from 50 to 100 (the September Dayton disorder, Detroit, Grand Rapids, Houston, Jackson, Pat-

erson, Phoenix and Plainfield; two major, five serious and one minor); in six cases from 100 to 200 (Cincinnati, the June Dayton disorder, Englewood, Nashville, Rockford and Tucson; one major, two serious and three minor); and in six cases from 200 to 1,000 (Atlanta, Houston, Jackson, Milwaukee, Newark and Tampa; three major and three serious).

52. Detroit, Englewood, Milwaukee, Nashville, New Haven, Paterson, Plainfield, Rockford, Tampa and Tucson (four major, three serious and three minor). Seven disorders began on Monday (Atlanta, Cambridge, Cincinnati, Elizabeth, Grand Rapids, Jersey City and New Brunswick; one major, three serious and three minor). Three began on Tuesday (the September Dayton disturbance, Houston and Phoenix; two serious and one minor), three on Wednesday (the June Dayton disturbance, Jackson and Newark; one major and two serious) and one Thursday (Bridgeton; minor).

53. Eighteen disorders for which temperature information was available occurred at the end of a day in which the temperature had reached a high of at least 79 degrees. In nine cases the temperature had reached 90 degrees or more during the day (Atlanta, Cambridge, Cincinnati, the June Dayton disturbance, Newark, Paterson, Phoenix, Tampa and Tucson; three major, five serious and one minor), in eight cases the temperature had been in the 80's (Detroit, Elizabeth, Englewood, Grand Rapids, Jersey City, New Brunswick, New Haven and Rockford; one major, two serious and five minor), and in one city the high temperature was 79 degrees (Milwaukee; a major disturbance).

54. See the annexed charts of levels of violence.

55. *Ibid.* Of New Haven's six cycles of violence, one occurred during early daylight hours and one began and reached its peak during the afternoon. In Plainfield (major) substantial violence began during one afternoon and continued, through a midnight peak, into the following day and evening. In Grand Rapids (serious) two cycles of violence occurred within one 24-hour period, one continuing into daylight hours and the other beginning in the afternoon.

56. In three disorders this was the pattern (Atlanta, Cambridge and Englewood; two serious and one minor). In a few cases these cycles were separated by one or more 24-hour periods in which little or no violence occurred, even during the first days of the disorder. Also see the charts annexed to this chapter.

57. Violence erupted within less than 30 minutes after the occurrence of the final incident in 11 disorders (Atlanta, Cincinnati, the June and September Dayton disturbances, Grand Rapids, Houston, Jackson, Milwaukee, Plainfield, Tampa and Tucson; four major, five serious and two minor).
In seven other disorders the violence erupted less than two hours after the occurrence of a final incident (Bridgeton, Cambridge, Detroit, Nashville, New Haven, Newark and Phoenix; two major, four serious and one minor). The time span between the final incident and the beginning of violence is not easily established for the disturbances in the five New Jersey cities in which the final incidents were reports of disorders in neighboring cities (Elizabeth, Englewood, New Brunswick, Jersey City and Paterson; one serious and four minor).

58. Violence in 11 disorders reached a peak for the first night, and in some cases an overall peak, in less than one hour after the initial outbreak (Atlanta, Bridgeton, the June and September Dayton disorders, Englewood, Milwaukee, Nashville, New Haven, Newark, Plainfield and Rockford; three major, five serious and three minor). In four other disorders violence reached a first night peak in less than two hours (Jersey City, New Brunswick, Paterson and Tampa; one major, one serious and two minor), and in eight disorders violence reached a first night peak in less than five hours (Cambridge, Cincinnati, Elizabeth, Grand Rapids, Houston, Jackson, Phoenix and Tucson; one major, five serious and two minor). In one disturbance (Detroit; major), violence continued to escalate over a period of 12 to 15 hours after the initial outbreak.

59. See the annexed charts of levels of violence.

60. *Ibid.* All except the June and September Dayton disturbances, Elizabeth, Houston and New Brunswick (two serious and three minor).

61. Bridgeton, Cambridge, Cincinnati, Englewood, Grand Rapids, Jersey City, Milwaukee, Nashville, Tampa and Tucson (two major, five serious and three minor).

62. Atlanta, Detroit, Jackson, Newark, New Haven, Paterson, Phoenix, Plainfield and Rockford (three major, five serious and one minor). See "Control Effort," *infra*, for a further discussion of violence levels.

63. Of 34 reported occasions of rock and bottle-throwing, 26 occurred in the first two cycles of violence. Of 31 reported occasions of window-breaking, 24 occurred in the first two cycles.

64. Of 30 reported occasions of looting, 20 occurred in the first two cycles and 28 in the first three cycles.

65. Of 24 reported occasions of fire bombs and Molotov cocktails, 12 occurred in the first two cycles and 12 in the second two.
66. Of 26 reported occasions of fires, 18 occurred in the second and third cycles and eight in the first and last.
67. Of 18 reported occasions, 13 occurred in the second and third cycles.
68. In only four instances did local police request and receive assistance in the initial response from an outside force (Bridgeton, Cambridge, Englewood and New Brunswick; one serious and three minor). In the case of Cambridge, the outside forces consisted of National Guardsmen, State police, and the county sheriff and constable. In the other three cases, they consisted of the police of neighboring towns or county or both.
69. In ten of the 24 disorders, this was the case (Atlanta, both Dayton disorders, Elizabeth, Houston, Jersey City, Nashville, Paterson, Phoenix and Tucson; six serious and four minor).
70. In a majority of cases for which we have such information, in 12 out of 22, the initial control force was either larger than the crowd on the street or no fewer than a ratio of one policeman to every five persons on the street (Bridgeton, Cambridge, both Dayton disorders, Elizabeth, Englewood, Grand Rapids, Jersey City, New Brunswick, Paterson, Phoenix and Rockford; five serious and seven minor).
In one of these instances almost the entire police force of 900 men was moved in before a single rioter appeared on the streets (Jersey City; minor). In the remaining ten cases the ratio varied; from one policeman to every six persons on the street (New Haven; serious), to one policeman to 300 people on the street (Tampa; major). The median ratio in these ten cases was one policeman to 25 persons on the street (Cincinnati, Detroit, Houston, Jackson, Nashville, Newark, Plainfield, and Tucson; four major, three serious and one minor).
71. In at least one case, the police rushed at the crowd with nightsticks (Newark; major). In only one case was a shot fired by the police during the initial response, and in that case it was a single shot (Cambridge; serious).
72. Englewood, Grand Rapids, Jersey City, Milwaukee, New Brunswick, New Haven, Newark, Paterson, Rockford and Tucson (two major, three serious and five minor).
In at least five of these cases, arrests were made (Englewood, Jersey City, New Brunswick, Paterson, and Tucson; one serious and four minor).
73. Atlanta, Bridgeton, Cincinnati, Detroit, Elizabeth, Houston, Phoenix and Tampa (three major, three serious and two minor).
74. Detroit, Houston, Phoenix and Tampa; two major and two serious.
75. Cambridge, both Dayton disturbances, Jackson, Nashville and Plainfield (one major, four serious and one minor).
76. See annexed charts of levels of violence. In at least 13 instances the initial control response appeared to fail, in this sense. The three control approaches, dispersal, reconnaissance containment, were almost equally represented in this group: six of these were cases of dispersal (Englewood, Grand Rapids, Milwaukee, New Haven, Newark and Tucson; two major, two serious and two minor); four cases of containment (Cambridge, both Dayton disorders and Jackson; three serious and one minor); and three were cases of reconnaissance (Detroit, Houston and Tampa; two major and one serious).
77. If violence continued, or resumed after a pause, the second control response by local police (and, in the instances we have noted, by the outside forces which by then had arrived) again was one of the three categories of dispersal, reconnaissance and containment. However, at this stage, dispersal was used in a slightly larger number of cases than at the stage of the initial response: twelve cases, two more than in the initial response (Atlanta, Bridgeton, Cambridge, Cincinnati, Detroit, Englewood, Milwaukee, Newark, New Brunswick, New Haven, Paterson and Rockford; four major, four serious and four minor). Containment was also now used in a slightly larger number of cases than at the earlier stage: nine cases, one more than before (both Dayton disturbances, Grand Rapids, Jackson, Nashville, Phoenix, Plainfield, Tampa and Tucson; two major, five serious and two minor). Reconnaissance, the most passive tactic and therefore understandably less tenable in the face of continued violence, was abandoned by half the forces which had used it initially but surprisingly was still employed by half: three forces (Cincinnati and Detroit, which turned to dispersal, and Tampa, which turned to containment; three major) abandoned reconnaissance for one of the other tactics, but reconnaissance was still used by three (Cambridge, Elizabeth, and Houston; two serious and one minor).
78. See footnote 22 to the section on "Levels of Violence and Damage" in Part I of this chapter. See also the Profiles on Newark and Detroit in Chapter 1.

168

79. This combination occurred in at least seven cases, two during the initial response (Englewood and Plainfield; one major and one minor) and five during a subsequent response (Cincinnati, Grand Rapids, Milwaukee, Nashville and New Haven; two major and three serious).

80. Atlanta, Detroit, Englewood, Grand Rapids, Jackson, Milwaukee, Newark, New Brunswick, New Haven, Phoenix and Plainfield (four major, five serious and two minor).

81. Cambridge, Nashville, Newark and New Haven (one major and three serious).

82. One major and one serious.

83. Cincinnati, Detroit, Jackson, New Haven, Newark, Plainfield, Phoenix, Rockford and Tampa (five major, three serious and one minor). In four of these nine disturbances (Detroit, Jackson, and, arguably, Phoenix and Rockford; one major, two serious and one minor) the entry of extra forces occurred after the first outbreak of violence. In four cities (Cincinnati, Newark, Plainfield, and Tampa; all major) extra forces were brought in after two outbreaks of violence. In one city (New Haven; serious) extra forces were brought in after three outbreaks of violence. See the annexed charts of levels of violence, and type and duration of law enforcement mobilization.

84. In all but two of these cities (Plainfield and, arguably, Rockford; one major and one minor) violence recurred thereafter on two occasions. In three cases, (Cincinnati, Tampa and Phoenix; two major and one serious) the subsequent violence was at lower levels than before the extra forces' arrival. But in the majority of cases (Detroit, Jackson, New Haven, Newark, Plainfield and Rockford; three major, two serious and one minor) the intensity of violence recurring after the arrival of extra forces was equal to or greater than that of the earlier violence.

85. Bridgeton, Cambridge, Englewood and New Brunswick (one serious and three minor).

86. In one city (Englewood; minor) four outbreaks followed; in four cities (Bridgeton, Cambridge, Grand Rapids, and Jersey City; two serious and two minor) two outbreaks followed; and in one city (New Brunswick; minor) a single outbreak followed.

87. In three of the six cities (Bridgeton, Englewood and Grand Rapids; one serious and two minor) the level of violence in one or more successive outbreaks was the same as or higher than that in the first outbreak of disorder. In three of these cities (Cambridge, Jersey City and New Brunswick; one serious and two minor) the later outbreak or outbreaks was of lower intensity than the first or there was no further outbreak of violence.

88. Atlanta, both Dayton disorders, Elizabeth, Houston, Nashville, Paterson and Tucson; five serious and three minor.

89. Two of these cities (Paterson and Tucson; one serious and one minor), had four outbreaks; one (Atlanta; serious) had three outbreaks; two (Elizabeth and Nashville; one serious and one minor), had two outbreaks; and three (both Dayton disorders and Houston; two serious and one minor), had one outbreak. Of the four cities which had multiple outbreaks, three (Atlanta, Paterson and Tucson; two serious and one minor), had subsequent outbreaks of violence at the same or a higher level of violence than the first outbreak.

90. There is evidence of a total of at least 68 such meetings in 21 of the 24 disturbances studied: only in three disorders (Cambridge, Milwaukee and Rockford; one major, one serious and one minor) is there no evidence of such meetings. The annexed charts include, on a horizontal line near the top, a depiction of such meetings through the period of disorder in the 21 cases.

91. In 17 of the 21 disturbances (excepting only Atlanta, Jackson, Jersey City and Paterson; three serious and one minor) the first meetings occurred either immediately before the disorder erupted or during the first or second day of disorders.
In only three of the 17 cases (Cincinnati, the Dayton September disturbance and New Brunswick; one major and two minor) did such meetings occur before the outbreak of violence.

92. Of the 16 disorders which had a duration of more than two days, the meetings also continued beyond that point in nine cases (Cincinnati, the Dayton June disturbance, Detroit, Englewood, Grand Rapids, New Haven, Newark, Plainfield and Tampa; five major, three serious and one minor). In five of these nine cases (the Dayton June disturbance, Detroit, Englewood, Grand Rapids and Tampa; two major, two serious and one minor), the meetings also continued through the final two days of the disorders.

93. Of the 21 disturbances in which such meetings occurred, established Negro leaders participated in meetings in 18 (all except Englewood, Jackson, and Phoenix; two serious and one minor).

94. Eight out of 21. In three cases (Englewood, Jackson and Phoenix; two serious and one minor), youths were the sole Negro participants in meetings with government officials.

95. Cincinnati, Nashville, New Brunswick, Plainfield and Tampa (three major, one serious and one minor). Of these five cases, the two elements of the Negro Community attended meetings together in two disorders (Cincinnati and Plainfield; one major, one serious) and in the remaining three disorders they attended such meetings separately.

96. This was the case in five disorders (Atlanta, Cincinnati, Houston, Plainfield and Phoenix; two major and three serious). In one of the five disorders (Phoenix; serious) the only meeting in which established Negro leadership participated was one with Negro youths. In the remaining four cases, established Negro leadership also met with government officials. In three of the five disorders, Negro youths also met with government officials (all except Atlanta and Houston; both serious).

97. This occurred in nine of the 21 disturbances in which such meetings took place (Atlanta, Bridgeton, Cincinnati, the Dayton June disturbance, Elizabeth, Grand Rapids, Newark, New Brunswick and New Haven; one major, five serious and three minor). Also involved were representatives of local human relations commissions (Bridgeton, Cincinnati, both Dayton disturbances, Elizabeth, Nashville, New Haven, Newark, Plainfield, Tampa and Tucson; four major, three serious and four minor); state community relations agencies (Jersey City, Newark, Plainfield and Tampa; three major and one minor) and federal agencies. In four cities (Cincinnati, Detroit, Jersey City and Newark; three major and one minor) officials of the Community Relations Service of the U.S. Department of Justice were participants in meetings.

98. Meetings during 19 of the 21 disorders followed this pattern (all except Houston and Tucson; one serious and one minor). In 13 cases the grievance related to the handling of the precipitating incident by the police (Bridgeton, Cincinnati, Elizabeth, Grand Rapids, Jackson, Jersey City, Nashville, Newark, New Brunswick, New Haven, Paterson, Plainfield and Phoenix; three major, six serious and four minor).

99. Meetings during 12 of the 21 disorders followed this pattern (all except Atlanta, Bridgeton, the Dayton September disturbance, Detroit, Elizabeth, Nashville, Newark, New Haven and Paterson; two major, four serious and three minor).
   In seven cases the pre-existing grievances related to unemployment and underemployment (Cincinnati, the Dayton June disturbance, Englewood, Jersey City, New Brunswick, Phoenix and Tucson; one major, two serious and four minor). In six cases they related to inadequate recreation facilities (the Dayton June disturbance, Jersey City, New Brunswick, Plainfield, Tampa and Tucson; two major, one serious and three minor).

100. This was the case in 10 of the 21 disorders in which meetings were held. In most of these cases (8 of 10), the earlier meetings or early stages of meetings focussed on disorder-related grievances and the later meetings, or stages of meetings, focussed on pre-existing grievances (Cincinnati, Englewood, Grand Rapids, Houston, Jackson, Jersey City, Phoenix and Tampa; two major, four serious and two minor). In only two cases (New Brunswick and Plainfield; one major and one minor), was the order of subjects reversed.

101. The only disorders in which counter-rioters were not active were Bridgeton, Cambridge, the Dayton September disorder, Englewood, Milwaukee and Rockford (one major, one serious and four minor).

102. For a discussion of this study and the characteristics of those who so identified themselves, as compared with rioters, see Part III, THE RIOT PARTICIPANT, *infra*.

103. Cincinnati, the Dayton June disorder, Detroit, Elizabeth, Grand Rapids, Houston, Nashville, Newark, New Brunswick, New Haven, Paterson, Plainfield, Phoenix, Tampa and Tucson (five major, seven serious and three minor).

104. For example, in Cincinnati the police opposed official recognition of counter-rioters, whereas in Detroit and Dayton there was close cooperation between police and counter-rioters.

105. Nine of 15 (Cincinnati, the Dayton June disorder, Detroit, Elizabeth, Grand Rapids, New Brunswick, Newark, Phoenix and Tampa; four major, three serious and two minor).

106. Houston, Nashville, New Haven, Paterson, Plainfield and Tucson (one major, four serious and one minor).

107. In Elizabeth and Newark the counter-rioters wore arm bands (one major and one minor).

108. Atlanta, Cincinnati, Detroit, Jackson, Jersey City and Newark (three major, two serious and one minor).

109. Examples are: employees of city agencies (Detroit and Cincinnati; two major); ministers (Atlanta, Phoenix and Tampa; one major and two serious); college students (Grand Rapids, Newark, Jackson and Nashville; one

170

major and three serious); civil rights leaders (Atlanta and Cincinnati; one major and one serious); young Negro militants (Phoenix, Jersey City and New Haven; two serious and one minor); poverty workers (Atlanta, Phoenix and Cincinnati; one major and two serious) and admitted former riot participants (Tampa; major).

110. Newark (major). In Paterson (serious) they held a block dance; in Phoenix (serious), they promised to make attempts to find jobs for rioters; in Jackson (serious) they kept nonstudents out of college dormitories; and in Atlanta (serious), they attempted to organize a Youth Corps Patrol, similar to Dayton's "White Hats." Counter-rioters used physical force to restrain rioters in two cities (Tampa and Nashville; one major and one serious). In neither case was the use of force officially authorized.

111. All four sources are subject to limitations, and we have therefore used each as a reliability check on the others. Eyewitness accounts are subject to retrospective distortion. Data on arrestees also involve built-in biases. The fact of arrest alone, without subsequent trial and conviction does not constitute evidence of the crime charged, and there has not been sufficient time for many of the 1967 riot arrestees to be brought to trial. Many of the most active rioters may have escaped arrest, while many of the uninvolved, or even counter-rioters, may have been arrested in the confusion. Finally, questions about riot activity in interview surveys may elicit overstatements of participation by some interviewees and under-statements by others.

We are conducting a continuing study of arrest records in a number of cities which experienced disorders in 1967 and in some earlier years as well. So far we have studied the records of 13,788 persons arrested during disturbances in 22 cities in 1967. The unpublished study of arrestees in Detroit, which was sponsored by the Department of Labor, Manpower Administration, involved interviews with 496 arrestees.

The Detroit and Newark surveys furnish the most comprehensive information on mass participation.

The Detroit survey data represent a reanalysis by Dr. Nathan S. Caplan and Jeffery M. Paige, Institute for Social Research, University of Michigan, of data collected during the two weeks following the disorder, in a study sponsored by the Detroit Urban League. The Newark study was conducted for the Commission by Dr. Caplan and Mr. Paige, approximately six months after the disorder.

The Detroit analysis is based on 393 interviews with Negroes aged 15 and over. The Newark data are based on 233 interviews with Negro males between the ages of 15 and 35. In both surveys, the sampling area was determined by identifying the 1960 census tracts in which violence and damage occurred. Newspaper accounts were used to identify the location of riot damage, fires and looting. In Detroit, the sample was drawn from two riot areas, the West Side and the East side, including the following census tracts: nine through 22, 26-28, 36-43, 115-123 and 152-188 (West Side); 759-778 and 789-793 (East Side). The Newark sample was drawn from an inner-city area consisting of census tracts 12, 29-33, 38-40, 58-67 and 81-82.

A probability sample was drawn for both cities so that the probability of inclusion for any household in Detroit was approximately 1/50th and Newark 1/44th. Blocks were selected at random from within the specified census tracts and constituted the primary sampling unit for each study. In Detroit, lists of all dwellings in the selected blocks were prepared from a city directory. Every fifteenth address was identified and assigned to an interviewer. In Newark, segments of approximately 10 dwelling units were constructed by field enumeration of blocks selected at random and assigned to interviewers. Both studies used techniques described by Leslie Kish in *Survey Sampling*, New York, Wiley, 1965, Chapter 9.

Each interviewer in Detroit was instructed to conduct interviews only at those dwelling units on his assignment sheet. Within households only Negroes were to be interviewed, and the interviewer was instructed to list all members of the household and then select every other one for interviewing. The interviewer was required to return twice if there was no answer to the initial call or if the respondent to be interviewed was not at home. This procedure yielded 437 interviews for 50 blocks, or 8.7 interviews per block.

In order to enlarge the sample of those who were likely to identify themselves as rioters, interviewers in Newark were told to interview only Negro males between the ages 15 and 35. They were instructed to interview all eligible respondents in each household. They were also required to return three times if there was no answer or if an eligible respondent was not at home. A total of 233 interviews were completed in 24 blocks, or 9.7 interviews per block.

In Detroit, 67.0 percent of all eligible respondents were interviewed; in Newark, 66.0 percent. While these response rates do not compare favorably

171

with the usual 80-85 percent response rate in white, middle-class samples, they are comparable to the rates in other ghetto area studies. A Negro response rate of 71.0 percent was reported in another study in approximately the same area of Newark. See Chernik, J., Indik, B., and Sternliev, G., "Newark-New Jersey: Population and Labor Force," Spring 1967, Institute of Management and Labor Relations, Rutgers—The State University, New Brunswick, New Jersey.

In both surveys, questions were designed to permit comparisons of the characteristics and attitudes of those who (a) admitted active participation in rioting, referred to as "self-reported rioters;" (b) those who said they had sought to stop the rioting, the "counter-rioters;" and (c) those who claimed not to have been involved, the "noninvolved." These classifications were based on the answers to two questions, one direct and one indirect. The indirect question asked how active the respondent had been during the riot, without specifying in particular what he had been doing. The second question, which appeared later in the questionnaire, asked whether the respondent had participated in various activities, such as trying to stop the riot, calling the fire department, or picking up goods and taking them home. Respondents were classified as "rioters" if they answered either that they were "active" or admitted one or more specific anti-social activities. They were classified as "counter-rioters" if they said that they were engaged in some pro-social activity whether or not they said they were "active." If they said that they had stayed home and also claimed not to have been "active," they were classified as "noninvolved." In the Detroit survey the analysis is based only on the answers of those 393 respondents who were willing to answer at least one of these classificatory questions. In the Newark survey the entire sample of 233 was used, and those who refused to answer either of the classificatory questions were included in the "noninvolved."

112. In Detroit, 11.2 percent (44) of the 393 respondents identified themselves as rioters, 15.8 percent (62) as counter-rioters, and the majority, 73 percent (287), as noninvolved. Bystanders included approximately 5 percent who admitted to having gone into the riot area but claimed not to have participated; and another 15 to 20 percent who claimed to have watched from the front steps or sidewalk in front of their homes. For purposes of analysis all of the 393 respondents other than the self-reported rioters and counter-rioters were treated as the "noninvolved." In the Newark survey, where the sample was restricted to Negro males between the ages of 15 and 35, 45.4 percent identified themselves as rioters, and 54.6 percent as noninvolved. About 5 percent of the respondents identified themselves as counter-rioters, but were included as noninvolved because the number of persons was so small. The proportion of respondents who admitted active participation does not necessarily indicate the levels of support for rioting among inner-city Negroes. In Detroit, 23.3 percent of those interviewed felt that more was to be gained than lost through rioting. In Newark 47.0 percent agreed that more was to be gained and 77.1 percent said that they were generally sympathetic to the rioters.

113. In the more detailed discussion which follows, only those characteristics of the counter-rioter which differed from those of the noninvolved are highlighted.

114. Of 13,012 arrestees in 22 cities (Atlanta, Bridgeton, Cincinnati, Dayton, Detroit, Elizabeth, Englewood, Grand Rapids, Houston, Jackson, Jersey City, Milwaukee, Nashville, New Brunswick, New Haven, Newark, Paterson, Phoenix, Plainfield, Rockford, Tampa and Tucson; six major, nine serious and seven minor) 10,792 (82.9 percent) were Negroes, 1967 (15.1 percent) were whites, 78 (.6 percent) were Puerto Ricans and 37 (.3 percent) were of other races. The ethnic origin of 138 arrestees (1.1 percent) was unknown.

A study of 348 arrestees in Grand Rapids (serious) divided the disorder in that city into two time segments of 4 hours and 36 hours. During the first 4 hours of the disorder, 95 percent were Negroes. The proportion of Negro arrestees declined to 66 percent during the remaining 48 hours of the disorder. See "Anatomy of a Riot," United Community Services, Research Department, Grand Rapids and Kent County, Michigan, 1967.

115.

Age Distribution

	Detroit Survey		Arrest Records 16 Cities*
Age	**R (44)	**NI (287)	**A (10,771)
15-24	61.3%	22.6%	52.5%
25-35	25.0	15.7	28.3
36-50	11.4	32.4	15.6
over 50	2.3	29.3	3.6
	100.0%	100.0%	100.0%

p< .001***

172

The Grand Rapids data indicate that during the first 4 hours of the disorder 82 percent of the arrestees were under 25 years of age. During the remaining 48 hours, the proportion of arrestees under 25 years of age declined to 58 percent. See "Anatomy of a Riot," *op cit.*

*Atlanta, Bridgeton, Cincinnati, Dayton, Detroit, Elizabeth, Jackson, Jersey City, New Brunswick, New Haven, Newark, Paterson, Plainfield, Rockford, Tampa and Tucson (five major, five serious and six minor)

**R —Rioters
NI —Noninvolved
A —Arrestees

***The symbol "p" represents the probability that a difference this great is a product of chance. The symbol ">" means greater than. The symbol "<" means less than.

116.   *Sex Distribution*

	Detroit Survey		Arrest Records 21 cities*
Sex	R (44)	NI (287)	A (11, 415)
Male	61.4%	43.9%	89.3%
Female	38.6	56.1	10.7
	100.0%	100.0%	100.0%

p< .025

The Grand Rapids data indicate that during the first 4 hours of the disorders, 45 of the 46 persons arrested (98 percent) were males. During the remaining 48 hours of the disorder female arrestees increased, comprising 10 percent of a total of 274 adults.

*Atlanta, Bridgeton, Cincinnati, Dayton, Detroit, Elizabeth, Englewood, Grand Rapids, Houston, Jackson, Jersey City, Nashville, New Brunswick, New Haven, Newark, Paterson, Phoenix, Plainfield, Rockford, Tampa and Tucson (five major, nine serious, and seven minor)

117.   *Marital Status*

Marital Status	Newark Survey		Detroit Arrest Study	Arrest Records 4 Cities*
	R(105)	NI(125)	A(496)	A(487)
Married	28.6%	44.0%	38.9%	19.3%
Single	56.2	49.6	47.8	73.9
Divorced/ Separated	14.2	6.4	11.3	0.2
Widowed	1.0	0.0	1.2	0.0
Undetermined	0.0	0.0	.8	6.6
	100.0%	100.0%	100.0%	100.0%

p< .10

*Atlanta, Cincinnati, New Brunswick and Tucson (one major, one serious, and two minor).

118.   *Family Structure in Newark Survey*

Adult Male Present in Family of Upbringing	R(106)	NI(126)
Yes	74.5	77.0
No	25.5	23.0
	100.0%	100.0%

p< .50

119.   *Region of Upbringing*

		Detroit Survey		Newark Survey	
Region	R(39)	NI(275)	CR(61)**	R(104)	NI(124)
South*	25.6%	64.0%	52.5%	26.0%	47.6%
North	74.4	36.0	47.5	74.0	52.4
	100.0%	100.0%	100.0%	100.0%	100.0%

*In the Detroit survey respondents were asked directly if they were brought up in the North or South; in Newark, South was defined as Alabama, Arkansas, Florida, Georgia, Kentucky, Louisiana. Maryland, Mississippi, Missouri, North Carolina, Oklahoma, South Carolina, Tennessee, Texas, Virginia, Washington, D. C., and West Virginia.

R-NI	p< .001
CR-NI	p< .025
R-CR	p< .05

**CR-Counter-Rioters

173

120. Of 266 arrestees in five cities (Atlanta, New Brunswick, Plainfield, Tampa and Tucson; two major, one serious and two minor), 106 (40 percent) were born in the state in which the disorder occurred, 98 (37 percent) were born in the South (but not in the state in which the disorder occurred in the cases of Atlanta and Tampa; one major and one serious) and 23 (8 percent) were born elsewhere. The state of birth of 39 persons (15 percent) was undetermined. For purposes of the sample, the South was defined as Alabama, Arkansas, Delaware, Florida, Georgia, Kentucky, Louisiana, Maryland, Mississippi, North Carolina, Oklahoma, South Carolina, Tennessee, Texas, Virginia, Washington, D.C., and West Virginia.

121. The discrepancy between the percentages of the non-involved brought up in the North in Newark and Detroit (two major) is not significant since the Detroit sample includes more older people than the Newark sample. This difference does not affect the validity of the figures for youthful rioters.

122.

Place of Birth

Born in Riot City	Detroit Survey		Newark Survey	
	R(43)	NI(285)	R(127)	NI(106)
Yes	59.4%	34.6%	53.5%	22.5%
No	40.6	65.4	46.5	77.5
	100.0%	100.0%	100.0%	100.0%
	p< .001		p< .001	

123. Of 3,395 arrestees in 15 cities (Atlanta, Bridgeton, Dayton, Elizabeth, Grand Rapids, Jackson, Jersey City, New Brunswick, New Haven, Newark, Paterson, Plainfield, Rockford, Tampa and Tucson; three major, seven serious and five minor) 3,054 (90 percent) resided in the city in which the disorder occurred, 228 (7 percent) resided in the state in which the disorder occurred, and 48 (1 percent) resided elsewhere. The residence of 65 persons (2 percent) was undetermined.

124.

Income Level

Annual Income*	Detroit Survey			Newark Survey	
	R(44)	NI(287)	CR(62)	R(104)	NI(126)
Less than 2,000	13.6%	12.9%	4.8%**	4.7%	3.2%
2,000-5,000	25.0	17.4	16.2**	27.9	26.2
5,000-7,500	13.6	20.6	22.6	27.9	30.1
7,500-10,000	18.2	13.9	17.7	14.4	11.1
10,000-12,500	2.3	3.8	14.5	1.0	4.0
12,500-15,000	0.0	1.7	1.6	1.0	1.6
More than 15,000	2.3	0.3	3.2	0.0	3.2
No answer	25.0	29.4	19.4	23.1	20.6
	100.0%	100.0%	100.0%	100.0%	100.0%
				p< .50	

R-NI p< .50
CR-NI p< .005
R-CR p< .25

*Annual income for Detroit based on individual income, for Newark on family income.
**All self-reported counter-rioters with incomes under $5,000 were female.

125. See the section on "The Pattern of Disadvantage" in Part IV of this chapter.

126.

Educational Level

Education	Detroit Survey			Newark Survey	
	R(43)	NI(272)	CR(59)	R(106)	NI(126)
Less than grades 1-6	2.3%	7.7%	1.7%	0.0%	3.2%
Grade school	4.7	20.2	18.6	1.9	11.1
Some high school	53.5	33.8	22.0	63.2	46.8
Graduated high school	23.3	26.1	32.2	29.2	31.0
Some college	14.0	10.3	22.1	5.7	6.3
Graduated college	0.0	1.5	0.0	0.0	1.6
Graduate work	2.2	0.4	3.4	0.0	0.0
	100.0%	100.0%	100.0%	100.0%	100.0%
				p< .06	

R-NI p< .05
CR-NI p< .025
R-CR p< .05

127.

	Employment Status			
	Detroit Survey*		Newark Survey**	
Currently Employed	R(27)	NI(127)	R(84)	NI(105)
Yes	70.4%	68.5%	70.3%	81.0%
No	29.6	31.5	29.7	19.0
	100.0%	100.0%	100.0%	100.0%
		p > .75	p < .50	

	Detroit Arrest Study	Arrest Records 4 cities***
Currently Employed	A (496)	A (310)
Yes	78.2%	66.8%
No	21.8	33.2
	100.0%	100.0%

*Males only
**Excludes students
***Atlanta, Cincinnati, New Brunswick and Tampa (two major, one serious and one minor)

128. Underemployment in Newark Survey

Have you been unemployed as long as a month during the last year?	R(104)	NI(124)
Yes	61.0%	43.4%
No	39.0	56.6
	100.0%	100.0%
		p < .05

129. Occupation Level in Newark Survey

Level	R(125)	NI(126)
Unskilled	50.0%	39.6%
Semiskilled or better	50.0	60.4
	100.0%	100.0%
		p < .06

130. Job Aspiration in Newark Survey

Do you feel your job is appropriate considering the education you have?	R (82)	NI (99)
Present job is about right	29.3%	44.4%
Should have job with more income and responsibility	70.7	55.6
	100.0%	100.0%
		p < .05

131. Perceived Job Opportunity in Newark Survey

Perceived opportunity	R (105)	NI (126)
Is possible to obtain desired job	32.4%	43.9%
Is not possible to obtain desired job	67.6	56.1
	100.0%	100.0%
		p < .06

132. Perceived Obstacles to Employment in Newark Survey

Obstacle	R (71)	NI (68)
Lack of Training	18.3%	41.2%
Lack of Experience	12.7	8.8
Discrimination	69.0	50.0
	100.0%	100.0%
		p < .025

175

133.

Is getting what you want out of life a matter of ability or being in the right place?	R (39)	NI (251)	CR (54)
Ability	76.9%	76.1%	88.9%
Right Place	23.1	23.9	11.1
	100.0%	100.0%	100.0%

R-NI	p < .90	
CR-NI	p < .05	
R-CR	p < .25	

134.

Racial Consciousness

	Detroit Survey		Newark Survey	
Who do you think are more dependable?	R (37)	NI (247)	R (91)	NI (108)
Negroes	48.6%	22.4%	45.0%	27.8%
Whites	21.7	27.6	35.2	49.1
About the same	29.7	50.0	19.8	23.1
	100.0%	100.0%	100.0%	100.0%
	p < .001		p < .05	

	Detroit Survey		Newark Survey	
Who do you think are nicer?	R (41)	NI (262)	R (96)	NI (110)
Negroes	61.0%	36.3%	78.1%	57.3%
Whites	4.9	5.0	21.9	37.3
About the same	34.1	58.7	0.0	5.4
	100.0%	100.0%	100.0%	100.0%
	p < .001		p < .025	

135.

Black Consciousness in Newark Survey

Self-description	R (105)	NI (126)
Black	52.4	33.3
Negro	28.6	34.9
Colored	10.4	17.5
No difference	8.6	14.3
	100.0%	100.0%
	p < .025	

	Newark Survey	
All Negroes should study African History and Language	R (125)	NI (104)
Agree	79.8%	68.8%
Disagree	20.2	31.2
	100.0%	100.0%
	p < .06	

136.

Anti-White Attitudes

	Detroit Survey		Newark Survey	
Civil rights groups which have white and Negro leaders would do better without whites	R (36)	NI (245)	R (105)	NI (124)
True	36.1%	21.1%	51.4%	33.1%
False	63.9	78.9	48.6	66.9
	100.0%	100.0%	100.0%	100.0%
	p < .1		p < .005	

	Newark Survey	
Sometimes I Hate White People	R (105)	NI (126)
Agree	72.4%	50.0%
Disagree	27.6	50.0
	100.0%	100.0%
	p < .001	

Negroes who make a lot
of money like .o think
they are better than other

Negroes	R(105)		NI(126)
Agree	71 4%		59.5%
Disagree	28.6		40.5
	100.0%		100.0%
		p< .06	

Negroes who make a lot
of money are just as bad

as whites	R(105)		NI(122)
Agree	50.5%		35.2%
Disagree	49.5		64.8
	100.0%		100.0%
		p< .05	

138. Half the arrestees were charged with one or more of three offenses: breaking and entering, trespassing, or curfew violation.

Of 13,112 offenses charged against 12.457 persons in 19 cities (Atlanta, Bridgeton, Cincinnati. Dayton. Detro't, Elizabeth, Englewood, Grand Rapids, Jackson, Jersey City, M.lwaukee, New Brunswick, Newark. Paterson, Phoenix, Plainfield, Rockford Tampa and Tucson; six major, six serious and seven minor), 4 108 (31 percent) were charges of breaking and entering or trespassing and 2 506 (19 percent) were charges of curfew violation. The breakdown of charges by categories was:

Charges*	Number	Percent
Breaking and entering or trespassing	4 108	31.3%
Curfew violation	2 506	19.1
Burgla:y, larceny robbery or theft	2 000	15.3
Disorderly conduct, disturbing the peace or rioting	807	6.2
Resisting arrest, drunk or traffic violations	550	4.2
Weapons charges	526	4.0
Assault	317	2.4
Vagrancy loitering. unlawful assembly, suspicious conduct	129	1.0
Narcotics charges	67	.5
Arson	56	.4
Juvenile delinquency	25	.2
Hom.cide	17	.1
Other charges	1,156	8.8
Unknown	848	6.5
	13,112	100.0%

*These arrest statistics should be interpreted with caution. Felony, misdemeanor and ordinance violat'on charges are combined. Later dispositions may change this distribution

139. *Political Information in Newark Survey*

Identification of Polit-
ical Figures—Kenneth

Gibson	R(105)		NI(125)
Negro	77.1%		61.6%
White	1.0		5.6
Don't Know	21.9		32.8
	100.0%		100.0%
		p< .025	

Political information

Test	R(106)		NI(127)
High Score	68.9%		51.2%
Low Score	31.1		48 8
	100.0%		100.0%
		p< .025	

140.

Frequency of Negro Rights Discussion

	R(106)	NI(126)
Nearly everyday	53.8%	34.9%
Once a week	12.3	7.9
From time to time	31.1	52.4
Never	0.0	0.0
Don't know	2.8	4.8
	100.0%	100.0%

p< .025

Attend meeting or participation in civil rights group

	R(89)	NI(113)
Yes	39.3%	25.7%
No	60.7	74.3
	100.0%	100.0%

p< .05

141. *Trust of the Government in Newark Survey*

How Much do you think you can trust the Newark government to do what is right?

	R(105)	NI(127)
Just about always	2.9%	1.6%
Most of the time	4.8	13.7
Some of the time	48.1	50.8
Almost never	44.2	33.9
	100.0%	100.0%

p< .1

142. *Political Grievances in Detroit Survey*

How much did anger with politicians have to do with causing riot?

	R(44)	NI(286)
Great deal	43.2%	19.6%
Something	31.8	39.1
Nothing	18.2	24.5
Don't know	6.8	16.8
	100.0%	100.0%

p< .05

How much did anger with police have to do with causing riot?

	R(44)	NI(287)
Great deal	70.5%	48.8%
Something	20.5	30.3
Nothing	2.2	14.3
Don't know	6.8	6.6
	100.0%	100.0%

p< .05

143. *Perception of Country as Not Worth Fighting For*

Country worth fighting for in major world war	Detroit Survey			Newark Survey	
	R(38)	NI(264)	CR(56)	R(106)	NI(126)
Worth fighting	55.3%	75.0%	86.9%	33.0%	50.8%
Not worth fighting	39.4	15.5	3.3	52.8	27.8
Don't know	5.3	9.5	9.8	14.2	21.4
	100.0%	100.0%	100.0%	100.0%	100.0%

p< .001

R-NI   p< .005
CR-NI   p< .05
R-CR   p< .001

144. For purposes of this section the three university-related riots, in Houston, Jackson and Nashville, have not been included.

145. See the discussion of Grievances in relation to the riot process in Part II of this chapter.

146. Our discussion relies heavily upon 1960 census data, which are always the most complete and usually the most recent data available. Nevertheless, 1960 statistics are outdated for describing American urban life in 1967 and consequently, we used more recent data wherever possible.

We have examined, for most purposes in this section, 20 of the 23 surveyed riot cities. Three cities (Houston, Jackson and Nashville; three serious) were excluded because their disturbances were more directly campus-related than city-related.

In each of 17 cities, we have compared conditions in the riot area with conditions elsewhere in (1) the city as a whole. and (2) the metropolitan area of which the city is a part, including the suburban areas. In addition, we have sought to determine whether racial differences affect these comparisons. To do this we have identified census tracts in which violence and damage occurred. This study of census tracts is limited to 17 cities because identification of the disturbance area for purposes of analysis was not possible for three cities (Bridgeton, Cambridge and New Brunswick; one serious and two minor). They are not divided into census tracts.

We recognize that participants in the disorders did not necessarily live in the area of disorder. However, we have attempted to learn whether the disturbance areas have characteristics which set them apart from the cities and metropolitan areas in which the disturbance areas are situated.

The disturbance areas were primarily commercial areas in a part of the city having a high concentration of Negro residents. These were usually characterized by a number of retail or wholesale shops, often with residences above the shops and with residential areas immediately adjacent to the commercial streets. In two cities (Atlanta and Tucson; one serious and one minor) the disturbance area was primarily residential.

147. After studying 100 cities, the Department of Labor reached the same conclusion: "Negroes living in non-poverty areas were not much better off than those in poverty areas; among whites, the differences were very sharp." (U.S. Department of Labor, Bureau of Labor Statistics, Special Labor Force Report No. 75, "Poverty Areas of Our Major Cities," October, 1966, p. 1105.)

148. The Bureau of the Census categorizes citizens as white and nonwhite. Since 92 percent of the nonwhites in the United States are Negroes, we have used the terms "Negro" and "nonwhites" interchangeably throughout this section. The numbers compared in the section are medians for the 17 cities.

149 In eight cities, white population also increased in that period however, it did so at a much lower rate. Only Englewood (minor) showed no change in white population during that period.

150. In 13 of 17 cities (Atlanta, Cincinnati, Dayton, Detroit, Grand Rapids, Jersey City, Milwaukee Newark, Paterson, Phoenix, Tucson, Rockford and Tampa; five major, five serious and three minor), including seven of the cities which experienced the most severe violence, the percentage of Negro population in the disturbance area was more than twice the percentage of Negro population in the entire city; in nine of the cities, the percentage of Negro population in the disturbance area was more than triple the city-wide percentage.

151. Comparing Negroes and whites in the cities: The percentage of Negro population 24 years of age or younger in all 17 cities exceeded the percentage of whites in that age group. The percentage of Negro population 65 years of age or older in all 17 cities except two (Phoenix and Tucson; one serious and one minor) was less than one-half the percentage of whites in that age group.

Comparing Negroes in the disturbance areas and Negroes in the cities: The percentage of Negro population 24 years of age or younger living in the disturbance area in approximately half the cities (Cincinnati Elizabeth, Englewood, Grand Rapids, Newark, Phoenix, Plainfield and Tucson; three major, two serious and three minor) exceeded the city-wide percentage. The percentages were equal only in Tampa (major).

The differences we have seen are even greater when the age distribution among Negroes in the disturbance areas is compared with the age distribution among whites in the Standard Metropolitan Statistical Areas (SMSA'S).

	Median Age Distribution (%)					
Age	Disturbance Areas		Cities		SMSA's	
	W.	N.W.	W.	N.W.	W.	N.W.
Male						
Under 25	37.5	50.4	41.4	51.8	45.0	53.1
Over 64	13.2	4.4	10.2	4.2	8.6	4.6
Female						
Under 25	36.6	49.2	38.6	53.7	43.0	50.0
Over 64	16,5	4.7	11.9	4.4	9.9	4.5

152. Comparing Negroes and whites in the cities: The number of median years of school completed by Negroes was less than the median number for whites

in all 17 cities. In 13 of 17 cities (Atlanta, Cincinnati, Dayton, Detroit, Elizabeth. Englewood, Grand Rapids, Milwaukee, Phoenix, Plainfield, Rockford, Tampa and Tucson; four major, five serious and four minor) there was a difference of at least one year.

The percentage of Negro population over 25 years of age having eight years or less of education in all 17 cities was greater than the percentage of white population.

Comparing Negroes in the disturbance areas and Negroes in the cities: The median years of school completed by Negroes in the disturbance area in more than half of the 17 cities (Dayton, Elizabeth, Englewood, Grand Rapids, Newark, Phoenix, Plainfield, Rockford and Tucson; two major, three serious and four minor) was lower than the median rate of education for Negroes in the entire city. In three of the 17 cities (Jersey City, Milwaukee and Tampa; two major and one minor) the median years completed by Negroes in the disturbance area and by Negroes in the city were equal. In the remaining five cities the median rate was slightly higher (less than a year's difference) for Negroes in the disturbance area. The difference between the median number of years completed was one-tenth of a year for the 17 cities. The percentage of Negro population in the disturbance area over 25 years of age having eight years or less education was slightly greater than the city-wide percentage in 11 of the 17 cities (Dayton, Elizabeth, Englewood, Grand Rapids, Milwaukee, Newark, Phoenix, Plainfield, Rockford, Tampa and Tucson; four major, three serious and four minor). The differences we have seen are even greater when comparing the level of education of Negroes in the disturbance areas with that of whites in the SMSA's:

Median Education

	Disturbance Areas		Cities		SMSA's	
	W.	N.W.	W.	N.W.	W.	N.W.
Median years of school completed	8.7	8.7	10.6	8.8	11.2	8.9
More than 8 years of schooling (%)	46.0	45.8	61.6	47.5	64.9	46.9

153. Comparing Negroes and whites in the cities: The percentage of Negro males in the labor force in nine of 17 cities (Elizabeth, Englewood, Jersey City, Milwaukee, New Haven, Newark, Paterson, Rockford and Tampa; three major, two serious and four minor) exceeded the percentage of white males. The proportion of Negro and white males employed or seeking employment was equal in Grand Rapids (serious).
The percentage of Negro females exceeded the percentage of white females in the labor force in all 17 cities.
Comparing Negroes in the disturbance area and Negroes in the cities: The percentage of Negro males in the disturbance area in the labor force, in all except seven cities (Dayton, Elizabeth, Englewood, Grand Rapids, Newark, Plainfield and Tucson; two major, two serious and three minor), exceeded the percentage of Negro males in the entire city in the labor force.
The percentage of Negro females in the labor force in the disturbance area, in all except ten cities (Atlanta, Dayton, Detroit, Elizabeth, Englewood, Grand Rapids, Jersey City, Paterson, Phoenix and Plainfield; two major, five serious and three minor) was larger than the percentage of Negro females in the entire city in the labor force.
The differences in the percentages of Negroes and whites in the labor force again can be seen to be small by comparing Negroes in the disturbance area with whites in the SMSA:

Median Labor Force Participation Rates (%)

	Disturbance Areas		Cities		SMSA's	
	W.	N.W.	W.	N.W.	W.	N.W.
Male	74.8	79.0	77.6	78.8	79.8	76.0
Female	38.0	46.6	38.0	46.7	35.2	45.0

154. Comparing Negroes and whites in the cities: The percentage of Negro male unemployment in all 20 cities was higher than the unemployment rate for white males. In 13 of the 20 cities (Bridgeton, Cambridge, Cincinnati, Detroit, Englewood, Grand Rapids, Milwaukee, New Brunswick, New Haven, Paterson, Phoenix, Plainfield and Rockford; four major, five serious and four minor) the rate of unemployment for Negroes was more than twice the rate for whites.

180

The unemployment rate for Negro females was more than the rate for white females in all of the 20 cities except Plainfield (major).

Comparing Negroes in the disturbance areas and Negroes in the cities: The unemployment rate for Negro males in the disturbance area was slightly more than the Negro citywide rate in 11 of 17 cities and slightly less in the remaining six (Atlanta, Cincinnati, Detroit, Englewood, New Haven and Paterson; two major, three serious and one minor).

The disturbance area unemployment rate for Negro females equalled or exceeded the citywide rate in seven of 17 cities (Cincinnati, Milwaukee, New Haven, Newark, Rockford, Tampa and Tucson; four major, two serious and one minor).

The differences are even greater when the unemployment rate among Negroes in the disturbance areas is compared with the unemployment rate among whites in the SMSA's:

Median Unemployment Rate (%)

	Disturbance Areas		Cities		SMSA's	
	W.	N.W.	W.	N.W.	W.	N.W.
Male	6.8	11.1	4.7	9.7	3.8	10.1
Female	5.8	9.9	5.1	9.4	4.8	9.5

More recent and complete data indicate that unemployment and underemployment of Negroes are even more serious than the 1960 census revealed. The Bureau of the Census estimates that one out of every six Negro males between ages 20 and 39 was not counted in the 1960 census. Unemployment is likely to be common among the uncounted men.

The Department of Labor, in November 1966, surveyed 10 slum areas in eight cities and obtained slightly earlier unemployment data for slums in four other cities. ("A Sharper Look at Unemployment in U.S. Cities and Slums," a summary report submitted to the President by the Secretary of Labor.) Two of these cities, Detroit and Phoenix (one major and one serious) were among the cities we surveyed.

The Department found, in the slum areas surveyed, that:

The unemployment rate was approximately three times the nationwide rate of 3.7 percent;

Six and nine-tenths percent of those listed as employed were working only part time although they were trying to find full-time work; the comparable figure for the nation as a whole was 2.3 percent;

Twenty-one percent of those working full time were earning less than $60 a week; the comparable figure for the nation as a whole was 15.4 percent;

One-third of the labor force was subemployed.

The Department of Labor included in its definition of subemployment (i) those unemployed in the sense that they are actively looking for work and unable to find it; (ii) those working only part time when they are trying to get full-time work; (iii) those heads of households under 65 who earn less than $60 per week working full time and those individuals under 65 who are not heads of households and earn less than $56 per week in a full-time job; (iv) half the number of "nonparticipants" (not in the labor force) in the male 20-64 age group; and (v) a conservative and carefully considered estimate of the male undercount group.

155. Labor Force Participation Increases as Better Job Opportunities Appear.

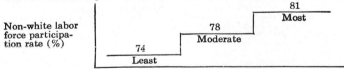

Non-white labor force participation rate (%)

74 Least
78 Moderate
81 Most

Cities with: least, moderate, and most opportunities for other than menial jobs.

156. Comparing Negroes and whites in the cities: The percentage of Negro male unskilled and service workers in ten of 17 cities (Atlanta, Cincinnati, Dayton, Englewood, Grand Rapids, Phoenix, Plainfield, Rockford, Tampa and Tucson; three major, four serious and three minor) was at least three times the rate of white men.

The percentage of Negro female unskilled and service workers in all but three of 17 cities (Englewood, Jersey City, and Milwaukee; one major and two minor) was at least three times the percentage of white females.

Comparing Negroes in the disturbance areas and Negroes in the cities: The percentage of Negro male unskilled and service workers in the disturbance areas in 11 of the 17 cities (Dayton, Englewood, Grand Rapids, Jersey City,

181

Newark, Paterson, Phoenix, Tucson, Plainfield, Rockford and Tampa; three major, four serious and four minor) slightly exceeded the percentage in the cities as a whole. The difference between the median of percentages in the disturbance areas and the median of percentages in the cities was 4.5 percent.

The percentage of Negro female unskilled and service workers in the disturbance areas in eight of the 17 cities (Atlanta, Cincinnati, Detroit, New Haven, Plainfield, Rockford, Tampa and Tucson; four major, two serious and two minor) was slightly smaller than the percentage of Negro female unskilled and service workers in the cities. The difference in 17 city medians was 3.6 percent.

The differences are even greater when comparing the percentage of Negro unskilled and service workers in the disturbance areas with whites in the SMSA's:

Median Workers in Unskilled and Service Jobs (%)

	Disturbance Areas		Cities		SMSA's	
	W.	N.W.	W.	N.W.	W.	N.W.
Male	17.9	41.1	12.5	38.7	10.5	38.9
Female	17.6	58.3	15.6	54.7	17.2	62.1

157. Comparing Negroes and whites in the cities in 1960: The median income of Negroes in 17 cities was 69.5 percent of the median income of whites. The 1966 nationwide median income earned by Negroes was 58 percent of the median income earned by whites. ("Social and Economic Conditions of Negroes in the United States," Joint Report by the Bureau of Labor Statistics and the Bureau of the Census, October, 1967, p. 15.

The percentage of Negro families in poverty (having an annual income under $3,000) in 14 of the 17 cities was twice the percentage of white families in poverty. In the other three cities (Englewood, Newark and Paterson; one major, one serious and one minor) the percentage was at least one and one half the percentage of white families.

Comparing Negroes in the disturbance areas and Negroes in the cities: The percentage of the families below the poverty line was slightly higher in the disturbance areas in almost two-thirds of 17 cities (Dayton, Elizabeth, Englewood, Grand Rapids, Milwaukee, New Haven, Newark, Phoenix, Plainfield, Tampa and Tucson; four major, four serious and three minor).

The differences are even greater when the income levels of Negroes in the disturbance areas are compared with the income levels of whites in the SMSA's:

Median Income

	Disturbance Areas		Cities		SMSA's	
	W.	N.W.	W.	N.W.	W.	N.W.
Income ($)	5335	4218	6243	4336	6697	4338
Families with annual income less than $3,000 (%)	21.6	32.0	14.0	29.0	11.6	32.8

158. Comparing Negroes and whites in the cities: The percentage of Negro children under 18 living with both parents in all 17 cities was less than the percentage of white children that age similarly situated.

Comparing Negroes in the disturbance areas and Negroes in the cities: The percentage of Negro children under 18 living with both parents in the disturbance area was greater than the city-wide percentage in seven of the 71 cities (Atlanta, Dayton, Milwaukee, New Haven, Newark, Rockford and Tucson; two major, three serious and two minor).

The differences are even greater when comparing the family status of Negroes in the disturbance areas and of whites in the SMSA's:

Family Status

	Disturbance Areas		Cities		SMSA's	
	W.	N.W.	W.	N.W.	W.	N.W.
Children under 18 living with both parents (%)	82	66	89	67	92	68

159. Family Stability Improves as Family Income Rises

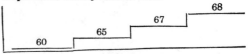

Non-white children
under 18 living
with both parents
(%)

60   65   67   68

Cities with: lowest . . . highest
median non-white family incomes.

160. Comparing Negroes and whites in the cities: The percentage of Negro owner-occupied units in all 17 cities was lower than that of whites. In ten of the cities (Atlanta, Cincinnati, Detroit, Elizabeth, Jersey City, Milwaukee, New Haven, Newark, Paterson and Tampa; five major, three serious and two minor) the proportion of white home ownership was at least one and one-half that of Negroes. In five of the ten cities (Cincinnati, Milwaukee, New Haven, Newark and Paterson; three major and two serious) the percentage of white home ownership was twice that of Negroes.

Although Negroes paid the same or slightly lower rents than did whites among non-home owners in 15 of the 17 cities (all except New Haven and Paterson; two serious), they paid a higher proportion of income for rent than whites. Median rent as a proportion of median income in 11 of 13 cities (Atlanta, Cincinnati, Dayton, Detroit, Grand Rapids, Jersey City, Milwaukee, Newark, Paterson, Plainfield and Tampa; six major, four serious and one minor) was higher for Negroes than for whites. Negroes paid the same proportion as whites in Phoenix (serious) and a smaller proportion than whites in Englewood (minor).

The percentage of overcrowded Negro-occupied homes (homes with more than 1.01 persons per room) in all of the 17 cities except Tucson (minor) was twice the percentage of overcrowded white-occupied homes. In nine of those cities (Elizabeth, Englewood, Grand Rapids, Milwaukee, New Haven, Paterson, Plainfield, Rockford and Tampa; three major, three serious and three minor) the percentage of overcrowded Negro-occupied homes was three times the percentage of white homes.

The percentage of homes occupied by whites which were sound and had adequate plumbing facilities was one and one-half times the proportion of Negro-occupied homes which met those criteria, in ten of 17 cities (Atlanta, Cincinnati, Elizabeth, Jersey City, Milwaukee, New Haven, Newark, Paterson, Phoenix and Tucson; three major, four serious and three minor).

Comparing Negro housing in the disturbance area and in the entire city: The percentage of Negro owner-occupied units in the disturbance area exceeded the Negro city-wide percentage in only six of 17 cities (Atlanta, Cincinnati, Jersey City, New Haven, Paterson and Tucson; one major, three serious and two minor). The city-wide median for 17 cities was 3.8 percentage points higher than the median for the disturbance area.

Negroes in the disturbance area paid more for rent than Negroes paid city-wide in eight of 13 cities (Atlanta, Cincinnati, Dayton, Detroit, Grand Rapids, Jersey City, Paterson and Plainfield; three major, four serious and one minor). In Milwaukee (major) they paid the same. In four cities they paid less (Englewood, Newark, Phoenix and Tampa; two major, one serious and one minor).

The proportion of income paid for rent by Negroes living in the disturbance area slightly exceeded the city-wide proportion paid by Negroes in eight of 13 cities (Cincinnati, Dayton, Englewood, Grand Rapids, Milwaukee, Newark, Plainfield and Tampa; four major, one serious and three minor). The proportions were equal in Detroit (major). The difference in medians was three-tenths of one percent.

The percentage of overcrowded homes in which Negroes lived in the disturbance area was slightly greater than the percentage of overcrowded homes in which Negroes lived city-wide in eight of the 17 cities (Cincinnati, Elizabeth, Englewood, Grand Rapids, Plainfield, Newark, Tampa and Tucson; four major, one serious and three minor). The median 17-city difference was 1.1 percentage points.

The percentage of sound homes in the entire city was slightly greater than in the disturbance area in 10 of 17 cities (Dayton, Englewood, Grand Rapids, Milwaukee, New Haven, Newark, Plainfield, Rockford, Tampa and Tucson; four major, three serious and three minor). The difference in medians was .7 percentage point. The differences are even greater when comparing the housing conditions of Negroes in the disturbance areas and of whites in the SMSA's:

Rent (13 cities only)

	Disturbance Areas		Cities		SMSA's	
	W.	N.W.	W.	N.W.	W.	N.W.
Median rent ($)	74	74	77	77	77	71
Median rent as a proportion of median income (%)	16.7	21.1	15.0	20.8	14.3	19.9

Median Housing Ownership

	Disturbance Areas		Cities		SMSA's	
	W.	N.W.	W.	N.W.	W.	N.W.
Owner-occupied units (%)	36.6	33.4	55.1	37.2	66.4	34.4

Median Housing Overcrowding and Condition

	Disturbance Areas		Cities		SMSA's	
	W.	N.W.	W.	N.W.	W.	N.W.
More than 1.01 persons per room (%)	9.2	21.4	7.6	22.5	8.8	24.0
Sound with all plumbing facilities (%)	68.6	54.4	85.0	53.7	86.1	50.5

161. For purposes of this section we have not included the three university communities.

162. Source: *The Municipal Year Book 1967*, The International City Managers' Association (Chicago 1967).

163. Detroit, Elizabeth, Jersey City, Newark, New Haven, Paterson, Rockford and Tampa (three major, two serious and three minor). In the case of Paterson, virtually no powers were left to the aldermen.

164. Atlanta, Bridgeton, Cambridge, Englewood and Plainfield (one major, two serious and two minor).

165. In the five cities having a council-city manager system, the city manager was appointed by the council, and the mayor's powers were limited (Cincinnati, Dayton, Grand Rapids, Phoenix and Tucson; one major, three serious and one minor).
In the one city having a commission form of government (New Brunswick; minor), the mayor was selected by the commission from its own membership and traditionally was the commissioner who received the largest popular vote. The mayor shared executive power with the other commissioners.

166. In three they were elected by the legislative bodies from their own membership (Cincinnati, Dayton and New Brunswick; one major, one serious; and one minor).

167. Bridgeton, Cambridge, Dayton, Englewood, Grand Rapids, New Brunswick, Plainfield and Tucson (one major, three serious and four minor). The part-time mayors had a variety of other occupations: in Bridgeton, the mayor was a clothing store clerk; in Cambridge, a plumbing contractor; in Dayton, a real estate investor; in Englewood, a businessman who worked in New York; in Grand Rapids, a part-owner of a restaurant supply business; in New Brunswick, a housewife; in Plainfield, a lawyer; and in Tucson, a pharmacist.

168. In 15 of the 20 cities, the principal executive, either the mayor or the city manager, earned an annual salary ranging from $15,000 to $35,000 (Atlanta, Cincinnati, Dayton, Detroit, Elizabeth, Grand Rapids, Jersey City, Milwaukee, Newark, New Haven, Paterson, Phoenix, Rockford, Tampa and Tucson; five major, six serious and four minor). The other five cities studied had no city manager and a part-time mayor whose annual salary was less than $2,000 in four cases and $5,500 in one case (Bridgeton, Cambridge, Englewood, New Brunswick and Plainfield; one major, one serious and three minor). In all five cities having a council-city manager system, the appointed city manager's salary was significantly higher than the salary of the elected mayor (Cincinnati, Dayton, Grand Rapids, Phoenix and Tucson; one major, three serious and one minor).

169. Thirteen mayors had terms of four years (Atlanta, Cambridge, Dayton, Detroit, Elizabeth, Grand Rapids, Jersey City, Milwaukee, Newark, New Brunswick, Rockford, Tampa and Tucson; four major, four serious and five minor). Two had terms of three years (Bridgeton and Paterson; one serious and one minor), and five had terms of two years (Cincinnati, Englewood, New Haven, Phoenix and Plainfield; two major, two serious and one minor). There appeared to be no pattern as to the length of time a mayor had been in office prior to the disturbance.

In four of the 20 cities the mayor had been in office for less than two years (Grand Rapids, New Brunswick, Paterson and Tampa; one major, two serious and one minor). In three cities the mayor had been in office for seven years or more (Milwaukee, New Haven and Rockford; one major, one serious and one minor). In the remaining cities, the mayor's tenure had ranged from two to seven years.

In two cities (Paterson and New Brunswick; one serious and one minor), the mayors had been in office for six months and two months respectively. In both cases the mayor appealed to people in the disturbance area to give the new administration a chance to solve the city's problems, and these appeals appeared to have had an effect in dampening the disorders.

170. Atlanta, Bridgeton, Cincinnati, Dayton, Detroit, New Brunswick, Phoenix and Tampa (three major, three serious and two minor).

171. Cambridge, Grand Rapids, Milwaukee, New Haven, Paterson, Rockford and Tucson (one major, four serious and two minor).

172. Elizabeth, Englewood, Jersey City, Newark and Plainfield (two major and three minor).

173. Of a total of 207 legislators in the 20 cities, 20 (or 10 percent) were Negroes.

174. Bridgeton, Elizabeth, Grand Rapids, Rockford, Tampa and Tucson (one major, one serious and four minor).

175. In Newark the budget director and the director of health and welfare were Negroes; in Cincinnati, the city solicitor was a Negro; in Jersey City, the director of health and welfare was a Negro; and in Detroit, an aide to the mayor was a Negro.

176. Atlanta, Cincinnati, Dayton, Detroit, Englewood, Newark and Phoenix (three major, three serious and one minor).

177. All except Milwaukee, Tampa and Tucson (two major and one minor). Of the 205 board of education members in those cities, 24 (or 11 percent) were Negro.

178. Excepting Englewood, New Brunswick and Paterson (one serious and two minor). In some instances it was called a "community relations commission" or "human rights commission."

179. Only the Equal Opportunities Commission in New Haven (serious) had the power to subpoena witnesses and enforce compliance with its decisions.

180. Thirteen councils had full-time, paid staff of two or more, responsible to the council itself (Atlanta, Cincinnati, Dayton, Detroit, Elizabeth, Grand Rapids, Milwaukee, Newark, New Haven, Phoenix, Plainfield, Tampa and Tucson; six major, five serious and two minor). In four cities, the councils had no paid staff (Bridgeton, Cambridge, Jersey City and Rockford; one serious and three minor).

Three of the four councils having no paid staff had been relatively inactive in the year prior to the 1967 summer disturbances. Cambridge (serious) held no meetings, and Jersey City (minor) had held one at which they decided their services were not needed during the summer. The council in Rockford (minor), which had not met for over a year, was in the process of being reorganized.

181. Of the 13 councils from which such information was available, five councils reported receiving more than 100 complaints annually (Atlanta, serious, 700 to 800; Detroit, major, 116; Elizabeth, minor, approximately 200; Newark, major, approximately 750; Plainfield, major, approximately 200). Three councils reported receiving 50 to 100 complaints (Cincinnati, major, approximately 50; New Haven, serious, approximately 60; Phoenix, serious, approximately 75). Five councils reported receiving less than 50 (Dayton, serious, 45; Grand Rapids, serious, approximately 25; Milwaukee, major, approximately 40; Tampa, major, 46; and Tucson, minor, 10).

The majority of the complaints from the 12 councils which reported this type of information were in the areas of housing discrimination, building and housing code enforcement, and discrimination in employment and promotion practices.

182. Two years ago in Rockford the 18-member human relations commission was asked to investigate an alleged incident of police brutality but, after a preliminary meeting to discuss the matter, held no further meetings. In the late spring of 1967, the Commission was reorganized with a number of new members.

In Plainfield, city agencies opposed an attempt by the Human Relations Commission to conduct its own investigation of complaints of police brutality prior to the 1967 disorder.

183. Cincinnati, Detroit, Elizabeth, Englewood, Newark, New Haven, Paterson, Phoenix and Tucson (three major, three serious and three minor). Only those in Detroit, New Haven and Tucson had been in existence more than two years prior to the disorder.

Four police departments (Paterson, Detroit, Rockford and New Haven; one major, two serious and one minor) had specialized complaint bureaus within the department, and in two cities (Paterson and Detroit) these bureaus had investigative authority.

In Milwaukee there was a Police and Fire Commission consisting of five members. Until recently only property owners were authorized by law to file complaints with the Commission. The law has since been amended to permit any registered voter to file complaints, but few complaints have been filed.

184. Eight of the nine, Englewood (minor) excepted.

185. Detroit and Newark (both major).

186. We have not attempted to analyze the often substantial social and economic programs of other levels of government.

Of necessity we have also restricted ourselves to only the most general quantitative comparisons, within each of the three cities, of the size of the selected federal programs, the number of people in need of them, and the number of people in any way reached by them. We have not attempted the far more difficult task of evaluating the efficiency of the programs or the quality of assistance provided to recipients or its impact on their lives. Qualitative evaluation is the responsibility of many other agencies of the Federal government and beyond our own mandate. Our evaluation necessarily assumes that all those reached are reached effectively. If the factor of effectiveness were taken into account, the magnitude of the still unmet needs might be even greater than our estimates.

As in "The Pattern of Disadvantage," supra, we have used 1960 Census data as the basis for most of our observations as to need. We are keenly aware of difficulties involved in comparing 1967 programs with 1960 needs and have used more recent data wherever available. In most instances the needs were even greater in 1967 than in 1960.

Various federal programs account for their expenditures in different ways and for different periods of time. We have generally used figures for fiscal year 1967, ending June 30, 1967, or calendar year 1967, as available in each case. We are cognizant also of the difficulties involved in considering only expenditures for 1967 as a measure of Federal efforts to deal with ghetto problems. Much was done in earlier years by these programs and more is being done now. We have generally chosen a single year's funding only as a measure of the level of Federal effort during the most recent period. The choice of a recent year for measuring Federal expenditures created a further problem, however. The amount of funds authorized or obligated for a particular program is usually higher than the actual disbursements for that program in a given time period, but data on disbursements is usually available only some time after the period has ended. With the exception of housing and welfare, we have relied upon the higher obligation figures.

187. Institutional training programs administered through local school boards under the Manpower Development and Training Act (MDTA) have been included instead with education programs.

188. Two of the programs had no fixed number of trainee positions. The following table further describes these programs.

Detroit

Programs	Federal Funds Obligated 1/1/67-9/30/67	Enrollee Positions Available
Urban Area Employment Project	$5,780,794	1,693
City of Detroit Neighborhood Youth Corps (NYC)	2,541,770	1,070
City of Detroit NYC (Summer)	1,106,980	2,700
City of Detroit On the Job Training (OJT) (2 Programs)	2,164,161	1,900

*Sources: Mayor's Committee on Human Resources Development and the U.S. Department of Labor. Funds were obligated from Department of Labor and Office of Economic Opportunity appropriations.

Programs	Federal Funds Obligated 1/1/67-9/30/67	Enrollee Positions Available
United Auto Workers OJT	$2,135,309	2,000
Trade Union Labor Council Pre-Apprentice	94,480	200
Urban Beautification	334,456	40
Board of Education NYC	1,528,640	1,800
Archdiocesan Opportunity	271,730	100
Program NYC	362,310	500
Northern Systems, Inc. OJT	1,200,000	450
Adult Youth Employment Project	759,000	1,000
Specialized Training Employment and Placement Service	749,000	**
Chrysler Motor OJT	53,625	55
Michigan Petroleum Association OJT	132,471	320
Chrysler OJT	182,070	**
Metropolitan Hospital OJT	6,022	21
Great Lakes Fabricating and Erecting OJT	113,963	50
Frank's Nursery OJT	20,000	40
Window Cleaners Local #139 OJT	9,508	20
TV Service Association OJT	40,506	20
Total	**$19,586,795**	**13,979**

**Number of trainees unavailable.

189. *Need*—In the spring of 1967 the labor force in Newark numbered 155,770 persons, of whom 90,358 were nonwhite. The unemployment rate during that period was 5.9 percent for whites, 11.5 percent for Negroes, and 13.4 percent for others (principally Spanish-speaking persons). A Rutgers University study in the spring of 1967 identified 3,859 unemployed whites, 8,932 unemployed Negroes, and 1,700 other unemployed nonwhites.
Programs—During the first two quarters of 1967, 12 job training programs in Newark were supported by $2,681,853 of Federal funds. These programs provided for 2,840 trainees.

Newark* Programs	Federal Funds Obligated 1/1/67-6/30/67	Enrollee Positions Available
Essex County Youth and Economic Rehabilitation Commission OJT	$ 107,997	200
City of Newark OJT	267,810	500
Food Service Industry Project OJT	29,443	20
Career Oriented Preparation for Employment	1,207,769	450
Work Training Program	246,000	200
Mountainside Hospital OJT	10,833	68
City of Newark OJT	296,506	500
Chrysler Corporation OJT	53,625	55
Painters' District Council #10 OJT	17,224	20
United Community Corporation OJT	262,313	500
Teamster's Local #97 OJT	168,288	300
Weldotron Corporation OJT	14,045	27
Total	**$2,681,853**	**2,840**

*Sources: Field Representative of the Bureau of Apprenticeship and Training, U. S. Department of Labor, and the United Community Corporation. Funds were obligated from Department of Labor and Office of Economic Opportunity appropriations.

190. *Need*—The Connecticut State Employment Service estimates there were approximately 145,000 to 150,000 nonagrarian workers in the labor force in New Haven and 12 surrounding towns during the first three quarters of 1967. The unemployment rate for the same period averaged approximately 3.5 percent.
Programs—During the first three quarters of 1967 there were 14 manpower programs in New Haven in various stages of operation. These provided $2,150,828 of Federal funds for 1,574 trainees. The number of trainees was not available for one program.

Programs	New Haven* Federal Funds Obligated 1/1/67–9/30/67	Enrollee Positions Available
Manpower Division, CPI, Administration	$ 284,227	None
NYC (Out-of-school)	379,300	109
NYC (In School)	370,060	550
Neighborhood Employment Centers	62,620	None
Elm Haven Employment Center	118,000	250
Skill Center	51,915	250
Basic Education	61,057	**
Community Progress, Inc. OJT	185,776	138
Burner Repair OJT	5,753	10
Refrigerator & Air Conditioning OJT	12,450	13
Health Aides Program	33,633	26
Adult Work Training	207,240	65
Foster Grandparents	222,832	85
Residential Youth Center	155,965	78
Total	$2,150,828	1,574

*Source: Community Progress, Inc. (CPI), the local community action agency. Funds were obligated from appropriations to the Department of Labor, the Department of Health, Education and Welfare, and the Office of Economic Opportunity.
**Information not available.

191. *Need*—There are more than 295,000 students in the Detroit public schools, of whom 43 percent are white and 56 percent Negro. Nearly 60 percent (about 175,000) are educationally disadvantaged within the definition of Title I. Thirty percent of the white students and 84.5 percent of the Negro students are in this group. There are approximately 180,000 functionally illiterate adults in Detroit.

The Detroit school board recently stated that it may cost twice as much to educate a ghetto child as it costs to educate a suburban child and produce the same educational result. The Superintendent of Detroit schools has estimated that, to educate inner-city children, as much as $500 or $600 per pupil is needed in addition to the present average state and local expenditure of $565 per pupil.

Programs—Detroit schools are scheduled to receive about $11 million during the 1967-68 school year under ESEA Title I. Of the estimated 175,000 low-income students, only about 55,000 are direct beneficiaries of Title I programs. Thus, while the $11 million represents $200 per student for the 55,000 direct recipients, 120,000 (or 69 percent) other educationally disadvantaged students are not participating in the programs.

The Adult Basic Education program is scheduled to receive $244,766 during the 1967-68 school year to serve about 3,900 adults.

Federal funding for public school students from kindergarten through high school for the 1967-68 school year will total $14,514,447. For a student population of 295,000, these funds add an average of about $49 per student to the state and local expenditures of approximately $565 per student.

*Detroit**
Federal Funds Obligated For
1967-1968 School Year

Funds designed to assist students in kindergarten through grade 12:

ESEA Title I (Compensatory Education Projects)	$11,221,537
ESEA Title II. (Library Materials)	695,352
ESEA Title III (Supplementary Educational Projects)	20,000
Vocational Education	2,337,558
Teacher Corps	240,000
Sub-Total	$14,514,447

Funds designed to assist pre-schoolers, out-of-school youths and adults:

MDTA	$ 2,819,943
Adult Basic Education	244,766
Head Start	1,280,000
Sub-Total	$ 4,344,709
Total	$18,859,156

*Source: Detroit Board of Education.
Funds were obligated from Department of Health, Education and Welfare and Office of Economic Opportunity appropriations.

192. *Need*—There are approximately 75,000 students in the Newark schools of whom 21 percent are whites and 79 percent are Negroes, Puerto Ricans and others. Approximately 33,000 (44 percent) of these students are from low-income families. In 1960 there were approximately 55,000 functionally illiterate adults in Newark.

Programs—Newark schools are scheduled to receive about $4 million during the 1967-68 school year under ESEA Title I. Of the estimated 33,000 educationally disadvantaged students, only about 24,000 (or 72 percent) are direct beneficiaries of the Title I programs. Thus, while $166 per student is spent for programs for the direct recipients, 9,000 educationally disadvantaged students are not receiving the benefits of the programs.

The Adult Basic Education program is scheduled to receive $169,000 during the 1967-68 school year to serve approximately 3,000 students at a cost of about $56 per person.

Federal funding for public school students from kindergarten through high school in Newark during the 1967-68 school year will total $4,554,098. For a student population of 75,000, these funds add an average of approximately $60 per student to the state and local expenditures of about $565.

Newark*
Federal Funds Obligated For
1967-1968 School Year

Funds designed to assist students in kindergarten through grade 12:

ESEA Title I (Compensatory Education Projects)	$4,049,498
ESEA Title II (Library Materials)	154,000
National Defense Education Act (NDEA) Title III (Improvement of Teaching Science and Languages)	43,600
NDEA Title V-a (Testing, Guidance and Counselling)	31,000
Vocational Education	276,000
Sub-Total	$4,554,098

Funds designed to assist pre-schoolers, out-of-school youths and adults:

MDTA	$ 296,000
Adult Basic Education	169,000
Head Start	791,000
Head Start Follow Through	63,000
Sub-Total	$1,319,000
Total	$5,873,098

*Source: Newark Board of Education.
Funds were obligated from Department of Health, Education and Welfare and Office of Economic Opportunity appropriations.

193. *Need*—There are more than 21,000 students in the New Haven public schools, of whom 47.9 percent are whites and 52.1 percent are Negroes, Puerto Ricans and others. In the middle and senior high schools an estimated 2,500 students are educationally disadvantaged. Of 33 elementary schools, 14 are designated as inner city or target schools for funds under ESEA Title I, and seven others reportedly could have been so designated. More than 50 percent of all elementary students (6,637 of 13,050) are in the 14 target schools. Twenty-two percent of the white students and more than 73 percent of the nonwhite students are in the target schools. There are an estimated 20,000 functionally illiterate adults in New Haven.

Programs—New Haven schools are scheduled to receive nearly $1 million in the 1967-68 school year under ESEA Title I. Of the 2,500 low-income students in middle and senior high schools, approximately 1,000 are beneficiaries of the programs. Because of the comprehensive nature of the Title I programs in New Haven, all 6,637 students in the 14 target elementary schools are recipients of the programs although not all are educationally disadvantaged. The number of educationally disadvantaged students who do not receive benefits from the programs because they attend the 19 non-target elementary schools is unknown.

The Adult Basic Education program is scheduled to receive $23,000 during the 1967-68 school year to serve almost 700 persons.

Federal funding for public school students from kindergarten through high school for the 1967-68 school year will total $1,090,260. For a student population of 21,000, these funds add an average of nearly $52 per student to the local and state expenditures of approximately $697 per student.

Federal Funds Obligated For
1967-1968 School Year
Funds designed to assist students in kindergarten through grade 12:

ESEA Title I (Compensatory Education Projects)	$ 992,000
ESEA Title II (Library Materials)	70,000
ESEA Title III (Supplementary Educational Projects)	28,260
Sub-Total	$1,090,260

Funds designed to assist pre-schoolers, out-of-school youths and adults:

Adult Basic Education	$ 23,000
Head Start	387,509
Sub-Total	$ 410,509
Total	$1,500,769

*Source: New Haven Board of Education.
Funds were obligated from Department of Health, Education and Welfare and Office of Economic Opportunity appropriations.

194. We have considered as substandard, in accordance with the definition of the Department of Housing and Urban Development, all units which were characterized by the census as dilapidated or as lacking one or more plumbing facilities. U. S. Bureau of Census, Measuring the Quality of Housing, *An Appraisal of Census Statistics and Methods*, Working Paper #25. Washington, D. C., 1967. We have treated as overcrowded all units identified by the census as having more than 1.01 persons per room, in accordance with the definition recently used by the Census Bureau and the Bureau of Labor Statistics. *Social and Economic Conditions of Negroes in the United States*, October, 1967, p. 57. Since many units are included in both categories, it is not possible to establish a total level of need by adding the numbers of units in the two categories, and we have therefore applied the two standards separately.

195. *Need*—In 1960 there were 553,198 housing units in Detroit. Of these, 36,810 were substandard and 45,126 were overcrowded.
  Programs—Federal funds in the amount of $78,656,000 were expended through September, 1967 for housing completed under the first three programs examined. An additional $41,000 were expended through December, 1967 under the Rent Supplements program. BMIR mortgages in the amount of $4,173,000 were insured by FHA through September, 1967. In the 1957-67 period, although no new public housing was constructed, 25 housing units were added as a result of FHA foreclosures. During this period, 346 units were constructed for the elderly and handicapped; families in 62 units were assisted through rent supplements; and mortgages on 325 units were insured under the BMIR program.

*Detroit**
Cumulative Through September 30, 1967
Except For Rent Supplements, Which Are Described
As Of December 31, 1967

Programs	Federal Funds Disbursed ($ 000)	Mortgages Insured ($ 000)	Maximum** No. of Low-Income Units or Accommodations Assisted	
			1937-56	1957-67
Housing for Elderly and Handicapped (completed units)	$ 3,961	—***	—	346
Urban Renewal, Title I (All projects)	44,318	—	0	0
Low-Rent Public Housing (Bond payments on completed projects)	30,380	—	8,180	25
Rent Supplements	41	—	—	62
Section 221, Below Market Interest Rate (BMIR)	—	$4,173	—	325
Total	$78,700	$4,173	8,180	758

*Sources: Department of Housing and Urban Development and Detroit Housing Commission.
**Middle and moderate income units are included in the totals, particularly in the cases of the BMIR and elderly and handicapped programs.
***Dashes indicate that the column is not applicable or the program was not in existence during time period indicated by the column heading.

196. *Need*—In 1960 there were 134,872 housing units in Newark. Of these, 23,743 were substandard and 16,600 were overcrowded.
Programs—Federal funds in the amount of $101,177,000 were expended through September, 1967 for housing completed under the first three programs examined. An additional $22,000 were expended through December, 1967 under the Rent Supplements program. BMIR mortgages in the amount of $20,308,000 were insured by FHA through September, 1967. Newark has 10,766 public housing units, of which 20 percent (2,174) were constructed after 1959. Since 1959, 299 units have been constructed for the elderly and handicapped; families in 59 units have been assisted through rent supplements; and mortgages on 1,228 units have been insured under the BMIR program.

Newark*
Cumulative Through September 30, 1967
Except For Rent Supplements, Which Are Described
As Of December 31, 1967

Programs	Federal Funds Disbursed ($ 000)	Mortgages Insured ($ 000)	Maximum** No. of Low-Income Units or Accommodations Assisted	
			1937-56	1960-67
Housing for Elderly and Handicapped (completed units)	$ 3,590	—***	—	299
Urban Renewal, Title I (For all projects)	40,002	—	0	0
Low-Rent Public Housing (Bond payments on completed projects)	57,585	—	8,592	2,174
Rent Supplements	22	—	—	59
Section 221, Below Market Interest Rate (BMIR)	—	$20,308	—	1,228
Total	$101,199	$20,308	8,592	3,760

*Sources: The Department of Housing and Urban Development and the Housing Authority of the City of Newark.

**Middle and moderate income units are included in the totals, particularly in the cases of the BMIR and elderly and handicapped programs.
***Dashes indicate that the column is not applicable or the program was not in existence during the period indicated by the column heading.

197. *Need*—In 1960 there were 51,471 housing units in New Haven. Of these, 6,667 were substandard and 4,278 were overcrowded.
Programs—Federal funds in the amount of $60,393,000 were expended through September 1967 for housing completed under the first four programs examined. BMIR mortgages in the amount of $6,045,000 were insured by FHA through September, 1967. Of the 2,074 public housing units in New Haven, only 469 were constructed after 1952. Mortgages on 482 units have been insured under the BMIR program.

New Haven*
Cumulative through September 30, 1967
Except For Rent Supplements Which Are Described
As Of December 31, 1967

Programs	Federal Funds Disbursed ($ 000)	Mortgages Insured ($ 000)	Maximum** No. of Low-Income Units or Accommodations Assisted	
			1937-52	1953-67
Housing for Elderly and Handicapped (For completed units)	0	—***	—	0
Urban Renewal, Title I (For all projects)	$53,588	—	0	0
Low-Rent Public Housing (Bond payments on completed projects)	6,805	—	1,605	469
Rent Supplements	0	—	—	0
Section 221, Below Market Interest Rate (BMIR)	—	$6,045	—	482
Total	$60,393	$6,045	1,605	951

191

*Sources: The Department of Housing and Urban Development and the New Haven Redevelopment Agency.
**Middle and moderate income units are included in the totals, particularly in the cases of the BMIR and elderly and handicapped programs.
***Dashes indicate that the column is not applicable or the program was not in existence in time period indicated by the column heading.

198. We have not included Medical Assistance to the Aged, because it is not limited to low-income persons.

199. *Need*—Of the 1,670,144 residents of Detroit in 1960, 361,348, or 21.6 percent of the city's population, including 204,820 nonwhites and 156,528 whites, were members of families with annual incomes of less than $3,000.
Programs—The estimated Federal contribution toward the four programs totalled $28,169,997. An estimated 69,310 poor persons received assistance. The average annual income of an AFDC family of four in Detroit was $1,752. By contrast, a "city worker's family budget for a moderate living standard" for a family of four in Detroit is $8,981 per year, according to the Department of Labor. (See p. 193.)

200. *Need*—Of the 405,220 residents of Newark in 1960, 89,949, or 22.2 percent of the city's population including 48,098 nonwhites and 41,851 whites, were members of families with annual income of less than $3,000.
Program—The estimated Federal contribution toward the four programs totalled $14,964,647. An estimated 48,319 poor persons received assistance. The average annual income of an AFDC family of four was $2,759. By contrast, the "city worker's family budget for a moderate living standard" for a family of four in Northern New Jersey is $10,195, according to the Department of Labor. (See p. 194.)

201. *Need*—Of the 152,048 residents of New Haven in 1960, 31,254, or 20.6 percent of the city's population, including 9,021 nonwhites and 22,233 whites, were members of families with annual incomes of less than $3,000.
Programs—The estimated Federal contribution toward the four programs totalled $3,889,487. An estimated 12,663 poor persons received assistance.

202. Data as to funding and persons reached have been obtained from Community Action Agencies (CAA's) in the three cities surveyed. Manpower and employment programs, such as Neighborhood Youth Corps, and Head Start programs have been included in other sections.

203. *Need*—As indicated in the section on Welfare, in 1960 there were 361,348 people in Detroit who were members of families with annual incomes of less than $3,000.
Programs—During fiscal year 1967, federal funds made available for community action programs, excepting manpower and Head Start, totalled $12,576,923. During that period the CAA estimates that these programs reached approximately 110,000 low-income persons.

*Detroit**
Fiscal Year 1967

Programs	Funds Obligated
Small Business Development Center	$ 89,220
Main Grant—Four Months	2,880,729
Medical	431,056
Five Year Human Capital Improvement Program	46,134
Small Business Development Center	115,850
Foster Grandparents	46,622
Main Grant—Eight Months	3,071,224
Legal Services	351,685
Moms & Tots	11,533
Youth Service Corps	63,529
Four Summer Programs	797,376
Summer Programs Supplement	249,721
Moms & Tots	31,242
Adult Basic Education	114,703
Summer Programs	934,184
Resource Allocation & Priority Analysis	49,752
Area Training and Technical Assistance Center	283,278
Comprehensive Health Services	2,859,924
Neighborhood Service Program Planning Grant	49,361
Emergency Loans for Families	100,000
Total	**$12,576,923**

*Source: Mayor's Committee for Human Resources Development. Funds were obligated from Office of Economic Opportunity appropriations.

Wayne County & Detroit* Fiscal Year 1967
Wayne County

Programs	Persons Assisted (1967 Monthly Average)	Monthly Average Payment Per Person	Federal & State Expenditures	Estimated Percentage of County Programs Attributed To Detroit
Aid to Aged	12,956	$71.48	$11,113,187	80.6%
Aid to Blind	674	90.43	730,850	83.3
Aid to Disabled	7,141	91.88	7,873,177	87.4
AFDC	77,235	40.87	37,882,244	88.8
Totals	98,006		$57,599,458	

City of Detroit
(Estimates)

Programs	Approximate Number Of Persons Assisted	Federal	Estimated Contributions State	Total
Aid to Aged	10,443	$ 5,982,588	$ 2,975,004	$ 8,957,592
Aid to Blind	561	337,882	270,914	608,796
Aid to Disabled	6,241	3,743,351	3,137,809	6,881,160
AFDC	52,065	18,106,176	15,533,256	33,639,432
Totals	69,310	$28,169,997	$21,916,983	$50,086,980

*Source: Michigan Department of Social Services, Research & Program Analysis Section

Essex County & Newark* Calendar Year 1967

Essex County

Programs	Persons Assisted In July 1967	Monthly Average Payment Per Person	Federal & State Expenditures	Estimated Percentage of County Programs Attributed To Newark
Aid to Aged	3,750	$75.00	$ 3,703,000	73%
Aid to Blind	270	105.04	329,000	74
Aid to Disabled	2,773	115.20	3,837,000	72
AFDC	51,041	55.55	35,198,000	85
Totals	57,834		$43,067,000	

City of Newark (Estimates)

Programs	Approximate Number Of Persons Assisted	Estimated Contributions			
		Federal	State	County	Total
Aid to Aged	2,738	$ 1,802,127	$ 675,797	$ 225,266	$ 2,703,190
Aid to Blind	200	115,888	63,786	63,786	243,460
Aid to Disabled	1,996	1,198,986	781,827	781,827	2,762,640
AFDC	43,385	11,847,646	9,035,327	9,035,327	29,918,300
Totals	48,319	$14,964,647	$10,556,737	$10,106,206	$35,627,590

*Source: Essex County Welfare Board.

New Haven* November, 1967 and Estimated Calendar 1967

Programs	Persons Assisted During November 1967	Average Payment Per Person	Federal & State Expenditures	Estimated Calendar 1967 Contributions**		
				Federal	State	Total
Aid to Aged	927	$72.21	$ 66,866	$ 540,144	$ 262,448	$ 802,592
Aid to Blind	35	95.37	3,338	20,989	19,067	40,056
Aid to Disabled	701	101.53	71,170	420,188	433,852	854,040
AFDC	11,000	56.77	624,606	2,908,166	4,587,106	7,495,272
Total	12,663		$765,980	$3,889,487	$5,302,473	$9,191,960

*Source: Connecticut Commission of Public Welfare, Chief of Research.
**Represents contributions for November, 1967, multiplied by 12.

204. *Need*—As indicated in the section on Welfare, in 1960 there were 89,949 people in Newark who were members of families with annual incomes of less than $3,000.

Programs—During fiscal year 1967, Federal funds made available for community action programs, excepting manpower and Head Start, totalled $1,901,130. During that period the CAA estimates that these programs reached approximately 39,796 low-income persons.

Newark*
Fiscal Year 1967

Programs	Federal Funds Obligated
League Youth Culture and Education Program	$ 16,544
United Community Corporation Central Administration	292,108
Community Action (Area Boards)	480,893
ENABLE (Family Development)	31,952
FOCUS (Spanish Information Center)	24,041
Small Business Center	22,613
Summer Block Recreation Program	268,148
Senior Citizens	399,831
Legal Services	365,000
Total	$1,901,130

*Source: United Community Corporation. Funds were obligated from Office of Economic Opportunity appropriations.

205. *Need*—As indicated in the section on Welfare, in 1960 there were 31,254 people in New Haven who were members of families with annual incomes of less than $3,000.

Programs—Federal funds made available for community action programs, excepting manpower and Head Start, during fiscal year 1967, totalled $2,251,042. During that period the CAA estimates that these programs reached 13,000 low-income persons.

New Haven*
Fiscal Year 1967

Programs	Federal Funds Obligated
Pre-kindergarten	$ 11,954
Tutorial	12,880
Remedial Reading	36,307
Under 16 Work Study	12,948
Legal Services	262,631
Community Schools	122,252
Community Services Division	422,036
Day Care	83,849
Central CAA Administration	332,433
Library Neighborhood Center	75,748
Union of Indigent People	35,887
CPI Manpower Division	701,304
Family Services Program	6,312
Youth Research Division	93,452
Police Youth Program	12,682
Juvenile Court Program	28,367
Total	$2,251,042

*Source: Community Progress, Incorporated. Funds were obligated from Office of Economic Opportunity appropriations.

206. Using this material we sought to identify and assign weights to the four types of grievances which appeared to have the greatest significance to the Negro community in each city. We made judgments with regard to the severity of particular grievances and assigned a rank to the four most serious. These judgments were based on the frequency with which a particular grievance was mentioned, the relative intensity with which it was discussed, references to incidents exemplifying the grievance, and estimates of severity obtained from the interviewees themselves. Each priority ranking was weighted by points (4 points for the first priority, 3 for second, 2 for third and 1 for fourth). The points for each grievance for all cities were added to create an inter-city ranking. Whenever two grievances were judged to be equally serious for a particular city, the points for the two rankings involved were divided equally (e.g., in case two were judged equally suitable for the first priority, the total points for first and second were divided and each received 3½ points).

195

Annexed are two sets of charts: Chart I shows the pervasiveness of types of grievances in 12 general categories, each of which is subdivided into several specific categories. Chart II shows only the general categories and indicates the number of times that grievances in each were ranked first, second, third, or fourth in terms of relative severity.

207. Education and recreation were ranked equally; municipal services and consumer and credit practices were also ranked equally.

208. *Ibid.*

209. *Ibid.*

210. *Ibid.*

211. In this survey 437 Negroes form the Detroit disturbance area were asked which of 23 grievances had a "great deal," "something" or "nothing" to do with the riot. The grievances which received the most responses of "a great deal" were: (1) police brutality, (2) overcrowded living conditions, (3) poor housing, (4) lack of jobs, (5) poverty, and (6) anger with business people. Interviewees who identified themselves as participants in the riot were singled out for special analysis and chose the same six causes but in a slightly different order. Overcrowded living conditions was first instead of police brutality.

212. We found significant grievances concerning police practices in each of 19 cities. Grievances concerning police practices were ranked first in eight cities, second in four cities, third in none, and fourth in two cities. Although such grievances were present in five other cities, they were not ranked in the first four orders of intensity.

213. Grievances in the employment area were ranked first in three cities, second in seven cities, third in four cities, and fourth in three cities. In only three cities was such a grievance present but not ranked among the highest four levels of intensity.

214. Grievances in the housing area were found in 18 cities and were ranked first in five cities, second in two cities, third in five cities, and fourth in two cities. In four cities where housing was a grievance, it was not ranked in the first four levels of intensity.

215. Educational grievances were found in 17 cities and were ranked first in two cities, second in two cities, third in two cities, and fourth in three cities. In eight cities where such a grievance was present, it was not ranked in the first four levels of priority.

216. Grievances relating to recreation were found in 15 cities and were ranked first in three cities, second in one city, third in four cities, and fourth in none. In seven cities where such a grievance was present, it was not ranked in the first four levels of priority.

217. Grievances relating to the political structure were found in 16 cities and were ranked first in two cities, second in one city, third in one city, and fourth in one city. In 11 cities where such a grievance was present, it was not ranked in the first four levels of priority.

218. Grievances relating to white attitudes were found in 15 cities and were ranked first in no city, second in one city, third in one city, and fourth in two cities. In 11 cities where such a grievance was present, it was not ranked in the first four levels of priority.

219. Grievances relating to the administration of justice were found in 15 cities and were ranked first in no city, second in none, third in two cities, and fourth in one city. In 12 cities where such a grievance was present, it was not ranked in the first four levels of priority.

220. Grievances relating to federal programs were found in 16 cities and were ranked first in no city, second in one city, third in none, and fourth in none. In 15 cities where such a grievance was present, it was not ranked in the first four levels of priority.

221. Grievances relating to municipal services were found in 11 cities and were ranked first in no city, second in none, third in one city, and fourth in none. In 10 cities where such a grievance was present, it was not ranked in the first four levels of priority.

222. Grievances relating to unfair commercial practices were found in 11 cities and were ranked first in no city, second in none, third in none and fourth in two cities. In nine cities where such a grievance was present, it was not ranked in the first four levels of priority.

223. We surveyed these cities shortly after the disturbances. Consequently, we are not in a position to assess more current events there. As noted elsewhere in this Report, the Commission is sponsoring two surveys which will measure the impact of the disorders on the attitudes of whites and Negroes. The surveys are being conducted in 15 cities and four suburban areas, including four of the 20 cities surveyed for this Report. The results of these surveys will be published separately and will provide a more complete treatment of the post-disorder situation.

224. We have noted earlier that no immunization took effect for the 25 cities which experienced two or more disorders in 1967. See "Levels of Violence and Damage" in Part I, *supra*. Six of the 20 cities we surveyed had more than one disorder (Atlanta (2), Cambridge (2), Cincinnati (3), Dayton (2), Rockford (2), and Tampa (2)). Houston had three disorders in 1967. However, the three cities which had campus-related disorders in our sample of 23 have not been included in our examination for the purpose of this section.

225. Bridgeton, Cincinnati, Tucson (one major and two minor). In Bridgeton, a white segregationist organization had become more active. In Cincinnati and Tucson, new black organizations tended to follow militant separatist policies.

226. In Atlanta, two new groups were formed, one composed largely of white ministers and lay members, and the other of black youths. Reportedly, the latter group is dedicated to the maintenance of law and order and the prevention of riots.

In Elizabeth, as a result of its leader's anti-riot activities during the disturbance, a relatively moderate religious sect, the Orthodox Moslems, appears to have gained stature in the Negro community.

227. In New Haven, at least two black militant organizations emerged after the riot and they seemed to have gained support from members of the moderate Negro community. In addition, an integrated group was formed several months after the riot to protest alleged police harassment and repression of the militant Negro leaders.

In Milwaukee, the NAACP Youth Commandoes, a militant but non-separatist group, appeared to have grown in influence in the Negro community after the riot. Also, a coalition of moderate Negro leaders was formed to develop economic and social programs.

228. Atlanta, Milwaukee, New Haven, Newark, Paterson, Plainfield, Rockford and Tucson (three major, three serious, and two minor).

In New Haven, the Police Department opened a store-front office in the disturbance area where citizens could make complaints or seek assistance. The office was also designed to serve as a "cooling-off" center to avoid the need for a trip to the central stationhouse in minor matters such as domestic quarrels.

In Milwaukee, the police department established a police-community relations division.

In Newark, the Negro captain, whose promotion was announced during the riot, has been appointed commanding officer of the fourth precinct in which the disorders of the summer started.

In Paterson, the program for the police community relations unit has been expanded to include a police-community relations board consisting of seven policemen and nine civilians. The civilians include representatives from the Negro community.

In Rockford, the mayor's commission on human relations planned a workshop on police-community relations to be conducted by experts from city, county, state and federal agencies. Each member of the Rockford police force was to be required to take 12 hours of instruction.

In Tucson, the police department planned to sponsor an institute of police-community relations, including seminars on the nature of prejudice and on the attitudes of Negroes, Mexican-Americans and Indians toward the police.

In Plainfield, the police department began actively recruiting Negro officers. The department also republished its complaint procedures.

229. Cambridge, Cincinnati, Detroit, Grand Rapids, New Brunswick, Paterson, Phoenix, Tampa and Tucson (three major, four serious and two minor). In Cambridge and Tampa, the local community relations commissions increased their efforts to induce employers to hire more Negroes. Tampa's commission employed a full-time job developer and established a job training program.

In Grand Rapids, a coalition of public and private organizations began a crash employment program to find 1,000 jobs in three months.

In New Brunswick, the business community sought to raise $75,000 for job training; $25,000 of this amount was contributed by one local pharmaceutical company.

In Phoenix, the anti-poverty program initiated a project to train 2,500 heads of households in ghetto areas.

After the Tampa disturbance, the local anti-poverty agency and area industries sponsored an on-the-job training program, and the Tampa Merchants Association established a job training course.

230. Cambridge, Cincinnati, Dayton, Detroit, Elizabeth, Milwaukee, Plainfield, Tampa and Rockford (five major, two serious and two minor).

In Cincinnati, the urban renewal agency established a complaint office in

197

the ghetto. The office, which was open three days a week, was closed after 38 days of operation. The city manager said the experiment was abandoned because citizens had failed to use it.

In Elizabeth, the city council approved the local housing authority's request to submit an application to the federal government for 400 low-income apartment units. The mayor also appointed a Negro to the local redevelopment agency.

In Milwaukee, the city council passed an open housing ordinance. However, Negro leaders denounced the ordinance on the ground that it merely restates the provisions of state law, which reportedly exclude 66 percent of the housing in Milwaukee from coverage. The lone Negro council member voted against the ordinance as "mere tokenism."

In Plainfield, a Negro was appointed to a five-year term as a member of the housing authority.

In Tampa, a block club staged a march on the Tampa housing authority's offices to publicize complaints against the authority, such as billing public housing residents for grass-cutting where there is no grass. The authority promised to consider the charges seriously.

In Rockford, the county housing authority is constructing a 75-unit housing development for the elderly in a Negro slum. The project was planned before the disturbance but construction began afterward. A community development corporation was also initiated before the disorder to encourage community self-help programs for home improvement, and local businesses contributed "seed money" to guarantee improvement loans. The city annexed the pilot project block in order to provide municipal services and planned to annex additional blocks as the program expands.

231. Newark is the headquarters office for two of the life insurance companies in the consortium of 350 which pledged to set aside $1 billion to finance ghetto housing under FHA insurance.

232. Dayton, Detroit, Elizabeth, Plainfield and Rockford (two major, one serious and two minor).
The Dayton board of education issued a policy statement that it would attempt to decrease *de facto* segregation in city schools.
Elizabeth's board of education instituted a program of free adult basic education.
The Plainfield board of education formalized its practice of permitting parents to have a third person present when talking to school officials. It also hired its first full-time Negro counsellor.

233. In Detroit, as aforementioned, the Michigan Bell Telephone Company plans to "adopt" one of the city's high schools and provide funds for special programs.

234. Atlanta, Cincinnati, Dayton and Tampa (two major and two serious).
In Atlanta, despite united resistance by local Negro leaders, the administration continued to build "portable" classrooms for use at predominantly black schools, maintained double sessions only in Negro schools, and refused to reconsider its "freedom of choice" desegregation procedures.
In Dayton and Tampa, bond issues for school construction were defeated. The Tampa referendum was opposed by local Negroes because most of the money was to be used in all-white, suburban schools.
Also in Tampa, the interscholastic athletic conference to which Tampa's white schools belong refused to admit the city's predominantly Negro schools to membership and made it impossible for the county schools to form a separate conference in which the Negro schools could participate in the highest class of competition.

235. Atlanta, Elizabeth, New Brunswick and Tampa (one major, one serious and two minor).
In Atlanta, immediately after the disturbance, work began on a playground for which area residents had been petitioning for two years.
In Elizabeth, shortly after the disturbance, the recreation department moved a playground closer to a poor Negro neighborhood.
In Tampa, a former local high school coach, popular among Negro youths, was hired as director of youth services for the neighborhood service centers of the county anti-poverty program.

236. Cincinnati, Englewood, Phoenix, Tampa and Tucson (two major, one serious and two minor).

237. President of city council in Englewood, member of civil service commission in Tucson and members of housing authority and board of adjustments in Plainfield (one major and two minor).
In elections for state office, the situation was mixed. A Negro candidate for state assemblyman from Newark was elected, but two incumbent Negro legislators from Newark were defeated. The incumbent Negro assemblyman whose district included Englewood was defeated by the candidate who had been mayor of that city during the disorder.

238. Cambridge and New Brunswick (one serious and one minor).
In Cambridge, the Governor of Maryland appointed a community relations committee immediately after the disturbance.
In New Brunswick, the mayor established an "open door" policy to facilitate the airing of grievances directly with her. A human relations commission, planned prior to the disturbance, was established, and several Negroes were appointed as commissioners.

239. In Tampa, some of the counter-rioters known as "White Hats" were hired by the city's commission on community relations to improve communication with ghetto youths. The program was recently terminated upon the indictment of several White Hats on felony charges not connected with the disorder.

240. Atlanta, Dayton, Detroit, Elizabeth, Englewood, New Haven, Newark and Tampa (three major, three serious and two minor).
In six of the cities surveyed (Atlanta, Dayton, Detroit, New Haven, Newark and Tampa) Model Cities applications have been approved by the Department of Housing and Urban Development.
In Elizabeth and Tampa, new legal services programs, funded by the Office of Economic Opportunity, were instituted.
A YMHA building, valued at $50,000, near Elizabeth's disturbance area was donated for use by the local community action agency as a community center.
The county community action agency opened an office in Englewood.

241. Tampa and Milwaukee (two major).
The nomination to the board of the county community action agency of the former commander of the Milwaukee police precinct which includes much of the ghetto area was resented by Negro residents. The nomination was never voted on as the nominee moved from the city before a vote was taken.
In Tampa, a highly-publicized controversy arose because a Negro neighborhood worker was fired by a local anti-poverty agency. The discharged employee filed charges of racial discrimination in the hiring and job placement practices of the county anti-poverty program.

242. Atlanta, Dayton, Elizabeth and New Brunswick (two serious and two minor).
Elizabeth opened a "little city hall" in the disturbance area.
In New Brunswick, the administration rented an armory for use as a neighborhood center.

243. In Elizabeth, the county legal services agency announced plans for one-day consumer clinics in various low-income neighborhoods for training and counselling on complaints about credit and other consumer practices.

244. Cincinnati and Detroit (two major).
In Detroit, as stated, CCAC began developing proposals for new businesses in the riot area, including a Negro-owned cooperative food market and a number of other cooperative business ventures.
In Cincinnati, newspapers reported that two Negroes who had long sought financing for a new business center in the disturbance area had succeeded since the disturbance.

245. Atlanta, Cincinnati, Detroit, Newark and Tampa (four major and one serious).
In Atlanta the police and fire departments announced the formulation of a confidential coordinated plan to cope with any future disturbance.
In Cincinnati, voters approved a bond issue to establish a countrywide police communications center and command post for normal conditions as well as riot conditions. The new city budget included $500,000 for 50 additional policemen.
In Newark, the city council appropriated $200,000 for the purchase of armored cars, riot guns, helmets and other riot control equipment.
In Tampa, city and county law enforcement departments prepared a detailed "After-action Report" describing the city's disorder and how it was controlled. The report recommended purchase of riot control equipment and suggested tactical improvements.

246. Dayton, Elizabeth, Paterson and Tampa (one major, two serious and one minor).
In Dayton, the organizers of the White Hats stated that the group would be used again if another riot occurred. The organizers also stated that they expected city officials to cooperate with them again as they had during the June disorder.
In Elizabeth, there was evidence that city officials planned to ask Negro community leaders to assist in future peace keeping as they did during the disorder.
In Paterson, the community action agency gave a leadership course for Negro teenagers in the hope that the youths will act as counter-rioters should the need arise.

247. In Tampa, as indicated above, the White Hats program, which had been continued after the disorder, ended with the indictment of several youths on non-riot-connected charges.

248. In Cincinnati, according to unofficial estimates, about 50 percent of the businesses damaged during that city's riot had reopened by mid-December, 1967.

In Dayton, where the total estimated property damage from the June disorder was relatively small, most of the storefronts damaged in the West Dayton business area were repaired.

249. Detroit and Plainfield (two major).

In Plainfield, two Negro organizations demanded that any new building be undertaken only after consultation with representatives of the Negro community.

In Detroit, CCAC insisted that no rebuilding be started until Negro citizens of the area decided how they want their neighborhoods redeveloped.

Chapter 3 / Organized Activity

The President directed the Commission to investigate "to what extent, if any, there has been planning or organization in any of the riots."

The President further directed the Federal Bureau of Investigation to provide investigative information and assistance to the Commission and authorized the Commission to request from any other executive department or agency any information and assistance which the Commission deemed necessary to carry out its functions.

The Commission obtained documents, numbering in the thousands, from the Federal Bureau of Investigation, the Department of State, the Department of Defense, the Department of the Treasury, the Internal Revenue Service, the Post Office Department, the Legislative Reference Service of the Library of Congress, and the Central Intelligence Agency. The Commission established a special investigating staff supplementing the Commission's field teams and related staff that made the general examination of the riots in 23 cities. The special investigating staff examined the data supplied by the field teams, by the several federal agencies, and by congressional investigating units, and maintained continuous liaison with these organizations throughout its investigation.

In addition to examining and evaluating intelligence and information from federal sources, the special investigating staff gathered information from local and state law enforcement agencies and officials. It also conducted its own field investigations in 15 cities with special emphasis on five that had experienced major disorders in 1967—Cincinnati, Newark, Detroit, Milwaukee, and New Haven. Special staff investigators employed by the Commission interviewed over 400 persons, including police officials, black militants, and ghetto residents.

The Commission studied the role of foreign and domestic organizations, and individuals, dedicated to the incitement or encouragement of violence. It considered the organizational affiliations of those who called for violence, their contacts, sources of financial support, travel schedules and, so far as possible, their effect on audiences.

The Commission considered the incidents that had triggered the disorders and the patterns of damage during disorders, particularly in Newark and Detroit. The Commission analyzed the extent of sniper activity and the use of fire bombs.

The Commission collected and investigated hundreds of rumors relating to possible organized activity. These included reports of arms caches, sniper gangs, guerrilla training camps, selection of targets for destruction, movement of armed individuals from one riot area to another, and pre-riot planning.

On the basis of all the information collected the Commission concludes that the urban disorders of the summer of 1967 were not caused by, nor were they the consequence of, any organized plan or "conspiracy." Specifically, the Commission has found no evidence that all or any of the disorders or the incidents that led to them were planned or directed by any organization or group, international, national or local.

Militant organizations, local and national, and individual agitators, who repeatedly forecast and called for violence, were active in the spring and summer of 1967. We believe that they deliberately sought to encourage violence, and that they did have an effect in creating an atmosphere that contributed to the outbreak of disorder.

We recognize that the continuation of disorders and the polarization of the races would provide fertile ground for organized exploitation in the future.

Since the disorders, intensive investigations have been conducted not only by this Commission but also by local police departments, grand juries, city and state committees, federal departments and agencies, and congressional committees. None thus far has identified any organized groups as having initiated any riots during the summer of 1967. The Commission appointed by Governor Richard J. Hughes to examine the disorders in New Jersey was unable to find evidence supporting a conclusion that there was a conspiracy or plan to organize the Newark or Plainfield riots.

Investigations are continuing at all levels of government, including committees of Congress. These investigations relate not only to the disorders of 1967 but also to the actions of groups and individuals, particularly in schools and colleges, during this last fall and winter. The Commission has cooperated in these investigations. They should continue.

PART II

WHY DID IT HAPPEN?

Chapter 4 / The Basic Causes

We have seen what happened. Why did it happen?

In addressing this question we shift our focus from the local to the national scene, from the particular events of the summer of 1967 to the factors within the society at large which have brought about the sudden violent mood of so many urban Negroes.

The record before this Commission reveals that the causes of recent racial disorders are imbedded in a massive tangle of issues and circumstances—social, economic, political, and psychological—which arise out of the historical pattern of Negro-white relations in America.

These factors are both complex and interacting; they vary significantly in their effect from city to city and from year to year; and the consequences of one disorder, generating new grievances and new demands, become the causes of the next. It is this which creates the "thicket of tension, conflicting evidence and extreme opinions" cited by the President.

Despite these complexities, certain fundamental matters are clear. Of these, the most fundamental is the racial attitude and behavior of white Americans toward black Americans. Race prejudice has shaped our history decisively in the past; it now threatens to do so again. White racism is essentially responsible for the explosive mixture which has been accumulating in our cities since the end of World War II. At the base of this mixture are three of the most bitter fruits of white racial attitudes:

Pervasive discrimination and segregation. The first is surely the continuing exclusion of great numbers of Negroes from the benefits of economic progress through discrimination in employment and education, and their enforced confinement in segregated housing and schools. The corrosive and degrading effects of this condition and the attitudes that underlie it are the source of the deepest bitterness and at the center of the problem of racial disorder.

Black migration and white exodus. The second is the massive and growing concentration of impoverished Negroes in our major cities resulting from Negro migration from the rural South, rapid population growth and the continuing movement of the white middle-class to the suburbs. The consequence is a greatly increased burden on the already depleted resources of cities, creating a growing crisis of deteriorating facilities and services and unmet human needs.

Black ghettos. Third, in the teeming racial ghettos, segregation and poverty have intersected to destroy opportunity and hope and to enforce failure. The ghettos too often mean men and women without jobs, families without men, and schools where children are processed instead of educated, until they return to the street—to crime, to narcotics, to dependency on welfare, and to bitterness and resentment against society in general and white society in particular.

These three forces have converged on the inner city in recent years and on the people who inhabit it. At the same time, most whites and many Negroes outside the ghetto have prospered to a degree unparalleled in the history of civilization. Through television—the universal appliance in the ghetto —and the other media of mass communications, this affluence has been endlessly flaunted before the eyes of the Negro poor and the jobless ghetto youth.

As Americans, most Negro citizens carry within themselves two basic aspirations of our society. They seek to share in both the material resources of our system and its intangible benefits —dignity, respect and acceptance. Outside the ghetto many have succeeded in achieving a decent standard of life, and in developing the inner resources which give life meaning and direction. Within the ghetto, however, it is rare that either aspiration is achieved.

Yet these facts alone—fundamental as they are—cannot be said to have caused the disorders. Other and more immediate factors help explain why these events happened now.

Recently, three powerful ingredients have begun to catalyze the mixture.

Frustrated hopes. The expectations aroused by the great judicial and legislative victories of the civil rights movement have led to frustration, hostility and cynicism in the face of the persistent gap between promise and fulfillment. The dramatic struggle for equal rights in the South has sensitized Northern Negroes to the economic inequalities reflected in the deprivations of ghetto life.

Legitimation of violence. A climate that tends toward the approval and encouragement of violence as a form of protest has been created by white terrorism directed against nonviolent protest, including instances of abuse and even murder of some civil rights workers in the South; by the open defiance of law and federal authority by state and local officials resisting desegregation; and by some protest groups engaging in civil disobedience who turn their backs on nonviolence, go beyond the Constitutionally protected rights of petition and free assembly, and resort to violence to attempt to compel alteration of laws and policies with which they disagree. This condition has been reinforced by a general erosion of respect for authority in American society and reduced effectiveness of social standards and community restraints on violence and crime. This in turn has largely resulted from rapid urbanization and the dramatic reduction in the average age of the total population.

Powerlessness. Finally, many Negroes have come to believe that they are being exploited politically and economically by the white "power structure." Negroes, like people in poverty everywhere, in fact lack the channels of communication, influence and appeal that traditionally have been available to ethnic minorities within the city and which enabled them—unburdened by color—to scale the walls of the white ghettos in an earlier era. The frustrations of powerlessness have led some to the conviction that there is no effective alternative to violence as a means of expression and redress, as a way of "moving the system." More generally, the result is alienation and hostility toward the institutions of law and government and the white society which controls them. This is reflected in the reach toward racial consciousness and solidarity reflected in the slogan "Black Power."

These facts have combined to inspire a new mood among Negroes, particularly among the young. Self-esteem and enhanced racial pride are replacing apathy and submission to "the system." Moreover, Negro youth, who make up over half of the ghetto population, share the growing sense of alienation felt by many white youth in our country. Thus, their role in recent civil disorders reflects not only a shared sense of deprivation and victimization by white society but also the rising incidence of disruptive conduct by a segment of American youth throughout the society.

Incitement and encouragement of violence. These conditions have created a volatile mixture of attitudes and beliefs which needs only a spark to ignite mass violence. Strident appeals to violence, first heard from white racists, were echoed and reinforced last summer in the inflammatory rhetoric of black racists and militants. Throughout the year, extremists crisscrossed the country preaching a doctrine of violence. Their rhetoric was widely reported in the mass media; it was echoed by local "militants" and organizations; it became the ugly background noise of the violent summer.

We cannot measure with any precision the influence of these organizations and individuals in the ghetto, but we think it clear that the intolerable and unconscionable encouragement of violence heightened tensions, created a mood of acceptance and an expectation of violence, and thus contributed to the eruption of the disorders last summer.

The police. It is the convergence of all these factors that makes the role of the police so difficult and so significant. Almost invariably the incident that ignites disorder arises from police action. Harlem, Watts, Newark and Detroit—all the major outbursts of recent years—were precipitated by arrests of Negroes by white police for minor offenses.

But the police are not merely the spark. In discharge of their obligation to maintain order and insure public safety in the disruptive conditions of ghetto life, they are inevitably involved in sharper and more frequent conflicts with ghetto residents than with the residents of other areas. Thus, to many Negroes police have come to symbolize white power, white racism and white repression. And the fact is that many police do reflect and express these white attitudes. The atmosphere of hostility and cynicism is reinforced by a widespread perception among Negroes of the existence of police brutality and corruption, and of a "double standard" of justice and protection—one for Negroes and one for whites.

*　　　*　　　*

To this point, we have attempted only to identify the prime components of the "explosive mixture." In the chapter that follows we seek to analyze them in the perspective of history. Their meaning, however, is already clear:

In the summer of 1967, we have seen in our cities a chain reaction of racial violence. If we are heedless, we shall none of us escape the consequences.

Chapter 5 / Rejection and Protest: An Historical Sketch

INTRODUCTION

The events of the summer of 1967 are in large part the culmination of 300 years of racial prejudice. Most Americans know little of the origins of the racial schism separating our white and Negro citizens. Few appreciate how central the problem of the Negro has been to our social policy. Fewer still understand that today's problems can be solved only if white Americans comprehend the rigid social, economic, and educational barriers that have prevented Negroes from participating in the mainstream of American life. Only a handful realize that Negro accommodation to the patterns of prejudice in American culture has been but one side of the coin—for as slaves and as free men, Negroes have protested against oppression and have persistently sought equality in American society.

What follows is neither a history of the Negro in the United States nor a full account of Negro protest movements. Rather, it is a brief narrative of a few historical events that illustrate the facts of rejection and the forms of protest.

We call on history not to justify, but to help explain, for black and white Americans, a state of mind.

THE COLONIAL PERIOD

Twenty years after Columbus reached the New World, African Negroes, transported by Spanish, Dutch, and Portuguese traders, were arriving in the Caribbean Islands. Almost all came as slaves. By 1600, there were more than half a million slaves in the Western Hemisphere.

In Colonial America the first Negroes landed at Jamestown in August 1619. Within 40 years Negroes had become a group apart, separated from the rest of the population by custom and law. Treated as servants for life, forbidden to intermarry with whites, deprived of their African traditions, and dispersed among Southern plantations, American Negroes lost tribal, regional, and family ties.

Through massive importation, their numbers increased rapidly. By 1776, some 500,000 Negroes were held in slavery and indentured servitude in the United States. Nearly one of every six persons in the country was a slave.

Americans disapproved a preliminary draft of the Declaration of Independence that indicted the King of England for waging "cruel war against human nature itself, violating its most sacred rights of life and liberty in the persons of a distant people who never offended him, captivating and carrying them into slavery in another hemisphere, or to incur miserable death in their transportation thither." Instead, they approved a document that proclaimed "all men are created equal."

The statement was an ideal, a promise. But it excluded the Negroes who were held in bondage, as well as the few who were free men.

The conditions in which Negroes lived had already led to protest. Racial violence was present almost from the beginning of the American experience. Throughout the 18th century, the danger of Negro revolts obsessed many white Americans. Slave plots of considerable scope were uncovered in New York in 1712 and 1714, and they resulted in bloodshed—whites and Negroes were slain.

Negroes were at first barred from serving in the Revolutionary Army, recruiting officers having been ordered in July 1775 to enlist no "stroller, Negro, or vagabond." Yet Negroes were already actively involved in the struggle for independence. Crispus Attucks, a Boston Negro, was perhaps the first American to die for freedom, and Negroes had already fought in the battles at Lexington and Concord. They were among the soldiers at Bunker Hill.

Fearing that Negroes would enlist in the British Army, which welcomed them, and facing a manpower shortage, the Continental Army accepted free Negroes. Many slaves did join the British, and according to an estimate by Thomas Jefferson, more than 30,000 Virginia slaves ran away in 1778 alone, presumably to enlist. The states were enrolling both free and slave Negroes, and finally Congress authorized military service for slaves, who were to be emancipated in return for their service. By the end of the war, about 5,000 Negroes had been in the ranks of the Continental Army. Those who had been slaves became free.

THE CONSTITUTION AND THE LAWS

Massachusetts abolished slavery in 1783, and Connecticut, Rhode Island, New Jersey, Pennsylvania, and New York soon provided for gradual liberation. But relatively few Negroes lived in these states. The bulk of the Negro population was in the South, where white Americans had fortunes invested in slaves. Although the Congress banned slavery in the Northwest Territory, delegates at the Constitutional Convention compromised—a slave was counted as three-fifths of a person for determining the number of representatives from a state to Congress; Congress was prohibited from restricting the slave trade until after 1808, and the free states were required to return fugitive slaves to their Southern owners.

Growing numbers of slaves in the South became permanently fastened in bondage, and slavery spread into the new Southern regions. When more slaves were needed for the cotton and sugar plantations in the Southwest, they were ordered from the "Negro-raising" states of the Old South or, despite Congressional prohibition of the slave trade, imported from Africa.

The laws of bondage became even more institutionalized. Masters retained absolute authority over their Negroes, who were unable to leave their masters' properties without written permission. Any white person, even those who owned no slaves—and they outnumbered slaveholders six to one—could challenge a truant slave and turn him over to a public official. Slaves could own no property, could enter into no contract, not even a contract of marriage, and had no right to assemble in public unless a white person was present. They had no standing in the courts.

DISCRIMINATION AS DOCTRINE

The situation was hardly better for free Negroes. A few achieved material success, some even owned slaves themselves, but the vast majority knew only poverty. Forbidden to settle in some areas, segregated in others, they were targets of prejudice and discrimination. In the South, they were denied freedom of movement, severely restricted in their choice of occupation, and forbidden to associate with whites or with slaves. They lived in constant danger of being enslaved—whites could challenge their freedom and an infraction of the law could put them into bondage. In both North and South, they were regularly victims of mobs. In 1829, for example, white residents invaded Cincinnati's "Little Africa," killed Negroes, burned their property, and ultimately drove half the colored population from the city.

Some Americans, Washington and Jefferson among them, advocated the gradual emancipation of slaves, and in the 19th century, a movement to abolish slavery grew in importance and strength. A few white abolitionist leaders wanted full equality for Negroes, but others sought only to eliminate the institution itself. And some anti-slavery societies, fearing that Negro members would unnecessarily offend those who were unsympathetic with abolitionist principles, denied entrance to Negroes.

Most Americans were, in fact, against abolishing slavery. They refused to rent their halls for anti-slavery meetings. They harassed abolitionist leaders who sought to educate white and Negro children together. They attacked those involved in the movement. Mobs sometimes killed abolitionists and destroyed their property.

A large body of literature came into existence to prove that the Negro was imperfectly developed in mind and body, that he belonged to a lower order of man, that slavery was right on ethnic, economic, and social grounds—and quoted the Scriptures in support.

Spreading rapidly during the first part of the 19th century, slavery held less than one million Negroes in 1800, but almost four million in 1860. Although some few white Americans had freed their slaves, most increased their holdings, for the invention of the cotton gin had made cotton the heart of the Southern economy. By mid-century, slavery in the South had become a systematic and aggressive way of treating a whole race of people.

The despair of Negroes was evident. Malingering and sabotage tormented every slaveholder. The problem of runaway slaves was endemic. Some slaves—Gabriel Prosser in 1800, Denmark Vesey in 1822, Nat Turner in 1831, and others—turned to violence, and the sporadic uprisings that flared demonstrated a deep protest against a demeaning way of life.

Negroes who had material resources expressed their distress in other ways. In 1816, Paul Cuffee, Negro philanthropist and owner of a fleet of ships, transported a group of Negroes to a new home in Sierra Leone. Forty years later Martin R. Delany, Negro editor and physician urged Negroes to settle elsewhere.

Equality of treatment and acceptance by the society at large were myths, and Negro protest during the first half of the 19th century took the form of rhetoric, spoken and written, which combined denunciation of undemocratic oppression together with pleas to the conscience of white Americans for the redress of grievances and the recognition of their constitutional rights.

A few Negroes joined white Americans who believed that only Negro emigration to Africa would solve racial problems. But most Negroes equated that program with banishment and felt themselves "entitled to participate in the blessings" of America. The National Negro Convention Movement, formed in 1830, held conferences to publicize on a national scale the evils of slavery and the indignities heaped on free Negroes.

The American Moral Reform Society, founded by Negroes in 1834, rejected racial separatism and advocated uplifting "the whole human race, without distinction as to . . . complexion." Other Negro reformers pressed for stronger racial consciousness and solidarity as the means to overcome racial barriers. Many took direct action to help slaves escape through the Underground Railroad. A few resisted discrimination by political action, even though most Negroes were barred from voting.

Frustration, disillusionment, anger, and fantasy marked the Negroes' protest against the place in American society assigned to them. "I was free," Harriet Tubman said, "but there was no one to welcome me in the land of freedom. I was a stranger in a strange land."

When Frederick Douglass, the distinguished Negro abolitionist, addressed the citizens of Rochester on Independence Day, 1852, he told them:

> The Fourth of July is *yours,* not mine. *You* may rejoice, *I* must mourn. To drag a man into the grand illuminated temple of liberty, and call upon him to join you in joyous anthems, were inhuman mockery and sacrilegious irony. . . . Fellow citizens, above your national tumultuous joy, I hear the mournful wail of millions, whose chains, heavy and grievous yesterday, are today rendered more intolerable by the jubilant shouts that reach them. . . .

THE PATH TOWARD CIVIL WAR

The 1850's brought Negroes increasing despair, as the problem of slavery was debated by the nation's leaders. The Compromise of 1850 and the Kansas-Nebraska Act of 1854 settled no basic issues. And the *Dred Scott* case in 1857 confirmed Negroes in their understanding that they were not "citizens" and thus not entitled to the Constitutional safeguards enjoyed by other Americans.

But the abolitionist movement was growing. "Uncle Tom's Cabin" appeared in 1852 and sold more than 300,000 copies that year. Soon presented on the stage throughout the North, it dramatized the cruelty of slave masters and overseers and condemned a culture based on human degradation and exploitation. The election of Abraham Lincoln on an anti-slavery platform gave hope that the end of slavery was near.

But by the time Lincoln took office, seven Southern states had seceded from the Union, and four more soon joined them.

The Civil War and Emancipation renewed Negro faith in the vision of a racially egalitarian and integrated American society. But Americans, after having been roused by wartime crisis, would again fail to destroy what abolitionists had described as the "sins of caste."

CIVIL WAR AND "EMANCIPATION"

Negroes volunteered for military service during the Civil War, the struggle, as they saw it, between the slave states and the free states. They were rejected.

Not until a shortage of troops plagued the Union Army late in 1862, were segregated units of "United States Colored Troops" formed. Not until 1864 did these men receive the same pay as white soldiers. A total of 186,000 Negroes served.

The Emancipation Proclamation of 1863 freed few slaves at first, but had immediate significance as a symbol. Negroes could hope again for equality.

But there were, at the same time, bitter signs of racial unrest. Violent rioting occurred in Cincinnati in 1862, when Negro and Irish hands competed for work on the riverboats. Lesser riots took place in Newark, New Jersey, and in Buffalo and Troy, New York, the result of combined hostility to the war and fear that Negroes would take white jobs.

The most violent of the troubles took place in New York City Draft Riots in July 1863, when white workers, mainly Irish-born, embarked on a three-day rampage.

Desperately poor and lacking real roots in the community, they had the most to lose from the draft. Further, they were bitterly afraid that even cheaper Negro labor would flood the North if slavery ceased to exist.

All the frustrations and prejudices the Irish had suffered were brought to a boiling point. . . . At pitiful wages, they had slaved on the railroads and canals, had been herded into the most menial jobs as carters and stevedores. . . . Their crumbling frame tenements . . . were the worst slums in the city.[1]

[1] Ladler, *New York's Bloodiest Week,* American Heritage, June 1959, p. 48.

Their first target was the office of the provost-marshal in charge of conscription, and 700 people quickly ransacked the building and set it on fire. The crowd refused to permit firemen into the area, and the whole block was gutted. Then the mob spilled into the Negro area, where many Negroes were slain and thousands forced to flee town. The police were helpless until federal troops arrived on the third day and restored control.

Union victory in the Civil War promised the Negroes freedom but not equality or immunity from white aggression. Scarcely was the war ended when racial violence erupted in New Orleans. Negroes proceeding to an assembly hall to discuss the franchise were charged by police and special troops who routed the Negroes with guns, bricks, and stones, killed some at once, pursued and killed others who were trying to escape.

Federal troops restored order. But 34 Negroes and four whites were reported dead and over 200 people were injured. General Sheridan later said:

> At least nine-tenths of the casualties were perpetrated by the police and citizens by stabbing and smashing in the heads of many who had already been wounded or killed by policemen . . . it was not just a riot but 'an absolute massacre by the police . . .' a murder which the mayor and police . . . perpetrated without the shadow of necessity.

RECONSTRUCTION

Reconstruction was a time of hope, the period when the 13th, 14th, and 15th Amendments were adopted, giving Negroes the vote and the promise of equality.

But campaigns of violence and intimidation accompanied these optimistic expressions of a new age, as the Ku Klux Klan and other secret organizations sought to suppress the emergence into society of the new Negro citizens. Major riots occurred in Memphis, Tennessee, where 46 Negroes were reported killed and 75 wounded, and in the Louisiana centers of Colfax and Coushatta, where more than 100 Negro and white Republicans were massacred.

Nevertheless, in 1875, Congress enacted the first significant civil rights law. It gave Negroes the right to equal accommodations, facilities, and advantages of public transportation, inns, theaters, and places of public amusement, but the law had no effective enforcement provisions and was, in fact, poorly enforced. Although bills to provide federal aid to education for Negroes were prepared, none passed, and educational opportunities remained meager. But Negroes were elected to every Southern legislature, 20 served in the U.S. House of Representatives, two represented Mississippi in the U.S. Senate, and a prominent Negro politician was Governor of Louisiana for 40 days.

Opposition to Negroes in state and local government was always open and bitter. In the press and on the platform they were described as ignorant and depraved. Critics made no distinction between Negroes who had graduated from Dartmouth and those who had graduated from the cotton fields. Every available means was employed to drive Negroes from public life. Negroes who voted or held office were refused jobs or punished by the Ku Klux Klan. One group in Mississippi boasted of having killed 116 Negroes and of having thrown their bodies into the Tallahatchie River. In a single South Carolina county, six men were murdered and more than 300 whipped during the first six months of 1870.

The federal government seemed helpless. Having withdrawn the occupation troops as soon as the Southern states organized governments, the President was reluctant to send them back. In 1870 and 1871, after the 15th Amendment was ratified, Congress enacted several laws to protect the right of citizens to vote. They were seldom enforced, and the Supreme Court struck down most of the important provisions in 1875 and 1876.

As Southern white governments returned to power, beginning with Virginia in 1869 and ending with Louisiana in 1877, the process of relegating the Negro to a subordinate place in American life was accelerated. Disenfranchisement was the first step. Negroes who defied the Klan and tried to vote faced an array of deceptions and obstacles—polling places were changed at the last minute without notice to Negroes, severe time limitations were imposed on marking complicated ballots, votes cast incorrectly in a maze of ballot boxes were nullified. The suffrage provisions of state constitutions were rewritten to disenfranchise Negroes who could not read, understand, or interpret the Constitution. Some state constitutions permitted those who failed the tests to vote if their ancestors had been eligible to vote on January 1, 1860—a date when no Negro could vote anywhere in the South.

In 1896, Negroes registered in Louisiana totalled 130,344. In 1900, after the state rewrote the suffrage provisions of its constitution, Negroes on the registration books numbered only 5,320. Essentially the same thing happened in the other states of the former Confederacy.

When the Supreme Court, in 1883, declared the Civil Rights Act of 1875 unconstitutional, Southern states began to enact laws to segregate the races. In 1896, the Supreme Court in *Plessy* v. *Ferguson* approved "separate but equal" facilities; it was then that segregation became an established fact, by law as well as by custom. Negroes and whites were separated on public carriers and in all places of public accommodation, including hospitals and churches. In courthouses, whites and Negroes took oaths on separate Bibles. In most communities, whites were separated from Negroes in cemeteries.

Segregation invariably meant discrimination. On trains all Negroes, including those holding first-class tickets, were allotted seats in the baggage car. Negroes in public buildings had to use freight elevators and toilet facilities reserved for janitors. Schools for Negro children were at best a weak imitation of those for whites, as states spent 10 times more to educate white youngsters than Negroes. Discrimination in wages became the rule, whether between Negro and white teachers of similar training and experience or between common laborers on the same job.

Some Northern states enacted civil rights laws in the 1880's, but Negroes in fact were treated little differently in the North than in the South. As Negroes moved north in substantial numbers toward the end of the century, they discovered that equality of treatment did not exist in Massachusetts, New York, or Illinois. They were crowded by local ordinances into sections of the city where housing and public services were generally sub-standard. Overt discrimination in employment was a general practice. Employment opportunities apart from menial tasks were few. Most labor unions excluded Negroes from membership—or granted membership in separate and powerless Jim Crow locals. Yet when Negroes secured employment during strikes, labor leaders castigated them for undermining the principles of trade unionism. And when Negroes sought to move into the mainstream of community life by seeking membership in the organizations around them—educational, cultural, and religious—they were invariably rebuffed.

By the 20th century, the Negro was at the bottom of American society. Disfranchised, Negroes throughout the country were excluded by employers and labor unions from white collar jobs and skilled trades. Jim Crow laws and farm tenancy characterized Negro existence in the South. About 100 lynchings occurred every year in the 1880's and 1890's; there were 161 lynchings in 1892. As increasing numbers of Negroes migrated to Northern cities, race riots became commonplace. Northern whites, even many former abolitionists, began to accept the white South's views on race relations.

That northern whites would resort to violence was made clear in anti-Negro riots in New York City, 1900; Springfield, Ohio, 1904; Greensburg, Ind., 1906; Springfield, Ill., 1908.

The latter was a three-day riot, initiated by a white woman's charge of rape by a Negro, inflamed by newspapers, intensified by crowds of whites gathered around the jail demanding that the Negro, arrested and imprisoned, be lynched. When the sheriff transferred the accused and another Negro to a jail in a nearby town, rioters headed for the Negro section and attacked homes and businesses owned by or catering to Negroes. White owners who showed handkerchiefs in their windows averted harm to their stores. One Negro was summarily lynched, others were dragged from houses and streetcars and beaten. By the time National Guardsmen could reach the scene, six persons were dead—four whites and two Negroes; property damage was extensive. Many Negroes left Springfield, hoping to find better conditions elsewhere, especially in Chicago.

PROTEST IN THE EARLY 1900's

Between his famous Atlanta Exposition Address in 1895 and his death in 1915, Booker T. Washington, principal of the Tuskegee Normal and Industrial Institute in Alabama and the most prominent Negro in America, privately spent thousands of dollars fighting disfranchisement and segregation laws; publicly he advocated a policy of accommodation, conciliation, and gradualism. Washington believed that by helping themselves, by creating and supporting their own businesses, by proving their usefulness to society through the acquisition of education, wealth, and morality, Negroes would earn the respect of the white man and thus eventually gain their constitutional rights.

Self-help and self-respect appeared a practical and sure, if gradual, way of ultimately achieving racial equality. Washington's doctrines also gained support because they appealed to race pride—if Negroes believed in themselves, stood together, and supported each other, they would be able to shape their destinies.

In the early years of the century, a small group of Negroes, led by W.E.B. Du Bois, formed the Niagara Movement to oppose Washington's program. Washington had put economic progress before politics, had accepted the separate-but-equal theory, and opposed agitation and protest. Du Bois and his followers stressed political activity as the basis of the Negro's future, insisted on the inequity of Jim Crow laws, and advocated agitation and protest.

In sharp language, the Niagara group placed responsibility for the race problem squarely on the whites. The aims of the movement were voting rights and "the abolition of all caste distinctions based simply on race and color."

Although Booker T. Washington tried to crush his critics, Du Bois and the Negro "radicals," as they were called, enlisted the support of a small group of influential white liberals and socialists. Together, in 1909-1910, they formed the National Association for the Advancement of Colored People.

The NAACP hammered at the walls of prejudice by organizing Negroes and well-disposed whites, by aiming propaganda at the whole nation, by taking legal action in courts and legislatures. Almost at the outset of its career, the NAACP prevailed upon the Supreme Court to declare unconstitutional two discriminatory statutes. In 1915, the Court struck down the Oklahoma "grandfather clause," a provision in several Southern state constitutions that, together with voting tests, had the effect of excluding from the vote those whose ancestors were ineligible to vote in 1860. Two years later, the Supreme Court outlawed residential segregation ordinances. These NAACP victories were the first legal steps in a long fight against disfranchisement and segregation.

During the first quarter of the 20th century, the federal government enacted no new legislation to ensure equal rights or opportunities for Negroes and made little attempt to enforce existing laws despite flagrant violations of Negro civil rights.

In 1913, members of Congress from the South introduced bills to federalize the Southern segregation policy. They wished to ban interracial marriages in the District of Columbia, segregate white and Negro federal employees, and introduce Jim Crow laws in the public carriers of the District. The bills did not pass, but segregation practices were extended in federal offices, shops, restrooms, and lunchrooms. The nation's capital became as segregated as any in the former Confederate states.

EAST ST. LOUIS, 1917

Elsewhere there was violence. In July 1917, in East St. Louis, a riot claimed the lives of 39 Negroes and nine whites, as a result of fear by white working men that Negro advances in economic, political and social status were threatening their own security and status.

When the labor force of an aluminum plant went on strike, the company hired Negro workers. A labor union delegation called on the mayor and asked that further migration of Negroes to East St. Louis be stopped. As the men were leaving City Hall, they heard that a Negro had accidentally shot a white man during a holdup. In a few minutes rumor had replaced fact: the shooting was intentional—a white woman had been insulted—two white girls were shot. By this time 3,000 people had congregated and were crying for vengeance. Mobs roamed the streets, beating Negroes. Policemen did little more than take the injured to hospitals and disarm Negroes.

The National Guard restored order. When the governor withdrew the troops, tensions were still high, and scattered episodes broke the peace. The press continued to emphasize the incidence of Negro crimes. White pickets and Negro workers at the aluminum company skirmished and, on July 1, some whites drove through the main Negro neighborhood firing into homes. Negro residents armed themselves. When a police car drove down the street Negroes riddled it with gunshot.

The next day a Negro was shot on the main street and a new riot was underway. The area became a "bloody half mile" for three or four hours; streetcars were stopped, and Negroes, without regard to age or sex, were pulled off and stoned, clubbed and kicked, and mob leaders calmly shot and killed Negroes who were lying in blood in the street. As the victims were placed in an ambulance, the crowds cheered and applauded.

Other rioters set fire to Negro homes, and by midnight the Negro section was in flames and Negroes were fleeing the city. There were 48 dead, hundreds injured, and more than 300 buildings destroyed.

World War I and Postwar Violence

When the United States entered World War I in 1917, the country again faced the question whether American citizens should have the right to serve, on an equal basis, in defense of their country. More than two million Negroes registered under the Selective Service Act, and some 360,000 were called into service.

The Navy rejected Negroes except as menials. The Marine Corps rejected them altogether. The Army formed them into separate units commanded, for the most part, by white officers. Only after great pressure did the Army permit Negro candidates to train as officers in a segregated camp. Mistreated at home and overseas, Negro combat units performed exceptionally well under French commanders, who refused to heed American warnings that Negroes were inferior people.

Negro soldiers returning home were mobbed for attempting to use facilities open to white soldiers. Of the 70 Negroes lynched during the first year after the war, a substantial number were soldiers. Some were lynched in uniform.

Reorganized in 1915, the Ku Klux Klan was flourishing again by 1919. Its program "for uniting native-born white Christians for concerted action in the preservation of American institutions and the supremacy of the white race," was implemented by flogging, branding with acid, tarring and feathering, hanging and burning. It destroyed the elemental rights of many Negroes, and of some whites.

Violence took the form of lynchings and riots, and major riots by whites against Negroes took place in 1917 in Chester, Pennsylvania, and Philadelphia; in 1919 in Washington, D.C., Omaha, Charleston, Longview, Texas, Chicago, and Knoxville; in 1921 in Tulsa.

The Chicago riot of 1919 flared from the increase in Negro population, which had more than doubled in 10 years. Jobs were plentiful, but housing was not. Black neighborhoods expanded into white sections of the city, and trouble developed. Between July 1917 and March 1921, 58 Negro houses were bombed, and recreational areas were sites of racial conflict.

The riot itself started on Sunday, July 27, with stone throwing and sporadic fighting at adjoining white and Negro beaches. A Negro boy swimming off the Negro beach drifted into water reserved for whites and drowned. Young Negroes claimed he had been struck by stones and demanded the arrest of a white man. Instead, police arrested a Negro. Negroes attacked policemen, and news spread to the city. White and Negro groups clashed in the streets, two persons died, and 50 were wounded. On Monday, Negroes coming home from work were attacked; later, when whites drove cars through Negro neighborhoods and fired weapons, Negroes retaliated. Twenty more were killed and hundreds wounded. On Tuesday, a handful more were dead, 129 injured. Rain began to fall; the mayor finally called in the state militia. After nearly a week of violence the city quieted down.

THE 1920's AND THE NEW MILITANCY

In the period between the two World Wars, the NAACP dominated the strategy of racial advancement. The NAACP drew its strength from large numbers of Southern Negroes who had migrated to Northern cities; from a small but growing Negro group of professionals and businessmen. It projected the image of the "New Negro," race-proud and self-reliant, believing in racial cooperation and self-help and determined to fight for his constitutional rights. This was reflected in the work of writers and artists known as the "Harlem Renaissance" who drew upon the Negro's own cultural tradition and experience. W. E. B. DuBois, editor of the *Crisis,* NAACP publication, symbolized the new mood and exerted great influence.

The NAACP did extraordinary service, giving legal defense to victims of race riots and unjust judicial proceedings. It obtained the release of the soldiers who had received life sentences on charges of rioting against intolerable conditions at Houston in 1917. It successfully defended Negro sharecroppers in Elaine, Arkansas, who in 1919 had banded together to gain fairer treatment, who had become the objects of a massive armed hunt by whites to put them "in their place," and who were charged with insurrection when they resisted. It secured the acquittal, with the help of Clarence Darrow, of Dr. Ossian Sweet and his family who had moved into a white neighborhood in Detroit, shot at a mob attacking their home, killed a man, and were eventually judged to have committed the act in self-defense.

Less successful were attempts to prevent school segregation in Northern cities. Gerrymandering of school boundaries and other devices by boards of education were fought with written petitions, verbal protests to school officials, legal suits and, in several cities, school boycotts. All proved of no avail.

The thrust of the NAACP was primarily political and legal, but the National Urban League, founded in 1911 by philanthropists and social workers, sought an economic solution to the Negroes' problems. Sympathetic with Booker T. Washington's point of view, believing in conciliation, gradualism, and moral suasion, the Urban League searched out industrial opportunities for Negro migrants to the cities, using arguments that appealed to the white businessman's sense of economic self-interest and also to his conscience.

Another important figure who espoused an economic program to ameliorate the Negroes' condition was A. Philip Randolph, an editor of the *Messenger*. He regarded the NAACP as a middle-class organization unconcerned about pressing economic problems. Taking a Marxist position on the causes of prejudice and discrimination, Randolph called for a new and radical Negro unafraid to demand his rights as a member of the working class. He advocated physical resistance to white mobs, but he believed that only united action of black and white workers against capitalists would achieve social justice.

Although Randolph addressed himself to the urban working masses, few of them ever read the *Messenger*. The one man who reached the masses of frustrated and disillusioned migrants in the Northern ghettos was Marcus Garvey.

Garvey, founder in 1914 of the Universal Negro Improvement Association (UNIA), aimed to liberate both Africans and American Negroes from their oppressors. His utopian method was the wholesale migration of American Negroes to Africa. Contending that whites would always be racist, he stressed racial pride and history, denounced integration, and insisted that the black man develop "a distinct racial type of civilization of his own and . . . work out his salvation in his motherland." On a more practical level he urged support of Negro businesses, and through the UNIA organized a chain of groceries, restaurants, laundries, a hotel, printing plant, and steamship line. When several prominent Negroes called the attention of the United States Government to irregularities in the management of the steamship line, Garvey was jailed, then deported for having used the mails to defraud.

But Garvey dramatized, as no one before, the bitterness and alienation of the Negro slum dwellers who, having come North with great expectations, found only overcrowded and deteriorated housing, mass unemployment, and race riots.

THE DEPRESSION

Negro labor, relatively unorganized and the target of discrimination and hostility, was hardly prepared for the depression of the 1930's. To a disproportionate extent, Negroes lost their jobs in cities and worked for starvation wages in rural areas. Although organizations like the National Urban League tried to improve employment opportunities, 65 percent of Negro employables were in need of public assistance by 1935.

Public assistance was given on a discriminatory basis, especially in the South. For a time Dallas and Houston gave no relief at all to Negro or Mexican families. In general, Negroes had more difficulty than whites in obtaining assistance, and the relief benefits were smaller. Some religious and charitable organizations excluded Negroes from their soup kitchens.

THE NEW DEAL

The New Deal marked a turning point in American race relations. Negroes found much in the New Deal to complain about: discrimination existed in many agencies; federal housing programs expanded urban ghettos; money from the Agricultural Adjustment Administration went in the South chiefly to white landowners, while crop restrictions forced many Negro sharecroppers off the land. Nevertheless, Negroes shared in relief, jobs, and public housing, and Negro leaders, who felt the open sympathy of many highly placed New Dealers, held more prominent political positions than at any time since President Taft's administration. The creation of the Congress of Industrial Organizations (CIO), with its avowed philosophy of non-discrimination, made the notion of an alliance of black and white workers something more than a visionary's dream.

The depression, the New Deal, and the CIO reoriented Negro protest to concern with economic problems. Negroes conducted "Don't Buy Where You Can't Work" campaigns in a number of cities, boycotted and picketed commercial establishments owned by whites, and sought equality in American society through an alliance with white labor.

The NAACP came under attack from some Negroes. Du Bois resigned as editor of the *Crisis* in 1934 in part because he believed in the value of collective racial economic endeavor and saw little point in protesting disfranchisement and segregation without more actively pursuing economic goals. Younger critics also disagreed with NAACP's gradualism on economic issues.

Undeterred, the NAACP broadened the scope of its legal work, fought a vigorous though unsuccessful campaign to abolish the poll tax, and finally won its attack on the white primaries in 1944 through the Supreme Court. But the heart of its litigation was a long-range campaign against segregation and the most obvious inequities in the Southern school systems: the lack of professional and graduate schools and the low salaries received by Negro teachers. Not until about 1950 would the NAACP make a direct assault against school segregation on the legal ground that separate facilities were inherently unequal.

WORLD WAR II

During World War II, Negroes learned again that fighting for their country brought them no nearer to full citizenship. Rejected when they tried to enlist, they were accepted into the Army according to the proportion of the Negro population to that of the country as a whole—but only in separate units—and those mostly noncombat. The United States thus fought racism in Europe with a segregated fighting force. The Red Cross, with the government's approval, separated Negro and white blood in banks established for wounded servicemen—even though the blood banks were largely the work of a Negro physician, Charles Drew.

Not until 1949 would the Armed Forces begin to adopt a firm policy against segregation.

Negroes seeking employment in defense industries were embittered by policies like that of a West Coast aviation factory which declared openly that "the Negro will be considered only as janitors and in other similar capacities. . . . Regardless of their training as aircraft workers, we will not employ them."

Two new movements marked Negro protest: the March on Washington, and the Congress of Racial Equality (CORE). In 1941, consciously drawing on the power of the Negro vote and concerned with the economic problems of the urban slum-dweller, A. Philip Randolph threatened a mass Negro convergence on Washington unless President Roosevelt secured employment for Negroes in the defense industries. The President's Executive Order 8802 establishing a federal Fair Employment Practices Commission forestalled the demonstration. Even without enforcement powers, the FEPC set a precedent for treating fair employment practice as a civil right.

CORE, founded in 1942-43, grew out of the Fellowship of Reconciliation, a pacifist organization, when certain leaders became interested in the use of nonviolent direct action to fight racial discrimination. CORE combined Gandhi's techniques with the sit-in, derived from the sit-down strikes of the 1930's. Until about 1959, CORE's main activity was attacking discrimination in places of public accommodation in the cities of the Northern and Border states, and as late as 1961, two-thirds of its membership and most of its national officers were white.

223

Meanwhile, wartime racial disorders had broken out sporadically—in Mobile, Los Angeles, Beaumont, Texas, and elsewhere. The riot in Detroit in 1943 was the most destructive. The Negro population in the city had risen sharply and more than 50,000 recent arrivals put immense pressures on the housing market. Neighborhood turnover at the edge of the ghetto bred bitterness and sometimes violence, and recreational areas became centers of racial abrasion. The federal regulations requiring employment standards in defense industries also angered whites, and several unauthorized walk-outs had occurred in automobile plants after Negro workers were upgraded. Activities in the city of several leading spokesmen for white supremacy—Gerald L. K. Smith, Frank J. Norris, and Father Charles Coughlin—inflamed many white southerners who migrated to Detroit during the war.

On Sunday, June 20, rioting broke out on Belle Isle, a recreational spot used by both races, but predominantly by Negroes. Fist fights escalated into a major conflict. The first wave of looting and bloodshed began in the Negro ghetto "Paradise Valley" and later spread to other sections of the city. Whites began attacking Negroes as they emerged from the city's all-night movie theatres in the downtown area. White forays into Negro residential areas by car were met by gunfire. By the time federal troops arrived to halt the racial conflict, 25 Negroes and nine whites were dead, property damage exceeded $2 million, and a legacy of fear and hate descended on the city.

In Harlem, New York, a riot erupted also in 1943, following the attempt of a white policeman to arrest a Negro woman defended by a Negro soldier. Negro rioters assaulted white passersby, overturned parked automobiles, tossed bricks and bottles at policemen, but the major emphasis was on destroying property, looting and burning stores. Six persons died, over 500 were injured, more than 100 were jailed.

THE POSTWAR PERIOD

White opinion in some quarters of America had begun to shift to a more sympathetic regard for Negroes during the New Deal, and the war had accelerated that movement. Thoughtful whites had been painfully aware of the contradiction in opposing Nazi racial philosophy with racially segregated military units. In the postwar years, American racial attitudes became more liberal as new nonwhite nations emerged in

224

Asia and Africa and took increasing responsibilities in international councils.

Against this background, the growing size of the Northern Negro vote made civil rights a major issue in national elections and, ultimately, in 1957, led to the establishment of the federal Civil Rights Commission, which had the power to investigate discriminatory conditions throughout the country and to recommend corrective measures to the President. Northern and Western states outlawed discrimination in employment, housing, and public accommodations, while the NAACP, in successive court victories, won judgments against racially restrictive covenants in housing, segregation in interstate transportation, and discrimination in publicly-owned recreational facilities. The NAACP helped register voters, and in 1954, *Brown* v. *Board of Education* became the triumphant climax to the NAACP's campaign against educational segregation in the public schools of the South.

CORE, which had been conducting demonstrations in the Border states, its major focus on public accommodations, began experimenting with direct-action techniques to open employment opportunities. In 1947, in conjunction with the Fellowship of Reconciliation, CORE conducted a "Journey of Reconciliation"—what would later be called a "Freedom Ride" —in the states of the Upper South to test compliance with the Supreme Court decision outlawing segregation on interstate buses. The resistance met by riders in some areas, the sentencing of two of them to 30 days on a North Carolina road gang, dramatized the gap between American democratic theory and practice.

But what captured the imagination of the nation and of the Negro community in particular, and what was chiefly responsible for the growing use of direct-action techniques, was the Montgomery, Alabama, bus boycott of 1955-1956, which catapulted into national prominence the Reverend Martin Luther King, Jr. Like the founders of CORE, King held to a Gandhian belief in the principles of pacifism.

Even before a court decision obtained by NAACP attorneys in November 1956 desegregated the Montgomery buses, a similar movement had started in Tallahassee, Florida. Afterward another one developed in Birmingham, Alabama. In 1957, the Tuskegee Negroes undertook a three-year boycott of local merchants after the state legislature gerrymandered nearly all of the Negro voters outside of the town's boundaries. In response to a lawsuit filed by the NAACP, the

225

Supreme Court ruled the Tuskegee gerrymander illegal.

These events were widely heralded. The "new Negro" had emerged in the South—militant, no longer fearful of white hoodlums or mobs, and ready to use his collective weight to achieve his ends. In this mood, King established the Southern Christian Leadership Conference in 1957 to coordinate direct-action activities in Southern cities.

Nonviolent direct action attained popularity not only because of the effectiveness of King's leadership but because the older techniques of legal and legislative action had had limited success. Impressive as the advances in the 15 years after World War II were, in spite of state laws and Supreme Court decisions, something was still clearly wrong. Negroes were disfranchised in most of the South, though in the 12 years following the outlawing of the white primary in 1944, the number of Negroes registered in Southern states had risen from about 250,000 to nearly a million and a quarter. Supreme Court decisions desegregating transportation facilities were still being largely ignored in the South. Discrimination in employment and housing continued, not only in the South but also in Northern states with model civil rights laws. The Negro unemployment rate steadily moved upward after 1954. The South reacted to the Supreme Court's decision on school desegregation by attempting to outlaw the NAACP, intimidating civil rights leaders, bringing "massive resistance" to the Court's decision, curtailing Negro voter registration, and forming White Citizens' Councils.

REVOLUTION OF RISING EXPECTATIONS

At the same time, Negro attitudes were changing. In what has been described as a "revolution in expectations," Negroes were gaining a new sense of self-respect and a new self-image as a result of the civil rights movement and their own advancement. King and others were demonstrating that nonviolent direct action could succeed in the South. New laws and court decisions and increasing support of white public opinion gave American Negroes a new confidence in the future.

Negroes no longer felt that they had to accept the humiliations of second-class citizenship. Ironically, it was the very successes in the legislatures and the courts that, more perhaps than any other single factor, led to intensified Negro expectations and resulting dissatisfaction with the limitations of legal and legislative programs. Increasing Negro impatience ac-

226

counted for the rising tempo of nonviolent direct action in the late 1950's, culminating in the student sit-ins of 1960 and the inauguration of what is popularly known as the "Civil Rights Revolution" or the "Negro Revolt."

Many believe that the Montgomery boycott ushered in this Negro Revolt, and there is no doubt that, in projecting the image of King and his techniques, it had great importance. But the decisive break with traditional techniques came with the college student sit-ins that swept the South in the winter and spring of 1960. In dozens of communities in the Upper South, the Atlantic coastal states, and Texas, student demonstrations secured the desegregation of lunch counters in drug and variety stores. Arrests were numbered in the thousands, and brutality was evident in scores of communities. In the Deep South the campaign ended in failure, even in instances where hundreds had been arrested, as in Montgomery; Orangeburg, South Carolina; and Baton Rouge. But the youth had captured the imagination of the Negro community and to a remarkable extent of the whole nation.

STUDENT INVOLVEMENT

The Negro protest movement would never be the same again. The Southern college students shook the power structure of the Negro community, made direct action temporarily pre-eminent as a civil rights tactic, speeded up the process of social change in race relations, and ultimately turned the Negro protest organizations toward a deep concern with the economic and social problems of the masses.

Involved in this was a gradual shift in both tactics and goals: from legal to direct action, from middle and upper class to mass action, from attempts to guarantee the Negro's constitutional rights to efforts to secure economic policies giving him equality of opportunity, from appeals to the sense of fair play of white Americans to demands based upon power in the black ghetto.

The successes of the student movement threatened existing Negro leadership and precipitated a spirited rivalry among civil rights oragnizations. The NAACP and SCLC associated themselves with the student movement. The organizing meeting of the Student Nonviolent Coordinating Committee (SNCC) at Raleigh, North Carolina, in April 1960 was called by Martin Luther King, but within a year the youth considered King too cautious and broke with him.

The NAACP now decided to make direct action a major

227

part of its strategy and organized and reactivated college and youth chapters in the Southern and Border states.

CORE, still unknown to the general public, installed James Farmer as national director in January 1961, and that spring joined the front rank of civil rights organizations with the famous Freedom Ride to Alabama and Mississippi that dramatized the persistence of segregated public transportation. A bus-burning resulted in Alabama, and hundreds of demonstrators spent a month or more in Mississippi prisons. Finally, a new order from the Interstate Commerce Commission desegregating all interstate transportation facilities received partial compliance.

ORGANIZATIONAL DIFFERENCES

Disagreement over strategy and tactics inevitably became intertwined with personal and organizational rivalries. Each civil rights group felt the need for proper credit in order to obtain the prestige and financial contributions necessary to maintain and expand its own programs. The local and national, individual and organizational clashes only stimulated competition and activity that further accelerated the pace of social change.

Yet there were differences in style. CORE was the most interracial. SCLC appeared to be the most deliberate. SNCC staff workers lived on subsistence allowances and seemed to regard going to jail as a way of life. The NAACP continued the most varied programs, retaining a strong emphasis on court litigation, maintaining a highly effective lobby at the national capital, and engaging in direct-action campaigns. The National Urban League, under the leadership of Whitney M. Young, Jr., appointed executive director in 1961, became more outspoken and talked more firmly to businessmen who had previously been treated with utmost tact and caution.

The role of whites in the protest movement gradually changed. Instead of occupying positions of leadership, they found themselves relegated to the role of followers. Whites were likely to be suspect in the activist organizations. Negroes had come to feel less dependent on whites, more confident of their own power, and they demanded that their leaders be black. The NAACP had long since acquired Negro leadership but continued to welcome white liberal support. SCLC and SNCC were from the start Negro-led and Negro-dominated. CORE became predominantly Negro as it expanded in 1962

228

and 1963; today all executives are Negro, and a constitutional amendment adopted in 1965 officially limited white leadership in the chapters.

A major factor intensifying the civil rights movement was widespread Negro unemployment and poverty; an important force in awakening Negro protest was the meteoric rise to national prominence of the Black Muslims, established around 1930. The organization reached the peak of its influence when more progress toward equal rights was being made than ever before in American history, while at the same time the poorest groups in the urban ghettos were stagnating.

The Black Muslims preached a vision of the doom of the white "devils" and the coming dominance of the black man, promised a utopian paradise of a separate territory within the United States for a Negro state, and offered a practical program of building Negro business through hard work, thrift, and racial unity. To those willing to submit to the rigid discipline of the movement, the Black Muslims organization gave a sense of purpose and dignity.

"Freedom Now!" and Civil Rights Laws

As the direct-action tactics took more dramatic form, as the civil rights groups began to articulate the needs of the masses and draw some of them to their demonstrations, the protest movement in 1963 assumed a new note of urgency, a demand for complete "Freedom Now!" Direct action returned to the Northern cities, taking the form of massive protests against economic, housing and educational inequities, and a fresh wave of demonstrations swept the South from Cambridge, Maryland, to Birmingham, Alabama. Northern Negroes launched street demonstrations against discrimination in the building trade unions and, the following winter, school boycotts against de facto segregation.

In the North, 1963 and 1964 brought the beginning of the waves of civil disorders in Northern urban centers. In the South, incidents occurred of brutal white resistance to the civil rights movement, beginning with the murders of Mississippi Negro leader Medgar Evers and four Negro schoolgirls in a church in Birmingham. These disorders and the events in the South are detailed in the introduction to Chapter 1, the *Profiles of Disorder*.

The massive anti-Negro resistance in Birmingham and numerous other Southern cities during the spring of 1963, compelled the nation to face the problem of race prejudice in the South. President Kennedy affirmed that racial discrimination was a moral issue and asked Congress for a major civil rights bill. But a major impetus for what was to be the Civil Rights Act of 1964 was the March on Washington in August 1963.

Early in the year, A. Philip Randolph issued a call for a March on Washington to dramatize the need for jobs and to press for a federal commitment to job action. At about the same time, Protestant, Jewish, and Catholic churches sought and obtained representation on the March committee. Although the AFL-CIO national council refused to endorse the March, a number of labor leaders and international unions participated.

Reversing an earlier stand, President Kennedy approved the March. A quarter of a million people, about 20 percent of them white, participated. It was more than a summation of the past years of struggle and aspiration. It symbolized certain new directions: a deeper concern for the economic problems of the masses; more involvement of white moderates; and new demands from the most militant, who implied that only a revolutionary change in American institutions would permit Negroes to achieve the dignity of citizens.

President Kennedy had set the stage for the Civil Rights Act of 1964. After his death President Johnson took forceful and effective action to secure its enactment. The law settled the public accommodations issue in the South's major cities. Its voting section, however, promised more than it could accomplish. Martin Luther King and SCLC dramatized the issue locally with demonstrations at Selma, Alabama, in the spring of 1965. Again the national government was forced to intervene, and a new and more effective voting law was passed.

FAILURES OF DIRECT ACTION

Birmingham had made direct action respectable, but Selma, which drew thousands of white moderates from the North, made direct action fashionable. Yet as early as 1964, it was becoming evident that, like legal action, direct action was of limited usefulness.

In deep South states like Mississippi and Alabama, direct action had failed to desegregate public accommodations in the sit-ins of 1960-1961. A major reason was that Negroes lacked the leverage of the vote. The demonstrations of the early 1960's had been successful principally in places like Atlanta, Nashville, Durham, Winston-Salem, Louisville, Savannah, New Orleans, Charleston, and Dallas—where Negroes voted and could swing elections. Beginning in 1961 Robert Moses of SNCC, with the cooperation of CORE and NAACP, established voter registration projects in the cities and county seats of Mississippi. He succeeded in registering only a handful of Negroes, but by 1964, he had generated enough support throughout the country to enable the Mississippi Freedom Democratic Party, which he had created, to challenge dramatically the seating of the official white delegates from the state at the Democratic National Convention.

In the black ghettos of the North direct action also largely failed. Street demonstrations did compel employers, from supermarkets to banks, to add Negroes to their work force in Northern and Western cities, and even in some Southern cities where the Negroes had considerable buying power. However, separate and inferior schools, slum housing, and police hostility proved invulnerable to direct attack.

NEW DIRECTIONS

But while Negroes were being hired in increasing numbers, mass unemployment and underemployment remained. As economist Vivian Henderson pointed out in his testimony before the Commission:

> No one can deny that all Negroes have benefited from civil rights laws and desegregation in public life in one way or another. The fact is, however, that the masses of Negroes have not experienced tangible benefits in a significant way. This is so in education and housing. It is critically so in the area of jobs and economic security. Expectations of Negro masses for equal job opportunity programs have fallen far short of fulfillment.
>
> Negroes have made gains. . . . There have been important gains. But . . . the masses of Negroes have been virtually untouched by those gains.

Faced with the intransigence of the deep South and the inadequacy of direct action to solve the problems of the slum dwellers, Negro protest organizations began to diverge. The momentum toward unity, apparent in 1963, was lost. At the very time that white support for the protest movement was rising markedly, militant Negroes felt increasingly isolated from the American scene. On two things, however, all segments of the protest movement agreed: (1) future civil rights

231

activity would have to focus on the economic and social discrimination in the urban ghettos and (2) while demonstrations would still have a place, the major weapon would have to be the political potential of the black masses.

By the middle of the decade, many militant Negro members of SNCC and CORE began to turn away from American society and the "middle-class way of life." Cynical about the liberals and the leaders of organized labor, they regarded compromise, even as a temporary tactical device, as anathema. They talked more of "revolutionary" changes in the social structure, of retaliatory violence, and increasingly rejected white assistance. They insisted that Negro power alone could compel the white "ruling class" to make concessions. Yet they also spoke of an alliance of Negroes and unorganized lower-class whites to overthrow the "power structure" of capitalists, politicians and bureaucratic labor leaders who exploited the poor of both races by dividing them through an appeal to race prejudice.

At the same time that their activities declined, other issues, particularly Vietnam, diverted the attention of the country, including some Negro leaders, from the issue of equality. In civil rights organizations, reduced financing made it increasingly difficult to support staff personnel. Most important was the increasing frustration of expectations that affected the direct-action advocates of the early 1960's—the sense of futility growing out of the feeling that progress had turned out to be "tokenism," that the compromises of the white community were sedatives rather than solutions and that the current methods of Negro protest were doing little for the masses of the race.

As frustration grew, the ideology and rhetoric of a number of civil rights activists became angrier. One man more than any other—a black man who grew up believing whites had murdered his father—became the spokesman for this anger: Malcolm X, who perhaps best embodied the belief that racism was so deeply ingrained in white America that appeals to conscience would bring no fundamental change.

"Black Power"

In this setting the rhetoric of "Black Power" developed. The precipitating occasion was the Meredith March from Memphis to Jackson in June 1966, but the slogan expressed tendencies that had been present for a long time and had been gaining strength in the Negro community.

Black Power first articulated a mood rather than a program —disillusionment and alienation from white America and independence, race pride, and self-respect, or "black consciousness." Having become a household phrase, the term generated intense discussion of its real meaning, and a broad spectrum of ideologies and programmatic proposals emerged.

In politics, Black Power meant independent action—Negro control of the political power of the black ghettos and its use to improve economic and social conditions. It could take the form of organizing a black political party or controlling the political machinery within the ghetto without the guidance or support of white politicians. Where predominantly Negro areas lacked Negroes in elective office, whether in the rural Black Belt of the South or in the urban centers, Black Power advocates sought the election of Negroes by voter registration campaigns, by getting out the vote, and by working for redrawing electoral districts. The basic belief was that only a well-organized and cohesive bloc of Negro voters could provide for the needs of the black masses. Even some Negro politicians allied to the major political parties adopted the term "Black Power" to describe their interest in the Negro vote.

In economic terms, Black Power meant creating independent, self-sufficient Negro business enterprise, not only by encouraging Negro entrepreneurs but also by forming Negro cooperatives in the ghettos and in the predominantly black rural counties of the South. In the area of education, Black Power called for local community control of the public schools in the black ghettos.

Throughout, the emphasis was on self-help, racial unity, and, among the most militant, retaliatory violence, the latter ranging from the legal right of self-defense to attempts to justify looting and arson in ghetto riots, guerrilla warfare and armed rebellion.

Phrases like "Black Power," "Black Consciousness," and "Black is Beautiful," enjoyed an extensive currency in the Negro community, even within the NAACP and among relatively conservative politicians, but particularly among young intellectuals and Afro-American student groups on predominantly white college campuses. Expressed in its most extreme form by small, often local, fringe groups, the Black Power ideology became associated with SNCC and CORE.

Generally regarded as the most militant among the important Negro protest organizations, they have developed different interpretations of the Black Power doctrine. SNCC calls for totally independent political action outside the established political parties, as with the Black Panther Party in Lowndes County, Ala.; rejects political alliances with other groups until Negroes have themselves built a substantial base of independent political power; applauds the idea of guerrilla warfare; and regards riots as rebellions.

CORE has been more flexible. Approving the SNCC strategy, it also advocates working within the Democratic Party; forming alliances with other groups and, while seeking to justify riots as the natural explosion of an oppressed people against intolerable conditions, advocates violence only in self-defense. Both groups favor cooperatives, but CORE has seemed more inclined toward job-training programs and developing a Negro entrepreneurial class, based upon the market within the black ghettos.

OLD WINE IN NEW BOTTLES

What is new about "Black Power" is phraseology rather than substance. Black Consciousness has roots in the organization of Negro churches and mutual benefit societies in the early days of the republic, the antebellum Negro convention movement, the Negro colonization schemes of the 19th century, Du Bois' concept of Pan-Africanism, Booker T. Washington's advocacy of race pride, self-help, and racial solidarity, the Harlem Renaissance, and the Garvey movement. The decade after World War I—which saw the militant, race-proud "new Negro," the relatively widespread theory of retaliatory violence, and the high tide of the Negro-support-of-Negro-business ideology—exhibits striking parallels with the 1960's.

The theme of retaliatory violence is hardly new for American Negroes. Most racial disorders in American history until recent years, were characterized by white attacks on Negroes. But Negroes retaliated violently in the past.

Black Power rhetoric and ideology actually express a lack of power. The slogan emerged when the Negro protest movement was slowing down, when it was finding increasing resistance to its changing goals, when it discovered that nonviolent direct action was no more a panacea than legal action, when CORE and SNCC were declining in terms of activity, membership, and financial support. This combination of circumstances provoked anger deepened by impotence. Powerless to make any fundamental changes in the life of the masses—powerless, that is, to compel white America to make those changes—many advocates of Black Power have retreated into an unreal world, where they see an outnumbered and poverty-stricken minority organizing itself separately from whites

234

and creating sufficient power to force white America to grant its demands. To date, the evidence suggests that the situation is much like that of the 1840's, when a small group of intellectuals advocated slave insurrections, but stopped short of organizing them.

The Black Power advocates of today consciously feel that they are the most militant group in the Negro protest movement. Yet they have retreated from a direct confrontation with American society on the issue of integration and, by preaching separatism, unconsciously function as an accommodation to white racism. Much of their economic program, as well as their interest in Negro history, self-help, racial solidarity and separation, is reminiscent of Booker T. Washington. The rhetoric is different, but the ideas are remarkably similar.

THE MEANING

By 1967, whites could point to the demise of slavery, the decline of illiteracy among Negroes, the legal protection provided by the constitutional amendments and civil rights legislation, and the growing size of the Negro middle class. Whites would call it Negro progress from slavery to freedom toward equality.

Negroes could point to the doctrine of white supremacy, its widespread acceptance, its persistence after emancipation, and its influence on the definition of the place of Negroes in American life. They could point to their long fight for full citizenship, when they had active opposition from most of the white population and little or no support from the government. They could see progress toward equality accompanied by bitter resistance. Perhaps most of all, they could feel the persistent, pervasive racism that kept them in inferior segregated schools, restricted them to ghettos, barred them from fair employment, provided double standards in courts of justice, inflicted bodily harm on their children, and blighted their lives with a sense of hopelessness and despair.

In all of this and in the context of professed ideals, Negroes would find more retrogression than progress, more rejection than acceptance.

Until the middle of the 20th century, the course of Negro protest movements in the United States, except for slave revolts, was based in the cities of the North, where Negroes enjoyed sufficient freedom to mount a sustained protest. It was in the cities, North and South, that Negroes had their greatest independence and mobility. It was natural, therefore, for black protest movements to be urban-based—and, until the last dozen years or so, limited to the North. As Negroes migrated from the South, the mounting strength of their votes in Northern cities became a vital element in drawing the federal government into the defense of the civil rights of Southern Negroes. White rural Negroes today face great racial problems, the major unsolved questions that touch the core of Negro life stem from discrimination embedded in urban housing, employment, and education.

Over the years the character of Negro protest has changed. Originally it was a white liberal and Negro upper class movement aimed at securing the constitutional rights of Negroes through propaganda, lawsuits, and legislation. In recent years the emphasis in tactics shifted first to direct action and then—among the most militant—to the rhetoric of "Black Power." The role of white liberals declined as Negroes came to direct the struggle. At the same time the Negro protest movement became more of a mass movement, with increasing participation from the working classes. As these changes were occurring, and while substantial progress was being made to secure constitutional rights for the Negroes, the goals of-the movement were broadened. Protest groups now demand special efforts to overcome the Negro's poverty and cultural deprivation—conditions that cannot be erased simply by ensuring constitutional rights.

The central thrust of Negro protest in the current period has aimed at the inclusion of Negroes in American society on a basis of full equality rather than at a fundamental transformation of American institutions. There have been elements calling for a revolutionary overthrow of the American social system or for a complete withdrawal of Negroes from American society. But these solutions have had little popular support. Negro protest, for the most part, has been firmly rooted in the basic values of American society, seeking not their destruction but their fulfillment.

Chapter 6 / The Formation of the Racial Ghettos

MAJOR TRENDS IN NEGRO POPULATION

Throughout the 20th century, and particularly in the last three decades, the Negro population of the United States has been steadily moving from rural areas to urban, from South to North and West.

In 1910, 2.7 million Negroes lived in American cities— 28 percent of the nation's Negro population of 9.8 million.

Today, about 15 million Negro Americans live in metropolitan areas, or 69 percent of the Negro population of 21.5 million. In 1910, 885,000 Negroes—9 percent—lived outside the South. Now, almost 10 million, about 45 percent, live in the North or West.

These shifts in population have resulted from three basic trends:

- A rapid increase in the size of the Negro population.
- A continuous flow of Negroes from Southern rural areas, partly to large cities in the South, but primarly to large cities in the North and West.
- An increasing concentration of Negroes in large metropolitan areas within racially segregated neighborhoods.

Taken together, these trends have produced large and constantly growing concentrations of Negro population within big cities in all parts of the nation. Because most major civil disorders of recent years occurred in predominantly Negro neighborhoods, we have examined the causes of this concentration.

THE GROWTH RATE OF THE NEGRO POPULATION

During the first half of this century, the white population of the United States grew at a slightly faster rate than the Negro population. Because fertility rates[1] among Negro women were more than offset by death rates among Negroes and by large-scale immigration of whites from Europe, the proportion of Negroes in the country declined from 12 percent in 1900 to 10 percent in 1940.

By the end of World War II—and increasingly since then—major advances in medicine and medical care, together with the increasing youth of the Negro population resulting from higher fertility rates, caused death rates among Negroes to fall much faster than among whites. This is shown in the following table:

Year	Death Rate/1,000 Population Whites	Nonwhites	Ratio of Nonwhite Rate to White Rate
1900	17.0	25 0	1.47
1940	10.4	13.8	1.33
1965	9.4	9.6	1.02

In addition, white immigration from outside the United States dropped dramatically after stringent restrictions were adopted in the 1920's.

[1] The "fertility rate" is the number of live births per year per 1,000 women age 15 to 44 in the group concerned.

Twenty-Year Period	Total Immigration (millions)
1901-1920	14.5
1921-1940	4.6
1941-1960	3.6

Thus, by mid-century, both factors which previously had offset higher fertility rates among Negro women no longer were in effect.

While Negro fertility rates, after rising rapidly to 1957, have declined sharply in the past decade, white fertility rates have dropped even more, leaving Negro rates much higher in comparison.

Year	Live Births Per 1,000 Women Aged 15-44		Ratio of Nonwhite to White
	White	Nonwhite	
1940	77.1	102.4	1.33
1957	117.4	163.4	1.39
1965	91.4	133.9	1.46

The result is that Negro population is now growing significantly faster than white population. From 1940 to 1960, the white population rose 34.0 percent, but the Negro population rose 46.6 percent. From 1960 to 1966, the white population grew 7.6 percent; whereas Negro population jumped 14.4 percent, almost twice as much.

Consequently, the proportion of Negroes in the total population has risen from 10.0 percent in 1950 to 10.5 percent in 1960, and 11.1 percent in 1966.[2]

In 1950, at least one of every ten Americans was Negro; in 1966, one of nine. If this trend continues, one of every eight Americans will be Negro by 1972.

Another consequence of higher birth rates among Negroes is that the Negro population is considerably younger than the white population. In 1966, the median age among whites was 29.1 years, as compared to 21.1 among Negroes. About 35 percent of the white population was under 18 years of age, compared with 45 percent for Negroes. About one of every six children under five and one of every six new babies are Negro.

Negro-white fertility rates bear an interesting relationship to educational experience. Negro women with low levels of education have more children than white women with similar schooling, while Negro women with four years or more of college education have fewer children than white women similarly educated. The following table illustrates this:

[2] These proportions are undoubtedly too low because the Census Bureau has consistently undercounted the number of Negroes in the U. S. by as much as 10 percent.

Education Level Attained	Number of Children Ever Born to All Women (Married or Unmarried) 35-39 Years Old, by Level of Education (Based on 1960 Census)	
	Nonwhite	White
Completed elementary school	3.0	2.8
Four years of high school	2.3	2.3
Four years of college	1.7	2.2
Five years or more of college	1.2	1.6

This suggests that the difference between Negro and white fertility rates may decline in the future if Negro educational attainment compares more closely with that of whites, and if a rising proportion of members of both groups complete college.

The Migration of Negroes from the South

The Magnitude of This Migration

In 1910, 91 percent of the nation's 9.8 million Negroes lived in the South. Twenty-seven percent of American Negroes lived in cities of 2,500 persons or more, as compared to 49 percent of the nation's white population.

By 1966, the Negro population had increased to 21.5 million, and two significant geographic shifts had taken place. The proportion of Negroes living in the South had dropped to 55 percent and about 69 percent of all Negroes lived in metropolitan areas compared to 64 percent for whites. While the total Negro population more than doubled from 1910 to 1966, the number living in cities rose five-fold (from 2.7 million to 14.8 million) and the number outside the South rose eleven-fold (from 885,000 to 9.7 million).

Negro migration from the South began after the Civil War. By the turn of the century, sizeable Negro populations lived in many large Northern cities—Philadelphia, for example, had 63,400 Negro residents in 1900. The movement of Negroes out of the rural South accelerated during World War I, when floods and boll weevils hurt farming in the South, and the industrial demands of the war created thousands of new jobs for unskilled workers in the North. After the war, the shift to mechanized farming spurred the continuing movement of Negroes from rural Southern areas.

The Depression slowed this migratory flow, but World War II set it in motion again. More recently, continuing mechanization of agriculture and the expansion of industrial employment in Northern and Western cities have served to sustain the movement of Negroes out of the South, although at a slightly lower rate.

Period	Net Negro Out-migration from the South	Annual Average Rate
1910-1920	454,000	45,400
1920-1930	749,000	74,900
1930-1940	348,000	34,800
1940-1950	1,597,000	159,700
1950-1960	1,457,000	145,700
1960-1966	613,000	102,500

From 1960 to 1963, annual Negro out-migration actually dropped to 78,000 but then rose to over 125,000 from 1963 to 1966.

Important Characteristics of this Migration

It is useful to recall that even the latest scale of Negro migration is relatively small when compared to the earlier waves of European immigrants. A total of 8.8 million immigrants entered the United States between 1901 and 1911, and another 5.7 million arrived during the following decade. Even during the years from 1960 through 1966, the 1.8 million immigrants from abroad were almost three times the 613,000 Negroes who departed the South. In these same six years, California alone gained over 1.5 million new residents from internal shifts of American population.

Three major routes of Negro migration from the South have developed. One runs north along the Atlantic Seaboard toward Boston, another north from Mississippi toward Chicago, and the third west from Texas and Louisiana toward California. Between 1955 and 1960, 50 percent of the nonwhite migrants to the New York metropolitan area came from North Carolina, South Carolina, Virginia, Georgia, and Alabama; North Carolina alone supplied 20 percent of all New York's nonwhite immigrants. During the same period, almost 60 percent of the nonwhite migrants to Chicago came from Mississippi, Tennessee, Arkansas, Alabama, and Louisiana; Mississippi accounted for almost one-third. During these years, three-fourths of the nonwhite migrants to Los Angeles came from Texas, Louisiana, Mississippi, Arkansas, and Alabama.

The flow of Negroes from the South has caused the Negro population to grow more rapidly in the North and West, as indicated below.

Total Negro Population Gains (Millions)

Period	North & West	South	Percent of Gain In North & West
1940-1950	1.859	0.321	85.2%
1950-1960	2.741	1.086	71.6%
1960-1966	2.119	0.517	80.4%

As a result, although a much higher proportion of Negroes still reside in the South, the distribution of Negroes throughout the United States is beginning to approximate that of whites, as the following tables show.

Percent Distribution of the Population By Region—1950, 1960 and 1966

	Negro			White		
	1950	1960	1966	1950	1960[3]	1966
United States	100	100	100	100	100	100
South	68	60	55	27	27	28
North	28	34	37	59	56	55
Northeast	13	16	17	28	26	26
North-central	15	18	20	31	30	29
West	4	6	8	14	16	17

Negroes as a Percentage of the Total Population in the United States and Each Region 1950, 1960, and 1966

	1950	1960	1966
United States	10	11	11
South	22	21	20
North	5	7	8
West	3	4	5

Negroes in the North and West are now so numerous that natural increase rather than migration provides the greater part of Negro population gains there. And even though Negro migration has continued at a high level, it comprises a constantly declining proportion of Negro growth in these regions.

Period	Percentage of Total North & West Negro Gain From Southern In-migration
1940-1950	85.9%
1950-1960	53.1%
1960-1966	28.9%

In other words, we have reached the point where the Negro populations of the North and West will continue to expand significantly even if migration from the South drops substantially.

[3] Rounds to 99.

Future Migration

Despite accelerating Negro migration from the South, the Negro population there has continued to rise.

Date	Negro Population in the South (millions)	Change from Preceding Date Total	Annual Average
1940	9.9	—	—
1950	10.2	321,000	32,100
1960	11.3	1,086,000	108,600
1966	11.8	517,000	86,200

Nor is it likely to halt. Negro birth rates in the South, as elsewhere, have fallen sharply since 1957, but so far, this decline has been offset by the rising Negro population base remaining in the South. From 1950 to 1960, Southern Negro births generated an average net increase of 254,000 per year, and from 1960 to 1966, an almost identical 188,000 per year. Even if Negro birth rates continue to fall, they are likely to remain high enough to support significant migration to other regions for some time to come.

The Negro population in the South is becoming increasingly urbanized. In 1950, there were 5.4 million Southern rural Negroes; by 1960, 4.8 million. But this decline has been more than offset by increases in the urban population. A rising proportion of inter-regional migration now consists of persons moving from one city to another. From 1960 to 1966, rural Negro population in the South was far below its peak, but the annual average migration of Negroes from the South was still substantial.

These facts demonstrate that Negro migration from the South, which has maintained a high rate for the past 60 years, will continue, unless economic conditions change dramatically in either the South or the North and West. This conclusion is reinforced by the fact that most Southern states in recent decades have also experienced outflows of white population. From 1950 to 1960, 11 of the 17 Southern states (including the District of Columbia) "exported" white population—as compared to 13 which "exported" Negro population. Excluding Florida's net gain by migration of 1.5 million, the other 16 Southern states together had a net loss by migration of 1.46 million whites.

THE CONCENTRATION OF NEGRO POPULATION IN LARGE CITIES

Where Negro Urbanization Has Occurred

Statistically, the Negro population in America has become more urbanized, and more metropolitan, than the white population. According to Census Bureau estimates, almost 70 percent of all Negroes in 1966 lived in metropolitan areas, compared to 64 percent of all whites. In the South, more than half the Negro population now lives in cities. Rural Negroes outnumber urban Negroes in only four states: Arkansas, Mississippi, North Carolina, and South Carolina.

Basic data concerning Negro urbanization trends, presented in tables at the conclusion of this chapter, indicate that:

- Almost all Negro population growth is occurring within metropolitan areas, primarily within central cities. From 1950 to 1966, the U. S. Negro population rose 6.5 million. Over 98 percent of that increase took place in metropolitan areas—86 percent within central cities, 12 percent in the urban fringe.
- The vast majority of white population growth is occurring in suburban portions of metropolitan areas. From 1950 to 1966, 77.8 percent of the white population increase of 35.6 million took place in the suburbs. Central cities received only 2.5 percent of this total white increase. Since 1960, white central-city population has actually declined by 1.3 million.
- As a result, central cities are steadily becoming more heavily Negro, while the urban fringes around them remain almost entirely white. The proportion of Negroes in all central cities rose steadily from 12 percent in 1950, to 17 percent in 1960, to 20 percent in 1966. Meanwhile, metropolitan areas outside of central cities remained 95 percent white from 1950 to 1960, and became 96 percent white by 1966.
- The Negro population is growing faster, both absolutely and relatively, in the larger metropolitan areas than in the smaller ones. From 1950 to 1966, the proportion of nonwhites in the central cities of metropolitan areas with one million or more persons doubled, reaching 26 percent, as compared with 20 percent in the central cities of metropolitan areas containing from 250,000 to one million persons, and 12 percent in the central cities of metropolitan areas containing under 250,000 persons.
- The 12 largest central cities (New York, Chicago, Los Angeles, Philadelphia, Detroit, Baltimore, Houston, Cleveland, Washington, D. C., St. Louis, Milwaukee, and San Francisco) now contain over two-thirds of the Negro population outside the South, and one-third of the total in the United States. All these cities have experienced rapid increases in Negro population since 1950. In six (Chicago, Detroit, Cleveland, St. Louis, Milwaukee, and San Francisco), the proportion of Negroes at least doubled. In two others (New York and Los Angeles), it probably doubled. In 1968, seven of these cities are over 30 percent Negro, and one (Washington, D. C.) is two-thirds Negro.

Factors Causing Residential Segregation
in Metropolitan Areas

The early pattern of Negro settlement within each metropolitan area followed that of immigrant groups. Migrants converged on the older sections of the central city because the lowest cost housing was there, friends and relatives were likely to be there; and the older neighborhoods then often had good public transportation.

But the later phases of Negro settlement and expansion in metropolitan areas diverge sharply from those typical of white immigrants. As the whites were absorbed by the larger society, many left their predominantly ethnic neighborhoods and moved to outlying areas to obtain newer housing and better schools. Some scattered randomly over the suburban area. Others established new ethnic clusters in the suburbs, but even these rarely contained solely members of a single ethnic group. As a result, most middle-class neighborhoods—both in the suburbs and within central cities—have no distinctive ethnic character, except that they are white.

Nowhere has the expansion of America's urban Negro population followed this pattern of dispersal. Thousands of Negro families have attained incomes, living standards, and cultural levels matching or surpassing those of whites who have "upgraded" themselves from distinctly ethnic neighborhoods. Yet most Negro families have remained within predominantly Negro neighborhoods, primarily because they have been effectively excluded from white residential areas.

Their exclusion has been accomplished through various discriminatory practices, some obvious and overt, others subtle and hidden. Deliberate efforts are sometimes made to discourage Negro families from purchasing or renting homes in all-white neighborhoods. Intimidation and threats of violence have ranged from throwing garbage on lawns and making threatening phone calls to burning crosses in yards and even dynamiting property. More often, real estate agents simply refuse to show homes to Negro buyers.

Many middle-class Negro families, therefore, cease looking for homes beyond all-Negro areas or nearby "changing" neighborhoods. For them, trying to move into all-white neighborhoods is not worth the psychological efforts and costs required.

Another form of discrimination just as significant is white withdrawal from, or refusal to enter, neighborhoods where large numbers of Negroes are moving or already residing. Normal population turnover causes about 20 percent of the residents of average United States neighborhoods to move out every year because of income changes, job transfers, shifts in life-cycle position or deaths. This normal turnover rate is even higher in apartment areas. The refusal of whites to move into changing areas when vacancies occur there

244

from normal turnover means that most of these vacancies are eventually occupied by Negroes. An inexorable shift toward heavy Negro occupancy results.

Once this happens, the remaining whites seek to leave, thus confirming the existing belief among whites that complete transformation of a neighborhood is inevitable once Negroes begin to enter. Since the belief itself is one of the major causes of the transformation, it becomes a self-fulfilling prophecy, which inhibits the development of racially integrated neighborhoods.

Thus, Negro settlements expand almost entirely through "massive racial transition" at the edges of existing all-Negro neighborhoods, rather than by a gradual dispersion of population throughout the metropolitan area.

Two points are particularly important:

- "Massive transition" requires no panic or flight by the original white residents of a neighborhood into which Negroes begin moving. All it requires is the failure or refusal of other whites to fill the vacancies resulting from normal turnover.
- Thus, efforts to stop massive transition by persuading present white residents to remain will ultimately fail unless whites outside the neighborhood can be persuaded to move in.

It is obviously true that some residential separation of whites and Negroes would occur even without discriminatory practices by whites. This would result from the desires of some Negroes to live in predominantly Negro neighborhoods and from differences in meaningful social variables, such as income and educational levels. But these factors alone would not lead to the almost complete segregation of whites and Negroes which has developed in our metropolitan areas.

The Exodus of Whites from Central Cities

The process of racial transition in central-city neighborhoods has been only one factor among many others causing millions of whites to move out of central cities as the Negro populations there expanded. More basic perhaps have been the rising mobility and affluence of middle-class families and the more attractive living conditions—particularly better schools—in the suburbs.

Whatever the reason, the result is clear. In 1950, 45.5 million whites lived in central cities. If this population had grown from 1950 to 1960 at the same rate as the nation's white population as a whole, it would have increased by eight million. It actually rose only 2.2 million, indicating an outflow of 5.8 million.[4]

From 1960 to 1966, the white outflow appears to have been even more rapid. White population of central cities declined 1.3 million instead of rising 3.6 million as it would if it had grown at the same rate as the entire white population. In theory, therefore, 4.9 million whites left central cities during these six years.

Statistics for all central cities as a group understate the relationship between Negro population growth and white outflow in individual central cities. The fact is, many cities with relatively few Negroes experienced rapid white-population growth, thereby obscuring the size of white out-migration that took place in cities having large increases in Negro population. For example, from 1950 to 1960, the 10 largest cities in the United States had a total Negro population increase of 1.6 million, or 55 percent, while the white population there declined 1.4 million. If we remove the two cities where the white population increased (Los Angeles and Houston), the nonwhite population in the remaining eight rose 1.4 million; whereas their white population declined 2.1 million. If the white population in these cities had increased at only half the rate of the white population in the United States as a whole from 1950 to 1960, it would have risen by 1.4 million. Thus, these eight cities actually experienced a white out-migration of at least 3.5 million, while gaining 1.4 million nonwhites.

The Extent of Residential Segregation

The rapid expansion of all-Negro residential areas and large-scale white withdrawal have continued a pattern of residential segregation that has existed in American cities for decades. A recent study[5] reveals that this pattern is present to a high degree in every large city in America. The authors devised an index to measure the degree of residential segregation. The index indicates for each city the percentage of Negroes who would have to move from the blocks where they now live to other blocks in order to provide a perfectly proportional, unsegregated distribution of population.

According to their findings, the average segregation index

[4] The outflow of whites may be somewhat smaller than the 5.8 million difference between these figures, because the ages of the whites in many central cities are higher than in the nation as a whole, and therefore the population would have grown somewhat more slowly.

[5] Negroes in Cities, Karl and Alma Taeuber, Aldine Publishing Co., Chicago (1965).

246

for 207 of the largest United States cities was 86.2 in 1960. This means that an average of over 86 percent of all Negroes would have had to change blocks to create an unsegregated population distribution. Southern cities had a higher average index (90.9) than cities in the Northeast (79.2), the North Central (87.7), or the West (79.3). Only eight cities had index values below 70, whereas over 50 had values above 91.7.

The degree of residential segregation for all 207 cities has been relatively stable, averaging 85.2 in 1940, 87.3 in 1950, and 86.2 in 1960. Variations within individual regions were only slightly larger. However, a recent Census Bureau study shows that in most of the 12 large cities where special censuses were taken in the mid-1960's, the proportions of Negroes living in neighborhoods of greatest Negro concentration had increased since 1960.

Residential segregation is generally more prevalent with respect to Negroes than for any other minority group, including Puerto Ricans, Orientals, and Mexican Americans. Moreover, it varies little between central city and suburb. This nearly universal pattern cannot be explained in terms of economic discrimination against all low-income groups. Analysis of 15 representative cities indicates that white upper- and middle-income households are far more segregated from Negro upper- and middle-income households than from white lower-income households.

In summary, the concentration of Negroes in central cities results from a combination of forces. Some of these forces, such as migration and initial settlement patterns in older neighborhoods, are similar to those which affected previous ethnic minorities. Others—particularly discrimination in employment and segregation in housing and schools—are a result of white attitudes based on race and color. These forces continue to shape the future of the central city.

TABLES

Proportion of Negroes in Each of the 30 Largest Cities, 1950, 1960, and Estimated 1965

	1950	*1960*	*(Estimate)*[6] *1965*
New York, N.Y.	10	14	18
Chicago, Ill.	14	23	28
Los Angeles, Calif.	9	14	17
Philadelphia, Pa.	18	26	31
Detroit, Michigan	16	29	34
Baltimore, Md.	24	35	38
Houston, Texas	21	23	23
Cleveland, Ohio	16	29	34
Washington, D.C.	35	54	66
St Louis, Mo.	18	29	36
Milwaukee, Wis.	3	8	11
San Francisco, Calif.	6	10	12
Boston, Mass.	5	9	13
Dallas, Texas	13	19	21
New Orleans, La.	32	37	41
Pittsburgh, Pa.	12	17	20
San Antonio, Tex.	7	7	8
San Diego, Calif.	5	6	7
Seattle, Wash.	3	5	7
Buffalo, N.Y.	6	13	17
Cincinnati, Ohio	16	22	24
Memphis, Tenn.	37	37	40
Denver, Colo.	4	6	9
Atlanta, Ga.	37	38	44
Minneapolis, Minn.	1	2	4
Indianapolis, Ind.	15	21	23
Kansas City, Mo.	12	18	22
Columbus, Ohio	12	16	18
Phoenix, Ariz.	5	5	5
Newark, N.J.	17	34	47

[6] Except for Cleveland, Buffalo, Memphis, and Phoenix, for which a special census has been made in recent years, these are very rough estimations computed on the basis of the change in relative proportions of Negro births and deaths since 1960.

Source: U. S. Department of Commerce, Bureau of the Census, BLS Report No. 332, p. 11.

Percent of All·Negroes in Selected Cities Living in Census Tracts
Grouped According to Proportion Negro in 1960 and 1964-1966 [7]

	Year	All census tracts	75 percent or more Negro	50 to 74 percent Negro	25 to 49 percent Negro	Less than 25 percent Negro
Cleveland,	1960	100	72	16	8	4
Ohio	1965	100	80	12	4	4
Phoenix,	1960	100	19	36	24	21
Ariz.	1965	100	18	23	42	17
Buffalo,	1960	100	35	47	6	12
N.Y.	1966	100	69	10	13	8
Louisville,	1960	100	57	13	17	13
Ky.	1964	100	67	13	10	10
Rochester,	1960	100	8	43	17	32
N.Y.	1964	100	16	45	24	15
Sacramento,	1960	100	9	—	14	77
Calif.	1964	100	8	14	28	50
Des Moines,	1960	100	—	28	31	41
Iowa	1966	100	—	42	19	39
Providence,	1960	100	—	23	2	75
R.I.	1965	100	—	16	46	38
Shreveport,	1960	100	79	10	7	4
La.	1966	100	90	—	6	4
Evansville,	1960	100	34	27	9	30
Ind.	1966	100	59	14	—	27
Little Rock,	1960	100	33	33	19	15
Ark.	1964	100	41	18	22	19
Raleigh,	1960	100	86	—	7	7
N.C.	1966	100	88	4	2	6

[7] Selected cities of 100,000 or more in which a special census was taken in any of the years 1964-1966. Ranked according to total population at latest census.

Source: U. S. Department of Commerce, Bureau of the Census, BLS Report No. 332, p. 12.

Population Change by Location, Inside and Outside Metropolitan Areas, 1950–1966 (numbers in millions)

Population

	Negro			White		
	1950	1960	1966	1950	1960	1966
United States	15.0	18.8	21.5	135.2	158.8	170.8
Metropolitan areas	8.4	12.2	14.8	80.3	99.7	109.0
Central cities	6.5	9.7	12.1	45.5	47.7	46.4
Urban fringe	1.9	2.5	2.7	34.8	52.0	62.5
Small cities, towns and rural	6.7	6.7	6.7	54.8	59.2	61.8

Change, 1950-1966

	Negro		White	
	Number	Percent	Number	Percent
United States	6.5	43	35.6	26
Metropolitan areas	6.4	77	28.7	36
Central cities	5.6	87	.9	2
Urban fringe	.8	42	27.7	79
Smaller cities, towns and rural	—[8]	1	7.0	13

Percent Distribution of Population by Location, Inside and Outside Metropolitan Areas, 1950, 1960 and 1966

	Negro			White		
	1950	1960	1966	1950	1960	1966
United States	100	100	100	100	100	100
Metropolitan areas	56	65	69	59	63	64
Central cities	43	51	56	34	30	27
Urban fringe	13	13	13	26	33	37
Smaller cities, towns and rural	44	35	31	41	37	36

Negroes as a Percentage of Total Population by Location, Inside and Outside Metropolitan Areas, and by Size of Metropolitan Areas—1950, 1960 and 1966

	Percent Negro		
	1950	1960	1966
United States	10	11	11
Metropolitan areas	9	11	12
Central cities	12	17	20
Central cities in metropolitan areas[9] of—			
1,000,000 or more	13	19	26[10]
250,000 to 1,000,000	12	15	20[10]
Under 250,000	12	12	12[10]
Urban fringe	5	5	4
Smaller cities, towns and rural	11	10	10

[8] Rounds to less than 50,000.

[9] In metropolitan areas of population shown as of 1960.

[10] Percent nonwhite; data for Negroes are not available. The figures used are estimated to be closely comparable to those for Negroes alone, using a check for Negro and nonwhite percentages in earlier years.

Source: U. S. Department of Commerce, Bureau of the Census.

Chapter 7 / Unemployment, Family Structure, and Social Disorganization

The Negro population in our country is as diverse in income, occupation, family composition, and other variables as the white community. Nevertheless, for purposes of analysis, three major Negro economic groups can be identified.

The first and smallest group consists of middle and upper-income individuals and households whose educational, occupational, and cultural characteristics are similar to those of middle and upper-income white groups.

The second and largest group contains Negroes whose incomes are above the "poverty level" but who have not attained the educational, occupational, or income status typical of "middle-class" Americans.

The third group has very low educational, occupational, and income attainments and lives below the "poverty level."

A recent compilation of data on American Negroes by the Departments of Labor and Commerce shows that although incomes of both Negroes and whites have been rising rapidly,

- Negro incomes still remain far below those of whites. Negro median family income was only 58 percent of the white median in 1966.
- Negro family income is not keeping pace with white family income growth. In constant 1965 dollars, median nonwhite income in 1947 was $2174 lower than median white income. By 1966, the gap had grown to $3036.
- The Negro upper-income group is expanding rapidly and achieving sizeable income gains. In 1966, 28 percent of all Negro families received incomes of $7000 or more, compared with 55 percent of white families. This was 1.6 times the proportion of Negroes receiving comparable incomes in 1960, and 4 times greater than the proportion receiving such incomes in 1947. Moreover, the proportion of Negroes employed in high-skill, high-status, and well-paying jobs rose faster than comparable proportions among whites from 1960 to 1966.
- As Negro incomes have risen, the size of the lowest-income group has grown smaller, and the middle and upper groups have grown larger—both relatively and absolutely.

251

Group	Percentage of Negro Families			Percentage of White Families
	1947	1960	1966	1966
$7,000 and over	7%	17%	28%	55%
$3,000 to $6,999	29	40	41	33
Under $3,000	65	44	32	13

• About two-thirds of the lowest-income group—or 20 percent of all Negroes—are making no significant economic gains despite continued general prosperity. Half of these hard-core disadvantaged—more than two million persons—living in central-city neighborhoods. Recent special censuses in Los Angeles and Cleveland indicate that the incomes of persons living in the worst slum areas/have not risen at all during this period, unemployment rates have declined only slightly, the proportion of families with female heads has increased, and housing conditions have worsened even though rents have risen.

Thus, between 2.0 and 2.5 million poor Negroes are living in disadvantaged neighborhoods of central cities in the United States. These persons comprise only slightly more than 1 percent of the nation's total population, but they make up about 16 to 20 percent of the total Negro population of all central cities, and a much higher proportion in certain cities.

UNEMPLOYMENT AND UNDEREMPLOYMENT

The Critical Significance of Employment

The capacity to obtain and hold a "good job" is the traditional test of participation in American society. Steady employment with adequate compensation provides both purchasing power and social status. It develops the capabilities, confidence, and self-esteem an individual needs to be a responsible citizen and provides a basis for a stable family life. As Daniel P. Moynihan has written:

The principal measure of progress toward equality will be that of employment. It is the primary source of individual or group identity. In America what you do is what you are: to do nothing is to be nothing; to do little is to be little. The equations are implacable and blunt, and ruthlessly public.

For the Negro American it is already, and will continue to be, the master problem. It is the measure of white bona fides. It is the measure of Negro competence, and also of the competence of American society. Most importantly, the linkage between problems of employment and the range of social pathology that afflicts the Negro community is unmistakable. Employment not only controls the present for the Negro American but, in a most profound way, it is creating the future as well.

For residents of disadvantaged Negro neighborhoods, obtaining good jobs is vastly more difficult than for most workers in society. For decades, social, economic, and psychological

252

disadvantages surrounding the urban Negro poor have impaired their work capacities and opportunities. The result is a "cycle of failure"—the employment disabilities of one generation breed those of the next.

Negro Unemployment

Unemployment rates among Negroes have declined from a post-Korean War high of 12.6 percent in 1958 to 8.2 percent in 1967. Among married Negro men, the unemployment rate for 1967 was down to 3.2 percent.[1]

Notwithstanding this decline, unemployment rates for Negroes are still double those for whites in every category, including married men, as they have been throughout the postwar period. Moreover, since 1954, even during the current unprecedented period of sustained economic growth, unemployment among Negroes has been continuously above the 6.0 percent "recession" level widely regarded as a sign of serious economic weakness when prevalent for the entire work force.

While the Negro unemployment rate remains high in relation to the white rate, the number of additional jobs needed to lower this to the level of white unemployment is surprisingly small. In 1967, approximately 3.0 million persons were unemployed during an average week, of whom about 638,000, or 21 percent, were nonwhites. When corrected for undercounting, total nonwhite unemployment was approximately 712,000 or 8 percent of the nonwhite labor force. To reduce the unemployment rate to 3.4 percent, the rate prevalent among whites, jobs must be found for 57.5 percent of these unemployed persons. This amounts to nearly 409,000 jobs, or about 27 percent of the net number of new jobs added to the economy in the year 1967 alone and only slightly more than ½ of 1 percent of all jobs in the United States in 1967.

THE LOW-STATUS AND LOW-PAYING NATURE OF MANY NEGRO JOBS

Even more important perhaps than unemployment is the related problem of the undesirable nature of many jobs open to Negroes. Negro workers are concentrated in the lowest-skilled and lowest-paying occupations. These jobs often involve substandard wages, great instability and uncertainty of tenure, extremely low status in the eyes of both employer and employee, little or no chance for meaningful advancement, and unpleasant or exhausting duties. Negro men in particular are

[1] Adjusted for Census Bureau undercounting.

more than three times as likely as whites to be in unskilled
or service jobs which pay far less than most:

Type of Occupation	Percentage of Male Workers in Each Type of Occupation —1966		Median Earnings of All Male Civilians in Each Occupation —1965
	White	Nonwhite	
Professional, Technical, Managerial	27%	9%	$7,603[2]
Clerical and sales	14	9	$5,532[2]
Craftsmen and foremen	20	12	$6,270
Operatives	20	27	$5,046
Service Workers	6	16	$3,436
Non-farm laborers	6	20	$2,410
Farmers and farm workers	7	8	$1,699[2]

This concentration in the least desirable jobs can be viewed
another way by calculating the changes which would occur
if Negro men were employed in various occupations in the
same proportions as the male labor force as a whole (not solely
the white labor force).

Type of Occupation	Number of Male Nonwhite Workers—1966			
	As Actually Distributed[3]	If Distributed the Same as All Male Workers	Difference	
			No.	Percent
Professional, technical, managerial	415,000	1,173,000	+758,000	+183%
Clerical and sales	415,000	628,000	+213,000	+51%
Craftsmen and foremen	553,000	894,000	+341,000	+62%
Operatives	1,244,000	964,000	—280,000	—23%
Service workers	737,000	326,000	—411,000	—56%
Non-farm laborers	922,000	340,000	—582,000	—63%
Farmers and farm workers	369,000	330,000	—39,000	—11%

Thus, upgrading the employment of Negro men to make
their occupational distribution identical with that of the labor
force as a whole would have an immense impact upon the
nature of their occupations. About 1.3 million nonwhite men—
or 28 percent of those employed in 1966—would move up the
employment ladder into one of the higher-status and higher-
paying categories. The effect of such a shift upon the incomes
of Negro men would be very great. Using the 1966 job distribution, the shift indicated above would produce about $4.8
billion more earned income for nonwhite men alone if they

[2] Average of two categories from normal Census Bureau categories as combined in data presented in *The Social and Economic Conditions of Negroes in
the United States* (BLS #332).

[3] Estimates based upon percentages set forth in BLS #332, page 41.

received the 1965 median income in each occupation. This would be a rise of approximately 30 percent in the earnings actually received by all nonwhite men in 1965 (not counting any sources of income other than wages and salaries).

Of course, the kind of "instant upgrading" visualized in these calculations does not represent a practical alternative for national policy. The economy cannot drastically reduce the total number of low-status jobs it now contains, or shift large numbers of people upward in occupation in any short period. Therefore, major upgrading in the employment status of Negro men must come through a faster relative expansion of higher-level jobs than lower-level jobs (which has been occurring for several decades), an improvement in the skills of nonwhite workers so they can obtain a higher proportion of those added better jobs, and a drastic reduction of discriminatory hiring and promotion practices in all enterprises, both private and public.

Nevertheless, this hypothetical example clearly shows that the concentration of male Negro employment at the lowest end of the occupational scale is greatly depressing the incomes of United States Negroes in general. In fact, this is the single most important source of poverty among Negroes. It is even more important than unemployment, as can be shown by a second hypothetical calculation. In 1966, there were about 724,000 unemployed nonwhites in the United States on the average, including adults and teenagers, and allowing for the Census Bureau undercount of Negroes. If every one of these persons had been employed and had received the median amount earned by nonwhite males in 1966 ($3,864), this would have added a total of $2.8 billion to nonwhite income as a whole. If only enough of these persons had been employed at that wage to reduce nonwhite unemployment from 7.3 to 3.3 percent—the rate among whites in 1966—then the income gain for nonwhites would have totaled about $1.5 billion. But if nonwhite unemployment remained at 7.3 percent, and nonwhite men were upgraded so that they had the same occupational distribution and incomes as all men in the labor force considered together, this would have produced about $4.8 billion in additional income, as noted above (using 1965 earnings for calculation). Thus the potential income gains from upgrading the male nonwhite labor force are much larger than those from reducing nonwhite unemployment.

This conclusion underlines the difficulty of improving the economic status of Negro men. It is far easier to create new jobs than either to create new jobs with relatively high status and earning power, or to upgrade existing employed or partly-employed workers into such better-quality employment. Yet only such upgrading will eliminate the fundamental basis of poverty and deprivation among Negro families.

Access to good-quality jobs clearly affects the willingness of Negro men actively to seek work. In riot cities surveyed by the Commission with the largest percentage of Negroes in skilled and semiskilled jobs, Negro men participated in the labor force to the same extent as, or greater than, white men. Conversely, where most Negro men were heavily concentrated in menial jobs, they participated less in the labor force than white men.

Even given similar employment, Negro workers with the same education as white workers are paid less. This disparity doubtless results to some extent from inferior training in segregated schools, and also from the fact that large numbers of Negroes are only now entering certain occupations for the first time. However, the differentials are so large and so universal at all educational levels that they clearly reflect the patterns of discrimination which charactrize hiring and promotion practices in many segments of the economy. For example, in 1966 among persons who had completed high school, the median income of Negroes was only 73 percent that of whites. Even among persons with an eighth-grade education. Negro median income was only 80 percent of white median income.

At the same time, a higher proportion of Negro women than white women participates in the labor force at nearly all ages except 16 to 19. For instance, in 1966, 55 percent of nonwhite women from 25 to 34 years of age were employed, compared to only 38 percent of white women in the same age group. The fact that almost half of all adult Negro women work reflects the fact that so many Negro males have unsteady and low-paying jobs. Yet even though Negro women are often better able to find work than Negro men, the unemployment rate among adult nonwhite women (20 years old and over) in 1967 was 7.1 percent, compared to the 4.3 percent rate among adult nonwhite men.

Unemployment rates are, of course, much higher among teenagers, both Negro and white, than among adults; in fact about one-third of all unemployed Negroes in 1967 were between 16 and 19 years old. During the first nine months of 1967, the unemployment rate among nonwhite teenagers was 26.5 percent; for whites, it was 10.6 percent. About 219,300 nonwhite teenagers were unemployed.[4] About 58,300 were still in school but were actively looking for jobs.

[4] After adjusting for Census Bureau undercounting.

Subemployment in Disadvantaged Negro Neighborhoods

In disadvantaged areas, employment conditions for Negroes are in a chronic state of crisis. Surveys in low-income neighborhoods of nine large cities made by the Department of Labor late in 1966 revealed that the rate of unemployment there was 9.3 percent, compared to 7.3 percent for Negroes generally and 3.3 percent for whites. Moreover, a high proportion of the persons living in these areas were "underemployed," that is they were either part-time workers looking for full-time employment, or full-time workers earning less than $3000 per year, or had dropped out of the labor force. The Department of Labor estimated that this underemployment is two and one-half times greater than the number unemployed in these areas. Therefore, the "subemployment rate," including both the unemployed and the underemployed, was about 32.7 percent in the nine areas surveyed, or 8.8 times greater than the overall unemployment rate for all U. S. workers. Since underemployment also exists outside disadvantaged neighborhoods, comparing the full subemployment rate in these areas with the unemployment rate for the nation as a whole is not entirely valid. However, it provides some measure of the enormous disparity between employment conditions in most of the nation and those prevalent in disadvantaged Negro areas in our large cities.

The critical problem is to determine the actual number of those unemployed and underemployed in central-city Negro ghettos. This involves a process of calculation which is detailed in the note at the end of this chapter. The outcome of this process is summarized in the following table:

Nonwhite Subemployment in Disadvantaged
Areas of All Central Cities—1967

Group	Unemployment	Underemployment	Total Subemployment
Adult men	102,000	230,000	332,000
Adult women	118,000	266,000	384,000
Teenagers	98,000	220,000	318,000
Total	318,000	716,000	1,034,000

Therefore, in order to bring subemployment in these areas down to a level equal to unemployment alone among whites, enough steady, reasonably-paying jobs (and the training and motivation to perform them) must be provided to eliminate all underemployment and reduce unemployment by 65 percent. For all three age groups combined, this deficit amounted to 923,000 jobs in 1967.

The Magnitude of Poverty in Disadvantaged Neighborhoods

The chronic unemployment problems in the central city, aggravated by the constant arrival of new unemployed migrants, is the fundamental cause of the persistent poverty in disadvantaged Negro areas.

"Poverty" in the affluent society is more than absolute deprivation. Many of the poor in the United States would be well-off in other societies. Relative deprivation—inequality—is a more useful concept of poverty with respect to the Negro in America because it encompasses social and political exclusion as well as economic inequality. Because of the lack of data of this type, we have had to focus our analysis on a measure of poverty which is both economic and absolute—the Social Security Administration's "poverty level"[5] concept. It is clear, however, that broader measures of poverty would substantiate the conclusions that follow.

In 1966 there were 29.7 million persons in the United States —15.3 percent of the nation's population—with incomes below the "poverty level," as defined by the Social Security Administration. Of these, 20.3 million were white (68.3 percent), and 9.3 million nonwhite (31.7 percent). Thus, about 11.9 percent of the nation's whites and 40.6 percent of its nonwhites were poor under the Social Security definition.

The location of the nation's poor is best shown from 1964 data as indicated by the following table:

| | Percentage of Those in Poverty in Each Group Living in: | | | |
| | Metropolitan Areas | | | |
Group	In Central Cities	Outside Central Cities	Other Areas	Total
Whites	23.8%	21.8%	54.4%	100%
Nonwhites	41.7	10.8	47.5	100
Total	29.4	18.4	52.2	100

Source: Social Security Administration

The following facts concerning poverty are relevant to an understanding of the problems faced by people living in disadvantaged neighborhoods.[6]

[5] $3335 per year for an urban family of four.

[6] Source: Social Security Administration; based on 1964 data.

- In central cities 30.7 percent of nonwhite families of two or more persons lived in poverty compared to only 8.8 percent of whites.
- Of the 10.1 million poor persons in central cities in 1964, about 4.4 million of these (43.6 percent) were nonwhites, and 5.7 million (56.4 percent) were whites. The poor whites were much older on the average than the poor nonwhites. The proportion of poor persons 65 years old or older was 23.2 percent among whites, but only 6.8 percent among nonwhites.
- Poverty was more than twice as prevalent among nonwhite families with female heads than among those with male heads, 57 percent compared to 21 percent. In central cities, 26 percent of all nonwhite families of two or more persons had female heads, as compared to 12 percent of white families.
- Among nonwhite families headed by a female, and having children under 6, the incidence of poverty was 81.0 percent. Moreover, there were 243,000 such families living in poverty in central cities—or over 9 percent of all nonwhite families in those cities.
- Among all children living in poverty within central cities, nonwhites outnumbered whites by over 400,000. The number of poor nonwhite children equalled or surpassed the number of white poor children in every age group.

Number of Children Living in Poverty (millions)

Age Group	White	Nonwhite	Percent of Total Nonwhite
Under 6	0.9	1.0	53%
6-15	1.0	1.3	57
16-21	0.4	0.4	50
Total	2.3	2.7	54%

Two stark facts emerge:

- 54 percent of all poor children in central cities in 1964 were nonwhites;
- Of the 4.4 million nonwhites living in poverty within central cities in 1964, 52 percent were children under 16, and 61 percent were under 21.

Since 1964, the number of nonwhite families living in poverty within central cities has remained about the same; hence, these poverty conditions are probably still prevalent in central cities in terms of absolute numbers of persons, although the proportion of persons in poverty may have dropped slightly.[7]

[7] For the nation as a whole, the proportion of nonwhite families living in poverty dropped from 39 percent to 35 percent from 1964 to 1966 (defining "family" somewhat differently from the definition used in the data above). The number of such families declined from 1.9 million to 1.7 million. However, the number and proportion of all nonwhites living in central cities rose in the same period. As a result, the number of nonwhite families living in so-called "poverty areas" of large cities actually rose from 1,561,000 in 1960 to 1,588,000 in 1966.

THE SOCIAL IMPACT OF EMPLOYMENT PROBLEMS IN DISADVANTAGED NEGRO AREAS

Unemployment and the Family

The high rates of unemployment and underemployment in racial ghettos are evidence, in part, that many men living in these areas are seeking but cannot obtain jobs which will support a family. Perhaps equally important, most jobs they can get are at the low end of the occupational scale, and often lack the necessary status to sustain a worker's self-respect, or the respect of his family and friends. These same men are also constantly confronted with the message of discrimination: "You are inferior because of a trait you did not cause and cannot change." This message reinforces feelings of inadequacy arising from repeated failure to obtain and keep decent jobs.

Wives of these men are forced to work, and usually produce more money. If men stay at home without working, their inadequacies constantly confront them and tensions arise between them and their wives and children. Under these pressures, it is not surprising that many of these men flee their responsibilities as husbands and fathers, leaving home, and drifting from city to city, or adopting the style of "street corner men."

Statistical evidence tends to document this. A close correlation exists between the number of nonwhite married women separated from their husbands each year and the unemployment rate among nonwhite males 20 years old and over. Similarly, from 1948 to 1962, the number of new Aid to Families with Dependent Children cases rose and fell with the nonwhite male unemployment rate. Since 1963, however, the number of new cases—most of them Negro children—has steadily increased even though the unemployment rate among nonwhite males has declined. The impact of marital status on employment among Negroes is shown by the fact that in 1967 the proportion of married men either divorced or separated

Unemployment Rate and Participation in Total Labor Force, 25 to 54-Year-Old Nonwhite Men, by Marital Status, March, 1967

	Unemployment Rate Nonwhite	Labor Force Participation (%) Nonwhite
Married, Wife Present	3.7	96.7
Other (Separated, Divorced, Widowed)	8.7	77.6

from their wives was more than twice as high among un-employed nonwhite men as among employed nonwhite men. Moreover, among those participating in the labor force, there was a higher proportion of married men with wives present than with wives absent.

Fatherless Families

The abandonment of the home by many Negro males affects a great many children growing up in the racial ghetto. As previously indicated, most American Negro families are headed by men, just like most other American families. Yet the pro-portion of families with female heads is much greater among Negroes than among whites at all income levels, and has been rising in recent years.

	Husband-Wife		Female Head	
Date	White	Nonwhite	White	Nonwhite
1950	88.0%	77.7%	8.5%	17.6%
1960	88.7	73.6	8.7	22.4
1966	88.8	72.7	8.9	23.7

Proportion of Families of Various Types

This disparity between white and nonwhite families is far greater among the lowest income families—those most likely to reside in disadvantaged big-city neighborhoods—than among higher income families. Among families with incomes under $3,000 in 1966, the proportion with female heads was 42 per-cent for Negroes but only 23 percent for whites. In contrast, among families with incomes of $7,000 or more, 8 percent of Negro families had female heads compared to 4 percent of whites.

The problems of "fatherlessness" are aggravated by the tendency of the poor to have large families. The average poor, urban nonwhite family contains 4.8 persons, as compared with 3.7 for the average poor, urban white family. This is one of the primary factors in the poverty status of nonwhite house-holds in large cities.

The proportion of fatherless families appears to be increas-ing in the poorest Negro neighborhoods. In the Hough section of Cleveland, the proportion of families with female heads rose from 23 to 32 percent from 1960 to 1965. In the Watts section of Los Angeles it rose from 36 to 39 percent during the same period.

The handicap imposed on children growing up without fathers, in an atmosphere of poverty and deprivation, is in-creased because many mothers must work to provide support.

The following table illustrates the disparity between the proportion of nonwhite women in the child-rearing ages who are in the labor force and the comparable proportion of white women:

| | Percentage of Women in the Labor Force | |
Age Group	Nonwhite	Wh
20-24	55%	51%
25-34	55	38
35-44	61	45

With the father absent and the mother working, many ghetto children spend the bulk of their time on the streets—the streets of a crime-ridden, violence-prone and poverty-stricken world. The image of success in this world is not that of the "solid citizen," the responsible husband and father, but rather that of the "hustler" who promotes his own interests by exploiting others. The dope sellers and the numbers runners are the "successful" men because their earnings far outstrip those men who try to climb the economic ladder in honest ways.

Young people in the ghetto are acutely conscious of a system which appears to offer rewards to those who illegally exploit others, and failure to those who struggle under traditional responsibilities. Under these circumstances, many adopt exploitation and the "hustle" as a way of life, disclaiming both work and marriage in favor of casual and temporary liaisons. This pattern reinforces itself from one generation to the next, creating a "culture of poverty" and an ingrained cynicism about society and its institutions.

The "Jungle"

The culture of poverty that results from unemployment and family disorganization generates a system of ruthless, exploitative relationships within the ghetto. Prostitution, dope addiction, casual sexual affairs, and crime create an environmental jungle characterized by personal insecurity and tension. The effects of this development are stark:

- The rate of illegitimate births among nonwhite women has risen sharply in the past two decades. In 1940, 16.8 percent of all nonwhite births were illegitimate. By 1950 this proportion was 18 percent; by 1960, 21.6 percent; by 1966, 26.3 percent. In the ghettos of many large cities, illegitimacy rates exceed 50 percent.
- The rate of illegitimacy among nonwhite women is closely related to low income and high unemployment. In Washington, D. C., for example, an analysis of 1960 census tracts shows that in tracts with unemployment rates of 12 percent or more among

nonwhite men, illegitimacy was over 40 percent. But in tracts with unemployment rates of 2.9 percent and below among nonwhite men, reported illegitimacy was under 20 percent. A similar contrast existed between tracts in which median nonwhite income was under $4,000 (where illegitimacy was 38 percent) and those in which it was $8,000 and over (where illegitimacy was 11 percent).

• Narcotics addiction is also heavily concentrated in low-income Negro neighborhoods, particularly in New York City. Of the 59,720 addicts known to the U. S. Bureau of Narcotics at the end of 1966, just over 50 percent were Negroes. Over 52 percent of all known addicts lived within New York State, mostly in Harlem and other Negro neighborhoods. These figures undoubtedly greatly understate the actual number of persons using narcotics regularly—especially those under 21.

• Not surprisingly, at every age from 6 through 19, the proportion of children from homes with both parents present who actually attend school is higher than the proportion of children from homes with only one parent or neither present.

• Rates of juvenile delinquency, venereal disease, dependency upon AFDC support, and use of public assistance in general are much higher in disadvantaged Negro areas than in other parts of large cities. Data taken from New York City contrasting predominantly Negro neighborhoods with the city as a whole clearly illustrate this fact.

Social Distress—Major Predominantly Negro
Neighborhoods in New York City and the City as a Whole

	Juvenile Delinquency[8]	Venereal Disease[9]	ADC[10]	Public Assistance[11]
Brownsville	125.3	609.9	459.0	265.8
East New York	98.6	207.5	148.6	71.8
Bedford-Stuyvesant	115.2	771.3	337.1	197.2
Harlem	110.8	1,603.5	265.7	138.1
South Bronx	84.4	308.3	278.5	165.5
New York City	52.2	269.1	120.7	60.8

In conclusion: in 1965, 1.2 million nonwhite children under 16 lived in central city families headed by a woman under 65. The great majority of these children were growing up in poverty under conditions that make them better candidates for crime and civil disorder than for jobs providing an entry into American society. Because of the immense importance of this fact—the potential loss to the society of these young people—we describe these conditions in the next chapter.

[8] Number of offenses per 1,000 persons 7-20 years (1965).

[9] Number of cases per 100,000 persons under 21 years (1964).

[10] Number of children in Aid to Dependent Children cases per 1,000 under 18 years, using 1960 population as base (1965).

[11] Welfare assistance recipients per 1,000 persons, using 1960 population as base (1965).

In 1967, total unemployment in the United States was distributed as follows, by age and color:

Group	Nonwhite	White	Total
Adult men (20 and over)	193,000	866,000	1,059,000
Adult women (20 and over)	241,000	837,000	1,078,000
Teenagers (16-19)	204,000	635,000	839,000
Total	638,000	2,338,000	2,976,000

Adjustment for the Census Bureau undercount of nonwhite males in the labor force amounting to 7.5 percent for the teenage group, 18 percent for the adult male group and approximately 10 percent for adult females result in the following revised total employment:

Group	Nonwhite	White	Total
Adult men	228,000	866,000	1,094,000
Adult women	265,000	837,000	1,102,000
Teenagers	219,000	635,000	854,000
Total	712,000	2,338,000	8,050,000

These figures cover the entire United States. To provide an estimate of the number of unemployed in disadvantaged neighborhoods within central cities, it is necessary to discover what proportion of the nonwhite unemployed are in central cities and what proportion of those in central cities are within the most disadvantaged neighborhoods. The Department of Labor survey in nine large central cities covering the first nine months of 1967 showed that these cities contained 27.3 percent of the total nonwhite labor force in the U. S., and 26.4 percent of total nonwhite unemployment. Hence, it is reasonable to assume that nonwhite unemployment is concentrated in central cities to about the same degree as the nonwhite labor force. In turn, the nonwhite labor force is located in central cities in about the same proportion as the nonwhite population, or 57.1 percent in 1967. Thus central city unemployment among nonwhites was presumably about 57.1 percent of the national figures:

Nonwhite Unemployment in All
Central Cities
(Rounded)

Adult men	130,000
Adult women	151,000
Teenagers	125,000
Total	406,000

Within large central cities, about 62 percent of all nonwhite familes lived in certain Census Tracts which have been designated "poverty areas." These tracts ranked lowest in U. S. cities over 250,000 persons in size, according to an index of "deprivation" based upon family income, children in broken homes, persons with low educational attainment, males in unskilled jobs, and substandard housing. On the assumption that conditions in these poverty areas are comparable to those in the nine disadvantaged areas surveyed by the Department of Labor in 1966, the number of unemployed nonwhites in disadvantaged areas of central cities is as follows:[12]

Nonwhite Unemployment in Disadvantaged
Areas of all Central Cities—1967

Adult men	102,000
Adult women	118,000
Teenagers	98,000
Total	318,000

The number of underemployed nonwhites in these areas was about 2.5 times larger than the number of unemployed. But we have already accounted for some underemployment in the adjustment for undercounting—so we will assume nonwhite underemployment was 2.25 times adjusted unemployment for all three age and sex groups. The resulting rough estimates are as follows:

Nonwhite Subemployment in Disadvantaged
Areas of All Central Cities—1967

Group	Unemployment	Underemployment	Total Subemployment
Adult men	102,000	230,000	332,000
Adult women	118,000	266,000	384,000
Teenagers	98,000	220,000	318,000
Total	318,000	716,000	1,034,000

[12] The number of nonwhite unemployed in the more disadvantaged areas was 26 percent higher than it would have been had it been proportional to the total population residing there. Therefore, the proportion of central city nonwhite unemployed in poverty areas is assumed to equal 78.1 percent (62 percent times 1.26).

Chapter 8 / Conditions of Life in the Racial Ghetto

The conditions of life in the racial ghetto are strikingly different from those to which most Americans are accustomed—especially white, middle-class Americans. We believe it important to describe these conditions and their effect on the lives of people who cannot escape from the ghetto.

(We have not attempted here to describe conditions relating to the fundamental problems of housing, education and welfare, which are treated in detail in later chapters.)

I. CRIME AND INSECURITY

Nothing is more fundamental to the quality of life in any area than the sense of personal security of its residents, and nothing affects this more than crime.

In general, crime rates in large cities are much higher than in other areas of our country. Within such cities, crime rates are higher in disadvantaged Negro areas than anywhere else.

The most widely-used measure of crime is the number of "index crimes" (homicide, forcible rape, aggravated assault, robbery, burglary, grand larceny, and auto theft) in relation to population. In 1966, 1,754 such crimes were reported to police for every 100,000 Americans. In cities over 250,000, the rate was 3,153, and in cities over one million, it was 3,630 —or more than double the national average. In suburban areas alone, including suburban cities, the rate was only 1,300, or just over one-third the rate in the largest cities.

Within larger cities, personal and property insecurity has consistently been highest in the older neighborhoods encircling the downtown business district. In most cities, crime rates for many decades have been higher in these inner areas than anywhere else, except in downtown areas themselves where they are inflated by the small number of residents.

High crime rates have persisted in these inner areas even though the ethnic character of their residents continually changed. Poor immigrants used these areas as "entry ports," then usually moved on to more desirable neighborhoods as soon as they acquired enough resources. Many "entry port" areas have now become racial ghettos.

The difference between crime rates in these disadvantaged neighborhoods and in other parts of the city is usually startling, as a comparison of crime rates in five police districts in Chicago for 1965 illustrates. These five include one high-income, all-white district at the periphery of the city, two very low-income, virtually all-Negro districts near the city core with numerous public housing projects, and two predominantly white districts, one with mainly lower-middle-income families, the other containing a mixture of very high-income and relatively low-income households. The table shows crime rates against persons and against property in these five districts, plus the number of patrolmen assigned to them per 100,000 residents, as follows:

Incidence of Index Crimes and Patrolmen Assignments per 100,000 Residents in 5 Chicago Police Districts, 1965

Number	High Income White District	Low-Middle-Income White District	Mixed High and Low-Income White District	Very Low Income Negro District No. 1	Very Low Income Negro District No. 2
Index crimes against persons	80	440	338	1,615	2,820
Index crimes against property	1,038	1,750	2,080	2,508	2,630
Patrolmen assigned	93	133	115	243	291

These data suggest the following conclusions:

- Variations in the crime rate against persons within the city are extremely large. One very low-income Negro district had 35 times as many serious crimes against persons per 100,000 residents as did the high-income white district.
- Variations in the crime rate against property are much smaller. The highest rate was only 2.5 times larger than the lowest.
- The lower the income in an area, the higher the crime rate there. Yet low-income Negro areas have significantly higher crime rates than low-income white areas. This reflects the high degree of social disorganization in Negro areas described in the previous chapter, as well as the fact that poor Negroes, as a group, have lower incomes than poor whites, as a group.
- The presence of more police patrolmen per 100,000 residents does not necessarily offset high crime in certain parts of the city. Although the Chicago Police Department had assigned over three times as many patrolmen per 100,000 residents to the highest-crime areas shown as to the lowest, crime rates in the highest-crime area for offenses against both persons and property combined were 4.9 times as high as in the lowest-crime area.

Because most middle-class Americans live in neighborhoods similar to the more crime-free district described above, they have little comprehension of the sense of insecurity that characterizes the ghetto resident. Moreover, official statistics normally greatly understate actual crime rates because the vast majority of crimes are not reported to the police. For example, studies conducted for the President's Crime Commission in Washington, D. C., Boston, and Chicago, showed that three to six times as many crimes were actually committed against persons and homes as were reported to the police.

Two facts are crucial to an understanding of the effects of high crime rates in racial ghettos: most of these crimes are committed by a small minority of the residents, and the principal victims are the residents themselves. Throughout the United States, the great majority of crimes committed by Negroes involve other Negroes as victims. A special tabulation made by the Chicago Police Department for the President's Crime Commission indicated that over 85 percent of the crimes committed against persons by Negroes between September 1965 and March 1966 involved Negro victims.

As a result, the majority of law-abiding citizens who live in disadvantaged Negro areas face much higher probabilities of being victimized than residents of most higher-income areas, including almost all suburbs. For nonwhites, the probability of suffering from any index crime except larceny is 78 percent higher than for whites. The probability of being raped is 3.7 times higher among nonwhite women, and the probability of being robbed is 3.5 times higher for nonwhites in general.

The problems associated with high crime rates generate widespread hostility toward the police in these neighborhoods for reasons described elsewhere in this Report. Thus, crime not only creates an atmosphere of insecurity and fear throughout Negro neighborhoods but also causes continuing attrition of the relationship between Negro residents and police. This bears a direct relationship to civil disorder.

There are reasons to expect the crime situation in these areas to become worse in the future. First, crime rates throughout the United States have been rising rapidly in recent years. The rate of index crimes against persons rose 37 percent from 1960 to 1966, and the rate of index crimes against property rose 50 percent. In the first nine months of 1967, the number of index crimes was up 16 percent over the same period in 1966 whereas the United States population rose about one percent. In cities of 250,000 to one million, index crime rose by over 20 percent, whereas it increased four percent in cities of over one million.[1]

Second, the number of police available to combat crime is rising much more slowly than the amount of crime. In 1966,

[1] The problem of interpreting and evaluating "rising" crime rates is complicated by the changing age distribution of the population, improvements in reporting methods, and the increasing willingness of victims to report crimes. Despite these complications, there is general agreement on the serious increase in the incidence of crime in the United States.

there were about 20 percent more police employees in the United States than in 1960, and per capita expenditures for police rose from $15.29 in 1960 to $20.99 in 1966, a gain of 37 percent. But over the six-year period, the number of reported index crimes had jumped 62 percent. In spite of significant improvements in police efficiency, it is clear that police will be unable to cope with their expanding workload unless there is a dramatic increase in the resources allocated by society to this task.

Third, in the next decade the number of young Negroes aged 14 to 24 will increase rapidly, particularly in central cities. This group is responsible for a disproportionately high share of crimes in all parts of the nation. In 1966, persons under 25 years of age comprised the following proportions of those arrested for various major crimes: murder—37 percent; forcible rape—64 percent; robbery—71 percent; burglary —81 percent; larceny—about 77 percent; and auto theft—over 89 percent. For all index crimes together, the arrest rate for Negroes is about four times higher than that for whites. Yet the number of young Negroes aged 14 to 24 in central cities will rise about 63 percent from 1966 to 1975, as compared to only 32 percent for the total Negro population of central cities.[2]

II. Health and Sanitation Conditions

The residents of the racial ghetto are significantly less healthy than most other Americans. They suffer from higher mortality rates, higher incidence of major diseases, and lower availability and utilization of medical services. They also experience higher admission rates to mental hospitals.

These conditions result from a number of factors.

Poverty

From the standpoint of health, poverty means deficient diets, lack of medical care, inadequate shelter and clothing, and often lack of awareness of potential health needs. As a result, about 30 percent of all persons with family incomes less than $2,000 per year suffer from chronic health conditions that adversely affect their employment—as compared with less than 8 percent of the families with incomes of $7,000 or more.

Poor families have the greatest need for financial assistance

[2] Assuming those cities will experience the same proportion of total United States Negro population growth that they did from 1960 to 1966. The calculations are derived from population projections in Bureau of the Census, *Population Estimates,* Current Population Reports, Series P-25, No. 381. Dec. 18, 1967, p. 63.

in meeting medical expenses. Only about 34 percent of families with incomes of less than $2,000 per year use health insurance benefits, as compared to nearly 90 percent of those with incomes of $7,000 or more.[3]

These factors are aggravated for Negroes when compared to whites for the simple reason that the proportion of persons in the United States who are poor is 3.5 times as high among Negroes (41 percent in 1966) as among whites (12 percent in 1966).

Maternal Mortality

Mortality rates for nonwhite mothers are four times as high as those for white mothers. There has been a sharp decline in such rates since 1940, when 774 nonwhite and 320 white mothers died for each 100,000 live births. In 1965, only 84 nonwhite and 21 white mothers died per 100,000 live births—but the relative gap between non-whites and whites actually increased.

Infant Mortality

Mortality rates among nonwhite babies are 58 percent higher than among whites for those under one month old, and almost three times as high among those from one month to one year old. This is true in spite of a large drop in infant mortality rates in both groups since 1940.

Number of Infants Who Died per 1,000 Live Births

| Year | Less Than One Month Old | | One Month to One Year Old | |
	White	Nonwhite	White	Nonwhite
1940	27.2	39.7	16.0	34.1
1950	19.4	27.5	7.4	17.0
1960	17.2	26.9	5.7	16.4
1965	16.1	25.4	5.4	14.9

Life Expectancy

To some extent because of infant mortality rates, life expectancy at birth was 6.9 years longer for whites (71.0 years) than for nonwhites (64.1 years) in 1965. Even in the prime

[3] Public programs of various kinds have been providing significant financial assistance for medical care in recent years. In 1964, over $1.1 billion was paid out by various governments for such aid. About 52 percent of medical vendor payments came from federal government agencies, 33 percent from states, and 12 percent from local governments. The biggest contributions were made by the Old Age Assistance program and the Medical Assistance for the Aged program. The enactment of Medicare in 1965 has significantly added to this flow of public assistance for medical aid. However, it is too early to evaluate the results upon health conditions among the poor.

working ages, life expectancy is significantly lower among nonwhites than among whites. In 1965, white persons 25 years old could expect to live an average of 48.6 more years; whereas nonwhites 25 years old could expect to live another 43.3 years, or 11 percent less. Similar but smaller discrepancies existed at all ages from 25 through 55; some actually increased slightly between 1960 and 1965.

Lower Utilization of Health Services

A fact that also contributes to poorer health conditions in the ghetto is that Negro families with incomes similar to those of whites spend less on medical services and visit medical specialists less often.

	Percent of Family Expenditures Spent for Medical Care 1960-61		Ratio White:
Income Group	White	Nonwhite	Nonwhite
Under $3,000	9	5	1.8:1
$3,000 to $7,499	7	5	1.4:1
$7,500 & over	6	4	1.5:1

Since the lowest income group contains a much larger proportion of nonwhite families than white families, the overall discrepancy in medical care spending between these two groups is very significant, as shown by the following table:

Health Expenses per Person per Year for the Period From July to December 1962

Income by Racial Group	Total Medical	Expenses				
		Hospital	Doctor	Dental	Medicine	Other
Under $2,000 per Family per Year:						
White	$130	$33	$41	$11	$32	$13
Nonwhite	63	15	23	5	16	5
$10,000 and More per Family per Year:						
White	$179	$34	$61	$37	$31	$16
Nonwhite	133	34	50	19	23	8

These data indicate that nonwhite families in the lower income group spent less than half as much per person on medical services as white families with similar incomes. This discrepancy sharply declines but is still significant in the higher income group, where total nonwhite medical expenditures per person equal, on the average, 74.3 percent of white expenditures.

Negroes spend less on medical care for several reasons. Negro households generally are larger, requiring larger nonmedical expenses for each household, and leaving less money

271

for meeting medical expenses. Thus lower expenditures per person would result even if expenditures per household were the same. Negroes also often pay more for other basic necessities such as food and consumer durables, as discussed in the next part of this chapter. In addition, fewer doctors, dentists, and medical facilities are conveniently available to Negroes than to most whites. This is a result both of geographic concentration of doctors in higher income areas in large cities and of discrimination against Negroes by doctors and hospitals. A survey in Cleveland indicated that there were 0.45 physicians per 1,000 people in poor neighborhoods, compared to 1.13 per 1,000 in nonpoverty areas. The result nationally is fewer visits to physicians and dentists.

Percent of Population Making One or More
Visits to Indicated Type of Medical
Specialist from July 1963 to June 1964

Type of Medical Specialist	Family Incomes of $2,000 to $3,999		Family Incomes of $7,000 to $9,999	
	White	Nonwhite	White	Nonwhite
Physician	64	56	70	64
Dentist	31	20	52	33

Although widespread use of health insurance has led many hospitals to adopt nondiscriminatory policies, some private hospitals still refuse to admit Negro patients or to accept doctors with Negro patients. And many individual doctors still discriminate against Negro patients. As a result, Negroes are more likely to be treated in hospital clinics than whites, and they are less likely to receive personalized service. This conclusion is confirmed by the following data:

Percent of All Visits to Physicians
from July 1963 to June 1964
Made in Indicated Ways

Type of Visit to Physician	Family Incomes of $2,000 to $3,999		Family Incomes of $7,000 to $9,999	
	White	Nonwhite	White	Nonwhite
In Physician's Office	68	56	73	66
Hospital clinic	17	35	7	16
Other (mainly telephone)	15	9	20	18
Total	100	100	100	100

Environmental Factors

Environmental conditions in disadvantaged Negro neighborhoods create further reasons for poor health conditions there. The level of sanitation is strikingly below that which is prevalent in most higher income areas. One simple reason is that residents often lack proper storage facilities for food—adequate refrigerators, freezers, even garbage cans which are sometimes stolen as fast as landlords can replace them.

In many areas where garbage collection and other sanitation services are grossly inadequate—commonly in the poorer parts of our large cities, rats proliferate. It is estimated that in 1965, there were over 14,000 cases of rat-bite in the United States, mostly in such neighborhoods.

The importance of these conditions was outlined for the Commission as follows:[4]

> Sanitation Commissioners of New York City and Chicago both feel this [sanitation] to be an important community problem and report themselves as being under substantial pressure to improve conditions. *It must be concluded that slum sanitation is a serious problem in the minds of the urban poor and well merits, at least on that ground, the attention of the Commission.* A related problem, according to one Sanitation Commissioner, is the fact that residents of areas bordering on slums feel that sanitation and neighborhood cleanliness is a crucial issue, relating to the stability of their blocks and constituting an important psychological index of "how far gone" their area is.
>
> . . . . There is no known study comparing sanitation services between slum and nonslum areas. The experts agree, however, that there are more services in the slums on a quantitative basis, although perhaps not on a per capita basis. In New York, for example, garbage pickups are supposedly scheduled for about six times a week in slums, compared to three times a week in other areas of the city; the comparable figures in Chicago are two-three times a week versus once a week.
>
> The point, therefore, is not the relative quantitative level of services, but the peculiarly intense needs of ghetto areas for sanitation services. This high demand is the product of numerous factors including: (1) higher population density; (2) lack of well managed buildings and adequate garbage services provided by landlords, number of receptacles, carrying to curbside, number of electric garbage disposals; (3) high relocation rates of tenants and businesses, producing heavy volume of bulk refuse left on streets and in buildings; (4) different uses of the streets —as outdoor living rooms in summer, recreation areas—producing high visibility and sensitivity to garbage problems; (5) large numbers of abandoned cars; (6) severe rodent and pest problems; (7) traffic congestion blocking garbage collection; and (8) obstructed street cleaning and snow removal on crowded, car-choked streets. Each of these elements adds to the problem and suggests a different possible line of attack.

---

[4] Memorandum to the Commission dated November 16, 1967, from Robert Patricelli, Minority Counsel, Subcommittee on Employment Manpower and Poverty, U.S. Senate.

III. Exploitation of Disadvantaged Consumers by Retail Merchants

Much of the violence in recent civil disorders has been directed at stores and other commercial establishments in disadvantaged Negro areas. In some cases, rioters focused on stores operated by white merchants who, they apparently believed, had been charging exorbitant prices or selling inferior goods. Not all the violence against these stores can be attributed to "revenge" for such practices. Yet it is clear that many residents of disadvantaged Negro neighborhoods believe they suffer constant abuses by local merchants.

Significant grievances concerning unfair commercial practices affecting Negro consumers were found in 11 of the 20 cities studied by the Commission. The fact that most of the merchants who operate stores in Negro areas are white undoubtedly contributes to the conclusion among Negroes that they are exploited by white society.

It is difficult to assess the precise degree and extent of exploitation. No systematic and reliable survey comparing consumer pricing and credit practices in all-Negro and other neighborhoods has ever been conducted on a nationwide basis. Differences in prices and credit practices between white middle-income areas and Negro low-income areas to some extent reflect differences in the real costs of serving these two markets (such as differential losses from pilferage in supermarkets), but the exact extent of these cost differences has never been estimated accurately. Finally, an examination of exploitative consumer practices must consider the particular structure and functions of the low-income consumer durables market.

Installment Buying

This complex situation can best be understood by first considering certain basic facts:

- Various cultural factors generate constant pressure on low-income families to buy many relatively expensive durable goods and display them in their homes. This pressure comes in part from continuous exposure to commercial advertising, especially on television. In January 1967, over 88 percent of all Negro households had TV sets. A 1961 study of 464 low-income families in New York City showed that 95 percent of these relatively poor families had TV sets.
- Many poor families have extremely low incomes, bad previous credit records, unstable sources of income, or other attributes which make it virtually impossible for them to buy merchandise

from established large national or local retail firms. These families lack enough savings to pay cash, and they cannot meet the standard credit requirements of established general merchants because they are too likely to fall behind in their payments.

- Poor families in urban areas are far less mobile than others. A 1967 Chicago study of low-income Negro households indicated their low automobile ownership compelled them to patronize neighborhood merchants. These merchants typically provided smaller selection, poorer services, and higher prices than big national outlets. The 1961 New York study also indicated that families who shopped outside their own neighborhoods were far less likely to pay exorbitant prices.

- Most low-income families are uneducated concerning the nature of credit purchase contracts, the legal rights and obligations of both buyers and sellers, sources of advice for consumers who are having difficulties with merchants, and the operation of the courts concerned with these matters. In contrast, merchants engaged in selling goods to them are very well informed.

- In most states, the laws governing relations between consumers and merchants in effect offer protection only to informed, sophisticated parties with understanding of each other's rights and obligations. Consequently, these laws are little suited to protect the rights of most low-income consumers.

In this situation, exploitative practices flourish. Ghetto residents who want to buy relatively expensive goods cannot do so from standard retail outlets and are thus restricted to local stores. Forced to use credit, they have little understanding of the pitfalls of credit buying. But because they have unstable incomes and frequently fail to make payments, the cost to the merchants of serving them is significantly above that of serving middle-income consumers. Consequently, a special kind of merchant appears to sell them goods on terms designed to cover the high cost of doing business in ghetto neighborhoods.

Whether they actually gain higher profits, these merchants charge higher prices than those in other parts of the city to cover the greater credit risks and other higher operating costs inherent in neighborhood outlets. A recent study conducted by the Federal Trade Commission in Washington, D. C., illustrates this conclusion dramatically. The FTC identified a number of stores specializing in selling furniture and appliances to low-income households. About 92 percent of the sales of these stores were credit sales involving installment purchases, as compared to 27 percent of the sales in general retail outlets handling the same merchandise.

The median income annually of a sample of 486 customers of these stores was about $4,200, but one-third had annual incomes below $3,600, about 6 percent were receiving welfare payments, and another 76 percent were employed in the lowest paying occupations (service workers, operatives, laborers, and domestics)—as compared to 36 percent of the total labor force in Washington in those occupations.

Definitely catering to a low-income group, these stores charged significantly higher prices than general merchandise outlets in the Washington area. According to testimony by Paul Rand Dixon, Chairman of the FTC, an item selling wholesale at $100 would retail on the average for $165 in a general merchandise store, and for $250 in a low-income specialty store. Thus, the customers of these outlets were paying an average price premium of about 52 percent.

While higher prices are not necessarily exploitative in themselves, many merchants in ghetto neighborhoods take advantage of their superior knowledge of credit buying by engaging in various exploitative tactics—high-pressure salesmanship, bait advertising, misrepresentation of prices, substitution of used goods for promised new ones, failure to notify consumers of legal actions against them, refusal to repair or replace substandard goods, exorbitant prices or credit charges, and use of shoddy merchandise. Such tactics affect a great many low-income consumers. In the New York study, 60 percent of all households had suffered from consumer problems (some of which were purely their own fault), about 23 percent had experienced serious exploitation. Another 20 percent, many of whom were also exploited, had experienced repossession, garnishment, or threat of garnishment.

Garnishment

Garnishment practices in many states allow creditors to deprive individuals of their wages through court action without hearing or trial. In about 20 states, the wages of an employee can be diverted to a creditor merely upon the latter's deposition, with no advance hearing where the employee can defend himself. He often receives no prior notice of such action and is usually unaware of the law's operation and too poor to hire legal defense. Moreover, consumers may find themselves still owing money on a sales contract even after the creditor has repossessed the goods. The New York study cited earlier in this chapter indicated that 20 percent of a sample of low-income families had been subject to legal action regarding consumer purchases. And the Federal Trade Commission study in Washington, D. C., showed that, on the average, retailers specializing in credit sales of furniture and appliances to low-income consumers resorted to court action once for every $2,200 of sales. Since their average sale was for $207, this amounted to using the courts to collect from one of every 11 customers. In contrast, department stores in the same area used court action against approximately one of every 14,500 customers.[5]

Variations in Food Prices

Residents of low-income Negro neighborhoods frequently claim that they pay higher prices for food in local markets than wealthier white suburbanites and receive inferior quality meat and produce. Statistically reliable information comparing prices and quality in these two kinds of areas is generally unavailable. The U. S. Bureau of Labor Statistics, studying food prices in six cities in 1966, compared prices of a standard list of 18 items in low-income areas and higher-income areas in each city. In a total of 180 stores, including independent and chain stores, and for items of the same type sold in the same types of stores, there were no significant differences in prices between low-income and high-income areas. However, stores in low-income areas were more likely to be small independents (which had somewhat higher prices), to sell low-quality produce and meat at any given price, and to be patronized by people who typically bought smaller-sized packages which are more expensive per unit of measure. In other words, many low-income consumers in fact pay higher prices, although the situation varies greatly from place to place.

Although these findings must be considered inconclusive, there are significant reasons to believe that poor households generally pay higher prices for the food they buy and receive lower quality food. Low-income consumers buy more food at local groceries because they are less mobile. Prices in these small stores are significantly higher than in major supermarkets because they cannot achieve economies of scale, and because real operating costs are higher in low-income Negro areas than in outlying suburbs. For instance, inventory "shrinkage" from pilfering and other causes is normally under 2 percent of sales, but can run twice as much in high-crime areas. Managers seek to make up for these added costs by charging higher prices for food, or by substituting lower grades.

These practices do not necessarily involve exploitation, but they are often perceived as exploitative and unfair by those who are aware of the price and quality differences involved, but unaware of operating costs. In addition, it is probable that genuinely exploitative pricing practices exist in some areas. In either case, differential food prices constitute another factor convincing urban Negroes in low-income neighborhoods that whites discriminate against them.

[5] Assuming their sales also averaged $207 per customer.

Chapter 9 / Comparing the Immigrant and Negro Experience

We have in the preceding chapters surveyed the historical background of racial discrimination and traced its effects on Negro employment, on the social structure of the ghetto community, and on the conditions of life that surround the urban Negro poor. Here we address a fundamental question that many white Americans are asking today: why has the Negro been unable to escape from poverty and the ghetto like the European immigrants?

THE MATURING ECONOMY

The changing nature of the American economy is one major reason. When the European immigrants were arriving in large numbers, America was becoming an urban-industrial society. To build its major cities and industries, America needed great pools of unskilled labor. The immigrants provided the labor, gained an economic foothold, and thereby enabled their children and grandchildren to move up to skilled, white collar, and professional employment.

Since World War II, especially, America's urban-industrial society has matured; unskilled labor is far less essential than before, and blue-collar jobs of all kinds are decreasing in number and importance as a source of new employment. The Negroes who migrated to the great urban centers lacked the skills essential to the new economy; and the schools of the ghetto have been unable to provide the education that can qualify them for decent jobs. The Negro migrant, unlike the immigrant, found little opportunity in the city; he had arrived too late, and the unskilled labor he had to offer was no longer needed.

THE DISABILITY OF RACE

Racial discrimination is undoubtedly the second major reason why the Negro has been unable to escape from poverty. The structure of discrimination has persistently narrowed his opportunities and restricted his prospects. Well before the high tide of immigration from overseas, Negroes were already relegated to the poorly paid, low status occupations. Had it not been for racial discrimination, the North might well have re-

278

cruited Southern Negroes after the Civil War to provide the labor for building the burgeoning urban-industrial economy. Instead, Northern employers looked to Europe for their sources of unskilled labor. Upon the arrival of the immigrants, the Negroes were dislodged from the few urban occupations they had dominated. Not until World War II were Negroes generally hired for industrial jobs, and by that time the decline in the need for unskilled labor had already begun. European immigrants, too, suffered from discrimination, but never was it so pervasive. The prejudice against color in America has formed a bar to advancement unlike any other.

ENTRY INTO THE POLITICAL SYSTEM

Political opportunities also played an important role in enabling the European immigrants to escape from poverty. The immigrants settled for the most part in rapidly growing cities that had powerful and expanding political machines, which gave them economic advantages in exchange for political support. The political machines were decentralized; and ward-level grievance machinery, as well as personal representation, enabled the immigrant to make his voice heard and his power felt. Since the local political organizations exercised considerable influence over public building in the cities, they provided employment in construction jobs for their immigrant voters. Ethnic groups often dominated one or more of the municipal services—police and fire protection, sanitation, and even public education.

By the time the Negroes arrived, the situation had altered dramatically. The great wave of public building had virtually come to an end; reform groups were beginning to attack the political machines; the machines were no longer so powerful or so well equipped to provide jobs and other favors.

Although the political machines retained their hold over the areas settled by Negroes, the scarcity of patronage jobs made them unwilling to share with the Negroes the political positions they had created in these neighborhoods. For example, Harlem was dominated by white politicians for many years after it had become a Negro ghetto; even today, New York's Lower East Side, which is now predominantly Puerto Rican, is strongly influenced by politicians of the older immigrant groups.

This pattern exists in many other American cities. Negroes are still underrepresented in city councils and in most city agencies.

Segregation played a role here too. The immigrants and their descendants, who felt threatened by the arrival of the

Negro, prevented a Negro-immigrant coalition that might have saved the old political machines. Reform groups, nominally more liberal on the race issue, were often dominated by businessmen and middle-class city residents who usually opposed coalition with any low-income group, white or black.

CULTURAL FACTORS

Cultural factors also made it easier for the immigrants to escape from poverty. They came to America from much poorer societies, with a low standard of living, and they came at a time when job aspirations were low. When most jobs in the American economy were unskilled, they sensed little deprivation in being forced to take the dirty and poorly paid jobs. Moreover, their families were large, and many breadwinners, some of whom never married, contributed to the total family income. As a result, family units managed to live even from the lowest paid jobs and still put some money aside for savings or investment, for example, to purchase a house or tenement, or to open a store or factory. Since the immigrants spoke little English and had their own ethnic culture, they needed stores to supply them with ethnic foods and other services. Since their family structures were patriarchal, men found satisfactions in family life that helped compensate for the bad jobs they had to take and the hard work they had to endure.

Negroes came to the city under quite different circumstances. Generally relegated to jobs that others would not take, they were paid too little to be able to put money in savings for new enterprises. In addition, Negroes lacked the extended family characteristics of certain European groups —each household usually had only one or two breadwinners. Moreover, Negro men had fewer cultural incentives to work in a dirty job for the sake of the family. As a result of slavery and of long periods of male unemployment afterwards, the Negro family structure had become matriarchal; the man played a secondary and marginal role in his family. For many Negro men, then, there were few of the cultural and psychological rewards of family life; they often abandoned their homes because they felt themselves useless to their families.

Although Negro men worked as hard as the immigrants to support their families, their rewards were less. The jobs did not pay enough to enable them to support their families, for prices and living standards had risen since the immigrants had come, and the entrepreneurial opportunities that had allowed some immigrants to become independent, even rich, had vanished. Above all, Negroes suffered from segregation, which denied them access to the good jobs and the right unions and which deprived them of the opportunity to buy real estate or obtain business loans or move out of the ghetto and bring up their children in middle-class neighborhoods. Immigrants were able to leave their ghettos as soon as they had the money; segregation has denied Negroes the opportunity to live elsewhere.

The Vital Element of Time

Finally, nostalgia makes it easy to exaggerate the ease of escape of the white immigrants from the ghettos. When the immigrants were immersed in poverty, they too lived in slums, and these neighborhoods exhibited fearfully high rates of alcoholism, desertion, illegitimacy, and the other pathologies associated with poverty. Just as some Negro men desert their families when they are unemployed and their wives can get jobs, so did the men of other ethnic groups, even though time and affluence has clouded white memories of the past.

Today, whites tend to contrast their experience with poverty-stricken Negroes. The fact is, among many of the Southern and Eastern Europeans who came to America in the last great wave of immigration, those who came already urbanized were the first to escape from poverty. The others who came to America from rural backgrounds, as Negroes did, are only now, after three generations, in the final stages of escaping from poverty. Until the last 10 years or so, most of these were employed in blue-collar jobs, and only a small proportion of their children were able or willing to attend college. In other words, only the third, and in many cases, only the fourth generation has been able to achieve the kind of middle-class income and status that allows it to send its children to college. Because of favorable economic and political conditions, these ethnic groups were able to escape from lower-class status to working class and lower middle-class status, but it has taken them three generations.

Negroes have been concentrated in the city for only two generations, and they have been there under much less favorable conditions. Moreover, their escape from poverty has been blocked in part by the resistance of the European ethnic groups; they have been unable to enter some unions and to move into some neighborhoods outside the ghetto because descendants of the European immigrants who control these unions and neighborhoods have not yet abandoned them for middle-class occupations and areas.

Even so, some Negroes have escaped poverty, and they have done so in only two generations; their success is less visible than that of the immigrants in many cases, for residential segregation has forced them to remain in the ghetto. Still, the proportion of nonwhites employed in white-collar, technical, and professional jobs has risen from 10.2 percent in 1950 to 20.8 percent in 1966, and the proportion attending college has risen an equal amount. Indeed, the development of a small but steadily increasing Negro middle class while the greater part of the Negro population is stagnating economically is creating a growing gap between Negro haves and have-nots.

This gap, as well as the awareness of its existence by those left behind, undoubtedly adds to the feelings of desperation and anger which breed civil disorders. Low-income Negroes realize that segregation and lack of job opportunities have made it possible for only a small proportion of all Negroes to escape poverty and the summer disorders are at least in part a protest against being left behind and left out.

The immigrant who labored long hours at hard and often menial work had the hope of a better future, if not for himself then for his children. This was the promise of the "American dream"—the society offered to all a future that was open-ended; with hard work and perseverance, a man and his family could in time achieve not only material well-being but "position" and status.

For the Negro family in the urban ghetto, there is a different vision—the future seems to lead only to a dead-end.

What the American economy of the late 19th and early 20th century was able to do to help the European immigrants escape from poverty is now largely impossible. New methods of escape must be found for the majority of today's poor.

PART III

WHAT CAN BE DONE?

Chapter 10 / The Community Response

INTRODUCTION

The racial disorders of last summer in part reflect the failure of all levels of government—federal and state as well as local —to come to grips with the problems of our cities. The ghetto symbolizes the dilemma: a widening gap between human needs and public resources and a growing cynicism regarding the commitment of community institutions and leadership to meet these needs.

The problem has many dimensions—financial, political and institutional. Almost all cities—and particularly the central cities of the largest metropolitan regions—are simply unable to meet the growing need for public services and facilities with traditional sources of municipal revenue. Many cities are structured politically so that great numbers of citizens—particularly minority groups—have little or no representation in the processes of government. Finally, some cities lack either the will or the capacity to use effectively the resources that are available to them.

Instrumentalities of federal and state government often compound the problems. National policy expressed through a very large number of grant programs and institutions rarely exhibits a coherent and consistent perspective when viewed at the local level. State efforts, traditionally focused on rural areas, often fail to tie in effectively with either local or federal programs in urban areas.

Meanwhile, the decay of the central city continues—its revenue base eroded by the retreat of industry and white middle-class families to the suburbs, its budget and tax rate inflated by rising costs and increasing numbers of dependent citizens and its public plant—schools, hospitals and correctional institutions —deteriorated by age and long deferred maintenance.

Yet to most citizens, the decay remains largely invisible.

283

Only their tax bills and the headlines about crime or "riots" suggest that something may be seriously wrong in the city.

There are, however, two groups of people that live constantly with the problem of the city: the public officials and the poor, particularly the residents of the racial ghetto. Their relationship is a key factor in the development of conditions underlying civil disorders.

Our investigations of the 1967 riot cities establishes that:

- Virtually every major episode of urban violence in the summer of 1967 was foreshadowed by an accumulation of unresolved grievances by ghetto residents against local authorities (often, but not always, the police). So high was the resulting underlying tension, that routine and random events, tolerated or ignored under most circumstances (such as the raid on the "Blind Pig" in Detroit and the arrest of the cab driver in Newark) became the triggers of sudden violence.
- Coinciding with this high level of dissatisfaction, confidence in the willingness and ability of local government to respond to Negro grievances was low. Evidence presented to this Commission in hearings, field reports and research analyses of the 1967 riot cities, establishes that a substantial number of Negroes were disturbed and angry about local governments' failures to solve their problems.

Several developments have converged to produce this volatile situation.

First, there is a widening gulf in communications between local government and the residents of the erupting ghettos of the city. As a result, many Negro citizens develop a profound sense of isolation and alienation from the processes and programs of government. This lack of communication exists for all residents in our larger cities; it is, however, far more difficult to overcome for low income, less educated citizens who are disproportionately supported by and dependent upon programs administered by agencies of local government. Consequently, they are more often subject to real or imagined official misconduct ranging from abrasive contacts with public officials to arbitrary administrative actions.

Further, as a result of the long history of racial discrimination, grievances experienced by Negroes often take on personal and symbolic significance transcending the immediate consequences of the event. For example, inadequate sanitation services are viewed by many ghetto residents not merely as instances of poor public service but as manifestations of racial discrimination. This perception reinforces existing feelings of alienation and contributes to a heightened level of frustration and dissatisfaction, not only with the administrators of the sanitation department, but with all the representatives of local

284

government. This is particularly true with respect to the police, who are the only public agents on duty in the ghetto 24 hours a day and who bear this burden of hostility for the less visible elements of the system.

The lack of communication and the absence of regular contacts with ghetto residents prevent city leaders from learning about problems and grievances as they develop. As a result, tensions which could have been dissipated if responded to promptly, mount unnecessarily and the potential for explosion grows inevitably. Once disorder erupts, public officials are frequently unable to fashion an effective response; they lack adequate information about the nature of the trouble and its causes and they lack rapport with local leaders who might be able to influence the community.

Second, many city governments are poorly organized to respond effectively to the needs of ghetto residents, even when these needs are made known to appropriate public officials. Most middle-class city dwellers have limited contacts with local government. When contacts do occur they tend to concern relatively narrow and specific problems. Furthermore, middle-class citizens, although subject to many of the same frustrations and resentments in dealing with the public bureaucracy as ghetto residents, find it relatively easy to locate the appropriate agency for help and redress. If they fail to get satisfaction, they can call on a variety of remedies—assistance of elected representatives, friends in government, a lawyer. In short, the middle-class city dweller has relatively fewer needs for public services and is reasonably well positioned to move the system to his benefit.

On the other hand, the typical ghetto resident has interrelated social and economic problems which require the services of several government and private agencies. At the same time, he may be unable to identify his problems to fit the complicated structure of government. Moreover, he may be unaware of his rights and opportunities under public programs and unable to obtain the necessary guidance from either public or private sources.

Current trends in municipal administration have had the effect of reducing the capacity of local government to respond effectively to these needs. The pressures for administrative efficiency and cost-cutting have brought about the withdrawal of many operations of city government from direct contact with neighborhood and citizen. Red tape and administrative complexity have filled the vacuum created by the centralization of local government. The introduction of a merit system and a professionalized civil service has made management of

the cities more businesslike, but it has also tended to deperson-
alize and isolate government. The rigid patterns of segregation
prevalent within the central city have widened the distance
between Negro citizens and city hall.

In most of the riot cities surveyed by the Commission, we
found little or no meaningful coordination among city agencies
either in responding to the needs of ghetto residents on an
ongoing basis or in planning to head off disturbances. The
consequences of this lack of coordination were particularly
severe for the police. Despite the fact that they were being
called upon increasingly to deal with tensions and citizen complaints having little, if anything, to do with police services, the
police departments of many large cities were isolated from
other city agencies, sometimes including the mayor and his
staff. In these cities, the police were compelled to deal with
ghetto residents angered over dirty streets, dilapidated housing, unfair commercial practices or inferior schools—grievances which they had neither the responsibility for creating,
nor the authority to redress.

Third, ghetto residents increasingly believe that they are
excluded from the decision-making process which affects their
lives and community. This feeling of exclusion, intensified by
the bitter legacy of racial discrimination, has engendered a
deep seated hostility toward the institutions of government. It
has severely compromised the effectiveness of programs intended to provide improved services to ghetto residents.

In part, this is the lesson of Detroit and New Haven where
well intentioned programs designed to respond to the needs
of ghetto residents were not worked out and implemented
sufficiently in cooperation with the intended beneficiaries. A
report prepared for the Senate Subcommittee on Employment,
Manpower and Poverty presented just prior to the riot in
Detroit, found that:

> Area residents . . . complain almost continually that . . . their de-
> mands for program changes are not heeded, that they have little
> voice in what goes on. . . . As much as the area residents are
> involved, listened to, and even heeded, . . . it becomes fairly
> clear that the relationship is still one of superordinate-subordi-
> nate, rather than one of equals . . . the procedures by which
> HRD (the Mayor's Committee for Human Resources Develop-
> ment, the Detroit Community Action Agency) operates by and
> large admit the contributions of area residents only after pro-
> grams have been written, after policies have already operated
> for a time or already been formulated, and to a large degree,
> only in formal and infrequent meetings rather than in day-to-
> day operations. . . . The meaningfulness of resident involvement

is reduced by its after-the-fact nature and by relatively limited resources they have at their disposal.[1]

Mayor Alfonso J. Cervantes of St. Louis was even more explicit. In testimony before this Commission, he stated that:

We have found that ghetto neighborhoods cannot be operated on from outside alone. The people within them should have a voice, and our experience has shown that it is often a voice that speaks with good sense, since the practical aspect of the needs of the ghetto people are so much clearer to the people there than they are to anyone else.

The political system, traditionally an important vehicle for minorities to participate effectively in decisions affecting the distribution of public resources, has not worked for the Negro as it has for other groups. The reasons are fairly obvious.

We have found that the number of Negro officials in elected and appointed positions in the riot cities is minimal in proportion to the Negro population. The alienation of the Negro from the political process has been exacerbated by his racial and economic isolation.

Specifically, the needs of ghetto residents for social welfare and other public services have swelled dramatically at a time when increased affluence has diminished the need for such services by the rest of the urban population. By reducing disproportionately the economic disability of other portions of the population, particularly other ethnic urban minorities, this affluence has left the urban Negro few potential local allies with whom to make common cause for shared objectives. The development of political alliances, essential to effective participation of minority groups in the political process, has been further impaired by the polarization of the races, which on both sides has transformed economic considerations into racial issues.

Finally, these developments have coincided with the demise of the historic urban political machines and the growth of the "city manager" concept of government. While this tendency has produced major benefits in terms of honest and efficient administration, it has eliminated an important political link between city government and low-income residents.

These conditions have produced a vast and threatening disparity in perceptions of the intensity and validity of Negro dissatisfaction. Viewed from the perspective of the ghetto resi-

Examination of War on Poverty, Staff and Consultants Reports, prepared by Center for Urban Studies, University of Chicago, for the Subcommittee on Employment, Manpower and Poverty, Senate Committee on Labor and Public Welfare, 90th Cong., 1st Sess., (Sept. 1967), vol. VI, pp. 1721 ff.

dent, city government appears distant and unconcerned, the possibility of effective change remote. As a result, tension rises perceptibly; the explosion comes as the climax to a progression of tension-generating incidents. To the city administration, unaware of this growing tension or unable to respond effectively to it, the outbreak of disorder comes as a shock.

No democratic society can long endure the existence within its major urban centers of a substantial number of citizens who feel deeply aggrieved as a group, yet lack confidence in the government to rectify perceived injustice and in their ability to bring about needed change.

We are aware that reforms in existing instruments of local government and their relationship to the ghetto population will mean little unless joined with sincere and comprehensive response to the severe social and economic needs of ghetto residents. Elsewhere in this Report we make specific recommendations with respect to employment, education, welfare, and housing which we hope will meet some of these needs.

We believe, however, that there are measures which can and should be taken now; that they can be put to work without great cost and without delay; that they can be built upon in the future and that they will effectively reduce the level of grievance and tension as well as improve the responsiveness of local government to the needs of ghetto residents.

BASIC STRATEGY AND GOALS

To meet the needs identified above, we recommend pursuit of a comprehensive strategy, which would accomplish the following goals:

- Effective communication between ghetto residents and local government.
- Improved ability of local government to respond to the needs and problems of ghetto residents.
- Expanded opportunities for indigenous leadership to participate in shaping decisions and policies which affect their community.
- Increased accountability of public officials.

We recognize that not all of the programs proposed below to implement the foregoing goals can be instituted with the immediacy which the problem requires. Because the need for action at the local level, where government impinges directly upon the ghetto resident, is particularly urgent, we propose that our suggested programs be implemented in two phases. It is vital, however, that the first phase programs not be regarded or perceived as short term, and anti-riot efforts calculated to cool already inflamed situations. These programs will have little

288

chance of succeeding unless they are part of a long-range commitment to action designed to eliminate the fundamental sources of grievance and tension.

Establishment of Neighborhood Action Task Forces

To open channels of communication between government and ghetto residents, improve the capacity of the city administration to respond effectively to community needs and provide opportunity for meaningful citizen participation in decision-making, we recommend establishment of joint government-community Neighborhood Action Task Forces covering each neighborhood within the city which has a high proportion of low-income minority citizens. While the exact form of these groups will depend upon the size and needs of each municipality, the following basic features should be incorporated:

Composition: Each Task Force should include a key official in the mayor's office with direct and immediate access to the mayor, ranking city officials from the operating agencies servicing the ghetto community, elected leaders, representatives from the local business, labor, professional and church communities and neighborhood leaders, including representatives of community organizations of all orientations and youth leaders. Each Task Force would be headed by the mayor's representative. In the larger cities, each of these chairmen would sit as a member of a city-wide Task Force.

Functions: The Neighborhood Action Task Forces should meet on a regular basis at a location accessible to ghetto residents. These meetings will afford an opportunity for ghetto leaders to communicate directly with the municipal administrators for their area to discuss problems and programs which affect the community. In effect, this device furnishes an interagency coordinating mechanism on the one hand and a "community cabinet" on the other.

Ghetto residents should be able to rely on the capacity of the Task Force to cut through the maze of red tape and to overcome bureaucratic barriers in order to make things—collection of garbage, removal of abandoned cars, installation of lights in the park, establishment of playstreets—happen. To accomplish this purpose, the participating city officials should be those with operational decision-making authority. Lower-staff or public relations personnel will not be able to provide the confrontation and interaction with the community representatives which is essential to the effective functioning of the Task

Force. Moreover, there is grave danger that opening channels of communication without providing opportunities for obtaining relief will further estrange ghetto residents. If this is not to happen, the Task Force should have a meaningful and realistic capacity for securing redress of grievances. For the same reason, it is essential that the Task Force have the full and energetic support of the mayor and the city council.

The potential for responding effectively to community needs is not limited to available public resources. Acting through business, labor and church members and local Urban Coalitions which have already been formed, the Task Force will have a capacity to involve the resources of the private sector in meeting needs within the ghetto. Possibilities range from support of special summer youth programs (weekend trips, recreation events, camping programs) to provision of cultural and employment opportunities on a year-round basis.

The Neighborhood Action Task Force can play a significant role with respect to youth activities. One approach which has worked in several cities involves the establishment of Youth Councils to employ young street leaders (regardless of previous police records) to develop community programs for other alienated youth. These activities might include organizing and operating libraries, neighborhood cleanup campaigns, police-community dialogues and sports competitions in their own neighborhoods.

Finally, such an organization can make a major contribution to the prevention of civil disorders. If the Task Force has been successful in achieving the objectives stressed above, its members will have gained the confidence of a wide spectrum of ghetto residents. This will enable them to identify potentially explosive conditions and, working with the police, to defuse them.

Similarly, the Task Force could have considerable effectiveness in handling threatening incidents identified by the police. To accomplish this objective, an early warning system could be instituted during the critical summer months. Operating on a 24-hour basis, such a system would have the capacity to receive and evaluate police reports of potentially serious incidents and to initiate an appropriate non-police response, utilizing community contacts and Task Force personnel. Any such operation must have the cooperation of the police, who will be in control of the overall disorder response. To avoid confusion and duplication of effort, the Task Force should have responsibility for coordinating the efforts of all agencies, other than police and fire, once a disturbance has occurred. An example will serve to illustrate how such a system might operate.

Following the slaying last summer of a Negro teen-ager by a Negro detective in the Bedford-Stuyvesant section of Brooklyn, New York, a rumor that the youth had been shot by a white policeman and that the police were trying to suppress this information began to circulate through an already tense neighborhood. The situation became threatening. Yet, within an hour, three white members of the mayor's summer task force group were able to convince a group of black militants that the police version was true. Walking the streets that night and the next two evenings, they worked to dispel the rumor and to restore community stability.

In the larger cities, the city-wide task force could have responsibility for coordinating the programs of various municipal agencies, concentrating their impact on poverty areas and planning for the more effective implementation of existing public efforts.

The Commission believes that the Task Force approach can do precisely what other forms of neighborhood organizations have not been able to do. It can connect the real needs and priorities of low-income residents with the energies and resources of both city government and the private sector. It can substantially improve the quality and timeliness of city services to these areas. It will fail unless all of the groups involved are prepared to deal fairly and openly with the problems of the community. But if it succeeds, it will not only produce improved services but help to generate a new sense of community, as well.

Establishment of Effective Grievance-Response Mechanisms

Effective implementation of the Neighborhood Action Task Forces will depend upon the continuing commitment of the city administration to its success. To ensure continuous attention to many of the sources of tension identified above, we recommend that formal mechanisms for the processing of grievances, many of which will relate to the performance of the city government, be established independent of the local administration.

We are convinced, on the record before this Commission, that the frustration reflected in the recent disorders results, in part at least, from the lack of accessible and visible means of establishing the merits of grievances against the agencies of local and state government, including but not limited to the police. Cities and states throughout the country now have under consideration various forms of grievance-response devices. While we are not prepared to specify the form which such a mechanism should take in any particular community, there are certain criteria which should be met. These include:

- *Independence:* This can be achieved by long term appointment of the administrator, subject to City Council removal. The grievance agency should be separate from operating municipal agencies.
- *Adequate staff and funding:* Exact costs will vary depending on the size and needs of the city's population. It is most important that the agency have adequate funds and staff to discharge its responsibilities.
- *Comprehensive coverage of grievances against public agencies and authorities:* General jurisdiction will facilitate access by grievants. Moreover, unlike specialized, complaint agencies, such as civilian review boards, all agencies would be brought equally under public scrutiny. This should facilitate its acceptance by public officials.
- *Power to receive complaints, hold hearings, subpoena witnesses, make public recommendations for remedial action to local authorities and, in cases involving violation of law, bring suit.* These powers are the minimum necessary to the effective operation of the grievance mechanism. As we envision it, the agency's principal power derives from its authority to investigate and make public findings and recommendations. It should, of course, have a conciliation process whereby complaints could be resolved without full investigation and processing.
- *Accessibility:* In large cities, ready access to grievants may require setting up neighborhood offices in ghetto areas. In others, local resident aides could be empowered to receive complaints. It should be possible to file a grievance orally or in writing. If forms are used, they should be easily understood and widely available.
- *Participation in grievance process:* Grievants should be given full opportunity to take part in all proceedings and to be represented by counsel. They should receive prompt advice of action taken, and results of investigations should be made public.

Expanded Legal Services

Among the most intense grievances underlying the riots of the summer of 1967 were those which derived from conflicts between ghetto residents and private parties, principally the white landlord and merchant. Though the legal obstacles are considerable, resourceful and imaginative use of available legal processes could contribute significantly to the alleviation of resulting tensions. Through the adversary process which is at the heart of our judicial system, litigants are afforded meaningful opportunity to influence events which affect them and their community. However, effective utilization of the courts requires legal assistance, a resource seldom available to the poor.

Litigation is not the only need which ghetto residents have for legal service. Participation in the grievance procedures suggested above may well require legal assistance. More importantly, ghetto residents have need of effective advocacy of their interests and concerns in a variety of other contexts, from representation before welfare agencies and other institutions of government to advocacy before planning boards and commissions concerned with the formulation of development plans. Again, professional representation can provide substantial benefits in terms of overcoming the ghetto resident's alienation from the institutions of government by implicating him in its processes. Although lawyers function in precisely this fashion for the middle-class clients, they are too often not available to the impoverished ghetto resident.

The Legal Services Program administered by the Office of Economic Opportunity has made a good beginning in providing legal assistance to the poor. Its present level of effort should be substantially expanded through increased private and public funding. In addition, the participation of law schools should be increased through development of programs whereby advanced students can provide legal assistance as a regular part of their professional training. In all of these efforts, the local bar bears major responsibility for leadership and support.

Assistance for Mayors and City Councils

In the chapters that follow we direct attention to broad strategies and programs of national action. Yet the capacity of the Federal Government to affect local problems depends to a great extent on the capacity of city government to respond competently to federal program initiatives.

In the face of the bewildering proliferation of both community demands and local, state and federal programs, mayors and city councils need to create new mechanisms to aid in decision making, program planning and coordination. At this time, however, no assistance is available to develop these new and critically necessary institutional capabilities or to support the required research, consultants, staff or other vital components of administrative or legislative competence.

The Commission recommends, therefore, that both the state and federal governments provide financial assistance to cities for these purposes as a regular part of all urban program funding.

*Hearings on Ghetto Problems and Enactment of
Appropriate Local Legislation*

Many of the grievances identified in our study of the conditions underlying civil disorders can be redressed only through legislative action. Accordingly, we recommend that the legislative body of each city with a substantial minority population hold, as soon as possible, a series of hearings on ghetto problems. In large cities, these hearings could well be held in the ghetto itself to facilitate full citizen participation.

In addition to establishing a foundation for needed legislative measures, these hearings would constitute a visible demonstration of governmental concern for the problems of ghetto residents. They would also provide a most useful means of bridging the communications gap, contributing to an improved understanding in the white community about the conditions of ghetto life.

Expanded Employment by City Government of Ghetto Residents

We strongly recommend that local government undertake a concerted effort to provide substantial employment opportunities for ghetto residents. Local governments now employ 6.4 million people full-time, most of whom live in urban areas; they comprise one of the fastest growing segments of the economy. This offers an opportunity of the greatest significance for local government to respond to one of the most critical needs of ghetto residents and, at the same time, to decrease the distance between city hall and the ghetto by deliberate employment, training and upgrading of Negroes.

To accomplish this goal, we recommend that municipal authorities review applicable civil service policies and job standards and take prompt action to remove arbitrary barriers to employment of ghetto residents. Re-evaluation is particularly necessary with respect to requirements relating to employment qualification tests and police records. Leadership by city government in this vital area is of urgent priority, not only because of the important public employment potential, but also to stimulate private employers to take similar action.

SECOND PHASE ACTIONS

Establishment of Neighborhood City Halls

The Neighborhood Action Task Force concept provides a basis on which lasting structures can be erected. The principal change required in order to transform the official component of the Task Force into a permanent instrument of local government involves the establishment of offices in the neighborhoods served. Depending on the size and composition of the neighborhood, the permanent staff should include an assistant mayor, representatives of the municipal agencies, the city councilman's staff and other institutions and groups included in the Task Force. This facility would function, in effect, as a "Neighborhood City Hall."

The Neighborhood City Hall would accomplish several interrelated objectives. It would contribute to the improvement of public services by providing an effective channel for low-income citizens to communicate their needs and problems to the appropriate public officials and by increasing the ability of local government to respond in a coordinated and timely fashion. It would serve as the eyes and ears of the mayor and council and furnish an informal forum for complaints and grievances. It would make information about government programs and services available to ghetto residents, enabling them to make more effective use of such programs and services and making clear the limitations on the availability of all such programs and services. It would expand opportunities for meaningful community access to and involvement in the planning and implementation of policy affecting the neighborhood. Most important, the Neighborhood City Hall, building on the Task Force approach, affords a significant opportunity to accomplish the democratic goal of making government closer and more accountable to the citizen.

Development of Multi-Service Centers

Frequently, services vital to the ghetto resident—job placement and location, health care, legal assistance—are inaccessible because they are located at considerable distance from the ghetto, a distance often made greater by the lack of efficient public transportation. This problem is compounded by the fact that many key service institutions are fragmented, requiring those seeking assistance to pursue it at various locations scattered throughout a large urban area.

To meet this need, the Office of Economic Opportunity has funded over 700 neighborhood centers in ghetto areas throughout the country since 1964. Many of these have been small store-front operations housing OEO-funded services. Some, as in Detroit, have had a fairly wide range of services and have served a large number of families.

The principal problem has been that most centers have not been comprehensive enough. They rarely include traditional city and state agency services. Many relevant federal programs are seldom located in the same center. Manpower and education programs from HEW and the Labor Department, for example, have been housed in separate centers without adequate consolidation or coordination either geographically or programmatically.

The resulting proliferation led the President to call upon the Department of Housing and Urban Development to establish comprehensive "one stop service centers." The experience thus far indicates the need for more effective coordination of federal programs at the national and regional levels. Legislation may be required to simplify grant procedures and assure such coordination.

Each center should have enough neighborhood workers to reach out into the homes of needy people who are not able to seek help. To assure that the service centers are relevant to the needs and styles of the neighborhood, ghetto residents should be trained and employed at all levels. This purpose can well be served through establishment and involvement of Community Service Center Councils to establish overall policy.

We recommend increased federal funding for comprehensive centers and implementation of the policy guidelines proposed above.

Improved Political Representation

It is beyond the scope of this Report to consider in detail the many problems presented by the existing distribution of political power within city governments. But it is plain that the Negro ghetto resident feels deeply that he is not represented fairly and adequately under the arrangements which prevail in many cities. This condition strikes at major democratic values.

To meet this problem, city government and the majority community should revitalize the political system to encourage fuller participation by all segments of the community. Whether this requires adoption of any one system of representation, we are not prepared to say. But it is clear that at-large representation, currently the practice in many American cities, does not give members of the minority community a feeling of involvement or stake in city government. Further, this form of representation dilutes the normal political impact of pressures generated by a particular neighborhood or district.

Negro representation and participation in the formal structure of government can also be furthered by a concerted effort to appoint Negroes to significant policy positions in city government.

More Effective Community Participation

One of the most difficult and controversial problems we have encountered relates to ghetto demands for "self-determination" or "community control." To a limited extent, this concept was made a matter of national policy in the Economic Opportunity

Act of 1964 which specified that community action programs should be developed, conducted and administered with "maximum feasible participation" of the residents of the areas and members of the groups served.

In the three years since the beginning of the war on poverty, the effort to put maximum feasible participation into effect has met with both success and failure. One measure of its success can be seen in the extent to which the demand for participation, even control, over a variety of programs affecting the ghetto has spilled over into the most traditional areas, such as public school administration.

But the demands made often seem intransigent and the time required for negotiation with residents extravagant. The pulling and hauling of different factions competing for control within the ghetto community sometimes makes it difficult to mount any program. Moreover, it is often easier to organize groups to oppose, complain, demonstrate and boycott than to develop and run programs.

Yet, the demand for a community voice represents a marked and desirable gain over the apathy that existed before. Despite its problems, we believe that meaningful community participation and a substantial measure of involvement in program development is an essential strategy for city government. The democratic values which it advances—providing a stake in the social system, improving the accountability of public officials— as well as the pragmatic benefits which it provides far outweigh these costs.

The essential question which city leadership must face is the ultimate goal of community participation. In this sense, community involvement is directly related to the strategy of decentralization, for with the support of the city, neighborhood groups may become an effective force for carrying on a variety of functions—such as physical renewal and redevelopment— which can be highly disruptive when imposed by outside authority.

If these principles are accomplished, then the choice of mechanisms will depend upon the needs of the particular community and the structure of the local government. We have described earlier in this section opportunities for meaningful community participation in the processes of government. Additional and diverse instrumentalities such as community neighborhood school boards, community planning boards, tenants' councils, youth councils, advisory committees and consumer trade organizations offer further ways of providing institutional channels for effective citizen participation in public decision-making. The crucial issue, however, is whether city government is willing to legitimate these organizations by dealing with them on a regular basis with respect to matters within their competence. We believe that such an approach offers substantial promise of improving the relationship between local government and ghetto residents.

The involvement of the ghetto community in the planning and operation of development programs need not be confined to the public arena. There is great potential in private community development corporations which can emerge from a combined public-private sponsorship and perform mixed functions for the community, including sponsorship of locally owned businesses.

A most promising approach is the neighborhood membership corporation, the first of which was established in Columbus, Ohio, in 1965—the East Central Citizens Organization (ECCO), under an OEO grant. Functioning as a town meeting, its members include all of the residents of a defined ghetto neighborhood (8,150 people). Its activities encompass day-care centers, credit unions, legal and medical services, newspapers, restaurants and business enterprises.

Both money and manpower will be needed from government, foundations and private business to create and assist these corporations and other new community institutions. Technical and professional support will be required. The opportunity that they offer to develop stable community leadership structures and constructive involvement should not be allowed to fail for lack of such support.

CONCLUSION

Finally, there remains the issue of leadership. Now, as never before, the American city has need for the personal qualities of strong democratic leadership. Given the difficulties and delays involved in administrative reorganization or institutional change, the best hope for the city in the short run lies in this powerful instrument. In most cities the mayor will have the prime responsibility.

It is in large part his role now to create a sense of commitment and concern for the problems of the ghetto community and to set the tone for the entire relationship between the institutions of city government and all the citizenry.

Part of the task is to interpret the problems of the ghetto community to the citizenry at large and to generate channels of communication between Negro and white leadership outside of government. Only if all the institutions of the community—those outside of government as well as those inside the structure—are implicated in the problems of the ghetto, can the alienation and distrust of disadvantaged citizens be overcome.

This is now the decisive role for the urban mayor. As leader and mediator, he must involve all those groups—employers, news media, unions, financial institutions and others—which only together can bridge the chasm now separating the racial ghetto from the community. His goal, in effect, must be to develop a new working concept of democracy within the city.

In this effort, state government has a vital role to play. It must equip city leadership with the jurisdictional tools to deal with its problems. It must provide a fuller measure of financial and other resources to urban areas. Most importantly, state leadership is in a unique position to focus the interests and growing resources, political as well as financial, of the suburbs on the physical, social, and cultural environment of the central cities. The crisis confronting city government today cannot be met without regional cooperation. This cooperation can take many forms—metropolitan government, regional planning, joint endeavors. It must be a principal goal, perhaps the over-riding concern, of leadership at the state level to fashion a lasting and mutually productive relationship between city and suburban areas.

Chapter 11 / Police and the Community

INTRODUCTION

We have cited deep hostility between police and ghetto communities as a primary cause of the disorders surveyed by the Commission. In Newark, in Detroit, in Watts, in Harlem—in practically every city that has experienced racial disruption since the summer of 1964—abrasive relationships between police and Negroes and other minority groups have been a major source of grievance, tension and, ultimately, disorder.

In a fundamental sense, however, it is wrong to define the problem solely as hostility to police. In many ways the policeman only symbolizes much deeper problems.

The policeman in the ghetto is a symbol not only of law, but of the entire system of law enforcement and criminal justice.

As such, he becomes the tangible target for grievances against shortcomings throughout that system: against assembly-line justice in teeming lower courts; against wide disparities in sentences; against antiquated corrections facilities; against the basic inequities imposed by the system on the poor —to whom, for example, the option of bail means only jail.

The policeman in the ghetto is a symbol of increasingly bitter social debate over law enforcement.

One side, disturbed and perplexed by sharp rises in crime and urban violence, exerts extreme pressure on police for tougher law enforcement. Another group, inflamed against police as agents of repression, tends toward defiance of what it regards as order maintained at the expense of justice.

The policeman in the ghetto is the most visible symbol, finally, of a society from which many ghetto Negroes are increasingly alienated.

At the same time, police responsibilities in the ghetto are even greater than elsewhere in the community since the other institutions of social control have so little authority: the schools, because so many are segregated, old, and inferior; religion, which has become irrelevant to those who have lost faith as they lost hope; career aspirations, which for many young Negroes are totally lacking; the family, because its bonds are so often snapped. It is the policeman who must deal with the consequences of this institutional vacuum and is then resented for the presence and the measures this effort demands.

Alone, the policeman in the ghetto cannot solve these problems. His role is already one of the most difficult in our society. He must deal daily with a range of problems and people that test his patience, ingenuity, character, and courage in ways that few of us are ever tested. Without positive leadership, goals, operational guidance, and public support, the individual policeman can only feel victimized. Nor are these problems the responsibility only of police administrators; they are deep enough to tax the courage, intelligence, and leadership of mayors, city officials, and community leaders. As Dr. Kenneth B. Clark told the Commission:

> This society knows . . . that if human beings are confined in ghetto compounds of our cities, and are subjected to criminally inferior education, pervasive economic and job discrimination, committed to houses unfit for human habitation, subjected to unspeakable conditions of municipal services, such as sanitation, that such human beings are not likely to be responsive to appeals to be lawful, to be respectful, to be concerned with property of others.

And yet, precisely because the policeman in the ghetto is a symbol—precisely because he symbolizes so much—it is of critical importance that the police and society take every possible step to allay grievances that flow from a sense of injustice and increased tension and turmoil.

In this work, the police bear a major responsibility for making needed changes. In the first instance, they have the prime responsibility for safeguarding the minimum goal of any civilized society—security of life and property. To do so, they are given society's maximum power—discretion in the use of force. Second, it is axiomatic that effective law enforcement requires the support of the community. Such support will not be present when a substantial segment of the community feels threatened by the police and regards the police as an occupying force.

At the same time, public officials also have a clear duty to help the police make any necessary changes to minimize so far as possible the risk of further disorders.

We see five basic problem areas:

- The need for change in police operation in the ghetto to ensure proper conduct by individual officers and to eliminate abrasive practices.
- The need for more adequate police protection of ghetto residents to eliminate the present high sense of insecurity to person and property.
- The need for effective mechanisms for resolving citizen grievances against the police.
- The need for policy guidelines to assist police in areas where police conduct can create tension.
- The need to develop community support for law enforcement.

Our discussion of each of these problem areas is followed by specific recommendations which relate directly to more effective law enforcement and to the prevention and control of civil disorders.[1]

I. POLICE CONDUCT AND PATROL PRACTICES

In an earlier era third-degree interrogations were widespread, indiscriminate arrests on suspicion were generally accepted, and "alley justice" dispensed with the nightstick was common.

Today, many disturbances studied by the Commission began with a police incident. But these incidents were not, for the most part, the crude acts of an earlier time. They were routine police actions such as stopping a motorist or raiding an illegal business. Indeed, many of the serious disturbances took place in cities whose police are among the best led, best organized, best trained and most professional in the country.

Yet some activities of even the most professional police department may heighten tension and enhance the potential for civil disorder. An increase in complaints of police mis-

[1] We wish to acknowledge our indebtedness to and reliance upon the extensive work done by the President's Commission on Law Enforcement and Administration of Justice (The "Crime Commission"). The reports, studies, surveys, and analyses of the Crime Commission have contributed to many of our conclusions and recommendations.

conduct, for example, may in fact be a reflection of professionalism; the department may simply be using law enforcement methods which increase the total volume of police contacts with the public. The number of charges of police misconduct may be greater simply because the volume of police-citizen contacts is higher.

Here we examine two aspects of police activities that have great tension-creating potential. Our objective is to provide recommendations to assist city and police officials in developing practices which can allay rather than contribute to tension.

Police Conduct

Negroes firmly believe that police brutality and harassment occur repeatedly in Negro neighborhoods. This belief is unquestionably one of the major reasons for intense Negro resentment against the police.

The extent of this belief is suggested by attitude surveys. In 1964, a New York Times study of Harlem showed that 43 percent of those questioned believed in the existence of police "brutality".[2] In 1965, a nationwide Gallup Poll found that 35 percent of Negro men believe there was police brutality in their areas; 7 percent of white men thought so. In 1966, a survey conducted for the Senate Subcommittee on Executive Reorganization found that 60 percent of Watts Negroes aged 15 to 19 believed there was some police brutality. Half said they had witnessed such conduct. A University of California at Los Angeles study of the Watts area found that 79 percent of the Negro males believed police lack respect for or use insulting language to Negroes and 74 percent believed police use unnecessary force in making arrests. In 1967, an Urban League study of the Detroit riot area found that 82 percent believed there was some form of police brutality.

The true extent of excessive and unjustified use of force is difficult to determine. One survey done for the Crime Commission suggests that when police-citizen contacts are systematically observed, the vast majority are handled without antagonism or incident. Of 5,339 police-citizen contacts observed in slum precincts in three large cities, in the opinion of the observer, only 20—about three-tenths of 1 percent—involved excessive or unnecessary force. And although almost all of those subjected to such force were poor, more than half were white. Verbal discourtesy was more common—15 percent of all such contacts began with a "brusque or nasty command"

[2] The "brutality" referred to in this and other surveys is often not precisely defined, and covers conduct ranging from use of insulting language to excessive and unjustified use of force.

on the part of the officer. Again, however, the objects of such commands were more likely to be white than Negro.

Such "observer" surveys may not fully reflect the normal pattern of police conduct. The Crime Commission Task Force concluded that although the study gave "no basis for stating the extent to which police officers used force, it did confirm that such conduct still exists in the cities where observations were made." Our investigators confirm this conclusion.

Physical abuse is only one source of aggravation in the ghetto. In nearly every city surveyed, the Commission heard complaints of harassment of interracial couples, dispersal of social street gatherings, and the stopping of Negroes on foot or in cars without obvious basis. These, together with contemptuous and degrading verbal abuse, have great impact in the ghetto. As one Commission witness said, these strip the Negro of the one thing that he may have left—his dignity, "the question of being a man."

Some conduct—breaking up of street groups, indiscriminate stops and searches—is frequently directed at youths, creating special tensions in the ghetto where the average age is generally under 21. Ghetto youths, often without work and with homes that may be nearly uninhabitable, particularly in the summer, commonly spend much time on the street. Characteristically, they are not only hostile to police, but eager to demonstrate their own masculinity and courage. The police, therefore, are often subject to taunts and provocations, testing their self-control and, probably, for some, reinforcing their hostility to Negroes in general. Because youths commit a large and increasing proportion of crime, police are under growing pressure from their supervisors—and from the community—to deal with them forcefully. "Harassment of youths" may therefore be viewed by some police departments—and members even of the Negro community—as a proper crime prevention technique.

In a number of cities the Commission heard complaints of abuse from Negro adults of all social and economic classes. Particular resentment is aroused by harassing Negro men in the company of white women—often their light-skinned Negro wives.

"Harassment" or discourtesy may not be the result of malicious or discriminatory intent of police officers. Many officers simply fail to understand the effects of their actions because of their limited knowledge of the Negro community. Calling a Negro teenager by his first name may arouse resentment because many whites still refuse to extend to adult Negroes the courtesy of the title, "Mister." A patrolman may take the arm of a person he is leading to the police car. Negroes are more likely to resent this than whites because the action implies that they are on the verge of flight and may degrade them in the eyes of friends or onlookers.

In assessing the impact of police misconduct we emphasize that the improper acts of a relatively few officers may create severe tensions between the department and the entire Negro community. Whatever the actual extent of such conduct, we concur in the Crime Commission's conclusion that:

> . . . all such behavior is obviously and totally reprehensible, and when it is directed against minority-group citizens it is particularly likely to lead, for quite obvious reasons, to bitterness in the community.

Police Patrol Practices

Although police administrators may take steps to attempt to eliminate misconduct by individual police officers, many departments have adopted patrol practices which in the words of one commentator, have ". . . replaced harassment by individual patrolmen with harassment by entire departments."

These practices, sometimes known as "aggressive preventive patrol," take a number of forms, but invariably they involve a large number of police-citizen contacts initiated by police rather than in response to a call for help or service. One such practice utilizes a roving task force which moves into high-crime districts without prior notice, and conducts intensive, often indiscriminate, street stops and searches. A number of obviously suspicious persons are stopped. But so also are persons whom the beat patrolman would know are respected members of the community. Such task forces are often deliberately moved from place to place making it impossible for its members to know the people with whom they come in contact.

In some cities aggressive patrol is not limited to special task forces. The beat patrolman himself is expected to participate and to file a minimum number of "stop-and-frisk" or field interrogation reports for each tour of duty. This pressure to produce, or a lack of familiarity with the neighborhood and its people, may lead to widespread use of these techniques without adequate differentiation between genuinely suspicious behavior, and behavior which is suspicious to a particular officer merely because it is unfamiliar.

Police administrators, pressed by public concern about crime, have instituted such patrol practices often without weighing their tension-creating effects and the resulting relationship to civil disorder.

Motorization of police is another aspect of patrol that has

affected law enforcement in the ghetto. The patrolman comes to see the city through a windshield and hear about it over a police radio. To him, the area increasingly comes to consist only of law breakers. To the ghetto resident, the policeman comes increasingly to be only an enforcer.

Loss of contact between the police officer and the community he serves adversely affects law enforcement. If an officer has never met, does not know, and cannot understand the language and habits of the people in the area he patrols, he cannot do an effective police job. His ability to detect truly suspicious behavior is impaired. He deprives himself of important sources of information. He fails to know those persons with an "equity" in the community—homeowners, small businessmen, professional men, persons who are anxious to support proper law enforcement—and thus sacrifices the contributions they can make to maintaining community order.

Recommendations

Police misconduct—whether described as brutality, harassment, verbal abuse, or discourtesy—cannot be tolerated even if it is infrequent. It contributes directly to the risk of civil disorder. It is inconsistent with the basic responsibility and function of a police force in a democracy. Police departments must have rules prohibiting such misconduct and enforce them vigorously. Police commanders must be aware of what takes place in the field, and take firm steps to correct abuses. We consider this matter further in the section on policy guidelines.

Elimination of misconduct also requires care in selecting police for ghetto areas, for there the police responsibility is particularly sensitive, demanding and often dangerous. The highest caliber of personnel is required if police are to overcome feelings within the ghetto community of inadequate protection and unfair, discriminatory treatment. Despite this need, data from Commission investigators and from the Crime Commission disclose that often a department's worst, not its best, are assigned to minority group neighborhoods. As Professor Albert Reiss, Director of the Center for Research on Social Organization, University of Michigan, testified before the Commission:

. . . I think we confront in modern urban police departments in large cities much of what we encounter in our schools, in these cities. The slum police precinct is like the slum school. It gets, with few exceptions, the worst in the system.

Referring to extensive studies in one city, Professor Reiss concluded:

305

In predominantly Negro precincts, over three-fourths of the white policemen expressed prejudice or highly prejudiced attitudes towards Negroes. Only one percent of the officers expressed attitudes which could be described as sympathetic towards Negroes. Indeed, close to one-half of all the police officers in predominantly Negro high crime rate areas showed extreme prejudice against Negroes. What do I mean by extreme racial prejudice? I mean that they describe Negroes in terms that are not people terms. They describe them in terms of the animal kingdom. . . .

Although some prejudice was displayed in only eight percent of police-citizen encounters:

The cost of such prejudiced behavior I suggest is much higher than my statistics suggest. Over a period of time, a substantial proportion of citizens, particularly in high crime rate areas, may experience at least one encounter with a police officer where prejudice is shown.

To ensure assignment of well-qualified police to ghetto areas, *the Commission recommends:*

- Officers with bad reputations among residents in minority areas should be immediately reassigned to other areas. This will serve the interests of both the police and the community.
- Screening procedures should be developed to ensure that officers with superior ability, sensitivity and the common sense necessary for enlightened law enforcement are assigned to minority. group areas. We believe that, with proper training in ghetto problems and conditions, and with proper standards for recruitment of new officers, in the long run, most policemen can meet these standards.
- Incentives, such as bonuses or credits for promotion should be developed wherever necessary to attract outstanding officers for ghetto positions.

The recommendations we have proposed are designed to help ensure proper police conduct in minority areas. Yet there is another facet of the problem: Negro perceptions of police misconduct. Even if those perceptions are exaggerated, they do exist. If outstanding officers are assigned to ghetto areas, if acts of misconduct, however infrequent, result in proper—and visible—disciplinary action, and if these corrective practices are made part of known policy, we believe the community will soon learn to reject unfounded claims of misconduct.

Problems stemming from police patrol cannot, perhaps, be so easily resolved. But there are two considerations which can help to allay such problems. The first consideration relates to law enforcement philosophy behind the use of techniques like aggressive patrol. Many police officials believe strongly that there are law enforcement gains from such techniques. However, these techniques can also have law enforcement liabilities. Their employment therefore should not be merely automatic, but the product of a deliberate balancing of pluses and minuses by command personnel.

We know that advice of this sort is easier to give than to act on. The factors involved are difficult to weigh. Gains cannot be measured solely in the number of arrests. Losses in police protection cannot be accepted solely because of some vague gain in diminished community tension. The kind of thorough, objective assessment of patrol practices and search for innovation we need will require the best efforts of research and development units within police departments, augmented if necessary by outside research assistance. The Federal Government can also play a major role in funding and conducting such research.

The second consideration concerning patrol is execution. There is more crime in the ghetto than in other areas. If the aggressive patrol clearly relates to the control of crime, the residents of the ghetto are likely to endorse the practice. What may arouse hostility is not the fact of aggressive patrol but its indiscriminate use so that it comes to be regarded not as crime control but as a new method of racial harassment. All patrol practices must be carefully reviewed to ensure they are properly carried out by individual officers.

New patrol practices must be designed to increase the patrolman's knowledge of the ghetto. Although motorized patrols are essential, means should be devised to get the patrolman out of the car and into the neighborhood and keeping him on the same beat long enough to get to know the people and understand the conditions. This will require training the patrolman to convince him of the desirability of such practices. There must be continuing administrative supervision. In practice as well as theory, all aspects of patrol must be lawful and conform to policy guidelines. Unless carried out with courtesy and with understanding of the community, even the most enlightened patrol practices may degenerate into what residents will come to regard as harassment. Finally, this concept of patrol should be publicly explained so that ghetto residents understand it and know what to expect.

II. THE PROBLEM OF POLICE PROTECTION

The strength of ghetto feelings about hostile police conduct may even be exceeded by the conviction that ghetto neighborhoods are not given adequate police protection.

This belief is founded on two basic types of complaint. The first is that the police maintain a much less rigorous standard of law enforcement in the ghetto, tolerating there illegal activities like drug addiction, prostitution and street violence that they would not tolerate elsewhere. The second is that police treat complaints and calls for help from Negro areas much less urgently than from white areas. These perceptions are widespread. As David Hardy, of the staff of *The New York Daily News,* testified:

> To put it simply, for decades little if any law enforcement has prevailed among Negroes in America, particularly those in the ghettos. If a black man kills another black man, the law is generally enforced at its minimum. Violence of every type runs rampant in a ghetto.

A Crime Commission study found that Negroes in Philadelphia and San Diego are convinced that the police apply a different standard of law enforcement in the ghettos. Another Crime Commission study found that about one white person in two believes police provide very good protection in his community; for Negroes, the figure is one in five. Other surveys have reported that Negroes in Harlem and South Central Los Angeles mention inadequate protection more often than brutality or harassment as a reason for their resentment toward the police.

The report of a New Haven community group summarizes the complaints:

> The problem of the adequacy of current police protection ranked with "police misconduct" as the most serious sore points in police-community relations. . . . When calls for help are registered, it is all too frequent that police respond too slowly or not at all. . . . When they do come, [they] arrive with many more men and cars than are necessary . . . brandishing guns and adding to the confusion.[8]

There is evidence to suggest that the lack of protection does not necessarily result from different basic police attitudes but rather from a relative lack of police personnel for ghetto areas, considering the volume of calls for police. As a consequence, the police work according to priorities. Because of the need for attention to major crimes, little, if any, attention can be accorded to reports of a suspicious person, for example, or a noisy party, or a drunk. And attention even to major crimes may sometimes be routine or skeptical.

Ghetto residents, however, see a dual standard of law enforcement. Particularly because many work in other areas of the city and have seen the nature of police responsiveness there, they are keenly aware of the difference. They come to believe

[8] "In Search of Fair and Adequate Law Enforcement," Report of the Hill-Dwight Citizens Commission on Police Community Relations, June, 1967, pp. 12-13.

that an assault on a white victim produces one reaction and an assault on a Negro quite another. The police, heavily engaged in the ghetto, might assert that they cannot cover serious offenses and minor complaints at the same time—that they cannot be two places at once. The ghetto resident, however, often concludes that the police respond neither to serious offenses nor to minor complaints.

Recent studies have documented the inadequacies of police response in some ghetto areas. A Yale Law Journal study of Hartford, Connecticut, found that:

> [T]he residents of a large area in the center of the Negro ghetto are victims of over one-third of the daylight residential burglaries in the city. Yet during the daytime only one of Hartford's eighteen patrol cars and none of its eleven foot patrolmen is assigned to this area. Sections in the white part of town about the same size as the central ghetto area receive slightly more intensive daytime patrol even though the citizens in the ghetto area summon the police about six times as often because of criminal acts.[4]

In a United States Commission on Civil Rights study, a review of police communications records in Cleveland disclosed that police took almost four times as long to respond to calls concerning robbery from the Negro district as for the district where response was next slowest. The response time for some other crimes was at least twice as long.

The Commission recommends:

- Police departments should have a clear and enforced policy that the standard of law enforcement in ghetto areas is the same as in other communities; complaints and appeals from the ghetto should be treated with the same urgency and importance as those from white neighborhoods.
- Because a basic problem in furnishing protection to the ghetto is the shortage of manpower, police departments should review existing deployment of field personnel to ensure the most efficient use of manpower. The Police Task Force of the Crime Commission stressed the need "to distribute patrol officers in accordance with the actual need for their presence." Communities may have to pay for more and better policing for the entire community as well as for the ghetto.

In allocating manpower to the ghetto, enforcement emphasis should be given to crimes that threaten life and property. Stress on social gambling or loitering, when more serious crimes are neglected, not only diverts manpower but fosters distrust and tension in the ghetto community.

[4] "Program Budgeting for Police Departments," 76 Yale L. J. 822 (1967).

III. The Problem of Grievance Mechanisms

A third source of Negro hostility to police is the almost total lack of effective channels for redress of complaints against police conduct. In Milwaukee, Wisconsin, and Plainfield, New Jersey, for example, ghetto residents complained that police reject complaints out of hand. In New Haven, a Negro citizens' group characterized a police review board as worthless. In Detroit, the Michigan Civil Rights Commission found that, despite well-intentioned leadership, no real sanctions are imposed on offending officers. In Newark, the mayor referred complaints to the FBI, which had very limited jurisdiction over them. In many of the cities surveyed by the Commission, Negro complaints focused on the continued presence in the ghetto of officers regarded as notorious for prejudice and brutality.

The 1967 Report of the Civil Rights Commission also states that a major issue in the Negro community is inadequate investigation of complaints against the police. It even reports threats of criminal actions designed to discourage complainants. A survey for the Crime Commission found substantial evidence that policemen in some cities have little fear of punishment for using unnecessary force because they appear to have a degree of immunity from their departments.

Recommendations

Objective evaluation, analysis, and innovation on this subject are vitally necessary. Yet attention has been largely, and unfortunately, diverted by protracted debate over the desirability of "civilian review boards." Research conducted by the Crime Commission and others shows that the benefits and liabilities of such boards have probably both been exaggerated.

In the context of civil disorder, appearances and reality are of almost equal importance in the handling of citizen complaints against the police. It is not enough that there are adequate machinery and procedures for handling complaints; it is also necessary that citizens believe these procedures are adequate. Some citizens will never trust an agency against which they have a grievance. Some irresponsible citizens will attempt to provoke distrust of every agency. Hence some police administrators have been tempted to throw up their hands and do nothing on the ground that whatever they do will be misunderstood. These sentiments may be understandable but the police should appreciate that Negro citizens also want to throw up their hands. For they believe that the "police stick together," that they will cover up for each other, that no officer ever receives more than token punishment for misconduct, and that even such expensive legal steps as false arrest or civil damage suits are foredoomed because "it is the officer's word against mine."

We believe that an internal review board—in which the police department itself receives and acts on complaints—regardless of its efficiency and fairness, can rarely generate the necessary community confidence, or protect the police against unfounded charges. We also believe, as did the Crime Commission, that police should not be the only municipal agency subject to outside scrutiny and review. Incompetence and mistreatment by any public servant should be equally subject to review by an independent agency.

The Crime Commission Police Task Force reviewed the various external grievance procedures attempted or suggested in this country and abroad. Without attempting to recommend a specific procedure, our Commission believes that police departments should be subject to external review. We discussed this problem in Chapter 10, The Community Response. Here, we highlight what we believe to be the basic elements of an effective system.

The Commission recommends:

- Making a complaint should be easy. It should be possible to file a grievance without excessive formality. If forms are used, they should be easily available and their use explained in widely-distributed pamphlets. In large cities, it should not be necessary to go to a central headquarters office to file a complaint but it should also be possible to file a complaint at neighborhood locations. Police officers on the beat, community service aides, or other municipal employees in the community, should be empowered to receive complaints.
- A specialized agency, with adequate funds and staff, should be created separate from other municipal agencies, to handle, investigate and to make recommendations on citizen complaints.
- The procedure should have a built-in conciliation process to attempt to resolve complaints without the need for full investigation and processing.
- The complaining party should be able to participate in the investigation and in any hearings, with right of representation by counsel, so that the complaint is fully investigated and findings made on the merits. He should be promptly and fully informed of the outcome. The results of the investigation should be made public.
- Since many citizen complaints concern departmental policies rather than individual conduct, information concerning complaints of this sort should be forwarded to the departmental unit which formulates or reviews policy and procedures. Information concerning all complaints should be forwarded to appro-

priate training units so that any deficiencies correctable by training can be eliminated.

Although we advocate an external agency as a means of resolving grievances, we believe that the basic need is to adopt procedures which will gain the respect and confidence of the entire community. This need can, in the end, be met only by sustained direction through the line of command, thorough investigation of complaints, and prompt, visible disciplinary action where justified.

IV. THE NEED FOR POLICY GUIDELINES

How a policeman handles day-to-day contacts with citizens will, to a large extent, shape the relationships between the police and the community. These contacts involve considerable discretion. Improper exercise of such discretion can needlessly create tension and contribute to community grievances.

Formally, the police officer has no discretion; his task is to enforce all laws at all times. Formally, the officer's only basic enforcement option is to make an arrest, or to do nothing. Formally, when a citizen resists arrest the officer's only recourse is to apply such reasonable force as he can bring with his hands, nightstick, and revolver.

Informally—and in reality—the officer faces an entirely different situation. He has and must have a great deal of discretion; there are not enough police or jails to permit the levels of surveillance that would be necessary to enforce all laws all the time—levels which the public would, in any event, regard as intolerable.

Patrick V. Murphy, now Director of Public Safety in the District of Columbia, told the Commission:

> The police, of course, exercise very broad discretion, and although in many states the law says or implies that all laws must be enforced and although the manuals of many police departments state every officer is responsible for the enforcement of all laws, as a practical matter it is impossible for the police to enforce all laws, and as a result they exercise very broad discretion. . . . [B]y failing to understand the fact that they do exercise important discretion every day, some police do not perceive just how they maintain the peace in different ways in different sections of a city.

The formal remedies of law, further, are inappropriate for many common problems. A family quarrel or a street fight, followed by an arrest, would give the parties a record and, typically, a suspended sentence; it would not solve the problem. And the appropriate legal grounds for making an arrest

312

are often not present, for the officer has not witnessed the incident nor does he have a sworn complaint from someone who has. Pacifying the dispute may well be the best approach, but many officers lack the training or experience to do so effectively. If the parties resist pacification or arrest, the officer, alone on the street, must either back down or use force—sometimes lethal.

Crime Commission studies and our police survey show that guidance for the exercise of discretion in many situations is often not available to the policeman. There are guidelines for the wearing of uniforms—but not for how to intervene in a domestic dispute; for the cleaning of a revolver—but not for when to fire it; for use of departmental property—but not for whether to break up a sidewalk gathering; for handling stray dogs—but not for handling field interrogations.

Recommendations

Contacts between citizens and the police in the ghetto require discretion and judgment which should be based upon carefully-drawn, written departmental policy. The Report of the Crime Commission and the Police Task Force Report considered this problem in detail, and recommended subjects for policy guidelines.

The Commission recommends the establishment of guidelines covering, at a minimum:

- The issuance of orders to citizens regarding their movements or activities—for example, when if ever should a policeman order a street gathering to break up or move on.
- The handling of minor disputes—between husband and wife, merchant and customer, or landlord and tenant. Guidelines should cover resources available in the community—family courts, probation departments, counseling services, welfare agencies—to which citizens can be referred.
- The decision whether to arrest in a specific situation involving a specific crime—for example, when police should arrest persons engaged in crimes such as social gambling, vagrancy and loitering, and other crimes which do not involve victims. The use of alternatives to arrest, such as a summons, should also be considered.
- The selection and use of investigative methods. Problems concerning use of field interrogations and "stop-and-frisk" techniques are especially critical. Crime Commission studies and evidence before this Commission demonstrate that these techniques have the potential for becoming a major source of friction between police and minority groups. Their constitutionality is presently under review in the United States Supreme Court. We also recognize that police regard them as important methods of preventing and investigating crime. Although we do not advocate

use or adoption of any particular investigative method, we believe that any such method should be covered by guidelines drafted to minimize friction with the community.

- Safeguarding the constitutional right of free expression such as rights of persons engaging in lawful demonstrations, the need to protect lawful demonstrators, and how to handle spontaneous demonstrations.
- The circumstances under which the various forms of physical force—including lethal force—can and should be applied. Recognition of this need was demonstrated by the regulations recently adopted by the City of New York further implementing the state law governing police use of firearms.
- The proper manner of address for contacts with any citizen.

The drafting of guidelines should not be solely a police responsibility. It is the duty of mayors and other elected and appointed executive officials to take the initiative, to participate fully in the drafting and to ensure that the guidelines are carried out in practice.

Police research and planning units should be fully used in identifying problem areas, performing the necessary studies and in resolving problems. Their product should be reviewed by the chief of police and city executives and representatives of the prosecution, courts, correction agencies and other criminal-justice agencies. Views of ghetto residents should be obtained, perhaps through police-community relations programs or human relations agencies. Once promulgated, the guidelines should be disseminated clearly and forcefully to all operational personnel. Concise, simply worded, and, if necessary, foreign language summaries of police powers and individual rights should be distributed to the public. Training the police to perform according to the guidelines is essential. Although conventional instruction is a minimum requirement, full understanding can only be achieved by intensive small-group training, involving simulation.

Guidelines, no matter how carefully drafted, will have little effect unless the department enforces them. This primarily requires command supervision and commitment to the guidelines. It also requires:

- A strong internal investigative unit to enforce compliance. Such a unit should not only enforce the guidelines on a case-by-case basis against individual officers, but should also develop procedures to deter and prevent violations. The Crime Commission discussed the various methods available.
- A fair and effective means to handle citizen complaints.

Finally, provision should be made for the periodic review of the guidelines to ensure that changes are made to take account of current court rulings and new laws.

V. Community Support for Law Enforcement

A fifth major reason for police-community hostility—particularly obvious since the recent disorders—is the general breakdown of communication between police and the ghetto. The contacts that do occur are primarily adversary contacts.

In the section on police patrol practices, we discussed one basic aspect of this problem. Here we consider how police forces have tried, with varying degrees of success, to deal with three issues underlying relations with ghetto communities.

Recruitment, Assignment and Promotion of Negroes

The Crime Commission Police Task Force found that for police in a Negro community to be predominantly white can serve as a dangerous irritant; a feeling may develop that the community is not being policed to maintain civil peace but to maintain the status quo. It further found that contact with Negro officers can help to avoid stereotypes and prejudices in the minds of white officers. Negro officers also can increase departmental insight into ghetto problems, and provide information necessary for early anticipation of the tensions and grievances that can lead to disorders. Commission witnesses confirm these conclusions.

There is evidence that Negro officers also can be particularly effective in controlling any disorders that do break out. In studying the relative performance of Army and National Guard forces in the Detroit disorder, we concluded that the higher percentage of Negroes in the Army forces contributed substantially to their better performance. As a result, last August, we recommended an increase in the percentage of Negroes in the National Guard. The need for increased Negro participation in police departments is equally acute.

Despite this need—and despite recent efforts to hire more Negro police—the proportion of Negroes on police forces still falls far below the proportion of Negroes in the total population. Of 28 departments which reported information of this kind in a Commission survey of police departments, the percentage of Negro sworn personnel ranged from less than 1 percent to 21 percent. The median figure for Negro sworn personnel on the force was 6 percent; the median figure for the Negro population was approximately 24 percent. In no case was the proportion of Negroes in the police department equal to the proportion in the population.[5] A 1962 survey of

[5] The data from this survey can be found in "Table A" at the end of this chapter of the Report.

the United States Civil Rights Commission, as reported in the Crime Commission Police Task Force Report, shows correspondingly low figures for other cities.

There are even more marked disproportions of Negro supervisory personnel. Our survey showed the following ratios:

- One in every 26 Negroes is a sergeant; the white ratio is one in 12.
- One in every 114 Negroes is a lieutenant; the white ratio is one in 26.
- One in every 235 Negroes is a captain or above; the white ratio is one in 53.

Public Safety Director Murphy testifying before the Commission described the problem and at least one of its causes:

I think one of the serious problems facing the police in the nation today is the lack of adequate representation of Negroes in police departments. I think the police have not recruited enough Negroes in the past and are not recruiting enough of them today. I think we would be less than honest if we didn't admit that Negroes have been kept out of police departments in the past for reasons of racial discrimination.

In a number of cities, particularly larger ones, police officials are not only willing but anxious to appoint Negro officers. There are obstacles other than discrimination. While these obstacles cannot readily be measured, they can be identified. One is the relatively high standards for police employment. Another is pay; better qualified Negroes are often more attracted by other, better paying positions. Another obstacle is the bad image of police in the Negro community. There also are obstacles to promotion apart from discrimination, such as the more limited educational background of some Negro officers.

Recommendations

The Commission recommends:

- Police departments should intensify their efforts to recruit more Negroes. The Police Task Force of the Crime Commission discussed a number of ways to do this and the problems involved. The Department of Defense program to help police departments recruit returning servicemen should be fully utilized. An Army report of Negro participation in the National Guard and Army reserves may also provide useful information.
- In order to increase the number of Negroes in supervisory positions, police departments should review promotion policies to ensure that Negroes have full opportunity to be rapidly and fairly promoted.
- Negro officers should be so assigned as to ensure that the police department is fully and visibly integrated. Some cities have adopted a policy of assigning one white and one Negro officer to

patrol cars, especially in ghetto areas. These assignments result in better understanding, tempered judgment and increased ability to separate the truly suspect from the unfamiliar.

Recruiting more Negro officers, alone, will not solve the problems of lack of communication and hostility toward police. A Negro's understanding of the ghetto is not enough to make him a good officer. He must also meet the same high standards as white officers and pass the same screening process. These requirements help create a dilemma noted by the Crime Commission. The need to develop better relations with minority group communities requires recruitment of police from these groups—groups handicapped by lack of educational opportunities and achievement. To require that police recruits have a high school diploma sets a standard too low in terms of the need for recruiting college graduates and perhaps too high in terms of the need for recruiting members of minority groups.

To meet this problem, the Crime Commission recommended creation of a new type of uniformed "community service officer." This officer would typically be a young man between 17 and 21 with the "aptitude, integrity, and stability necessary to perform police work." He would perform a variety of duties short of exercising full law enforcement powers, with primary emphasis on community service work. While so serving, he would continue his studies in order to be promoted as quickly as possible to the status of a police officer.

The Commission recommends:

● The community service officer program should be adopted. Use of this program to increase the number of Negroes in police departments will help to establish needed channels of communication with the Negro community; will permit the police to perform better their community service functions, especially in the minority group neighborhoods; and will also create a number of badly needed jobs for Negro youths.

The standards of selection for such community service officers or aides should be drawn to ensure that the great majority of young Negro males are eligible to participate in the program. As stated in the Crime Commission Task Force Report, selection should not be based on inflexible educational requirements, but instead ". . . should be made on an individual basis with priority being given to applicants with promising aspirations, honesty, intelligence, a desire and a tested capacity to advance his education, and an understanding of the neighborhood and its problems." An arrest record or a minor conviction record should not in itself be a bar to employment.

The Commission recommends:

● The federal government should launch a program to establish community service officers in cities with populations over 50,000. Eligible police departments should be reimbursed for 90 percent of the costs of employing one aide for every 10 full-time police officers.

We emphasize, however, that recruitment of community service aides must complement, not replace, efforts to recruit more Negroes as police officers.

Community Service Functions

Because police run almost the only 24-hour day, seven-day-a-week emergency service, they find it very hard not to become involved in a host of nonpolice services. Complaints about a wide range of matters, from noisy neighbors and deteriorated streets to building code violations, at best, are only peripheral to police work. Because these are often not police matters and because police increasingly face serious shortages of manpower and money, police administrators have systematically resisted becoming involved in such matters. This resistance, coupled with centralization and motorization of the police, has resulted in the police becoming more distant from the people they serve.

Recommendations

The Commission believes that police cannot, and should not resist becoming involved in community service matters.[6] There will be benefits for law enforcement no less than for public order.

First, police, because of their "front line position" in dealing with ghetto problems, will be better able to identify problems in the community that may lead to disorder. Second, they will be better able to handle incidents requiring police intervention, particularly marital disputes that have a potential for violence. How well the police handle domestic disturbances affects the incidence of serious crimes, including assaults and homicides. Third, willing performance of such work can gain police the respect and support of the community. Finally, development of nonadversary contacts can provide the police with a vital source of information and intelligence concerning the communities they serve.

[6] We join in the Crime Commission's caveat that police should not become involved in service tasks which involve neither policing nor community help (such as tax collection, licensing and dog-pound duties).

A variety of methods have been devised to improve police performance of this service function. We comment on two of special interest. The first is the New York Police Department's experimental "Family Crisis Intervention" program to develop better police response to marital disputes; if results develop as expected, this may serve as a model for other departments.

Second, neighborhood service centers have been suggested, and opened in some cities. These centers typically are established in tense, high-crime areas, in easily accessible locations such as store-fronts or public housing projects. Staffed by a civilian city employee as well as a police officer, their task is to provide information and service—putting a citizen in touch with the right agency, furnishing general advice. This gives the beat patrolman somewhere to refer a marital dispute. It gives the local resident a clear, simple contact with official advice. It gives the police in general the opportunity to provide services, not merely to enforce the law. The needed additional manpower for such centers could be provided by the community service aides recommended earlier, or by continuing to employ experienced policemen who have reached the age of retirement.

Community Relations Programs

Many police departments have established programs to deal specifically with police-community relations. The Crime Commission recommended a number of such programs, and federal funds have been made available for putting them into operation. Although of great potential benefit, the results thus far have been disappointing. This is true partly because the changes in attitude sought by such programs can only be achieved over time. But there are other reasons, as was shown by Detroit's experience with police-community meetings: minimum participation by ghetto residents; infrequent meetings; lack of patrolmen involvement; lack of attention to youth programs; lack of coordination by police leadership either within the department or with other city programs.

More significantly, both the Detroit evaluation and studies carried on for the Commission show that too often these are not community relations programs, but public relations programs, designed to improve the department's image in the community. In one major city covered by the Commission's study, the department's plan for citizen observers of police work failed because people believed that the citizen observer was allowed to see only what the police thought he should see. Similarly, the police chief's "open house," an opportunity for discussion, was considered useless by many who regarded him as unsympathetic and unresponsive.

Moreover, it is clear that these programs have little support among rank and file officers. In Detroit, more than a year after instructions were sent out to establish such programs, several precincts still had failed to do so. Other cities have had similar experiences. On the command level, there is often little interest. Programs are not integrated into the departments; units do not receive adequate budgetary support.

Nevertheless, some programs have been successful. In Atlanta, a Crime Prevention Bureau has within two years established a good relationship with the community, particularly with the young people. It has concentrated on social services, persuading almost 600 dropouts to return to school, assisting some 250 hardship cases with food and work, arranging for dances and hydrant showers during the summer, working quickly and closely with families of missing persons. The result is a close rapport with the community—and recruits for the department. Baltimore and Winston-Salem are reported to have equally successful programs.

Recommendations

Community relations programs and training can be important in increasing communication and decreasing hostility between the police and the ghetto. Community relations programs can also be used by police to explain new patrol practices, law enforcement programs, and other police efforts to reduce crime. Police have a right to expect ghetto leaders to work responsibly to reduce crime. Community relations programs offer a way to create and foster these efforts.

We believe that community relations is an integral part of all law enforcement. But it cannot be made so by part-time effort, peripheral status, or cliche methods.

One way to bolster community relations is to expand police department award systems. Traditionally, special awards, promotional credit, bonuses and selection for special assignments are based on heroic acts and arrest activity. Award systems should take equal cognizance of the work of officers who improve relations with alienated members of the community and by so doing minimize the potential for disorder.

However, we see no easy solution to police-community relations and misunderstandings and are aware that no single procedure or program will suffice. Improving community relations is a full-time assignment for every commander and every officer—an assignment that must include the development of an attitude, a tone, throughout the force that conforms with the ultimate responsibility of every policeman: public service.

TABLE A
NONWHITE PERSONNEL IN SELECTED POLICE DEPARTMENTS

Name of Dept.	Number Sworn Pers.	Number Non-White Sworn Pers.	Number Sergeants		Number Lieuts.		Number Capts.		Number Above Captain	
			N.W.	W.	N.W.	W.	N.W.	W.	N.W.	W.
Atlanta	968	98	2	12	3	56	0	15	0	6
Baltimore	3,046	208	7	389	3	105	1	17	1	21
Boston	2,508	49	1	228	0	80	0	20	0	12
Buffalo	1,375	37	1	60	1	93	1	24	0	32
Chicago	11,091	1,842	87	1,067	2	266	1	73	6	66
Cincinnati	891	54	2	68	2	34	0	13	0	7
Cleveland	2,216	165	6	155	0	78	0	26	0	17
Dayton	417	16	1	58	0	13	0	6	0	4
Detroit	4,326	227	9	339	2	156	0	0	1	62
Hartford	342	38	0	32	1	16	0	9	0	2
Kansas City	927	51	7	158	0	36	0	11	1	14
Louisville	562	35	1	42	1	29	0	10	1	7
Memphis	869	46	0	0	4	192	0	45	0	44
Mich. St. Pol.	1,502	1	0	135	0	24	0	19	0	3
New Haven	446	31	0	20	0	16	0	12	0	6
New Orleans	1,308	54	7	107	1	51	0	27	0	10
New York	27,610	1,485	65	1,785	20	925	2	273	3	157
New Jersey S.P.	1,224	5	0	187	0	43	1	17	0	4
Newark	1,869	184	5	97	3	95	1	22	0	0
Oakland	658	27	1	95	0	25	1	10	0	3
Oklahoma City	438	16	0	32	1	19	0	11	0	6
Philadelphia	6,890	1,377	26	314	8	139	3	46	0	23
Phoenix	707	7	0	88	1	22	0	10	0	4
Pittsburgh	1,558	109	3	137	3	47	0	4	1	6
St. Louis	2,042	224	21	201	3	46	4	17	0	11
San Francisco	1,754	102	0	217	0	66	0	15	0	10
Tampa	511	17	0	50	0	12	0	13	0	8
Washington, D.C.	2,771	559	19	216	3	107	3	37	0	31
Totals	80,621	7,046	271	6,289	62	2,791	16	802	14	576

321

Name of Dept.	% Non-White pop.	% Non-White Police Officers	Ratio: Serg. to Officers		Ratio: Lieut. to Officers		Ratio: Capt. to Officers		Ratio: Above Capt. to Officers	
			N.W.	W.	N.W.	W.	N.W.	W.	N.W.	W.
Atlanta, Ga.	38*	10	1:49	1:73	1:33	1:16	0:98	1:58	0:98	1:145
Baltimore, Md.	41*	7	1:30	1:7	1:69	1:27	1:208	1:167	1:208	1:135
Boston, Mass.	11*	2	1:49	1:11	0:49	1:31	0:49	1:123	0:49	1:205
Buffalo, N.Y.	18*	3	1:37	1:22	1:37	1:14	0:37	1:56	0:37	1:42
Chicago, Ill.	27*	17	1:21	1:9	1:921	1:35	1:1842	1:127	1:307	1:140
Cincinnati, Ohio	28*	6	1:27	1:12	1:27	1:25	0:54	1:64	0:54	1:120
Cleveland, Ohio	34*	7	1:28	1:13	1:165	1:26	0:165	1:79	0:165	1:121
Dayton, Ohio	26*	4	1:16	1:7	0:16	1:30	0:16	1:67	0:16	1:100
Detroit, Mich.	39*	5	1:25	1:12	1:114	1:26	No such rank		1:227	1:66
Hartford, Conn.	20**	11	0:38	1:10	1:38	1:20	0:38	1:34	0:38	1:152
Kansas City, Mo.	20**	6	1:7	1:6	0:51	1:24	0:51	1:80	1:51	1:63
Louisville, Ky.	21*	.6	1:35	1:13	1:35	1:18	0:35	1:53	1:35	1:75
Memphis, Tenn.	38*	a¹	No such rank		1:12	1:4	0:46	1:18	0:46	1:19
Mich. St. Pol.	9***	7	0:1	1:11	0:1	1:63	0:1	1:79	0:1	1:500
New Haven, Conn.	19**	4	0:31	1:21	0:31	1:26	0:31	1:35	0:31	1:69
New Orleans, La.	41*	4	1:8	1:12	1:54	1:25	0:54	1:46	0:54	1:125
New York, N.Y.	16*	5	1:23	1:15	1:74	1:28	1:748	1:96	1:495	1:166
New Jersey St. Pol.	9***	a¹	0:5	1:7	0:5	1:28	0:5	1:72	0:5	1:305
Newark, N.J.	40*	10	1:37	1:17	1:61	1:18	1:184	1:77	None Listed	
Oakland, Calif.	31*	4	1:27	1:25	0:27	1:25	1:27	1:63	0:27	1:210
Oklahoma City, Okla.	15*	4	0:16	1:13	1:16	1:22	0:16	1:38	0:16	1:70
Philadelphia, Pa.	29*	20	1:53	1:18	1:172	1:40	1:459	1:120	0:1377	1:240
Phoenix, Ariz.	8*	1	0:7	1:8	1:7	1:32	0:7	1:70	0:7	1:175
Pittsburgh, Pa.	19*	7	1:36	1:11	1:36	1:31	0:109	1:362	1:109	1:242
St. Louis, Mo.	37*	11	1:11	1:9	1:75	1:40	1:56	1:107	0:224	1:165
San Francisco, Calif.	14*	6	0:102	1:8	0:102	1:25	0:102	1:110	0:102	1:165
Tampa, Fla.	17*	3	0:17	1:10	0:17	1:41	0:17	1:38	0:17	1:62
Washington, D.C.	63*	21	1:29	1:10	1:186	1:20	1:186	1:58	0:559	1:70

a¹ Less than ½ of 1%

* % Negro population figures, 1965 estimates by the Center for Research in Marketing, Cong. Quarterly, Weekly Report, No. 36, Sept. 8, 1967.

** % Negro population figures, 1966 estimates, Office of Economic Opportunity
*** % Negro population figures for states of Michigan and New Jersey, 1960 Census Figures

Chapter 12 / Control of Disorder

To analyze the complex social causes of disorder, to plumb the impact of generations of deprivation, to work for broad and sensitive efforts at prevention are vital tasks, but they are slow and difficult. When, in the meantime, civil disorder breaks out, three simple principles emerge.

First: Preserving civil peace is the first responsibility of government.

Individuals cannot be permitted to endanger the public peace and safety and public officials have a duty to make it clear that all just and necessary means to protect both will be used. Our society is founded on the rule of law. That rule must prevail; without it, we will lack not only order but the environment essential to social and economic progress.

Second: In maintaining the rule of law, we must be careful not to sacrifice it in the name of order.

In our concern over civil disorder we must not mistake lawful protest for illegal activities. The guardians of the law are also subject to the law they serve. As the FBI states in its riot manual for law enforcement officers:

A peaceful or lawful demonstration should not be looked upon with disapproval by a police agency; rather, it should be considered as a safety valve possibly serving to prevent a riot. The police agency should not countenance violations of law. However, a police agency does not have the right to deny the demonstrator his constitutional rights.

Third: Maintaining civil order is the responsibility of the entire community.

Not even the most professional and devoted law enforcement agency alone can quell civil disorder any more than it alone can prevent civil disorder. A thin blue line is too thin. Maintaining civil peace is the responsibility of the entire community, particularly public officials. The guidance, assistance, and support of the mayor can be decisive.

This does not deny the very great responsibility which is and should be borne by the police. In the Supplement on Control of Disorder we offer specific comments which we hope

323

will help law enforcement agencies regain control after major disorders have developed. In this chapter, however, the Commission considers ways by which the police—with the leadership and support of the civil authorities—can suppress and restrain potentially major disorders in their initial phases.[1]

I. The Initial Incident

Last summer, almost 150 cities experienced some form of civil disorder. Most remained minor disturbances, effectively controlled by the local police and civil authorities. In some cities similar incidents led to serious disorder. Why?

Testimony and evidence studied by the Commission point to the preeminent role of police reaction to the initial incident. How the police and the community respond to and deal with such incidents may well determine whether they remain relatively minor police problems—or balloon into major disorders.

Initial Police Response

When police receive word of an accident, fight, or similar incident, a patrolman is routinely sent to the scene. He is called on to exercise technical and professional skills at which he is practiced—investigation, individual control and perhaps

[1] In arriving at these assessments and recommendations, the Commission has relied heavily on information and advice supplied by many police, military and other leading authorities. In addition to the studies conducted for the Commission by the International Association of Chiefs of Police, a number of outstanding authorities worked closely with the Commission staff and provided invaluable assistance. In particular, we wish to thank John Ingersoll, Chief of Police of Charlotte, North Carolina, and former Director of Field Services of the International Association of Chiefs of Police; Daryl F. Gates, Deputy Chief of Police, Los Angeles Police Department, who was one of the commanders in the field during the Watts riot; and Major General George M. Gelston, Adjutant General of Maryland and former Police Commissioner of Baltimore.

In addition to the testimony and reports received on the cities studied by the Commission and which had experienced disorders, the Commission drew upon the valuable information and material furnished by the Boston, Chicago, Cincinnati, Kansas City, Los Angeles, New York City and Oakland Police Departments. Valuable guidance also was provided by Colonel Orlando W. Wilson, until recently Superintendent of Police of Chicago and formerly Dean of the School of Criminology, University of California.

The Commission also was markedly assisted by material made available by the Federal Bureau of Investigation and its pamphlet, "The Prevention and Control of Mobs and Riots," related reports by the Crime Commission, and information supplied by the Office of Public Safety, Agency for International Development. The Commission also received the active cooperation and assistance of the Department of Defense and in particular from the special Army task force established in the Office of the Deputy Chief of Staff for Military Operations to study and make recommendations relative to the role of the Army and National Guard in controlling civil disorders.

arrest. Infrequently, he may have to call for assistance. In any event, his judgments, while important, normally have an impact only on the immediate participants.

In the densely populated ghetto, however, particularly when summer heat drives many residents into the streets, even the most routine incident may call for far more than a technical assessment. The responding officer's initial judgment here is critical in two respects. First, it will guide his own conduct. Second, it will guide the response of his superiors. What orders, if any, should they give him? What help should they send if he asks for help? An assessment of this sort may be difficult for the best-informed officer. What makes it even more difficult is that police often do not know what to expect when they respond to incidents in ghetto areas where virtually all the 1967 disorders occurred.

The average police officer has little knowledge of understanding of the underlying tensions and grievances that exist in the ghetto. Yet this information is vital if the police officer is to decide correctly what police or other control measures should be taken to deal with the incident. The task is to find ways to inform his judgment to the maximum extent possible.

While good judgment cannot be institutionalized, some broad considerations can be offered.

The Basic Factors

Five factors, often inseparable, recurred in the major disorders of last summer: (1) crowded ghetto living conditions, worsened by summer heat; (2) youth on the streets; (3) hostility to police; (4) delay in appropriate police response; and (5) persistent rumors and inadequate information.

On hot summer nights, the front steps and the street become a refuge from the stifling tenements of the ghetto. Detroit's 12th Street, New Haven's Congress Street, and the grim public housing blocks of Newark illustrate how ghetto streets come alive with people, especially on summer nights and weekends —when many of the disorders of 1967 began. The people on the streets invariably include a very high proportion of youth.

It takes little to attract a crowd in this setting. Making an arrest is a routine matter to many police officers. In the ghetto, it can draw a crowd instantly—quick to misunderstand, quick to characterize the police action as unfair, quick to abandon curiosity for anger.

Crowded ghetto living conditions and youth on the streets —the first two factors—cannot be remedied by the police. But the police must take these conditions into account in assessing even the most routine ghetto incident. Every police officer responding to a call in tense, heavily-populated areas must be sensitive to tension situations. Here more than in any other type of police duty, the individual officer must exercise good judgment and common sense. The Chicago Police Department issued the following training bulletin to all its personnel:

> Preventing civil disorders is always easier than suppressing them. The police officer, by disciplining his emotions, recognizing the rights of all citizens, and conducting himself in the manner his office demands can do much to prevent a tension situation from erupting into a serious disturbance.[2]

There are, however, steps police can take to eliminate or minimize the effects of the remaining three factors.

In the preceding chapter, we have already discussed the factor of hostility to police.

As to delay, sufficient manpower is a prerequisite for controlling potentially dangerous crowds; the speed with which it arrives may well determine whether the situation can be controlled. In the summer of 1967 we believe that delay in mobilizing help permitted several incidents to develop into dangerous disorders, in the end requiring far more personnel and creating increased hazards to life and property.

Rumors significantly aggravated tension and disorder in more than 65 percent of the disorders studied by the Commission. Sometimes, as in Tampa and New Haven, rumor served as the spark which turned an incident into a civil disorder. Elsewhere, notably Detroit and Newark, even where they were not precipitating or motivating factors, inflaming rumors made the job of police and community leaders far more difficult.

Experience also has shown that the harmful effect of rumors can be offset if police, public officials, and community leaders quickly and effectively circulate the facts. The Commission recommends that loudspeakers should be available to police at the scene of an incident. Radio and television announcements and special telephone networks to reach many neighborhood residents have been effective.

An innovative method is that of a "Rumor Central"—an office responsible for the collection, evaluation, and countering of rumors which could lead to civil disorder.[3] To be

[2] Training Bulletin—Tension Situations, 24 April, 1967, The Chicago Police Department.

[3] The "Rumor Central" unit is discussed in the Supplement on Control of Disorder.

most effective, such units might be located outside police departments. In any event, they should work closely with police and other public officials.

II. Control Capabilities

Whenever an initial incident erupts into a major crowd control problem, most police departments are confronted with a difficult manpower problem. A police department normally has only about 13 percent of its uniformed force on duty during the peak 4 p.m. to midnight watch, when nearly all the riots studied by the Commission began. For example, a city like Cincinnati, with a population of about 500,000 and an area of 77 square miles, would normally have fewer than 100 uniformed policemen available if trouble broke out. A city like Peoria, Illinois, with a population of about 100,000, would have less than 25 uniformed patrolmen on hand.[4]

Dispersal is also a factor. Normal police operations require personnel to be distributed over the entire geographical area of a city. When disorder breaks out, the task of mobilizing all available manpower is enormous. The police administrator must weigh the need for police to control the riot against the risks of leaving vital areas of the city without police protection.

It is apparent that most American cities would not have enough policemen quickly available to assure control in the event of a sudden large disorder. A high premium must hence be placed on the capability to prevent disorders—or to contain them before they develop into serious proportions.

Training

Despite the obvious importance of well-trained police in controlling disorder, the Commission survey of the capabilities of selected police departments disclosed serious deficiencies. For example, riot-control training is usually given to recruits. This averaged 18 hours for the departments surveyed, ranging from 62 hours to only two. Little additional training is provided for command-level officers. By contrast, the National Guard now receives a minimum of 32 hours of riot control

[4] The majority of American cities between 50,000 and 100,000 population have less than 100 policemen. Of those with over 100,000 population, 71 percent have less than 500 policemen. Only 19 cities have more than 1000. As suggested by the cited figure of 13 percent manpower available, these figures are deceptively reassuring. Considering three shifts, days off, vacations and sick leave, five men are required to keep one police post manned 24 hours a day. In addition, manpower for regular police services like administration, records and detective work must be taken into account.

training under new U.S. Army regulations and National Guard officers receive 16 hours of command training for disorder situations.

The deficiencies in police training for disorders are magnified by the fact that standard police training and operations differ radically from training needed for the control of riots. Traditional training and emphasis have been on the individual policeman. His routine duties involve isolated incidents and dealings with small numbers of people at one time. The nature of his work—riding or walking mostly alone or in pairs—means that he has considerable individual discretion.

The control of civil disturbances, on the other hand, requires large numbers of disciplined personnel, comparable to soldiers in a military unit, organized and trained to work as a team under a highly unified command and control system. Thus when a civil disturbance occurs, a police department must suddenly shift into a new type of organization with different operational procedures. The individual officer must stop acting independently and begin to perform as a member of a closely supervised, disciplined team. Our survey disclosed that training in practically all departments is limited to the individual.

Last year's disorders demonstrated that the control problems encountered were different even from those for which riot-control training had been designed. Violence often involved small groups and hit-and-run tactics. Except in the later stages of the largest disorders, the crowds included large numbers of spectators not active in looting or destruction. Since they were mostly residents of the area, dispersal alone was futile. As a result, training in conventional riot-control formations and tactics, designed primarily to control and disperse mobs, was often inapplicable and ineffective.

Few departments have the resources and expertise to provide adequate and relevant training for control of serious disorders. We discuss this problem in greater detail in our Supplement on the Control of Disorder, and set forth additional recommendations.

Discipline and Command

As the Riot Profiles in the opening chapter of the Report have shown, discipline of the control force is a crucial factor. Officers at the scene of a ghetto disorder are likely to suffer vilification, and to be the targets for rocks or bottles. Nevertheless, police discipline must be sufficiently strong so that an individual officer is not provoked into unilateral action. He must develop sufficient confidence in himself and his fellow officers to avoid panic or the indiscriminate—and inflammatory—use of force that has sometimes occurred in the heat of disorders. Discipline of this sort depends on the leadership of seasoned commanders and the presence in the field of sufficient supervisory officers to make major decisions.

The ability of police commanders to maintain command and control of units at the scene of disorder is severely handicapped by deficiencies in police communications. Police departments usually can communicate with their personnel only through radios in police vehicles. Once the officer leaves his police car or motorcycle, he loses communication with his superiors and is outside their effective control.

The military has field communications systems which make it possible to achieve effective command and control. The nation's police departments do not. A more complete discussion of this problem and the Commission's recommendations are contained in the Supplement.

Police Tactics

There are no all-purpose control tactics. Last summer's disorders demonstrated repeatedly that tactics which are effective in one situation may be totally ineffective in another. The cardinal requirement is to have enough men and control equipment available to carry out effectively whatever tactics are necessary and appropriate according to the dictates of sound judgment.

Tactical operations are dealt with in the Supplement. Specific riot control tactics are discussed in the Model Operations Plan, described in the Supplement, which has been prepared for separate distribution to police departments.

III. The Use of Force

Justification of Deadly Force

There are at least three serious problems involved in the use of deadly weapons in a civil disorder. The first is the risk of killing or wounding innocent persons—bystanders or passersby who may in fact be hundreds of feet away when a shot is fired.

The second is the justification for the use of deadly force against looting or vandalism. Are bullets the correct response to offenses of this sort? Major General George Gelston[5] told the Commission: . . . "I am not going to order a man killed for

---

[5] Adjutant General of Maryland, commander of National Guard forces in Cambridge, Maryland last summer, and former Police Commissioner of Baltimore.

stealing a six-pack of beer or a television set." Instead, he said, a non-lethal tear gas can stop any looting.

The third problem is that the use of excessive force—even the inappropriate display of weapons—may be inflammatory and lead to even worse disorder. As the FBI riot control manual states:

> The basic rule, when applying force, is to use only the minimum force necessary to effectively control the situation. Unwarranted application of force will incite the mob to further violence, as well as kindle seeds of resentment for police that, in turn, could cause a riot to recur. Ill-advised or excessive application of force will not only result in charges of police brutality, but also may prolong the disturbance.

Such counsel with respect to disorders accords with the clearly established legal and social principle of minimum use of force by police.

The major difficulty in dealing with all these problems, however, is the limited choice still presented to police in mass disorders: to use too much force or too little. The police who were faced with the New York riot of 1863 were equipped with two weapons—a wooden stick and a gun. For the most part, the police faced with urban disorders last summer had to rely on two weapons—a wooden stick and a gun.

Our police departments today require a middle range of physical force with which to restrain and control both more humanely and more effectively.

Alternatives to Deadly Force

The dilemma regarding force has endured for more than a century for two reasons. One is that police are inhibited from using even the new tools which have been developed. The second is that the improvement and perfection of these tools is proceeding far too slowly.

As pointed out in the Supplement, fear of public reaction and other policy considerations have tended to inhibit police use of nonlethal chemical agents in civil disorders. The U.S. Army, on the other hand, relies heavily on the use of CS, a chemical agent, for controlling riots. The Army has found it to be both much more effective and safer than the more traditional tear gas, CN. The use of CS is prescribed in the standard military sequence of force prior to the employment of any lethal firearms. Moreover, new developments now make it possible to use chemical agents selectively against individuals and small groups with minimum danger to innocent persons. Thus the understandable concern of many police and public officials as to the wisdom of using massive amounts of gas in densely populated areas need no longer prove a barrier.

The value and effectiveness of chemical agents in restoring law and order, with minimum danger to lives and property, is also attested by the FBI's riot control manual: "Chemical agents . . . can negate the numerical superiority the mob has over the police force. They are the most effective and most humane means of achieving temporary, neutralization of a mob with a minimum of personal injury."

The Commission recommends that in suppressing disorder, the police, whenever possible, follow the example of the U.S. Army in requiring the use of chemical agents before the use of deadly weapons.

The experience of many police forces has demonstrated, however, that the value and community acceptance of new nonlethal methods may be jeopardized if police officers employ them in an indiscriminate way. In some of the cities we studied, reports of improper use of some chemical weapons by individual police officers have led to charges that these weapons are brutalizing or demeaning. To assure public confidence and prevent misuse, police administrators should issue clear guidelines on where and how police may employ such control measures.

The Commission has received many suggestions for other nonlethal control equipment. Distinctive marking dyes or odors and the filming of rioters have been recommended both to deter and positively identify persons guilty of illegal acts. Sticky tapes, adhesive blobs, and liquid foam are advocated to immobilize or block rioters. Intensely bright lights and loud distressing sounds capable of creating temporary disability may prove to be useful. Technology will provide still other tools.

There is need for additional experience and evaluation before the police and the public can be reasonably assured that these control innovations meet the performance and safety standards required for use in civilian communities. The Commission believes, however, that the urgent need for nonlethal alternatives requires immediate attention and federal support. We discuss this further in the Supplement.

IV. COMMUNITY ASSISTANCE IN DISORDER CONTROL

Commission studies have shown that in a number of instances both police and other responsible civil authorities were forced to make decisions without adequate facts in an atmosphere charged by rumor.

Police administrators consulted by the Commission emphasized the importance of employing trained police intelligence officers to collect, evaluate and disseminate information. The use of undercover police officers, reliable informants and the assignment of police personnel to provide fast, accurate, on-the-scene reports were all cited as essential.

During the early stage of a disorder when lawlessness is still relatively restricted, the cooperation and assistance of Negro leaders and other community residents with a common interest in the maintenance of order can be extremely valuable. They can provide the police with the kind of pertinent, reliable information essential for decision-making during the disorder. Many agencies and organizations in the area, public and private, have valuable contacts and channels of communication. These also can serve as important information resources.

In some cities, "counter-rioters" have played an important role in dampening disturbance. Volunteers have assisted in restoring order by patrolling their neighborhoods and trying independently to persuade others to go home. Sometimes local authorities have actively recruited ghetto residents to perform these missions. The Commission believes that mayors and police chiefs should recognize and assess carefully the potential benefit such efforts can sometimes provide, restoring the peace in a way that will earn public support and confidence.

The larger question, however—whether police should withdraw from the disorder area and let the community leaders or forces seek to cool the rioting—raises a number of critical issues. The first and most important is whether by so doing the police are abdicating their basic responsibility to maintain order and protect lives and property.

Some police administrators are deeply convinced that it is a dereliction of duty for police to delegate complete authority to individuals or groups who lack legal responsibility. In their judgment, such actions creates the danger of vigilante groups.

The Commission shares this concern; a sanctioned control group could use its position to intimidate or terrorize. Those who come forward to discourage rioting may have no influence with the rioters. If they fail, they may well blame officials, creating new enforcement problems.

The Commission believes that only the mayor—who has the ultimate responsibility for the welfare and safety of the community—can, with the advice of the police administrator, make the critical judgment.

The Role of Public Officials

The Commission believes incidents are less likely to escalate into larger violence if ghetto residents know they have effective political channels of protest. We discussed formal grievance outlets at length in the preceding chapters. Here we are particularly concerned with the role of the mayor or city manager or police chief.

Civil disorders are fundamental governmental problems, not simply police matters. As the chief elected official, the mayor must take ultimate responsibility for all governmental action in times of disorder. To make this meaningful, he must have the corresponding authority and control. He must become fully involved in disorder planning and operations. He must understand the nature of the problems posed by a disorder, the strategy of response and the pattern of field operations.

In some cities, mayors have taken the view that disorders were entirely police matters. This represents a failure to accept a fundamental responsibility. The unwillingness of a mayor to become personally involved and negotiate grievances with local residents may cut off a vital outlet for peaceful protest.

Similarly, police chiefs should understand this responsibility and involve the mayor in their planning activities and operations. Only regular participation by the mayor in police problems, in cold winters as well as hot summers, will educate both the mayor and the police to the mutually reinforcing nature of their relationship.

Parallel responsibilities exist at the state level. Governors and other civilian officials with responsibility over state law enforcement activities, such as attorneys general, have an obligation to supervise planning and operations for civil disorders.

One of the most important responsibilities of local officials is to maintain close personal contact with the ghetto. The importance of creating channels of communication with ministers, with community organizations, with Negro leaders including young activists and militants cannot be overestimated. Given such contacts, officials become more sensitive to ghetto reactions to particular episodes and frictions. They also create acquaintanceships which can be used to help alleviate tensions that might otherwise heighten.

As the Riot Profiles indicate, in a number of the disorders studied by the Commission, efforts were made to respond to grievances. In some instances, Negro leaders took the initiative. In others, mayors and state officials did so. In New

Brunswick, for example, discussion alleviated tension and led to a peaceful settlement. Often the determination of civilian officials, especially the mayor, to seek out these opportunities may be decisive in avoiding violence.

Having determined that it will try to resolve its problems by political means, the city must then decide with whom to negotiate—often a difficult question. Large meetings open to the general public or small meetings limited to established, older Negro leaders were rarely found to be effective. City officials are often faced with a fragmented Negro community. If they have failed to keep open broad channels of communication, city officials will have great difficulty identifying leaders with sufficient influence to get through to those on the streets.

Even after contacts are made, negotiations may be extremely difficult. Younger, militant leaders are often distrustful of city government, fearful of compromising their militancy or their leadership by allying themselves too closely with "the power structure," particularly when that structure may have nothing to deliver.

Civil disorders require the maximum coordination of the activities of all governmental agencies. Such cooperation can only be brought about by the chief executive. Examples are joint operations by the police and fire departments, mutual assistance agreements with neighboring communities, and state and federal assistance. These problems are discussed in the Supplement.

V. DANGER OF OVERREACTION

Emergencies are anticipated in police planning. They range from natural threats like floods and storms to man-made incidents like the recent disorders. Until 1964, most civil disorders were regarded as difficult but basically manageable police problems of an essentially local nature. The events of the last few summers, however, particularly the events of 1967, have radically changed this view. Disturbances in densely populated, predominantly Negro areas which might earlier have been labelled brawls became characterized as "riots," with racial overtones. A national climate of tension and fear developed, particularly in cities with large Negro populations.

Were relatively minor incidents inflated or escalated into serious disturbances? Did such inflation result from overly aggressive law enforcement action? Did it stem from unwarranted fears on the part of the ghetto community? Precise answers are impossible. What can be said, however, is that there was widespread misunderstanding and exaggeration of what did occur.

The most notable example is the belief widely held across the country last summer that riot cities were paralyzed by sniper fire. Of 23 cities surveyed by the Commission, there had been reports of sniping in at least 15. What is probable, although the evidence is fragmentary, is that there was at least some sniping. What is certain is that the amount of sniping attributed to rioters—by law enforcement officials as well as the press—was highly exaggerated.

According to the best information available to the Commission, most reported sniping incidents were demonstrated to be gunfire by either police or National Guardsmen.

The climate of fear and expectation of violence created by such exaggerated, sometimes totally erroneous, reports demonstrates the serious risks of overreaction and excessive use of force. In particular, the Commission is deeply concerned that, in their anxiety to control disorders, some law enforcement agencies may resort to indiscriminate, repressive use of force against wholly innocent elements of the Negro community. The injustice of such conduct—and its abrasive effects—would be incalculable.

Elected officials, police and National Guard officials must take effective steps to prevent false assessments and the tragic consequences that could follow. This will require improved communications. It will require reliable intelligence about ghetto problems and incidents. It will require, equally, assurance of steadfast discipline among control personnel.

FUNDING OF RECOMMENDATIONS FOR PREVENTION AND CONTROL OF DISORDERS

Many of the recommendations in this and the preceding chapter will be costly. Studies of police practices, intensified recruitment of Negro officers, increased planning and training for disorder control—all would impose heavy financial burdens on communities already hard-pressed by the increasing costs of their present systems of criminal justice.

The Commission recommends that the federal government bear a part of this burden.

Federal funding need not and should not in any way infringe on the principle of local law enforcement authority. The federal government already finances a variety of law enforcement assistance programs without such infringement. The Department of Justice provides direct grants for research, planning and demonstration through the Office of Law Enforcement Assistance, and the FBI conducts training programs for state and local police officers. The Department of Health, Education and Welfare administers juvenile delinquency control programs and educational grants for law enforcement studies. The Department of Labor helps pay for Police Cadet Training programs. The Office of Economic Opportunity assists in police-community relations activities. We commend and endorse these efforts. But we believe more federal financial assistance is needed.

Such assistance should take two forms. First, in this chapter, the preceding one, and in the Supplement, we specifically recommend federal funding for certain programs—community service officers, development of portable communications equipment, a national clearing house for training information, and nonlethal weapons development.

Second, we also believe that more federal support is necessary to help local communities improve the overall quality of their criminal justice systems. With the Crime Commission, we believe that the federal government ". . . can make a dramatic new contribution to the national effort against crime by greatly expanding its support of the agencies of justice in the states and in the cities."

These remarks are in no way intended to excuse local governments from their financial responsibilities. Improved law enforcement at the local level, including increased capacity to prevent and control civil disorders, is possible only if local citizens are willing to put their tax money where their desires are. But this Commission believes that not even the most devoted and willing community can succeed acting alone. Only the federal government is in a position to provide expertise, conduct and evaluate comprehensive test programs, and pay for the large capital investment necessary to develop experimental programs and new equipment.

The Crime Commission outlined a broad program of federal funding, advice, and assistance to meet major criminal justice needs. It estimated that in the next decade, several hundred million dollars could be profitably spent each year on this program. The increased demands imposed on law enforcement agencies by the recent disorders have intensified the urgency and increased the cost of such a program.

Nevertheless, 14 months have now passed since the Crime Commission's exhaustive study and recommendations; 13 months have passed since the President first urged the Congress to enact such a program; that urgent request was renewed by the President in his Public Safety Message of February 7, 1968. No final action has yet been taken. It should be taken—and taken promptly. Because law enforcement is a local responsibility, whatever legislation is adopted should permit direct grants to municipal governments. Funding should be at least as high as that requested by the President in his Message.

Chapter 13 / The Administration of Justice Under Emergency Conditions

I. The Condition in Our Lower Courts

A riot in the city poses a separate crisis in the administration of justice. Partially paralyzed by decades of neglect, deficient in facilities, procedures and personnel, overwhelmed by the demands of normal operations, lower courts have staggered under the crushing new burdens of civil disorders.

Some of our courts, moreover, have lost the confidence of the poor. This judgment is underwritten by the members and staff of this Commission, who have gone into the courthouses and ghettos of the cities torn by the riots of 1967. The belief is pervasive among ghetto residents that lower courts in our urban communities dispense "assembly-line" justice; that from arrest to sentencing, the poor and uneducated are denied equal justice with the affluent, that procedures such as bail and fines have been perverted to perpetuate class inequities. We have found that the apparatus of justice in some areas has itself become a focus for distrust and hostility. Too often the courts have operated to aggravate rather than relieve the tensions that ignite and fire disorders.

The quality of justice which the courts dispense in time of civil crisis is one of the indices of the capacity of a democratic society to survive. To see that this quality does not become strained is therefore a task of critical importance.

"No program of crime prevention," the President's Commission on Law Enforcement and the Administration of Justice found, "will be effective without a massive overhaul of the lower criminal courts."[1] The range of needed reforms recommended in their report is broad: increasing judicial manpower and reforming the selection and tenure of judges; providing more prosecutors, defense counsel, and probation officers and training them adequately; modernizing the physical facilities and administration of the courts; creating unified

[1] The President's Commission on Law Enforcement and the Administration of Justice, *The Challenge of Crime in a Free Society*, A Report, 1967, p. 128; and Task Force on Administration of Justice, *Task Force Report: The Courts*, 1967, p. 29.

state court systems; coordinating statewide the operations of local prosecutors; improving the informational basis for pretrial screening and negotiated pleas; revising the bail system and setting up systems for station-house summons and release for persons accused of certain offenses; revising sentencing laws and policies toward a more just structure.

If we are to provide our judicial institutions with sufficient capacity to cope effectively with civil disorders, these reforms are vitally necessary. They are long overdue. The responsibility for this effort will rest heavily on the organized bar of the community. The prevalence of "assembly-line" justice is evidence that in many localities, the bar has not met its leadership responsibilities.

II. THE EXPERIENCE OF SUMMER 1967

In the cities shaken by disorders during the summer of 1967, there were recurring breakdowns in the mechanisms for processing, prosecuting and protecting arrested persons. In the main, these resulted from the communities' failure to anticipate, and plan for, the emergency judicial needs of civil disorders, and from longstanding structural deficiencies in criminal court systems distended grotesquely to process a massive influx of cases. In many instances tensions and hostilities from the streets infected the quality of justice dispensed by the courts.

While final information on the processing of riot offenders is not yet assembled, the information presently available provides valuable guidelines for future planning.

The goals of criminal justice under conditions of civil disorder are basic:

- To insure the apprehension and subsequent conviction of those who riot, incite to riot or have committed acts of physical violence or caused substantial property damage.
- To insure that law violators are subjected to criminal process, and that disposition of their cases is commensurate with the severity of the offense; to provide, at the same time, for just but compassionate disposition of inadvertent, casual, or minor offenders.
- To provide prompt, fair judicial hearings for arrested persons under conditions which do not aggravate grievances within the affected areas.

In the summer of 1967, these goals too often were disregarded or unattainable.

338

Few Successful Prosecutions for Serious Crimes Committed During the Riot Period

In Detroit, 26 alleged snipers were charged with assault with intent to commit murder. Twenty-three of those charges were subsequently dismissed. As of September 30, 1967, one out of seven homicide arrests had resulted in a conviction; two were still pending. Of 253 assault arrests only 11 convictions were produced; 58 were still pending. Twenty-one out of 34 arson arrests, and 22 out of 28 inciting to riot arrests, had been dropped by the prosecution.[2]

Three elements impaired successful prosecution of persons arrested for major offenses:

First, the technique of mass arrest was sometimes used to clear the streets. Those arrested often included innocent spectators and minor violators along with major offenders. In Newark and Detroit, mass street arrests were made in sectors where sniping was reported and extensive looting occurred.

Second, the obstacles to deliberate, painstaking, on-the-scene investigations during a riot are formidable. Thus, insufficient evidence was obtained to insure conviction on many of the most serious charges.

Third, the masses of arrestees in the major riots so overwhelmed processing and pre-trial procedures that facilities and personnel were not free to deal adequately with serious offenders or with evidence of their crimes. Personnel in police stations were overwhelmed by the sheer numbers of accused persons to be booked, screened, detained, and eventually brought to court. Minor and major offenders were herded unselectively through the process.[3]

Assembly-line booking operations in the Detroit precincts and at the jail—20 to 30 employees assigned to 12 hour shifts—proved inadequate. Records necessary to identify defendants or to check for past criminal records could not be obtained. Follow-up investigation, essential to secure convictions in serious cases, proved difficult or impossible.

With lesser crimes as well, the system displayed an inability to produce successful prosecutions. Looting charges comprised 84% of the felony arrests in Detroit.[4] Yet almost half of the

[2] In the 1965 Watts riot, of seven persons arrested on homicide charges, five were subsequently released. None has yet been convicted. A total of 120 adult arrests for assault produced only 60 convictions; 27 adult arson arrests: seven convictions. In Newark, one homicide indictment and 22 assault indictments (none for sniping) have been returned.

[3] In Detroit 7,231 arrests were made during the nine day riot, in Newark 1,510 in five days. In one week, the Detroit Recorder's Court handled a month's quota of misdemeanor cases and a six months' quota of felony cases.

[4] Fifty-five percent of all prosecuted arrests were for looting. Twenty-four percent of all riot arrests for felonies were not prosecuted.

felony charges that went to court were dismissed at preliminary hearing for lack of evidence.[5]

Serious Overcrowding of Facilities

From the point of arrest on, accused persons in Detroit and Newark suffered the abuses of an overtaxed and harassed system of justice. In Detroit, inability to maintain a centralized system of arrest records meant that families and defense attorneys could not locate arrested persons confined in widely scattered emergency detention facilities. In one day alone, 790 persons were booked at the Wayne County Jail and 1,068 sent on to other detention facilities, usually without opportunity to notify or consult family or counsel.

Regular detention facilities were swamped. Detroit's main city jail, built for 1,200 persons, was crammed wtih over 1,700. Precinct lockups built for 50 prisoners received 150 or more. The juvenile detention home built for 120 held over 600 during the riot. Makeshift detention facilities were commandeered; 1,000 arrestees were held in an underground police garage for several days, many without adequate food or water. Others were held for over 24 hours in city buses. Adults of both sexes were sometimes locked up together. In Newark, a large portion of those arrested were held in an armory without proper food, water, toilet or medical facilities. Prisoners had no way to contact lawyers or relatives. Members of the press or official observers were unable to reassure those on the outside. In the absence of information about arrestees, new rumors and fears added to the tensions of the riot.

Judicial Procedures Oriented to Mass Rather Than Individualized Justice

Normal screening procedures were overrun in the chaos of the major disorders. Rational decisions to prosecute, to delay prosecution on good behavior, to dismiss, to release with or without bail pending trial, to accept a plea to a lesser charge or to press for conviction on the original charge, and to impose a just sentence require access to a comprehensive file of information on the offender contributed by police, prosecution, defense counsel, bail interviewers and probation officers. Orderly screening requires time, personnel, deliberation. These elements were absent in the court processing of those arrested in the major riots.

[5] Sixty percent of felony riot charges went to preliminary hearing. At this stage, 49 percent of those charges were dismissed, as compared with only 23 percent of felony charges dismissed during 1966.

In Detroit defendants were herded to arraignment in groups.[6] There was little chance to screen out those cases that could best be handled out of court or which could not survive trial. Defense counsel were not allowed to represent defendants at this stage in Detroit. Some judges failed to advise the defendants of their legal rights. After one group-arraignment, a Detroit judge told the next group of defendants, "You heard what I said to them. The same things apply to you."

Arraignments in the major riot cities were often delayed several days, thus denying defendants the right to prompt bail. In Detroit many persons arrested for minor ordinance violations were jailed for a number of days before going to court. When the judicial process was finally activated for them, most judges tended to set inordinately high bail so as to frustrate release.[7] Pressure on detention facilities thus remained at intolerable levels for several days. Bail for offenses such as looting and property destruction was set as high as $50,000; for assault up to $200,000. Bond for curfew violations was rarely set at less than $10,000—often as high as $15,000 to $25,000.[8] In Newark bail was uniformly set at $500 for curfew offenses, $250 for loitering and at $2,500 and up for property offenses. No attempt was made in most cases to individualize the bail setting process. Pressured by unattainably high bail, many indigent defendants pleaded guilty or accepted immediate trial when offered.

In both Newark and Detroit, detention pressures finally forced a more lenient bail policy. In what were essentially duplications of earlier bail hearings, prisoners were interviewed

---

[6] One thousand defendants were arraigned in a single day in the Detroit Recorder's Court (250 per six-hour shift). Information usually available to the judge at arraignment on the warrant—i.e., fingerprint checks, interviews, investigative reports, formal complaints—was often missing due to the logjam in the warrant clerk's office. Grand jury proceedings suffered similarly. Mass indictments naming 100 or more defendants were handed down in all-day sessions in Newark after average deliberation of less than two minutes per case.

[7] In Detroit, the prosecutor announced this policy publicly and most of the judges acceded. The Recorder's Court in 1966 released 26 percent on their own bond. During the riot the figure was 2 percent. Acceptance of money bonds in any amount was suspended during one 24-hour period. Offers of defense counsel to represent defendants at bail hearings were rejected.

[8] A survey of Detroit riot defendants held in Jackson State Prison for lack of bail, showed only 9 percent with bond set below $1,500; 14 percent with bond set between $1,500 and $2,500; 20 percent between $5,000 and $10,000; 44 percent between $10,000 and $25,000. Another survey of defendants imprisoned in Milan federal penitentiary who were arrested on the first day of the riot for property offenses, showed 90 percent with bond set between $10,000 and $50,000.

and released without bail in large numbers.[9] In Newark, an ROR (release on the defendant's own recognizance) program initiated in the last days of the riot interviewed over 700 prisoners (at least half of all those arrested) and secured the release of between 65 and 80 percent.

Courts in several of the smaller cities successfully experimented with release of offenders on their own recognizance from the beginning of the riot. Dayton continued its release on recognizance policy during its September disorder. Most of the 203 people arrested were released without money bail, In New Haven—out of 550 arrested—80 percent were released on their own recognizance.

COUNSEL

The riots underscored other deficiencies in local court systems. Most prominent in the major outbreaks was the shortage of skilled defense lawyers to handle the influx of cases in any fashion approximating individual representation. Even where volunteer lawyers labored overtime, the system was badly strained. Individual counsel was rarely available. Inexperienced lawyers in Detroit were given briefings by experienced criminal attorneys and were handed procedural handbooks before entering the court rooms.[10] They had no opportunity to bargain for pleas before arraignment, or even to see police files before preliminary hearings. In several cities (Detroit, Newark, and New Brunswick), volunteer attorneys were denied access to prisoners in jail—in one case because they did not know the prisoners' names. While individual lawyers and legal organizations in several cities provided counsel to represent minor violators (Milwaukee, the Legal Services program; New Haven, the Legal Assistance Association; Cincinnati, the American Civil Liberties Union, National Association for the Advancement Of Colored People and Legal Aid Society); in others (Rock-

[9] The prosecutor finally initiated the lenient bail policy in Detroit. (One judge, however, used bail examiners throughout the riot and released 10 percent of defendants who came before him on their own recognizance.) Over 3,000 were released within a few days through bail review; by August 4, only 1,200 remained in detention. Files were flown to the FBI for checking to expedite release. Only one known re-arrest (for curfew violation) was reported from among such persons released. When preliminary examinations began on August 1, most defendants were released on $500 personal bond, except in violent crimes or cases of serious prior records.

In Newark, on the Sunday following the Wednesday the riot began, the judges went into the jails to conduct bail review hearings.

[10] The Detroit Bar Association mustered over 700 lawyers (10 to 15 percent of its membership) to serve as defense counsel. They were used primarily at preliminary hearings and arraignments on the information—not at initial bail hearings.

ford, Illinois; Atlanta, Georgia and Dayton, Ohio) those defendants normally not eligible for assigned counsel went unrepresented.

The need for prompt, individual legal counsel is particularly acute in riot situations. This is because of the range of alternative charges, the severity of penalties that may be imposed in the heat of riot, the inequities that occur where there is mass, indiscriminate processing of arrested persons, and the need for essential information when charges are made by the prosecutor and bail is set. The services of counsel at the earliest stage, preferably at the precinct station, are essential. Provision of effective counsel at an early stage will also protect against a rash of post-conviction challenges and reversals.

SENTENCING

Trial and sentencing proved equally vulnerable to the tyranny of numbers. Sentences meted out during the riots tended to be harsher than in those cases disposed of later. Some judges in the early days of the riots openly stated that they would impose maximum penalties across-the-board as deterrents. One Cincinnati judge announced that any person brought before him on a riot-connected offense would receive the maximum penalty. Circumstances of the arrest, past record, age, family responsibilities or other mitigating factors were not considered.

The burden of this policy fell on the poorest defendants—those unable to raise bail—who agreed to immediate trials. Those who could raise bail and wait out the riot often received more lenient sentences. Once the riots were over, defendants were frequently sentenced to time already spent in detention, if they consented to plead guilty.

In those cities where the riots were less extensive and the number of arrests allowed normal trial procedures to remain largely intact, sentences did not markedly vary from the norm. In Dayton, where most of the 203 law violators were charged with minor offenses such as disorderly conduct and destruction of property, the standard penalty was a fine of $15 to $50. In Rockford, Illinois, where all arrests were for disorderly conduct or curfew violations, fines were assessed within a $20 to $250 range according to the individual's ability to pay.

A primary function of criminal justice in a riot situation is effectively to apprehend, prosecute and punish the purposeful inciters to riot, and to assure the community at large—rioters and nonrioters alike—that law violators will be prosecuted and sentenced according to an ordered system of justice.

Dispassionate objectivity on the part of both the bench and the bar—always required and always difficult—becomes even more necessary when civil disorders occur. The passions of the street must not enter the courtroom to affect any step in the administration of justice, particularly sentencing. During a riot emergency, it is highly important that courts adhere to established criteria for sentencing. This did not always occur in Detroit and Newark in the summer of 1967. In smaller disorders, such as Dayton, Atlanta, and New Haven, arrests were fewer, arraignments were prompt, release policies were fair and sentences were within normal ranges.

III. Guidelines for the Future

In a period of civil disorder, it is essential that our judicial system continue firmly to protect the individual constitutional rights upon which our society is based.

Our criminal jurisprudence has developed important safeguards based on the arrest process as the mechanism which activates the full judicial machinery. Thus, arrest brings into play carefully developed procedures for the protection of individual rights.

Some suggest that the judicial system must respond to the riot emergency by short-cutting those procedures. Such suggestions, usually referred to as "preventive arrest" or "preventive detention," involve extending the police power to include detention without formal arrest, broadening summary enforcement procedures, and suspending bail hearings and pre-trial procedures for sorting out charges and defendants.

We reject such suggestions. Rather, we urge each community to undertake the difficult but essential task of reform and emergency planning necessary to give its judicial system the strength to meet emergency needs. We make the following recommendations.

The Community Should Prepare a Comprehensive Plan for Emergency Operation of the Judicial System

A comprehensive plan for the emergency operation of the judicial system during a riot should involve many public and private agencies in the community. It must include:

- A review of applicable statutes and ordinances (and their amendment and revision if necessary) to ensure that there are well drawn, comprehensive laws sufficient to deter and punish the full range of riot behavior.[11]

- Compilations and interpretations of the laws relied on to control such an emergency must be made available to police, prosecutors and, through the press, to the community at large well in advance. When a disorder arises there must be no doubt what citizens are supposed to do and not do. Citizens are more likely to remain calm and resist the provocations of unfounded rumors if they are already familiar with the laws applicable to riot conditions.

- Regulatory guidelines should be drawn in advance detailing interaction of police with other law enforcement personnel (such as state police and National Guard), specifying who can make arrests and how they should be handled,[12] the charges to enter for prohibited acts, and how certain minor violations may be handled without formal arrest and detention. Booking, screening and bail setting will proceed more efficiently when there are established guidelines for processing large numbers of cases.

- Basic policy decisions for each step in the judicial process must be made: which charges will become eligible for summons and release after arrest, with trial postponed until the emergency is over? Will any defendants be released during a riot and on what conditions? Which charges require immediate court processing? Which charges require an immediate follow-through investigation in order to support subsequent prosecution?

- Bail and sentencing policies applicable during emergencies should be defined by the judiciary with consistency and justice as a goal. Bail interviewers and probation officers should be instructed as to the kind of information required for release or sentencing decisions in a riot situation.

- Administrative techniques should be established by the court to ensure that eligible indigent defendants will be represented by counsel at the earliest stage.

- Arrangements for night and weekend court sessions should be made.

- Public and volunteer defenders can be more effectively utilized if there are prior allocations to each group of specific classes of cases; and if there are agreed procedures for assigning counsel to each defendant and for determining how long they will remain on the case. For instance, volunteer lawyers may be provided to represent riot participants who normally would not be eligible to obtain public defenders because of the minor nature of their

[11] For example: it has been suggested that rather than relying on vague disorderly conduct or loitering statutes in riot situations, specific laws or ordinances be enacted which, upon declaration of emergency, deal with possession of incendiary devices (even before they are used), interference with police, firemen or other emergency workers, storage of firearms, restrictions on access to riot areas, restriction on sale of liquor or firearms during emergencies, imposition of curfews, and crowd dispersal. Laws designed to meet such emergency circumstances must be specific and uniform regarding conditions which must exist to invoke their application, who may proclaim such an emergency, and what activities or powers such a declaration limits or permits. Provision should also be made for judicial review of the invocation of such emergency laws. See Supplement on Control of Disorders.

[12] During the Detroit riot, processing difficulties arose because National Guardsmen, who could not make arrests under state law, handed prisoners over to local police without sufficiently recording circumstances of the arrests.

violations. The entire organized bar of the city and even the state
—and particularly Negro or other minority members of the bar—
should be involved in emergency planning. Adequate provision
must be made for individual counseling of clients in order that
effective representation does not deteriorate, as it did in many
cities last summer. There must be training courses in advance to
ensure that all participating lawyers are prepared for the task.
Defense strategy on such basic issues as plea negotiation, bail review, and habeas corpus needs to be planned ahead of time. A
control center where volunteer lawyers may get advice and investigative help during a riot is an essential component of planning.

- Sufficient facilities as near as possible to the court must be found
to house, in a humane fashion, those detained during riots. Civic
and service groups have vital roles to play in this aspect of riot
planning. Temporary detention centers can generate terrible conditions if proper medical care, communication with the outside,
food and sanitary facilities are not provided. Juveniles require
special handling aimed toward early return to their parents. Community organizations and volunteers willing to temporarily shelter or supervise juveniles and adults from the riot area must be
enlisted, coordinated, and assigned according to plan.

- Press coverage and impartial observers to report to the community on all stages of processing should be provided. Information centers, accessible by a well publicized phone number, must
be set up to locate defendants promptly and to assure continual
contact with their families.

- Emergency planning should also include agreements between different levels of courts and among courts in different jurisdictions
to facilitate emergency transfers of judges, prosecutors, and probation officers. Where necessary, laws should be passed allowing
the appointment of members of the bar as special judges during
such an emergency. Auxiliary courtrooms need to be readied. A
master list of all competent clerical personnel in the area to help
process defendants' records quickly is needed.

We think it probable that a highly visible plan, in which
basic procedures for handling riots are established and publicized beforehand, and in which ghetto leaders and citizens
are full participants, will have a reassuring effect during a disorder. People need to know where they stand—what they can
and cannot do and what will happen to them if they are
arrested in a riot situation.

Prevention is paramount, but experience has shown that
refusal to plan is foolhardy and can only compound the human
agonies of civil outbreak.

The organized bars of our cities and states have a special
responsibility in planning for the administration of justice during a riot. Their responsibility does not stop with providing
defense counsel for rioters; they must assist the overloaded
prosecutors as well. Their participation cannot be confined to
a small segment—the defense bar or legal aid lawyers—it must

also include the large law firms, the corporate counselors and those who are leaders in the local bar. Lawyers must take the lead in showing the community that orderly justice is a priority item in any plan for riot prevention and control.

Recommended Policies in Processing Arrested Persons

ARRESTS

Alternatives to arrest. In any riot, the first priority is to enforce the law. This may require clearing the streets and preventing persons from entering or leaving the riot area. The authority of local police and other law enforcement officials should be spelled out in carefully drawn laws with a range of alternatives to arrest. Persons in the riot area should be permitted to "move on" or "out"—to go back to their homes voluntarily before police resort to arresting them. Discriminating use of such options by the police would tend to reduce the number of innocent bystanders or minor curfew violators picked up, and thereby alleviate congestion of judicial machinery.[13]

There are other situations during a riot when alternatives to arrest and detention may prove useful. One such alternative is a summons or notice to appear (like a traffic ticket). It may be handed to a citizen on the spot and requires him to appear later for processing at the police station or in court. Situations do arise such as curfew violations or where the act of arrest itself threatens to set off a new chain of violence, when the police should be given the discretionary power to issue on-the-street notices to minor violators. The primary advantage of the summons is that it avoids congestion of facilities and frees police personnel to remain on the street.

Guidelines for police discretion to use the summons must be drawn up in advance and the police instructed in proper exercise of such discretion. The summons will be most useful in emergencies if the police are already accustomed to using it as a routine law enforcement tool.

Follow-up in serious arrests. Just as essential as avoiding unnecessary arrests is the formulation of special measures to ensure the effectiveness of arrests for serious violations. On-the-spot photos have been found useful in some jurisdictions.

---

[13] In Detroit there were 935 adult arrests for curfew violations; 570 in Milwaukee; 335 in New Haven; 95 in Newark; 264 in Watts. A survey of 1,014 males in Detroit's Jackson Prison who had been arrested for riot offenses showed 120 were there for curfew offenses.

They fix the accused's identity and help to refresh the police officer's recollection after he has made scores of arrests for different offenses within a matter of hours.

In the serious case the arresting officer should fill out a reasonably detailed incident report as soon as feasible. At the station house, serious offenders might be turned over to a special follow-up detail, who can conduct early interrogation, check fingerprints and police records, or even revisit the scene for additional necessary evidence. Thus, serious cases will be separated at the outset for special processing designed to produce effective prosecution.[14]

POST-ARREST PROCESSING

Processing facilities. Some experts have suggested that all persons arrested during a riot be taken to a central processing center, preferably near the court, where available resources can most efficiently be used and intelligence activities can be coordinated (lawyers and relatives looking for arrested persons would at least know where to start). Others point out that a single location would impose a hardship on residents of widely dispersed communities; that neighborhood processing centers should be used. A two-step process may be preferable —screening for immediate release at the local precinct or neighborhood center, with later transportation to a single detention center for those who are not released or who cannot be taken immediately to court.

The proper choice of single or multiple processing centers will be determined by community size, location of available facilities in relation to the courts, the dimensions of the disturbance, and the number of arrested persons. But the facilities themselves must be arranged in advance and equipped for emergency conversion. Alternate plans may be necessary, since many factors cannot be predicted in advance. If multiple detention or processing centers are used, a central arrest and disposition record system is essential, so that prisoners can be located by their families and lawyers. The phone number of the central information post should be well publicized, and the telephone should be manned on a 24-hour basis. In Detroit there were nine separate detention centers; in Newark there

[14] Fifty-seven percent of adults booked on felonies in the Watts riots were convicted as compared with 72 percent on misdemeanors. A total of 732 were given jail sentences, only 36 of which exceeded six months. According to the report of the California Bureau of Criminal Statistics "These case dispositions have . . . suggested that there was little before the court in the form of evidence or positive proof of specific criminal activity." (p. 37)

were five. No centralized arrest record system was maintained. Confusion and distress over "lost" persons was widespread.

Screening for release. The most important function of post-arrest screening is promptly to separate different classes of offenders so they can be treated on rationally different bases: some summoned and released at the station house; some released on their own recognizance for later prosecution; some held until arraignment and further disposition by a judicial officer. It is, therefore, critically important that prosecutors, defense counsel, and bail interviewers be present in sufficient numbers at the initial processing center. Serious violators accused of murder, arson, sniping, aggravated assault, robbery, possession of explosives or incitement to riot must be separated at this early point, necessary follow-up investigations begun and preparations made for prompt presentment in court. Most minor offenders swept up in dragnet arrests should be issued a summons and released. Curfew offenders or hotheads picked up for failure to disperse at the scene, but now cooled down and cooperative, might be released without further detention, postponing a decision whether later to prosecute. Juveniles should be immediately separated for disposition by juvenile judges or by probation officers authorized under local law to release them to parents or to place them in separate juvenile facilities.[15]

Between the innocent person and the dangerous offender lies a mass of arrestees, brought in on felony charges relating to offenses against property—breaking and entering, burglary, looting.[16] Handling these cases requires broad and sensitive discretion. Some looters may be professional thieves systematically exploiting the riot chaos. Some looters are normally law abiding citizens. In Detroit, after the riot had subsided, many persons returned looted merchandise. These people usually have no significant prior criminal records.[17] Although prosecution may still be justified, in most instances they may safely be released back into the community to pursue their

[15] In the Watts riot, 556 juveniles (14 percent of all arrests) were taken into custody: 448 (16 percent) in Newark; 105 (20 percent) in New Haven; 62 (30 percent) in Dayton; 23 (6 percent) in Cincinnati; 703 (10 percent) in Detroit.

[16] In Detroit, 84 percent of felony charges were for forms of looting. In Watts, 82 percent were arrested on felony charges, most of them "burglary."

[17] Statistics on arrested persons in the Watts riots show that 38 percent had no major record (i.e., they had never been sentenced to more than 90 days) and 27 percent had no record at all). In Detroit, 51 percent of the arrestees had no arrest records. A sample of those arrested on the first day of the riot— 76 percent for looting—showed 41 percent with no record at all and only 17 percent with any felony record. In Newark, less than 45 percent of the arrestees had any police record.

livelihood and prepare their defense.[18] According to predetermined standards agreed upon by police, courts, and prosecutors they should be interviewed promptly for issuance of a summons and release at the station house. Where they have solid roots in the community,[19] and no serious criminal record they should be allowed to return to their homes and jobs. The station-house summons after arrest might also be reinforced by a law providing more severe penalties for those who commit new violations while awaiting their court appearances.

Several cities have had favorable experience in using station-house summonses in nonriot situations and in small scale demonstrations. This technique, pioneered by the Vera Institute of Justice in New York City in conjunction with the New York Police Department, permits the police to release defendants after booking and station-house processing with a summons to appear in court at a later time. The summons is issued on the basis of information about the defendant—obtained from an interview and verified only in exceptional cases—showing that he has substantial roots in the community and is likely to appear for trial. Station-house summonses are now used in all New York City precincts and have measurably improved police efficiency—an average of five man hours saved in every case—while 94 percent of defendants summoned have appeared voluntarily in court.[20] New Haven, where the station-house summons was routine under non-riot conditions, employed the technique during the riot with notable

[18] It has been pointed out by defense counsel in Detroit that in widespread searches in private homes, any new goods found were often confiscated as loot. The accused looter's defense would be to produce a bill of sale, or in some cases alibi witnesses as to his whereabouts at the time of the alleged looting. In either event, the accused was severely prejudiced if he could not return to his home or neighborhood before trial.

[19] Analysis of 1,057 convicted Watts arrestees referred for pre-sentence reports showed 85 percent lived with family or friends; 73 percent were employed; 75 percent had lived in the community five years or more. In Jackson State Prison near Detroit, a survey of riot defendants showed 83 percent charged with some form of breaking, looting, or larceny; 73 percent had lived at the same address over a year; 80 percent were employed; 47 percent had no arrest record and 67 percent no conviction record. In Detroit 887 females were arrested, mostly for looting; 74 percent of the females had no prior record. Many had young children to care for. The Newark analysis of arrestees showed only 10 percent from out of the city.

[20] In its first six months of city-wide operations, New York police issued more than 5,500 station-house summonses to about 25 percent of all persons arrested for summonsable offenses. The default rate was below 6 percent. The police have not issued summonses in some cases of picketing or protests because they were able to centrally book and arraign the number involved immediately. On the other hand, they cite marked success in summonsing up to 100 demonstrators in a school busing protest, and report that "further use of the summons process will be made in like instances."

success. At least 40 percent of all arrestees were released in this manner, including some charged with felony offenses.

Successful employment of this technique requires a corps of bail interviewers, and procedures for checking quickly into an arrestee's past record.[21] It also means providing transportation to deliver defendants either back to their homes or to shelters outside the riot area. With adequate planning there will be a registry of churches, civic organizations, neighborhood groups, and poverty centers to supervise persons released or to provide temporary shelter if necessary.

In using these procedures at the station house or screening center, wide discretion must be left to police and prosecution to refuse to summons and release riot participants who appear to pose a substantial risk to the community. Persons rearrested after release, for any but the most trivial violations, should be disqualified from further summons and release without judicial sanction.

The desirability of using defense lawyers in the station-house screening process is suggested by the New Haven experience. The lawyers can contribute information about the defendants; help to make release arrangements; negotiate on the charges with the prosecutors and guard against any overcharging which would prevent early release; insure that the defendants understand their legal rights and the reason for cooperation in summons interviews.

Booking procedures. The ordinary mechanics of booking and record keeping must be simplified at the emergency screening center. Special techniques must be devised to record necessary information about arrestees. The multiple-use form devised by the United States Department of Justice for large protest demonstrations may provide a prototype.

Single copies of this form are sent to key points in the process through which arrestees pass. One copy is sent to the

[21] During the riots, some cities such as Cincinnati which already had R.O.R. programs, suspended them because of the difficulty of identifying and verifying information about arrested persons. Other cities such as Dayton continued to use the program. In Newark, which began releasing persons in large numbers toward the end of the riot, verification of interview information was not required. The New York station-house summons program does not ordinarily verify interview information; as a result, the average time expended on a summons case is only one hour. While checks of local criminal records might be necessary, FBI fingerprint checks delay any release process for a considerable time, and are not required in present station-house summons procedures. In the riot situation, such requirement should be confined to serious cases where false identity is strongly suspected.

The shortage of police trained in identification procedures at the Detroit processing centers has been commented upon by the judges there. It has been suggested that a list of all such trained ID officers be drawn ahead of time for emergency use. Such help is needed so that arrest records, fingerprint checks, photo identifications, and other information can be provided quickly for use in station-house summons interviews and court bail hearings.

351

Bureau of Prisons where a central record of arrested persons is kept. Another is sent to the detention center where arrestees are taken. The first copy contains all information necessary to present a formal charge against a defendant in a hearing before a United States Commissioner: defendant's name, basic facts of the alleged offense, time and date of the offense, name of the arresting officer.

At the processing station where the arrestee is first detained, the arresting officer fills out the form and swears to its facts. He is then freed to return immediately to his duty station. A notary public is present at the processing station to notarize the forms as required by law.

The arrestee's picture is taken at the time the form is filled out if this has not already been done on the scene. The picture is attached to a copy of the arrest form. Thus, the arrestee can later be identified, even if he refuses to give his name. A docket number is also assigned to the case which is used thereafter throughout each phase of processing. Docket numbers are assigned consecutively. The number of persons arrested can thus readily be ascertained.

The Commission recommends that cities adopt this type of form.

DETENTION AND BAIL SETTING

Court personnel. For those arrested persons who are not considered safe risks for station-house summons and release, detention facilities must be provided until such time as they can be brought to court for arraignment. By means of extra judges and court sessions, arraignments and bail hearings should be arranged as quickly as is consistent with individualized attention.[22]

To meet the extraordinary case load encountered during riots, judges from courts of record can be asked to volunteer for lower court arraignments and bail hearings. Emergency plans should provide for service by out-of-town judges, judges from other courts, and if necessary specially appointed judges

[22] In many jurisdictions normal processing time will have to be speeded up to avoid intolerable congestion. The President's Commission on Law Enforcement and Administration of Justice recommended as a norm that first court appearances follow arrest within hours, with preliminary hearings and formal charges three days later for jailed defendants; and that the delay between arraignment and trial be no longer than nine weeks. On the other hand, jurisdictions which impose maximum time limits on various stages of the court process for all defendants may want to provide for relaxation during an emergency. As a result of a 10-day preliminary hearing rule in Detroit, defendants freed on bail had to be processed as quickly as those detained in makeshift facilities. Authorization to handle those detained on a priority basis would have alleviated the harsh congestion problem in those facilities.

sitting on a temporary basis. A statewide prosecutor system—another recommendation of the Crime Commission—would also be valuable in providing a reserve force of additional prosecutors with experience in local and state law. In the absence of this flexibility, former prosecutors and private attorneys should be specially deputized and trained in advance for emergency service.

Provision should be made for exchange of court personnel among communities in a metropolitan area or in a regional council. Authorities might also provide an emergency corps of court clerical personnel to move swiftly into riot torn cities for immediate service.

Detention facilities. At the detention centers, teams of defense lawyers, social workers, interviewers and medical personnel should be on hand to gather pertinent information about detainees to present to the judge at bail hearings. Defense counsel should be prepared to propose reasonable conditions for release of each prisoner which will guard against renewal of riot activity.

Bail setting. When the riot defendant comes before the court, he should receive an individual determination of bail. He should be represented by counsel and the judge should ascertain from counsel, client, and bail interviewer the relevant facts of his background, age, living arrangements, employment, and past record. Uniform bail amounts based on charges and riot conditions alone should be shunned as unfair.

With the constitutional imperatives of bail and pre-conviction release well in mind, we are fully aware that some rioters, if released, will commit new acts of violence. This is an aggravated extension of a problem which has engaged law enforcement officials and criminal law authorities for many years. Although the number of dangerous offenders to be processed, even in a riot,[23] may not be sizable, how to determine and detain them before trial poses a problem of great perplexity. The Commission realizes that in riot situations the temptation is strong to detain offenders by setting money bail in amounts beyond their reach. In the past, such high money bail has been indiscriminately set, often resulting in the detention of every-

[23] In the Detroit riot there were seven arrests and three prosecutions for homicide; nine arrests and two prosecutions for rape; 108 arrested and 18 prosecutions for robbery; 206 arrests and 55 prosecutions for assault; 34 arrests and 13 prosecutions for arson; 28 arrests and six prosecutions for inciting to riot; 21 arrests and 18 prosecutions for possessing and placing explosives. In Newark there were arrests for one murder, two arsons, 46 assaults, 91 weapons offenses, and four robberies. In Watts, there were 120 booked and 60 convicted for aggravated assault, 94 booked and 46 convicted for robbery, 27 arrested and seven convicted for arson; seven booked for homicide, none convicted and two cases pending.

one arrested during a riot without distinction as to the nature of the alleged crime or the likelihood of repeated offenses.

The purposes of bail in our system of law have always been to prevent confinement before conviction and to insure appearance of the accused in court. The purpose has not been to deter future crime. Yet some have difficulty adhering to the doctrine when it results in releasing a dangerous offender back into the riot area.

We point out that, as to the dangerous offender, there already exists a full range of permissible alternatives to outright release as a hedge against his reentry into the riot.

These include: release on conditions of third-party custody; forbidding access to certain areas or at certain times; part-time release with a requirement to spend nights in jail; use of surety or peace bonds on a selective basis.[24] In cases where no precautions will suffice, trial should be held as soon as possible so that a violator can be adjudicated innocent and released or found guilty and lawfully confined pending sentencing. Finally, special procedures should be set up for expedited bail review by higher courts so that defendants' rights will not be lost by default.

RIGHT TO COUNSEL

The right to counsel is a right to effective counsel. An emergency plan should provide that counsel be available at the station house to participate in the charging and screening operations, to provide information for station-house summons and release officers and to guard against allegations of brutality or fraudulent evidence. All accused persons who are not released during post-arrest processing should be represented at the bail hearing, whether or not local law provides this as a matter of right. During any detention period, defense counsel must be able to interview prisoners individually at the detention center; privacy must be provided for these lawyer-client consultations.

The number of lawyers needed for this kind of individual representation is obviously great, thus furnishing another argument for screening out early as many innocent persons and

---

[24] We are aware that predicating the condition of release upon danger of renewed riot activity represents some departure from existing law and may also be challenged in the courts. It has, however, been recommended by the President's Commission on Law Enforcement and Administration of Justice as a preferable alternative to preventive detention. *The Challenge of Crime in a Free Society*—A Report, 1967, pp. 131-2.

minor offenders as possible, and releasing as many of the rest as can be relied upon to create no new disturbance and to return for trial. Local bar associations, public defender offices, legal aid agencies, neighborhood legal services staffs, rosters of court-assigned counsel, law schools and military establishments are sources of manpower. They can be pre-trained in the procedures of an emergency plan and called into volunteer service. Assigning one lawyer to a group of defendants should be discouraged. If possible, each defendant should have his own lawyer ready to follow the case to conclusion. Case quotas can be established ahead of time, with teams of lawyers prepared to take over in relays. Law students can be used as investigators and case assistants. Legal defense strategy and sources of experienced advice for the volunteers should be planned ahead of time.

Any community plan must make adequate provision for fair representation whenever the trials are held, whether during the heat of riot or at a later, more deliberate time.

There must be no letdown of legal services when trials and arraignments are postponed until the riot runs its course. The greatest need for counsel may come when the aura of emergency has dissipated. Volunteers then may be less willing to drop their daily obligations to represent riot defendants. If this occurs, assembly-line techniques may be resorted to in an effort to complete all pending matters cheaply and quickly. In one city this letdown had unfortunate results: up to 200 post-trial arraignments were assigned to one lawyer each day. Courtroom "regulars" were given such group assignments in preference to the volunteers' more individualized representation.

TRIAL AND SENTENCING

Important policies are involved in deciding whether judicial emphasis during the riot should be placed on immediate trials of minor offenders, prompt trials of serious offenders, or arraignment and bail-setting only. In the case of some serious offenders, prompt trials may be the only legal route to detention. A defendant, however, will often prefer later trial and sentencing in the post-riot period, when community tensions are eased (if he is not detained during the delay). Witnesses may also be difficult to locate and bring to court while riot controls are in effect. Arresting officers cannot be easily spared from their duty stations. Unprejudiced juries will be difficult to empanel. Prosecutors may be more receptive at a later date to requests for dismissal, reduction of charges or negotiated pleas.[25] The most rational allocation of judicial manpower, as well as basic fairness, suggests that decisions at such vital stages as prosecution, plea negotiation, preliminary examination and trials be postponed until the riot is over in all but the most minor cases. At the same time, it is necessary to avoid congesting the jails and detention centers with masses of arrestees who might safely be released. Both can be accomplished only with a workable post-arrest screening process and pre-trial release of all except dangerous defendants.

Trails of minor offenses, involving detained defendants should be scheduled quickly, so that pre-conviction confinement will not stretch jail time beyond authorized penalties. Arraignments and bail hearings for those not summoned and released at the station house should be held as soon as possible. Trials and preliminary examinations of released offenders can be postponed until the emergency ends, unless the defendants pose a present danger to the community.

Sentencing is often best deferred until the heat of the riot has subsided, unless it involves only a routine fine which the defendant can afford. Riot defendants should be considered individually. They are less likely to be hardened, experienced criminals. A pre-sentence report should be prepared in all cases where a jail sentence or probation may result. The task of imposing penalties for many riot defendants which will deter and rehabilitate is a formidable one. A general policy should be adopted to give credit on jail sentences for pre-conviction detention time in riot cases.

After the riot is over, a residue of difficult legal tasks will remain: proceedings to litigate and compensate for injustices —false arrests, physical abuse, property damage—committed under the stress of riot;[26] actions to expunge arrest records acquired without probable cause; restitution policies to encourage looters to surrender goods. Fair, even compassionate, attention to these problems will help reduce the legacy of post-riot bitterness in the community.

[25] For whatever reasons—policy or evidentiary problems—in the Watts riot, 43 percent of adult felony arrests and 30 percent of adult misdemeanor arrests did not result in convictions. In Detroit, 25 percent of all arrests and 24 percent of the felony arrests were not prosecuted, including 57 percent of the homicide arrests, 74 percent of the aggravated assault arrests, 83 percent of the robbery arrests, 43 percent of the stolen property arrests, and 62 percent of the arson arrests. Only 29 percent of the curfew arrests were not prosecuted. Reportedly, plea bargaining in Detroit was based almost entirely on a defendant's past record.

[26] The Newark Legal Services Program reported 29 complaints after the riot from ghetto residents concerning personal indignities; 57 about physical abuses; 104 about indiscriminate shooting; and 96 about destruction of property.

IV. Summary of Recommendations

The Commission recommends:

- That communities undertake, as an urgent priority, the reform of their lower criminal court systems to insure fair and individual justice for all. The 1967 report of the President's Commission on Law Enforcement and the Administration of Justice provides the blueprint for such reform.
- That communities formulate a plan for the administration of justice in riot emergencies. Under the leadership of the organized bar, all segments of the community, including minority groups, should be involved in drawing up such a plan. The plan should provide clear guidelines for police on when to arrest or use alternatives to arrest. Adequate provision must be made for extra judges, prosecutors, defense counsel, court and police personnel to provide prompt processing, and for well-equipped detention facilities. Details of the plan should be publicized so the community will know what to expect if an emergency occurs.
- That existing laws be reviewed to insure their adequacy for riot control and the charging of riot offenders, and for authority to use temporary outside help in the judicial system.
- That multiple-use processing forms (such as those used by the Department of Justice for mass arrests) be obtained. Centralized systems for recording arrests and locations of prisoners on current basis should be devised, as well as fast systems to check fingerprint identification and past records. On-the-spot photographing of riot defendants may also be helpful.
- That communities adopt station-house summons and release procedures (such as are used by the New York City Police Department) in order that they be operational before an emergency arises. All defendants who appear likely to return for trial and not to engage in renewed riot activity should be summonsed and released.
- That recognized community leaders be admitted to all processing and detention centers to avoid allegations of abuse or fraud and to reassure the community about the treatment of arrested persons.
- That the bar in each community undertake mobilization of all available lawyers for assignment so as to insure early individual legal representation to riot defendants through disposition, and to provide assistance to prosecutors where needed. Legal defense strategies should be planned and volunteers trained in advance. Investigative help and experienced advice should be provided.
- That communities and courts plan for a range of alternative conditions to release, such as supervision by civic organizations or third party custodians outside the riot area, rather than to rely on high money bail to keep defendants off the streets. The courts should set bail on an individual basis and provide for defense counsel at bail hearings. Emergency procedures for fast bail review are needed.
- That no mass indictments or arraignments be held, and reasonable bail and sentences be imposed, both during or after the riot. Sentences should be individually considered and pre-sentence reports required. The emergency plan should provide for transfer of probation officers from other courts and jurisdictions to assist in the processing of arrestees.

357

Chapter 14 / Damages: Repair and Compensation

The President, in his charge to the Commission, requested advice on the "proper public role in helping cities repair the damage" suffered in the recent disorders.

Damage took many forms. In Detroit alone, 43 persons were killed, many of whom were heads of families. Over 600 persons were injured. Fire destroyed or badly damaged at least 100 single and two-family dwellings. Stores of all kinds were looted and burned. Hundreds of businesses lost revenue by complying with a curfew, and thousands of citizens lost wages because businesses were closed. As the riot came to an end, streets and sidewalks were strewn with rubble, and citizens were imperiled by the shells of burned-out buildings verging on collapse.

In most other disorders, the extent of damage was far less, but in almost all, a few persons suffered severe physical or financial injury.

Some of the losses, such as pain and suffering, cannot be repaired or compensated. Others are normally handled through private insurance. The Commission believes that legislation should be enacted to provide fuller assistance to communities and to help expand the private insurance mechanism to compensate individuals for their losses.

AMENDING THE FEDERAL DISASTER ACT

The Federal Government has traditionally played a central role in responding to community needs that follow such disasters as hurricanes, tornadoes, floods and earthquakes. Until 1950, this federal response was accomplished through special legislation after each disaster. In 1950, Congress enacted the Federal Disaster Act to enable the President, in cases of "major disaster," to invoke a broad range of emergency relief and repair measures without awaiting special legislation. This Act, with subsequent amendments, has, however, been interpreted administratively to apply only to natural disasters and not to civil disorders.

The Commission recommends that Congress amend the Federal Disaster Act to permit assistance during and following major civil disorders. The hardships to a community can be as serious as those following natural catastrophes, and local government resources to meet these hardships are likely to be inadequate regardless of their cause.

Applying the Disaster Act to disorders would permit the federal government to provide—during the critical period while the disorder is still going on or just ending—food, medical and hospital supplies, emergency equipment such as beds and tents, and temporary shelters and housing. It would also permit the loan of equipment and manpower for clearing debris and repairing or temporarily replacing damaged public facilities.

In 1967, these necessities were largely provided through the prompt and laudable actions of local and state government agencies and of private organizations, including churches and neighborhood groups.[1] Provision for additional help is desirable. Though some food and medical assistance can now be provided by the federal government outside the Disaster Act, adequate and comprehensive federal assistance to supplement private and local response can be assured only by amending the statute.

Perhaps even more important than the provisions for immediate response are those that would aid long-term repair. In cases of natural disaster, the Disaster Act in its present form permits adjustments on many federal loans where financial hardship has resulted to the borrower; gives priority status to grant or loan applications for public facilities, public housing, and public works; provides grants and matching grants for the repair or reconstruction of key public facilities; permits low interest loans by the Small Business Administration to businesses that have suffered serious economic damage; and extends to individuals and businesses tax deductions beyond those normally available for catastrophe losses.[2] The Act should be amended to make all these kinds of relief available following major civil disorders.

---

[1] The kinds of planning recommended at a state and local level to meet human needs during the course of a disorder and the coordination of such planning with the planning of control forces are considered in the Supplement on Control of Disorders, pp. 484 ff.

[2] A few kinds of long-term assistance are already available under acts other than the Federal Disaster Act. The Small Business Administration can provide long-term loans up to the actual tangible loss suffered by business concerns. Loans of this kind were made by SBA in Detroit. The Department of Housing and Urban Development is authorized to insure mortgages of families in certain low and moderate income housing if it determines that the dwelling is situated in an area in which "rioting or other civil disorders" have occurred or are threatened and that certain other conditions are satisfied.

In the aftermath of the summer's riots in 1967, insurance protection was an important source of security and reimbursement for innocent victims who suffered property damage.

We believe that a well-functioning private insurance mechanism is the proper method for paying individuals for losses suffered in disorders. Property insurance should be available at reasonable cost to residents and businessmen for property in reasonable condition regardless of location. If insurance is so available, it will function more equitably and efficiently to pay riot losses than a program of direct government payments to individuals.[3]

The private insurance industry can market policies widely and collect premiums commensurate with the risks. It can develop and recommend loss-prevention techniques and assess and pay large numbers of claims on an individual basis. Standard property insurance contracts presently include damage from civil disorders in their coverage, just as they provide compensation for losses due to natural disasters such as fire and windstorm. They should continue to do so.

Early in our deliberations, however, we received many reports that property insurance was unavailable, or was available only at prohibitive cost, in center cities. This did not appear to be simply a riot problem but a long-term, pervasive problem of center city areas. Since a separate and expert group could best examine the problems of the high cost and availability of property insurance in center city areas, the President, on the Commission's behalf, appointed a National Advisory Panel on Insurance in Riot-Affected Areas on August 10, 1967. The Panel's work is now complete.[4]

The Panel found:

> There is a serious lack of property insurance in the core areas of our nation's cities. For a number of years, many urban residents and businessmen have been unable to purchase the insurance protection they need. Now, riots and the threat of riots are aggravating the problem to an intolerable degree. Immediate steps must be taken to make insurance available to responsible persons in all areas of our cities.

---

[3] Over a dozen states have statutes which impose varying degrees of liability on municipalities for private losses suffered during disorders. In addition to problems posed in litigating claims, it is questionable, given competing needs for the limited municipal financial resources, whether these statutes will be allowed to continue in force.

[4] The report of the Panel is available from the Superintendent of Documents, U.S. Government Printing Office, Washington, D.C. 20402.

The Panel also found that:

The insurance problems created by riots cannot be allowed to jeopardize the availability of property insurance in center-city areas. But the problem of providing adequate and reasonable insurance in the urban core cannot be solved merely by supplying financial assistance to protect insurance companies against catastrophic riot losses. It is clear that adequate insurance was unavailable in the urban core even before the riots. We are dealing with an inner-city insurance problem that is broad in scope and complicated in origin, and riots are only one aspect of it.

In order to assure the availability of property insurance in all areas, the Panel recommended a five-part program of mutually supporting actions to be undertaken immediately by all who have a responsibility for solving the problem:

We call upon the insurance industry to take the lead in establishing voluntary plans in all states to assure all property owners fair access to property insurance.

We look to the states to cooperate with the industry in establishing these plans; and to supplement the plans, to whatever extent may be necessary, by organizing insurance pools and taking other steps to facilitate the insuring of urban core properties.

We urge that the federal government enact legislation creating a National Insurance Development Corporation (NIDC) to assist the insurance industry and the states in achieving the important goal of providing adequate insurance for inner cities. Through the NIDC, the state and federal governments can provide backup for the remote contingency of very large riot losses.

We recommend that the federal government enact tax deferral measures to increase the capacity of the insurance industry to absorb the financial costs of the program.

We suggest a series of other necessary steps to meet the special needs of the inner city insurance market—for example, programs to train agents and brokers from the core areas; to assure the absence of discrimination in insurance company employment on racial or other grounds; and to seek out better methods of preventing losses and of marketing insurance in low-income areas.

The fundamental thrust of our program is cooperative action. Thus, only those companies that participate in plans and pools at the local level, and only those states that take action to implement the program, will be eligible to receive the benefits provided by the National Insurance Development Corporation and by the federal tax deferral measures. We firmly believe that all concerned must work together to meet the urban insurance crisis. Everyone must contribute; no one should escape responsibility.

361

The Commission endorses the proposals of the Panel and recommends they be put into effect by appropriate state and federal measures.

Chapter 15 / The News Media and the Disorders

INTRODUCTION

The President's charge to the Commission asked specifically: "What effect do the mass media have on the riots?"

The question is far reaching and a sure answer is beyond the range of presently available scientific techniques. Our conclusions and recommendations are based upon subjective as well as objective factors; interviews as well as statistics; isolated examples as well as general trends.

Freedom of the press is not the issue. A free press is indispensable to the preservation of the other freedoms this nation cherishes. The recommendations in this chapter have thus been developed under the strong conviction that only a press unhindered by government can contribute to freedom.

To answer the President's question, the Commission:

- Directed its field survey teams to question government officials, law enforcement agents, media personnel, and ordinary citizens about their attitudes and reactions to reporting of the riots;
- Arranged for interviews of media representatives about their coverage of the riots;
- Conducted special interviews with ghetto residents about their response to coverage;
- Arranged for a quantitative analysis of the content of television programs and newspaper reporting in 15 riot cities during the period of the disorder and the days immediately before and after;
- From November 10-12, 1967, sponsored and participated in a conference of representatives from all levels of the newspaper, news magazine, and broadcasting industries at Poughkeepsie, New York.

Finally, of course, the Commissioners read newspapers, listened to the radio, watched television, and thus formed their own impressions of media coverage. All of these data, impressions, and attitudes provide the foundation for our conclusions.

The Commission also determined, very early, that the answer to the President's question did not lie solely in the performance

362

of the press and broadcasters in reporting the riots proper. Our analysis had to consider also the overall treatment by the media of the Negro ghettos, community relations, racial attitudes, urban and rural poverty—day by day and month by month, year in and year out.

On this basis, we have reached three conclusions:

First, that despite instances of sensationalism, inaccuracies, and distortions, newspapers, radio and television, on the whole, made a real effort to give a balanced, factual account of the 1967 disorders.

Second, despite this effort, the portrayal of the violence that occurred last summer failed to reflect accurately its scale and character. The overall effect was, we believe, an exaggeration of both mood and event.

Third, and ultimately most important, we believe that the media have thus far failed to report adequately on the causes and consquences of civil disorders and the underlying problems of race relations.

With these comments as a perspective, we discuss first the coverage of last summer's disturbances. We will then summarize our concerns with overall coverage of race relations.

Coverage of the 1967 Disturbances

We have found a significant imbalance between what actually happened in our cities and what the newspaper, radio, and television coverage of the riots told us happened. The Commission, in studying last summer's disturbances, visited many of the cities and interviewed participants and observers. We found that the disorders, as serious as they were, were less destructive, less widespread, and less a black-white confrontation than most people believed.

Lacking other sources of information, we formed our original impressions and beliefs from what we saw on television, heard on the radio, and read in newspapers and magazines. We are deeply concerned that millions of other Americans, who must rely on the mass media, likewise formed incorrect impressions and judgments about what went on in many American cities last summer.

As we started to probe the reasons for this imbalance between reality and impression, we first believed that the media had sensationalized the disturbances, consistently overplaying violence and giving disproportionate amounts of time to emotional events and militant leaders. To test this theory, we commissioned a systematic, quantitative analysis, covering the content of newspaper and television reporting in 15 cities where disorders occurred. The results of this analysis do not support our early belief. Of 955 television sequences of riot and racial news examined, 837 could be classified for predominant atmosphere as either "emotional," "calm," or "normal." Of these, 494 were classified as calm, 262 as emotional, and 81 as normal. Only a small proportion of all scenes analyzed showed actual mob action, people looting, sniping, setting fires, or being injured, or killed. Moderate Negro leaders were shown more frequently than militant leaders on television news broadcasts.

Of 3,779 newspaper articles analyzed, more focused on legislation which should be sought and planning which should be done to control ongoing riots and prevent future riots than on any other topic. The findings of this content analysis are explained in greater detail in Section I. They make it clear that the imbalance between actual events and the portrayal of those events in the press and on the air cannot be attributed solely to sensationalism in reporting and presentation.

We have, however, identified several factors which, it seems to us, did work to create incorrect and exaggerated impressions about the scope and intensity of the disorders.

First, despite the overall statistical picture, there were instances of gross flaws in presenting news of the 1967 riots. Some newspapers printed "scare" headlines unsupported by the mild stories that followed. All media reported rumors that had no basis in fact. Some newsmen staged "riot' events for the cameras. Examples are included in the next section.

Second, the press obtained much factual information about the scale of the disorders—property damage, personal injury, and deaths—from local officials, who often were inexperienced in dealing with civil disorders and not always able to sort out fact from rumor in the confusion. At the height of the Detroit riot, some news reports of property damage put the figure in excess of $500 million.[1] Subsequent investigation shows it to be $40 to $45 million.[2]

The initial estimates were not the independent judgment of reporters or editors. They came from beleaguered government officials. But the news media gave currency to these errors. Reporters uncritically accepted, and editors uncritically published, the inflated figures, leaving an indelible impression of

[1] As recently as February 9, 1968, an Associated Press dispatch from Philadelphia said "damage exceeded $1 billion" in Detroit.

[2] Michigan State Insurance Commission Estimate, December, 1967. See also *Meeting the Insurance Crisis of Our Cities,* a Report by the President's National Advisory Panel on Insurance in Riot-Affected Areas, January, 1968.

damage up to more than ten times greater than actually occurred.

Third, the coverage of the disorders—particularly on television—tended to define the events as black-white confrontations. In fact almost all of the deaths, injuries and property damage occurred in all-Negro neighborhoods, and thus the disorders were not "race riots" as that term is generally understood.

Closely linked to these problems is the phenomenon of cumulative effect. As the summer of 1967 progressed, we think Americans often began to associate more or less neutral sights and sounds (like a squad car with flashing red lights, a burning building, a suspect in police custody) with racial disorders, so that the appearance of any particular item, itself hardly inflammatory, set off a whole sequence of association with riot events. Moreover, the summer's news was not seen and heard in isolation. Events of these past few years—the Watts riot, other disorders, and the growing momentum of the civil rights movement—conditioned the responses of readers and viewers and heightened their reactions. What the public saw and read last summer thus produced emotional reactions and left vivid impressions not wholly attributable to the material itself.

Fear and apprehension of racial unrest and violence are deeply rooted in American society. They color and intensify reactions to news of racial trouble and threats of racial conflict. Those who report and disseminate news must be conscious of the background of anxieties and apprehension against which their stories are projected. This does not mean that the media should manage the news or tell less than the truth. Indeed, we believe that it would be imprudent and even dangerous to downplay coverage in the hope that censored reporting of inflammatory incidents somehow will diminish violence. Once a disturbance occurs, the word will spread independently of newspapers and television. To attempt to ignore these events or portray them as something other than what they are, can only diminish confidence in the media and increase the effectiveness of those who monger rumors and the fears of those who listen.

But to be complete, the coverage must be representative. We suggest that the main failure of the media last summer was that the totality of its coverage was not as representative as it should have been to be accurate. We believe that to live up to their own professed standards, the media simply must exercise a higher degree of care and a greater level of sophistication than they have yet shown in this area—higher, perhaps, than the level ordinarily acceptable with other stories.

This is not "just another story." It should not be treated like one. Admittedly, some of what disturbs us about riot coverage last summer stems from circumstances beyond media control. But many of the inaccuracies of fact, tone and mood were due to the failure of reporters and editors to ask tough enough questions about official reports, and to apply the most rigorous standards possible in evaluating and presenting the news. Reporters and editors must be sure that descriptions and pictures of violence, and emotional or inflammatory sequences or articles, even though "true" in isolation, are really representative and do not convey an impression at odds with the overall reality of events. The media too often did not achieve this level of sophisticated, skeptical, careful news judgment during last summer's riots.

The Media and Race Relations

Our second and fundamental criticism is that the news media have failed to analyze and report adequately on racial problems in the United States and, as a related matter, to meet the Negro's legitimate expectations in journalism. By and large, news organizations have failed to communicate to both their black and white audiences a sense of the problems America faces and the sources of potential solutions. The media report and write from the standpoint of a white man's world. The ills of the ghetto, the difficulties of life there, the Negro's burning sense of grievance, are seldom conveyed. Slights and indignities are part of the Negro's daily life, and many of them come from what he now calls "the white press"—a press that repeatedly, if unconsciously, reflects the biases, the paternalism, the indifference of white America. This may be understandable, but it is not excusable in an institution that has the mission to inform and educate the whole of our society.

Our criticisms, important as they are, do not lead us to conclude that the media are a cause of riots, any more than they are the cause of other phenomena which they report. It is true that newspaper and television reporting helped shape people's attitudes toward riots. In some cities people who watched television reports and read newspaper accounts of riots in other cities later rioted themselves. But the causal chain weakens when we recall that in other cities, people in very much the same circumstances watched the same programs and read the same newspaper stories but did not riot themselves.

366

The news media are not the sole source of information and certainly not the only influence on public attitudes. People obtained their information and formed their opinions about the 1967 disorders from the multiplicity of sources that condition the public's thinking on all events. Personal experience, conversations with others, the local and long-distance telephone are all important as sources of information and ideas and contribute to the totality of attitudes about riots.

No doubt, in some cases, the knowledge or the sight on a television screen of what had gone on elsewhere lowered inhibitions or kindled outrage or awakened desires for excitement or loot—or simply passed the word. Many ghetto residents we interviewed thought so themselves. By the same token, the news reports of riots must have conditioned the response of officials and police to disturbances in their own cities. The reaction of the authorities in Detroit was almost certainly affected in some part by what they saw or read of Newark a week earlier. The Commission believes that none of these private or official reactions was decisive in determining the course of the disorders. Even if they had been more significant than we think, however, we cannot envision a system of governmental restraints that could successfully eliminate these effects. And an effort to formulate and impose such restraints would be inconsistent with fundamental traditions in our society.

The failings of the media must be corrected and the improvement must come from within the media. A society that values and relies on a free press as intensely as ours, is entitled to demand in return responsibility from the press and conscientious attention by the press to its own deficiencies. The Commission has seen evidence that many of those who supervise, edit, and report for the news media are becoming increasingly aware of and concerned about their performance in this field. With that concern, and with more experience, will come more sophisticated and responsible coverage. But much more must be done, and it must be done soon.

The Commission has a number of recommendations designed to stimulate and accelerate efforts toward self-improvement. And we propose a privately organized, privately funded Institute of Urban Communications as a means for drawing these recommendations together and promoting their implementation.

I. News Coverage of Civil Disorders— Summer 1967

The Method of Analysis

As noted, the Commission has been surveying both the reporting of disorders last summer and the broader field of race relations coverage. With respect to the reporting of disorders, we were trying to get a sense of content, accuracy, tone, and bias. We sought to find out how people reacted to it and how reporters conducted themselves while carrying out their assignments. The Commission used a number of techniques to probe these matters and to provide cross checks on data and impressions.

To obtain an objective source of data, the Commission arranged for a systematic, quantitative analysis of the content of newspapers, local television, and network coverage in 15 cities for a period from three days before to three days after the disorder in each city.[3]

The cities were chosen to provide a cross-section in terms of the location and scale of the disorders and the dates of their occurrence.

Within each city, for the period specified, the study was comprehensive. Every daily newspaper and all network and local television news films were analyzed, and scripts and logs were examined. In all, 955 network and local television sequences and 3,779 newspaper articles dealing with riot and race relations news were analyzed. Each separate analysis was coded and the cards were cross-tabulated by computer to provide results and comparisons for use by the Commission. The material was measured to determine the amount of space devoted to news of riot activity; the nature of the display given compared with other news coverage; and the types of stories, articles, and television programming presented. We sought specific statistical information on such matters as the amount of space or time devoted to different kinds of riot stories, the types and identities of persons most often depicted or interviewed, the frequency with which race relations problems were mentioned in riot stories or identified as the cause of riot activity.

The survey was designed to be objective and statistical.

[3] Detroit, Michigan; Milwaukee, Wisconsin; Cincinnati, Ohio; Dayton, Ohio; Tampa, Florida; Newark, New Jersey; Plainfield, New Jersey; Elizabeth, New Jersey; Jersey City, New Jersey; East Orange, New Jersey; Paterson, New Jersey; New Brunswick, New Jersey; Englewood, New Jersey; New Haven, Connecticut; Rochester, New York.

Within its terms of reference, the Commission was looking for broad characterizations of media tone and content.

The Commission is aware of the inherent limitations of content analysis techniques. They cannot measure the emotional impact of a particular story or television sequence. By themselves, they provide no basis for conclusions as to the accuracy of what was reported. Particular examples of good or bad journalistic conduct, which may be important in themselves, are submerged in a statistical average. The Commission therefore sought through staff interviews and personal contact with members of the press and the public to obtain direct evidence of the effects of riot coverage and the performance of the media during last summer's disturbances.

Conclusions About Content [4]

TELEVISION

1. Content analysis of television film footage shows that the tone of the coverage studied was more "calm" and "factual" than "emotional" and "rumor-laden." Researchers viewed every one of the 955 television sequences and found that twice as many "calm" sequences as "emotional" ones were shown. The amount and location of coverage were relatively limited, considering the magnitude of the events. The analysis reveals a dominant, positive emphasis on control of the riot and on activities in the aftermath of the riot (53.8 percent of all scenes broadcast) rather than on scenes of actual mob action, or people looting, sniping, setting fires, or being injured or killed (4.8 percent of scenes shown). According to participants in our Poughkeepsie conference, coverage frequently was of the postriot or interview variety because newsmen arrived at the scene after the actual violence had subsided. Overall, both network and local television coverage was cautious and restrained.

2. Television newscasts during the periods of actual disorder in 1967 tended to emphasize law enforcement activities, thereby overshadowing underlying grievances and tensions. This conclusion is based on the relatively high frequency with which television showed and described law enforcement agents, police, national guardsmen, and army troops performing control functions.

Television coverage tended to give the impression that the riots were confrontations between Negroes and whites rather than responses by Negroes to underlying slum problems. The

[4] What follows is a summary of the major conclusions drawn from the content analysis conducted for the Commission.

control agents were predominantly white. The ratio of white male adults[5] to Negro male adults shown on television is high (1:2) considering that the riots took place in predominantly Negro neighborhoods. And some interviews with whites involved landlords or proprietors who had lost property or suffered business losses because of the disturbances and thus held strongly antagonistic attitudes.

The content analysis shows that by far the most frequent "actor" appearances on television were Negro male adults, white male adults, law enforcement agents, and public officials. We cannot tell from a content analysis whether there was any preconceived editorial policy of portraying the riots as racial confrontations requiring the intervention of enforcement agents. But the content analysis does present a visual three-way alignment of Negroes, white bystanders, and public officials or enforcement agents. This alignment tended to create an impression that the riots were predominantly racial confrontations between black and white citizens.

3. About one-third of all riot-related sequences for network and local television appeared on the first day following the outbreak of rioting, regardless of the course of development of the riot itself. After the first day there was, except in Detroit, a very sharp decline in the amount of television time devoted to the disturbance. In Detroit, where the riot started slowly and did not flare out of control until the evening of July 24, 48 hours after it started, the number of riot-related sequences shown increased until July 26, and then showed the same sharp drop-off as noted after the first day of rioting in the other cities.[6] These findings tend to controvert the impression that the riot intensifies television coverage, thus in turn intensifying the riot. The content analysis indicates that whether or not the riot was getting worse, television coverage of the riot decreased sharply after the first day.

4. The Commission made a special effort to analyze television coverage of Negro leaders. To do this, Negro leaders were divided into three categories: (a) celebrities or public figures, who did not claim any organizational following (e.g., social scientist Dr. Kenneth B. Clark, comedian Dick Gregory); (b) "moderate" Negro leaders, who claim a political or organizational following; and (c) "militant" Negro leaders who claim a political or organizational following. During the riot periods surveyed, Negro leaders appeared infrequently on

[5] The white male adult category in this computation does *not* include law enforcement agents or public officials.

[6] Detroit news outlets substantially refrained from publicizing the riot during the early part of Sunday, the first day of rioting.

network news broadcasts and were about equally divided among celebrity or public figures, moderate leaders, and militant leaders. On local television, Negro leaders appeared more often. Of the three categories, "moderate" Negro leaders were shown on local stations more than twice as often as Negro leaders identified primarily as celebrities or public figures, and three times more frequently than militant leaders.

NEWSPAPERS

1. Like television coverage, newspaper coverage of civil disturbances in the summer of 1967 was more calm, factual and restrained than outwardly emotional or inflammatory. During the period of the riot there were many stories dealing exclusively with nonriot racial news. Considering the magnitude of the events, the amount of coverage was limited. Most stories were played down or put on inside pages. Researchers found that almost all the articles analyzed (3,045 of 3,770) tended to focus on one of 16 identifiable subjects. Of this group, 502 articles (16.5 percent) focused primarily on legislation which should be sought and planning which could be done to control ongoing riots and prevent future riots. The second largest category consisted of 471 articles (15.5 percent) focusing on containment or control of riot action. Newspaper coverage of the disorders reflects efforts at caution and restraint.

2. Newspapers tended to characterize and portray last summer's riots in national terms rather than as local phenomena and problems, especially when rioting was taking place in the newspaper's own city. During the actual disorders, the newspapers in each city studied tended to print many stories dealing with disorders or racial troubles in other cities. About 40 percent of the riot or racial stories in each local newspaper during the period of rioting in that city came from the wire services. Furthermore, most newspaper editors appear to have given more headline attention to riots occurring elsewhere than to those at home during the time of trouble in their own cities.

Accuracy of the Coverage

We have tested the accuracy of coverage by means of interviews with local media representatives, city and police officials, and residents of the ghettos. To provide a broad base, we used three separate sources for interview data: the Commission's field survey teams, special field teams, and the findings of a special research study.

As is to be expected, almost everyone had his own version

of "the truth," but it is noteworthy that some editors and reporters themselves, in retrospect, have expressed concern about the accuracy of their own coverage. For example, one newspaper editor said at the Commission's Poughkeepsie conference:

> We used things in our leads and headlines during the riot I wish we could have back now, because they were wrong and they were bad mistakes . . . We used the words "sniper kings" and "nests of snipers." We found out when we were able to get our people into those areas and get them out from under the cars that these sniper kings and these nests of snipers were the constituted authorities shooting at each other, most of them. There was just one confirmed sniper in the entire eight-day riot and he was . . . drunk and he had a pistol, and he was firing from a window.

Television industry representatives at the conference stressed their concern about "live" coverage of disorders and said they try, whenever possible, to view and edit taped or filmed sequences before broadcasting them. Conference participants admitted that live television coverage via helicopter of the 1965 Watts riot had been inflammatory, and network news executives expressed doubts that television would ever again present live coverage of a civil disorder.

Most errors involved mistakes of fact, exaggeration of events, overplaying of particular stories, or prominently displayed speculation about unfounded rumors of potential trouble. This is not only a local problem; because of the wire services and networks, it is a national one. An experienced riot reporter told the Commission that initial wire service reports of a disturbance tend to be inflated. The reason, he said, is that they are written by local bureau men who in most cases have not seen a civil disorder before. When out-of-town reporters with knowledge in the field, or the wire services' own riot specialists arrive on the scene, the situation is put into a more accurate context.

Some examples of exaggeration and mistakes about facts are catalogued here. These examples are by no means exhaustive. They represent only a few of the incidents discovered by the Commission and, no doubt, are but a small part of the total number of such inaccuracies. But the Commission believes that they are representative of the kinds of errors likely to occur when, in addition to the confusion inherent in civil disorder situations, reporters are rushed and harried or editors are superficial and careless. We present these as examples of mistakes that we hope will be avoided in the future.

In particular, we believe newsmen should be wary of how

they play rumors of impending trouble. Whether a rumor is reliable and significant enough to deserve coverage is an editorial decision. But the failure of many headlined rumors to be borne out last summer suggests that these editorial decisions often are not as carefully made as the sensitivity of the subject requires.

- In Detroit, a radio station broadcast a rumor, based on a telephone tip, that Negroes planned to invade suburbia one night later; if plans existed, they never materialized.
- In Cincinnati, several outlets ran a story about white youths arrested for possessing a bazooka; only a few reports mentioned that the weapon was inoperable.
- In Tampa a newspaper repeatedly indulged in speculation about impending trouble. When the state attorney ruled the fatal shooting of a Negro youth justifiable homicide, the paper's news columns reported: "There were fears today that the ruling would stir new race problems for Tampa tonight." The day before, the paper quoted one "top lawman" as telling reporters "he now fears that Negro residents in the Central Avenue Project and in the West Tampa trouble spots feel they are in competition, and are trying to see which can cause the most unrest—which area can become the center of attraction."
- A West Coast newspaper put out an edition headlined: "Rioting Erupts in Washington, D.C. / Negroes Hurl Bottles, Rocks at Police Near White House." The story did not support the headline. It reported what was actually the fact: that a number of teenage Negroes broke store windows and threw bottles and stones at police and firemen near downtown Washington, a mile or more from the White House. On the other hand, the same paper did not report unfounded local rumors of sniping when other news media did.

Television presents a different problem with respect to accuracy. In contrast to what some of its critics have charged, television sometimes may have leaned over too far backward in seeking balance and restraint. By stressing interviews, many with whites in predominantly Negro neighborhoods, and by emphasizing control scenes rather than riotous action, television news broadcasts may have given a distorted picture of what the disorders were all about.

The media—especially television—also have failed to present and analyze to a sufficient extent the basic reasons for the disorders. There have, after the disorders, been some brilliant exceptions.[7] As the content analysis findings suggest, however,

[7] As examples, less than a month after the Detroit riot, the Detroit *Free Press* published the results of a landmark survey of local Negro attitudes and grievances. *Newsweek* Magazine's November 20, 1967 special issue on "The Negro American—What Must Be Done" made a significant contribution to public understanding.

coverage during the riot period itself gives far more emphasis to control of rioters and black-white confrontation than to the underlying causes of the disturbances.

Ghetto Reactions to the Media Coverage

The Commission was particularly interested in public reaction to media coverage; specifically, what people in the ghetto look at and read and how it affects them. The Commission has drawn upon reports from special teams of researchers who visited various cities where outbreaks occurred last summer. Members of these teams interviewed ghetto dwellers and middle-class Negroes on their responses to news media. In addition, we have used information from a statistical study of the mass media in the Negro ghetto in Pittsburgh.[8]

These interviews and surveys, though by no means a complete study of the subject, lead to four broad conclusions about ghetto, and to a lesser degree middle-class Negro, reactions to the media.

Most Negroes distrust what they refer to as the "white press." As one interviewer reported:

The average black person couldn't give less of a damn about what the media say. The intelligent black person is resentful at what he considers to be a totally false portrayal of what goes on in the ghetto. Most black people see the newspapers as mouthpieces of the "power structure."

These comments are echoed in most interview reports the Commission has read. Distrust and dislike of the media among ghetto Negroes encompass all the media, though in general, the newspapers are mistrusted more than the television. This is not because television is thought to be more sensitive or responsive to Negro needs and aspirations, but because ghetto residents believe that television at least lets them see the actual events for themselves. Even so, many Negroes, particularly teenagers, told researchers that they noted a pronounced discrepancy between what they saw in the riots and what television broadcast.

Persons interviewed offered three chief reasons for their attitude. First, they believed, as suggested in the quotation above, that the media are instruments of the white power structure. They thought that these white interests guide the entire white community, from the journalists' friends and neighbors to city officials, police officers, and department store

[8] The Commission is indebted, in this regard, to M. Thomas Allen for his document on *Mass Media Use Patterns and Functions in the Negro Ghetto in Pittsburgh.*

owners. Publishers and editors, if not white reporters, supported and defended these interests with enthusiasm and dedication.

Second, many people in the ghettos apparently believe that newsmen rely on the police for most of their information about what is happening during a disorder and tend to report much more of what the officials are doing and saying than what Negro citizens or leaders in the city are doing and saying. Editors and reporters at the Poughkeepsie conference acknowledged that the police and city officials are their main—and sometimes their only—source of information. It was also noted that most reporters who cover civil disturbances tend to arrive with the police and stay close to them—often for safety, and often because they learn where the action is at the same time as the authorities—and thus buttress the ghetto impression that police and press work together and toward the same ends (an impression that may come as a surprise to many within the ranks of police and press).

Third, Negro residents in several cities surveyed cited as specific examples of media unfairness what they considered the failure of the media:

- To report the many examples of Negroes helping law enforcement officers and assisting in the treatment of the wounded during disorders;
- To report adequately about false arrests;
- To report instances of excessive force by the National Guard;
- To explore and interpret the background conditions leading to disturbances;
- To expose, except in Detroit, what they regarded as instances of police brutality;
- To report on white vigilante groups which allegedly came into some disorder areas and molested innocent Negro residents.

Some of these problems are insoluble. But more first-hand reporting in the diffuse and fragmented riot area should temper easy reliance on police information and announcements. There is a special need for news media to cover "positive" news stories in the ghetto before and after riots with concern and enthusiasm.

A multitude of news and information sources other than the established news media are relied upon in the ghetto. One of our studies found that 79 percent of a total of 567 ghetto residents interviewed in seven cities[9] first heard about the outbreak in their own city by word of mouth. Telephone and word of mouth exchanges on the streets, in churches, stores, pool halls, and bars, provide more information—and rumors—

[9] Detroit, Newark, Atlanta, Tampa, New Haven, Cincinnati, Milwaukee.

375

about events of direct concern to ghetto residents than the more conventional news media.

Among the established media, television and radio are far more popular in the ghetto than newspapers. Radios there, apparently, are ordinarily listened to less for news than for music and other programs. One survey showed that an overwhelmingly large number of Negro children and teenagers (like their white counterparts) listen to the radio for music alone, interspersed by disc jockey chatter. In other age groups, the response of most people about what they listen to on the radio was "anything," leading to the conclusion that radio in the ghetto is basically a background accompaniment.

But the fact that radio is such a constant background accompaniment can make it an important influence on people's attitudes, and perhaps on their actions once trouble develops. This is true for several reasons. News presented on local "rock" stations seldom constitutes much more than terse headline items which may startle or frighten but seldom inform. Radio disc jockeys and those who preside over the popular "talk shows" keep a steady patter of information going over the air. When a city is beset by civil strife, this patter can both inform transistor radio-carrying young people where the actions is, and terrify their elders and much of the white community. "Burn, baby, burn," the slogan of the Watts riot, was inadvertently originated by a radio disc jockey.

Thus, radio can be an instrument of trouble and tension in a community threatened or inundated with civil disorder. It can also do much to minimize fear by putting fast-paced events into proper perspective. We have found commendable instances, for example, in Detroit, Milwaukee, and New Brunswick, of radio stations and personalities using their air time and influence to try to calm potential rioters. In Section II, we recommend procedures for meetings and consultations for advance planning among those who will cover civil disorders. It is important that radio personnel, and especially disc jockeys and talk show hosts, be included in such preplanning.

Television is the formal news source most relied upon in the ghetto. According to one report, more than 75 percent of the sample turned to television for national and international news, and a larger percentage of the sample (86 percent) regularly watched television from 5 to 7 p.m., the dinner hours when the evening news programs are broadcast.

The significance of broadcasting in news dissemination is seen in Census Bureau estimates that in June 1967, 87.7 percent of nonwhite households and 94.8 percent of white households had television sets.

When ghetto residents do turn to newspapers, most read tabloids, if available, far more frequently than standard size newspapers and rely on the tabloids primarily for light features, racing charts, comic strips, fashion news and display advertising.

Conduct of Press Representatives

Most newsmen appear to be aware and concerned that their very physical presence can exacerbate a small disturbance, but some have conducted themselves with a startling lack of common sense. News organizations, particularly television networks, have taken substantial steps to minimize the effect of the physical presence of their employees at a news event. Networks have issued internal instructions calling for use of unmarked cars and small cameras and tape recorders, and most stations instruct their cameramen to film without artificial light whenever possible. Still, some newsmen have done things "for the sake of the story" that could have contributed to tension.

Reports have come to the Commission's attention of individual newsmen staging events, coaxing youths to throw rocks and interrupt traffic, and otherwise acting irresponsibly at the incipient stages of a disturbance. Such acts are the responsibility of the news organization as well as of its individual reporter.

Two examples occurred in Newark. Television cameramen, according to officials, crowded into and in front of police headquarters, interfering with law enforcement operations and "making a general nuisance of themselves." In a separate incident, a New York newspaper photographer covering the Newark riot repeatedly urged and finally convinced a Negro boy to throw a rock for the camera. Crowding may occasionally be unavoidable; staging of events is not.

We believe every effort should be made to eliminate this sort of conduct. This requires the implementation of thoughtful, stringent staff guidelines for reporters and editors. Such guidelines, carefully formulated, widely disseminated, and strictly enforced, underlie the self-policing activities of some news organizations already, but they must be universally adopted if they are to be effective in curbing journalistic irresponsibility.

The Commission has studied the internal guidelines in use last summer at the Associated Press, United Press International, the Washington Post, and the Columbia Broadcasting System. Many other news organizations, large and small, have similar guidelines. In general, the guidelines urge extreme care to ensure that reporting is thorough and balanced and that words and statistics used are appropriate and accurate. The AP guidelines call for broad investigation into the immediate and underlying causes of an incident. The CBS guidelines demand as much caution as possible to avoid the danger of camera equipment and lights exacerbating the disturbance.

Internal guidelines can, and all those studied do, go beyond problems of physical presence at a disturbance to the substantive aspects of searching out, reporting, and writing the story. But the content of the guidelines is probably less important than the fact that the subject has been thoughtfully considered and hammered out within the organization, and an approach developed that is designed to meet the organization's particular needs and solve its particular problems.

We recommend that every news organization that does not now have some form of guidelines—or suspects that those it has are not working effectively—designate top editors to (a) meet with its reporters who have covered or might be assigned to riots, (b) discuss in detail the problems and procedures which exist or are expected and (c) formulate and disseminate directives based on the discussions. Regardless of the specific provisions, the vital step is for every newsgathering organization to adopt and implement at least some minimal form of internal control.

II. A Recommendation to Improve Riot Coverage

A Need for Better Communication

A recurrent problem in the coverage of last summer's disorders was friction and lack of cooperation between police officers and working reporters. Many experienced and capable journalists complained that policemen and their commanding officers were at best apathetic and at worst overtly hostile toward reporters attempting to cover a disturbance. Policemen, on the other hand, charged that many reporters seemed to forget that the task of the police is to restore order.

After considering available evidence on the subject, the Commission is convinced that these conditions reflect an absence of advance communication and planning among the people involved. We do not suggest that familiarity with the other's problems will beget total amity and cooperation. The interests of the media and the police are sometimes necessarily at variance. But we do believe that communication is a vital step toward removing the obstacles produced by ignorance, confusion, and misunderstanding of what each group is actually trying to do.

Mutual Orientation

What is needed first is a series of discussions, perhaps a combination of informal gatherings and seminar-type workshops. They should encompass all ranks of the police, all levels of media employees, and a cross-section of city officials. At first these would be get-acquainted sessions—to air complaints and discuss common problems. Working reporters should get to know the police who would be likely to draw duty in a disorder. Police and city officials should use the sessions for frank and candid briefings on the problems the city might face and official plans for dealing with disturbances.

Later sessions might consider procedures to facilitate the physical movement of personnel and speed the flow of accurate and complete news. Such arrangements might involve nothing more than a procedure for designating specific locations at which police officers would be available to escort a reporter into a dangerous area. In addition, policemen and reporters working together might devise better methods of identification, communication, and training.

Such procedures are infinitely variable and depend on the initiative, needs, and desires of those involved. If there is no existing institution or procedure for convening such meetings, we urge the mayor or city manager to do so in every city where experience suggests the possibility of future trouble. To allay any apprehension that discussions with officials might lead to restraints on the freedom to seek out and report the news, participants in these meetings should stipulate beforehand that freedom of access to all areas for reporters will be preserved.

Designation of Information Officers

It is desirable to designate and prepare a number of police officers to act as media information officers. There should be enough of these so that, in the event of a disturbance, a reporter will not have to seek far to find a policeman ready and able to give him information and answer questions. Officers should be of high enough rank within the police department to have ready access to information.

Creation of Central Information Center

A nerve center for reliable police and official government information should be planned and ready for activation when a disturbance reaches a predetermined point of intensity. Such a center might be located at police headquarters or city hall. It should be directed by an experienced, high-ranking information specialist with close ties to police officials. It is imperative, of course, that all officials keep a steady flow of accurate information coming into the center. Ideally, rooms would be set aside for taping and filming interviews with public officials. Local television stations might cut costs and relieve congestion by pooling some equipment at this central facility. An information center should not be thought of as replacing other news sources inside and outside the disturbance area. If anything, our studies suggest that reporters are already too closely tied to police and officials as news sources in a disorder. An information center should not be permitted to intensify this dependence. Properly conceived, however, a center can supplement on-the-spot reporting and supply news about official action.

Out-of-Town Reporters

Much of the difficulty last summer apparently revolved around relations between local law enforcement officials and out-of-town reporters. These reporters are likely to be less sensitive about preserving the "image" of the local community.

Still, local officials serve their city badly when they ignore or impede national media representatives instead of welcoming them, informing them about the city, and cooperating with their attempts to cover the story. City and police officials should designate liaison officers and distribute names and telephone numbers of police and other relevant officials, the place they can be found if trouble develops, and other information likely to be useful.

National and other news organizations, in turn, could help matters by selecting a responsible home office official to act as liaison in these cases and to be accessible by phone to local officials who encounter difficulty with on-the-spot representatives of an organization.

General Guidelines and Codes

In some cases, if all parties involved were willing, planning sessions might lead to the consideration of more formal undertakings. These might include: (a) agreements on specific procedures to expedite the physical movement of men and equipment around disorder areas and back and forth through police lines; (b) general guidelines on the behavior of both media and police personnel, and (c) arrangements for a brief moratorium on reporting news of an incipient disturbance. The Commission stresses once again its belief that though each of these possibilities merits consideration, none should be formulated or imposed by unilateral government action. Any procedure finally adopted should be negotiated between police and media representatives and should assure both sides the flexibility needed to do their respective jobs. Acceptance of such arrangements should be frankly based on grounds of self-interest, for negotiated methods of procedure can often yield substantial benefits to each side—and to the public which both serve.

At the request of the Commission, the Community Relations Service of the Department of Justice surveyed recent experiences with formal codes. Most of the codes studied: (a) set forth in general terms common sense standards of good journalistic conduct, and (b) establish procedures for a brief moratorium (seldom more than 30 minutes to an hour) on reporting an incipient disturbance.

In its survey, the Community Relations Service described and analyzed experiences with codes in eleven major cities where they are currently in force. Members of the CRS staff conducted interviews with key citizens (newsmen, city officials, and community leaders) in each of the eleven cities, seeking comments on the effectiveness and practicality of the codes and guidelines used. CRS's major findings and conclusions are:

- All codes and guidelines now in operation are basically voluntary arrangements usually put forward by local authorities and accepted by the news media after consultation. Nowhere has an arrangement or agreement been effected that binds the news media without their assent.
- No one interviewed in this survey considered the code or guidelines in effect in his city as useless or harmful. CRS thought that, where they were in effect, the codes had a constructive impact on the local news media. Observers in some cities, however, thought the increased sense of responsibility manifested by press and television was due more to experience with riot coverage than to the existence of the codes.
- The more controversial and often least understood aspect of guidelines has been provision for a brief voluntary moratorium on the reporting of news. Some kind of moratorium is specified in the codes of six cities surveyed (Chicago, Omaha, Buffalo, Indianapolis, Kansas City, and Toledo), and the moratorium was invoked last summer in Chicago and Indianapolis. In each case, an effort to prevent quite minor racial incidents from escalating into more serious trouble was successful, and many thought the moratorium contributed.
- The confusion about a moratorium, and the resulting aversion to it, is unfortunate. The specific period of delay is seldom more than 30 minutes. In practice, under today's conditions of reporting and broadcasting, this often will mean little if any

delay before the full story gets into the paper or on the air. The time can be used to prepare and edit the story and to verify and assess the reports of trouble. The only loss is the banner headline or the broadcast news bulletin that is released prematurely to avoid being beaten by "the competition." It is just such reflexive responses that can lead to sensationalism and inaccuracy. In cities where a moratorium is part of the code, CRS interviewers detected no discontent over its presence.

- The most frequent complaint about shortcomings in existing codes is that many of them do not reach the underpinnings of crisis situations. Ghetto spokesmen, in particular, said that the emphasis in the codes on conduct during the crisis itself tended to lead the media to neglect reporting the underlying causes of racial tension.

At the Poughkeepsie Conference with media representatives, there was considerable criticism of the Chicago code on grounds that the moratorium is open ended. Once put into effect it is supposed to be maintained until "the situation is under control." There were doubts about how effective this code had been in practice. The voluntary news blackout in Detroit for part of the first day of the riot—apparently at the request of officials and civil rights groups—was cited as evidence that suppression of news of violence does not necessarily de-fuse a riot situation.

On the basis of the CRS survey and other evidence, the Commission concludes that codes are seldom harmful, often useful, but no panacea. To be of any use, they must address themselves to the substance of the problems that plague relations between the press and officialdom during a disorder, but they are only one of several methods of improving those relations. Ultimately, no matter how sensitive and comprehensive a code or set of guidelines may be, efficient, accurate reporting must depend on the intelligence, judgment, and training of newsmen, police, and city officials together.

III. REPORTING RACIAL PROBLEMS IN THE UNITED STATES

A Failure to Communicate

The Commission's major concern with the news media is not in riot reporting as such, but in the failure to report adequately on race relations and ghetto problems and to bring more Negroes into journalism. Concern about this was expressed by a number of participants in our Poughkeepsie conference. Disorders are only one aspect of the dilemmas and difficulties of race relations in America. In defining, explaining, and reporting this broader, more complex and ultimately far more fundamental subject, the communications media, ironically, have failed to communicate.

They have not communicated to the majority of their audience—which is white—a sense of the degradation, misery, and hopelessness of living in the ghetto. They have not communicated to whites a feeling for the difficulties and frustrations of being a Negro in the United States. They have not shown understanding or appreciation of—and thus have not communicated—a sense of Negro culture, thought, or history.

Equally important, most newspaper articles and most television programming ignore the fact that an appreciable part of their audience is black. The world that television and newspapers offer to their black audience is almost totally white, in both appearance and attitude. As we have said, our evidence shows that the so-called "white press" is at best mistrusted and at worst held in contempt by many black Americans. Far too often, the press acts and talks about Negroes as if Negroes do not read the newspapers or watch television, give birth, marry, die, and go to PTA meetings. Some newspapers and stations are beginning to make efforts to fill this void, but they have still a long way to go.

The absence of Negro faces and activities from the media has an effect on white audiences as well as black. If what the white American reads in the newspapers or sees on television conditions his expectation of what is ordinary and normal in the larger society, he will neither understand nor accept the black American. By failing to portray the Negro as a matter of routine and in the context of the total society, the news media have, we believe, contributed to the black-white schism in this country.

When the white press does refer to Negroes and Negro problems it frequently does so as if Negroes were not a part of the audience. This is perhaps understandable in a system where whites edit and, to a large extent, write news. But such attitudes, in an area as sensitive and inflammatory as this, feed Negro alienation and intensify white prejudices.

We suggest that a top editor or news director monitor his news production for a period of several weeks, taking note of how certain stories and language will affect black readers or viewers. A Negro staff member could do this easily. Then the staff should be informed about the problems involved.

The problems of race relations coverage go beyond incidents of white bias. Many editors and news directors, plagued by shortages of staff and lack of reliable contacts and sources of information in the city, have failed to recognize the significance of the urban story and to develop resources to cover it adequately.

We believe that most news organizations do not have direct access to diversified news sources in the ghetto. Seldom do they have a total sense of what is going on there. Some of the blame rests on Negro leaders who do not trust the media and will not deal candidly with representatives of the white press. But the real failure rests with the news organization themselves. They—like other elements of the white community—have ignored the ghettos for decades. Now they seek instant acceptance and cooperation.

The development of good contacts, reliable information, and understanding requires more effort and time than an occasional visit by a team of reporters to do a feature on a newly-discovered ghetto problem. It requires reporters permanently assigned to this beat. They must be adequately trained and supported to dig out and tell the story of a major social upheaval —among the most complicated, portentous and explosive our society has known. We believe, also, that the Negro Press— manned largely by people who live and work in the ghetto— could be a particularly useful source of information and guidance about activities in the black community. Reporters and editors from Negro newspapers and radio stations should be included in any conference between media and police-city representatives, and we suggest that large news organizations would do well to establish better lines of communication to their counterparts in the Negro press.[10]

In short, the news media must find ways of exploring the problems of the Negro and the ghetto more deeply and more meaningfully. To editors who say "we have run thousands of inches on the ghetto which nobody reads" and to television executives who bemoan scores of underwatched documentaries, we say: find more ways of telling this story, for it is a story you, as journalists, must tell—honestly, realistically, and imaginatively. It is the responsibility of the news media to tell the story of race relations in America, and with notable exceptions, the media have not yet turned to the task with the wisdom, sensitivity, and expertise it demands.

Negroes in Journalism

The journalistic profession has been shockingly backward in seeking out, hiring, training, and promoting Negroes. Fewer than 5 percent of the people employed by the news business in editorial jobs in the United States today are Negroes. Fewer than 1 percent of editors and supervisors are Negroes, and most of them work for Negro-owned organizations. The lines

[10] We have not, in this report, examined the Negro press in detail. The thrust of our studies was directed at daily mass circulation, mass audience media which are aimed at the community as a whole.

of various news organizations to the militant blacks are, by admission of the newsmen themselves, almost nonexistent. The plaint is, "We can't find qualified Negroes." But this rings hollow from an industry where, only yesterday, jobs were scarce and promotion unthinkable for a man whose skin was black. Even today, there are virtually no Negroes in positions of editorial or executive responsibility and there is only one Negro newsman with a nationally syndicated column.

News organizations must employ enough Negroes in positions of significant responsibility to establish an effective link to Negro actions and ideas and to meet legitimate employment expectations. Tokenism—the hiring of one Negro reporter, or even two or three—is no longer enough. Negro reporters are essential, but so are Negro editors, writers and commentators. Newspaper and television policies are, generally speaking, not set by reporters. Editorial decisions about which stories to cover and which to use are made by editors. Yet, very few Negroes in this country are involved in making these decisions, because very few, if any, supervisory editorial jobs are held by Negroes. We urge the news media to do everything possible to train and promote their Negro reporters to positions where those who are qualified can contribute to and have an effect on policy decisions.

It is not enough, though, as many editors have pointed out to the Commission, to search for Negro journalists. Journalism is not very popular as a career for aspiring young Negroes. The starting pay is comparatively low and it is a business which has, until recently, discouraged and rejected them. The recruitment of Negro reporters must extend beyond established journalists, or those who have already formed ambitions along these lines. It must become a commitment to seek out young Negro men and women, inspire them to become—and then train them as—journalists. Training programs should be started at high schools and intensified at colleges. Summer vacation and part-time editorial jobs, coupled with offers of permanent employment, can awaken career plans.

We believe that the news media themselves, their audiences and the country will profit from these undertakings. For if the media are to comprehend and then to project the Negro community, they must have the help of Negroes. If the media are to report with understanding, wisdom and sympathy on the problems of the cities and the problems of the black man— for the two are increasingly intertwined—they must employ, promote and listen to Negro journalists.

The Negro in the Media

Finally, the news media must publish newspapers and produce programs that recognize the existence and activities of the Negro, both as a Negro and as part of the community. It would be a contribution of inestimable importance to race relations in the United States simply to treat ordinary news about Negroes as news of other groups is now treated.

Specifically, newspapers should integrate Negroes and Negro activities into all parts of the paper, from the news, society and club pages to the comic strips. Television should develop programming which integrates Negroes into all aspects of televised presentations. Television is such a visible medium that some constructive steps are easy and obvious. While some of these steps are being taken, they are still largely neglected. For example, Negro reporters and performers should appear more frequently—and at prime time—in news broadcasts, on weather shows, in documentaries, and in advertisements. Some effort already has been made to use Negroes in television commercials. Any initial surprise at seeing a Negro selling a sponsor's product will eventually fade into routine acceptance, an attitude that white society must ultimately develop toward all Negroes.

In addition to news-related programming, we think that Negroes should appear more frequently in dramatic and comedy series. Moreover, networks and local stations should present plays and other programs whose subjects are rooted in the ghetto and its problems.

IV. Institute of Urban Communications

The Commission is aware that in this area, as in all other aspects of race relations, the problems are great and it is much easier to state them than to solve them. Various pressures— competitive, financial, advertising—may impede progress toward more balanced, in-depth coverage and toward the hiring and training of more Negro personnel. Most newspapers and local television and radio stations do not have the resources or the time to keep abreast of all the technical advances, academic theories, and government programs affecting the cities and the lives of their black inhabitants.

During the course of this study, the Commission members and the staff have had many conversations with publishers, editors, broadcasters, and reporters throughout the country. The consensus appears to be that most of them would like to do much more but simply do not have the resources for independent efforts at either training or coverage.

The Commission believes that some of these problems could be resolved if there were a central organization to develop, gather and distribute talent, resources, and information and to keep the work of the press in this field under review. For this reason, the Commission proposes the establishment of an Institute of Urban Communications on a private, non-profit basis. The Institute would have neither governmental ties nor governmental authority. Its board would consist in substantial part of professional journalists and, for the rest, of distinguished public figures. The staff would be made up of journalists and students of the profession. Funding would be sought initially from private foundations. Ultimately, it may be hoped, financial support would be forthcoming from within the profession.

The Institute would be charged, in the first instance, with general responsibility for carrying out the media recommendations of the Commission, though as it developed a momentum and life of its own it would also gain its own view of the problems and possibilities. Initial tasks would include:

1. *Training and education for journalists in the field of urban affairs.* The Institute should organize and sponsor, on its own and in cooperation with universities and other institutions, a comprehensive range of courses, seminars and workshops designed to give reporters, editors and publishers the background they need to cover the urban scene. Offerings would vary in duration and intensity from weekend conferences to grants for year-long individual study on the order of the Nieman Fellowships.

All levels and all kinds of news outlets should be served. A most important activity might be to assist disc jockeys and commentators on stations that address themselves especially to the Negro community. Particularly important would be sessions of a month or more for seasoned reporters and editors, comparable to middle management seminars or mid-career training in other callings. The press must have all of the intellectual resources and background to give adequate coverage to the city and the ghetto. It should be the first duty of the Institute to see that this is provided.

2. *Recruitment, training and placement of Negro journalists.* The scarcity of Negroes in responsible news jobs intensifies the difficulties of communicating the reality of the contemporary American city to white newspaper and television audiences. The special viewpoint of the Negro who has lived through these problems and bears their marks upon him is, as we have seen, notably absent from what is, on the whole, a white press. But full integration of Negroes into the journalistic profession is imperative in its own right. It is unacceptable that the press, itself the special beneficiary of fundamental constitutional protections, should lag so far behind other fields in giving effect to the fundamental human right to equality of opportunity.

To help correct this situation, the Institute will have to undertake far-ranging activities. Providing educational opportunities for would-be Negro journalists is not enough. There will have to be changes in career outlooks for Negro students and their counselors back to the secondary school level. And changes in these attitudes will come slowly unless there is a change in the reality of employment and advancement opportunities for Negroes in journalism. This requires an aggressive placement program, seeking out newspapers, television and radio stations that discriminate, whether consciously or unconsciously, and mobilizing the pressures, public, private and legal, necessary to break the pattern. The Institute might also provide assistance to Negro newspapers, which now recruit and train many young journalists.

3. *Police-press relations*. The Commission has stressed the failures in this area, and has laid out a set of remedial measures for action at the local level. But if reliance is placed exclusively on local initiative we can predict that in many places—often those that need it most—our recommended steps will not be taken. Pressure from the federal government for action along the lines proposed would be suspect, probably, by both press and local officials. But the Institute could undertake the task of stimulating community action in line with the Commission's recommendations without arousing local hostility and suspicion. Moreover, the Institute could serve as a clearing house for exchange of experience in this field.

4. *Review of media performance on riots and racial issues*. The Institute should review press and television coverage of riot and racial news and publicly award praise and blame. The Commission recognizes that government restraints or guidelines in this field are both unworkable and incompatible with our Constitution and traditions. Internal guidelines or voluntary advance arrangements may be useful, but they tend to be rather general and the standards they prescribe are neither self-applying nor self-enforcing. We believe it would be healthy for reporters and editors who work in this sensitive field to know that others will be viewing their work and will hold them publicly accountable for lapses from accepted standards of good journalism. The Institute should publicize its findings by means of regular and special reports. It might also set a series of awards for especially meritorious work of individuals or news organizations in race relations reporting.

5. *An urban affairs service*. Whatever may be done to improve the quality of reporting on urban affairs, there always will be a great many outlets that are too small to support the specialized investigation, reporting and interpreting needed in this field. To fill this gap, the Institute could organize a com-

prehensive urban news service, available at a modest fee to any news organization that wanted it. The Institute would have its own specially trained reporters, and it would also cull the national press for news and feature stories of broader interest that could be reprinted or broadcast by subscribers.

6. *Continuing research.* Our own investigations have shown us that academic work on the impact of the media on race relations, its role in shaping attitudes, and the effects of the choices it makes on people's behavior, is in a rudimentary stage. The Commission's content analysis is the first study of its type of contemporary riot coverage, and it is extremely limited in scope. A whole range of questions needs intensive scholarly exploration, and indeed the development of new modes of research and analysis. The Institute should undertake many of these important projects under its own auspices and could stimulate others in the academic community to further research.

* * *

Along with the country as a whole, the press has too long basked in a white world, looking out of it, if at all, with white men's eyes and a white perspective. That is no longer good enough. The painful process of readjustment that is required of the American news media must begin now. They must make a reality of integration—in both their product and personnel. They must insist on the highest standards of accuracy—not only reporting single events with care and skepticism, but placing each event into meaningful perspective. They must report the travail of our cities with compassion and in depth.

In all this, the Commission asks for fair and courageous journalism—commitment and coverage that are worthy of one of the crucial domestic stories in America's history.

Chapter 16 / The Future of the Cities

INTRODUCTION

We believe action of the kind outlined in preceding pages can contribute substantially to control of disorders in the near future. But there should be no mistake about the long run. The underlying forces continue to gain momentum.

The most basic of these is the accelerating segregation of low-income, disadvantaged Negroes within the ghettos of the largest American cities.

By 1985, the 12.1 million Negroes segregated within central cities today will have grown to approximately 20.3 million—an increase of 68 percent.

Prospects for domestic peace and for the quality of American life are linked directly to the future of these cities.

Two critical questions must be confronted: Where do present trends now lead? What choices are open to us?

I. The Key Trends

Negro Population Growth[1]

The size of the Negro population in central cities is closely related to total national Negro population growth. In the past 16 years, about 98 percent of this growth has occurred within metropolitan areas, and 86 percent in the central cities of those areas.

A conservative projection of national Negro population growth indicates continued rapid increases. For the period 1966 to 1985, it will rise to a total of 30.7 million, gaining an average of 484,000 a year, or 7.6 percent more than the increase in each year from 1960 to 1966.

CENTRAL CITIES

Further Negro population growth in central cities depends upon two key factors: in-migration from outside metropolitan areas, and patterns of Negro settlement within metropolitan areas.

From 1960 to 1966, the Negro population of all central cities rose 2.4 million, 88.9 percent of total national Negro population growth. We estimate that natural growth accounted for 1.4 million, or 58 percent of this increase, and in-migration accounted for 1 million, or 42 percent.

As of 1966, the Negro population in all central cities totaled 12.1 million. By 1985, we have estimated that it will rise 68 percent to 20.3 million. We believe that natural growth will account for 5.2 million of this increase and in-migration for 3.0 million.

Without significant Negro out-migration, then, the combined Negro populations of central cities will continue to grow by an average of 274,000 a year through 1985, even if no further in-migration occurs.

Growth projected on the basis of natural increase and in-

[1] Tables and explanations of the projections on which they are based appear at the end of the chapter.

migration would raise the proportion of Negroes to whites in central cities by 1985 from the present 20.7 percent to between an estimated 31 and 34.7 percent.

These, however, are national figures. Much faster increases will occur in the largest central cities where Negro growth has been concentrated in the past two decades. Washington, D. C., Gary, and Newark are already over half Negro. A continuation of recent trends would cause the following 10 major cities to become over 50 per cent Negro by the indicated dates:

New Orleans	1971	St. Louis	1978
Richmond	1971	Detroit	1979
Baltimore	1972	Philadelphia	1981
Jacksonville	1972	Oakland	1983
Cleveland	1975	Chicago	1984

These cities, plus Washington, D. C., (now over 66 percent Negro) and Newark, contained 12.6 million people in 1960, or 22 percent of the total population of all 224 American central cities. All 13 cities undoubtedly will have Negro majorities by 1985, and the suburbs ringing them will remain largely all white, unless there are major changes in Negro fertility rates,[2] in-migration, settlement patterns or public policy.

Experience indicates that Negro school enrollment in these and other cities will exceed 50 percent long before the total population reaches that mark. In fact, Negro students already comprise more than a majority in the public elementary schools of 12 of the 13 cities mentioned above. This occurs because the Negro population in central cities is much younger and because a much higher proportion of white children attend private schools. For example, St. Louis' population was about 36 percent Negro in 1965; its public elementary school enrollment was 63 percent Negro. If present trends continue, many cities in addition to those listed above will have Negro school majorities by 1985, probably including:

Dallas	Louisville
Pittsburgh	Indianapolis
Buffalo	Kansas City, Mo.
Cincinnati	Hartford
Harrisburg	New Haven

Thus, continued concentration of future Negro population

[2] The fertility rate is the number of live births each year per 1,000 women aged 15 to 44.

growth in large central cities will produce significant changes in those cities over the next 20 years. Unless there are sharp changes in the factors influencing Negro settlement patterns within metropolitan areas, there is little doubt that the trend toward Negro majorities will continue. Even a complete cessation of net Negro in-migration to central cities would merely postpone this result for a few years.

Growth of the Young Negro Population

We estimate that the nation's white population will grow 16.6 million, or 9.6 percent, from 1966 to 1975, and the Negro population 3.8 million, or 17.7 percent, in the same period. The Negro age group from 15 to 24 years of age, however, will grow much faster than either the Negro population as a whole, or the white population in the same age group.

From 1966 to 1975, the number of Negroes in this age group will rise 1.6 million, or 40.1 percent. The white population aged 15 to 24 will rise 6.6 million, or 23.5 percent.

This rapid increase in the young Negro population has important implications for the country. This group has the highest unemployment rate in the nation, commits a relatively high proportion of all crimes, and plays the most significant role in civil disorders. By the same token, it is a great reservoir of underused human resources which are vital to the nation.

The Location of New Jobs

Most new employment opportunities do not occur in central cities, near all-Negro neighborhoods. They are being created in suburbs and outlying areas—and this trend is likely to continue indefinitely. New office buildings have risen in the downtowns of large cities, often near all-Negro areas. But the out-flow of manufacturing and retailing facilities normally offsets this addition significantly—and in many cases has caused a net loss of jobs in central cities while the new white collar jobs are often not available to ghetto residents.

Providing employment for the swelling Negro ghetto population will require society to link these potential workers more closely with job locations. This can be done in three ways: by developing incentives to industry to create new employment centers near Negro residential areas; by opening suburban residential areas to Negroes and encouraging them to move closer to industrial centers; or by creating better transportation between ghetto neighborhoods and new job locations.

All three involve large public outlays.

The first method—creating new industries in or near the ghetto—is not likely to occur without government subsidies on a scale which convinces private firms that it will pay them to face the problems involved.

The second method—opening up suburban areas to Negro occupancy—obviously requires effective fair housing laws. It will also require an extensive program of federally-aided, low-cost housing in many suburban areas.

The third approach—improved transportation linking ghettos and suburbs—has received little attention from city planners and municipal officials. A few demonstration projects show promise, but carrying them out on a large scale will be very costly.

Although a high proportion of new jobs will be located in suburbs, there are still millions of jobs in central cities. Turnover in those jobs alone can open up a great many potential positions for Negro central city residents—if employers cease racial discrimination in their hiring and promotion practices.

Nevertheless, as the total number of Negro central city jobseekers continues to rise, the need to link them with emerging new employment in the suburbs will become increasingly urgent.

The Increasing Cost of Municipal Services

Local governments have had to bear a particularly heavy financial burden in the two decades since the end of World War II. All United States cities are highly dependent upon property taxes that are relatively unresponsive to changes in income. Consequently, growing municipalities have been hard-pressed for adequate revenues to meet rising demands for services generated by population increase. On the other hand, stable or declining cities have not only been faced with steady cost increases but also with a slow-growing, or even declining, tax base.

As a result of the population shifts of the post-war period, concentrating the middle class in residential suburbs while leaving the poor in the central cities, the increasing burden of municipal taxes frequently falls upon that part of the urban population least able to pay them.

Increasing concentrations of urban growth have called forth greater expenditures for every kind of public service: education, health, police protection, fire protection, parks, sanitation, etc. These expenditures have strikingly outpaced tax revenues. The story is summed up below:

Local Government Revenues, Expenditures and Debt
(Billions of dollars)

	1950	1966	Increase
Revenues	11.7	41.5	+29.8
Expenditures	17.0	60.7	+43.7
Debt outstanding	18.8	77.5	+58.7

Despite the growth of federal assistance to urban areas under various grant-in-aid programs, the fiscal plight of many cities is likely to grow even more serious in the future. Local expenditures inevitably will continue to rise steeply as a result of several factors, including the difficulty of increasing productivity in the predominantly service activities of local governments, and the rapid technologically-induced increases in productivity in other economic sectors.

Traditionally, individual productivity has risen faster in the manufacturing, mining, construction, and agricultural sectors than in those involving personal services.

However, all sectors compete with each other for talent and personnel. Wages and salaries in the service-dominated sectors generally must keep up, therefore, with those in the capital-dominated sectors. Since productivity in manufacturing has risen about 2.5 percent per year compounded over many decades, and even faster in agriculture, the basis for setting costs in the service-dominated sectors has gone up, too.

In the postwar period, costs of the same units of output have increased very rapidly in certain key activities of local government. For example, education is the single biggest form of expenditure by local governments (including school districts), accounting for about 40 percent of their outlays. From 1947 to 1967, costs per pupil-day in United States public schools rose at a rate of 6.7 percent per year compounded—only slightly less than doubling every ten years.[8] This major cost item is likely to keep on rising rapidly in the future, along with other government services like police, fire, and welfare activities.

Some increases in productivity may occur in these fields, and some economies may be achieved through use of assistants such as police and teachers' aides. Nevertheless, the need to keep pace with private sector wage scales will force local government costs to rise sharply.

This and other future cost increases are important to future relations between central cities and suburbs. Rising costs will inevitably force central cities to demand more and more assistance from the federal government. But the federal government can obtain such funds through the income tax only

---

[8] It is true that the average pupil-teacher ratio declined from 28 to about 25, and other improvements in teaching quality may have occurred. But they cannot account for anything approaching this rapid increase in costs.

from other parts of the economy. Suburban governments are, meanwhile, experiencing the same cost increases along with the rising resentment of their constituents.

II. Choices for the Future

The complexity of American society offers many choices for the future of relations between central cities and suburbs and patterns of white and Negro settlement in metropolitan areas. For practical purposes, however, we see two fundamental questions:

- Should future Negro population growth be concentrated in central cities, as in the past 20 years, thereby forcing Negro and white populations to become even more residentially segregated?
- Should society provide greatly increased special assistance to Negroes and other relatively disadvantaged population groups?

For purposes of analysis, the Commission has defined three basic choices for the future embodying specific answers to these questions:

The Present Policies Choice

Under this course, the nation would maintain approximately the share of resources now being allocated to programs of assistance for the poor, unemployed and disadvantaged. These programs are likely to grow, given continuing economic growth and rising federal revenues, but they will not grow fast enough to stop, let alone reverse, the already deteriorating quality of life in central-city ghettos.

This choice carries the highest ultimate price, as we will point out.

The Enrichment Choice

Under this course, the nation would seek to offset the effects of continued Negro segregation and deprivation in large city ghettos. The Enrichment Choice would aim at creating dramatic improvements in the quality of life in disadvantaged central-city neighborhoods—both white and Negro. It would require marked increases in federal spending for education, housing, employment, job training, and social services.

The Enrichment Choice would seek to lift poor Negroes

and whites above poverty status and thereby give them the capacity to enter the mainstream of American life. But it would not, at least for many years, appreciably affect either the increasing concentration of Negroes in the ghetto or racial segregation in residential areas outside the ghetto.

The Integration Choice

This choice would be aimed at reversing the movement of the country toward two societies, separate and unequal.

The Integration Choice—like the Enrichment Choice—would call for large-scale improvement in the quality of ghetto life. But it would also involve both creating strong incentives for Negro movement out of central-city ghettos and enlarging freedom of choice concerning housing, employment, and schools.

The result would fall considerably short of full integration. The experience of other ethnic groups indicates that some Negro households would be scattered in largely white residential areas. Others—probably a larger number—would voluntarily cluster together in largely Negro neighborhoods. The Integration Choice would thus produce both integration and segregation. But the segregation would be voluntary.

Articulating these three choices plainly oversimplifies the possibilities open to the country. We believe, however, that they encompass the basic issues—issues which the American public must face if it is serious in its concern not only about civil disorder, but the future of our democratic society.

III. The Present Policies Choice

Powerful forces of social and political inertia are moving the country steadily along the course of existing policies toward a divided country.

This course may well involve changes in many social and economic programs—but not enough to produce fundamental alterations in the key factors of Negro concentration, racial segregation, and the lack of sufficient enrichment to arrest the decay of deprived neighborhoods.

Some movement towards enrichment can be found in efforts to encourage industries to locate plants in central cities, in increased federal expenditures for education, in the important concepts embodied in the "War on Poverty," and in the Model Cities Program. But congressional appropriations for even present federal programs have been so small that they fall short of effective enrichment.

As for challenging concentration and segregation, a national commitment to this purpose has yet to develop.

Of the three future courses we have defined, the Present Policies Choice—the choice we are now making—is the course with the most ominous consequences for our society.

The Probability of Future Civil Disorders

We believe that the Present Policies Choice would lead to a larger number of violent incidents of the kind that have stimulated recent major disorders.

First, it does nothing to raise the hopes, absorb the energies, or constructively challenge the talents of the rapidly-growing number of young Negro men in central cities. The proportion of unemployed or underemployed among them will remain very high. These young men have contributed disproportionately to crime and violence in cities in the past, and there is danger, obviously, that they will continue to do so.

Second, under these conditions, a rising proportion of Negroes in disadvantaged city areas might come to look upon the deprivation and segregation they suffer as proper justification for violent protest or for extending support to now isolated extremists who advocate civil disruption by guerrilla tactics.

More incidents would not necessarily mean more or worse riots. For the near future, there is substantial likelihood that even an increased number of incidents could be controlled before becoming major disorders, if society undertakes to improve police and National Guard forces so that they can respond to potential disorders with more prompt and disciplined use of force.

In fact, the likelihood of incidents mushrooming into major disorders would be only slightly higher in the near future under the Present Policies Choice than under the other two possible choices. For no new policies or programs could possibly alter basic ghetto conditions immediately. And the announcement of new programs under the other choices would immediately generate new expectations. Expectations inevitably increase faster than performance: in the short run, they might even increase the level of frustration.

In the long run, however, the Present Policies Choice risks a seriously greater probability of major disorders, worse, possibly, than those already experienced.

If the Negro population as a whole developed even stronger feelings of being wrongly "penned in" and discriminated against, many of its members might come to support not only riots, but the rebellion now being preached by only a handful.

397

If large-scale violence resulted, white retaliation could follow. This spiral could quite conceivably lead to a kind of urban *apartheid* with semi-martial law in many major cities. enforced residence of Negroes in segregated areas, and a drastic reduction in personal freedom for all Americans, particularly Negroes.

The same distinction is applicable to the cost of the Present Policies Choice. In the short run, its costs—at least its direct cash outlays—would be far less than for the other choices.

Any social and economic programs likely to have significant lasting effect would require very substantial annual appropriations for many years. Their cost would far exceed the direct losses sustained in recent civil disorders. Property damage in all the disorders we investigated, including Detroit and Newark, totalled less than $100 million.

But it would be a tragic mistake to view the Present Policies Choice as cheap. Damage figures measure only a small part of the costs of civil disorder. They cannot measure the costs in terms of the lives lost, injuries suffered, minds and attitudes closed and frozen in prejudice, or the hidden costs of the profound disruption of entire cities.

Ultimately, moreover, the economic and social costs of the Present Policies Choice will far surpass the cost of the alternatives. The rising concentration of impoverished Negroes and other minorities within the urban ghettos will constantly expand public expenditures for welfare, law enforcement, unemployment and other existing programs without arresting the decay of older city neighborhoods and the breeding of frustration and discontent. But the most significant item on the balance of accounts will remain largely invisible and incalculable —the toll in human values taken by continued poverty, segregation and inequality of opportunity.

Polarization

Another and equally serious consequence is the fact that this course would lead to the permanent establishment of two societies: one predominantly white and located in the suburbs, in smaller cities, and in outlying areas, and one largely Negro located in central cities.

We are well on the way to just such a divided nation.

This division is veiled by the fact that Negroes do not now dominate many central cities. But they soon will, as we have shown, and the new Negro mayors will be facing even more difficult conditions than now exist.

As Negroes succeed whites in our largest cities, the proportion of low-income residents in those cities will probably increase. This is likely even if both white and Negro incomes continue to rise at recent rates, since Negroes have much lower incomes than whites. Moreover, many of the ills of large central cities spring from their age, their location, and their obsolete physical structures. The deterioration and economic decay stemming from these factors have been proceeding for decades and will continue to plague older cities regardless of who resides in them.

These facts underlie the fourfold dilemma of the American city:

- Fewer tax dollars come in, as large numbers of middle-income taxpayers move out of central cities and property values and business decline;
- More tax dollars are required, to provide essential public services and facilities, and to meet the needs of expanding lower-income groups;
- Each tax dollar buys less, because of increasing costs;
- Citizen dissatisfaction with municipal services grows as needs, expectations and standards of living increase throughout the community.

These are the conditions that would greet the Negro-dominated municipal governments that will gradually come to power in many of our major cities. The Negro electorates in those cities probably would demand basic changes in present policies. Like the present white electorates there, they would have to look for assistance to two basic sources: the private sector and the federal government.

With respect to the private sector, major private capital investment in those cities might have ceased almost altogether if white-dominated firms and industries decided the risks and costs were too great. The withdrawal of private capital is already far advanced in most all-Negro areas of our large cities.

Even if private investment continued, it alone would not suffice. Big cities containing high proportions of low-income Negroes and block after block of deteriorating older property need very substantial assistance from the federal government to meet the demands of their electorates for improved services and living conditions.

By that time, however, it is probable that Congress will be more heavily influenced by representatives of the suburban and outlying city electorate. These areas will comprise 40 percent of our total population by 1985, compared with 31 percent in 1960, Central cities will decline from 32 percent to 27 percent.[4]

[4] Based on Census Bureau Series D projections.

Yet even the suburbs will be feeling the squeeze of higher local government costs. Hence, Congress might resist providing the extensive assistance which central cities will desperately need.

Thus the Present Policies Choice, if pursued for any length of time, might force simultaneous political and economic polarization in many of our largest metropolitan areas. Such polarization would involve large central cities—mainly Negro, with many poor, and nearly bankrupt—on the one hand, and most suburbs—mainly white, generally affluent, but heavily taxed—on the other hand.

Some areas might avoid political confrontation by shifting to some form of metropolitan government designed to offer regional solutions for pressing urban problems such as property taxation, air and water pollution and refuse disposal, and commuter transport. Yet this would hardly eliminate the basic segregation and relative poverty of the urban Negro population. It might even increase the Negro's sense of frustration and alienation if it operated to prevent Negro political control of central cities.

The acquisition of power by Negro-dominated governments in central cities is surely a legitimate and desirable exercise of political power by a minority group. It is in an American political tradition exemplified by the achievements of the Irish in New York and Boston.

But such Negro political development would also involve virtually complete racial segregation and virtually complete spatial separation. By 1985, the separate Negro society in our central cities would contain almost 21 million citizens. That is almost 68 percent larger than the present Negro population of central cities. It is also larger than the current population of every Negro nation in Africa except Nigeria.

If developing a racially integrated society is extraordinarily difficult today when 12.1 million Negroes live in central cities, then it is quite clearly going to be virtually impossible in 1985 when almost 21 million Negroes—still much poorer and less educated than most whites—will be living there.

Can Present Policies Avert Extreme Polarization?

There are at least two possible developments under the Present Policies Choice which might avert such polarization. The first is a faster increase of incomes among Negroes than has occurred in the recent past. This might prevent central cities from becoming even deeper "poverty traps" than they now are. It suggests the importance of effective job programs and higher levels of welfare payments for dependent families.

The second possible development is migration of a growing Negro middle class out of the central city. This would not prevent competition for federal funds between central cities and outlying areas, but it might diminish the racial undertones of that competition.

There is, however, no evidence that a continuation of present policies would be accompanied by any such movement. There is already a significant Negro middle class. It grew rapidly from 1960 to 1966. Yet in these years, 88.9 percent of the total national growth of Negro population was concentrated in central cities—the highest in history. Indeed, from 1960 to 1966, there was actually a net total in-migration of Negroes from the urban fringes of metropolitan areas into central cities.[5] The Commission believes it unlikely that this trend will suddenly reverse itself without significant changes in private attitudes and public policies.

IV. The Enrichment Choice

The Present Policies Choice plainly would involve continuation of efforts like Model Cities, manpower programs, and the War on Poverty. These are in fact enrichment programs, designed to improve the quality of life in the ghetto.

Because of their limited scope and funds, however, they constitute only very modest steps toward enrichment—and would continue to do so even if these programs were somewhat enlarged or supplemented.

The premise of the Enrichment Choice is performance. To adopt this choice would require a substantially greater share of national resources—sufficient to make a dramatic, visible impact on life in the urban Negro ghetto.

The Effect of Enrichment on Civil Disorders

Effective enrichment policies probably would have three immediate effects on civil disorders.

First, announcement of specific large-scale programs and the demonstration of a strong intent to carry them out might persuade ghetto residents that genuine remedies for their problems were forthcoming, thereby allaying tensions.

Second, such announcements would strongly stimulate the aspirations and hopes of members of these communities—

[5] Although Negro population on the urban fringe of metropolitan areas did increase slightly (0.2 million) from 1960 to 1966, it is safe to assume an actual net in-migration to central cities from these areas based upon the rate of natural increase of the Negro population.

possibly well beyond the capabilities of society to deliver and to do so promptly. This might increase frustration and discontent, to some extent cancelling the first effect.

Third, if there could be immediate action on meaningful job training and the creation of productive jobs for large numbers of unemployed young people, they would become much less likely to engage in civil disorders.

Such action is difficult now, when there are about 585,000 young Negro men aged 14 to 24 in the civilian labor force in central cities—of whom 81,000 or 13.8 percent, are unemployed and probably two or three times as many are underemployed. It will not become easier in the future. By 1975, this age group will have grown to nearly 700,000.

Given the size of the present problem, plus the large growth of this age group, creation of sufficient meaningful jobs will require extensive programs, begun rapidly. Even if the nation is willing to embark on such programs, there is no certainty that they can be made effective soon enough.

Consequently, there is no certainty that the Enrichment Choice would do much more in the near future to diminish violent incidents in central cities than would the Present Policies Choice. However, if enrichment programs can succeed in meeting the needs of residents of disadvantaged areas for jobs, education, housing and city services, then over the years this choice is almost certain to reduce both the level and frequency of urban disorder.

The Negro Middle Class

One objective of the Enrichment Choice would be to help as many disadvantaged Americans as possible—of all races—to enter the mainstream of American prosperity, to progress toward what is often called middle-class status. If the Enrichment Choice were adopted, it could certainly attain this objective to a far greater degree than would the Present Policies Choice. This could significantly change the quality of life in many central city areas.

It can be argued that a rapidly enlarging Negro middle class would also promote Negro out-migration, and thus the Enrichment Choice would open up an escape hatch from the ghetto. This argument, however, has two weaknesses.

The first is experience. Central cities already have sizable and growing numbers of middle-class Negro families. Yet only a few have migrated from the central city. The past pattern of white ethnic groups gradually moving out of central-city areas to middle-class suburbs has not applied to Negroes. Effective open-housing laws will help make this possible. It is probable, however, that other more extensive changes in policies and attitudes will be required—and these would extend beyond the Enrichment Choice.

The second weakness in the argument is time. Even if enlargement of the Negro middle class succeeded in encouraging movement out of the central city, it could not do so fast enough to offset the rapid growth of the ghetto. To offset even *half* the growth estimated for the ghetto by 1975 would call for the out-migration from central cities of 217,000 persons a year. This is eight times the annual increase in suburban Negro population—including natural increase—which occurred from 1960 to 1966. Even the most effective enrichment program is not likely to accomplish this.

A corollary problem derives from the continuing migration of poor Negroes from the Southern to Northern and Western cities.

Adoption of the Enrichment Choice would require large-scale efforts to improve conditions in the South sufficiently to remove the pressure to migrate. Under present conditions, slightly over a third of the estimated increase in Negro central-city population by 1985 will result from in-migration—3.0 million out of total increase of 8.2 million.

Negro Self-Development

The Enrichment Choice is in line with some of the currents of Negro protest thought that fall under the label of "Black Power." We do not refer to versions of Black Power ideology which promote violence, generate racial hatred, or advocate total separation of the races. Rather, we mean the view which asserts that the American Negro population can assume its proper role in society and overcome its feelings of powerlessness and lack of self-respect only by exerting power over decisions which directly affect its own members. A fully integrated society is not thought possible until the Negro minority within the ghetto has developed political strength—a strong bargaining position in dealing with the rest of society.

In short, this argument would regard predominantly Negro central cities and predominantly white outlying areas not as harmful, but as an advantageous future.

Proponents of these views also focus on the need for the Negro to organize economically as well as politically, thus tapping new energies and resources for self-development. One of the hardest tasks in improving disadvantaged areas is to discover how deeply deprived residents can develop their own capabilities by participating more fully in decisions and activities which affect them. Such learning-by-doing efforts are a vital part of the process of bringing deprived people into the social mainstream.

Separate But Equal Societies?

The Enrichment Choice by no means seeks to perpetuate racial segregation. In the end, however, its premise is that disadvantaged Negroes can achieve equality of opportunity with whites while continuing in conditions of nearly complete separation.

This premise has been vigorously advocated by Black Power proponents. While most Negroes originally desired racial integration, many are losing hope of ever achieving it because of seemingly implacable white resistance. Yet they cannot bring themselves to accept the conclusion that most of the millions of Negroes who are forced to live racially segregated lives must therefore be condemned to inferior lives—to inferior educations, or inferior housing, or inferior status.

Rather, they reason, there must be some way to make the quality of life in the ghetto areas just as good—or better—than elsewhere. It is not surprising that some Black Power advocates are denouncing integration and claiming that, given the hypocrisy and racism that pervade white society, life in a black society is, in fact, morally superior. This argument is understandable, but there is a great deal of evidence that it is unrealistic.

The economy of the United States and particularly the sources of employment are preponderantly white. In this circumstance, a policy of separate but equal employment could only relegate Negroes permanently to inferior incomes and economic status.

The best evidence regarding education is contained in recent reports of the Office of Education and Civil Rights Commission which suggest that both racial and economic integration are essential to educational equality for Negroes. Yet critics point out that, certainly until integration is achieved, various types of enrichment programs must be tested, and that dramatically different results may be possible from intensive educational enrichment—such as far smaller classes, or greatly expanded pre-school programs, or changes in the home environment of Negro children resulting from steady jobs for fathers.

Still others advocate shifting control over ghetto schools from professional administrators to local residents. This, they say, would improve curricula, give students a greater sense of their own value, and thus raise their morale and educational achievement. These approaches have not yet been tested sufficiently. One conclusion, however, does seem reasonable: any real improvement in the quality of education in low-income, all-Negro areas will cost a great deal more money than is now being spent there—and perhaps more than is being spent per pupil anywhere. Racial and social class integration of schools may produce equal improvement in achievement at less total cost.

Whether or not enrichment in ghetto areas will really work is not yet known, but the Enrichment Choice is based on the yet-unproved premise that it will. Certainly, enrichment programs could significantly improve existing ghetto schools if they impelled major innovations. But "separate but equal" ghetto education cannot meet the long-run fundamental educational needs of the central-city Negro population.

The three basic educational choices are: providing Negro children with quality education in integrated schools; providing them with quality education by enriching ghetto schools; or continuing to provide many Negro children with inferior education in racially segregated school systems, severely limiting their life-time opportunities.

Consciously or not, it is the third choice that the nation is now making, and this choice the Commission rejects totally.

In the field of housing, it is obvious that "separate but equal" does not mean really equal. The Enrichment Choice could greatly improve the quantity, variety, and environment of decent housing available to the ghetto population. It could not provide Negroes with the same freedom and range of choice as whites with equal incomes. Smaller cities and suburban areas together with the central city provide a far greater variety of housing and environmental settings than the central city alone. Programs to provide housing outside central cities, however, extend beyond the bounds of the Enrichment Choice.

In the end, whatever its benefits, the Enrichment Choice might well invite a prospect similar to that of the Present Policies Choice: separate white and black societies.

If enrichment programs were effective, they could greatly narrow the gap in income, education, housing, jobs, and other qualities of life between the ghetto and the mainstream. Hence the chances of harsh polarization—or of disorder—in the next 20 years would be greatly reduced.

Whether they would be reduced far enough depends on the scope of the programs. Even if the gap were narrowed from the present, it still could remain as a strong source of tension. History teaches that men are not necessarily placated even by great absolute progress. The controlling factor is relative progress—whether they still perceive a significant gap between themselves and others whom they regard as no more deserving. Widespread perception of such a gap—and consequent resentment—might well be precisely the situation 20 years from now under the Enrichment Choice, for it is essentially another way of choosing a permanently divided country.

V. The Integration Choice

The third and last course open to the nation combines enrichment with programs designed to encourage integration of substantial numbers of Negroes into the society outside the ghetto.

Enrichment must be an important adjunct to any integration course. No matter how ambitious or energetic such a program may be, relatively few Negroes now living in central-city ghettos would be quickly integrated. In the meantime, significant improvement in their present environment is essential.

The enrichment aspect of this third choice should, however, be recognized as interim action, during which time expanded and new programs can work to improve education and earning power. The length of the interim period surely would vary. For some it may be long. But in any event, what should be clearly recognized is that enrichment is only a means toward the goal; it is not the goal.

The goal must be achieving freedom for every citizen to live and work according to his capacities and desires, not his color.

We believe there are four important reasons why American society must give this course the most serious consideration. First, future jobs are being created primarily in the suburbs, while the chronically unemployed population is increasingly concentrated in the ghetto. This separation will make it more and more difficult for Negroes to achieve anything like full employment in decent jobs. But if, over time, these residents began to find housing outside central cities, they would be exposed to more knowledge of job opportunities. They would have to make much shorter trips to reach jobs. They would have a far better chance of securing employment on a self-sustaining basis.

Second, in the judgment of this Commission, racial and social-class integration is the most effective way of improving the education of ghetto children.

Third, developing an adequate housing supply for low-income and middle-income families and true freedom of choice in housing for Negroes of all income levels will require substantial out-movement. We do not believe that such an out-movement will occur spontaneously merely as a result of increasing prosperity among Negroes in central cities. A national fair housing law is essential to begin such movement. In many suburban areas, a program combining positive incentives with the building of new housing will be necessary to carry it out.

Fourth, and by far the most important, integration is the only course which explicitly seeks to achieve a single nation rather than accepting the present movement toward a dual society. This choice would enable us at least to begin reversing the profoundly divisive trend already so evident in our metropolitan areas—before it becomes irreversible.

VI. CONCLUSIONS

The future of our cities is neither something which will just happen nor something which will be imposed upon us by an inevitable destiny. That future will be shaped to an important degree by choices we make now.

We have attempted to set forth the major choices because we believe it is vital for Americans to understand the consequences of our present drift.

Three critical conclusions emerge from this analysis:

1. The nation is rapidly moving toward two increasingly separate Americas.

Within two decades, this division could be so deep that it would be almost impossible to unite:

- a white society principally located in suburbs, in smaller central cities, and in the peripheral parts of large central cities; and
- a Negro society largely concentrated within large central cities.

The Negro society will be permanently relegated to its current status, possibly even if we expend great amounts of money and effort in trying to "gild" the ghetto.

2. In the long run, continuation and expansion of such a permanent division threatens us with two perils.

The first is the danger of sustained violence in our cities. The timing, scale, nature, and repercussions of such violence cannot be foreseen. But if it occurred, it would further destroy our ability to achieve the basic American promises of liberty, justice, and equality.

The second is the danger of a conclusive repudiation of the

traditional American ideals of individual dignity, freedom, and equality of opportunity. We will not be able to espouse these ideals meaningfully to the rest of the world, to ourselves, to our children. They may still recite the Pledge of Allegiance and say "one nation . . . indivisible." But they will be learning cynicism, not patriotism.

3. We cannot escape responsibility for choosing the future of our metropolitan areas and the human relations which develop within them. It is a responsibility so critical that even an unconscious choice to continue present policies has the gravest implications.

That we have delayed in choosing or, by delaying, may be making the wrong choice, does not sentence us either to separatism or despair. But we must choose. We will choose. Indeed, we are now choosing.

NOTE ON NEGRO POPULATION PROJECTIONS

1. The Census Bureau publishes four projections of future population growth based upon differing assumptions about future fertility rates (i.e., the rate is the annual number of live births per 1,000 women aged 15 to 44). Series A assumes fertility rates similar to those prevalent from 1962 to 1966. Series B through D assume lower rates. Assuming that Negro fertility rates will continue to decline, we have used the average of Series C and D—which are based on the lowest assumptions about such rates. We have also converted the Census Bureau's nonwhite population projections into Negro projections by assuming Negroes will continue to comprise about 92 percent of all nonwhites. If, however, fertility rates remain at their present levels, then the total Negro population in 1985 would be 35.8 million rather than 30.7 million. The average annual rate of increase from 1966 to 1985 would be 753,000, rather than 484,000—56 percent higher. The projection is as follows:

Date	Total U.S. Negro Population (in millions)	Negroes As % of Total U.S. Population	Increase from the Previous Date Shown		
			Total Increase		Annual Average
			Number (in millions)	Percent	
1960	18.8 (actual)	10.4%	—	—	—
1966	21.5 (actual)	10.9	2.7	14.4	450,000
1970	23.2	11.3	1.7	7.9	425,000
1975	25.3	11.6	2.1	9.1	420,000
1980	28.1	12.0	2.5	9.9	500,000
1985	30.7	12.4	2.9	10.9	580,000

2. The general concept of a metropolitan area is of an integrated, economic and social unit with a recognized large population nucleus. Statistically, it is called a Standard Metropolitan Statistical Area—one which contains at least one central city of at least 50,000 inhabitants. It covers the county of the central city and adjacent counties found to be economically and socially integrated with that county.

A Central City is the largest city of an SMSA and which gives the SMSA its name.

"Core city" or "inner city" is a popular expression sometimes meaning central city and sometimes meaning the central business district and densely populated downtown neighborhoods of generally poorer residents.

The array of statistical materials for metropolitan areas by "central city" and "outside central city" categories carries with it some dangers. The general proposition made in such displays is that the Negro population is concentrated in the central city and is kept out of the suburbs. Certainly this is true.

The danger arises from the inference which the reader may make about the character of "outside central city" and "suburb." "Outside central city" means the whole metropolitan area outside the city or cities whose names are given to the Standard Metropolitan Statistical Area. This is not a homogeneous, affluent, white-only collection of bedroom communities or housing developments. It is a wide-ranging assortment of these and more. Some are attractive communities with trees, grass and fresh air. Others are grimy, industrial towns with all the problems commonly associated with the central city. There are, in fact, 246 cities of over 25,000 "hidden" in the concept "outside central city." Seventy-seven of these had over 50,000 population in 1960. Many are white only or close to it. Many are not. Some even have higher proportions of Negroes to total population than the central cities of the metropolitan areas of which they are a part. Some of these cities are new. Some are old and have to fight the same battles against urban blight as the central cities of many metropolitan areas.

3. We have considered two projections of this population. The first projection assumes no further in-migration or out-migration of Negroes to or from central cities. This assumption is unrealistic, but it provides a measure of how much the central-city Negro population is likely to expand through natural increase alone. The second projection assumes that central cities will continue to contain 88.9 percent of all Negro population growth, as they did from 1960 to 1966.

| | Total U.S. Central-City Negro Population (in millions) | |
Date	Based on Natural Increase from the Existing Base Only	Based on 88.9% of All Future Negro Growth In Central Cities
1966 (actual)	12.1	12.1
1970	13.1	13.6
1975	14.2	15.5
1980	15.6	17.7
1985	17.3	20.3

Thus, even assuming no Negro migration into central cities, the total Negro population would increase six million, 43.0 percent, by 1985. Under the more realistic assumption of both continued in-migration (at present rates) and natural growth, total Negro population of central cities would increase by 8.2 million Negroes, 68 percent.

4. We have arrived at these estimates by making three different assumptions about future white central-city population shifts: (a) that it will remain constant at its 1966 level of 46.4 million; (b) that it will decline, as it did from 1960 to 1966, by an amount equal to half the increase in central-city Negro population; and (c) that it will decline by an absolute amount equal to the total gains in central-city Negro population. In all three cases, we assume that Negro central-city population will continue to account for 88.9 percent of all Negro population growth. The full projections are as follows:

		Proportion of Total Central City Population Negro if:	
		White Population Declines at an Absolute Annual Rate Equal to:	
	White Population Remains Constant	One-Half Negro	Total Negro
Date	at 1966 Level	Population Gains	Population Gains
1966 (actual)	20.7%	20.7%	20.7%
1975	25.0	25.7	26.5
1985	30.4	32.4	34.7

The first assumption requires a rise in total central-city population from 58.5 million in 1966 to 66.7 million in 1985. Since many of the largest central cities are already almost fully developed, so large an increase is probably unrealistic. On the other hand, the third assumption involves no change in the 1966 central-city population figure of 58.5 million. This may be unrealistically low. But in any event, it seems likely that continued concentration will cause the total proportion of Negroes in central cities to reach at least 25 percent by 1975 and 30 percent by 1985.

Chapter 17 / Recommendations for National Action

The Commission has already addressed itself to the need for immediate action at the local level. Because the city is the focus of racial disorder, the immediate responsibility rests on community leaders and local institutions. Without responsive and representative local government, without effective processes of interracial communication within the city, and without alert, well-trained and adequately supported local police, national action—no matter how great its scale—cannot be expected to provide a solution.

Yet the disorders are not simply a problem of the racial ghetto or the city. As we have seen, they are symptoms of social ills that have become endemic in our society and now affect every American—black or white, businessman or factory worker, suburban commuter or slum dweller.

None of us can escape the consequences of the continuing economic and social decay of the central city and the closely related problem of rural poverty. The convergence of these conditions in the racial ghetto and the resulting discontent and disruption threaten democratic values fundamental to our progress as a free society.

The essential fact is that neither existing conditions nor the garrison state offer acceptable alternatives for the future of this country. Only a greatly enlarged commitment to national action —compassionate, massive and sustained, backed by the will and resources of the most powerful and the richest nation on this earth—can shape a future that is compatible with the historic ideals of American society.

It is this conviction that leads us, as a commission on civil disorders, to comment on the shape and dimensions of the action that must be taken at the national level.

In this effort we have taken account of the work of scholars and experts on race relations, the urban condition and poverty. We have studied the reports and work of other commissions, of congressional committees and of many special task forces and groups both within the government and within the private sector.

Financing the Cost

The Commission has also examined the question of financing; although there are grave difficulties, we do not regard them as insoluble. The nation has substantial financial resources —not enough to do everything some might wish, but enough to make an important start on reducing our critical "social deficit," in spite of a war and in spite of current budget requirements.

The key factors having a bearing on our ability to pay for the cost are the great productivity of the American economy, and a Federal revenue system which is highly responsive to economic growth. In combination, these produce truly astounding automatic increases in Federal budget receipts, provided only that the national economy is kept functioning at capacity, so that actual national income expands in line with potential.

These automatic increases—the "fiscal dividend"—from the Federal revenue system range from $11 billion to $14 billion under conditions of steady economic growth.

The tax surcharge requested by the President, including continuation of excise taxes, would add about $16 billion to a fiscal dividend of about $28.5 billion over a two-year period.

While competing demands are certain to grow with every increase in federal revenues, so that hard choices are inevitable, these figures demonstrate the dimension of resources—apart from changes in tax rates—which this country can generate.

Federal Program Coordination

The spectacle of Detroit and New Haven engulfed in civil turmoil despite a multitude of federally-aided programs raised basic questions as to whether existing "delivery system" is adequate to the bold new purposes of national policy. Many who voiced these concerns overlooked the disparity between the size of the problems at which the programs are aimed and the level of funding provided by the federal government.

Yet there is little doubt that the system through which federal programs are translated into services to people is a major problem in itself. There are now over 400 grant programs operated by a broad range of federal agencies and channeled through a much larger array of semi-autonomous state and local government entities. Reflective of this complex scheme, federal programs often seem self-defeating and contradictory: field officials unable to make decisions on their own programs and unaware of related efforts; agencies unable or unwilling to work together; programs conceived and administered to achieve different and sometimes conflicting purposes.

The new social development legislation has put great strain upon obsolescent machinery and administrative practices at all levels of government. It has loaded new work on federal de-

411

partments. It has required a level of skill, a sense of urgency, and a capacity for judgment never planned for or encouraged in departmental field offices. It has required planning and administrative capacity rarely seen in statehouses, county courthouses and city halls.

Deficiencies in all of these areas have frustrated accomplishment of many of the important goals set by the President and the Congress.

In recent years serious efforts have been made to improve program coordination. During the 1961-1965 period, almost 20 executive orders were issued for the coordination of federal programs involving intergovernmental administration. Some two dozen interagency committees have been established to coordinate two or more federal aid programs. Departments have been given responsibility to lead others in areas within their particular competence—OEO, in the poverty field, HUD in Model Cities. Yet, despite these and other efforts, the Federal Government has not yet been able to join talent, funds and programs for concentrated impact in the field. Few agencies are able to put together a comprehensive package of related programs to meet priority needs.

There is a clear and compelling requirement for better coordination of federally funded programs, particularly those designed to benefit the residents of the inner city. If essential programs are to be preserved and expanded, this need must be met.

The Commission's Recommendations

We do not claim competence to chart the details of programs within such complex and interrelated fields as employment, welfare, education and housing. We do believe it is essential to set forth goals and to recommend strategies to reach these goals.

That is the aim of the pages that follow. They contain our sense of the critical priorities. We discuss and recommend programs not to commit each of us to specific parts of such programs but to illustrate the type and dimension of action needed.

Much has been accomplished in recent years to formulate new directions for national policy and new channels for national energy. Resources devoted to social programs have been greatly increased in many areas. Hence, few of our program suggestions are entirely novel. In some form, many are already in effect.

All this serves to underscore our basic conclusion: the need is not so much for the government to design new programs as it is for the nation to generate new will. Private enterprise, labor unions, the churches, the foundations, the universities— all our urban institutions—must deepen their involvement in the life of the city and their commitment to its revival and welfare.

Objectives for National Action

Just as Lincoln, a century ago, put preservation of the Union above all else, so should we put creation of a true union —a single society and a single American identity—as our major goal. Toward that goal, we propose the following objectives for national action:

- Opening up all opportunities to those who are restricted by racial segregation and discrimination, and eliminating all barriers to their choice of jobs, education and housing.
- Removing the frustration of powerlessness among the disadvantaged by providing the means for them to deal with the problems that affect their own lives, and by increasing the capacity of our public and private institutions to respond to these problems.
- Increasing communication across racial lines to destroy stereotypes, to halt polarization, to end distrust and hostility, and to create common ground for efforts toward common goals of public order and social justice.

There are those who oppose these aims as "rewarding the rioters." They are wrong. A great nation is not so easily intimidated. We propose these aims to fulfill our pledge of equality and to meet the fundamental needs of a democratic, civilized society—domestic peace, social justice, and urban centers that are citadels of the human spirit.

There are others who say that violence is necessary—that fear alone can prod the nation to act decisively on behalf of racial minorities. They too are wrong. Violence and disorder compound injustice; they must be ended and they will be ended.

Our strategy is neither blind repression nor capitulation to lawlessness. Rather it is the affirmation of common possibilities, for all, within a single society.

I. Employment

Introduction

Unemployment and underemployment are among the most persistent and serious grievances of our disadvantaged minorities. The pervasive effect of these conditions on the racial ghetto is inextricably linked to the problem of civil disorder.

In the Employment Act of 1946, the United States set for itself a national goal of a useful job at a reasonable wage for all who wish to work. Federal expenditures for manpower development and training have increased from less than $60 million in 1963 to $1.6 billion in 1968. The President has proposed a further increase to $2.1 billion in 1969 to provide work experience, training and supportive services for 1.3 million men and women. Despite these efforts, and despite sustained general economic prosperity and growing skill demands of automated industry, the goal of full employment has become increasingly hard to attain.

Today there are about two million unemployed, and about ten million underemployed, 6.5 million of whom work full time and earn less than the annual poverty wage.

The most compelling and difficult challenge is presented by some 500,000 "hard-core" unemployed who live within the central cities, lack a basic education, work not at all or only from time to time, and are unable to cope with the problems of holding and performing a job. A substantial part of this group is Negro, male, and between the ages of approximately 18 and 25. Members of this group are often among the initial participants in civil disorders.

A slum employment study by the Department of Labor in 1966 showed that, as compared with an unemployment rate for all persons in the United States of 3.8 percent, the unemployment rate among 16 to 19 year-old nonwhite males was 26.5 percent, and among 16 to 24 year-old nonwhite males 15.9 percent. Data collected by the Commission in cities where there were racial disorders in 1967 indicate that Negro males between the ages of 15 and 25 predominated among the rioters. More than 20 percent of the rioters were unemployed; and many of those who were employed worked in intermittent, low status, unskilled jobs—jobs which they regarded as below their level of education and ability.

In the riot cities which we surveyed, Negroes were three times as likely as whites to hold unskilled jobs, which are often part time or seasonal, and "dead end"—a fact that's as significant for Negroes as unemployment.

Goals and Objectives

We propose a comprehensive national manpower policy to meet the needs of both the unemployed and the underemployed. That policy will require:

• Continued emphasis on national economic growth and job creation so that there will be jobs available for those who are newly trained, without displacing those already employed.

- Unified and intensive recruiting to reach those who need help with information about available job, training and supportive aids.
- Careful evaluation of the individual's vocational skills, potentials and needs; referral to one or more programs of basic education, job training and needed medical, social and other services; provision for transportation between the ghetto and outlying employment areas, and continued follow-up on the individual's progress until he no longer needs help.
- Concentrated job training efforts, with major emphasis on on-the-job training by both public and private employers, as well as public and private vocational schools and other institutional facilities.
- Opening up existing public and private job structures to provide greater upward mobility for the underemployed, without displacing anyone already employed at more advanced levels.
- Large-scale development of new jobs in the public and private sectors to absorb as many as possible of the unemployed, again without displacement of the employed.
- Stimulation of public and private investment in depressed areas, both urban and rural, to improve the environment, to alleviate unemployment and underemployment and, in rural areas, to provide for the poor alternatives other than migration to large urban centers.
- New kinds of assistance for those who will continue to be attracted to the urban centers, both before and after they arrive.
- Increasing small business and other entrepreneurial opportunities in poverty areas, both urban and rural.

Basic Strategies

To achieve these objectives, we believe the following basic strategies should be adopted:

- Existing programs aimed at recruiting, training and job development should be consolidated according to the function they serve at the local, state and federal levels, to avoid fragmentation and duplication.

We need comprehensive and focused administration of a unified group of manpower programs.

- High priority should be placed on the creation of new jobs in both the public and private sectors.

In the public sector a substantial number of such jobs can be provided quickly, particularly by government at the local level, where there are vast unmet needs in education, health, recreation, public safety, sanitation, and other municipal services. The National Commission on Technology, Automation, and Economic Progress estimated that there are 5.3 million potential jobs in public service. But the more difficult task is to provide jobs in private industry for the hard-core unemployed. Both strategies must be pursued simultaneously, with some arrangements for a flow of trainees from public sector jobs to on-the-job training in private companies.

● Creation of jobs for the hard-core unemployed will require substantial payments to both public and private employers to offset the extra costs of supportive services and training.

Basic education and counseling in dress, appearance, social relationships, money management, transportation, hygiene and health, punctuality, and good work habits—all of which employers normally take for granted—may have to be provided. Productivity may be low for substantial periods.

● Special emphasis must be given to motivating the hard-core unemployed.

A sure method for motivating the hard-core unemployed has not yet been devised. One fact, however, is already clear from the experience of the Job Corps, Neighborhood Youth Corps, and Manpower Development and Training projects: the previously hard-core unemployed trainee or employee must understand that he is not being trained for or offered a "dead-end" job. Since, by definition, he is not eligible even for an entry-level position, he must be given job training. He must be convinced that, if he performs satisfactorily, after the training period he will be employed and given an opportunity to advance, if possible, on a clearly defined "job ladder," with step increases in both pay and responsibility.

● Artificial barriers to employment and promotion must be removed by both public agencies and private employers.

Racial discrimination and unrealistic and unnecessarily high minimum qualifications for employment or promotion often have the same prejudicial effect. Government and business must consider for each type of job whether a criminal record should be a bar, and whether a high school diploma is an inflexible prerequisite. During World War II, industry successfully employed large numbers of the previously unemployed and disadvantaged by lowering standards and by restructuring work patterns so that the job fit the level of available skills. We believe that too often government, business and labor unions fail to take into account innate intelligence and aptitudes which are not measurable.

Present recruitment procedures should be reexamined. Testing procedures should be revalidated or replaced by work sample or actual job tryouts. Applicants who are rejected for immediate training or employment should be evaluated and counseled by company personnel offcers and referred to either company or public remedial programs. These procedures have already been initiated in the steel and telephone industries.

● Special training is needed for supervisory personnel.

Support needed by the hard-core unemployed during initial job experience must be provided by specially-trained supervisors. A new program of training entry-level supervisors should be established by management, with government assistance if necessary.

Suggested Programs

We are proposing programs in six areas in order to illustrate how we believe the basic strategies we have outlined can be put into effect:

● Consolidating and concentrating employment efforts.
● Opening the existing job structure.
● Creating one million new jobs in the public sector in three years.
● Creating one million new jobs in the private sector in three years.
● Developing urban and rural poverty areas.
● Encouraging business ownership in the ghetto.

● CONSOLIDATING AND CONCENTRATING EMPLOYMENT EFFORTS

RECRUITMENT

There is an urgent need for a comprehensive manpower recruitment and services agency at the community level. The Federal-State Employment Service is not serving this function in many urban areas and cannot do so unless it is substantially restructured and revitalized. This was recommended in 1965 by the Employment Service Task Force but has been only partially achieved by the Employment Services' new Human Resources Development Program.

We believe that every city should establish such a comprehensive agency, with authority to direct the coordination of all manpower programs, including those of the Employment Service, the community action agencies, and other local groups.

The Concentrated Employment Program established by the Department of Labor last year and now operating in the ghettos of 20 cities and in two rural areas is an important beginning toward a unified effort at the local level. A related effort by the Department of Housing and Urban Development is under way in the Model Cities Program, now in the planning stage in some 63 cities.

PLACEMENT

In order to match men to jobs, we need more effective interchange of information. A computerized nationwide service should be established, as recommended in 1966 by the National Commission on Technology, Automation, and Economic Progress, with priority of installation given to the large urban centers.

An information system of this sort would simplify placement—including inter-area placement and placement from ghetto to suburb. This in turn will often require transportation assistance and counseling.

The existing experimental mobility program, under the Manpower Development and Training Act, should be greatly expanded, and should support movement from one part of a metropolitan area to another. Aid to local public transportation under the Mass Transportation Program should be similarly expanded on the basis of an existing experiment with subsidies for routes serving ghetto areas.

Job development and placement in private industry is critical to our proposed strategies, and is now handled separately by a variety of agencies and programs: the Manpower Development and Training Act program, the vocational education programs, the Vocational Rehabilitation program, the Job Corps and, recently, the Neighborhood Youth Corps and several new adult work experience and training programs. All seek to place trainees with private employers, sometimes with and sometimes without training assistance, through a wide variety of local agencies, as well as through the Employment Service, community action agencies and others.

A single cooperative national effort should be undertaken with the assistance of business, labor and industrial leaders at national, regional and local levels. It should reach both individual companies and trade associations, systematically and extensively, with information about incentive programs and aids, and with authority to negotiate contractual arrangements and channel incentive funds to private employers.

The recently created Urban Coalition, with its local affiliates, brought together many of the interested parties in the private sector. The National Alliance of Businessmen just established by the President will be concentrating private industry efforts in on-the-job training of the hard-core unemployed. We believe that it may be helpful now to create a federally-chartered corporation with authority to undertake the coordination of the private sector job program outlined below.

● OPENING THE EXISTING JOB STRUCTURE

Arbitrary barriers to employment and promotion must be eliminated.

Federal, state and local efforts to ensure equal opportunity in employment should be strengthened by:

(a) Including federal, state and local government agencies as employers covered by Title VII of the 1964 Civil Rights Act, the federal anti-discrimination-in-employment law, which now covers other employers of 50 or more employees (and as of July, 1968 will cover employers of 25 or more employees), labor unions, and employment agencies.

(b) Granting to the Equal Employment Opportunity Commission, the federal enforcement agency under Title VII, cease and desist power comparable to the enforcement power now held by other federal agencies administering regulatory national policies.

(c) Increasing technical and other assistance now provided through the Equal Employment Opportunity Commission to state and local anti-discrimination commissions under the provisions of Title VII.

(d) Undertaking, through the Equal Employment Opportunity Commission, an industry and areawide enforcement effort based not only upon individual complaints but upon employer and union reports showing broad patterns of discrimination in employment and promotion.

(e) Linking enforcement efforts with training and other aids to employers and unions, so that affirmative action to hire and promote may be encouraged in connection with investigations of both individual complaints and charges of broad patterns of discrimination.

(f) Substantially increasing the staff and other resources of the Equal Employment Opportunity Commission to enable it to perform effectively these additional functions.

Equal opportunity for employment by federal contractors under Executive Order 11246 should be enforced more vigorously against both employers and unions. This is particularly critical in regard to federal construction contracts. Staff and other resources of the Office of Contract Compliance in the Department of Labor should be increased so that withholding federal contracts is made a meaningful sanction.

The efforts of the Department of Labor to obtain commitments from unions to encourage Negro membership in apprenticeship programs are especially noteworthy and should be intensified.

Title VI of the 1964 Civil Rights Act, which provides for

withholding federal grant-in-aid funds from activities which discriminate on grounds of color or race, should be supported fully, particularly in regard to recruitment for federally-assisted job training in hospitals, universities, colleges and schools. The staff and other resources of the Department of Health, Education and Welfare, which has primary jurisdiction over these functions, should be expanded for this purpose.

The federal government, through the Civil Service Commission and other agencies, should undertake programs of recruitment, hiring and on-the-job training of the disadvantaged and should reexamine and revalidate its minimum employment and promotion standards. In this regard the federal government should become a model for state and local government and the private business community. To enlist the full cooperation of federal agencies, they should be reimbursed by internal allowances for the extra costs of training disadvantaged employees.

One way to improve the condition of the under-employed, on a national basis, would be to increase the federal minimum wage and widen its coverage. The recent increase to $1.60 per hour yields an annual wage only slightly above the poverty level and only for those employed full time. As an alternative, we recommend consideration be given to an experimental program of wage supplements or other methods for achieving the same income goals.

● CREATING ONE MILLION NEW JOBS IN THE PUBLIC SECTOR IN THREE YEARS

Existing public employment programs should be consolidated and substantially increased. The Neighborhood Youth Corps last year involved approximately 300,000 youths between the ages of 14 and 22 in three programs of work experience. NYC offers either full-time positions year-round or during the summer, or part-time positions during the school year. Several similar but considerably smaller public employment programs involve chronically unemployed adults, generally in subprofessional community betterment work: Operation Mainstream in small towns and rural areas; New Careers and Special Impact in urban areas; and Work Experience and Training for Welfare recipients under the 1967 Amendments to Title IV of the Social Security Act.

Emphasis in the expanded public employment programs should be shifted, so far as possible, from work experience to on-the-job training, and additional federal assistance, above the present payment of 90 percent of wages, should be provided to pay for the additional costs of training and supportive services

420

to trainees. Federal assistance should be scaled so that it does not terminate abruptly; the public employer should pay a progressively larger share of the total cost as trainees' productivity increases.

Emphasis should also be placed on employing trainees to improve run-down neighborhoods and to perform variety of other socially useful public services which are not "make-work," including Community Service Officers in police departments, as recommended by the President's Commission on Law Enforcement and Administration of Justice and as discussed above in Chapter 11.

Public employers should be required to pay on-the-job trainees not less than the minimum wage or the prevailing wage in the area for similar work, whichever is higher. We recommend a three-year program, aimed at creating 250,000 new public service jobs in the first year and a total of one million such jobs over the three-year period.

The Department of Defense should (a) continue its emphasis on (and consider expansion of) "Project 100,000" under which it accepts young men with below standard test scores; (b) intensify its recruiting efforts in areas of high unemployment so that young men living there are fully aware of the training and service opportunities open to them and (c) substantially expand Project Transition which began on a pilot basis in 1967 and involves training and counseling for servicemen scheduled to return to civilian life.

- CREATING ONE MILLION NEW JOBS IN THE PRIVATE SECTOR IN THREE YEARS [1]

Eighty-four percent of the nation's 73 million civilian workers are at work in 11.5 million private enterprises. The involvement of only 5 percent of all private companies would represent the use of more than 500,000 enterprises and provide a massive additional spur to job development.

Based on experience with training by private employers, primarily under the Manpower Development and Training Act, our recommendations are aimed at inducing a substantially expanded number of companies to hire and train the hard-core unemployed.

Recruitment and referral of the disadvantaged unemployed should be undertaken by a public body such as the manpower service agency we have already described. The manpower service agency would determine eligibility and certify a chronically unemployed person for on-the-job training by issuing to him a

[1] The text of the report to the Commission by its Advisory Panel on Private Enterprise is set forth as an appendix to this Report.

certificate of eligibility or similar identifying document. This would entitle the private employer to reimbursement for certain costs. A similar technique was used under the G. I. Bill for training veterans of World War II and the Korean conflict.

The direct reimbursement system currently used in on-the-job training programs should be expanded and the existing programs should be consolidated under a single administration. These programs include the Manpower Development and Training Act and the new Work Training in Industry components of the Neighborhood Youth Corps, New Careers and Special Impact programs. Under these programs a federal agency contracts to reimburse each employer for a negotiated average cost of training and supportive services for each trainee.

If a corporation is chartered by Congress to serve as the government's primary instrument for job development in the private sector, the corporation, through regional and local subsidiaries, would:

(a) systematically work with trade groups, companies and labor unions;
(b) arrange for any necessary supportive services and prevocational educational training which employers are unable to provide; and
(c) enter into contracts with employers providing for their reimbursement for the extra costs of training.

The employer would of course undertake not to dismiss existing employees in order to hire trainees; to provide job training along with supportive services: and to give reasonable assurance that the employee would be fairly promoted if he successfully completed his training period.

To serve as an incentive to widespread business involvement the average amount of the reimbursement must exceed substantially the approximately $1,000 per year payment now made under federal on-the-job training programs and, for the hard-core unemployed, should at least equal the $3,500 recommended by the President in his Manpower Message of January 23, 1968.

An additional and potentially lower cost method of stimulating on-the-job training and new job creation for the hard-core unemployed is through a tax credit system, provided that guidelines are adopted to ensure adequate training and job retention. The Commission believes this alternative holds promise. With respect to the tax credit device, we note that since its enactment in 1962 the existing 7 percent incentive credit for investment in new equipment and machinery has been highly successful as a technique for reaching a large number of individual enterprises to effectuate a national policy. During the 1962-65 period the credit was taken on 1,239,000 corporate tax returns representing new investment in the amount of approximately $75 billion.

To assure comparable simplicity in administration, the tax credit should be geared to a fixed amount for each certificated employee hired and retained at least for a six-month period, with decreasing credits for retention for additional periods totaling another 18 months. No credit would be allowed if existing employees are displaced, or if the turnover rate among certificated employees during each period exceeds more than twice the employer's usual turnover rate.

The corporation chartered by Congress would establish performance guidelines, compare and evaluate the results of job training operations by contract and under the tax credit and arrange to share with all participating employers the experiences of other companies with techniques for training the hardcore unemployed and holding them on the job.

The Commission recommends a three-year program, aimed at creating 300,000 new private sector jobs in the first year and a total of one million such jobs over the three-year period, provided that the tax credit is enacted at an early date. If the tax credit is not so enacted, a realistic goal would be 150,000 such jobs in the first year and one million jobs over a three to five-year period.

● DEVELOPING URBAN AND RURAL POVERTY AREAS [2]

A tax credit should also be provided for the location and renovation of plants and other business facilities in urban and rural "poverty areas," as already defined jointly by several federal departments and agencies.

The existing incentive tax credit for investment in new equipment (but not for real property or plant) is available without regard to where the investment is made. For investment in poverty areas, the existing credit should be increased substantially and extended to investments in real property and plant, whether for the construction of a new plant or the acquisition of an existing facility. Plant and equipment in these areas should also be eligible for rapid amortization, within as little as five years.

These incentives would be designed to attract to the poverty areas the kind of industrial and commercial development which would create new jobs and provide other economic benefits for

[2] The Commission invites particular attention to Chapters 3 and 4 of "The People Left Behind," a Report by the President's National Advisory Commission on Rural Poverty, September, 1967.

the disadvantaged community surrounding the enterprise. An employer eligible for the poverty area investment credit would also be eligible—if he employed certificated trainees—for the hard-core employment credit. The two credits are designed to meet separate needs and different costs to investors and employers.

To begin an intensified national effort to improve rural economic conditions and to stem the flow of migration from these areas to large urban centers, the new investment credit should also be available for firms investing or expanding in rural poverty areas.

The authority and the resources of the Economic Development Administration should be enlarged to enable it to expand its operations into urban poverty areas on a substantial scale.

● ENCOURAGING BUSINESS OWNERSHIP IN THE GHETTO

We believe it is important to give special encouragement to Negro ownership of business in ghetto areas. The disadvantaged need help in obtaining managerial experience and in creating for themselves a stake in the economic community. The advantages of Negro entrepreneurship also include self-employment and jobs for others.

Existing Small Business Administration equity and operating loan programs, under which almost 3,500 loans were made during fiscal year 1967, should be substantially expanded in amount, extended to higher risk ventures and promoted widely through offices in the ghetto. Loans under Small Business Administration guarantees, which are now authorized, should be actively encouraged among local lending institutions.

Counseling and managerial assistance should also be provided. The new Department of Commerce program under which Negro small businessmen are assisted in creating associations for pooling purchasing power and sharing experience, should be expanded and consolidated with the Small Business Administration loan program. The Interracial Council for Business Opportunity and other private efforts to provide counseling by successful businessmen outside the ghetto should be supported and enlarged.

II. EDUCATION

Introduction

Education in a democratic society must equip the children of the nation to realize their potential and to participate fully in

American life. For the community at large, the schools have discharged this responsibility well. But for many minorities, and particularly for the children of the racial ghetto, the schools have failed to provide the educational experience which could help overcome the effects of discrimination and deprivation.

This failure is one of the persistent sources of grievance and resentment within the Negro community. The hostility of Negro parents and students toward the school system is generating increasing conflict and causing disruption within many city school districts.

But the most dramatic evidence of the relationship between educational practices and civil disorder lies in the high incidence of riot participation by ghetto youth who had not completed high school. Our survey of riot cities found that the typical riot participant was a high school dropout. As Superintendent Briggs of Cleveland testified before the Commission:

> "Many of those whose recent acts threaten the domestic safety and tear at the roots of the American democracy are the products of yesterday's inadequate and neglected inner-city schools. The greatest unused and underdeveloped human resources in America are to be found in the deteriorating cores of America's urban centers."

The bleak record of public education for ghetto children is growing worse. In the critical skills—verbal and reading ability—Negro students fall further behind whites with each year of school completed. For example, in the metropolitan Northeast Negro students on the average begin the first grade with somewhat lower scores on standard achievement tests than white, are about 1.6 grades behind by the sixth grade, and have fallen 3.3 grades behind white students by the twelfth grade.[3] The failure of the public schools to equip these students with basic verbal skills is reflected in their performance on the Selective Service Mental Test. During the period June 1964-December 1965, 67 percent of Negro candidates failed the examination. The failure rate for whites was 19 percent.

The result is that many more Negro than white students drop out of school. In the metropolitan North and West, Negro students are more than three times as likely as white students to drop out of school by age 16-17.[4] As reflected by the high unemployment rate for graduates of ghetto schools and the

[3] "Equality of Educational Opportunity," U. S. Department of HEW, Office of Education (1966), p. 20. This report, generally referred to as the "Coleman Report," was prepared pursuant to Section 402 of the Civil Rights Act of 1964.

[4] The actual nonenrollment rate for Negro students in these areas is 20 percent, as opposed to 6 percent for white students. Coleman Report, p. 31.

even higher proportion of employed workers who are in low-skilled, low-paid jobs, many of those who do graduate are not equipped to enter the normal job market, and have great difficulty securing employment.[5]

Several factors have converged to produce this critical situation.

Segregation

The vast majority of inner-city schools are rigidly segregated. In 75 major central cities surveyed by the U.S. Commission on Civil Rights in its study, "Racial Isolation in the Public Schools," 75 percent of all Negro students in elementary grades attended schools with enrollments that were 90 percent or more Negro. Almost 90 percent of all Negro students attended schools which had a majority of Negro students. In the same cities, 83 percent of all white students in those grades attended schools with 90 to 100 percent white enrollments.

Racial isolation in the urban public schools is the result principally of residential segregation and widespread employment of the "neighborhood school" policy, which transfers segregation from housing to education. The effect of these conditions is magnified by the fact that a much greater proportion of white than Negro students attend private schools. Studies indicate that in America's twenty largest cities approximately four out of ten white students are enrolled in nonpublic schools, as compared with only one out of ten Negro pupils. The differential appears to be increasing.[6]

Segregation in urban schools is growing. In a sample of 15 large Northern cities, the Civil Rights Commission found that the degree of segregation rose sharply from 1950 to 1965. As Negro enrollments in these 15 cities grew, 97 percent of the increase was absorbed by schools already over 50 percent Negro and 84 percent by schools more than 90 percent Negro.[7] By 1975, it is estimated that, if current policies

[5] Employment figures reflect discriminatory practices as well. The contribution of inadequate education to unemployment, while not quantified, is clearly substantial.

[6] "Big City School Desegregation: Trends and Methods," Dentler and Elsbery, National Conference on Equal Educational Opportunity, November, 1967, p. 3.

[7] While the proportion of Negroes attending all-Negro schools in Southern and border states has declined in the 14 years since the Supreme Court's school desegregation decision, the number of Negro students attending schools with all or nearly all Negro enrollments has risen. "Racial Isolation in the Public Schools," p. 10.

and trends persist, 80 percent of all Negro pupils in the twenty largest cities, comprising nearly one-half of the nation's Negro population, will be attending 90 to 100 percent Negro schools.[8]

Segregation has several major effects that have acted to reduce the quality of education provided in schools serving disadvantaged Negro neighborhoods.

Most of the residents of these areas are poor. Many of the adults, the product of the inadequate, rural school systems of the South,[9] have low levels of educational attainment. Their children have smaller vocabularies, and are not as well equipped to learn rapidly in school—particularly with respect to basic literary skills—as children from more advantaged homes.

When disadvantaged children are racially isolated in the schools, they are deprived of one of the more significant ingredients of quality education: exposure to other children with strong educational backgrounds. The Coleman Report and the Report of the Civil Rights Commission establish that the predominant socio-economic background of the students in a school exerts a powerful impact upon achievement. Further, the Coleman Report found that "if a minority pupil from a home without much educational strength is put with schoolmates with strong educational backgrounds, his achievement is likely to increase."[10]

Another strong influence on achievement derives from the tendency of school administrators, teachers, parents and the students themselves to regard ghetto schools as inferior. Reflecting this attitude, students attending such schools lose confidence in their ability to shape their future. The Coleman Report found this factor—destiny control—"to have a stronger relationship to achievement than . . . all the 'school' factors together" and to be "related, for Negroes, to the proportion of whites in the schools."[11]

In other words, both class and race factors have a strong

[8] "Big City School Desegregation: Trends and Methods," *supra*.

[9] The poor quality of education offered in these schools, located in the most poverty stricken section of the country, is attested to by the fact that "the 12th-grade Negro in the nonmetropolitan South is 0.8 standard deviation below—or, in terms of years, 1.9 years behind—the Negro in the Metropolitan Northeast . . . " Coleman Report, p. 21.

[10] This finding was limited to performance of students from minority groups. The Coleman Report states:
"if a white pupil from a home that is strongly and effectively supportive of education is put in a school where most pupils do not come from such homes, his achievement will be little different than if he were in a school composed of others like himself." p. 22

[11] Coleman Report, p. 23.

bearing on educational achievement; the ghetto student labors under a double burden.

Teachers

The schools attended by disadvantaged Negro children commonly are staffed by teachers with less experience and lower qualifications than those attended by middle-class whites.[12] For example, a 1963 study ranking Chicago's public high schools by the socio-economic status of surrounding neighborhoods found that in the 10 lowest-ranking schools only 63.2 percent of all teachers were fully certified and the median level of teaching experience was 3.9 years. In three of these schools, the median level was one year. Four of these lowest ranking schools were 100 percent Negro in enrollment and three were over 90 percent Negro. By contrast eight of the ten highest ranking schools had nearly total white enrollments, and the other two were more than 75 percent white. In these schools, 90.3 percent of the teachers were fully certified and the median level of teaching experience was 12.3 years.

Testifying before the Commission, Dr. Daniel Dodson, Director of the New York University Center for Human Relations and Community Services, stated that:

"Inner-city schools have not been able to hold teaching staff. Between 1952 and 1962 almost half the licensed teachers of New York City left the system. Almost two out of every five of the 50,000 teaching personnel of New York City do not hold regular permanent licenses for the assignments they have.

"In another school system in one of the large cities, it was reported of one inner-city school that of 84 staff members, 41 were temporary teachers, 25 were probationaries and 18 [were] tenure teachers. However, only one of the tenure teachers was licensed in academic subjects."

U.S. Commissioner of Education, Harold Howe, testified that many teachers are unprepared for teaching in schools serving disadvantaged children, "have what is a traumatic experience there and don't last." Moreover, the more experi-

[12] The Civil Rights Commission's survey found no major national differences in the educational attainment (years completed) of teachers in majority-Negro or majority-white schools. However, many large cities did not take part in the basic studies which supplied the data for this conclusion. It is precisely in these cities that teachers of disadvantaged Negro students tend to be the least experienced. Moreover, the Commission did conclude that Negro students, more often than whites, had teachers with non-academic college majors and lower verbal achievement levels.

enced teachers normally select schools in white neighborhoods, thereby relegating the least experienced teachers to the disadvantaged schools. This process reinforces the view of ghetto schools as inferior.

As a result, teachers assigned to these schools often begin with negative attitudes toward the students, and their ability and willingness to learn. These attitudes are aggravated by serious discipline problems, by the high crime rates in areas surrounding the schools, and by the greater difficulties of teaching students from disadvantaged backgrounds. These conditions are reflected in the Coleman Report's finding that a higher proportion of teachers in schools serving disadvantaged areas are dissatisfied with their present assignments and with their students than are their counterparts in other schools.[13]

Studies have shown that the attitudes of teachers toward their students have very powerful impacts upon educational attainment. The more teachers expect from their students— however disadvantaged those students may be—the better the students perform. Conversely, negative teacher attitudes act as self-fulfilling prophecies: the teachers expect little from their students; the students fulfill the expectation. As Dr. Kenneth Clark observed, "Children who are treated as if they are uneducable invariably become uneducable."[14]

In disadvantaged areas, the neighborhood school concept tends to concentrate a relatively high proportion of emotionally disturbed and other problem children in the schools. Disadvantaged neighborhoods have the greatest need for health personnel, supplementary instructors and counsellors to assist with family problems, provide extra instruction to lagging students and deal with the many serious mental and physical health deficiencies that occur so often in poverty areas.

These conditions which make effective teaching vastly more difficult, reinforce negative teacher attitudes. A 1963 survey of Chicago public schools showed that the condition creating the highest amount of dissatisfaction among teachers was lack of adequate provision for the treatment of maladjusted, retarded and disturbed pupils. About 79 percent of elementary school teachers and 67 percent of high school teachers named this item as a key factor. The need for professional support for teachers in dealing with these extraordinary problems is seldom, if ever, met.

Although special schools or classes are available for emo-

[13] Coleman Report, p. 12.

[14] Dr. Kenneth Clark, *Dark Ghetto*, Harper & Row, New York (1965), p. 128.

tionally disturbed and mentally handicapped children, many pupils requiring such help remain in regular classes because of negligence, red tape or unavailability of clinical staff. An example is provided by a National Education Association Study of Detroit:[15]

> Before a disturbed child can receive psychological assistance, he must receive diagnostic testing. But before this happens, the teacher must fill in a form . . . to be submitted . . . to a central office committee . . . If the committee decides that psychological testing is in order, the teacher must fill out a second form . . . to be submitted to the psychological clinic. The child may then be placed on the waiting list for psychological testing. The waiting period may last for several weeks, several months, or several years. And while he waits, he 'sits in' the regular classroom . . . Since visiting teachers are scarce and special classes insufficient in number, the child who has been tested is usually returned to the regular classroom to serve more time as a 'sit-in.'

Teaching in disadvantaged areas is made more difficult by the high rate of student turnover. In New York City during 1963-1964, seven of ten students in the average, segregated Negro-Puerto Rican elementary school either entered or left during the year.[16] Similar conditions are common to other inner-city schools. Continuity of education becomes exceedingly difficult—the more so because many of the students entering ghetto schools during the school year come from rural southern schools and are behind even the minimum levels of achievement attained by their fellow northern-born students.

Enrollments

In virtually every large American city, the inner city schools attended by Negroes are the most overcrowded. We have cited the vast population exchange—relatively affluent whites leaving the city to be replaced by Negroes—which has taken place over the last decade. The impact on public education facilities has been severe.

Despite an overall decrease in the population of many cities, school enrollment has increased. Over the last 15 years, Detroit has lost approximately 20,000 to 30,000 families. Yet during that same period the public school system gained approximately 50,000 to 60,000 children. Between 1961 and 1965, Detroit's Negro public school enrollment increased by 31,108, while white enrollment dropped 23,748. In Cleveland

---

[15] "Detroit, Michigan: A Study of Barriers to Equal Educational Opportunity in a Large City," National Commission on Professional Rights and Responsibilities of the National Education Association of the United States, March, 1967, p. 66.

[16] The comparable rate in the white schools was four out of ten.

430

between 1950 and 1965, a population loss of 130,000 coincided with a school enrollment increase of 50,000. Enrollment gains in New York City and Chicago were even larger.

Although of lesser magnitude, similar changes have occurred in the public school systems of many other large cities. As white students withdraw from a public school, they are replaced by a greater number of Negro students. This reflects the fact that the Negro population is relatively younger, has more children of school age, makes less use of private schools, and is more densely concentrated than the white population.

As a result, Negro school enrollments have increased even more rapidly than the total Negro population in central cities. In Cincinnati, for example, between 1960 and 1965 the Negro population grew 16 percent, while Negro public school enrollment increased 26 percent.[17] The following data for four other cities illustrate how the proportion of Negroes in public schools has outgrown the Negro proportion of the total city population.[18]

Negro Population and Public School Enrollment

	Negro % of Population			Negro % of Public School Enrollment		
	1950	1965	Change	1950	1965	Change
Atlanta	36.6	43.5	+ 6.9	39.1	53.7	+14.6
Milwaukee	3.5	10.8	+ 7.3	6.6	22.9	+16.3
Oakland	12.4	30.0	+17.6	14.0	45.0	+31.0
Washington	35.0	55.0	+20.0	50.1	89.4	+39.3

Negroes now comprise a majority or near majority of public school students in seven of the ten largest American cities, as well as in many other cities. The following table illustrates the percentage of Negro students for the period 1965-1966 in the public elementary schools of 42 cities, including the 28 largest, 17 of which have Negro majorities:

[17] Cincinnati report for U. S. Commission on Civil Rights, pp. 8-9, 11.

[18] Figures for Atlanta, Milwaukee and Oakland are from their reports to the Civil Rights Commission: Atlanta, pp. 2-3, 25; Milwaukee, pp. 19, 37, 42; Oakland, pp. 7, 11-15A; and the Bureau of the Census. Washington figures are from the District of Columbia Board of Education.

Proportion of Negro Students in Total Public
Elementary School Enrollment, 1965-1966

City	Percent Negro
Washington, D.C.	90.9%
Chester, Pa.	69.3
Wilmington, Del.	69.3
Newark	69.1
New Orleans	65.5
Richmond	64.7
Baltimore	64.3
East St. Louis	63.4
St. Louis	63.3
Gary	59.5
Philadelphia	58.6
Detroit	55.3
Atlanta	54.7
Cleveland	53.9
Memphis	53.2
Chicago	52.8
Oakland	52.1
Harrisburg	45.7
New Haven	45.6
Hartford	43.1
Kansas City	42.4
Cincinnati	40.3
Pittsburgh	39.4
Buffalo	34.6
Houston	33.9
Flint	33.1
Indianapolis	30.8
New York City	30.1
Boston	28.9
San Francisco	28.8
Dallas	27.5
Miami	26.8
Milwaukee	26.5
Columbus	26.1
Los Angeles	23.4
Oklahoma City	21.2
Syracuse	19.0
San Antonio	14.2
Denver	14.0
San Diego	11.6
Seattle	10.5
Minneapolis	7.2

Source: U. S. Commission on Civil Rights,
"Racial Isolation in the Public Schools."

Because this rapid expansion of Negro population has been concentrated in segregated neighborhoods, ghetto schools have experienced acute overcrowding. Shortages of textbooks and supplies have developed. Double shifts are common; hallways and other non-classroom space have been adapted for class instruction; and mobile classroom units are used. Even programs for massive construction of new schools in Negro neighborhoods cannot always keep up with increased overcrowding.

From 1951 to 1963, the Chicago Board of Education built 266 new schools or additions, mainly in all-Negro areas. Yet a special committee studying the schools in 1964 reported that 40 percent of the Negro elementary schools had more than 35 students per available classroom, as compared to 12 percent of the primarily white elementary schools. Of the eight Negro high schools, five had enrollments over 50 percent above designed capacity. Four of the 10 integrated high schools, but only four of the 26 predominantly white high schools, were similarly overcrowded. Comparable conditions prevail in many other large cities.

The Civil Rights Commission found that two-thirds of the predominantly Negro elementary schools in Atlanta were overcrowded. This compared with 47 percent of the white schools. In 1965, all Atlanta Negro high schools were operating beyond their designed capacity; only one of three all-white high schools, and six of eight predominantly white schools were similarly overcrowded.[19]

Washington, D. C. elementary schools with 85-100 percent Negro enrollments operated at a median of 115 percent of capacity. The one predominantly white high school operated at 92.3 percent, an integrated high school at 101.1 percent, and the remaining schools—all predominantly Negro—at 108.4 percent to 127.1 percent of capacity.

Overcrowded schools have severe effects on education, the most important of which is that teachers are forced to concentrate on maintaining classroom discipline, and thus have little time and energy to perform their primary function—educating the students.

Facilities and Curricula

Inner-city schools are not only overcrowded, they also tend to be the oldest and most poorly equipped.

In Detroit, 30 of the school buildings still in use in these areas were dedicated during the administration of President Grant.[20] In Cincinnati, although from 1950 to 1965, Negro student population expanded at a faster pace than white, most additional school capacity planned and constructed was in predominantly white areas. According to a Civil Rights Commission report on Cincinnati, the added Negro pupil population was housed, for the most part, in the same central-city schools vacated by the whites.[21]

[19] Atlanta report for Civil Rights Commission, pp. 32-34.
[20] Testimony of Norman Drachler, Superintendent of Schools, Detroit.
[21] Cincinnati report tor the Civil Rights Commission, pp. 21-25.

With respect to equipment, the Coleman Report states that "Negro pupils have fewer of some of the facilities that seem most related to achievement: They have less access to physics, chemistry, and language laboratories; there are fewer books per pupil in their libraries; their textbooks are less often in sufficient supply."[22]

The quality of education offered by ghetto schools is diminished further by use of curricula and materials poorly adapted to the life-experiences of their students. Designed to serve a middle-class culture, much educational material appears irrelevant to the youth of the racial and economic ghetto. Until recently, few texts featured any Negro personalities. Few books used or courses offered reflected the harsh realities of life in the ghetto, or the contribution of Negroes to the country's culture and history. This failure to include materials relevant to their own environment has made students skeptical about the utility of what they are being taught. Reduced motivation to learn results.

Funds

Despite the overwhelming need, our society spends less money educating ghetto children than children of suburban families. Comparing the per capita education costs for ghetto and suburban schools—one educator, in testimony before this Commission, said:

> If the most educated parents with the highest motivated children find in their wisdom that it costs $1,500 per child per year to educate their children in the suburbs, isn't it logical that it would cost an equal amount to educate the less well motivated, low-income family child in the inner city? Such cost would just about double the budget of the average inner-city school system.[23]

Twenty-five school boards in communities surrounding Detroit spent up to $500 more per pupil per year to educate their children than the city. Merely to bring the teacher/pupil ratio in Detroit in line with the state average would require an additional 1,650 teachers at an annual cost of approximately $13 million.[24]

There is evidence that the disparity in educational expenditures for suburban and inner-city schools has developed in parallel with population shifts. In a study of twelve metropolitan areas, the Civil Rights Commission found that, in

[22] Coleman report, pp. 9-12.

[23] Testimony of Dr. Dodson.

[24] Testimony of Norman Drachler, Superintendent of Schools, Detroit.

1950, 10 of the 12 central cities spent more per pupil than the surrounding suburbs; by 1964, in seven of the 12 the average suburb spent more per pupil than the central city in seven.[25]

This reversal reflects the declining or stagnant city tax base, and increasing competition from nonschool needs (police, welfare, fire) for a share of the municipal tax dollar. The suburbs, where nonschool needs are less demanding, allocate almost twice the proportion of their total budgets to education as the cities.[26]

State contributions to city school systems have not had consistent equalizing effects. The Civil Rights Commission found that, although state aid to city schools has increased at a rate proportionately greater than for suburban schools, states continue to contribute more per pupil to suburban schools in seven of the twelve metropolitan areas studied. The following table illustrates the findings:

Revenues per Pupil from State sources

Place	Amount Per Pupil 1950	1964	Percent Increase 1950-64
Baltimore City	$ 71	$171	140.8
Suburbs	90	199	121.1
Birmingham City	90	201	123.3
Suburbs	54	150	177.7
Boston City	19	52	173.7
Suburbs	30	75	150.0
Buffalo City	135	284	110.4
Suburbs	165	270	63.6
Chattanooga City	62	136	119.4
Suburbs	141	152	7.8
Chicago City	42	154	266.6
Suburbs	32	110	243.8
Cincinnati City	51	91	78.4
Suburbs	78	91	16.7
Cleveland City	50	88	76.0
Suburbs	39	88	125.6
Detroit City	135	189	40.0
Suburbs	149	240	61.1
New Orleans City	152	239	57.2
Suburbs	117	259	121.4
St. Louis City	70	131	87.1
Suburbs	61	143	134.4
San Francisco City	122	163	33.6
Suburbs	160	261	63.1

Source: U. S. Commission on Civil Rights, "Racial Isolation in the Public Schools."

[25] "Racial Isolation in the Public Schools," p. 27.
[26] "Racial Isolation in the Public Schools," p. 26.

Federal assistance, while focused on the innercity schools, has not been at a scale sufficient to remove the disparity. In the 1965-1966 school year, federal aid accounted for less than 8 percent of total educational expenditures. Our survey of federal programs in Detroit, Newark and New Haven during the school year 1967-1968 found that a median of approximately half the eligible school population is receiving assistance under Title I of the Elementary and Secondary Education Act (ESEA).

Community-School Relations

Teachers of the poor rarely live in the community where they work and sometimes have little sympathy for the life styles of their students. Moreover, the growth and complexity of the administration of large urban school systems has compromised the accountability of the local schools to the communities which they serve, and reduced the ability of parents to influence decisions affecting the education of their children. Ghetto schools often appear to be unresponsive to the community, communication has broken down, and parents are distrustful of education officials.

The consequences for the education of students attending these schools are serious. Parental hostility to the schools is reflected in the attitudes of their children. Since the needs and concerns of the ghetto community are rarely reflected in educational policy formulated on a citywide basis, the schools are often seen by ghetto youth as being irrelevant.

On the basis of interviews of riot area residents in Detroit, Dr. Charles Smith, of the U.S. Office of Education's comprehensive elementary and secondary education program, testified that "one of the things that came through very clearly to us is the fact that there is an attitude which prevails in the inner city that says in substance we think education is irrelevant."

Dr. Dodson explained this phenomenon as follows:

"This divergence of goals [between the dominant class and ghetto youth] makes schools irrelevant for the youth of the slum. It removes knowledge as a tool for groups who are deviant to the ethos of the dominant society. It tends to destroy the sense of self-worth of minority background children. It breeds apathy, powerlessness and low self-esteem. The majority of ghetto youth would prefer to forego the acquisition of knowledge if it is at that cost. One cannot understand the alienation of modern ghetto youth except in the context of this conflict of goals."

The absence of effective community-school relations has

436

deprived the public education system of the communication required to overcome this divergence of goals. In the schools, as in the larger society, the isolation of ghetto residents from the policy-making institutions of local government is adding to the polarization of the community and depriving the system of its self-rectifying potential.

Ghetto Environment

All of the foregoing factors contribute substantially to the poor performance of ghetto schools. Inadequate and inefficient as these schools are, the failure of the public education system with respect to Negro students cannot fully be appraised apart from the constant and oppressive ghetto environment.

The interaction of the ghetto environment and the schools is well described in the testimony of Superintendent Briggs of Cleveland:

"But what about the child of the ghetto? It is he whom we must save for we cannot afford to lose this generation of young Americans.

"If this child of despair is a young adult, there is a better than a 50 percent chance that he is a high school dropout. He is not only unemployed, but unemployable, without a salable skill. Neither of his parents went beyond the eighth grade. Preschool or nursery school was out of the question when he was four, and when he was five he was placed on a kindergarten waiting list. . . . At six he entered school; but could only attend for half a day because of the big enrollment. . . . During his six years in elementary school, he attended four different schools because the family moved often, seeking more adequate housing for the six children. When he got to high school he wanted vocational training, but none was available.

"The family was on relief and he couldn't afford a good lunch at noon because Cleveland schools at that time were not participating in the federal hot lunch program and the average cost of lunches amounted to 70 cents.

"Of his few friends who were graduated from high school none had found jobs and they couldn't afford to go to college.

"Here he is now, discouraged and without hope—economically incompetent at a time in life when, traditionally, young Americans have entered the economic mainstream as job holders.

"A younger brother, age 9, is now in the fourth grade. He attends a new school, opened in 1964. Though he lives one mile from Lake Erie, he has never seen it. He has never taken a bus ride, except when his class at school went on a field trip. The family still does not subscribe to a daily newspaper. The television set is broken and there is no money to have it repaired. His mother has never taken him downtown shopping.

"He has never been in the office of a dentist and has seen a physician only at the local clinic when he was injured playing in an abandoned house in the neighborhood.

"At home there are no books. His toys, if any, are secondhand. His shoes are too small and his sweat shirt, bought for 25 cents at a rummage sale, bears the insignia of a suburban school system.

"Each morning he looks forward anxiously to the free milk he gets at school because there is no breakfast at home.

"He can't study well at home because of the loud blare of rock-and-roll music from the bar up the street. There are nine bars in his rather compact neighborhood. . . .

"The screaming police siren is a very familiar sound to him for he hears it regularly in his neighborhood, where the crime rate is Cleveland's highest.

"These boys both have better than average intelligence but they are the victims of neglect and are lost in the maze of statistics. Their plight and that of thousands like them in America's ghettos can certainly be considered the most pressing unattended business on America's agenda."

Basic Strategies

To meet the urgent need to provide full equality of educational opportunity for disadvantaged youth, we recommend pursuit of the following strategies:

● Increasing efforts to eliminate de facto segregation.

We have cited the extent of racial isolation in our urban schools. It is great and it is growing. It will not easily to overcome. Nonetheless, we believe school integration to be vital to the well-being of this country.

We base this conclusion not on the effect of racial and economic segregation on achievement of Negro students, although there is evidence of such a relationship; nor on the effect of racial isolation on the even more segregated white students, although lack of opportunity to associate with persons of different ethnic and socio-economic backgrounds surely limits their learning experience.

We support integration as the priority education strategy because it is essential to the future of American society. We have seen in this last summer's disorders the consequences of racial isolation, at all levels, and of attitudes toward race, on both sides, produced by three centuries of myth, ignorance and bias. It is indispensable that opportunities for interaction between the races be expanded. "The problems of this society will not be solved unless and until our children are brought

438

into a common encounter and encouraged to forge a new and more viable design of life." [27]

● Provision of quality education for ghetto schools.

We recognize that the growing dominance of pupils from disadvantaged minorities in city populations will not soon be reversed. No matter how great the effort toward desegregation, many children of the ghetto will not, within their school careers, attend integrated schools.

If existing disadvantages are not to be perpetuated, we must improve dramatically the quality of ghetto education. Equality of results with all-white schools in terms of achievement must be the goal.

We see no conflict between the integration and quality education strategies we espouse. Commitment to the goal of integrated education can neither diminish the reality of today's segregated and unequal ghetto schools nor sanction the tragic waste of human resources which they entail.

Far from being in conflict, the strategies are complementary. The aim of quality education is to compensate for and overcome the environmental handicaps of disadvantaged children. The evidence indicates that integration, in itself, does not wholly achieve this purpose. Assessing his report in light of interpretation by others of its findings, Dr. Coleman concludes that:

> "it is also true that even in socially or racially integrated schools a child's family background shows a very high relation to his performance. The findings of the [Coleman] Report are quite unambiguous on this score. Even if the school is integrated, the heterogeneity of backgrounds with which children enter school is largely preserved in the heterogeneity of their performance when they finish. As the Report indicates, integration provides benefits to the underprivileged. But it takes only a small step toward equality of educational opportunity." [28]

Moreover, most large integrated schools retain a form of ability grouping, normally resulting in resegregation along racial lines. The Civil Rights Commission found that "many Negro students who attend majority-white schools in fact are in majority-Negro classrooms." [29]

In short, compensatory education is essential not only to improve the quality of education provided in segregated ghetto schools, but to make possible both meaningful integration and maximum achievement in integrated schools.

[27] Testimony of Dr. Dodson.
[28] "Towards Open Schools," James S. Coleman, *The Public Interest,* Fall 1967, p. 23.
[29] "Racial Isolation in the Public Schools," p. 162.

Attainment of this goal will require adoption of a comprehensive approach designed to reconstruct the ghetto child's social and intellectual environment, compensate for disadvantages already suffered and provide necessary tools for development of essential literary skills. This approach will entail adoption of new and costly educational policies and practices beginning with early childhood and continuing through elementary and secondary schools. It will require extraordinary efforts to reconnect parents with the schools. It will also require unique experimentation with new methods to bring back into the educational process street-oriented teenagers and subteenagers who have lost all connection with existing school institutions.

- Improving community-school relations.

In an atmosphere of hostility between the community and the schools, education cannot flourish. A basic problem stems from the isolation of the schools from the other social forces influencing youth. Changes in society—mass media, family structure, religion—have radically altered the role of the school. New links must be built between the schools and the communities they serve. The schools must be related to the broader system which influences and educates ghetto youth.

Expansion of opportunities for community and parental participation in the school system is essential to the successful functioning of the inner-city schools.

- Expanding opportunities for higher and vocational opportunities.

To increase the relevance of education to the needs and aspirations of disadvantaged youth and to prepare them for full participation in American society, we recommend expanding opportunities both for higher education and for vocational training.

Suggested Programs

- INCREASING EFFORTS TO ELIMINATE DE FACTO SEGREGATION

  INCREASED AID TO SCHOOL SYSTEMS SEEKING TO ELIMINATE DE FACTO SEGREGATION EITHER WITHIN THE SYSTEM OR IN COOPERATION WITH NEIGHBORING SCHOOL SYSTEMS

Local school boards have experimented with a variety of techniques designed to accomplish desegregation. Among those commonly employed are school pairing, busing, open enrollment, boundary changes, strategic use of site selection, enlargement of attendance areas, and consolidation of schools to overcome racial imbalance. The results have not been uniform. Much appears to depend on the size and racial composition of the city and the attitudes of its suburbs.

Some of the smaller cities have achieved considerable success. In many of our larger cities, however, the population shift earlier described has proceeded so far that integration is not feasible without the active cooperation of suburban communities. In others, distances between the white and Negro populations living within city boundaries make these methods of accomplishing integration unfeasible. While the desegregation technique best suited for it should be determined by each community we believe substantial federal assistance should be provided.

TITLE IV

Under Title IV of the Civil Rights Act of 1964, the U.S. Commissioner of Education is authorized to provide "technical assistance to . . . [state and local education agencies] in the preparation, adoption, and implementation of plans for the desegregation of public schools." However, such aid is not available in support of locally-designed programs to overcome racial imbalance in the schools. Moreover, this program has never been adequately funded, even to accomplish its limited objectives. Applications for Title IV funds have consistently exceeded the amounts requested by the Administration and the far lower sums appropriated by the Congress.

We believe that the Title IV program should be reoriented and expanded into a major federal effort to provide comprehensive aid to support state and local desegregation projects.

To accomplish this purpose, Title IV should become the vehicle for a comprehensive federal construction, technical assistance and operating grant program. Successful implementation of such a program will require repeal of the present statutory prohibition against provision of assistance to support and encourage desegregation through "assignment of students to public schools in order to overcome racial imbalance." To stimulate needed planning, formulation of long-term integration plans by applicant state and local agencies should be required as a condition to receiving assistance. Title IV aid would be available only for projects which promote integrated education in accordance with such plans.

As an additional incentive to integration, the Title IV program might well be modified to provide substantially increased support upon attainment of specified levels of racial integration. Such bonus assistance should be large enough to enable each recipient school to attain a clearly superior quality of education in comparison with non-integrated schools.

EXEMPLARY SCHOOLS

The Title IV program should stimulate development of exemplary city or metropolitan schools offering special courses and programs designed to attract, on a voluntary basis, students of varying racial and socio-economic backgrounds on a full or part-time basis.[30] These model programs should make extensive and imaginative use of resources uniquely available to city schools—the city itself, its museums, galleries, governmental institutions, and other public and private facilities.

To the extent that the quality of city schools influences migration to the suburbs, development of exemplary schools could operate to retain middle-class white families in the city and induce others to return, so increasing opportunities for integration. Through educational planning on a metropolitan basis, fostered by direct federal grants to cooperative planning bodies encompassing city and suburban school districts, opportunities for engaging central-city and suburban students in common educational experiences can be provided.

Specific methods of providing integrated educational experiences under this program could include the following:

- Establishment of major educational magnet schools: depending upon the size and racial character of the city and its suburbs, these schools could serve all the students of a small city, students living in different sections of a large city or subdivisions of a metropolitan area. Special curricula could include intensive instruction or specialized educational programs (for example, science or commerce).
- Establishment of supplemental education centers: these centers would offer specialized facilities and instruction to students from different schools for a portion of the school day. It is most important that courses be developed and scheduled to provide racially integrated educational experiences.

[30] Limited funds have been provided for this purpose under Title III of the Elementary and Secondary Education Act (ESEA). This aspect of the Title III program could be used to supplement the Title IV program here proposed or could be discontinued, releasing limited ESEA funds for other purposes.

Such a reoriented Title IV program could provide support, including construction funds, for communities choosing to develop the promising but costly educational parks now under consideration in several cities.

As contrasted with the magnet schools and supplementary centers described above, educational parks would consolidate or cluster existing schools, thereby broadening attendance areas to bring within the school zone a racially and economically heterogenous population. These parks could be developed in conjunction with metropolitan plans to serve students from the suburbs, as well as the city. Their location should be selected to accomplish this objective.

Because of the economies of size made possible through consolidation, the quality of education offered all of the students attending educational parks could be improved. Problems raised by the size of such institutions could be overcome through inclusion of smaller sub-unit schools and individualized instruction made feasible by educational technology (computers, television) and savings resulting from the school consolidation program.

ELIMINATING DISCRIMINATION IN NORTHERN SCHOOLS

While racial isolation in the urban public schools results largely from residential segregation, there is evidence that racial discrimination also plays a part in reducing opportunities for integration.

For example, the Civil Rights Commission found that, when crowding in certain Cleveland and Milwaukee Negro schools became acute, school authorities began busing students to nearby underutilized white schools, where they were segregated in separate classrooms and luncheon facilities. When Negro residents objected, school officials in Milwaukee canceled busing altogether as "educationally undesirable," even though white students had been bussed and integrated into receiving-school classrooms for years. In Cincinnati, to relieve overcrowding in a Negro school, students were bused past several nearby white schools with available space to a 98 percent Negro school, 5.5 miles away.

The Civil Rights Commission also reported that in many cities school attendance boundaries and location of new schools have been designed to perpetuate racial segregation.

Under Title VI of the Civil Rights Act of 1964, the Congress prohibited federal financial aid to any program or activity which practices racial discrimination.

Federal law requires that Title VI be applied uniformly in all states. Implementing this provision, the Department of Health, Education and Welfare has recently instituted a survey to examine compliance with Title VI in school districts of all 50 states. The Department has made clear that its investigation is not directed at *de facto* segregation arising from reasonable application of neighborhood attendance policies.

We support this survey and urge that it be followed by vigorous action to assure full compliance with federal law in all sections of the country. Sufficient staff and resources should be provided HEW, so that this program can be effectively carried out without reducing the Title VI effort in the South.

● PROVIDING QUALITY EDUCATION IN GHETTO SCHOOLS

IMPROVING THE QUALITY OF TEACHING IN GHETTO SCHOOLS

The teaching of disadvantaged children requires special skills and capabilities. Teachers possessing these qualifications are in short supply. We need a national effort to attract to the teaching profession well-qualified and highly motivated young people, and to equip them to work effectively with disadvantaged students.

The Teacher Corps program is a sound instrument for such an effort. Established by the Higher Education Act of 1965, it provides training in local colleges or universities for college graduates interested in teaching in poverty areas. Corpsmen are assigned to poverty area schools at the request of local school systems and with approval of state education agencies. They are employed by the school system and work in teams headed by experienced teachers.

The National Advisory Council on the Education of Disadvantaged Children and the National Education Association found the Teacher Corps to have succeeded in attracting dedicated young people to the teaching profession, training them to work effectively in poverty areas, and making substantial contributions to the education of students.

The impact of this highly promising program has been severely restricted by limited and late funding. There are now only 1,406 interns and 330 team leaders in the entire nation.

The Teacher Corps should be expanded into a major national program.

The Education Professions Development Act ("EPDA") provides grants and fellowships to attract qualified persons to the field of education, and improve the ability of teachers through advanced training and retraining. The Act also provides funds for institutes and workshops for other educational personnel, including guidance counselors, social workers, teacher aides and administrators. Finally, EPDA offers grants to local educational agencies experiencing critical shortages of teachers and teacher aides.

We recommend that the EPDA program focus on the special need for expanding the supply and improving the quality of teachers working in schools serving disadvantaged students and that it be substantially funded.

Concomitantly teacher training institutions should place major emphasis on preparing teachers for work in schools serving disadvantaged children. Courses should familiarize teacher candidates with the history, culture and learning problems of minority group pupils.

Class work alone, however, cannot be expected adequately to equip future teachers of disadvantaged children. Intensive in-service training programs designed to bring teacher candidates into frequent and sustained contact with inner-city schools are required. Other professionals and non-professionals working in ghetto-related activities—social workers, street workers—could be included as instructors in teacher training programs.

YEAR-ROUND EDUCATION FOR DISADVANTAGED STUDENTS

The present, anachronistic practice of releasing hundreds of thousands of children from a relatively full school schedule to idleness in the summer months is both a substantial factor in producing disorders and a tragic waste of time and facilities. Financing should be provided, through ESEA, for large-scale year-round programs in the disadvantaged areas of our cities. The testimony before this Commission, including that of Cabinet members and public educators, was unanimous in its support of this proposal.

What is needed is not 12 months of the same routine, but innovative programs tailored to total educational needs, and providing a wide range of educational activities (verbal skills, culture and arts, recreation, job training, work experience and camps).

Planning on a 12-month basis will be required. ESEA assistance should be provided through a single grant program (rather than separate 10-month and summer grants) and conditioned on development of year-round educational plans. Technical assistance should be made available for such planning.

As a step toward year-round education, federal funds should be made available for school and camp programs this summer.

The National Advisory Council on Education of Disadvantaged Children studied summer programs set up with ESEA funds and found that they offer special opportunities for new approaches to teaching disadvantaged children.

Summer camp programs offer significant educational and recreational opportunities, and should be encouraged. Educational components, particularly verbal-skills projects, should be incorporated. It is essential that federal aid for such projects be committed well before the end of this school year, so that adequate time is available to design effective programs.

EARLY CHILDHOOD EDUCATION

Early childhood education is the very heart of the effort to reconstruct the environment which incapacitates disadvantaged children educationally, even before they enter the school system. Comprehensive preschool programs are essential to overcome the early language deprivation and conceptual disabilities of these children. Yet no more than 40 percent of the eligible school population in most disadvantaged central-city areas is receiving even one year (age 4) of preschool training.

We believe that the time has come to build on the success of the Head Start and other preschool programs in order to bring the benefits of comprehensive early childhood education to all children from disadvantaged homes, and to extend the reach to younger children. For this purpose, the Office of Economic Opportunity should receive substantially increased funds.

Effective implementation of this expanded program will be vital to its success. We recommend the following guidelines:

● Early childhood education programs should provide comprehensive educational support tailored to the needs of the child, and should not be simply custodial care. Both day care and Head Start components are part of comprehensive early childhood education; each should be designed to overcome the debilitating effect on learning ability of a disadvantaged environment.
● Parents and the home environment have a critical impact on a child's early development. Early childhood programs should involve parents and the home, as well as the child. This can be accomplished through community education classes, and use of

446

community aides and mothers' assistants. To reduce the incidence of congenital abnormalities, these community-based programs should be tied in with prenatal training.

- Since adequate facilities are scarce in many disadvantaged communities, where schools are overcrowded, and other buildings deteriorated, the program should provide funds for special early childhood education facilities.
- There is a need for maximum experimentation and variety. Funding should continue to support early childhood programs operated by community groups and organizations, as well as by the school system.
- Early childhood education programs should include provisions for medical care and food, so that the educational experience can have its intended impact.

IMPROVING EDUCATIONAL PRACTICES—ELEMENTARY SCHOOLS

Without major changes in educational practices, greater expenditures on existing elementary schools serving disadvantaged neighborhoods will not significantly improve the quality of education. Moreover, current assessments of preschool programs indicate that their gains are lost in the elementary grades, unless the schools themselves are improved.

We suggest adoption of the following educational practices to improve school performance:

- Extra incentives for highly qualified teachers working in ghetto and economically and culturally deprived rural area schools. The most effective means to attract such teachers is to make these schools exciting and attractive places to work. The recommended practices set forth below contribute toward this end. In addition, we suggest that opportunities for creative and imaginative teaching be expanded by allowing the teacher greater discretion in selection and presentation of materials. Such an approach is likely to produce benefits in terms of attraction and retention of excellent teachers and improved student performance. Rewards related to attainment of career objectives should be provided for teachers working in schools serving disadvantaged children. For example, all school systems should consider requiring service in such schools as a condition to advancement to administrative positions, where the experience gained would be of great value.
- Reduction in maximum class size: It is clear that disadvantaged students require more attention and exert greater demands on teacher time than middle-class students. While reduction of class size may not in itself improve pupil achievement, it will free teachers to devote more time to educating disadvantaged students. It is of vital importance, therefore, that efforts to reduce the maximum class size in schools serving disadvantaged students be coupled with programs designed to improve the skills and capacities of teachers of disadvantaged children.
- Recognition of the history, culture and contribution of minority groups to American civilization in the textbooks and curricula of

447

all schools: In addition, school curricula should be adapted to take advantage of student experiences and interests in order to stimulate motivation.

- Provision of supplementary services in the schools for severely disadvantaged or disturbed students: Such services should be made available within the schools, rather than at centralized facilities, and should include medical and psychiatric care.

- Individualized instruction through extensive use of nonprofessional personnel: There is impressive evidence that these workers can make a meaningful educational contribution by providing individualized tutoring and incentive lacking in segregated schools.

In the Homework Helper program in New York City, pupils in the fourth through sixth grades were tutored after school by senior high school students. Tutoring was provided four afternoons a week under the supervision of a master teacher; the tutors received training on the fifth day. Initiated with a grant from the Ford Foundation primarily to provide employment for high school students, the program had significant educational impact on both the pupils and the tutors.

The Neighborhood Youth Corps and the College Work-Study programs provide the tools for reproducing this program in every major city. In some cities, NYC students are already working in these schools. But in many, NYC job assignments are far less stimulating. Colleges and universities should be encouraged to assign more students participating in the College Work-Study program to tutorial projects.

Both programs, NYC and College Work-Study should be expanded and reoriented for this purpose.

- Intensive concentration on basic verbal skills: A basic problem in schools in large cities is the low achievement in the fundamental subjects of students from disadvantaged areas. This has been documented in the HARYOU Studies in New York, the study prepared for the McCone Commission following the Watts riot of 1965 and nationally in the Coleman Report. The lack of reading and writing ability affects detrimentally every other aspect of the later school program. Intensive assistance in literacy skills, including remedial assistance, should be provided in all schools serving disadvantaged children.

We recognize that the enrichment programs we recommend will be very costly. ESEA provides financial assistance for such programs, but the amounts available do not match the need. To make a significant improvement in the quality of education provided in schools serving disadvantaged students, ESEA funding should be substantially increased from its current level.

In addition, Title I should be modified to provide for greater concentration of aid for school districts having the greatest proportion of disadvantaged students. This can be accomplished by altering the formula governing eligibility to exclude affluent school districts with less than specified minimum levels of poor students.

Many of the educational practices recommended with respect to the elementary schools are applicable at the secondary level. In addition, secondary school students require extensive guidance, counseling and advice in planning their education program and future careers. Such assistance, routinely provided by middle-class families, is lacking for the ghetto student. To promote its acceptance, indigenous personnel—college students, returning Vietnam veterans—should be utilized.

The new Stay in School program, for which the President recently requested an appropriation of $30 million, could provide funds for this and other projects designed to motivate disadvantaged high school students to pursue their education. We recommend that this program be fully funded.

INTENSIVE NATIONAL PROGRAM TO INCREASE VERBAL SKILLS OF GHETTO RESIDENTS

For the products of the ghetto schools, many of them unemployed and functionally illiterate, these efforts will come too late. To compensate for educational disadvantages already incurred, we recommend a substantial appropriation to support an intensive year-round program beginning in the summer of 1968 to improve the verbal skills of people in low-income areas, with primary emphasis on the language problems of minority groups.

The present effort simply does not match the need. Current estimates indicate that there are approximately 16,300,000 educationally disadvantaged Americans (those who have less than an 8th grade education). While exact figures are not available, it is highly likely that a disproportionate number of the educationally disadvantaged are Negroes. Census data establishes that 36.9 percent of Negroes over 25 years of age, but only 14.8 percent of whites, are functionally illiterate.

The principal federal literacy program—Adult Basic Education—is meeting only a small fraction of this need; as of June 1966, it had provided assistance to some 373,000 people.

The Adult Basic Education program is a sound instrument for implementing an intensive literacy program. By affording both the public schools and community-based organizations the opportunity to conduct literacy projects, this program provides desired flexibility. It should be strengthened and expanded to make a major impact on illiteracy.

To concentrate its effect where the need is greatest and the potential payoff high, we suggest that priority be given to the unemployed and underemployed, and to welfare mothers. Increasing the literacy levels of these groups would eliminate a major barrier to productive employment, and improve support for education in the home.

The high school dropouts should be brought into the program by lowering the age limit from 18 to 16, as proposed by the President. Course offerings should be expanded to include matters of interest and concern to residents of low-income areas.

EXPANDED EXPERIMENTATION, EVALUATION, AND RESEARCH

Much remains to be learned about the most effective methods of teaching disadvantaged children in schools segregated by race and class. Research efforts should be increasingly oriented in this direction.

In addition to research, federal support should be provided for promising, but as yet unvalidated, experimental programs designed to involve the talents and resources of the entire community in support of education of disadvantaged children, and develop new and better educational techniques particularly adapted to the interests and needs of these students.

Among the educational approaches which we believe should be considered and evaluated are the current efforts to develop new patterns of education (such as storefront schools and street academies) for students who do not fit the traditional pattern, possible forms of competitive education (such as the use of businesses, universities and neighborhood corporations as subcontractors for the operation of certain education programs), concentration of assistance to a few schools serving ghetto children in order to test the effects of a maximum compensatory education effort, development of model experimental subsystems (high school and several feeder schools to provide specialized instruction) and teaching English as a second language to ghetto students whose dialect often constitutes a first language.

Finally, there is great need to evaluate not only these experimental programs but the entire enrichment effort. The Elementary and Secondary Education Act should be amended to require recipient school systems to undertake a thorough evaluation of their compensatory education effort, as a condition to receiving ESEA funds.

● IMPROVING COMMUNITY-SCHOOL RELATIONS

COMMUNITY PARTICIPATION IN THE EDUCATIONAL PROCESS SHOULD BE ENCOURAGED

The school systems of our largest cities have become highly

centralized, with decision-making responsibility for a large and disparate population concentrated in a central board of education. While this process has produced substantial benefits—city-wide tax base and nonpolitical administration—it has sometimes entailed serious sacrifices in terms of accountability and community participation. What is necessary is to preserve the worthwhile features present in the existing system while eliminating the liabilities thus far encountered. The objective must be to make public education more relevant and responsive to the community, and to increase support for it in the home.

This can be accomplished through maintaining centralized control over educational standards and the raising of revenue, while decentralizing control over other aspects of educational policy. The precise mix must be determined locally. However, specific mechanisms for seeking the advice and consultation of students and parents such as Parents Advisory Councils or other similar bodies should be adopted.

GHETTO SCHOOLS SHOULD SERVE AS COMMUNITY CENTERS

School facilities should be available during and after normal school hours for a variety of community service functions, delivery of social services by local agencies (including health and welfare), adult and community training and education programs, community meetings, recreational and cultural activities Decentralization and the establishment of Parents Advisory Councils will afford the community a means through which to communicate needs for such services and to play an active role in shaping activities. In addition to making better use of the major capital investment in school plants, this approach will encourage ghetto residents to regard their schools not as alien institutions but as vital community centers.

USE OF LOCAL RESIDENTS AS TEACHER AIDES AND TUTORS

We have noted the educational gains accomplished through use of local, subprofessional personnel in the schools. These workers can contribute to improving community-school relations by providing a close link between the school system and the parents.

RESULTS OF ACHIEVEMENT AND OTHER TESTS SHOULD BE MADE PUBLIC ON A REGULAR BASIS

To increase the accountability of the public schools, the

results of their performance should be made available to the public. Such information is available in some, but not all, cities. We see no reason for withholding useful and highly relevant indices of school (but not individual student) performance and recommend that all school systems adopt a policy of full public disclosure.

● EXPANDING OPPORTUNITIES FOR HIGHER EDUCATION

By enactment of the Higher Education Act of 1965, the Congress committed this nation to the goal of equal opportunity for higher education for all Americans, regardless of race or economic circumstance. While progress has been made, this goal, the key to virtually all managerial and professional jobs, remains for the disadvantaged student an unfulfilled promise.

Mr. Harvey Oostdyck, Educational Director of the New York Urban League, testified that less than one percent of the youth in Harlem go to college. In the nation, approximately eight percent of disadvantaged high school graduates, many of whom are Negro, attend college; the comparable figure for all high school graduates is more than 50 percent.

The fundamental reasons for this disparity lie in the cost of higher education and the poor quality of the elementary and secondary education available to minorities. In the preceding sections, we have recommended programs which we believe will ultimately eliminate these differences. But the full effect of these changes will not be felt for some years. In the interim, if we are to provide equality of opportunity for that segment of disadvantaged youth with college potential, special programs are needed.

EXPANSION OF UPWARD BOUND AND ESTABLISHMENT OF SPECIAL ONE-YEAR POSTGRADUATE COLLEGE PREPARATORY SCHOOLS

The Upward Bound program of the Office of Economic Opportunity, under which students from poverty backgrounds attend intensive six to eight week summer sessions on college campuses and receive special assistance throughout the school year, is designed to motivate and prepare disadvantaged youth for college. The program has been effective. Of the 23,000 students covered in 1967 (52 percent of whom were Negro), 83 percent went on to college. However, the size of the Upward Bound program is far short of the need. Estimates indicate that some 600,000 poverty-area students could usefully be included.

We believe that the Upward Bound concept is sound and recommend that the program be substantially expanded.

Even an expanded Upward Bound program will not compensate for the poor level of secondary school education attained by ghetto youth. We recommend that federal funds be available for special one-year educational programs with the function of providing college preparatory training for disadvantaged youth. These programs could be operated by community colleges or local boards of education.

REMOVING FINANCIAL BARRIERS TO HIGHER EDUCATION

The effort to assist qualified but needy young people to obtain a higher education should be strengthened and expanded.

Through the Educational Talent Search program, the Federal Government provides financial assistance to public and nonprofit agencies to identify and encourage disadvantaged young people with college potential to enter or re-enter educational programs. The President's proposed Educational Opportunity Act of 1968 would provide combined grant, work and loan aid to poor college-bound students in need of financial assistance. Such assistance should be sufficiently flexible and substantial to accommodate the differing needs of individual students.

These programs can make an important contribution to realization of the goal set by the President in his 1968 Education Message to the Congress "that every qualified young person . . . have all the education he wants and can absorb." If this promise is to become a reality, these programs must be funded at a level commensurate with need.

The benefit gained by increasing opportunities for disadvantaged students to seek and obtain higher education can be amplified by providing incentives for college-trained public service personnel (particularly, teachers and health workers) needed to work in poverty areas. This can be accomplished by providing for the cancellation of loans at a reasonable annual rate, if the recipient works in a low-income area. Such a forgiveness feature is included in the National Defense Education Act loan program.

● EXPANDING OPPORTUNITIES FOR VOCATIONAL EDUCATION

Despite substantially increased efforts made possible by the Vocational Education Act of 1963, quality vocational education is still not available to all who need it. The recent report of the Advisory Council on Vocational Education, established to evaluate the Act, concluded that, although five out of six youths never achieve a college education, only a quarter of the total high school population in the country received vocational education. Similarly, a 1964 Labor Department survey found that less than one-half of the non-college-trained labor force had any formal preparation for the jobs they held.

Existing vocational training programs are not effectively linked to job opportunities. The Advisory Council found "little evidence of much effort to develop programs in the area where critical manpower shortages exist"—examples are the health occupations and technical fields.[31]

The special need of the dropout is still being neglected. With an unemployment rate for Negro youth more than twice that for white youth, this need is particularly acute.

To improve the quality and expand the availability of vocational education, provision of additional funds as recommended by the Advisory Council may well be required. The federal vocational education program should be strengthened by enactment of the proposed Partnership for Learning and Earning Act of 1968.

Significant improvement of vocational education, however, will depend on the use made locally of federal and other funds. We suggest the following guidelines:

- Inclusion of intensive literacy training: literacy skills are obviously indispensable to productive employment. All vocational education programs should provide literacy training, either directly or in conjunction with Adult Basic Education or other programs.
- Greater emphasis on part-time cooperative education programs combining formal instruction and on-the-job training through use of release time: the Advisory Council found that these programs, which provide students with jobs upon completion of the course, are the best available in the vocational education field. They consistently yield high placement records, high employment stability and high job satisfaction. The most important factor in improving vocational education is that training be linked to available jobs with upward mobility potential. To accomplish this goal, the active cooperation of the business community in defining job needs and effective training practices should be fully engaged. Consideration should be given to releasing students to attend pretraining Opportunities Industrialization Centers.
- Full implementation of vocational training programs for high school dropouts: the Advisory Council found that assistance available under the Vocational Education Act for the training of this group is not being adequately utilized. The need for doing so is critical.

[31] "Vocational Education: The Bridge Between Man and His Work," Report of the Advisory Council on Vocational Education, 1968, p. 29.

- Elimination of barriers to full participation of ghetto youth in vocational education programs: some vocational schools attempt to improve the quality of their student body and enhance their prestige by raising entrance requirements. This policy eliminates those in greatest need. This practice should be discontinued and support for these students expanded.
- Follow-up support and assistance to ghetto youth receiving vocational training: the Advisory Council reported that "the most successful vocational programs are those which assume responsibility for placing their graduates and thus get feedback on their strengths and weaknesses."[32] Vocational educators should continue to provide counselling and guidance for their students until they have been successfully placed in jobs related to their training.
- Increased training to meet the critical need for more workers in professional, semi-professional and technical fields: demand for public service workers alone exceeds supply by five to one. Preparation of disadvantaged students for these desirable positions should be greatly intensified.

Implementation of These Programs

The Federal Role—The principal burden for funding the programs we have proposed will fall upon the Federal Government. Caught between an inadequate and shrinking tax base and accelerating demands for public expenditures, the cities are not able to generate sufficient financing. Although there is much more that state governments can and should do, the taxing resources available at this level are far from adequate.

The Federal Government has recognized and responded to this need. Federal expenditures for education, training and related services have increased from $4.7 billion in fiscal 1964 to $12.3 billion in fiscal 1969. These figures include aid for preschool, elementary, secondary and higher education, vocational education, work-training and activities not related to the education of disadvantaged students. This network of federal educational programs provides a sound and comprehensive basis for meeting the interrelated educational needs of disadvantaged students. We need now to strengthen that base, as we have proposed, and to build upon it by providing greatly increased federal funds for the education of the disadvantaged.

The State Role—Many states provide more support for suburban and rural schools than for inner-city education systems. Designed at a time when the suburban school systems were poorer than those in the cities, state aid formulas now operate to reinforce existing inequities.

We urge that every state reexamine its present method of allocating funds to local school districts, not merely to provide equal funds for all political subdivisions on a per-pupil

[32] *Ibid.*, p. 62.

basis, but to assure more per-student aid to districts having a high proportion of disadvantaged students. Only if equalization formulas reflect the need to spend larger amounts per pupil in schools predominantly populated by disadvantaged students will state aid be allocated on an equitable basis.

To assist the states in devising equalization formulas which would accomplish this objective, we recommend that the Office of Education develop prototype formulas. Federal programs should require allocation of federal aid to education within each state in accordance with formulas which conform with the criteria set forth above.

We recognize that virtually all school districts need more money than they now receive. Provision of expanded state aid to education may well be justified. Whatever the amounts may be, we believe that allocation should be made in accordance with the standards described above.

Finally, the states and, in particular, the state education agencies, have a key role to play in accomplishing school integration. The states are in a unique position to bring about urban-suburban cooperation and metropolitan planning. We urge that the efforts of state educational agencies in this area be given clear direction through adoption of state-wide, long-term integration plans and intensified through active promotion of such plans.

The Local Role—We have emphasized that more money alone will not suffice. Accomplishment of the goal of meaningful educational opportunity for all will require exercise of enlightened and courageous leadership by local government. The programs which we have proposed can succeed only if imaginative and effective use is made locally of funds provided by Federal and State governments. Mayors, city councils, school boards and administrators must lead the community toward acceptance of policies which promote integration while improving the quality of education in existing, racially segregated schools. The cooperation of their suburban counterparts is no less essential.

This responsibility is not limited to public officials. It is shared by the private community—business leaders, professionals, clergymen, civic organizations. Attainment of the goal of equal and integrated educational opportunity will require the leadership, support, talents and energies of the entire community.

III. The Welfare System

Introduction

The Commission believes that our present system of public assistance contributes materially to the tensions and social disorganization that have led to civil disorders. The failures of the system alienate the taxpayers who support it, the social workers who administer it, and the poor who depend on it. As one critic told the Commission, "The welfare system is designed to save money instead of people and tragically ends up doing neither."

The system is deficient in two critical ways:

First, it excludes large numbers of persons who are in great need, and who, if provided a decent level of support, might be able to become more productive and self-sufficient;

Second, for those who are included, it provides assistance well below the minimum necessary for a humane level of existence, and imposes restrictions that encourage continued dependency on welfare and undermine self-respect.

In short, while the system is indispensable simply because for millions—mostly children—it supports basic needs, drastic reforms are required if it is to help people free themselves from poverty.

The existing welfare programs are a labyrinth of federal, state and local legislation. Over 90 percent of national welfare payments are made through programs that are partly or largely federally funded. These reach an average of 8 million persons each month:

- 2.8 million are over 65, blind or otherwise severely handicapped.
- 3.9 million are children in the Aid for Dependent Children (AFDC), whose parents do not or cannot provide financial support.
- 1.3 million are the parents of children on AFDC. Of these, over one million are mothers and less than 200,000 are fathers; about two-thirds of the fathers are incapacitated. Only 60,000 fathers are in the special program called "Aid to Families with Dependent Children (Unemployed Parents)" (AFDC-UP) operating in 22 states.

Among all welfare programs, AFDC and AFDC-UP have clearly the greatest impact on youths and families in central cities areas; for this reason, they will be the principal focus for discussion here.

States and local governments contribute an average of about 45 percent of the cost of supporting the AFDC program, with each state setting the level of grants for its own residents.

457

Accordingly, monthly payments vary widely from state to state. They range from $9.30 per AFDC recipient monthly in Mississippi to a high of $62.55 in New York. In fiscal year 1967, the total annual cost of the AFDC program, including federal, state and local contributions, was approximately $2.0 billion, providing an average of about $36 monthly for each recipient.

This sum is well below the poverty subsistence level under almost any standard. The National Advisory Council on Public Welfare has commented:

> "The national average provides little more than half the amounts admittedly required by a family for subsistence; in some low-income states, it is less than a quarter of that amount. The low public assistance payments contribute to the perpetuation of poverty and deprivation that extend into future generations."

Over the last six years, despite the longest sustained period of economic progress in the history of this country, the AFDC caseload has risen each year while the unemployment rate has fallen. Cases increased nationally by 319,000 during fiscal year 1967 and will, under present HEW estimates, increase by another 686,000 during fiscal year 1968. The burden of welfare—and the burden of the increases—will fall principally on our central cities. In New York City alone, 525,000 people receive AFDC support and 7,000 to 10,000 more are added each month. And it is estimated that in 1965, nationwide, over 50 percent of persons eligible to receive assistance under welfare programs were not enrolled.[33]

In addition to the AFDC program, almost all states have a program of general assistance to provide minimum payments based largely or entirely on need. During calendar year 1966, the states spent $336 million on general assistance. No federal funds have ever been available for this program. In fact, no federal funds have ever been available for the millions of unemployed or underemployed men or women in the United States who are in need but are neither aged, severely handicapped nor the parents of minor children.

The dimension of the "pool" of poor but unassisted individuals and families—either ineligible under present programs or eligible but unenrolled—is indicated by the fact that in 1966 there were 21.7 million nonaged persons in the United States with incomes below the "poverty level" as defined by the Social Security Administration. Only a third of these received assistance from major public welfare programs:

[33] Testimony before the Commission of Lisle C. Carter, Jr., Assistant Secretary for Individual and Family Services, Department of Health, Education and Welfare.

458

"[T]he bulk of the nonaged poor live in families where there is a breadwinner who works either every day or who had worked a part of the year, so that the picture that people have of who the poor are is quite a different thing from an analysis of the poverty population. And what we have done in effect is carve out, because of our categorical approach to public assistance, a certain group of people within that overall poverty population to give help to.

"Seventy per cent of the nonaged poor families were headed by men, and 50 per cent of these held full-time jobs and 86 per cent of them worked at least part of the year, so that the typical poor family is much like the typical American family, except they don't make enough money. And they have been historically excluded from the AFDC program."[84]

The gaps in coverage and low levels of payments are the source of much of the long-term dissatisfaction with the system. The day-to-day administration of the system creates even sharper bitterness and dissatisfaction, because it repeatedly serves to remind recipients that they are considered untrustworthy, ungrateful, promiscuous and lazy. Among the most troublesome statutory requirements, administrative practices and regulations are the following:

First, in most states benefits are available only when a parent is absent from the home. Thus, in these states an unemployed father whose family needs public assistance in order to survive, must either abandon his family or see them go hungry. This so-called "Man-in-the-House" rule was intended to prevent payments to children who have an alternative potential source of support. In fact, the rule seems to have fostered the breakup of homes and perpetuated reliance on welfare. The irritation caused by the rule is aggravated in some states by regular searches of recipients' homes to ferret out violations.

Second, until recently all amounts earned by adult welfare recipients on outside jobs, except for small allowances for expenses, were deducted directly from the welfare payments they would otherwise have received. This practice, required by federal law, appears to have taken away from many recipients the incentive to seek part- or full-time employment. The 1967 amendments to the welfare laws permit retention of the first $30 earned by a recipient each month and one-third of all earnings above that amount. This is a start in the right direction but does not go nearly far enough. New York City has, for example, begun experimenting with a promising program that allows welfare mothers to keep the first $85 of earnings each month and a percentage of amounts above that.

Third, in most states, there is a residency requirement, generally averaging around a year, before a person is eligible

[84] *Ibid.*

to receive welfare. These state regulations were enacted to discourage persons from moving from one state to another to take advantage of higher welfare payments. In fact, they appear to have had little, if any, impact on migration and have frequently served to prevent those in greatest need—desperately poor families arriving in a strange city—from receiving the boost that might give them a fresh start.

Fourth, though large amounts are being spent on social service programs for families, children and young people, few of these programs have been effective. In the view of the Advisory Council on Public Welfare, the inadequacies in social services:

> "are themselves a major source of such social evils as crime and juvenile delinquency, mental illness, illegitimacy, multi-generational dependency, slum environments, and the widely deplored climate of unrest, alienation, and discouragement among many groups in the population."

A final example of the system's inadequacy is the brittle relationship that exists between many welfare workers and the poor. The cumulative abrasive effects of the low levels of assistance, the complicated eligibility requirements, the continuing efforts required by regulations to verify eligibility—often by means that constitute flagrant invasions of privacy—have often brought about an adversary relationship between the case worker and the recipient family. This is intensified by the fact that the investigative requirements not only force continuing confrontations but, in those states where the same worker performs both investigative and service functions, leave the worker little time to provide service.

As was stated by Lisle Carter, Assistant Secretary of Health, Education and Welfare, in testimony before the Commission:

> "[W]e think [it] is extremely important that welfare recipients begin to feel that the welfare worker is on their side instead of on the side of the agency. There have been statements made that the welfare workers are among the most hated persons in the ghetto, and one of the studies shows that the recipients tend to feel that what the worker says is something that cannot be challenged. Nowhere do you get the feeling that . . . the worker is there to really go to bat for recipients in dealing with the other pressures that they face in the community. . . ."

One manifestation of the tension and dissatisfaction created by the present system has been the growth of national and local welfare protest groups. Some are seeking to precipitate a national welfare crisis, in part by bringing on the welfare rolls so many new recipients that America will be forced to face the enormity of its poverty problem. Others, often composed of welfare recipients or welfare workers, seek expanded welfare programs and attack day-to-day inequities in the administration of the system.

On the other hand, many Americans who advocate better housing, better schools, and better employment opportunities for disadvantaged citizens oppose welfare programs of all kinds in the belief that they subsidize people who should be working. The fact is, as we have pointed out, that all but a small fraction of welfare recipients are disabled because of age, ill health or the need to care for their children. Even more basic is the fact that the heads of most poor families who can work are working, and are not on welfare. For both of these groups ⌐f people in need—those who cannot work and those who can and do—the problem in at least one vital respect is the same: lack of sufficient income to provide them with the kind of base on which they can begin building a path out of poverty, if not for themselves, at least for their children.

An altered and expanded welfare system by extending support to more of those in need, by raising levels of assistance on a uniform national basis, and by eliminating demeaning restrictions, could begin to recapture the rich human resources that are being wasted by poverty.

Basic Strategies

In framing strategies to attack welfare problems, the Commission recognizes that a number of fundamental questions remain to be answered. Although many of the present inadequacies in the system can be identified, and specific changes recommended, long-term measures for altering the system are still untested.

A first strategy is to learn more about how welfare affects people and what its possibilities for creative use are. We endorse the recommendation of the Advisory Council on Public Welfare for greatly expanded research. We also commend the experimental incentive programs being carried out through the Department of Health, Education and Welfare and the Office of Economic Opportunity, as well as the Model Cities Program through which some cities hope to develop integrated programs of income supplementation, job training and education. We further commend the President's recent creation of a Commission on Income Maintenance Programs, which may provide answers to the complex problems here presented.

Despite the questions left open, we believe that many specific inadequacies in the present structure can and should be corrected.

• The most important basic strategy we would recommend is to overhaul the existing categorical system to:

461

(a) provide more adequate levels of assistance on the basis of uniform national standards.

(b) reduce the burden on state and local government by financing the cost of assistance almost entirely with federal funds.

(c) create new incentives to work and eliminate the features that cause hardship and dependency.

(d) improve family-planning and other social services to welfare recipients.

- Our longer-range strategy, one for which we can offer only tentative guides, is the development of a national system of income supplementation to provide a basic floor of economic and social security for all Americans.

Suggested Programs

Overhauling the Present System

To repair the defects in the existing categorical system is not simply a matter of changing one or two aspects. Major changes are needed in at least seven areas.

- STANDARDS OF ASSISTANCE

The federal government should develop a minimum income standard for individuals and families enrolled in AFDC. The standard for AFDC recipients should be at least as high as the subsistence "poverty" level periodically determined by the Social Security Administration. Only a few states now approach this "poverty" level, which is currently set at $3,335 for an urban family of four. The amending legislation should, if feasible, also permit cost of living variations among the states and within "high-cost" areas in each state.

As a critical first step toward raising assistance levels, the Commission recommends that the present provision under which the federal government pays fifteen-eighteenths of the first $18 of AFDC monthly payments be amended to provide that the federal government assume the entire first $15 and the same proportion of payments beyond $15 presently applied to that above $18. Taken together with existing legislation that requires the states to maintain levels of support when federal assistance rates are increased, the effect of this change would be to raise by over one-third the monthly welfare payments in eight states of the Deep South. In Mississippi, payments would be more than doubled.

- EXTENSION OF AFDC-UP

The Commission strongly urges that the temporary legislation, enacted in 1961, which extends the AFDC programs to include needy families with two unemployed parents be made permanent and mandatory on all states and that the new federal definition of "unemployment" be broadened. This program, which reaches the family while it is still intact, has been put into effect in only 22 states. Even in states where it has been implemented, the numbers participating have been small, partly because many states have narrowly defined the term "unemployment" and partly because the number of broken homes makes many children eligible under the regular form of AFDC.

● FINANCING

Because the states are unable to bear substantially increased welfare costs, the federal government should absorb a far greater share of the financial burden than presently. At least two methods are worth considering. The first would be to rearrange payment formulas so that, even at the highest levels of payments, the federal government absorbed 90 percent or more of the costs. A second method would be to have the federal government assume 100 percent of the increment in costs that would be encountered through raising standards of assistance and rendering AFDC-UP mandatory. Under either of these approaches, the share of costs presently imposed on municipal governments should be removed to release their limited resources for other uses.

● WORK INCENTIVES AND TRAINING

In three important ways, steps were taken in the 1967 amendments to the Federal Welfare Act to encourage—or compel—welfare recipients to seek employment. Each of these controversial steps had some salutary aspects but each requires substantial further attention:

(a) *Job training.* The amendments provide substantially greater funds for job training. This was in principle a wise step. The amendments also, however, require the states to condition grants to "appropriate" adult welfare recipients on their willingness to submit to job training. Though the Commission agrees that welfare recipients should be encouraged to accept employment or job training, we strongly disagree with compelling mothers of small children to work or else lose welfare support. Many mothers, we believe, will want to work. A recent study of about 1,500 welfare mothers in New York indicated that 70 percent of all mothers—and 80 percent of Negro mothers—would prefer to work for pay than stay at home.[35]

[35] Podell, Families on Welfare in New York City, Preliminary Report No. 3, "Mother's Education and Employment," p. 7 (1967).

(b) *Day-care centers for children.* The 1967 amendments provide funds for the first time for day-care programs for children of working mothers. Further expansion is desirable to make centers an effective means of enabling welfare recipients to take advantage of training and employment opportunities. Efforts should be made to ensure that centers are open in the evening and that more education features are built into center programs. State and federal standards that prevent centers from employing subprofessional workers, including welfare recipient mothers, should be removed.

Welfare mothers themselves should be encouraged to set up cooperative centers with one or more mothers tending children of other mothers and with welfare funds available for salaries. Such "living room" day care can only be effective if the mother taking care of the children can be paid without losing any substantial portion of her welfare check.

(c) *Retention of part of earnings.* The amendments permit an AFDC or AFDC-UP recipient to retain the first $30 of earned income monthly and one-third of the balance. Both the sums that can be kept without penalty, and the percentage of the balance that can be retained, should be raised substantially to maximize incentive to work. Some experimental programs are now going forward, but expanded efforts are needed to test different combinations and approaches. These programs should be supported at all levels of government.

● REMOVAL OF FREEZE ON RECIPIENTS

The 1967 welfare amendments freeze, for each state, the percentage of children who can be covered by federal AFDC grants to the percentage of coverage in that state in January 1968. The anticipated effect of this new restriction will be to prevent federal assistance during 1968 to 475,000 new applicants otherwise eligible under present standards. In the face of this restriction, states and cities will have to dig further into already depleted local resources to maintain current levels. If they cannot bear the increased costs, a second alternative, less feasible under existing federal requirements, will be to tighten eligibility requirements for everyone or reduce per capita payments. We strongly believe that none of these alternatives are acceptable, and that the freeze should be eliminated.

● RESTRICTIONS ON ELIGIBILITY

The so-called "Man-in-the-House" rule and restrictions on new residents of states should be eliminated. Though these restrictions are currently being challenged in the courts, we believe that legislative and administrative action should be taken to eliminate them now.

● OTHER FEATURES OF THE SYSTEM THAT SHOULD BE
ALTERED OR STRENGTHENED

(a) *Clear and enforceable rights.* These include prompt determinations of eligibility and rights to administrative appeal with representation by counsel. A recipient should be able to regard assistance as a right and not as an act of charity.

Applicants should be able to establish initial eligibility by personal statements or affidavits relating to their financial situation and family composition, subject to subsequent review conducted in a manner that protects their dignity, privacy and constitutional rights. Searches of welfare recipients' homes, whether with or without consent, should be abandoned. Such changes in procedures would not only accord welfare recipients the respect to which they are entitled but also release welfare workers to concentrate more of their time on providing service. They would also release a substantial portion of the funds spent on establishing eligibility for the more important function of providing support.

(b) *Separation of administration of AFDC and welfare programs for the disabled.* The time that welfare workers have available for the provision of services would be increased further by separating the administration of AFDC and general assistance programs from aid to aged and physically incapacitated. The problems of these latter groups are greatly different and might better be handled, at the federal level, through the Social Security Administration. Any such change would, of course, require that programs for the disabled and aged continue to be paid out of general funds and not impair the integrity of the Social Security Trust Fund.

(c) *Special neighborhood welfare contact and diagnostic centers.* Centers to provide the full complement of welfare services should be combined into the multi-purpose neighborhood service facilities being developed by the Office of Economic Opportunity and the Department of Housing and Urban Development. Federal funds should be provided to help local welfare agencies decentralize their programs through these centers, which would include representatives of all welfare, social, rehabilitation and income-assistance services.

(d) *Expansion of family-planning programs.* Social workers have found that many women in poverty areas would like to limit the size of their families and are either unaware of existing birth control methods, or do not have such methods

465

available to them. Governments at all levels—and particularly the federal—should underwrite broader programs to provide family-planning information and devices to those who desire them. Through such programs, the Commission believes that a significant contribution can be made to breaking the cycle of poverty and dependency.

Toward a National System of Income Supplementation

In 1949, Senator Robert A. Taft described a system to provide a decent level of income for all citizens:

"I believe that the American people feel that with the high production of which we are now capable, there is enough left over to prevent extreme hardship and maintain a minimum standard floor under subsistence, education, medical care and housing, to give to all a minimum standard of decent living and to all children a fair opportunity to get a start in life."

Such a "minimum standard of decent living" has been called for by many other groups and individuals, including the AFL-CIO, major corporate executives, and numerous civil rights and welfare organizations. The study of the new Commission on Income Maintenance Programs, and the Model Cities Program will be of particular importance in providing direction. We believe that efforts should be made to develop a system of income supplementation with two broad and basic purposes:

- To provide for those who can work or who do work, any necessary supplements in such a way as to develop incentives for fuller employment;
- To provide for those who cannot work and for mothers, who decide to remain with their children, a minimum standard of decent living, to prevent deprivation and aid in saving children from the prison of poverty that has held their parents.

Under this approach, then, all present restrictions on eligibility—other than need—would be eliminated. In this way, two large and important groups not covered by present federal programs would be provided for: employed persons working at substandard hours or wages, and unemployed persons who are neither disabled nor parents of minor children.

A broad system of supplementation would involve substantially greater federal expenditures than anything now contemplated. The cost will range widely depending on the standard of need accepted as the "basic allowance" to individuals and families, and on the rate at which additional income above this level is taxed. Yet if the deepening cycle of poverty and dependence on welfare can be broken, if the children of the poor can be given the opportunity to scale the wall that now separates them from the rest of society, the return on this investment will be great indeed.

IV. HOUSING

Introduction

The passage of the National Housing Act in 1934 signalled a new federal commitment to provide housing for the nation's citizens. Fifteen years later Congress made the commitment explicit in the Housing Act of 1949, establishing as a national goal, the realization of "a decent home and suitable environment for every American family."

Today, after more than three decades of fragmented and grossly under-funded federal housing programs, decent housing remains a chronic problem for the disadvantaged urban household. Fifty-six percent of the country's non-white families live in central cities today, and of these, nearly two-thirds live in neighborhoods marked by substandard[36] housing and general urban blight. For these citizens, condemned by segregation and poverty to live in the decaying slums of our central cities, the goal of a decent home and suitable environment is as far distant as ever.

During the decade of the 1950's, when vast numbers of Negroes were migrating to the cities, only 4 million of the 16.8 million new housing units constructed throughout the nation were built in the central cities. These additions were counterbalanced by the loss of 1.5 million central-city units through demolition and other means. The result was that the number of nonwhites living in substandard housing increased from 1.4 to 1.8 million, even though the number of substandard units declined.

Statistics available for the period since 1960 indicate that the trend is continuing. There has been virtually no decline in the number of occupied dilapidated units in metropolitan areas, and surveys in New York City and Watts actually show an increase in the number of such units. These statistics have led the Department of Housing and Urban Development to conclude that while the trend in the country as a whole is toward less substandard housing, "There are individual neighborhoods and areas within many cities where the housing situation continues to deteriorate."[37]

[36] The Department of Housing and Urban Development classifies substandard housing as that housing reported by the United States Census Bureau as (1) sound but lacking full plumbing, (2) deteriorating and lacking full plumbing, or (3) dilapidated.

[37] Hearings before the Subcommittee on Executive Reorganization of the Committee on Government Operations, United States Senate, 89th Congress, 2nd session, August 16, 1966, p. 148.

Inadequate housing is not limited to Negroes. Even in the central cities the problem affects two and a half times as many white as nonwhite households. Nationally, over 4 million of the nearly 6 million occupied substandard units in 1966 were occupied by whites.

It is also true that Negro housing in large cities is significantly better than that in most rural areas—especially in the South. Good quality housing has become available to Negro city dwellers at an increasing rate since the mid-1950's when the postwar housing shortage ended in most metropolitan areas.

Nevertheless, in the Negro ghetto, grossly inadequate housing continues to be a critical problem.

Substandard, Old and Overcrowded Structures

Nationwide, 25 percent of all nonwhites living in central cities occupied substandard units in 1960 compared to 8 percent of all whites. Preliminary Census Bureau data indicate that by 1966, the figures had dropped to 16 and 5 percent respectively. However, if "deteriorating" units and units with serious housing code violations are added, the percentage of nonwhites living in inadequate housing in 1966 becomes much greater.

In 14 of the largest U.S. cities, the proportions of all nonwhite housing units classified as deteriorating, dilapidated, or lacking full plumbing in 1960 (the latest date for which figures are available), were as follows:

City	Percentage of Non-white Occupied Housing Units Classified Deteriorating or Dilapidated, 1960	Percentage of Non-white Occupied Housing Units Classified Deteriorating, Dilapidated, or Sound but Without Full Plumbing, 1960
New York	33.8%	42.4%
Chicago	32.1%	42.8%
Los Angeles	14.7%	18.1%
Philadelphia	28.6%	32.0%
Detroit	27.9%	30.1%
Baltimore	30.5%	31.7%
Houston	30.1%	36.7%
Cleveland	29.9%	33.9%
Washington, D.C.	15.2%	20.8%
St. Louis	40.3%	51.6%
San Francisco	21.3%	34.0%
Dallas	41.3%	45.9%
New Orleans	44.3%	56.9%
Pittsburgh	49.1%	58.9%

Source: U.S. Department of Commerce Bureau of the Census

Conditions were far worse than these city-wide averages in many specific disadvantaged neighborhoods. For example, a study of housing in Newark, New Jersey, before the 1967 disorders, showed the following situation in certain predominantly Negro neighborhoods as of 1960:[38]

Percentage of Housing Units Dilapidated or Deteriorated in Selected Areas of Newark, 1960

Area Number	Population	Percentage Nonwhite	Percentage of All Housing Units Dilapidated or Deteriorating
1	25.300	75.5%	91.0%
2	48,200	64.5%	63.8%
3A	48,300	74.8%	43.1%

These three areas contained 30 percent of the total population of Newark in 1960. and 62 percent of its nonwhite population.

The Commission carried out special analyses of 1960 housing conditions in three cities, concentrating on all Census Tracts with 1960 median incomes of under $3,000 for both families and individuals. It also analyzed housing conditions in Watts. The results showed that the vast majority of people living in the poorest areas of these cities were Negroes, and that a high proportion lived in inadequate housing:

Item	Detroit	Washington D.C.	Memphis	Watts Area of Los Angeles
Total population of study area	162,375	97,084	150,827	49,074
Percentage of study area nonwhite	67.5%	74.5%	74.0%	87.3%
Percentage of Housing Units in study area:				
—Substandard by HUD definition	32.7%	23.9%	35.0%	10.5%
—Dilapidated, deteriorating or sound but lacking full plumbing	53.1%	37.3%	46.5%	29.1%

Source: U.S. Department of Commerce, Bureau of Census

Negroes, on the average, also occupy much older housing than whites. In each of ten metropolitan areas analyzed by the Commission, substantially higher percentages of nonwhites than whites occupied units built prior to 1939.

[38] Source: George Sternlieb, *The Tenement Landlord*, New Brunswick, New Jersey: Rutgers (1966), pp. 238-241.

Percentage of White and Nonwhite Occupied Housing Units
Built Prior to 1939 in Selected Metropolitan Areas

Metropolitan Area	White Occupied Units	Nonwhite Occupied Units
Cleveland	33.2	90.6
Dallas	31.9	52.7
Detroit	46.2	86.1
Kansas City	54.4	89.9
Los Angeles—Long Beach	36.6	62.4
New Orleans	52.9	62.2
Philadelphia	62.0	90.8
Saint Louis	57.9	84.7
San Francisco—Oakland	51.3	67.6
Washington, D.C.	31.9	64.9

Source: U.S. Department of Commerce Bureau of the Census

Finally, Negro housing units are far more likely to be overcrowded than those occupied by whites. In U.S. metropolitan areas in 1960, 25 percent of all nonwhite units were overcrowded by the standard measure (that is, they contained 1.01 or more persons per room). Only 8 percent of all white-occupied units were in this category. Moreover, 11 percent of all nonwhite-occupied units were seriously overcrowded (1.51 or more persons per room), compared with 2 percent for white-occupied units. The figures were as follows in the ten metropolitan areas analyzed by the Commission.

Percentage of White and Nonwhite Occupied Units With 1.01
or More Persons Per Room in Selected Metropolitan Areas

Metropolitan Area	White Occupied Units	Nonwhite Occupied Units
Cleveland	6.9	19.3
Dallas	9.3	28.8
Detroit	8.6	17.5
Kansas City	8.7	18.0
Los Angeles—Long Beach	8.0	17.4
New Orleans	12.0	36.1
Philadelphia	4.9	16.3
Saint Louis	11.8	28.0
San Francisco—Oakland	6.0	19.7
Washington, D.C.	6.2	22.6

Source: U.S. Department of Commerce Bureau of the Census

Higher Rents for Poorer Housing

Negroes in large cities are often forced to pay the same rents as whites and receive less for their money, or pay higher rents for the same accommodations.

The first type of discriminatory effect—paying the same amount but receiving less—is illustrated by data from the 1960 Census for Chicago and Detroit.

In certain Chicago census tracts, both whites and nonwhites paid median rents of $88, and the proportions paying various specific rents below that median were almost identical. But the units rented by nonwhites were typically:

- Smaller (the median number of rooms was 3.35 for nonwhites versus 3.95 for whites).
- In worse condition (30.7 percent of all nonwhite units were deteriorated or dilapidated units versus 11.6 percent for whites).
- Occupied by more people (the median household size was 3.53 for nonwhites versus 2.88 for whites).
- More likely to be overcrowded (27.4 percent of nonwhite units had 1.01 or more persons per room versus 7.9 percent for whites).

In Detroit, whites paid a median rental of $77 as compared to $76 among nonwhites. Yet 27.0 percent of nonwhite units were deteriorating or dilapidated, as compared to only 10.3 percent of all white units.

The second type of discriminatory effect—paying more for similar housing—is illustrated by data from a study of housing conditions in disadvantaged neighborhoods in Newark, New Jersey. In four areas of that city (including the three areas cited previously), nonwhites with housing essentially similar to that of whites paid rents that were from 8.1 percent to 16.8 percent higher. Though the typically larger size of nonwhite households, with consequent harder wear and tear, may partially justify the difference in rental, the study found that nonwhites were paying a definite "color tax" of apparently well over 10 percent on housing. This condition prevails in most racial ghettos.

The combination of high rents and low incomes forces many Negroes to pay an excessively high proportion of their income for housing. This is shown by the following chart, showing the percentage of renter households paying over 35 percent of their incomes for rent in ten metropolitan areas:

Percentages of White and Nonwhite Occupied Units With
Households Paying 35 Percent or More of Their Income
For Rent in Selected Metropolitan Areas

Metropolitan Area	White Occupied Units	Nonwhite Occupied Units
Cleveland	8.6	33.8
Dallas	19.2	33.8
Detroit	21.2	40.5
Kansas City	20.2	40.0
Los Angeles—Long Beach	23.4	28.4
New Orleans	16.6	30.5
Philadelphia	19.3	32.1
Saint Louis	18.5	36.7
San Francisco—Oakland	21.2	25.1
Washington, D.C.	18.5	28.3

Source: U.S. Department of Commerce Bureau of the Census

The high proportion of income that must go for rent leaves less money in such households for other expenses. Undoubtedly, this hardship is a major reason many Negro households regard housing as one of their worst problems.

Discrimination in Housing Code Enforcement

Thousands of landlords in disadvantaged neighborhoods openly violate building codes with impunity, thereby providing a constant demonstration of flagrant discrimination by legal authorities. A high proportion of residential and other structures contain numerous violations of building and housing codes. Refusal to remedy these violations is a criminal offense, one which can have serious effects upon the victims living in these structures. Yet in most cities, few building code violations in these areas are ever corrected, even when tenants complain directly to municipal building departments.

There are economic reasons why these codes are not rigorously enforced. Bringing many old structures up to code standards and maintaining them at that level often would require owners to raise rents far above the ability of local residents to pay. In New York City, rigorous code enforcement has already caused owners to board up and abandon over 2,500 buildings rather than incur the expense of repairing them. Nevertheless, open violation of codes is a constant source of distress to low income tenants and creates serious hazards to health and safety in disadvantaged neighborhoods.

Housing Conditions and Disorder

Housing conditions in the disorder cities surveyed by the Commission paralleled those for ghetto Negroes generally.

Many homes were physically inadequate. Forty-seven percent of the units occupied by nonwhites in the disturbance areas were substandard.

Overcrowding was common. In the metropolitan areas in which disorders occurred, 24 percent of all units occupied by nonwhites were overcrowded, against only 8.8 percent of the white-occupied units.

Negroes paid higher percentages of their income for rent than whites. In both the disturbance areas and the greater metropolitan areas of which they were a part, the median rent as a proportion of median income was over 25 percent higher for nonwhites than for whites.

The result has been widespread discontent with housing conditions and costs. In nearly every disorder city surveyed, grievances related to housing were important factors in the structure of Negro discontent.

Poverty and Housing Deterioration

The reasons many Negroes live in decaying slums are not difficult to discover. First and foremost is poverty. Most ghetto residents cannot pay the rent necessary to support decent housing. This prevents private builders from constructing new units in the ghettos or from rehabilitating old ones, for either action involves an investment that would require substantially higher rents than most ghetto dwellers can pay. It also deters landlords from maintaining units that are presently structurally sound. Maintenance too requires additional investment, and at the minimal rents that inner-city Negroes can pay, landlords have little incentive to provide it.

The implications of widespread poor maintenance are serious. Most of the gains in Negro housing have occurred through the turnover which occurs as part of the "filtering down" process—as the white middle class moves out, the units it leaves are occupied by Negroes. Many of these units are very old. Without proper maintenance, they soon become dilapidated, so that the improvement in housing resulting from the filtering-down process is only temporary. The 1965 New York City survey points up the danger. During the period that the number of substandard units was decreasing, the number of deteriorating units increased by 95,000.

Discrimination

The second major factor condemning vast numbers of Negroes to urban slums is racial discrimination in the housing market. Discrimination prevents access to many nonslum areas, particularly the suburbs, and has a detrimental effect on ghetto housing itself. By restricting the area open to a growing population, housing discrimination makes it profitable for landlords to break up ghetto apartments for denser occupancy, hastening housing deterioration. Further, by creating a "back pressure" in the racial ghettos, discrimination keeps prices and rents of older, more deteriorated housing in the ghetto higher than they would be in a truly free and open market.

Existing Programs

To date, federal building programs have been able to do comparatively little to provide housing for the disadvantaged. In

473

the 31-year history of subsidized federal housing, only about 800,000 units have been constructed, with recent production averaging about 50,000 units a year. By comparison, over a period only three years longer, FHA insurance guarantees have made possible the construction of over ten million middle and upper-income units.

Federal programs also have done little to prevent the growth of racially segregated suburbs around our cities. Until 1949, FHA official policy was to refuse to insure any unsegregated housing. It was not until the issuance of Executive Order 11063 in 1962 that the Agency required nondiscrimination pledges from loan applicants.

It is only within the last few years that a range of programs has been created that appears to have the potential for substantially relieving the urban housing problem. Direct federal expenditures for housing and community development have increased from $600 million in fiscal 1964 to nearly $3 billion in fiscal 1969. To produce significant results, however, these programs must be employed on a much larger scale than they have been so far. In some cases the constraints and limitations imposed upon the programs must be reduced. In a few instances supplementary programs should be created. In all cases, incentives must be provided to induce maximum participation by private enterprise in supplying energy, imagination, capital and production capabilities.

Federal housing programs must also be given a new thrust aimed at overcoming the prevailing patterns of racial segregation. If this is not done, those programs will continue to concentrate the most impoverished and dependent segments of the population into the central-city ghettos where there is already a critical gap between the needs of the population and the public resources to deal with them. This can only continue to compound the conditions of failure and hopelessness which lead to crime, civil disorder and social disorganization.

Basic Strategies

We believe the following basic strategies should be adopted:

● The supply of housing suitable for low-income families should be expanded on a massive basis.

The basic reason many Negroes are compelled to live in inadequate housing is the failure of the private market to produce decent housing at rentals they can afford to pay. Programs we have recommended elsewhere are directed toward raising income levels. Yet it is obvious that in the foreseeable

474

future there will continue to be a gap between the income of many Americans and the price of decent housing produced by normal market mechanisms. Thus, the implementation of the strategy depends on programs which not only generate more lower cost housing, but also raise the rent-paying capability of low-income households.

- Areas outside of ghetto neighborhoods should be opened up to occupancy by racial minorities.

Provision of decent low-cost housing will solve only part of the problem. Equally fundamental is the elimination of the racial barrier in housing. Residential segregation prevents equal access to employment opportunities and obstructs efforts to achieve integrated education. A single society cannot be achieved as long as this cornerstone of segregation stands.

Suggested Programs

We propose programs in ten areas to illustrate how we believe the basic strategies we have outlined can be put into effect:

- Provision of 600,000 low- and moderate-income housing units next year, and 6 million units over the next five years.
- An expanded and modified below-market interest rate program.
- An expanded and modified rent supplement program, and an ownership supplement program.
- Federal write-down of interest rates on loans to private builders.
- An expanded and more diversified public housing program.
- An expanded Model Cities Program.
- A reoriented and expanded urban renewal program.
- Reform of obsolete building codes.
- Enactment of a national, comprehensive and enforceable open-occupancy law.
- Reorientation of federal housing programs to place more low- and moderate-income housing outside of ghetto areas.

The Supply of Housing Suitable for Low-Income Families Should Be Expanded

The Commission Recommends

- PROVISION OF 600,000 LOW- AND MODERATE-INCOME HOUSING UNITS NEXT YEAR, AND 6 MILLION UNITS OVER THE NEXT FIVE YEARS

Some 6 million substandard housing units are occupied in the United States today, and well over that number of families lack sufficient income to rent or buy standard housing, without spending over 25 percent of their income and thus sacrificing other essential needs. The problem promises to become more critical with the expanded rate of family formation on the immediate horizon and the increasing need to replace housing which has been destroyed or condemned.

In our view, the dimension of the need calls for an unprecedented national effort. We believe that the nation's housing programs must be expanded to bring within the reach of low- and moderate-income families 600,000 new and existing units next year, and 6 million units over the next five years.

This proposal can only be implemented if present subsidy programs are extended so that (a) a part of the existing housing inventory can be brought within the reach of lower income families, and (b) private enterprise can become a major factor in the low-cost housing field, both in terms of the construction capabilities of private developers and the capital of private institutional lenders.

In the sections that follow, we discuss specific programs that must be part of this expanded national effort.

● AN EXPANDED AND MODIFIED BELOW-MARKET INTEREST RATE PROGRAM

The below-market interest rate program, which makes long-term, low-interest financing available to nonprofit and limited profit sponsors, is the best mechanism presently available for engaging private enterprise in the task of providing moderate and lower-income housing.

Several limitations, however, prevent the program from providing the quantity of housing that is needed. Nonprofit sponsors are deterred by lack of seed money to finance pre-construction costs, limited profit corporations are deterred by the statutory prohibition on transfer or refinancing of projects for 20 years without FHA permission. Funding levels are inadequate to launch a national program.

We recommend that legislation be enacted to permit interest-free loans to nonprofit sponsors to cover preconstruction costs, and to allow limited profit corporations to sell projects to nonprofit corporations, cooperatives, or condominiums. We also recommend that funding levels of the program be substantially increased.

Though the potential of the program is great, it presently serves few truly low-income families. Current costs average $14,400 per unit, making the typical rental for a two-bedroom unit $110 per month, thereby in effect requiring a minimum annual income of $5,300. Only with rent supplements can poor families afford housing commanding rents of this amount, but the amount of rent supplement funds which can be used in such developments is limited by statute to 5 percent of the total appropriation for the rent supplement program.

In order to make below-market interest rate housing available to low as well as moderate-income families, we recommend that the 5 percent limitation be removed, and that the overall funding of rent supplements be greatly expanded. We also recommend that serious consideration be given to expanding the interest subsidy under the program in order to lower the rate for sponsors.

● AN EXPANDED AND MODIFIED RENT SUPPLEMENT PROGRAM, AND AN OWNERSHIP SUPPLEMENT PROGRAM

The rent supplement program offers a highly flexible tool for subsidizing housing costs, because it permits adjustment of the subsidy according to the income of the tenant. The project financing is at market rates, so that tenants who do not qualify for supplements must pay market rentals. Potentially, therefore, these developments can provide an alternative to public housing for low-income families, while still attracting middle-income families.

We believe, however, that several changes are necessary if the full potential of this program is to be realized.

First, we recommend that existing regulations restricting architectural design, imposing rigid unit cost standards, and limiting tenant income to amounts lower than required by statute be removed. These regulations diminish the attractiveness of the program to private developers, and represent a major barrier to substantial expansion of the program.

Second, the statutory limitation of rent supplements to new or rehabilitated housing should be changed to permit use of rent supplements in existing housing. In many areas, removal of the restriction would make possible a major increase of the program without requiring investment in new construction. This option must be made available if the program is to be expanded to its fullest potential.

Third, the rent supplement concept should be extended to provide home ownership opportunities for low-income families. The ambition to own one's own home is shared by virtually all Americans, and we believe it is in the interest of the nation to permit all who share such a goal to realize it. Home ownership would eliminate one of the most persistent problems facing low-income families in rental housing—poor maintenance by absentee landlords—and would provide many low-income families with a tangible stake in society for the first time.

The Senate Banking and Currency Committee recently approved a bill that would establish a program to pay a portion of the mortgage payments of low-income families seeking to purchase homes. As with rent supplements, subsidy payments would decrease as the purchasers income rose. The income limits of the program—70 percent of the below-market interest rate eligibility limits—would, in our opinion, greatly impair its usefulness and should be eliminated. With that reservation, we strongly endorse the concept, urge that such a program of ownership supplements be enacted, and recommend that it be funded on a basis that will permit its wide use in achieving the goal of 6 million units for low- and moderate-income families over the next five years.

● FEDERAL WRITE-DOWN OF INTEREST RATES ON LOANS TO PRIVATE BUILDERS

To make private loan capital available, we recommend direct federal write-down of interest rates on market rate loans to private construction firms for moderate-rent housing. This program would make it possible for any qualified builder to enter the moderate-rent housing field on the basis of market rate financing, provided that the project meets necessary criteria. The federal government would enter into a contract with the financing institution to supply the difference between the mortgage payment at the market interest rate and 20 percent of the tenant's monthly income, to a specified maximum "write-down" which would make the interest rate paid by the tenant equivalent to 1 or 2 percent.

● AN EXPANDED AND MORE DIVERSIFIED PUBLIC HOUSING PROGRAM

Since its establishment in 1937, the public housing program has produced only some 650,000 low-rent housing units. Insufficient funding has prevented construction of a quantity more suited to the need, and unrealistic unit-cost limitations have mandated that most projects be of institutional design and mammoth size. The resulting large concentration of low-income families has often created conditions generating great resistance in communities to new projects of this type.

We believe that there is a need for substantially more public housing, but we believe that the emphasis of the program should be changed from the traditional publicly-built, slum-based, high-rise project to smaller units on scattered sites. Where traditional high-rise projects are constructed, facilities for social services should be included in the design, and a broad range of such services provided for tenants.

To achieve the shift in emphasis we have recommended, we urge first, expansion of present programs under which public housing authorities lease existing scattered site units. Present statutory restrictions on long-term leasing should be eliminated to provide incentives for private construction and financing. Families whose incomes increase above the public housing limit should be permitted to take over the leases of their units from the housing authority.

We also urge expansion of present "turnkey" programs, under which housing authorities purchase low-rent units constructed by private builders instead of constructing the units themselves. Here too, families whose incomes rise above the public housing limits should be permitted to stay in the units at market rentals.

● AN EXPANDED MODEL CITIES PROGRAM

The Model Cities Program is potentially the most effective weapon in the federal arsenal for a long-term, comprehensive attack on the problems of American cities. It offers a unique means of developing local priorities, coordinating all applicable government programs—including those relating to social development (e.g., education and health) as well as physical development—and encouraging innovative plans and techniques. Its "block grant" multi-purpose funding feature allows the city to deploy program funds with much greater flexibility than is possible under typical categorical grant programs. The statutory requirement that there be widespread citizen participation and maximum employment of area residents in all phases of the program promises to involve community residents in a way we think most important.

The full potential of the program can be achieved, however, only if (a) the Model Cities Program is funded at a level which gives the cities involved an opportunity and incentive to produce significant results, and (b) the various programs which can be brought into play under Model Cities, such as urban renewal, below-market interest rate housing, and health, education and welfare programs, are independently supported at levels which permit Model Cities' funds to be used for essentially innovative purposes. Appropriations must also be sufficient to expand coverage far beyond the 63 cities that are currently funded.

The President has recommended that $1 billion be appropriated for Model Cities. We strongly support this recommendation as a minimum start, noting that a much greater scale of funding will ultimately be necessary if the program proves successful and if it is to be made available to all the cities that require such aid.

● A REORIENTED AND EXPANDED URBAN RENEWAL PROGRAM

Urban renewal has been an extremely controversial program since its inception. We recognize that in many cities it has demolished more housing than it has erected, and that it has often caused dislocation among disadvantaged groups.

Nevertheless, we believe that a greatly expanded, though re-oriented, urban renewal program is necessary to the health of our cities. Urban renewal is an essential component of the Model Cities Program and, in its own right, is an essential tool for any city attempting to preserve social and economic vitality.

Substantially increased funding will be necessary if urban renewal is to become a reality in all the cities in which renewal is needed. A reorienting of the program is necessary to avoid past deficiencies. The Department of Housing and Urban Development has recognized this, and has promulgated policies giving top priority to urban renewal projects that directly assist low-income households in obtaining adequate housing. Projects aimed primarily at bolstering the economic strength of down-town areas, or at creating housing for upper-income groups while reducing the supply of low-cost housing, will have low priority, unless they are part of balanced programs including a strong focus on needs of low-income groups. It is with these priorities in mind that we recommend substantial expansion of the program.

● REFORM OF OBSOLETE BUILDING CODES

Approximately 5,000 separate jurisdictions in the United States have building codes. Many of these local codes are antiquated and contain obsolete requirements that prevent builders from taking advantage of new technology. Beyond the factor of obsolesence, the very variety of the requirements prevents the mass production and standardized design that could significantly lower building costs.

Opinions differ as to whether a uniform national code is yet feasible, but it is clear that much greater uniformity is pos-sible than presently exists. We urge state and local govern-ments to undertake the task of modernizing their codes at once, and recommend that the Department of Housing and Urban Development design, for their guidance, a model na-tional code. We can no longer afford the waste caused by arbitrary and archaic building codes.

Areas Outside of Ghetto Neighborhoods Should Be Opened Up to Occupancy by Racial Minorities

The Commission Recommends

● ENACTMENT OF A NATIONAL, COMPREHENSIVE AND ENFORCE-ABLE OPEN-OCCUPANCY LAW

The federal government should enact a comprehensive and enforceable open-occupancy law making it an offense to discriminate in the sale or rental of any housing—including single family homes—on the basis of race, creed, color, or national origin.

In recent years, various piecemeal attempts have been made to deal with the problem of housing discrimination. Executive Order 11063, issued by President Kennedy in 1962, provided that agreements for federally assisted housing made after the date of the Order must be covered by enforceable nondiscrimination pledges. Congress, in enacting Title VI of the Civil Rights Act of 1964, promulgated a broad national policy of nondiscrimination with respect to programs or activities receiving federal financial assistance—including public housing and urban renewal. Eighteen states and more than 40 cities have enacted fair housing laws of varying degrees of effectiveness.

Despite these actions, the great bulk of housing produced by the private sector remains unaffected by anti-discrimination measures. So long as this continues, public and private action at the local level will be inhibited by the argument that local action produces competitive disadvantage.

We have canvassed the various alternatives, and have come to the firm opinion that there is no substitute for enactment of a federal fair housing law. The key to breaking down housing discrimination is universal and uniform coverage, and such coverage is obtainable only through federal legislation.

We urge that such a statute be enacted at the earliest possible date.

Open housing legislation must be translated into open housing action. Real estate boards should work with fair housing groups in communities where such groups exist, and help form them in areas where they do not exist. The objective of voluntary community action should be (1) the full dissemination of information concerning available housing to minority groups, and (2) providing information to the community concerning the desirability of open housing.

● REORIENTATION OF FEDERAL HOUSING PROGRAMS TO PLACE MORE LOW- AND MODERATE-INCOME HOUSING OUTSIDE OF GHETTO AREAS

481

Enactment of a national fair housing law will eliminate the most obvious barrier limiting the areas in which nonwhites live, but it will not deal with an equally impenetrable barrier, the unavailability of low and moderate income housing in nonghetto areas.

To date, housing programs serving low-income groups have been concentrated in the ghettos. Nonghetto areas, particularly suburbs, for the most part have steadfastly opposed low-income, rent supplement, or below-market interest rate housing, and have successfully restricted use of these programs outside the ghetto.

We believe that federally aided low- and moderate-income housing programs must be reoriented so that the major thrust is in nonghetto areas. Public housing programs should emphasize scattered site construction, rent supplements should, wherever possible, be used in nonghetto areas, and an intensive effort should be made to recruit below-market interest rate sponsors willing to build outside the ghettos.

The reorientation of these programs is particularly critical in light of our recommendation that 6 million low and middle-income housing units be made available over the next five years. If the effort is not to be counter-productive, its main thrust must be in nonghetto areas, particularly those outside the central city.

Conclusion

One of the first witnesses to be invited to appear before this Commission was Dr. Kenneth B. Clark, a distinguished and perceptive scholar. Referring to the reports of earlier riot commissions, he said:

> I read that report . . . of the 1919 riot in Chicago, and it is as if I were reading the report of the investigating committee on the Harlem riot of '35, the report of the investigating committee on the Harlem riot of '43, the report of the McCone Commission on the Watts riot.
>
> I must again in candor say to you members of this Commission —it is a kind of Alice in Wonderland—with the same moving picture re-shown over and over again, the same analysis, the same recommendations, and the same inaction.

These words come to our minds as we conclude this Report.

We have provided an honest beginning. We have learned much. But we have uncovered no startling truths, no unique insights, no simple solutions. The destruction and the bitterness of racial disorder, the harsh polemics of black revolt and white repression have been seen and heard before in this country.

It is time now to end the destruction and the violence, not only in the streets of the ghetto but in the lives of people.

This morning I have welcomed the members of the Commission on Civil Disorders to the White House for its first meeting. The Commission is chaired by Governor Kerner of Illinois. The Vice Chairman is Mayor Lindsay of New York. They are both here with me.

I have commended these 11 citizens for what they have agreed to do for this Nation. They are undertaking a responsibility as great as any in our society.

The civil peace has been shattered in a number of cities. The American people are deeply disturbed. They are baffled and dismayed by the wholesale looting and violence that has occurred both in small towns and great metropolitan centers.

No society can tolerate massive violence, any more than a body can tolerate massive disease. And we in America shall not tolerate it.

But just saying that does not solve the problem. We need to know the answers, I think, to three basic questions about these riots:

— What happened?
— Why did it happen?
— What can be done to prevent it from happening again and again?

Beyond these basic questions there are others—the answers to which can help our Governors and our mayors, our chiefs of police and our citizens all over the country to cope with their immediate and their long-range problems of maintaining order:

— Why riots occur in some cities and do not occur in others?
— Why one man breaks the law, while another, living in the same circumstances, does not?
— To what extent, if any, there has been planning and organization in any of the riots?
— Why have some riots been contained before they got out of hand and others have not?
— How well equipped and trained are the local and State police, and the State guard units, to handle riots?
— How do police-community relationships affect the likelihood of a riot—or the ability to keep one from spreading once it has started?
— Who took part in the riots? What about their age, their level of education, their job history, their origins, and their roots in the community?
— Who suffered most at the hands of the rioters?
— What can be done to help innocent people and vital institutions escape serious injury?
— How can groups of lawful citizens be encouraged, groups that can help to cool the situation?

- What is the relative impact of the depressed conditions in the ghetto—joblessness, family instability, poor education, lack of motivation, poor health care—in stimulating people to riot?
- What Federal, State and local programs have been most helpful in relieving those depressed conditions?
- What is the proper public role in helping cities repair the damage that has been done?
- What effect do the mass media have on the riots?

What we are really asking for is a profile of the riots—of the rioters, of their environment, of their victims, of their causes and effects.

We are asking for advice on
- short-term measures that can prevent riots,
- better measures to contain riots once they begin,
- and long-term measures that will make them only a sordid page in our history.

I know this is a tall order.

One thing should be absolutely clear: this matter is far, far too important for politics. It goes to the health and safety of all American citizens—Republicans and Democrats. It goes to the proper responsibilities of officials in both of our Parties. It goes to the heart of our society in a time of swift change and of great stress. I think the composition of this Commission is proof against any narrowness or partisanship.

You will have all the support and cooperation you need from the Federal government, as the Chairman and the Vice Chairman lead this Commission in this study.

Sometimes various Administrations have set up commissions that were expected to put the stamp of approval on what the Administration believed.

This is not such a commission. We are looking to you, not to approve our own notions, but to guide us and to guide the country through a thicket of tension, conflicting evidence and extreme opinion.

So, Mr. Chairman and Mr. Vice Chairman, let your search be free. Let it be untrammeled by what has been called the "conventional wisdom." As best you can, find the truth, the whole truth, and express it in your report.

I hope you will be inspired by a sense of urgency but also conscious of the danger that lies always in hasty conclusions.

The work that you do ought to help guide us not just this summer, but for many summers to come and for many years to come.

Thank you.

OTTO KERNER, CHAIRMAN—Governor of Illinois, 1961-   ;
Springfield, Ill. Born August 15, 1908, Chicago, Ill. A.B., Brown
University, 1930; Trinity College, Cambridge University, 1930-
31; J.D., Northwestern University, 1934. Attorney, Chicago, 1934-
47; U. S. District Attorney, Northern District of Illinois, 1947-
54; County Judge, Cook County, 1954-61. Illinois National
Guard, 1934-41; 1946-54, advancing from Private to Captain,
9th Infantry Division, European Theater of Operations; Field
Artillery School, Fort Sill, Oklahoma; and 32nd Infantry Division, Pacific Theater of Operations, 1941-46, retiring as Major
General; Soldier's Medal, Bronze Star, Army Commendation,
Ribbon, Presidential Unit Citation (34th Field Artillery Bat-
talion).

JOHN V. LINDSAY, VICE CHAIRMAN—Mayor of New York
City, 1966-   . Born November 24, 1921, New York City. A.B.
Yale University, 1944; LL.B., Yale Law School, 1948. Attorney,
New York City, 1945-1955; Executive Assistant to the Attorney
General of the United States, 1955-1957; elected U. S. Repre-
sentative, 86th Congress, 1958; reelected to the 87th, 88th and
89th Congresses. U. S. Navy, 1943-46. Member Council on For-
eign Relations; Citizens Committee for Children of New York
City, Inc.; former board member, Freedom House; former mem-
ber Executive Committee, Association of the Bar of the City of
New York; elected to the Yale Corporation, 1964; Elected Chairman of the Political Committee of the NATO Parliamentarians
Conference, 1964.

I. W. ABEL—President, United Steelworkers of America
(AFL-CIO), 1965-   ; Pittsburgh, Pa. Born August 11, 1908,
Magnolia, Ohio. Canton, Ohio Business College. Employed by
American Sheet and Tin Plate Company and Timken Roller
Bearing Co., Canton, 1922-38; Staff of United Steelworkers,
1938-42; Director, Canton-Massillon Area, District 27 of the
United Steelworkers, 1942-53; Secretary-Treasurer, United Steel-
workers, 1953-65.

EDWARD W. BROOKE—U. S. Senator from Massachusetts,
1966-   ; Newton Centre, Mass. Born October 26, 1919, Washington, D. C. B.S., Howard University, 1941; LL.M., Boston University Law School, 1950 (editor of Law Review, 1946-48);
Honorary Degrees: Doctor of Public Administration, North-
eastern University, Boston, 1964; Doctor of Laws, Emerson
College, Boston, 1965; Doctor of Laws, George Washington University, Washington, D. C., 1967; Doctor of Science, Lowell
Technological Institute, Lowell, Mass., 1967. Attorney, Boston,
1948-61; Chairman of Finance Commission, City of Boston, 1961-
62; Attorney General of the Commonwealth of Massachusetts,

1962-66; elected to the U. S. Senate November 8, 1966; Republican. Five years active duty, U. S. Army, World War II; Captain, Infantry, European Theater of Operations; Bronze Star, Combat Infantryman's Badge; served with "Partisans" in Italy. Fellow, American Academy of Arts and Sciences; Fellow, American Bar Association for excellence in law, 1963; Trustee, Boston University; Chairman of the Board, The Opera Company of Boston, Inc.; Member, American Veterans of World War II (AMVETS), National Council of Boy Scouts of America, National Board of Boys' Clubs of America, Board of Overseers of Harvard College, National Sponsors Committee of The Clarke School for the Deaf and Hampton Institute, and member of the American, Massachusetts and Boston Bar Associations. Recipient of one of the Ten Outstanding Young Men of Greater Boston awards of the Junior Chamber of Commerce, 1952; Distinguished Service Award, AMVETS; National Judge Advocate, AMVETS, 1955-57, and Massachusetts Department Commander AMVETS 1954-55. Recipient of The Spingarn Medal, NAACP, 1967, and the Charles Evans Hughes Award, National Conference of Christians and Jews, 1967.

JAMES C. CORMAN—U. S. Representative from California, 22nd District, 1960-   ; Van Nuys, Calif. Born October 20, 1920, Galena, Kansas. B.A., University of California at Los Angeles, 1942; LL.B., University of Southern California, 1948. Attorney, Los Angeles, 1948-50 and 1952-57; Member of the Los Angeles City Council, 1957-60; elected November 8, 1960 to the 87th Congress; reelected to the 88th, 89th, and 90th Congresses. Democrat. U. S. Marine Corps, 3rd Marine Division, at Bougainville, Guam, and Iwo Jima, 1942-46; subsequent service 1950-52. Member of the Methodist Church, Lions International, American Legion, Veterans of Foreign Wars, Elks; the American, California, Los Angeles and San Fernando Valley Bar Associations, Los Angeles Community Relations Conference. Awards from the Jewish Federation-Council of Greater Los Angeles for "outstanding service in fostering good will and understanding among religious and racial groups," and from the California Congressional Recognition Plan, Claremont College for "exemplary service" on the House Judiciary Committee.

FRED R. HARRIS—U. S. Senator from Oklahoma, 1964-   ; Lawton, Okla. Born November 13, 1930, Walters, Okla. B.A. in political science and history, University of Oklahoma, 1952; LL.B. "with distinction," University of Oklahoma, 1954. Practiced law, 1954-64; Member of Oklahoma State Senate, 1956-64; elected to U. S. Senate November 3, 1964, to fill unexpired term of Robert S. Kerr; reelected November 8, 1966, for term ending January 3, 1973. Democrat. Recipient, Oklahoma Junior Chamber of Commerce "Outstanding Young Man of Oklahoma" award, 1959; one of the U. S. Jaycee "Ten Outstanding Young Men" awards, 1965.

HERBERT JENKINS—Chief of Police, Atlanta, Georgia, 1947-   . Born 1907, Lithonia, Georgia. Atlanta public schools and Atlanta Law School. Joined Atlanta Police Department, 1931; elected Chief of Atlanta Police Department, 1947. President, International Association of Chiefs of Police, 1965; Member, Attorney General's Advisory Panel on Grants, 1964; Baptist Church; Past Worshipful Master of Atlanta Masonic Lodge; charter member of Northside Atlanta Kiwanis Club; Board of Directors of the Atlanta Boys Club and other civic organizations. Awards include: 1962 Outstanding Citizen Award by Jewish War Veterans of United States of America, Atlanta Post 112; Atlanta Jaycee Good Government Award, 1962; Alpha Chapter of Delta Kappa Gamma Society award for leadership in maintaining public education, 1962; Silk Hat Award by Northside Atlanta Kiwanis Club, 1962; Boys Club Bronze Keystone for Long and Devoted Service to Boys by the Boys Clubs of America, 1963.

WILLIAM M. McCULLOCH—U. S. Representative from the State of Ohio, 4th District, 1947-   ; Piqua, Ohio. Born November 24, 1901, Holmes County, Ohio. LL.B. Ohio State University, 1925; Honorary LL.D., Ohio Northern University; Member Ohio House of Representatives six terms, serving as Republican leader 1936-39, and as Speaker for three terms; Elected to 80th Congress, November 4, 1947, reelected to each succeeding Congress. Republican. Veteran, World War II. Member, American Political Science Association; Recipient, Congressional Distinguished Service Award, APSA, and the Distinguished Alumni Award, College of Wooster, Wooster, Ohio.

KATHERINE GRAHAM PEDEN—Commissioner of Commerce, State of Kentucky, 1963-67; Hopkinsville, Ky. Born January 2, 1926, Hopkinsville, Ky. Traffic Department, Radio Station WHOP, Hopkinsville, 1944-49; Vice President and Director, WHOP, 1949-   ; Owner-President, Radio Station WNVL, Nicholasville. President, National Federation of Business and Professional Women, 1961-62; Member, the Defense Advisory Committee of Women in the Service (DACOWITS); the National Advisory Council of the Small Business Administration; the Governor's Commission on the Status of Women—Kentucky; Board of Directors, Kentucky Chamber of Commerce; the American Industrial Development Council; the Southern Industrial Development Council; President, Kentucky Federation of Business and Professional Women, 1955-56; Director, Mental Health Association, and Co-Chairman, Western State Hospital Chapel Fund, 1956-   ; Trustee, Business and Professional Women's Foundation, 1958-   ; Member, Kentucky Federation of Business and Professional Women, Kentucky Broadcasters Association, First Christian Church of Hopkinsville, and Hopkinsville Chamber of Commerce, 1951-   ; Recipient, Woman of the Year Award, Hopkinsville, 1951.

CHARLES B. THORNTON—Chairman of the Board and Chief Executive Officer, Litton Industries, Inc., 1953-   ; Los Angeles, Calif. Born July 22, 1913, Knox County, Texas. B.C.S., Columbus University, 1937; Honorary D.C.S., George Washington University, 1964; Honorary Jur.D., Texas Technological College, 1957. Director of Planning, Ford Motor Company, 1946-48; Vice President and Assistant General Manager, Hughes Aircraft Company, Culver City, Calif., 1948-53; Vice President,

Hughes Tool Company, 1948-53; President, Litton Industries, 1953-61. Colonel, USAF, World War II; Consultant to Commanding General, 1946; Distinguished Service Medal, Legion of Merit, Commendation Ribbon with two oakleaf clusters. Director and member of the executive committee: United California Bank, Western Bancorporation, Times Mirror Company, (1959-67); Director: Union Oil Company of California, Lehman Corporation, General Mills, Inc. (1963-67); Director and Executive Committee Member, Cyprus Mines, Inc.; Director, MCA, Inc.; Director and Finance Committee Member, Trans World Airlines, Inc.; Trustee, University of Southern California; Trustee, Harvey Mudd College of Science and Engineering; Member, California Institute Associates; Member, University of Southern California Associates; Member, The Visiting Committee, Harvard Business School; Board of Governors, Welfare Federation of Los Angeles (1960-63); National Professional and Civic Organizations: Member, The Business Council; Defense Industry Advisory Council to the Department of Defense; Air Force Academy Advisory Council; Director, National Committee for International Development; Trustee, Committee for Economic Development; Trustee, National Security Industrial Association; Member, West Coast Advisory Group of American Management Association; prior affiliation with numerous other local and national civic and governmental bodies.

ROY WILKINS—Executive Director, National Association for the Advancement of Colored People, 1955-   ; New York, New York. Born August 30, 1901, St. Louis, Mo. A.B., University of Minnesota, 1923. Managing Editor, Kansas City Call, 1923-31; Assistant Secretary, NAACP, 1931-49; Acting Secretary, NAACP, 1949-50; Administrator, NAACP, 1950; Editor, *Crisis* Magazine, 1934-49. Recipient, the Spingarn Medal, NAACP, 1964.

INDEX

A

Abel, I. W., biographical sketch of, 486
Abolition Movement
  19th century, 209ff
Addonizio, Hugh, Mayor, Newark, N.J., 57
Administration of Justice, *see* Justice, Administration of
Advertising, effect on poor, 274
Affluence of non-ghetto residents affects social services, 287
Aftermath of Disorder, The, 151
Aid for Dependent Children (AFDC), "man-in-the-house" rule, 459
Agency for International Development, Office of Public Safety, cited, 324
Alcoholism, 281
Alienation, feeling of, among ghetto residents, 284
Allen, Ivan, Mayor, Atlanta, Ga., 53
American Federation of Labor (AFL-CIO), 222f
American Revolution, 1776; *see* history
Army, U.S.
  Negroes in, 315
    1917-18, 218
    1941-45, 223
  performance in Detroit civil disorder, 315
Arrest
  age data of rioters, non-involved, 129
  during disorder, *see* Justice, Administration of
  lack of grounds for, 312
  of student demonstrators, 227
  record data, Detroit
    sex of riot participants, 130
  record data
    racial factor in, 129
  records
    as riot participant data, 128
    data re arrest charges, 134
    employment data, correlation to riot participation, 132
    marital status data from four cities, 130
    riot participant residence data, 131
  summons as alternative to, 313
Arrest and booking system, Detroit, 107
Arrestees
  family structure statistics on, 130
  racial, age, sex, and residence data on, 129ff
Atlanta, Ga.
  1967, 52ff

Crime Prevention Bureau, 320
  municipal services in disturbance area, 156
  precipitating incident, 54
  withdrawal of police patrols, 154
  Youth Patrol in, 55f
Attitudes, influenced by more than mass media, 376
Auto theft, 266, 269

B

Bachrach, Mayor Walton H., Cincinnati, Ohio, 50f
Back-to-Africa Movement, 211
Background of Civil Disorders, 135f, 151
Bail, during riots, *see* Justice, Administration of
Bail setting, program for, outlined, 353f
Baltimore, Md.
  over half Negro by 1972, 391
  success of community relations programs in, 320
Baton Rouge, La., arrest of student demonstrators, 227
Beaumont, Tex., civil disorders, World War II, 224
Bedford-Stuyvesant
  1964, 36
  Task Force and incident in, 291
Birmingham, Ala.
  1963, 35
  church explosion, 229
  direct action in, 230
"Black Consciousness"
  see "Black Power"
Black Muslims, 229
Black Panther Party, Lowndes County, Ala., 233f
"Black Power," 205
  concept of Commission, 403f
  Congress of Racial Equality (CORE), 234
  defined, 232ff
  extremist doctrine, 205
  false premises of, 404
  Student Nonviolent Coordinating Committee (SNCC), 233f
Blackman's Volunteer Army of Liberation in Newark, 60
Bogalusa, La., 1965, 37
Booking procedures, outline recommendation, 351f
Boston, Mass.
  crime reported, 268
  police department, 324
Boycott
  bus
    Birmingham, Ala., 1957, 225
    Montgomery, Ala., 225, 227
    Tallahassee, Fla., 1957, 225
  schools, 229

490

Tuskegee Civil Assoc., 1957-1960, 225
white businesses discriminating in the 1930's depression, 222
Brooke, Senator Edward W., biographical sketch of, 486 f
Brown, H. "Rap"
in Atlanta, 56
in Cincinnati, 52
Brown v. *Board of Education,* 225
Buffalo, N.Y.
Civil War disorders, 212
Negro school majority in, by 1985, 391
Building trades unions, demonstrations in, 229
Bureau of the Census
Negroes in metropolitan areas, 390, 402
projections explained, 408f
Bureau of Labor Statistics, food price study in six cities, 1966, 277
Burglaries, police response to, in Hartford, Conn., 309
Burglary, index crime, 266ff, 269
Businesses
lost revenue due to curfew, 358
as victims of disorders
see civil disorders; exploitation by retail merchants

C

Cambridge, Md., 1963, 35
Carmichael, Stokely
1967, 40
in Atlanta, Ga., 55
Catholic charities, low-cost homes in New Jersey cities, 155
Causes of disorder, 203ff
Cavanagh, Mayor Jerome, Detroit, Mich., 86
Census projections, explained, 408f
Central cities
compared to suburb, by 1985, 400
defined, 408f
deteriorating property in, and Federal government assistance, 399
the Negro and jobs in, 392
Negro middle class in, 402f
Negro population in, 390
Negro population growth producing changes in, 391f
net loss of jobs in, 392
proportion of Negroes to whites by 1985, 390
reasons for decay in, 283
Central Information Centers, creation of, urged, 379f
Central Intelligence Agency (CIA), 201

Cervantes, Mayor Alfonso J., St. Louis, Mo., quoted, 287
Charleston, S.C., civil disorder, 1919, 219
Chester, Pa., civil disorder, 1917, 219
Chemical agents, use of in riot control, 330f
Chicago, Ill.
1963, 35
1964, 35f
1966, 38f
civil disorders, 1919, 219f
code, criticism of, by media, 382
crime rate, 1965 (five police districts), 266f
crime reported, 268
low-income neighborhoods, 1967 study, 274
Negro migration, 1955-60 to, from South, 240
over half Negro by 1984, 391
police department, 324
assignment of patrolmen in highest crime areas, 267-268
training bulletin, quoted, 326
"Rumor Central" concept, 326f
slum sanitation, 273
Churches, aid during disorders, 359
Cincinnati, Ohio
1967, 47ff
civil disorders in "Little Africa," 1829, 209
Civil War disorders, 212
estimate of damage, 109
fires in, 51
injuries in, 52
media coverage, 373
National Guard mobilized in, 51
Negro school majority in, by 1985, 391
organized activity, study of, 201
police-community relations, 154
police department, 324
police on duty, 4:00 p.m. to midnight, 327
precipitating incident, 49
school board election, 155
school incident, 155
tension in, 47
Cities
dilemma of, 399
future of, 389ff
problems of tax dollars enumerated, 399
worsening of financial plight, 394
see also community response
Citizens' complaints, police guidelines, 314
City administration, generally unaware of tension, 287
City councils, Negro underrepresentation, 279
City government

crisis confronting, 299
viewed by ghetto resident, 287
City governments, poorly organized for needs of ghetto residents, 285
City leadership, community involvement, 297
Civil damage suits, against police, 310f
Civil disorders—see disorder
Civil order
entire community responsibility, 323
first responsibility of government, 323
Civil Rights Act of 1875, 213
declared unconstitutional, 214
Civil Rights Act of 1964, 230
Lyndon B. Johnson, and, 230
Civil Rights Commission
1962 survey, cited, 315f
1967 report, cited, 310
power of, 225
report of, cited, 404f
report of, Racial Isolation in the Public Schools, 426
Civil rights leaders, view of, 133
Civil service, hiring of ghetto residents, review of, 294
Civil War, 211
Civilian review boards, Crime Commission research on, 294f
Clark, Dr. Kenneth B., quoted, 300, 429, 483
Clark, Attorney General Ramsey, Detroit, 95
Cleveland, Ohio
1964, 36
Civil Rights Commission, study of, cited, 310
doctor scarcity in poor areas, 272
fatherless families in Hough section, 261
over half Negro by 1975, 391
Clustering of disorders, 114
CN (tear gas), chemical agent in riot control, 330
Colfax, La., Reconstruction, civil disorders, 213
Codes, building or housing see housing
Coleman Report, 425
Columbus, Ohio, East Central Citizens Organization (ECCO), 298
Commerce, Department of, economic data on Negroes, 251f
Commercial practices, as Negro grievance, 145
Commission see National Advisory Commission on Civil Disorders
Commission survey information on sex of riot participants, 130
racial factor in participation, 130
residence data on rioter, non-involved, 131

Commissioners, biographical sketches of, 486 ff
Communication
importance of, between government and ghetto, 333f
special problem for deprived citizens, 284
see also Media
Communities, recommendations for assistance, 358f
Community action groups, establishing legitimacy of, 297
Community action programs, 296f
effectiveness of,
in Detroit, Mich., 143
in Newark, N.J., 143
list of, 143
"Community cabinet," establishment, recommended, 289
Community participation
by ghetto residents encouraged, 296
neighborhood city halls, 295
Community relations
general failure of, 319
programs,
as part of public service function of police, 320
decrease of ghetto hostility, 320
problems of, 319f
Community Relations Service study, findings on media outlined, 381
Community response
conclusion, 298
recommendations for, 289
Community Service Center Councils, recommended establishment of, 296
Community, size of, 114
Community service officer
endorsed by Civil Disorders Commission, 317
Negroes in police work, 317
qualifications and functions of, 317
recommended by Crime Commission, 317
Community service officers
criteria for selection, 317
Federal financing to establish, 318
Conditions, Negro unemployment in Detroit, 1967, 141
Conditions, pre-riot
city government structure, 137ff
comparison, Negro and non-Negro conditions, 136f
education programs
effectiveness of, 141
Detroit, Mich., funding, 141
list of, 141
Newark, N.J., funding, 141
Federal programs; public opinion of, 136

local government structure and capability; public opinion of, 136

Negro-community political relations, 137ff

Negro grievances; public opinion of, 136

Negro, white homeowners, rents, 137

Negro, white semi-skilled, skilled work opportunities, 137

Negro population increase (1950-60), 136

proportion of Negro government officials to population, 137

social and economic; public opinion of, 136

see also under disorder; ghetto

Congress of Industrial Organizations (CIO), 222

Congress of Racial Equality (CORE), 223ff
Black Power, 234
inadequacy of, 233
increases militancy, 232
Negro led and dominated, 228
voter registration drive in Mississippi, 1961 on, 231

Conspiracy, 201f
see also organized activity

Control of disorder, 323ff
basis of information discussed, 324
present policy choice, 397f

Conyers, Congressman John, Jr., in Detroit, 88

CORE
see Congress of Racial Equality

Corman, Congressman James C., biographical sketch, 487

Coughlin, Father Charles, white supremacy spokesman, 224

Counsel, right to, in emergency disorder situations, 354f

Counter-rioter
as part of riot process, 116f
birthplace, regional data on, 130
compared to non-involved, 111, 129
see also disorder; investigations
economic status of, 129
education as participation factor, 132
social institution supporter, 129
use of, in disorders, 332
vital economic, education factors, 111f
see also disorder; investigations
see also riot process

Courts, *see* Justice, Administration of

Courts, lower, conditions in, 337f

Credit buying and uneducated low-income families
see exploitation by retail merchants

Crime
effect of income and race, 267
increase, Negro youth a factor, 269
impact on ghetto life, 266ff
Negroes principal victims of crime by Negroes, 268
rate
high in Negro ghettos, 268f
immigrants in "entry ports," 266
in Chicago, Ill., 1965, 266
suburban, 266
urban, Index Crime, 268f
reported
Boston, Mass., 268
Chicago, Ill., 268
rise in and police, 300
statistics understating of, 267

Criminal justice, goals of, in disorder, outlined, 338

Crowds
sizeable, 213
see also disorders, major
the ghetto, 325f

CS, chemical agent for riot control, 330f

Cuffee, Paul, Back-to-Africa movement, 1816, 210

Curfew, revenue loss due to, 358

Crime Commission, 268
outline of federal funds and assistance, 336
recommendations cited, 313
survey of, cited, 310
Task Force, quoted, 303

D

Dallas, Negro school majority, by 1985, 391

Damage
accidental, 116
see also Detroit
by fire, 115
by fire, with heavy wind as a factor, 116
caused by fire department's control efforts, 116
caused by police control efforts, 116
deliberately inflicted by Negroes on white businesses, 116
early estimates, 115
forms of, 358
from retributive police action, 116, 120
see also Newark, N.J.
occurrences during disturbances, 114
to police and fire equipment, 116
to property, 115
to public institutions, 116
see also violence, victims of
to residences in Detroit, 116

Death, occurrences during disturbances, 115

Declaration of Independence, 207

Defense, Department of
Office of Chief of Operations, cited, 324

Delany, Martin R., urges fellow Negroes to settle elsewhere, 210

Democratic National Convention, seating of Mississippi delegation, 231

Demonstrations
against unions (building trades), 229
lawful, police guidelines for, 314
most successful early 1960's, 231
spontaneous and police guidelines for, 314

Denver, Colo.

Depression
history, 1930's, 221f
Negro migration, 239f

Deprived areas, decay in and current policy, 396

Deprived citizen
special problems of communication, 284
see also ghetto residents

Detention and bail setting, court personnel for, described, 352ff

Detention facilities described, 353

Detroit, Mich., 84ff, 114
accidental damages, 116
adoption of public high school by Michigan Bell Telephone Company, 152
Army performance in disorder, 315
arrest and booking system, 106f
arrestee study as riot participant data, 128
City-wide Citizens Action Committee, 153
civil disorder, 1943, 224
Common Council passage of fair housing ordinance, 152
conduct of Federal troops in, 97
damage to residences, 116
see also damage
development of violence in, 123
estimate of damage, 115
excessive damage, reports of, 364
factors in disorder, 325
failure of police-community relations programs in, 319
Federal troops into, requested, 95
Federal troops leave, 108
final incident, July 23, 1967, 3:45 a.m., 120
firefighting in, 92
insurance losses in, 107
looting in, 93
media coverage of rumors, 372f
National Education Association (NEA) study of, 430
National Guard called in, 93
National Guard leaves, 108
National Guard performance in disorder, 315
New Detroit Committee, 152
occurrences of death and injuries, 115
persons killed in disorders, 358
plans to improve administration of justice, 157
police-citizen conflicts, 85
police commando unit in, 87
police-minority relations, 299
prior incidents, 118
problems of programs in, 286
purchases of riot equipment, 152f
rebuilding of residences, 157
sanctions on offending police officers in, 311
Senate Report, quoted, 286
sniping in, 93ff
study of organized activity, 201
suit by school board against State of Michigan, 152
surveys of participants, non-participation
age data of rioters, non-involved, 105
education data, correlation to riot participation, 132
employment data, correlation to riot participation, 132
family structure data from, 130
income data, correlation to riot participation, 131
racial self-image data of riot participants, non-participants, 133
residence data from, rioter, non-involved, 131
riot participant, non-participant, region of upbringing, 130
rioter, non-involved, political attitudes involvement, 134
sex factor, riot participants, 130
time severe levels of violence reached, 123
TV coverage in, 370
typical sequence of riot events described, 118ff
Urban League study in, 302
see also clustering of disorders

Direct action, failures in North, 230f

Disaffection (urban), problems

494

of democracy, 288
Discrimination
  in North, 215
  in South, 214f
  outlawed in employment, 225
  poor services seen as, 284
Disfranchisement, 214
Disorder
  against commercial establishments in disadvantaged areas, 274
  and Reconstruction, 213
  arrests for minor offenses predominate, 339
  as protest, 40
  background of
    Federal programs in, 112
    general factors in, 112
    grievance reservoir in, 112
  causes of, pervasive discrimination and segregation, 203
    violent mood of urban Negroes, 203
  characterization
    as non-"inter-racial," 110
    as "racial," 112
  cities survey, generalizations found in, 115
  civil definition of, 112
  classification, 113
  climate, 113
  community assistance control of, 331ff
  conduct of police officer, 326
  control
    Negro community participation, 109
    use of chemical agents, 330f
    stages, uniform set, 125
    training for police recruits, 327f
  control of, 323ff
  coordination of efforts in, 334
  coverage, recommendations for, 378ff
  crowded ghetto living conditions, 325ff
  danger of overreaction, 334f
  dispersal of crowds in, 328
  environment
    see background; conditions, pre-riot; ghetto; Negro conditions
  events, typical sequence, described, 118ff
  factors causing ghetto conditions, 109
  goals of criminal justice in, outlined, 338
  hostility to police, and, 325
  ignited by police action, 109, 206
  in major U.S. cities, police personnel inadequate for, 327f
  location, 112
  major, defined, 113
  mayor's responsibility, 333
  media failure to analyze, 373

minor defined, 113
Negro attitude toward, 128
participant
  assumed characteristics, 127f
  attitude toward employment discrimination, 128f
  data
    regions of upbringing and birthplace, 130
    residence, 131
  determining research data, 128
  marital status statistics, 130
  partial information, 128
  political awareness, 129
  racial attitudes, 129, 133ff
  see arrestee; rioter, profile of; rioter, self-reported
participants, comparison of rioter, non-involved, controllers, 110
participants
  family structure data sources, 130
  income statistics, 131
  number (according to survey), 128
  racial, age and sex characteristics, 129f
police approach to initial outbreak, 125
popular conceptions of
  conception validation, 109f
  participants, stages, in, description of, 110
  profile of participant, 111
    characteristics (general), age, marital status, residential status, economic position, 129f
  characteristics sought in investigation, 110
profiles studied by Commission, 333f
relation of high crime rate, 268
role of public officials in, 333f
rumor and inadequate information, 325
slaves in New York, N.Y., 18th cenutry, 207
sniping and looting, arrests, in, 339
"typical," definition of, 116
  see also riot process
youth on the streets, 325
Disorder coverage
  exaggeration and error, 372
  TV conclusions about content of discussed, 369
  TV timing of, 370
Disorder police control, dispersal of manpower a factor, 327
Distortion, of news coverage of disorders, 363

Disturbances, guidelines for discretion in, not available, 313
Douglass, Frederick, quoted, 210
Drew, Charles, 223
Drug addiction, toleration of in ghetto, 307f
see also narcotics
Du Bois, W. E. B., 216-217, 220

E

East Central Citizens Organization (ECCO), community action group neighborhood membership corporation, 298
East St. Louis, Ill., civil disorders, 1917, 217f
Education
adult basic education program, purpose of, 141
as a determining factor in employment, 254
as riot participation factor, 132
bonus support for integrated schools, 441f
community participation in educational process, 450
community-school relations, 436
de facto segregation, elimination of, 440
discrimination, 203
early childhood, recommended, 446
educational parks, 442
Educational Professions Development Act (EPDA), discussed, 444f
efforts to improve by local governments, 155
elementary, improvement of, 447
Enrichment Choice, 404f
enrollments, increase of, 430
equality of for ghetto schools, 439
exemplary schools and, 442
experimentation, evaluation and research, recommended, 450
facilities and curricula in ghetto schools, 433
funding of, 434
ghetto environment and, 437
headstart, 446
higher, and ghetto youth, 440
higher, equal opportunity for, 452
higher, financial barriers to, 453
magnet schools, 443
National Teacher Corps, 444
neighborhood school policy, 426
northern schools, discrimination in, 443
problems of overcrowding in schools, 433

programs
implementation
Federal, 455
Local, 456
State, 455
racial and economic integration of, 404f
Rockford, Ill., 155
school dropouts, 425
schools and testing process, 451
secondary, improvement of, 449
segregation, de facto, programs to eliminate, 440
segregation in, continuing, 426f
suggested programs, 440
supplemental education centers, 442
teacher aides and tutors in ghetto, 451
teachers in, 428
teaching effectiveness and student turnover, 430
Title I program, 141
Title IV, Civil Rights Act of 1964 and, 441
Title VI, Civil Rights Act of 1964, 443
Upward Bound, expansion of, 452
vocational, 453
year-round and disadvantaged students, 445
youthful rioters, 425
Effective utilization of courts needed, 292
Elaine, Ark., defense of Negro sharecroppers, 220
Elizabeth, N.J.
1964, 36
1967, 71
outbreaks, warned, 70
school board
donation of building by Standard Oil Company of New Jersey, 155
Emancipation, 211f
Emergency relief, cases of major disaster, 358
Employment
adult-teenage differentials, 254
as riot participation factor, 132
attitudes of rioters and nonrioters, 132
city governments of ghetto residents, recommended, 294
Commission goals and objectives outlined, 414f
critical significance, 252f
discrimination, 203
ghetto businesses, 424
"hard core" unemployed, 414
immediate programs stressed, 417
job placement, 418
jobs

private sector, 421
public sector, creating, 426
local governments, 294
Negro businesses, 424
Negro, in general, 253ff
Negro-white education levels, 254
net loss, in central cities, 392
opportunities, in central cities, 392
poverty areas and, 423
problems of, discussed, 414
programs, extensive, 402
recruitment for, 417
sex as a factor, 254
strategies outlined, 415
strengthening job structure, 419-420
subemployment, disadvantaged neighborhoods, 257f
training for insurance agents from core areas, 361
undesirable jobs open to Negroes, 253
unemployed men, rejection by families, 280
"unemployment" defined, 254f
unemployment, suburban versus urban, 406f
Enforcement of equal opportunities, 213
Englewood, N.J., disturbances in, 73
Enrichment
defined, 401
interim action, 406
Enrichment Choice
discussed, 401ff
education, 404f
housing, 405
implications of segregation, 404
middle-class status for disadvantaged Americans, 402
the Southern Negro, 403
Equal opportunities, legislation, 1900-25, 217
Equipment
see damages; police; violence, victims of
European immigrants — compared to Negro, 278
Evers, Medgar, 229
Executive Order
11063, on housing discrimination cited, 481
Expanded legal service to the poor, 292
Exploitation by retail merchants, 274ff
credit buying and the uneducated low-income family, 275
garnishment, 276
installment buying, 274
problems in assessing, 274
variations in food prices, 277

Eyewitness accounts/NACCD investigations as riot participant data, 128

F

Fair Employment Practices Commission, Executive Order, 223
Fair housing law, national, essential, 407
Family Crisis Intervention, program of New York Police Department, 319
Family planning, 465
Fatherless families, effect on children, 260
Federal assistance programs
as Negro grievance, 145
cities reviewed, 140
community action, 143
description of research programs, 140
education, 141
effect on ghetto conditions, 109, 140ff
housing, 142
improved in eight cities, 156
manpower, 140
research conclusions, 140
welfare, 142
Federal Bureau of Investigation, complaints against Newark police, 310
riot manual quoted, 323f, 330f
to assist Commission, 201
Federal Disaster Act
amending, 358f
applicable to natural disasters, 359
Federal forces, 113
see also disorders, major
Federal funding, increased for centers, 296
Federal housing, in suburban areas, 392f
Federal programs see Federal assistance programs
Federal Trade Commission, study, 275
Federal troops
conduct of in Detroit, 97
enter Detroit, 97
leave Detroit, 108
Federally-aided programs, coordination of discussed, 411
Female head of families, 259f
Fertility rate
Negro, in U.S., 391
relation to educational experience, 238
Finances, problem of in central city, 283
Fires, see major disorders, 113
see also disorder; violence, patterns of
First phase programs, 288

not short term anti-riot efforts, 288
part of long range commitment, 289
Force
  excessive, problem of, 330
  excessive use of, on poor, 302
  justification of, discussed, 329f
  "middle range of," needed by police departments, 330
  non-lethal chemicals as alternative to, 330f
  problems of, killing or wounding innocent persons, 329
  tools for (police weaponry), 330
  use of, against looting, 329
  use of, in disorders, 329f
  use of, 113
    non-lethal methods, 331
    see also disorders, major
Ford Foundation, aid to Commission by, 578
Ford Motor Company, ghetto employment program, 152
"Freedom Rides," 225, 227f
Free press, problems of and civil disorder, not an issue, 362
Fugitive slaves,
  see slavery

G

Gambling, enforcement of laws on, 309
Garbage collectors
  see health and sanitation conditions
Garnishment
  see exploitation by retail merchants
Garvey, Marcus, 221
Gary, Ind., over half Negro by 1973, 391
Gates, Daryl F., cited, 324
Gelston, Major General George M., 324
  quoted, 329
Ghetto
  adequate police protection in, recommended, 301
  community factions, 297
  conditions, post-riot, little basic change, 112
  coordination lacking in response to needs of, 286
  defined, 237
  dramatic impact on, outlined, 401ff
  dual standard of law enforcement in, 308
  growth of, 236ff
  hostility in, focuses on police, 286
  inclusion in community structure encouraged, 298
  increased per capita aid to, in Detroit, 152

lack of police personnel in, 308
media portrayal lacking, 366
personal contact in and disorder prevention, 333
police in, 299
quality of life in, 404
reactions to media coverage, 374
relation to disorders, 284
relations with TV and press, 377
spread of, widens gap between citizen and government, 287f
subsidies to establish new industries, 392
volume of police calls in, 309
Ghetto children, improvement in education of, necessary, 406f
Ghetto leaders, reduction of crime, 320
Ghetto problems
  hearings on, on local level, 293
    recommended, 293
  legislation to improve, 293
  Negro officers, better insight into, 315
  police compelled to tackle even those not responsible for, 286
Ghetto residents
  adequate representation of, necessary, 296
  advocacy of their interests needed, 293
  breakdown of communications with police, 315
  complicated problems of, and need for public services, 285
  contacts with public officials, 284
  control of ghetto schools by, 405
  deep hostility toward institutions of government, 286
  excluded from planning of programs to aid them, 286
  feel excluded from decision-making process, 286
  feeling of isolation and alienation among, 284
  fuller participation in government encouraged, 296
  grievances against local authorities a cause of disorder, 284
  hiring of by cities a stimulant to private employers, 294
  legal assistance, 292
  limited awareness of public programs, 286
  needs for public services grow, 287
  participation in legal processes necessary, 292
  problems with government differ from middle-class city dweller, 285

reforms in local government to aid, 288

review of civil service requirements for hiring, 294

verbal skills of, program to improve, 449

view of city government, 287f

Ghetto schools
  control by ghetto residents, 405
  quality of education in, 444ff
  teachers in, 428
  total community and, 451
  see also education

Ghetto youths
  crime rate, 303
  police conduct, 303
  problems of, 303

Governors, responsibility, in disorders, 333

Grand larceny, Index Crime, 266, 269

Grants, simplification of procedures for, 296

Greensburg, Ind., civil disorders, 1906, 215

Grievance mechanisms
  adequacy of, 310
  against local government
    accessibility assured, 292
    alleviate frustrations, 291
    comprehensive coverage of grievances against public agencies and authorities, 292
    conciliation in, 292
    criteria for, 292
    existing structures, 138f
    grievants participate in the process fully, 292
    need for adequate staff and funding, 292
    need independence, 292
    power to bring legal action necessary, 292
  against police
    complaints on policy matters, handling of, 312
    ease of filing complaint a necessity, 311
    effective recommended, 301
    improved in two cities, 156
    problem of, 310
    recommendations on, 310
    separate agency to review complaints necessary, 311
    training programs, 312
    trust of police, 310

Grievances
  levels of intensity, 143
  participation of, by rioters and non-rioters, 117
    see also incidents, precipitating
  Negro, basis of, 111
  reservoir, as aspect of riot process, 117
    see also riot process
  reservoir of, defined, 117
  types of, 144

Growth, rate, Negro population, 237

H

Hardy, David, N.Y. *Daily News,* quoted, 308

Harlem
  1964, 35ff
  civil disorder ignited by police action, 206
  narcotics, 262
    see also New York City
  Negro attitude toward police protection in, 308
  New York Times study of 1964, 302
  police-minority relations, 299

Harris, Fred R., biographical sketch of, 487

Harrisburg, Pa., Negro school majority in, by 1985, 391

Hartford, Conn.
  Negro school majority in, by 1985, 391
  police protection in ghetto, 309
  Yale Law Journal, study of, quoted, 309

Health and sanitation conditions
  environmental factors, 272f
  health insurance, 272
    benefits, 282
  health services not well used by Negroes, 271ff
  infant mortality, 270
  life expectancy, 270f
  maternal mortality, 270
  of the ghetto, 269ff
  poverty, 269f
  sanitation as indicator of neighborhood stability, 273

Health, Education and Welfare, Department of (HEW)
  juvenile delinquency control problems, 335
  manpower and education programs, 295
  Newark, N.J., medical center, 155

Health insurance
  see health and sanitation conditions

Health services
  see health and sanitation conditions

Hearings on ghetto problems, 294

Henderson, Vivian, quoted, 231

Hill-Dwight Citizens Commission on Police Community Relations, report of, quoted, 308

History, of Negro, 206ff

Hostility in ghetto focuses on police, 285

Hough
  see Cleveland, Ohio

Housing
  adequate for low and middle
    incomes, 407
  below market interest rates
    for, needed, 476f
  building codes obsolete, re-
    form recommended, 480
  Cambridge, Md., 154
  central cities, 467f
  Dayton, Ohio
    concentrated housing code
      enforcement, 154
    moratorium on building
      public units, 155
  deterioration of, poverty, dis-
    cussed, 473
  discrimination in, 473, 481
  Enrichment Choice and, 405
  existing programs, review of,
    473f
  Federal programs, reorienta-
    tion of, recommended,
    481
  Federal write-down of inter-
    est rates to private
    builders urged, 478
  high rents for poor, 470
  low rent, five year program for
    building, 476
  Model Cities Program, 479
  old structures, 468
  open occupancy outside ghet-
    to, recommended, 482
  overcrowding, 470
  problems discussed, 467ff
  public, expanded and diversi-
    fied program of, 478
  rent supplements and owner
    supplements recom-
    mended, 477
  segregation, 203
  strategy to achieve objectives
    outlined, 474
  substandard, 467
  substandard and the Negro,
    467ff
  substandard, old, and over-
    crowded, 468
  suggested programs for, out-
    lined, 475
  urban renewal, expansion and
    reorientation of pro-
    gram, 468f
  variety of, and Negro, 405
Housing and Urban Develop-
    ment, Department of
    (HUD)
  insurance of mortgage by, 359
  Newark medical center, 155
  service centers, President
    calls for, 296
Housing code, discrimination in,
    enforcement of, 472
Houston, Texas
  1967, 41
  NAACP, defense of soldiers,
    1917, 220
  violence in, 118
    see also incidents, precip-
      itating

Hughes, Governor Richard J.,
    64, 202
Human Relations Councils
  Negro representation, 138
  see also grievance mechanisms
Humphrey, Hubert H., Vice
    President, 95

I

Illegal exploitation rewarded, 261
Illegitimacy, 261f, 281
Immigrants, crime rate "entry
    ports," 266
Immigration, 278ff
  Negro migration compared,
    240
  settlement patterns, 243f
Incident, initial, 324ff
  community response to, 324
  control capabilities, 327ff
  police reaction to, crucial, 324
  problems of, police response
    to, 324
Incidents, relation to tension
    level, 288
Incidents, precipitating
  an aspect of riot process, 116
    see also riot process
  defined, 117f
Incitement to violence, 205
Income
  and riot participation, 131
  statistics, 266f
Income supplement, national
    system of, recommend-
    ed, 466f
"Index Crimes"
  aggravated assault, auto theft,
    burglary, forcible rape,
    grand larceny, homicide,
    robbery, 266
  percentage of Negro, as com-
    pared to white victims,
    268
Indianapolis, Ind., Negro school
    majority in, by 1985, 391
Industry, jobs in Negro areas,
    392
Infant mortality
  see health and sanitation con-
    ditions
Ingersoll, John, cited, 324
Injury, occurrences during dis-
    turbances, 115
Inner city
  see central cities
Installment buying
  see exploitation by retail
    merchants
Institute of Urban Communica-
    tions, proposed, 367
Insurance
  private, handles some losses,
    360
  property, at reasonable cost,
    regardless of location,
    360
Integrated society, Negro polit-
    ical strength, 403f

Integration
  new questions of, and the future, 404
  see also Education
Integration Choice
  discussed, 406f
  overview of, 396
Internal review board, police, inadequacy of, 311
International Association of Chiefs of Police (IACP), 324
Interracial couples, harassing of by police, 303
Interview surveys, as non-participant data, 128
Investigations of death, injury and damage, 115
  see also Permanent Subcommittee on Investigations of the Senate Committee on Government Operations
Irish, New York draft riots, 1863, 212
Isolation, feeling of, among ghetto residents, 284

J

Jacksonville, Fla.
  1964, 55f
  over half Negro by 1972, 391
Jails, use during disorders, 353
Jefferson, Thomas
  emancipation advocate, 209
  estimate re-run away slaves, 208
Jenkins, Herbert, biographical sketch of, 487f
Jersey City, N.J.
  1964, 36
  outbreaks in, warned, 70
Jim Crow laws, 216
Job programs,
  see employment
Johnson, President Lyndon B.
  address to nation on civil disorders, 484f
  appoints Insurance Panel, 360
  charge regarding organization or planning in riots, 201
  charge to Commission, 358
  Civil Rights Act of 1964, 230
  HUD service centers, calls for, 296
  Public Safety Message, 1968, 336
  tension, quoted, 203
Justice
  assembly-line, effect on ghetto, 299
  attitude of ghetto residents toward, 337
  emergency conditions and, 337ff
  new demands on, by disorder, 337
Justice, administration of
  arraignment
    large numbers create most
    problems, 340
    not conform with due process, 341f
  arrest, recommendations, 347
  arrests
    during riots, indiscriminate, 339
    for minor offenses predominate, 339
    not on basis of evidence, 339
    number in Detroit, Mich., 339
    used as control rather than for convictions, 339
  attitudes toward, during disorder, 345
  bail, 338
    recognizance bonds usual where disorders small, 342
    set to detain defendants, unusually high, 341
  booking, Detroit, Mich., 340
  counsel
    ACLU volunteers, 342
    lack of court appointed, 342f
    lack of effective, 342f
    NAACP volunteers, 342
  criminal justice and riots, 337f
  delay and confusion after arrest, 340
  demands upon by disorders, new, 338
  detention
    facilities overloaded, 340
    large numbers create problems, 340
  identification and recording, biggest problem of arrests, 340
  inadequacies penalize poor man, 337
  institutional shortcomings in criminal justice system, 337f
  processing and detention facilities, recommendations for, 348ff
  prosecutional discretion, recommendations for, 347
  recommendations by Crime Commission, 337
  recommendations to improve, 344ff
  riot cases, many dismissed for lack of evidence, 339
  riot cases still pending, 338
  speed of, affects sentences, 343
  summary of recommendations outlined, 357
  trial sentence affected by delay in trial, 343
  trial sentence, affected by nature of disorders, 343
  trials, lesser riots, normal sentencing, 343
Justice, Department of
  grants by, 335

K

Kansas City, Mo.
  Negro school majority by 1985, 391
  police department, 324
Kennedy, John F.
  Civil Rights Bill, asks for, 230
  Executive Order on housing discrimination, 481
Kerner, Otto, Foreword
  biographical sketch of, 486
King, Rev. Martin Luther, Jr.
  establishes Southern Christian Leadership Conference (SCLC), 225
  Montgomery bus boycott, 225
  nonviolence, 226f
  SCLC, Selma, Ala., demonstrations, 1965, 230
Kirk, Gov. Claude, Tampa, 45
Knoxville, Tenn., civil disorders, 1919, 219
Ku Klux Klan, 213f, 219

L

Labor, Department of
  Disadvantaged Area Survey, 1966, (9 Disadvantaged Areas), 257
  economic data on Negroes, 251f
  estimates of underemployment, "subemployment rate," 254f
  manpower and education programs, 295f
  police cadet training, 336
Law enforcement
  community relations an integral part of, 320
  community support for, 315ff
  dual standard of, in ghetto, 308f
  new role of police in, 300
  recommendations on, and police departments, 316f
  recommendations on standards of, in ghetto, 309
  see Justice, adminstration of; police
Law, rule of, foundation of society, 323
Lawful citizens, participation in riot control, 109f
Leadership, an issue in community response, 298
Legal services
  participation of law schools in, 293
  program of OEO, 293
Legislation to improve ghetto problems, 293f
Life expectancy, 270f
  see also health and sanitation conditions
Lindsay, John V., biographical sketch of, 486
Local government
  affected by current trends in municipal administration, 286f
  reforms in, to aid ghetto resident, 298
  relation to ghetto residents crucial, 284ff
  response to ghetto problems, 294ff
  structure of, in riot cities, 137
Loitering
  enforcement of laws on, 309
  police discretion in, 313
Longview, Tex.
  civil disorder, 1919, 219
Looting
  in Detroit, Mich., 93
  intensive, 113
  isolated, as riot factor, 113
Los Angeles, Calif.
  1965, 37
  1966, 38
  census, special, 248
  civil disorders, World War II, 224
  fatherless families in Watts, 261
  Negro attitude toward police protection in, 308
  Negro migration, 1955-60, 240
  police department, 324
  see also Watts
Louisville, Ky., Negro school majority in, by 1985, 391
Lowndes County, Ala., Black Panther Party, 233
Lynchings, 215f
  1880's-1890's, 216
  post World War I, 219

M

McCulloch, Wm. M., biographical sketch of, 488
Malcolm X, 232
Major disorders
  see disorders, major
Manpower
  see training
March on Washington, 230
  1941, 223
  1963, 230
  A. Phillip Randolph, 223
Marines, U.S.
  Negroes
    1917-1918, 218
    1941-1945, 223
Maternal mortality, 270
  see also health and sanitation conditions
Mayors
  city councils, assistance for, 293
  role of, in ghetto community action, 298f
  to judge use of riot control groups, 332
Media
  accuracy of, coverage of, 371ff
  continuing research in, 389

corrections of, from within, 367
coverage
  Commission ideas on, 367
  ghetto reactions to, 374ff
  Negro needs for, outlined, 385f
duty of, stressed, 389
failure to communicate ghetto problems to whites, 382f
information, police as a source of, 374f
mass
  codes of conduct in disorders, 377f
  cooperation in disorder problems, 380ff
  coverage of Negroes, 382ff
  editorial comment by Negro staff members, 383
  emphasis on disorders to public, 363f
  journalists
    recruitment by, 387f
    training of, 387
  liaison with police, ghetto idea of, 375
  local community recommendations for, 379ff
  need for good contacts in ghetto, 384
  Negro
    mistrusts, 374f
    newspapers and, 384
  Negroes in, as employees, 382f
  newspapers
    ghetto lack of interest in, 376
    ghetto reads tabloids, 377
    reporting style, 363f
    outlook basically "white," 374f
  police-press relations, 378ff
  relations with ghetto, 376f
  staging of events, 377
  study of disorder coverage of, explained, 363f
  TV most relied upon by ghetto, 374
  urban affairs service of, 388f
not a cause of riots, 366f
orientation sessions for, by police, 379
race relations, 366f
reports and white outlooks, 366
"unfairness" Negro view of, 375
Medical assistance, provided by Federal government, 359
Medical facilities, availability, 272
Medicare, 270
Memphis, Tenn., reconstruction, civil disorders, 213
Merchants credit risks, 275
Merchants operating costs, 275
Meredith, James, Memphis to Jackson march in June, 1966, 232f

Methods, riot suppression by lawful citizens, 109
  see also lawful citizens
Metropolitan area, problems of definition, 408f
Metropolitan government
  see regional government
Michigan Civil Rights Commission, findings of, in Detroit, 310
Middle-class citizen
  fewer needs for public services, 285
  finds help for problems more easily than ghetto resident, 285
  system moves more easily for, 285
Migration rates, discussed, 240
Milwaukee, Wis.
  complaints against police in, 310
  violence in, 123
Minorities, political system, 287
Minority groups
  dilemma of hiring as police officers, 317
  lack of representation in government, 283
  participation in city government encouraged, 296
Mississippi, prison terms for demonstrators (Freedom Ride), 228
Mississippi Freedom Democratic Party, created by Robert Moses of SNCC, 230f
Mobile, Ala., civil disorders, World War II, 224
Model Cities program
  cited, 396
  expanded, recommended, 478ff
Montgomery, Ala.
  bus boycott, 225
  student demonstrators arrests, 227
Moses, Robert
  creates Mississippi Freedom Democratic Party, 230f
  SNCC voter registration drive, 1961, in Mississippi, 231
Moynihan, Daniel P., employment, quoted, 252
Multi-Service Centers, development of, recommended, 295f
Municipal administration, current trends in, affecting local government, 285f
Municipal governments, 283ff
  crisis confronting, 299
  Negro-dominated, future of, 399
  Negro officials in, 138
  Negro political alienation, 138
  political accountability, 138
Municipal services, increasing cost of, 393f
Municipal tax base, 393
Murder, Index Crime, 266, 269
Murphy, Patrick V., quoted, 312, 316

N

Narcotics
  addiction, 263
  use of, 204
National Advisory Commission
    on Civil Disorders
  national recommendations of,
    410ff
National Advisory Panel on In-
    surance in Riot-Affected
    Areas, 360
  findings of, 361
  members listed, Foreword
  proposals endorsed, 362
National Association for the
    Advancement of Colored
    People (NAACP)
  achievements, 1920-40, 219ff
  attempts to end school segre-
    gation, 220f, 224f
  Black Power, 233
  boycotts, 225
  campaign to abolish poll tax,
    222
  early program, 217
  founded, 217
  Negro leadership, white sup-
    port, 228
  strategy, change to direct ac-
    tive, 227
National Guard
  Federal mission, 97, 500
  Negroes in units, increase,
    recommended, 315
  performance in
    Cincinnati, Ohio, 51
    Detroit, Mich., 93, 107, 315
    East St. Louis, Ill., 1917,
      217f
    Newark, N.J., 64f
    Plainfield, N.J., 81
    Springfield, Ill., 1908, 215
    Tampa, Fla., 46
    training, 327
  use, in serious disorders, 113
National Insurance Develop-
    ment Corporation (NI-
    DC), creation of,
  recommended, 361
National Negro Convention
    Movement, 1830, 211
National Urban League
  changes, tactics, outspoken,
    228
  founded in 1911, 220
Navy, U.S., Negroes, 1917-1918,
    218
Negotiation difficulties, 334
Negro
  areas of cities, withdrawal of
    white capital, 399
  as police officers, 315ff
  central city job-seekers, 393
  children of fatherless homes,
    lower intelligence quo-
    tients, 261
  city government, increased in-
    volvement, 296, 400

combat units, French com-
    manders, 218
community response to riot,
    110
concentration, current policy,
    396
conditions
  compared with non-Negro,
    137
  housing
    Federally financed, 142
    need for low-income, 142
    New Haven, Conn., 142
    Newark, N.J., 142
  local government structure,
    137
  social and economic pat-
    terns of disadvantage,
    136
dissatisfaction, disparity in
    perception, 287f
family
  instability, unemployment,
    260
  matriarchal structure, 280
grievances
  additional aggravation fac-
    tors, 110f
  as part of negotiations, 112
  in incident-grievance rela-
    tionship, 111
  investigation results, 143
  levels of intensity, 143f
  list of, 143f
  major topics, 143
  reinforcement process, 111
  transcend immediate event,
    284f
in the ghetto, political
    strength of, 403f
in the media, 385f
incomes, faster increase, 401
in-migration offsetting out-
    migration, 403
leaders
  established in Negro-white
    negotiations, 112
  TV coverage, 369ff
mayors in Cleveland, and
    Gary, 156
men, employment, discussed,
    392f, 402
middle class, 282
  central cities, 403
  ghetto residence forced on,
    281f
  Negro out-migration, 403
  rapid growth, 401
migrants, lack of skills, 278
migration
  from South, magnitude, 239f
  future, 241f
  immigration compared, 240
  slowed by Depression, 239
  World War I, industrial de-
    mands, 239
  World War II, 239
militant organizations, influ-
    ence of, 153
militants, in disorder negotia-
    tions, 112

504

opinions, of police brutality, 302
organizations, participation in rebuilding, 157
out-migration
  Negro middle-class, 402
political development, racial and spatial segregation, 400
population
  birth rate in South, 242
  growth, projected, 390
  growth rate and trends, 237f
  in central cities
    factors, 390ff
    migration, a factor, 390
  median age, 238
  public school enrollment, 431
  trends and future, 391f
  young, growth, faster than white, 392
protest movements, 236
  changing character, 236
  evaluated, meaning, 235f
racial pride, Garvey, Marcus, 221
rebellion concept, 398
reporters needed, 231
revolts (violence)
  see civil disorders
role in American society, 403f
self-development
  discussed, 403f
  economic and political, 404
students, majority in urban schools, 391
urban population centers, 243
urbanization, 242f
youth
  crimes, high share, 269
  unemployment, 392
  see also employment
view poor services as racial discrimination, 284f
Negro-white
  confrontations, TV impressions of, 369ff
  negotiations (officials)
    as civil disorder process factor, 112
    characteristics, 112
    "terms of peace," 112
  polarization, Present Policies Choice, 398ff
Neighborhood
  city halls
    establishment, recommended, 294f
    functions, described, 295
  membership corporation, functions, 298
  merchants, patronization by poor, 274f
  schools
    see education
Neighborhood Action Task Force
  city officials, role, 289f
  composition, 289
  function, 289ff

see also Task Force
New Brunswick, N. J., 82ff
  initiative of Negro leaders in calming disorders, 333f
  vandalism, 83
New Haven, Conn.
  factors in disorder, 325
  Negro school majority in by 1985, 391
  police protection, cited, 308
  police review board, 310
  problems of programs in, 286
  rumors as spark to disorder, 326
New Jersey
  clustering of disorders, 69ff, 114
  Governor's Select Commission on Civil Disorders, 202
New Orleans, La.
  fire department, 493
  over half Negro by 1971, 391
  racial violence, 1860's, 212f
New York City
  1964, 36
  civil disorders, 1900, 215
  civil disorders, World War II, 224f
  colonial slave revolts, 207
  consumer problems, 276
  draft riots, Civil War, 212, 330
  guidelines for police use of firearms established, 314
  libel action, consumer purchase (study), 277
  migration from North Carolina, 1955-60, 240
  police
    department, 323f
    family crisis intervention program, 319
  slum sanitation, 273
  social ills in Negro neighborhoods, 263
  television use by the poor, 274f
  see also Bedford-Stuyvesant; Harlem
New York Times, 1964 study of Harlem, 302
Newark, N.J., 56ff
  arrest of cab driver, trigger to violence, 284
  civil disorder ignited by police action, 206
  Civil War disorders, 212
  clustering of disorders, 114
  Committee of Concern, 153
  complaints against police in, 310
  damage estimate, 115
  damage to property, 116
  death and injuries, 115
  fire damage less than in Detroit, 358
  Governor Hughes in, 64
  initial incident, 119
  initial violence, 119
  looting, 64f
  Medical Center Project, 155
  National Guard

in, 64
 withdrawn, 68
Negro militants, 153
over half Negro, 391
police action against Negro
 property, 116f, 120
police-minority relations, 299
police mobilization in, 6
prior incidents, 118f
problem of rumors in, 326
sniping in, 65f
study of organized activity,
 201
survey
 attitude toward Negro middle class, 134
 education, employment data
  and, 132
 employment attitudes and
  riot participation, 132
 family structure data, 130
 income data, 131
 political attitudes and involvement, 134
 racial self-image data, 133
 region of upbringing data,
  130
 time of severe levels of violence, 123
 trigger incident, 60
 typical sequence of riot events
  described, 118ff
 white segregationists, 153
News media
 analysis of disorder coverage
  of, by Commission, 363f
 conclusions on, 363
 disorders overblown by, 363f
 methodology of gathering information on, explained,
  362f
 overall treatment of urban and
  racial problems, 362f
 riots, 362ff
 see also media, mass; newspapers; radio; TV
Newspapers
 coverage of disorders discussed, 371ff
 local, saw riots in national
  terms, 371
 see Media
Newsweek, "Negro American—
  What Must Be Done,"
  cited, 373
Niagara Movement, 216f
Non-involved
 age characteristics of, 129
 attitude on employment, 132
 compared to involved, 129
 employment data on, 132
 income data on, 131
 racial attitudes of, 133
 racial, sex, age characteristics, 129f
 regional, birthplace data on,
  130
 residence data on, 131
 see also counter-rioter
 see also disorders, investigations

Non-lethal control of disorder,
  more experience and
  evaluation needed, 331
Non-violent direct action, 226
Norris, Frank J., white supremacy spokesman, 224

O

Oakland, Calif.
 over half Negro by 1983, 391
 police department, 323f
Office of Economic Opportunity
  (OEO)
 Community Action Programs,
  297
 Detroit, Mich., multi-service
  centers, 295
 legal services program, 293
 multi-service centers established, 295
 police-community relations
  programs, 336
Office of Education, report, cited,
  404
Ohio, 114
 see also clustering of disorders
Omaha, Nebr., civil disorder
  1919, 219
Open housing
 in suburbs and Negro jobs,
  392f, 403
 necessity, emphasized, 475
Open occupancy law, recommended, 481f
Orangeburg, S.C., student demonstrators' arrest, 227
Organizations, militant, 202
Organized activity, 201f
 conclusions, 202
 foreign influence, 201
 staff study, 201
Overreaction to disorders, problems discussed, 334f

P

Participants, active, 113
 see rioter
Paternalism, bias of media toward, 366
Paterson, N.J., 1964, 36
Patricelli, Robert, quoted, 273
Peden, Katherine G., biographical sketch of, 488
Peoria, Ill., police on duty, 327
Permanent Subcommittee on Investigations of the Senate Committee on Gov-
  ernment Operations, 115
Philadelphia, Miss., 1964, 36
Philadelphia, Pa.
 1963, 35
 1964, 37
 civil disorders, 1917, 219
 Negro
  attitude toward police protection, 308f
  over half Negro by 1981, 391

population, 1900, 239
Pittsburgh, Pa., Negro school majority by 1985, 391
Plainfield, N.J.
  civil disorder, 75ff
  complaints against police, 310
  National Guard, 81
  New Jersey Commission, 202
  new organization, 153
  police mobilization, 78
  trigger incident, 77
  weapons, 80
Polarization
  an immediate danger, stressed, 407
  avoidance of and Present Policies Choice, 401
  economic, in metropolitan areas, 400
  Enrichment Choice, 405
  of races as a result of political problems, 287
  political, in metropolitan areas, 400
Police
  action as a cause of disorders, 206
  activities, an increase to tension, 301f
  alternatives to force, 331f
  arrest, Harlem civil disorder, 1943, 224
  as source of media information, 375
  as symbol of white racism, 206
  breakdown of communications with ghetto residents, 315
  brutality, 302f
  chiefs' role in planning for disorders, 333
  citizen conflicts, Detroit, Mich., history of, 85
  citizen contacts, 312
    prejudices of police shown in, instances quoted, 306
    written departmental policy for, necessary, 313f
  civil disorders in East St. Louis, Ill., 1917, 217f
  commanders, 207
  communications
    communications system, recommended, 329
  community service
    functions, explained, 318
  complaints against, 310
  conduct
    ghetto youths, 303
    Negro attitudes toward, 302
    patrol practices, 301ff
    redress of complaints against, 310f
  confidence, necessary for discipline, 328
  control
    capability in event of disorder, 157
    of disorder under Present

Policies Choice, 397
department
  award systems discussed, 320
departments
  increase of Negroes in supervisory positions recommended, 317
  recruiting of more Negroes recommended, 317
dogs, failure to purchase, 154
evidence of racial prejudice in, 305f
external review of, recommended, 311
focus of hostility of ghetto, 284f
guidelines, 312ff
  arrest decisions, 313
  dissemination
    to personnel, 314
    to public, 314
  enforcement necessary, 314
  firearms, use of, 314
  for stop-and-frisk techniques, 313f
  handling of minor disputes, 313
  internal investigative unit necessary for, 314
  investigative methods, selection and use of, 313f
  periodic review necessary, 314
  physical force, 314
  responsibility of drafting, 314
  right of free expression (lawful demonstrations), 314
  small-group training of police in use of, 314
hampered by ineffective communication, 329
harassment, 303f
  intent of, 303
lack of understanding by police, 303
high crime rate, general hostility, 268f
hostility to, 299, 325
incentives to outstanding officers in ghetto, 306
Information Officers, advocated, 379
initial phase of disorder, 324
interrogations, 301
involvement in community service matters necessary, 318f
isolated from other city agencies, 286
knowledge of ghetto problems and initial response, 325
liaison with mass media, ghetto ideas of, 374f
local, use of, 113
minority relations in major cities, 299
misconduct
  factors in elimination, 305
  ghetto attitude toward po-

507

lice punishment, 311
Negro perceptions, 306
recommendations, 305ff
relation to professionalism, 302
neighborhood service centers, 319
officers
  as Negro supervisory personnel, 316
  assignment of best-qualified to ghetto, recommended, 306
  Negro, below percentage in population, 315f
  Negro, recruitment of, 316
  Negroes, problems of hiring, 316
patrol
  practices, 304f
    as a Negro grievance, 144
    new and police knowledge of ghetto, 307
    reassessment, recommended, 307
    review and execution, recommended, 307
patrols
  "aggressive preventive patrols," 304
  as source of friction, 304
personnel
  inadequate for disorder, 328
  lack of in ghetto, 308
press relations
  functions of remedial measures, 388
  relations with non-local reporters, 380
protection
  adequate in ghetto, recommended, 301
  Negro attitudes toward, 307ff
  priorities on calls from ghetto, 308f
  versus diminished community tension, 307
  volume of calls in ghetto, 308
redress of grievance, self-investigatory, 139
response to initial incident crucial, 324
responsibility for making changes emphasized, 300f
retired, as neighborhood service center workers, 319
screening procedures for new officers necessary, 306
state
  use in serious disorders, 113
tactics, discussed, 329
Task Force
  Crime Commission, quoted, 310
  Report
    recommendations, cited, 313f
training
  recruit level, 327
use of force, 301
verbal abuse, 302f

viewed as "occupying force," 301
work, nature of disorders, 342
Police-community relations, 154, 319f
Political
attitudes and involvement of rioters and non-involved, 134f
machines, decline of, 287
organization, ethnic group domination, 279
structure, as a Negro grievance, 144f
system, minorities. 287
Population
Negro
  see Negro migration, post-World War II, 393
Poverty
areas, based on index of deprivation, 259
as a cause of poor health, 269f
escape from, 278, 280
  by European immigrant, 279
in disadvantaged neighborhoods, extent of, 257f
Negro children in poverty areas, 259
Social Security Administration data, 1964, 258
War on, accomplishments, 297
"Poverty Level," defined by Social Security Administration, 258, 462
Pre-riot Conditions, see education
Present Policies Choice
attitudes of Negro men, 397
continued disorder, 397f
control of disorder, 397f
Negro-white polarization, 398ff
overview, 395
short and long run costs, 398
President's Commission on Law Enforcement and the Administration of Justice, see Crime Commission
Press, see Media
Prevention and Control of Mobs and Riots, The, 324
Private
community development corporations, potential of, 298
enterprise, role, 399
organizations, actions of, 359
sectors, Task Force must involve in ghetto needs, 290
Programs
large-scale, effects on ghetto, 401f
social and economic, Present Policies Choice, 398
Progress, ghetto attitude toward, 406
Property

crimes threatening, 309
damage, 1967 disorders, 398
taxes, dependence of cities on,
393
Prosser, Gabriel, slave uprising
led by, 210
Prostitution, tolerance of in
ghetto, 307
Protest movements, Negro, discussed, 235f
Protests
lawful, non-interference with,
323
Negro, 19th century, 211
Public assistance
contributions to tension and
social disorder, 457
Depression, 221f
for Negroes and whites, two
sources, 399
see Welfare System
Public institutions
as targets of attacks, 116
damages to, 116
Public officials
duties, outlined, 301
incitement by mass media, 367
see also local government
Public services
account for rising local government costs, 394
complicated needs by ghetto
residents, 285
expenditure, increased, and
urban growth, 393
fewer needs for among middle
class, 285
inadequacy in central city, 283
needs diminish by non-ghetto
residents, 287
needs grow by ghetto residents, 287
poor public transportation, 295

R

Race problems, failure of communications, 382ff
Race relations
failure of media to analyze
and report, 366
importance of media, 385f
see also Negro
Racial attitudes
intensity of riot participants,
133f
of whites, as a Negro grievance, 144f
survey data, Detroit, Mich.,
and Newark, N.J., 133
Radio
as an instrument of tension
and trouble, 376
influence on disorders, 376
popularity in ghetto, 376
Randolph, A. Phillip, 221
March on Washington, 1941,
223
March on Washington, 1964,
230

Rape, Index Crime, 266, 269
Rats, proliferation
see health and sanitation conditions
Recommendations, chapters 10-
17
effective grievance response
mechanisms, 291f
financing of, 410f
funding, discussed, 335f
police in ghettos, 306
State and Federal financial
assistance to cities, 293
use of chemical agents before
use of deadly weapons,
331
Reconstruction, 213
Negro political officeholders,
213f
Recreation, improved in four
cities, 155
Recruitment, see employment
Redress of Negro grievance
see grievance mechanisms;
Human Relations Coun-
cils
Regional government
no solution to
polarization, 400
problems as Negro sees
them, 400
Reiss, Albert, University of
Michigan, quoted, 306
Rent supplements
see housing
Reporters, inexperienced, covering disorders, 364
see media
Response, level of law enforcement, 113
Richmond, Va., over half Negro
by 1971, 391
Riot
see disorder
Rioter
as element of riot process, 117
profile of, 111
characteristics sought in investigation, 110
characteristics (general),
age, marital status, residential status, economic
position, 128
see also disorder, participant
self-reported
data on family structure,
130
education characteristics of,
132
employment data, 132
see counter-rioter
Riot process, 116
control effort, 124
precipitating violence, 117
reservoir of grievances, 117
Riots
see civil disorders
Robbery
Index Crime, 277

police response in Cleveland, Ohio, 309
Rochester, N.Y., 1964, 36
Romney, Governor George, visits Detroit, Mich., 92
Roosevelt, Franklin D., Fair Employment Practices Commission (FEPC), 223
Rumors
civil disorder, East St. Louis, Ill., 1917, 217f
disorder, 326
dispelling with radio and TV, 326
media, credence, 372f
offsetting crucial, 326
reported by media as fact, 364
sparks to disorder in Tampa, Fla., and New Haven, Conn., 326
units to dispel discussed, 326
Rural poverty, problems of, 410

S

St. Augustine, Fla., 1964, 36
St. Louis, Mo.
mayor of, quoted, 287
Negro population versus school enrollment, 391
over half Negro by 1978, 391
San Diego, Calif., Negro attitude toward police protection, 308
Savannah, Ga., 1963, 35
SCLC
see Southern Christian Leadership Conference
School segregation in the North, 220
Schools
organization by militants, 202
parent hostility toward, 436
segregation, 203
see also education
Segregation, 203, 217
by law, 214ff
future, Black Power advocates, 404
increased aid to systems eliminating segregation, 440
job opportunities, 280ff
Negroes in politics, 279
public schools, 215
racial, current policy, 396
urban
residences, 243ff
residential, extent, 246f
white exodus, 245f
Selective Service Act, 1917, 218
Selma, Ala.
1965, 37
SCLC with Rev. Martin Luther King, Jr., 1965, 230
Senate Subcommittee on
Employment, Manpower and Poverty, report, quoted, 286f
Executive Reorganization, report on Watts, 302

"Separate but Equal"
Plessy v. Ferguson, 214
Separatism, 219ff
Service institutions, fragmentation of, a problem, 295
Services
of municipal government, as a Negro grievance, 145
poor, viewed as racial discrimination, 284
public, problem of wages of employees, 394
Sheehan, Mayor Patricia Q., New Brunswick, N.J., quoted, 69
Shuttlesworth, Rev. Fred, Cincinnati, Ohio, 48
Sit-in movement, 226f
CORE, from Gandhi, 223f
failures in Mississippi and Alabama, 230f
Slave revolts
see civil disorders
Slavery
early laws, 209
runaways, 210
three-fifths compromise, Constitution, 208
Slums
see ghetto
Small Business Administration, 359
SNCC
see Student Non-Violent Coordinating Committee
Sniping, in Detroit, Mich., 93
Social Security Administration, poverty level defined, 258
Southern Christian Leadership Conference (SCLC)
at Selma, Ala., 1965, 230
established by Rev. Martin Luther King, Jr., 225
Negro led and dominated, 228
Southern college student, 227
Southern Negro, the Enrichment Choice, 403
Special schools in ghetto, 429f
Springfield, Ill., civil disorders, 1908, 215
"Staging" of disorders by newsmen, 364
Standard Metropolitan Statistical Area (SMSA), defined, 408f
States, rural-oriented, 283
Stop-and-frisk, police patrol device, 304
Student
demonstrations, 226f
involvement, 227
Student Non-Violent Coordinating Committee (SNCC)
Black Power, 233
increases militancy, 231f
Negro led and dominated, 228
Robert Moses and Mississippi voter registration drive, 1961, 230f
"Subemployment" rate defined, 257

Subsidies, to establish new industries in ghetto, 392
Substandard and overcrowded housing
    see housing
Suburbs
    crime rate, 266
    higher taxes, a problem for urban aid, 400
    versus central city, by 1985, 400
Summer youth programs, recommended, 290
Summons, as alternative to arrest, 313
Supreme Court decisions
    against Negro rights, 214
    desegregation of Montgomery, Ala., buses, 225
    desegregation of transportation facilities decreed, 381
    Oklahoma "Grandfather Clause" overruled, 217
    Plessy v. *Ferguson*, 214
    school desegregation decreed, 226
    segregation ordinances outlawed, 217
    "separate but equal," 214
    Tuskegee gerrymander, 225

T

Tampa, Fla., 42ff
    1967
        Black Muslims, 46
        coverage of disorder in, 372f
        crowds gather, 42
        National Guard, 46
        police-community relations, 44
        precipitating incident, 42
        rumors spark disorder, 326
        Youth Patrol, 46f.
Task Force
    coordinates activities in a disturbance, 290f
    fills needs other groups cannot, 291
    in Bedford-Stuyvesant incident, 291
    "incidents," 290
    involves private sector in needs of ghetto, 290
    made permanent by neighborhood city halls, 294f
    prevention of civil disorders, 290
    provides relief for ghetto residents 290
    realistic capacity to redress grievances, 290
    warning system, 290
    youth activities, 290
Tax deferral measures recommended for property insurance industry, 361
Tax dollar problems of cities enumerated, 399
Taxes, 410f

Teachers
    not living in ghetto, problems created by, 436
    qualifications of, a problem, 428
Tear gas
    see chemical agents
Teenagers, unemployment rate, 256
Television
    conclusions about content of disorder coverage, discussed, 369ff
    coverage
        emphasis, 369
        "live," problem of, 372
        of Negro leaders, 370f
        timing, 370
    most relied on in ghetto, 376f
    pressure to buy expensive goods, 274f
    self-restraint, a problem, 373
    universal ghetto appliance as status symbol, 204
    see also media
Temperature, at time violence erupted, 123
Tension
    aggravation by rumor, 330
    as a riot process, 118
    grows with lack of communication, 285
    lack of response of city government to, 288
Thornton, Charles B., biographical sketch of, 488f
Throckmorton, Lt. General John T., in Detroit, Mich., 95f
"Tokenism," 232
Training programs
    manpower programs, research, 140
    Newark, N. J., and New Haven, Conn., 141
Transportation
    between ghetto and jobs, 392
    improved, large urban problems, 392f
Trial sentencing, outline of procedures for, 355f
Trigger incident
    see incident, initial; incidents, precipitating
Troy, N. Y., Civil War disorders, 212
Tucson, Ariz., employment effort by public agencies and private industry, 154
Tulsa, Okla., civil disorders, 1921, 219
Turner, Nat, 210
"Typical"
    civil disorders, viewed in national framework, 110
    riot, 109
    see also civil disorders; disorder, popular conceptions of

U

"Underemployed," outside ghetto areas, 257

see also "subemployment"
Underemployment, 257
  as a Negro grievance, 144
  cities survey, research, 140
  effect on family structure, 260
  Labor, Department of, study, 140
  see also employment; disorder, participant
Unemployment
  as participation factor, 132
  effect on family structure, 260
  Negro men in ghetto, problem of, 402
  Negro youth, 392
  rate after 1954, 226
  social impact in ghettos, 260ff
Union discrimination, 281f
Unions, civil disorders in East St. Louis, Ill. 1917, 217
Universal Negro Improvement Association (UNIA), Marcus Garvey, 221
University of California, Los Angeles (UCLA) study of Watts, 302
Urban
  areas, federal assistance to, a reflection of national problem, 393f
  ghettos, Present Policies Choice, 398
  growth, increased public service expenditures, 393
  mayor, role in community problems, 299
  occupations, Negroes displaced by immigrants, 279
  problems, reflected in disorders, 283
  renewal, expansion and reorientation of, recommended, 479f
  society after World War II, 278
  violence, rise in, and police, 300
Urban Communications, Institute of, 386ff
  duties, recommended, 387
  establishment, recommended, 386f
Urban League
  study of Detroit, Mich., 302
  see also National Urban League
Urban Renewal, see housing

V

Vagrancy, police discretion in, 313
Vance, Cyrus R.
  in Detroit, Mich., 95f
Vesey, Denmark, slave uprising led by, 210
Vietnam, 232
  rioter, non-involved attitude toward, 135

Violence
  as riot definition factor, 113
  categories of, 113
  development
    aspect of riot process, 116
    described, 123
  duration, 113
  during 1967, 112f
  encouraged, 205f
  increase of, and present policies, 397
  initial, in Detroit, Mich., 119
  legitimatized, 204f
  patterns of classification utilized in study, 110, 112
  sequential occurrence, 123
  sustained, in U.S. cities, danger of, 407f
  victims of, 116
  white retaliation to, 398
  see also disorder
Voter registration drive, 1961, Mississippi, 230f
Voting Rights Act of 1965, 230

W

War on Poverty, accomplishments of, 297, 396
Washington, Booker T., 216, 234f
Washington, D.C.
  civil disorders, 1919, 219
  Federal Trade Commission study, 276
  illegitimacy statistics from analysis, Census, 1960, 262
  media, stories about, 373
  over half Negro, 391
  segregation extended to, 217
Washington, George, advocated emancipation, 209
Watts
  1965, 38
  civil disorder, ignited by police action, 206
  fatherless families, 261
  pattern of damage similar to Detroit, 358
  police-minority relations, 299
  Senate Subcommittee on Executive Reorganization, 302
  UCLA study of, 302
Welfare system, 457ff
  AFDC-UP, extension, 462f
  Aid For Dependent Children (AFDC), 457f
  alteration and expansion, recommended, 461
  case workers, 460
  correction of, specific inadequacies, 461f
  day-care centers, 463f
  deficiencies, 457ff
  family-planning, 465f
  financing increased costs, 463f
  income supplements, 462, 466f
  job training, 463
  partial retention, outside earnings, 464
  standards of assistance, 462
  strategies to improve, 461f

512

suggested programs, 462
work incentives and training, 464
White Citizens' Councils, 226
White population decline in central cities, 245f
Whites, role of, in Negro movements, 228
White supremacy spokesmen, 224
Wilkins, Roy, biographical sketch of, 489
Wilson, Orlando W., cited, 324
Winston-Salem, N.C., success of community relations programs in, 320

World War I, 218f
Negro migration accelerated, 239
World War II
Negro migration expended, 240
Negroes in industrial jobs, 279

Y

Yale Law Journal, study of Hartford, Conn., quoted, 309
Young, Whitney M., Jr., appointed Executive Director, National Urban League, 1961, 228